COGNITIVE PSYCHOLOGY

WAYNE A. WICKELGREN

University of Oregon

Prentice-Hall, Inc., Englewood Cliffs, New Jersey 07632

Library of Congress Cataloging in Publication Data

WICKELGREN, WAYNE A. (date)
   Cognitive psychology.

   Bibliography: p.
   Includes index.
      1. Cognition.   I. Title.   [DNLM: 1. Cognition.
   2. Psychology.   BF311 W636c]
   BF311.W573   153.4   78–11301
   ISBN 0–13–139543–2

Printed in the United States of America

10 9 8 7 6 5 4 3 2 1

Editorial/production supervision and interior design by Lynda Heideman
Cover design by Judi Katz

PRENTICE-HALL INTERNATIONAL, INC., *London*
PRENTICE-HALL OF AUSTRALIA PTY. LIMITED, *Sydney*
PRENTICE-HALL OF CANADA, LTD., *Toronto*
PRENTICE-HALL OF INDIA PRIVATE LIMITED, *New Delhi*
PRENTICE-HALL OF JAPAN, INC., *Tokyo*
PRENTICE-HALL OF SOUTHEAST ASIA PTE. LTD., *Singapore*
WHITEHALL BOOKS LIMITED, *Wellington, New Zealand*

This book is dedicated to George Miller, the genius who did so much to shape the field of cognitive psychology, both by his creative ideas (especially the concepts of chunking and plans) and by his critical judgment of promising directions for thinking and research (he did indeed mill a lot of the flour that others baked into ideas—some fully, others less so). Although our research philosophies differ somewhat, he probably bent my twig more than any other single individual vis-à-vis theoretical approaches to cognitive psychology.

CONTENTS

PREFACE   ix

CHAPTER 1
INTRODUCTION   1

Objectives *1*   Overview of Cognitive Psychology *2*
Coding *6*   Cognitive Processes *11*
Cognitive Modalities *17*   Summary *26*

CHAPTER 2
VISUAL PERCEPTION   27

Objectives *27*
Hierarchical Features: Conjunction, Disjunction,
and Negation *28*
Inhibition *36*   Adaptation *42*
Grouping: Figures and Grounds *48*
Object Concepts and Form Perception *56*
Expectation and Feedback in Perception *64*
Perceptual Responses *64*   Summary *65*

CHAPTER 3
SPATIAL COGNITION AND IMAGERY   67

Objectives *67*   Spatial Memory *69*   Imagery *73*
Image Operations *82*   Summary *92*

CHAPTER 4
AUDITORY PERCEPTION

94

Objectives *94*   Sound *96*   Hierarchical Features *99*
Inhibition *107*   Adaptation *109*
Grouping in Auditory Perception *111*
Perception of Temporal Order *114*
Object Concepts and Auditory Pattern Perception *116*
Expectation and Feedback in Perception *116*
Perceptual Responses *117*   Music *117*   Aesthetics *119*
Summary *120*

CHAPTER 5
SPEECH AND READING

122

Objectives *122*   Verbal Levels and Units *124*
Speech Recognition *131*   Articulation *139*
Reading *147*   Summary *159*

CHAPTER 6
ATTENTION

161

Objectives *161*
Theoretical Analysis of Attention and Set *164*
Attention *167*   Attentional Set *176*
Summary *186*

CHAPTER 7
SHORT-TERM MEMORY

188

Objectives *188*   Iconic Memory *190*
Echoic Memory *198*   Graphic Short-Term Memory *201*
Phonetic Short-Term Memory *202*   Active Memory *210*
Working Memory *211*   Summary *212*

CHAPTER 8
ASSOCIATIVE LONG-TERM MEMORY

214

Objectives *214*
Associative and Nonassociative Memory *216*
Long-Term Conceptual Memory Is Associative *220*
Chunking and Vertical Association *227*
Three Phases of Memory *234*   Summary *246*

CHAPTER 9
RETRIEVAL: RECALL AND RECOGNITION 249

Objectives *249*
Elementary and Complex Retrieval Tasks *250*
Perceptual Recognition and Recognition Memory *252*
Item Memory and Associative Memory *253*
Two Memory Output Stages: Retrieval and Decisions *254*
Decision Rules and Strength Measurement *256*
Retrieval: Direct Access or Search? *259*
Recognition and Recall Compared *267*
Retrieval Dynamics *270*
Summary *281*

CHAPTER 10
SEMANTIC MEMORY CODING:
CONCEPTS, PROPOSITIONS, AND SCHEMATA 283

Objectives *283*   Concepts *286*   Concept Learning *301*
Phrases *315*   Propositions *317*
Schemata and Networks *325*   Summary *327*

CHAPTER 11
SEMANTIC MEMORY PROCESSES:
RETRIEVAL, LEARNING, AND UNDERSTANDING 330

Objectives *330*   Retrieval: Recognition and Recall *333*
Learning *340*   Understanding *349*   Summary *353*

CHAPTER 12
THINKING: PLANS, INFERENCE,
PROBLEM SOLVING, AND CREATIVITY 355

Objectives *355*   Plans and Procedural Knowledge *356*
Inference *360*   Problem Solving *370*   Creativity *381*
Summary *387*

REFERENCES 391

INDEXES 425

Name Index *425*   Subject Index *432*

PREFACE

Cognitive psychology is concerned with the general principles of how the mind works. In synthesizing the scientific literature to write this text, I came to realize just how much we now know about this subject. Thinkers in philosophy, linguistics, and artificial intelligence, as well as in cognitive psychology, have combined to produce an understanding of the mind that, while far from complete and certain to be revised, is nevertheless conceptually deep and rich and enjoys a considerable degree of empirical support. There is no need to apologize for the state of development of the field. We know a lot about how the mind works, and this book attempts to summarize the most important parts of that knowledge within an integrated theoretical framework that is a consistent (not an eclectic) combination of what I consider the best parts of associative, structural-linguistic, and information-processing approaches to the mind. In addition, I have tried throughout to indicate clearly the degree and nature of the empirical support for these principles of cognitive psychology, and to pose some important and as yet unanswered questions concerning how the mind works.

The primary objective of this book is to teach the theoretical concepts and principles of cognitive psychology. In doing this, it is essential to begin with what the student already knows about the mind and to use that common knowledge to explain more precise scientific concepts and principles. Accordingly, I have made extensive use of everyday experiences and practical applications to illustrate the important concepts and principles of cognitive psychology. In addition, it is helpful to explain some of the methods and facts derived from laboratory experiments that illustrate these concepts and principles and provide empirical support for them. However, this is not a "how to do it" research book for future professors of cognitive psychology. Experimental methodology is presented only to the extent that it is needed to understand a fact, concept, or principle; to explain the nature of the evidence for it; or, on occasion, to illustrate experimental scientific methods in cognitive psychology. The focus in this text is primarily on how the mind works and only secondarily on how to do research on how the mind works.

Some people believe that we don't know much about how the mind works but that we know a lot about how to do research on how the mind works. The logic of this position escapes me. How could we know we had good research methods if those methods had not produced a lot of worthwhile knowledge? Scientific methods, like any other methods, must be judged by the quality and quantity of what they produce. In the case of cognitive psychology, that product is knowledge of the mind. The only good reason for believing that the methods are worth teaching is that they have produced knowledge worth teaching, however incomplete and subject to future modification that knowledge may be. All students of cognitive psychology need to know how the mind works. Only a small minority will ever need to know how to do research on how the mind works. Accordingly, while this text does present general principles of both theoretical and experimental scientific methods, because these general principles are an aid to clear thinking, it does not present detailed descriptions of experiments as the standard approach to explaining our knowledge in each and every area of cognitive psychology. My standard approach is to describe scientific concepts, facts, and principles in everyday terms already familiar to the reader, relying at least as much on experiential as on experimental examples.

I also believe in applying what is known about the mind to writing texts, subject of course to my skills and limitations as a writer. First, learning new concepts is absolutely basic to understanding in any area, and this text stresses learning the important concepts for understanding the mind.

Second, learning new concepts is not an all-or-nothing affair—the more we know about a concept, the more we know about relations between it and other concepts. There is no glossary in this book because I do not want to encourage the naive and false notion that you know a lot about a concept when you know a one- or two-sentence definition of it. This text teaches the meaning of concepts by using them over and over again in propositions that richly relate these concepts to other concepts.

Third, spaced repetition is highly beneficial for learning and memory. Accordingly, I do not assume in a later chapter that the reader necessarily remembers the meanings of specialized terms introduced in earlier chapters. I try to remind the reader often of the meanings of technical terms that occur throughout the book. This makes each chapter somewhat more self-contained, permitting chapters to be read out of sequence. It also aids the reader who has forgotten the meaning of some important term introduced earlier.

Finally, repetition provides spaced reviews for the reader who does remember the concept.

Fourth, organization is highly beneficial for learning. To assist the reader in organizing the material and to provide spaced review, every chapter begins with a list of objectives and ends with a summary of the basic concepts and principles discussed in that chapter. The objectives and summaries foretell and retell the contents of the chapters in ways that I hope will help the reader to distinguish the forest from the trees—the general concepts and principles from the supporting evidence and illustrative examples. If you find yourself remembering the general principles but have trouble remembering all the specific examples, that's terrific. Don't sweat it; it only proves you are a member of the human race!

Fifth, motivation and arousal are essential for learning, if only because they guarantee that the reader will pay attention to the material. To increase your enjoyment of this text, I have done several things. I discuss topics of general significance for understanding the human mind, rather than narrow technical details. I speculate concerning the functional purposes of cognitive processes and coding principles. I discuss applications of cognitive psychology to life experiences and problems. Finally, I have tried to write in an informal, personal, emotional style, relating personal experiences, expressing my feelings, and making jokes and light-hearted asides. To purge any field of study of everything but the purest intellectual motivation contributes little to objectivity, and besides, it bores the reader. Furthermore, recent studies indicate that material presented in close conjunction with humor is remembered better than material presented in a straight, unemotional, scholarly fashion. Not only is "many a truth spoken in jest," but also jesting truths are better remembered than the sober truths of which professors are so fond. My only regret is that, for many reasons, I was unable to take more than a small step in this direction.

ACKNOWLEDGMENTS

I am very grateful for the helpful criticisms and suggestions of my reviewers: Carlton James, Rutgers College; Roberta Klatzky, University of California at Santa Barbara; Lester A. Lefton, University of South Carolina; Richard Mayer, University of California at Santa Barbara; Peter G. Polson, University of Colorado; Henry L. Roediger III, Purdue University; Wayne Shebilske, University of Virginia; and W. Edgar Vinacke, State University of New York at Buffalo. As always, I want to acknowledge my children, Ingrid and Abe, who fill my life with love and are the stimulus for many ideas. Finally, I want to thank the following people for their help in publishing the book: Irene Elmer, copy editor; and John Isley, Ted Jursek, and Lynda Heideman, Prentice-Hall editors.

CHAPTER 1
INTRODUCTION

OBJECTIVES

1 To explain how understanding depends first on *analysis* of a topic into parts and then on *synthesis* of the parts by specifying relations among them.

2 To describe how cognitive psychology is related to experimental psychology and to psychology in general.

3 To explain three ways of analyzing cognitive psychology into parts: *function* (perception, learning and memory, language, and thinking); *modality* and *level of processing* (visual, auditory, verbal); and *coding* vs. *cognitive processes.*

4 To distinguish among sensory, motor, and cognitive modalities. To point out that the highest-level cognitive modalities are specialized to represent not particular stimuli or motor responses but to represent concepts (language, forms, spatial relations, music) that can be cued by a variety of different stimuli in various sensory modalities and that can govern responses in various motor modalities.

5 To discuss network theories of coding in which specific elements (nodes) in the network represent ideas (percepts, images, attributes, concepts, propositions), and associations (links) between these nodes account for the flow of thought.

6 To distinguish among three types of associations—upward, downward, and horizontal—that may represent logically different kinds of relations between nodes (ideas) in the mind.

7 To discuss how vertical (upward and downward) associations endow the mind with the capacity to define new (chunk) nodes to represent combinations of previously defined nodes. Such a memory has a growing, rather than a static, representational (coding) capacity.

1

8 To point out the critical importance of asking and answering your own questions as you read or listen. You understand the material much more fully when you read or listen actively rather than passively.

9 To describe briefly some major types of cognitive processes: learning; storage (consolidation and forgetting); activation (perception, retrieval, and thinking); and priming (partial activation in attentional set and short-term memory).

10 To discuss the modality concept, including physiological evidence that supports subdivision of the brain into different processing modalities and some possible psychological functions that might be served by such subdivision.

It is May Day as I begin to write this first chapter, and it is a very beautiful day. As I sit here searching for a beginning to the book, it occurs to me that my experiences at this moment are a microcosm of what cognition is all about. I'm continually looking out at the woods I live in, the patterns of sunshine and shade, and the blue sky. I recognize a hawk soaring high above me. The sounds of a baseball game on television drift in from the next room, and I catch snatches of the game from time to time, especially when something exciting is occurring.

How do I recognize the trees, the hawk, the words of the sportscaster? How am I able to attend to one aspect of my environment for a time and then shift my attention to another aspect or to the task at hand? How do I manage, more or less, to maintain an attentional set for my goal of writing this chapter? How do I manage even to remain awake and alert on this peaceful, dreamy day? How am I able to draw on my perception and memory to construct grammatical and meaningful sentences, and to spell words correctly? How is it that you are able to read these words, understand what I am saying, and encode the meaning in your memory?

What controls the flow of thought? How is it that we can learn new concepts and propositions and retrieve what we have learned later when these memories are needed? How do we make inferences from presented or retrieved information, solve problems, and create new ideas? Answering all these questions and many more like them is what cognition is all about.

OVERVIEW OF COGNITIVE PSYCHOLOGY

What do you wish to learn from reading this book? I hope your answer was something equivalent to "to acquire an understanding of cognitive psychology." What do you think such an understanding would consist of? The question itself suggests the first part of the answer. Understanding any topic means *analyzing* the whole topic into parts and then *synthesizing* the whole from the parts by explicitly encoding a rich set of relations among the parts and between each part and the whole. Deeper understanding of a topic is achieved by further constituent analysis of each major part into its parts (constituents) accompanied by synthesis of the relations among the parts, and so on for as long as seems possible and worthwhile. One need not start at the top in this hierarchy of understanding. One could start anywhere in the hierarchy to construct a network of concepts and relations for understanding a topic. However, the beautiful Witch of the North was right—"It's always best to start at the beginning"—whether the road is paved with yellow brick or only good intentions.

A good beginning in this case is the analysis of all of psychology into parts, of which cognitive psychology is one. Psychology may first be subdivided into applied and theoretical psychology. Applied psychology is concerned with the practical use of psychology by individuals and society. It includes such areas as clinical, counseling, industrial, engineering, environmental, and educational psychology. Theoretical psychology is concerned with the basic principles of how the mind controls behavior. It includes such areas as perception, learning and memory, thinking, psycholinguistics, and cognitive, physiological, comparative, developmental, social, and personality psychology. Cognitive psychology is a relative newcomer to this list. It overlaps extensively with perception, learning and memory, thinking, and psycholinguistics, being essentially a synthesis of the principles common to all four areas of what has been called "experimental psychology." Experimental psychology is now a rather poor name for these four areas, since other areas of psychology are also experimental to varying degrees. And experimental psychology should not, and does not, exclude either nonexperimental *observations* of behavior or *theories* of how the mind controls behavior. Many people are coming to consider *cognitive psychology* a more apt name for all of the fields included in experimental psychology. To other people, cognitive psychology means the study of only the "higher" mental processes, namely, thinking and language. This latter, more specific meaning is losing ground to the former, more inclusive meaning, because we are discovering that all areas of cognitive psychology share many common theoretical principles.

Cognitive psychology was born out of a desire to synthesize all of "experimental" psychology under a common set of concepts and principles. However, a fruitful synthesis begins first with analysis, so how can we break up cognitive psychology into more manageable parts? Of course, one way is the traditional division among various *functions* of the mind: perception, learning and memory, language (speech and reading), and thinking. This book tends to cover these functions in the order given, but the final organization reflects a compromise between this functional analysis and two somewhat newer analyses. The first of these is based on cognitive modality and levels of processing. The second is based on the distinction between coding and processes.

Cognitive *modalities* may be visual, auditory, sensory-motor, or verbal. Each modality has several levels of processing. The earliest sensory levels (e.g., the retina of the eye and several levels of the visual nervous system beyond the retina) are common to several modalities (e.g., the nonverbal visual-image, sensory-motor, and verbal modalities). Figure 1.1 illustrates one plausible (but not proved) analysis of several levels of processing that analyze sensory input from the eye and control motor output to the hand (both in writing verbal symbols and in drawing or grasping objects). Of course, many levels of many modalities have been left out of figure 1.1, but there are enough left to make all the points I wish to make here. First, there is a strong vertical, hierarchical organization to the mind—hence the term *levels*. Second, there are three basic types of levels: sensory (which only receive upward input and only produce upward output), motor (which only receive downward input and only produce downward output), and cognitive (which receive and produce both upward and downward input and output). Sensory levels represent stimuli; motor levels represent responses; cognitive levels attempt to represent the world. In between S(timulus) and R(esponse) for human beings is an abstract cognitive model of the world that is neither purely sensory nor purely motor in its function. Third, the modalities (integrated sets of levels) are all headed (topped) by an abstract cognitive level. The verbal graphic modality that allows us to read and write letters and words includes the cognitive sensory-motor segment level (which represents lines and angles) and also every sensory and motor level below the cognitive segment level. The nonverbal image and spatial modalities that allow us to perceive and draw pictures of familiar objects and to find our way around town also contain the sensory-motor segment level and the visual and motor feature levels below it.

The distinction between *coding* and *process* is somewhat analogous to the distinction between statics and dynamics in physics or between structure (anatomy) and function (physiology) in biology. You know what a *code* is. If I write a word, substituting for each letter the next letter in the alphabet (so that "code," for example, would be written "dpef"), that's a (very simple) code. A code is a system for representing ideas or concepts. The term *code* is commonly used to mean a private system for representing ideas that insiders use so that outsiders won't be able to understand them—unless they can "break the code" (figure out the system). Cognitive psychologists and information scientists in general use the term *code* more generally to mean any system for representing ideas (including concepts, propositions, images, events, and so forth). The English language is a code for representing ideas. To the extent that you know English vocabulary words (know what concepts the words represent), and understand the rules of grammar (syntax) by which words are combined into sentences to represent propositions, you understand messages written or spoken in the English code.

Mental (cognitive) *processes* are concerned with how we *learn* these mental codes in the first place, how we *remember* them (store them in our memories), and how we *use* them in perception, thought, and action (includ-

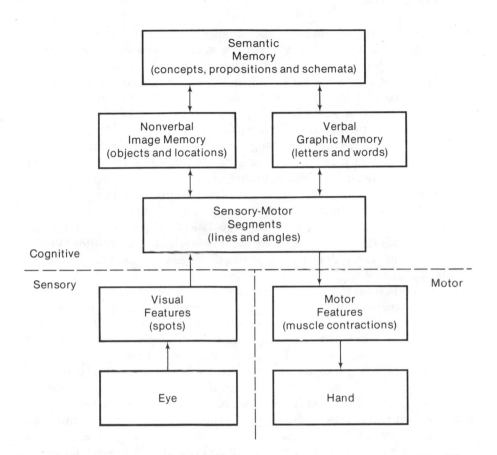

Fig. 1.1 Flowchart of some sensory, motor, and cognitive levels of mental processing that analyze input from the eye and control output to the hand.

ing the act of communicating to others). Psychologists have esoteric names for these three types of processes, namely, *acquisition, storage,* and *retrieval* of memories. Not all mental coding is learned. Coding at lower sensory and motor levels is largely innate, modifiable by experience only in very special and limited ways. Coding at higher cognitive levels is almost certainly largely learned, but the innate nature of the human mind constrains it to follow certain principles.

Learning and memory are important parts of cognitive psychology, but its primary focus is on the usage processes. Usage includes memory retrieval in elementary *recall* and *recognition,* but it also includes the activation of innate codes at lower sensory and motor levels in *perception* and *motor response* and the activation of cognitive codes in complex sequences characteristic of *language and thinking.* One of the goals of cognitive psychology is to formulate general principles concerning cognitive processes that are true at all levels and modalities of processing. This book will organize current knowledge of *usage* processes in terms of three basic types of processes. The first type is *activation* of codes (in perception, attention, recognition, memory, recall, inference, understanding, thinking, and speaking). The second type is *priming* of codes (partial activation as in positive attentional set and short-term memory—the unconscious penumbra of thought). The third type of process is *inhibition* of codes (as in negation, contradiction, and negative attentional set). Learning, memory, activation, priming, and inhibition may not turn out to be the ideal typology of cognitive processes, but this five-process typology serves to integrate current understanding of a wide range of phenomena in cognitive psychology, and therefore it is highly useful. The study of mental *coding* is concerned with the objects of thought: the nature of representation in the mind. Coding refers to the "language" we use to perceive and remember (think about) our experience in various levels and modalities. Verbal language is one such coding modality, visual imagery is another, and musical coding is still another.

The book is organized as follows: chapters 2, 3, and 4 are concerned with nonverbal visual and auditory perception, imagery, and spatial cognition. The remaining chapters focus primarily on the coding and processing of verbal symbols. This focus is not exclusive; some nonverbal processing is included in chapters 6 through 9, which are concerned with general principles of higher-level coding and cognitive processes. Chapter 5 integrates coding and process to discuss the functions of speech recognition, speech articulation, and reading. This discussion focuses on lower featural and segmental levels but pays some attention to the role of higher-level semantic (meaningful) memory. Chapters 6 and 7 are concerned with the general cognitive processes of attention and short-term memory. Chapters 8 and 9 present the basic principles of *associative memory* as a theory of higher mental coding and discuss long-term memory processes of learning, storage (consolidation and forgetting), and retrieval (recall and recognition memory). They offer empirical support drawn primarily from studies of verbal learning and memory but also from studies of image memory. Semantic memory is discussed in the last three chapters. Chapter 10 is concerned with coding; chapter 11 is concerned with the acquisition, retrieval, and understanding processes; and chapter 12 is concerned with thinking, including basic semantic inferences, more complex processing plans, problem solving, and creativity. The result, I hope, provides a proper balance between analytic simplicity and synthetic adequacy.

CODING

A mental code is a system for representing thoughts of any kind (e.g., ideas, percepts, images, features, segments, responses, concepts, propositions, schemata). Can you think of some system for representing thoughts? Pretty general question, isn't it? It's hard to get a grip on it. Well, how do you represent anything—for instance the concept *cat?* You speak a specific word or write a specific word or draw a specific diagram. You use some specific symbol or element to stand for *cat* that is different from all the other specific elements you use to represent other concepts. It is the same way with the mind. There must be a specific element in the mind that represents any thought we can think of, and it must be different from the element that stands for any other thought. The term *node* has been chosen to stand for the specific element in the mind that represents a thought (Quillian 1967, 1968, 1969; Rumelhart, Lindsay, and Norman 1972; Anderson and Bower 1973). We are sometimes consciously thinking about a given idea and sometimes not. The node representing that idea must therefore have at least two potential states: it can be *activated* (during conscious thinking) and *not activated.* Actually, it appears more consistent with the facts to assume various degrees of activation for a node. Thus we may be *primed* (set, prepared) to perceive or think of some concepts more than other concepts that are not currently at the focus of conscious thought. Primed concepts (partially activated nodes) constitute our subconscious thoughts.*

One thought tends to activate other thoughts—hence the need to assume associations among the nodes. When one node is associated to another node, activation of the first node tends to activate the second node after some brief delay (Rashevsky 1938; McCulloch and Pitts 1943; Quillian 1967, 1968, 1969; Anderson and Bower 1973; Collins and Loftus 1975; Anderson 1976). Thus nodes represent thoughts, and associations represent the connections that account for the flow of thought. Actually, there are a number of different conceptions of networks. These conceptions seek to answer two questions: (1) whether a single thought is represented by a single node or by a set of nodes and (2) whether associations between nodes differ only in strength or represent several qualitatively different kinds of relations between the concept nodes they link. We shall largely ignore these complex issues in this book, because for almost all of the topics we shall discuss it is sufficient to use a fairly simple network model of the mind in which nodes represent thoughts, and three types of associations represent the flow of thought. Relations are thoughts and can always be represented as nodes; you do not need to represent relations by many different types of links (that is, by qualitatively different types of associations) (Anderson and Bower 1973, pp. 88–90).

However, there are two distinctions, which define three types of associations, that the student must understand. This holds true even if it should turn out that, physiologically, there is really only one basic type of link

---

*At this stage in our understanding of the neural mechanisms of cognition, it is easiest to think of psychological nodes as single neurons. However, this hypothesis is by no means established, nor is it necessarily the most plausible. A node may be a single neuron, a small system of neurons, or a pattern of firing in a large system of neurons.

between nodes. First, there is the distinction between *horizontal* and *vertical association.* Horizontal association is the time-honored conception of associative memory that has been around at least since Aristotle. Vertical association is a new idea, parts of which were developed by a number of psychologists. This idea began with the most famous paper ever written in cognitive psychology—George Miller's paper on chunking—and has continued with research on semantic memory over the last decade or so (Miller 1956; Wickelgren 1969*c*, 1976*d*, 1977*b*; Estes 1972; Anderson and Bower 1973). As is often the case, an example provides the best initial explanation of the difference between horizontal and vertical associations. Figure 1.2 illustrates the encoding of the proposition *Del Jager can't swim* both by horizontal associations between nodes and by vertical associations between nodes.

In a horizontal associative memory, the concept node for *Del Jager* is directly associated to the concept node for *can't swim,* and vice versa. No new nodes are formed. In a vertical associative memory, the learning process associates both *Del Jager* and *can't swim* to a new (previously undefined) node that now represents the entire proposition *Del Jager can't swim.* The critical difference between the two conceptions of associative memory is that according to the vertical theory the memory possesses Miller's chunking type of learning, while according to the horizontal theory it does not. Chunking requires a large pool of genetically unspecified (free) nodes that come to represent some new thought (concept, proposition, image, or whatever) as a result of learning. Since a vertical associative memory does also establish a chain of links in both directions from *Del Jager* to and from *can't swim,* it can do everything a horizontal associative memory can do and more. A vertical associative memory is thus more powerful than a horizontal associative memory, and there is strong evidence to indicate that humans do have this more powerful kind of memory.

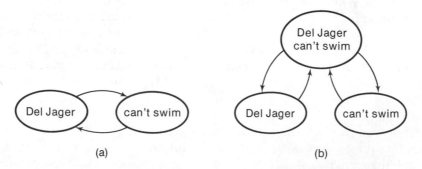

(a) (b)

Fig. 1.2   Encoding of the proposition *Del Jager can't swim* according to a nonhierarchical (horizontal) associative theory in (a) and a hierarchical (vertical) associative theory in (b). In both cases it is assumed that there are both forward and backward associations between the two constituents.

In some cases we shall talk about associations between two nodes as if these were direct horizontal associations. We do so because it is not relevant to the phenomenon in question whether or not there is any indirect vertical mediation of these associations. In fact, all that is really established is that we have the more powerful vertical associative memory. Whether there are also direct horizontal associations in our vertical associative memory or whether all apparently horizontal associations are indirectly mediated by vertical associations is not known at present.

The second important distinction between types of associations concerns *upward* vs. *downward* direction in a vertical associative memory. Horizontal associations are often assumed to be symmetrical *occurred-with* relations between nodes. In figure 1.2(a) the horizontal associations between the nodes *Del Jager* and *can't swim* represent the fact that these concepts *occurred with* each other in the same proposition. Vertically *upward* associations from the *constituent* nodes (e.g., *Del Jager* and *can't swim*) to the chunk node (e.g., *Del Jager can't swim*) are logically *is-a-constituent-of* relations, while the vertically *downward* associations from the chunk to the constituents are *has-as-a-constituent* relations. Thus the concept node for *Del Jager* is a constituent of the proposition node for *Del Jager can't swim,* and the upward association represents this relation. In the reverse direction, the downward association represents the fact that the proposition node for *Del Jager can't swim* has as a constituent the node for the concept *Del Jager.* Think about these distinctions in relation to the example and get the notion clearly in your head that concepts (represented in verbal language by words or phrases) are constituents of propositions (often represented in verbal language by sentences). The concept node for *Del Jager* simply means "whatever thing in the mind is activated when we think of this person Del Jager." It's called a concept node (rather than a word node) because we are referring to the Del Jager node that can be activated by any of various Del Jager signs: his name as written or spoken words, the sound of his voice, the sight of his face from the front, the sight of the back of his head, and so on.

In chapter 8 we will consider evidence supporting both the (hierarchical) vertical associative theory of coding and the theory that much learning consists of the formation of associations to new *chunk nodes* that represent the *combination* of the concepts to be associated in a unitary proposition or image. For now it suffices to cite two arguments in favor of this vertical associative theory.

First, the hierarchical associative theory of learning results in the same sort of associations at higher cognitive levels as those found in the more peripheral levels of sensory and motor modalities, which are largely specified genetically. Both innate and learned associations are logical *constituency relations* in the hierarchical (vertical) associative theory, whereas learned associations in the nonhierarchical (horizontal) associative theory are *occurred-with* relations.

Second, the vertical associative theory permits easy encoding of embedded propositions (where one proposition is a constituent of a higher-order proposition), such as *Peter knows that Del Jager can't swim.* The encoding of such embedded propositions is by specification of higher-order nodes, as illustrated in figure 1.3(b). Merely forming new horizontal *(occurred-with)* associations between the conceptual elements of this sentence, as illustrated in figure 1.3(a), fails to represent its syntactic (grammatical) structure. Failure

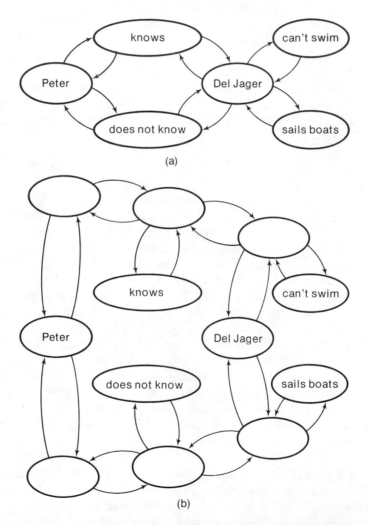

Fig. 1.3 Nonhierarchical associative theory illustrated in (a) with equal opportunity for retrieving false and true propositions. Hierarchical associative theory illustrated in (b) with new nodes specified to provide separate representation of each true proposition and avoid associative interference.

to encode in memory the syntactic structure of a proposition results in disastrous *associative interference.* For example, suppose it is also true that Del Jager sails boats, but Peter does not know that. With a vertical associative theory, you can encode both propositions *Peter knows Del Jager can't swim* and *Peter does not know Del Jager sails boats* in your memory by specifying new propositional nodes for each. With a horizontal associative memory, you would have *Del Jager* associated to both *can't swim* and *sails boats,* but you would have no way to differentiate those facts Peter knows from those he does not know. See figure 1.3(a). Since human beings can keep facts such as these differentiated in their memories, it seems very likely that our memories are of the vertical type, though, as was discussed earlier, one can also have horizontal associations in a vertical associative memory. For both pedagogical and theoretical simplicity, we shall assume three kinds of associations in this book: upward, downward, and horizontal.

COGNITIVE PROCESSES

Your nervous system is constantly doing things—perceiving stimuli inside and outside your body, controlling internal and external responses, and thinking long and short thoughts that may be only indirectly tied to present stimuli or responses. If we are to understand the cognitive processes that account for all this mental activity, we must first do—what? I hope you said something equivalent to "analyzing cognitive processes (or mental processing or the dynamics of thought) into parts." One of the commonest methods of analysis is subdivision into types (classes, categories, or whatever). Ideally, such a classification is *mutually exclusive* (e.g., there is no overlap between different types of cognitive processes) and *exhaustive* (e.g., no cognitive processes are left out). This ideal may be pretty hard to achieve in the beginning, so let's start with any typology that gets you going. Stop reading and think a bit about what sort of classification you could impose on cognitive processes. What are the basic types of cognitive processes?

I hope you did stop and think a bit about this question and that you will often take time out to think about what you are reading. Asking and answering questions actively while you are reading is critical to understanding any area of science. If you read passively, trying to memorize the words on the page or letting understanding be something that "just happens" when you read, you are wasting your time. Try to anticipate what's going to be said next in a text or in class. Keep on asking and answering your own self-posed questions as you read or listen. Ask "stupid" questions (they're often not so stupid) or hopelessly vague, general questions, if you can't think of questions that precisely delineate what you want to know. You can learn to ask good questions, but you must practice a lot if you want to improve— just as with any skill.

After all that, I hope you did generate a list of cognitive processes. It doesn't matter too much how well your list agrees with mine. Just having generated your own basic typology of cognitive processes will considerably deepen your understanding of the typology used in this book—and maybe one of you will come up with a creative idea that will one day force a major change in the way we think about cognitive processes. My list is as follows: learning; memory (consolidation and forgetting); activation (perception, retrieval, and thinking, including attentional limits on these processes); priming (partial activation in attentional set and short-term memory); and inhibition (negation, contradiction, and negative attentional set in perception, memory retrieval, and thinking). All these terms probably have some meaning for you from your common knowledge and your courses in introductory psychology, but they will acquire considerably more meaning as you read this book. For now I will say just a little about each type of cognitive process.

Learning

Learning is the process by which associations between nodes get strengthened. It includes the chunking process. In the chunking process a new (free, unspecified) node that previously had no strong associations to (or from) other nodes comes to have strong associations to and from some combination of constituent nodes. By virtue of these newly formed associations, the chunk node now represents the combined constituent nodes. To be physiologically reasonable, we assume that the associations between all nodes exist anatomically prior to learning, but that they are very weak. Learning strengthens them.

Memory Storage

Learned associations must persist in strengthened form to have any later effect on mental functioning. The evidence indicates that the learning process is followed by a *consolidation process* that decreases the susceptibility of long-term memory traces to decay. The *decay process* decreases the strength of unused associations as a function of time, though this decay probably occurs as a result of general neural activity, since it appears to vary with level of arousal. There is also an *interference process* that decreases the strength of association from node A to node B as a result of learning a new association to node A. Thus, while our hierarchical associative memories have the ability to encode a multiplicity of propositions involving the same concepts without disastrous associative interference, there is apparently some limit on this capacity. Learning new associations to a concept does appear to weaken slightly the strength of previously learned associations, unless the prior associations are reviewed (rehearsed). This permits us to maintain frequently used (retrieved) associations to a node while gradually eliminating unused associations. If a node has limited (though probably fairly large) connective capacity, forgetting (whether due to decay or interference) would appear to be functional. Furthermore, to the extent that we are limited in the number of associations we can think of at one time, weakening unused associations by the interference process facilitates fast retrieval of frequently used associations.

Activation

How do we use the system of strengthened associations that we have acquired and stored? We use it in several basic ways, all of which make use of the *activation* process. Nodes can be considered to have various degrees of activation, just as neurons have various rates of firing.

Perception. Some nodes are relatively directly connected to sensory input from the external world. Nodes in the most peripheral levels of sensory modalities probably can only be activated by appropriate external stimuli and not by internal thoughts. That is, these receptor nodes may have no central associative input. The analysis of sensory events proceeds through a number of levels. At the lowest levels, the connections between nodes are considered to be primarily *upward* (from lower-level to upper-level nodes) or *lateral* (among nodes at the same level). There are few or no *downward* connections (from nodes at higher levels to nodes at lower levels). At somewhat higher levels of perceptual analysis, it is likely that nodes receive downward activation from nodes representing higher-level *expectations;* they also receive upward and lateral activation from stimuli.

Top-down processing derived from expectations based on prior context plays an extensive role in perception. To a large extent we see and hear what we expect to see and hear. I experienced a vivid demonstration of this fact about a month ago. I was staying in a motel that had rooms 1–10 along one hall and 11–20 along another hall. I was in room 17. I turned into what I thought was the correct hall; then, rather absentmindedly, I glanced at a room number as I passed it. "Room 4?! Oh good grief, I'm in the wrong hall." By this time I was passing what I perceived as rooms 5 and 6. "Wrong hall all right. But I'm sure I took the correct turn—very confusing!" I looked more closely at the next room number—17! "That's my room; I *am* in the right hall. What's going on?" I went back to check the prior room numbers—and found that they were 16 and 15 (not 6 and 5 as I had perceived them at the time), but then came 14 with the 1 missing. Seeing this had created so strong an expectation of being in the wrong hall that I had misperceived the next two room numbers. Only when I asked myself how I could possibly have made this mistake did I finally perceive my own room number correctly. It's the same way with hearing. People make speech errors (slips of the tongue) rather frequently, but we generally fail to notice such errors unless we are explicitly listening for them. I was totally unaware of the fact that my six-year-old son rarely pronounced the /r/ sound at all adequately until his mother and a speech therapist pointed it out to me. I processed his speech for meaning and had simply not noticed a major speech defect over thousands of hours of listening to him talk! Our meaningful (semantic) expectations bias our perception so that we see or hear what we expect (what makes sense) on the basis of the context. If an umpire at the start of a baseball game yelled, "Blay pawl," I very much doubt whether anyone would notice, but if someone said "blay" to you in an experiment on nonsense syllable recognition, you would probably perceive it as "blay," not "play."

We are able to have expectations only because we have coded a present stimulus as similar to previously encountered stimuli that we have stored in our memory. When we recognize a stimulus as familiar, we are using our previously stored memory to encode the present stimulus. When we generate an expectation regarding the next stimulus to be perceived after "Mary had a little—," for instance, we are recalling from our memory. Memory retrieval (recognition and recall) plays an extremely important role in perception. Indeed, memory retrieval is an essential part of all adult perception.

Retrieval.   The memory retrieval process includes more than *recognizing* the incoming stimulus in the sense of mapping it onto some portion of the node structure in memory. It also frequently includes *recalling* portions of the node structure that represent elements not present in the test stimulus but strongly associated to the test stimulus as a result of prior learning. Recognizing *Del Jager* in figure 1.2(b) involves vertically upward activation of the *Del Jager* concept node through all lower-level word and letter nodes and possibly some downward feedback activation through this same nodal hierarchy. But it need not (though it may sometimes) involve upward activation of the proposition node *Del Jager can't swim,* or downward activation from the proposition node to the *can't swim* predicate constituent. Recall of the predicate *can't swim* to the subject cue *Del Jager* obviously requires this additional memory retrieval. Recall is activation due to purely central (downward) associative input. It lacks the peripheral sensory source of activation (to the nodes being recalled) that is present to support recognition memory. However, it is parsimonious to assume that the same basic memory retrieval (activation) process is the basis of both recognition and recall.

Thinking.   Thinking takes place in those parts of the mind that are concerned with perception and memory. Complex thinking, decision making, and problem solving are sequences of elementary acts of memory retrieval, inference, and decision. They are not thought to involve any basically different types of processes. Nevertheless, some new principles are relevant to this more complex and temporally extended area of human cognitive functioning.

These principles are discussed in chapters 3, 11, and 12. The boundary line between elementary cognitive processes and sequences of elementary processes is unclear. Some of the *inferences* we make in understanding a sentence may be either elementary acts of memory retrieval or basic processes in and of themselves, distinct from the retrieval of directly stored information. Other inferences require a complex sequence of elementary inferential processes. One of the important unsolved problems in cognitive psychology is to develop a viable theory of basic inference processes and other cognitive operations, such as those which allow us to manipulate mental images in our heads.

Attention.   One process that cognitive psychology has focused on recently is attention. There appear to be limits to our capacity to process many pieces of information simultaneously—whether in perception, retrieval, or thinking. The field of attention is concerned with learning the nature of these limitations. If the same basic activation process underlies perception, recognition memory, recall, and thinking, it is reasonable to expect that the same principles of limited attentional capacity will apply to all these subdivisions of cognitive processing. To the extent that we find basic differences among these processes, we might expect to find different limitations on attentional capacity.

Priming

Short-term memory.   It takes time to retrieve a memory: to activate selectively those nodes that are associated to previously activated nodes. Even when no new long-term associative learning takes place, the state of a memory trace must be different after it has been retrieved (activated). Otherwise there would be no point in having a retrieval process; no time would be required for retrieval; and we would be thinking all our thoughts at once. Retrieval is the process by which an inactive, stored association is converted into an active, retrieved association. Once an association is in the retrieved state, it can be maintained in that state virtually indefinitely by rehearsal (subject to boredom and fatigue factors). For example, I might ask you to retrieve a predicate about *Del Jager* (e.g., that he *can't swim*), but withhold your response until I gave some auxiliary signal. You would require perhaps one second to initiate your response if I signaled you to respond immediately. However, once you had retrieved *can't swim* (in about one second), you could delay your response for two, five, ten seconds or whatever, and then initiate your response in perhaps half a second after I gave the signal to respond. This is the *priming effect* in memory retrieval.

There is evidence to indicate that a retrieved (primed) association does not instantly return to the stored (unprimed) state as soon as one stops thinking about it and begins thinking about something else. Under some conditions, the priming consequences of prior activation may persist for a second or longer. During this time, a primed association can be retrieved faster than an unprimed association. It is parsimonious to assume that this priming trace is identical to what has been called *short-term memory* for recently presented information, such as immediate memory span for a telephone number. The real issue is whether the short-term memory trace established by perception, or learning, or both is the same as the short-term memory trace established by retrieval. We will assume that it is, since there is no evidence to suggest that it is not. Chapter 7 will discuss short-term memory, and chapter 9 will discuss priming effects on retrieval.

Attentional set.   Chapter 6 will discuss attentional set. Attentional set is the ability to prepare oneself for a particular class of stimuli, such as sounds coming from a certain direction, visual stimuli falling on a particular part of the retina, words belonging to a particular conceptual category or associated to previously presented material, and so on. Attentional set speeds up *reaction times* to stimuli falling within the expected set and often retards responses to unexpected stimuli. It is still unclear whether attentional set affects the *accuracy* of perception as well as the reaction time.

One theory holds that attentional set results from short-term memory (priming) traces established by the prior activation of sets of nodes and associations in the connection network that correspond to the set of expected stimuli. According to this theory, attentional set is the activation of a higher-order node in memory that has downward associations to those portions of the network structure that are appropriate for recognizing stimuli in the expected set. Activation of this node partially activates, and therefore primes, all of the (lower-order) nodes to which it is associated. This facilitates all activation (perception, memory retrieval, and thinking) within the primed set. It may also inhibit processing in some portions of memory outside the primed set.

Inhibition

The nervous system is known to contain both excitatory and inhibitory connections between neurons. In chapters 2 and 4 we will review some of the known neural evidence and plausible hypotheses concerning the role of inhibition in visual and auditory perception. In these and other chapters we will consider what little psychological evidence and speculation there is concerning the possible role of inhibition in perception, attention, memory retrieval, and thinking. How, for example, are we able to focus attention on certain thoughts and away from other thoughts? One plausible hypothesis is that the most strongly activated nodes, representing the thoughts at the focus of attention, inhibit all other thoughts. It is also plausible to hypothesize that inhibition plays an important role in negative attentional set—as when I couldn't see the 1 digit in room numbers 15 and 16. Finally, it seems reasonable to guess that inhibition plays a role in negation and contradiction in thinking. Chicago is not in Pennsylvania, because Chicago is in Illinois and being in Illinois implies not being in Pennsylvania. There isn't much direct psychological evidence for most of these speculations. However, we know for an absolute certainty that inhibition occurs throughout the nervous system, so it is hiding one's head in the sand to ignore its probable role in virtually all cognitive processing. Therefore, despite the wildly speculative character of all psychological hypotheses concerning inhibition, I have bent over backwards to include a discussion of its possible role wherever anyone has made reasonable suggestions.

COGNITIVE MODALITIES

Earlier in the chapter we defined a *modality* as a system of codes that operate at several levels in a hierarchy. That's fine as far as it goes. But now let's examine (1) the precise definition of the modality concept in general and the principal cognitive modalities humans are alleged to possess; (2) the neuroanatomical localization of these modalities; and (3) some possible psychological reasons why the mind is subdivided into modalities.

Modality Defined

The visual modality could be defined as all the nodes in the mind (or neurons in the brain) that can be activated by visual input. I will use a less inclusive definition. I define the visual modality as that set of nodes that can *only* be activated by visual input. This may limit the visual modality to the lower levels of visual featural analysis (spots and lines). It certainly excludes concept and proposition nodes from the visual modality, even if these nodes are activated by reading. And it probably excludes nodes representing forms and words, if these nodes can also be activated by tactile or auditory input for example. If there are purely visual word nodes that feed into a higher, more abstract word node, then the purely visual word nodes are of course part of the visual modality.

If upward and downward associations are profoundly different, and if some visual nodes receive downward *expectation* or *imaging* input from abstract concept nodes, one might nonetheless still want to classify them as part of the visual modality. Ideally, the visual modality might be defined as all nodes whose upward input comes only from visual stimulation. I will adopt that definition in this book and leave the extent of downward expectational input as an important open question.

However, to think clearly, we must use more abstract terms—such as semantic, verbal, spatial, and imagery modalities—to refer to our systems of encoding propositions, concepts, words, cognitive maps, and so on. The nodes in these modalities integrate information from a variety of sensory modalities. The knowledge encoded in these cognitive modalities is about the world in general, not just the visual world alone, or the auditory world, or the kinesthetic world. Indeed, one of the major functions of a cognitive modality is to integrate information from different sensory modalities. For one thing, such integration can aid perceptual recognition, as when we watch someone's lips while listening to him speak. Conversely, when these two sources of information—visual and auditory—are out of synchronization, as in a dubbed movie, we may have trouble recognizing what is being said, even though audition is clearly the dominant input modality in understanding speech. These cognitive modalities also serve to direct actions and to store knowledge acquired through the senses and otherwise—for example, by inferential reasoning. We will briefly treat the basic principles of the visual and auditory sensory modalities at the beginnings of chapters 2 and 4. We will then give primary consideration to the coding and processes that characterize the abstract cognitive modalities.

What are these abstract cognitive modalities? No one knows, but certain distinctions have proved useful. These distinctions will be used in this book to subdivide the mind into more manageable parts. They are the spatial (location, cognitive map) modality; the imagery (form, object) modality; the music modality; the verbal phonetic and graphic modalities; and the verbal semantic modality. The spatial and imagery modalities are discussed in chapter 3. The music modality is discussed in chapter 4. The phonetic and graphic modalities are discussed in chapters 5 and 7, and the semantic modality is discussed in chapters 10, 11, and 12.

The *spatial modality* is concerned with knowledge concerning locations and their relations one to another; this knowledge is stored in *cognitive maps* of various parts of the world. The *imagery modality* is concerned with representing *what* rather than *where.* Images of complex scenes are encoded as objects in various relations to one another, and images of objects are encoded as forms in various relations to one another. There is some evidence to support the distinction between these two modalities, but it is far from definitive.

The final nonverbal modality is *music.* As we shall see, music is neuroanatomically classed with the other nonverbal modalities. But since it appears to have little psychological association with the other nonverbal modalities, it seems safest to consider music as a separate modality.

The structural levels of the *verbal modality* are the *phonetic modality,* which encodes spoken language, and the *graphic modality,* which encodes written language. The phonetic modality must receive upward input from auditory feature nodes and provide downward output to articulatory (speech motor) nodes. The phonetic modality itself may have abstract (both sensory and motor) feature nodes. It must have some type of abstract segmental nodes —for example, for phonemes, allophones (variants of phonemes), or syllables. Likewise, the graphic system is presumed to receive upward input from vision and to provide downward output to control the writing motor modality. The phonetic and graphic modalities may be extensively interconnected; thus people who read by subvocalizing, for example, make extensive use of the graphic-to-phonetic associations. The phonetic and graphic modalities must have direct or indirect associations to the *semantic* (memory) *modality*.

Semantic memory is often considered a verbal modality. It is seen as being connected to the phonetic and graphic modalities, but also as being extensively interconnected with the nonverbal spatial and imagery modalities. It is probably equally reasonable to view semantic memory as the highest-level, most abstract, cognitive modality, which integrates the verbal and nonverbal strands that are separate at lower levels. For present purposes, it doesn't matter which way you look at it. However, it is clear that the brain has an anatomical differentiation between verbal and nonverbal modalities. In most humans the verbal modalities are located in the left hemisphere and the spatial and imagery modalities in the right hemisphere. (The hemispheric localization of the musical modality is controversial.) This neuroanatomical differentiation between verbal and nonverbal modalities is the subject of the next section.

Neuroanatomical Localization

The human cerebral cortex is divided into left and right hemispheres. Presumably, both hemispheres normally function cooperatively in human thinking. However, we now know that the two hemispheres are not equivalent. Each has its own capacities and deficiencies. When the communication channel between the two hemispheres, the corpus collosum, is absent due to surgery or genetic abnormality, each hemisphere can process information independently of the other. Like cases of multiple personality, such *split-brain* patients demonstrate dual consciousness—it's as if two minds were housed in the same skull. Unlike cases of multiple personality, a split-brain patient has two simultaneously conscious "personalities"—each capable of controlling his behavior. On occasion, the two hemispheres of a split-brain patient may disagree. If the right hand, which is controlled by the left hemisphere, makes a choice that the right hemisphere thinks is inappropriate, the right hemisphere may direct the left hand to slap the right hand.

In nearly all right-handed individuals (and many left-handers as well), the left hemisphere is specialized for verbal cognition and memory, including language and most areas of mathematics. The right hemisphere is specialized for nonverbal cognition and memory, including spatial relations and imagery, but also music and other nonverbal sounds. Each hemisphere receives input from the visual, auditory, kinesthetic, and tactile sensory modalities and provides motor output to all the muscles of the body. There are some differences between the hemispheres in sensory input and motor output. For example, the left hemisphere receives visual stimuli only from the right visual field, and the right hemisphere receives information only from the left visual field. However, the differences between the hemispheres are not to be understood in terms of sensory or motor specializations. Rather, they are abstractly cognitive—that is, they relate to the type of information that is represented and the way it is represented, rather than to the input or output channels. Most verbal and mathematical intelligence tests tend to assess the capacities of the left hemisphere. By contrast, spatial relations tests tend to assess right-hemisphere functions. Spatial relations tests have virtually zero correlation with verbal and mathematical aptitude tests.

The evidence for hemisphere specialization comes from four basic sources. The first source is split-brain patients. The second source is lesions —surgical or accidental removals of part or all of one hemisphere. The third source is temporary (reversible) impairments of one hemisphere. These may be caused by unilateral administration of electroconvulsive shock or by unilateral drugging of one hemisphere. The fourth source is differences in the speed of processing material presented to each ear or visual field. The studies of ear and field differences in normal subjects generally support the conclusions derived from the first three sources; however, they are more complex to interpret (Kimura 1973). Hence we shall concentrate on studies of split-brain patients and permanently or reversibly lesioned patients.

Split brains. Split-brain patients lack cortical communication between the two hemispheres because the neural pathway that normally connects them (the corpus collosum) has been severed. Because sensory information from the right half of the visual field and from the right hand goes exclusively to the left hemisphere, while material presented to the left field and hand goes to the right hemisphere, it is possible to present a task for processing by a particular hemisphere, without help from the other, in split-brain patients. Thus one can investigate the cognitive capabilities of each hemisphere separately.*

The results of such studies (on right-handed subjects) show that the left hemisphere has an essentially normal capacity to produce and comprehend language. The right hemisphere generally cannot speak or write, though in some subjects it may be able to produce a few digits, letters, and simple words. However, the right hemisphere can match spoken words or visually presented words or objects to objects touched with the left hand. Thus the right hemisphere is able to associate single, concrete, spoken or written nouns with the objects they represent. The evidence is less clear that the right

*The results discussed in this section come from Gazzaniga 1970; Nebes 1974; Sperry 1968; and Teng and Sperry 1973.

hemisphere associates concrete verbs with the actions they represent, but it probably can do this. Right hemisphere comprehension of language also includes the ability to pick up the correct object upon hearing a phrase describing the properties or use of the object. For example, it can choose a coin from the property description "round, thin object made of metal," or a magnifying glass from the use description "makes things look bigger." However, only the left hemisphere can comprehend propositions that are at all complex. The right hemisphere can distinguish between positive and negative statements, but not between active and passive voice, present and future tense, or singular and plural.

The left hemisphere has a normal capacity to perform arithmetic operations; it can add, subtract, multiply, and divide. It probably has a normal capacity to solve most of the more complicated mathematical problems as well. In some subjects the right hemisphere is able to add or multiply two single digits whose sum or product is less than twenty. The right hemisphere is superior to the left on spatial relations tests, on recognizing part-whole relationships in forms, on recognizing faces, on reconstructing jigsaw puzzles, and the like.

Lesions. Individuals who suffer brain damage primarily to the left hemisphere exhibit deficits in verbal cognition and memory. Right hemisphere damage produces deficits in nonverbal imagery and in spatial cognition and memory. It has been known for a long time that lesions in particular locations in the left hemisphere typically produce expressive or comprehension *aphasia* (inability to produce or understand speech), *alexia* (inability to read), and *agraphia* (inability to write). More recently it has been demonstrated that lesions of the right hemisphere produce deficits in perceptual matching and memory for nonsense forms, textures, complex geometric designs, faces, mazes, maps, and places. Left hemisphere lesions generally leave such faculties unimpaired. There is even some support for a distinction between an imagery modality for representing objects, forms, faces, and so on (the *what* system) and a spatial modality for representing locations, cognitive maps, and so on (the *where* system). This distinction would seem to be justified, since there tends to be a zero or even negative correlation between these two classes of deficits across different right hemisphere lesions (Penfield and Roberts 1959; Luria 1970; Milner 1971, 1973; Newcombe and Russell 1969; Warrington and James 1967).*

Over a period of time following injury to the left or right hemisphere, there is often some recovery of function. This recovery of function is most marked in young children, in whom the functional specialization is thought to be at an early stage of development. Infants with complete decortication of either the left or right cerebral hemisphere develop both verbal and non-

---

*Also see Attneave (1974) for psychological evidence favoring this distinction.

verbal spatial skills in the remaining hemisphere. This demonstrates that both hemispheres have a capacity for at least elementary verbal and nonverbal information processing. However, even when decortication occurs at a very early age, individuals who lose their right hemisphere are impaired on complex imagery and spatial tasks. This suggests some genetic differences in the structure of each hemisphere that make the left hemisphere more suited to verbal representation and the right hemisphere more suited to nonverbal spatial representation. We know that this assignment of functions to hemispheres is not invariant, since some individuals (especially left-handers) appear to have their assignments to hemispheres switched. More interesting are the cases of bilateral representation of language in some left-handed and ambidextrous individuals (Kohn and Dennis 1974; Milner 1973; Smith and Burkland 1966; Milner, Branch, and Rasmussen 1964).

Unilateral ECS or drugging. Temporary selective impairment of predominantly verbal memory is produced by administering electroconvulsive shock (ECS) to the left hemisphere, while ECS to the right hemisphere impairs nonverbal memory primarily. (Cohen et al. 1968; Gottlieb and Wilson 1965). Similarly, injection of a drug (sodium amytal) into the common carotid artery serving the left hemisphere temporarily inactivates that hemisphere and in over 90% of right-handers produces a severe disruption of verbal language ability (Milner 1973; Milner, Branch, and Rasmussen 1966).

Psychological Functions

Density of interconnection. What is the psychological significance of distinguishing a certain set of nodes as belonging to one modality and another set as belonging to a different modality? The most obvious answer is that the nodes within a given modality are concerned with concepts that are relatively highly interconnected in a dense associative network; whereas associations between nodes in different modalities are sparse.

Interference, inhibition, and attention. Nodes and associations within a modality may also have greater potential for interference with one another than nodes or associations that cross modalities. Cohen and Granström (1970) demonstrated that recognition memory for complex geometric figures suffered greater interference when the retention interval was filled with image material consisting of human faces than when it was filled with verbal material consisting of people's names. For recall of the verbal descriptions of the geometric forms, these findings were reversed. Murray and Newman (1973) showed that memory for the *names* of shapes appearing in the cells of a three-by-four matrix was more seriously disrupted by a verbal interfering task (rapid counting by ones) than by a nonverbal imagery task (copying lines pointing in different directions). By contrast, memory for the *locations* of the shapes within the cells of the matrix was disrupted more by the imagery task than by the verbal task.

Diana Deutsch (1970) distinguished between verbal and musical modalities by demonstrating that recognition memory for the pitch of a tone suffered greater interference from subsequently presented tones than from subsequently presented digits. Memory for digits was not affected by the need to retain a tone in short-term memory. These results indicate one of the psychological bases for distinguishing between different coding modalities: memory traces within a modality are subject to much greater storage interference from the learning or processing of other material coded in the same modality than from material coded in a different modality.

Processing of other material coded in the same modality also causes greater interference with memory retrieval. An extensive series of experiments by Lee Brooks showed that recall of a line diagram (image) was faster by speaking (using the verbal modality) than by pointing to correct items in a column of symbols (which presumably uses the image or spatial modality). For recall of a sentence the results were reversed—pointing was faster than verbal output. Such findings are obtained when the verbal output is incompatible with the words being recalled and when the image-controlled output is incompatible with the image being recalled. Speaking the actual words in a sentence or drawing the image being recalled are compatible and fast retrieval modes. To demonstrate that interference between different nodes is greater within than across modalities, it is necessary to create interference. Brooks did this by having subjects categorize each word in a sentence as a noun or nonnoun either by saying *yes* or *no* or by pointing at *yes* or *no* on successive lines of a page. In recall of an image, he had subjects categorize each corner in a diagram as vertically extreme (at the top or bottom) or not; they did this either verbally or by pointing. When the responses were different from the nodes most directly activated by recall, there was greater retrieval interference between different nodes in the same modality than between different nodes in different modalities (Brooks 1968).

Brooks also showed that acquisition is subject to greater interference from activation of different nodes in the same modality than from activation of different nodes in different modalities. Specifically, the act of reading a written description of spatial relations interfered more with acquiring the correct image than did listening to the same verbal description. Many controls were run to rule out alternative interpretations (Brooks 1967). The general result seems well established: in learning, storage, and retrieval there is greater interference between nodes within a modality than between nodes across modalities.

Syntax of coding. The preceding two ways of differentiating modalities are quantitative. They refer to ways of dividing an associative network into parts by means of partitions that cut the fewest associations, or that maximize the average extent of association within a part. Although the information coded in each modality is different, the basic rules of encoding are not necessarily different for different modalities. To take it to the extreme, one might, for example, distinguish the "baseball" and the "politics" modalities because there is much more interconnection within each system of nodes than there is between them. Perhaps typical modality distinctions, such as that between verbal and image modalities, are merely large-scale versions of distinctions based on subject matter. However, it seems somewhat more plausible (and certainly more exciting) to assume that the major modality distinctions are based on differences in the language of coding, especially its syntax (grammar). There is no direct evidence in support of this hypothesis, though.

The most frequently hypothesized difference between the encoding languages of verbal versus nonverbal spatial or image modalities is as follows: the verbal modality is somehow specialized for the representation of simple linear orderings, especially temporally ordered events. The nonverbal spatial or image modalities are specialized for the representation of multidimensional relations, especially two- or three-dimensional spatial relations (Paivio and Csapo 1969). There is good evidence to indicate that the auditory sensory modality is specialized for precise representation of temporal relations between successive events, while vision is specialized for representing spatial relations (Freides 1974). However, such specialization of sensory input modalities must not be confused with specialization of high-level cognitive modalities. There is every reason to believe that at least at the semantic level of the verbal modality, the representation of propositions is multidimensional in the semihierarchical way described earlier. Some theorists have claimed that multidimensional spatial relations are represented in the same semihierarchical propositional language (Anderson and Bower 1973).

On the whole, the evidence does not support the hypothesis that the verbal modality is specialized for (unidimensional) sequential information and the image modality for (multidimensional) simultaneous information (Davies 1969; Nelson, Brooks, and Borden 1973; Snodgrass and Antone 1974).

Serial versus parallel processing. Some theorists also speculate that the verbal modality is specialized for rapid serial activation of nodes, while the nonverbal modality is specialized for somewhat slower but parallel activation of many nodes at once. This hypothesis regarding a cognitive processing difference between verbal and nonverbal modalities should not be confused with another, superficially similar hypothesis: that the verbal modality is specialized for coding simple, serially ordered items, while the nonverbal modalities are specialized for coding multidimensional relationships. This latter hypothesis concerns a difference in the syntax of coding. The former hypothesis concerns a difference in the nature of cognitive processes such as learning or retrieval. Gillian Cohen (1973) obtained evidence consistent with the former hypothesis, but on the whole there is little evidence to support it. Thus the only established psychological reason for subdividing the mind into modalities is that there are many more excitatory and inhibitory interconnections within a modality than between modalities. However, there are probably more profound differences between both coding and processes in different modalities—differences that as yet we know nothing about.

SUMMARY

1 To understand any area of science, one must first *analyze* it into parts, defining concepts and assigning words to represent these concepts. One must then *synthesize* the whole by defining other concepts that relate the parts to each other. To understand an area, it is critically important to learn the basic vocabulary of that area because vocabulary learning is concept learning, and understanding these analytic concepts is the first step towards understanding the synthetic principles of the area.

2 Cognitive psychology includes all of the psychological subject matter of what has been called "experimental psychology." But cognitive psychology emphasises theory and facts, rather than experimental methods and facts, and focuses on those theoretical principles that are common to perception, learning, memory, language, and thinking.

3 There are three different levels of processing: sensory levels, which represent stimuli; motor levels, which represent responses; and cognitive levels, which represent concepts and propositions concerning the world. Cognitive levels both receive sensory input and direct motor systems to perform responses. S and R do not meet at the top of the mind; they meet at the bottom of several levels of abstract cognitive representation.

4 Networks are composed of nodes and associations (links) between nodes. In network theories of coding, a *node* means *whatever represents any idea* (percept, image, attribute, concept, proposition, or whatever). Nodes are logically necessary in any theory of coding. Network theories differ in the number and logical character of the associations that they posit, in how these associations are learned, stored, and used in perception, memory retrieval, and thinking.

5 Evidence strongly supports the theory that the human mind has the learning capacity to define new (chunk) nodes to represent thoughts that are combinations of already defined nodes (simpler thoughts). For example, we can define a new node to represent an entire proposition such as *Del Jager can't swim* by forming associations between the new propositional node and its constituent nodes *Del Jager* and *can't swim.*

6 In this book we shall distinguish three types of associations. These are (a) vertically upward *(is-a-constituent-of)* and (b) vertically downward *(has-as-a-constituent)* associations, which are involved in the formation of new nodes via the chunking process, and (c) the older, *occurred-with* horizontal (lateral) associations. The vertical associations have all the conceptual power of horizontal associations and more, which may render horizontal associations superfluous. However, for many purposes, the extra power in the hierarchical associative

memory is irrelevant to the issue at hand. Therefore, it is simpler just to talk as if there were a direct horizontal link between two nodes, instead of a chain of upward and downward links.

7 If you are serious about learning any area of science, you must begin now to ask and answer your own questions. Good questions specify precisely what you know about a topic and what you don't know. Good questions are narrow, specific, answerable. You want to learn how to ask good questions, but this skill, like any other skill, takes practice. First you crawl, then you walk. First you ask too-general and vague questions. Then you learn how to sharpen them up to focus on the specific areas you don't understand.

8 The major cognitive processes can be classified into five groups. The first is learning—strengthening associations between nodes. The second is memory storage—consolidation, interference, and decay of these associations after learning and prior to retrieval. The third is activation—of nodes, due to some combination of upward sensory input and downward or lateral associative input in perception, memory retrieval, and thinking. The fourth is priming—partial activation of nodes in attentional set and short-term memory for previously activated nodes. And the fifth is inhibition—negation, contradiction, and negative attentional set.

9 There is strong neuroanatomical and psychological evidence for the distinction between verbal and nonverbal modalities. There is also some evidence for finer-grain distinctions within these categories. From a psychological standpoint, we know that nodes within a modality have much more extensive interconnection and interaction (excitatory and inhibitory) than nodes from different modalities. It is attractive to suppose that there are some important differences in the nature (syntax) of coding in different modalities, but there is little or no evidence to support this conjecture.

CHAPTER 2
VISUAL PERCEPTION

OBJECTIVES

1 To illustrate the principle of specific node (neuron) encoding of visual features such as spots, lines, corners, and gratings in the nervous system. How do we encode visual stimuli of varying size and illumination with different grains of resolution? Can our visual system be broken down into parts concerned with form versus location and form versus color and texture? How may complex feature nodes be built up from sets of simple feature nodes?

2 To discuss the possible existence of spatial-frequency (grating) detectors in the visual system.

3 To discuss the concept of constituent structure. To discuss how higher-order neurons (nodes) may compute approximately logical functions (e.g., A_1 and A_2 and A_3, A_1 or A_2 or A_3) of their lower-level constituent attributes (e.g., A_1, A_2, A_3).

4 To discuss the functions that neural inhibition may serve in the visual modality. These include positive representation of dark spots and lines, enhancing contrast and deblurring, light adaptation, focusing attention, and attentional set.

5 To discuss several different types of visual adaptation within a common theoretical framework that emphasizes some possible similarities of function for neural and receptor light-dark adaptation, figural adaptation, and movement adaptation. To discuss the role of adaptation in all psychophysical absolute judgments and in the perception of ambiguous figures.

6 To present the grouping principles (both innate and learned) by which the mind segregates attributes into separate figures distinct from each other and from the background. The important general principle of context-sensitive coding (redundant, overlapping, interlocking coding) is introduced in the context of line and angle detectors in form perception. The chapter discusses how such coding may achieve a unitary focus of attention on context-sensitive attributes that group (interlock) to compose an object (form). The chunking of a set of constituent attribute nodes into a higher-order chunk node is also discussed.

7 To describe the conjunctive (chunking or ANDing) and disjunctive (ORing) aspects of the constituent structure of object concepts. To discuss our ability to recognize a familiar object over a wide range of levels of illumination, retinal positions, distance (and therefore retinal size), and even to some extent orientations (rotational perspectives).

8 To point out our substantial capacity for processing several visual attributes simultaneously (in parallel). To point out an apparent limitation on this capacity where two highly similar types of stimulus dimensions may force successive (serial) processing by the same analyzer system.

9 To discuss the important role of context and expectations in perception. To some extent, we see what we expect to see. Our expectations also drive the perceptual responses such as eye and head movements by which we selectively acquire new information.

Seeing is believing. So indeed are hearing, touching, and every other modality of perception. Our conscious perception of the world almost certainly occurs in the same high levels of the mind that learn, think, and remember. These levels of the mind perceive object concepts and relations between objects in an abstract representation that receives input from many sensory modalities as well as from its own associative memory. We don't just *see* a movie, we use both our visual and our auditory sensory modalities and our expectations to *perceive* what is happening in an abstract cognitive modality that encodes new events in the context of all of our prior knowledge of the world. Furthermore, an important part of perception is the information-gathering responses we perform. These responses include orienting our eyes to a stimulus, scanning it, moving over to it, touching it, kicking it, tracking its movements with our eyes, and so forth. Perception, then, is not a purely passive analysis of the sensations of the eye or ear. But it does start out with the analysis of a sensory event into combinations of features—and so does this chapter.

HIERARCHICAL FEATURES: CONJUNCTION, DISJUNCTION, AND NEGATION

In 1826, the physiologist Johannes Müller formulated the basic principle of encoding in sensory neurons, which is also the basic principle of encoding in motor neurons and probably throughout the nervous system. This principle may be stated as follows: events are represented by the specific neurons that are activated. They are not represented by the temporal pattern or by any other characteristics besides frequency of firing (Müller in Herrnstein and Boring 1968, pp. 26–33). Activation of a visual receptor or neuron produces visual sensations, not tactile or auditory sensations, regardless of how the receptor or neuron is activated (visually, tactually, electrically, chemically), and regardless of the temporal pattern of activation. No pattern of activation of the motor nerve to the biceps will produce leg movement rather than arm movement. This is the doctrine of specific nerve energies, which I have renamed the principle of *specific node encoding,* to reflect a vastly extended meaning—that the representation of any specific concept, image, thought, idea, percept, or response is by *which* particular nodes (neurons) are activated strongly and not by their temporal pattern of activation or any other code. This is a reasonably (though not completely) precise, simple, and general hypothesis for which there is a great deal of support—within sensory and motor modalities. Extension of the principle to higher levels of encoding in the nervous system is plausible and parsimonious, but there is only a little direct neural evidence to support it. However, there is now a great deal of evidence to support specific node encoding in the visual nervous system from the retina to the visual cortex.

Retinal Spot Detectors

Light falling on the retina is captured by special pigment molecules in the rods and cones (receptor cells). Capture of a photon of light by a pigment molecule changes that molecule to a different molecule (bleaches it). This sets up a rather long-lasting electrical generator potential in the (first-order) receptor cell. Receptor cells excite (activate) a set of second-order cells (neurons), which are interconnected by both excitatory and inhibitory links. The exact system of excitatory and inhibitory interconnection in the mammalian retina is unknown. It could be different for different species (Glezer et al. 1971). However, the result of this processing in the retina is the activation of (third-order) retinal ganglion cells. In cats and monkeys, these cells appear to be light- and dark-*spot detectors* with receptive fields consisting of two concentric regions, as shown in figure 2.1 (see review by Robson 1975).

The receptive field of a visual neuron is that part of the retina where visual stimulation can either excite or inhibit the firing rate of the neuron. In the case of a light-spot detector, light in a center region excites the cell, while light in the concentric surrounding region inhibits the cell. This situation is reversed for dark-spot detectors. Thus the best stimulus for a light-spot detector is a light spot on a dark background, and the best stimulus for a dark-spot detector is the reverse (Kuffler 1953).

Spot detectors come in a wide variety of sizes. They range from fine-grain to course-grain representation of the pattern on the retina. This varia-

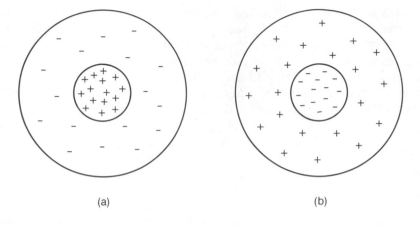

Fig. 2.1   Receptive fields of a light-spot detector in (a) and a dark-spot detector in (b).
Light shown on the retina in the regions indicated by + signs will excite the neuron,
while light in the regions indicated by − signs will inhibit the neuron.

tion occurs partly because the average size of the receptive field increases as
the distance increases from the fovea (center of vision)—where visual resolution is sharpest due to the small size of receptive fields—to the retinal periphery—where resolution is poor but light detection capacity is high. However,
not all of the variation in receptive field size is explainable in this way (Kuffler
1953). Receptive field size also varies substantially in the fovea. This variation
may serve to provide an economical representation of patterns of different
size, using spot detectors with a different grain of resolution. There is also
some evidence to indicate that the central portion of the receptive field of spot
detector neurons decreases with increasing light adaptation and increases
with increasing dark adaptation. On the one hand, this permits us to resolve
the finer details under strong illumination. On the other hand, it makes us
more sensitive in dim illumination, although the perception of fine detail is
necessarily sacrificed (Barlow, Fitzhugh, and Kuffler 1975; Glezer et al. 1971).*

All of these neurons encode the *contrast* between a spot and its immediate background. They do not encode the absolute intensity with which either
is illuminated. Such neurons are ideally suited to the recognition of objects
regardless of the level of illumination. That is, they are suited to quality or
form perception rather than to intensity perception. However, there is another, rather rare, type of retinal ganglion neuron whose maintained discharge frequency varies quite regularly with the level of illumination. These
neurons are thought to be involved in the control of pupil diameter rather
than in the perception of brightness (Barlow and Levick 1969; Cleland and
Levick 1974).

*See also Bitterman, Krauskopf, and Hochberg (1954) at a psychological level.

Cortical Simple Line Detectors

According to Hubel and Wiesel, the first-level form analyzers in the cat visual cortex are neurons whose receptive fields are either straight-line slits or edges (fig. 2.2). Hubel and Wiesel called them simple cells because they had the simplest receptive field properties of all the linear form detectors they found in the cortex. *Edge detectors* have receptive fields composed of two areas, one excitatory and the other inhibitory, with a straight-line boundary between them. The straight edge must be oriented at a particular angle to fire the cell at the maximum rate. The contrast between the lighter and darker sides of the edge must be correct (e.g., light below dark in figure 2.2[a]), and the edge must be located in the appropriate part of the visual field. *Slit detectors* have just slightly more complex receptive fields composed of a central excitatory area in the shape of an elongated slit flanked by two inhibitory regions. Again the boundary between the regions is an approximately straight line. Orientation is critical, as is the position in the visual field. Some simple slit detectors respond to light slits flanked by dark; others to dark slits flanked by light (Hubel and Wiesel 1962).

Hubel and Wiesel theorize that a simple cortical line detector receives its input from a conjunction of light-spot and dark-spot detectors whose receptive field centers fall in the appropriate areas of the simple cortical cell's receptive field. You might think that a simple light-slit detector could receive purely excitatory input from a conjunction of linearly oriented light-spot detectors and flanking dark-spot detectors. But this purely excitatory input would not have the same degree of contrast-enhancement as a combination of excitatory and inhibitory input has. Hubel and Wiesel suggest that the simple line detectors might receive appropriate inhibitory input from light-spot detectors in the area of the receptive field that should be dark, and from

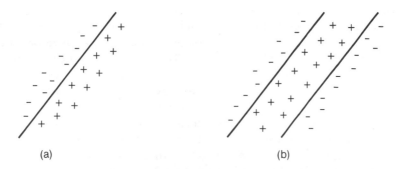

(a)   (b)

Fig. 2.2   Receptive fields of the two types of cortical simple line detectors. The best
    stimulus for the edge detector in (a) is an edge oriented at 45° with light below and
    dark above. The best stimulus for the slit detector in (b) is a slit of light of a certain
    width oriented at 60° to the horizontal and flanked by dark regions on both sides.
    There are also light-above-dark edge detectors and dark-slit detectors.

dark-spot detectors in the area of the receptive field that should be light. We know that inhibition operates at earlier levels of analysis in the visual modality to enhance contrast, and there is every reason to expect it to continue to operate at higher levels.

Receptive field sizes of simple line detectors increase with distance from the center of vision, but they also vary considerably at a given position in the visual field. The narrowest slit widths (10 to 15 minutes of arc) are comparable to the diameter of the center of the smallest single-spot detectors. But other simple cortical slit detectors are much wider—suited to encoding thicker lines at a coarser grain of representation. The length of a simple receptive field is always considerably greater than its width (e.g., 3° in length for 1/4° in width), and if the length of a slit is increased up to the optimum length of the receptive field, rate of firing is increased also. Beyond that optimum length there is no further summation, but neither is there any inhibition. Thus the simple cortical cells really do encode lines (of indefinite length) rather than rays (lines with one specified end and one unspecified end) or segments (lines with two specified ends and therefore of definite length).

Cortical Complex Line Detectors

The primary visual cortex also contains what Hubel and Wiesel call complex cells. Like simple cells, complex cells respond best to lines (edges or slits) of a particular orientation, but unlike simple cells, complex cells respond at any of about five positions over a rather wide receptive field. Complex line detectors have approximately the same range of optimum line lengths as simple cells, but lines at any of several positions over a 1° to 20° range drive the cell. Again, the receptive field widths get larger in the periphery, but there is a considerable range of complex receptive field widths at any place in the visual field. An example of the receptive field of a complex slit detector is shown in figure 2.3(a).

As described by Hubel and Wiesel, complex line detectors appear to represent a disjunction of similarly oriented lines over a range of adjacent spatial positons (line A_1 or line A_2 or line A_3 . . .). Complex line detectors thus provide a certain degree of generalization of similar stimuli over translation in position in the visual field. This kind of generalization might occur while either the observer or the observed object was moving. In fact, moving an optimally oriented line through the receptive field perpendicular to the optimum axis is almost always a more effective stimulus than just flashing the line at one place in the receptive field. Some complex line detectors are activated equally well by moving the line in either of the two directions perpendicular to its axis. Other complex line detectors appear to encode direction of movement as well. They do so by responding much more actively to movement of the line in one direction than the other. Finally, different cells are maximally activated by different rates of movement. This raises the possi-

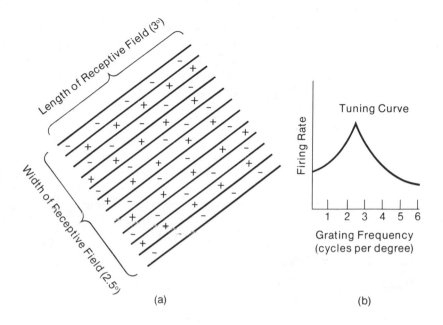

Fig. 2.3 (a) The receptive field of a complex slit detector for which the best stimulus is one or more slits 3° of visual angle in length oriented at an angle of 45° to the horizontal at any of the five positions indicated by a line of + signs. The lines of – signs are the inhibitory surrounds. (b) The tuning curve of the response of such a cell to gratings (alternating light and dark stripes) of different frequency in cycles per degree, where one cycle is a light and a dark stripe. Note that the best response for this hypothetical cell is obtained when the grating frequency is about two cycles per degree (exactly matching the strip widths, which have about five cycles in 2½ degrees).

bility that many different velocities, rather than just two (back and forth), are encoded by the cells (Hubel and Wiesel 1962).

Cortical Ray and Segment Detectors

Line detectors, whether simple or complex, represent lines in the mathematical sense. A line in this sense has a particular orientation but no definite end. (Complex cells represent a disjunction of lines). In higher cortical levels of the visual modality, there are ray and segment detectors. These represent lines with one or two definite ends, respectively. Whereas with line detectors one gets no inhibition of response for increases in line lengths beyond the limits of the receptive field, with a ray detector increases in length beyond a certain point at one end of the receptive field produce pronounced inhibition. A segment detector represents a slit or edge that is stopped at both ends by inhibitory fields. Ray and segment detectors respond to similarly oriented rays and segments over a range of positions in the visual field; in this respect they are analogous to complex line detectors. Thus ray and segment detectors may represent a disjunction of similarly oriented rays and segments over a spatially contiguous range of positions. Hence they also provide a certain degree of invariant encoding of form with translation in the visual field. Hubel and Wiesel theorize that a ray detector arises from the conjunction of excitatory input from one complex line detector and inhibitory input from one or more complex detectors whose fields lie at one end of the excitatory field. Segment detectors would be a conjunction of excitatory input from a central complex line detector with inhibitory input from line detectors at both ends (Hubel and Wiesel 1965). However, there is some reason to believe that ray and segment detectors receive input from complex combinations of simple cells.

Cortical Corner Detectors

Hubel and Wiesel found a few cells that appeared to represent a corner. The best stimulus for such a corner cell was a conjunction of two edges intersecting at or near their ends; these edges were roughly perpendicular to each other. Hubel and Wiesel theorize that such cells could represent the conjunction of excitatory input from two complex (line, ray, or segment) edge detectors with optimum orientation 90° apart. But again it is possible that corner detectors receive input from a complex combination of simple cells.

Spatial-Frequency Analyzers
(Grating Detectors)

According to the Hubel-Wiesel theory of the encoding of form, single lines (or rays or segments) and their combinations (corners and who knows what else) are the fundamental visual features at the primary visual cortical level. An alternative feature system for the encoding of form is provided by any of several systems for two-dimensional spatial-frequency analysis of visual input. Such a system is analogous to what is achieved by the one-dimensional temporal-frequency (spectrographic) analysis of auditory input, which the ear performs right at the periphery. Since the auditory nervous system deals with spectral features, there is every reason to believe that the visual nervous system could, too. This is not to say that the visual modality *does* preform such a spatial-frequency analysis. The nature of the transduction from sound energy to neural firing by the ear more or less forces the auditory modality to deal with spectrographic features. The eye does not directly transduce light energy into a pattern of activation of spatial-frequency analyzers. Hence if such a spatial-frequency analysis is to be performed by the visual modality, it must be done neurally. Nevertheless, there are some substantial advantages to spatial-frequency analysis, and there is both psychological and neural evidence to support the existence of such an analysis.*

The basic assumption at the neural level is that there are *grating detectors* in the visual cortex. A multiple-cycle grating detector has exactly the same structure of receptive field as that illustrated for the complex cell in figure 2.3 —except that it represents the *conjunction* (line L_1 AND line L_2 AND . . .) of the excitatory (and lack of inhibitory) input from the parallel strips, rather than the *disjunction* (line L_1 OR line L_2 OR . . .) of such inputs. One cycle of a grating consists of an excitatory strip and an adjacent inhibitory strip.

A neuron is a threshold device, not a logical AND or OR gate. Thus when one speaks of a neuron representing a conjunction of inputs, one means that the neuron increases in firing rate with additional inputs. One may mean that the neuron requires all of a conjunction of inputs in order to fire above its spontaneous rate. Only in the latter case does the neuron represent a conjunction in the strict logical sense. In this sense, all of several constituent features are required to provide sufficient input to exceed a (high) threshold and to cause the neuron to fire above spontaneous background rate. To be an ideal AND gate, such a neuron should fire at only two levels—spontaneous (background) rate and maximum rate. For a neuron to serve as a pure inclusive OR gate, it should go from spontaneous to maximum rate when any one of the specified features is present, and it should show neither an increase nor a decrease in rate when more than one of the specified features are present. A neuron serving as an exclusive OR gate (e.g., A_1 OR A_2, but not both) would go from spontaneous to maximum rate in the presence of one of the specified alternative features, but would reduce its firing rate to the spontaneous level in the presence of two or more of these features. No one asserts that any feature-detector neurons are functioning strictly as either logical AND or OR gates. But the logical operators help us to envision neurons functioning as different types of threshold devices—acting as if they were computing a conjunction of their inputs (AND gate) or an inclusive or exclusive disjunction of their inputs (OR gate).

A grating detector tuned to respond best to a frequency of about 2 cycles/degree should decrease its rate of firing for gratings with frequencies greater than the optimum (finer gratings = narrower stripes) and less than the optimum (coarser gratings = wider stripes). Such a grating detector is shown in figure 2.3; it has 5-1/2 cycles in 2-1/2°. The function that relates firing rate to some physical stimulus variable such as strip width or grating frequency is called a *tuning curve.* An example of a hypothetical curve is shown in figure 2.3(b) for the complex receptive field of figure 2.3(a). One of the lines of evidence favoring the hypothesis that some cortical neurons are grating detectors tuned to different spatial frequencies is that they have tuning curves

---

*See reviews by Campbell (1974) and Pollen and Taylor (1974). Also see Glezer et al. (1976) and Pollen and Ronner (1975).

that are peaked at a particular frequency (Glezer et al. 1976). Russell DeValois and his associates have found many neurons in primary visual cortex that show a much greater change in firing rate as a function of frequency of gratings than they do as a function of the line width of single strips. Such neurons therefore appear to be encoding gratings of particular frequencies rather than single slits of particular widths. Furthermore, the firing rate of such neurons to more complex visual input appears to be most accurately predicted by the assumption that such neurons are grating detectors. The neurons characterized as grating detectors by DeValois appear to be the neurons characterized as edge and slit detectors by Hubel and Wiesel. There is an unresolved conflict here, but it is less sharp than it might appear at first sight, for DeValois claims that these simple grating detectors have only about 1-1/2 cycles (presumably corresponding to Hubel and Wiesel's edge detectors) or 2-1/2 cycles (presumably corresponding to Hubel and Wiesel's slit detectors). Figure 2.4 compares the two models.* My tentative conclusion is that DeValois has modified the Hubel and Wiesel theory of simple cells in two basic ways. First, he more accurately characterizes the quantitative structure of their receptive fields. This reveals slightly more complexity than was revealed by Hubel and Wiesel's pioneering first approximation. Second, he notes many of the theoretical properties of such miniature spatial-frequency detectors and confirms them experimentally. This is not so much scientific conflict as cumulative scientific progress. However, DeValois's work is too recent to have been adequately evaluated by others, and earlier neurophysiological research by others on spatial-frequency (grating) detectors is less definitive and highly controversial. So the proper attitude at present is "wait and see."

It is very attractive to imagine two different systems in the visual modality for the representation of objects (figures, forms) and textures (backgrounds). Textures may well be ideally represented by conjunctions of grating detectors that respond optimally to periodic repetition of elements, while objects may be ideally represented by conjunctions and disjunctions of contour detectors (line segments, corners, and so forth). However, grating detectors could also provide the featural basis for object perception.

INHIBITION

Neurons generally receive input from other neurons over two different types of synapses—excitatory and inhibitory. Excitatory input acts to increase the firing rate of a neuron, while inhibitory input acts to reduce the sensitivity of the neuron to excitatory input. In a neuron with a high spontaneous firing rate, inhibition can reduce the spontaneous firing rate. In a neuron with a low

*DeValois 1977: personal communication.

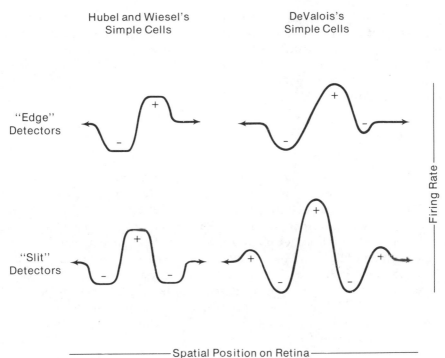

Hubel and Wiesel's
Simple Cells

DeValois's
Simple Cells

"Edge"
Detectors

"Slit"
Detectors

Firing Rate

Spatial Position on Retina

Fig. 2.4   Hubel and Wiesel's and DeValois's respective characterization of the receptive
fields of simple cortical cells. Note the high degree of similarity between the two
characterizations. Note, too, that Hubel and Wiesel's original characterization can be
viewed as a good first approximation of DeValois's characterization.

spontaneous firing rate, the principal effect of inhibition is to reduce the
sensitivity of the neuron to any subsequent excitatory input.

Jerzy Konorski has distinguished four functionally different inhibitory
systems that are known to occur in the nervous system (Konorski 1972). First,
there is *reciprocal inhibition,* in which pairs of nervous centers are antagonistic
to each other so that excitation of one center inhibits the other and vice versa.
Examples include flexion versus extension of the limbs, expiration versus
inspiration in breathing, sleep versus waking, and hunger versus satiation.
Second, there are *antagonisms* between centers that are not specifically paired.
One example is antagonisms of one drive to a variety of other drives. Third,
there is *unidirectional inhibition,* in which one center exerts inhibitory effects
on other centers, but these centers do not inhibit it. One example is the
inhibition that the cerebral cortex exerts on lower levels of the nervous
system. Finally, there is *lateral inhibition,* in which each neuron inhibits all of
its neighbors, usually in proportion to their proximity.

Inhibition probably plays an important role in at least five visual perceptual phenomena: positive representation of dark contours, contrast enhancement, light adaptation, attention (perceptual choice), and attentional set. There is solid neurophysiological evidence for the role of inhibition in the first three of these phenomena. For the last two the evidence is primarily theoretical plausibility.

Positive Representation
of Dark Contours

Inhibition plays an important role in the receptive field properties of virtually every neuron in the visual modality at the levels studied thus far. Line, ray, and segment detectors have linear excitatory regions flanked on one or both sides by linear inhibitory regions. Spot detectors have concentric excitatory and inhibitory regions. One function of having both excitatory and inhibitory input to visual feature neurons is to permit the representation of dark spots and dark lines. Normal humans have four types of visual receptor elements—rods and three types of cones. All four generate electric potentials in response to light of various wavelengths. None generates a potential in response to a dark spot falling on them. The logic of the nervous system works fundamentally on positive neuronal firing. Therefore, in order to see a dark object, it is probably important for that object to be represented by the positive firing of some neurons, rather than by the lack of firing of some neurons. The process of neural inhibition accomplishes this objective. The dark-spot detectors receive inhibitory input from the central region of their receptive field and excitatory input from the concentric surround region. In this way a homogeneous light distribution over the receptive field evokes little or no response, but a dark spot in the center of a lighter background removes the inhibition from the center and permits the excitatory input from the surround to drive the neuron in a positive way.

Contrast, Contour Enhancement,
and Mach Bands

To an organism, the most important aspect of vision is the ability to recognize objects. Objects are often darker than their background—hence the importance of the positive representation of dark contours. However, enormous changes take place in incident illumination, due to the fluctuation from day to twilight to night among other things. Therefore, the precise encoding of absolute light intensity would be of little value for object recognition. (However, it is of value for regulating pupil diameter, and there are neurons that encode the overall intensity of retinal illumination.) What is invariant over changes in incident illumination is the contrast (relative reflectance) of adjacent areas of the visual field. Antagonistic excitatory and inhibitory regions of receptive fields provide us with feature detectors of the contrast (relative light intensity) between adjacent areas. This is accomplished in a manner that is largely independent of the absolute light intensity over an enormous dynamic range below glare level. As long as both excitatory and inhibitory areas are receiving the same incident illumination, this contrast is a direct measure of an invariant property of the object, namely, the relative reflectance of these adjacent areas.

Antagonistic excitatory and inhibitory regions of receptive fields probably do more than record the relative contrast level on the retina. They probably also serve to correct for the slight imperfection of the lens of the eye, which produces a very small degree of blurring of the image on the retina. Blurring takes an abrupt light-dark border and converts this step function illumination gradient into a ramp function illumination gradient, as illustrated in figure 2.5(a). The early levels of the visual nervous system, using inhibition to enhance the contrast of such blurred contours, convert the ramp function on the eye back into a step function at the level of the firing rates of visual neurons. In this way the imperfection of the lens is compensated for by the properties of the visual nervous system.

This contrast-enhancing deblurring mechanism works virtually perfectly for abrupt (step function) contrasts between adjacent regions. However, the mechanism is fooled a bit by actual ramp functions of illumination, which the lens converts to slightly more gradual ramps, as illustrated in figure 2.5(b). The nervous system overcompensates for blurring in this case and not

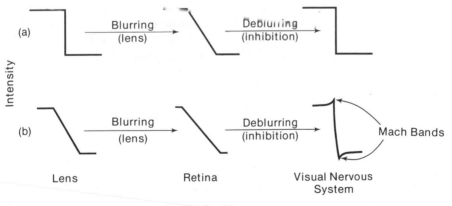

Fig. 2.5 The lens of the eye blurs images slightly, changing illumination step functions to ramps and ramps to more gradual ramps on the retina. The visual nervous system uses inhibition to deblur the image, converting steep ramps on the retina back to step functions in the spot detectors. However, the system does not work in a perfectly veridical manner for incident ramp functions, which are converted into steeper ramps with bordering light and dark (Mach) bands.

only steepens the ramp but actually produces distinctly brighter and darker bands at the light and dark edges of the ramp. These are called Mach bands after Ernst Mach, the man who first described them (see Ratliff 1965). It is not known whether this contrast enhancement of illumination ramps is useful for detecting gradual contrast changes, or whether it is a minor flaw in a system designed to deblur what are in reality abrupt contrast changes.

Light Adaptation

The antagonistic excitatory center and inhibitory surround structure of spot detectors accomplishes another amazing objective in visual perception. It changes the sensitivity and acuity of visual representation in response to changes in level of illumination. As we have seen, when illumination is poor, the excitatory center of the receptive field of spot detectors is larger than when illumination is good. This is functional, since it permits sharp acuity (resolution of differences between the intensity levels of very small regions) when illumination is high, but preserves the detectability of contrasts between larger regions when illumination is low.

The nervous system accomplishes these changes in the receptive field center by the following mechanism, illustrated for a light-spot detector. The excitatory and inhibitory inputs to the spot detector come from overlapping regions of the receptive field. In fact, there is reason to believe that both the excitatory and the inhibitory input to a spot detector contribute their peak input at the center of the receptive field (fig. 2.6). The field has an excitatory center and an inhibitory surround because the magnitude of the excitatory input is more sharply peaked at the center, where it exceeds the inhibitory input. However, the inhibitory gradient falls off much more gradually, so that it exceeds the excitatory gradient in the surround region (Wagner, MacNichol, and Wolbarsht 1963; Enroth-Cugell and Robson 1966).

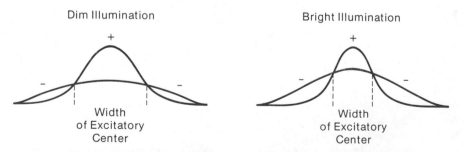

Fig. 2.6 Both the excitatory and the inhibitory input peak at the center of the receptive field of a spot detector. Increases in illumination increase the level of inhibition more than the level of excitation, reducing the size of the receptive field center and increasing acuity. In dim illumination the receptive field center increases to increase sensitivity.

By varying the relative magnitude of the excitatory and inhibitory input, one can vary the size of the receptive field center (fig. 2.6). In bright illumination the magnitude of the inhibitory input is increased relative to the excitatory input, reducing the size of the excitatory center and increasing visual acuity. In dim illumination the magnitude of the inhibitory input is decreased relative to the excitatory input, increasing the size of the center. This increases the eye's ability to detect larger features, although fine grain detail is necessarily lost because it is below the sensitivity of the visual system in dim illumination. Increasing receptive field centers in dark adaptation gives us a brighter, but somewhat blurred, neural representation of the visual field instead of absolute darkness (Enroth-Cugell and Lennie 1975). Once again, scientific psychology confirms a commonly known fact of human nature— that we're less inhibited in the dark. (Sorry about that.)

Attention (Perceptual Choice)

Attention will be discussed in more detail later in this chapter and in chapter 6. The purpose of the present discussion is to highlight the possible role of inhibition in focusing our attention on certain features or objects in the visual field. The basic hypothesis is that under certain conditions, at one or more levels of the visual modality, we can greatly amplify small differences in the level of of activation of different sets of features or objects. According to this hypothesis, deciding what to attend to (perceptual choice) is a process of increasing the differences in firing rates of different neurons so that, eventually, relatively small differences in activation will be transformed into large differences. The relative contributions of upward (forward) and lateral (horizontal or same-level) inhibition in determining the input structure of the receptive fields of feature detectors is not known in most cases. Probably it differs for different levels and species. However, the prevailing neural conception of attention defines it as lateral inhibition among all the neurons in some set (Konorski 1967; Walley and Weiden 1973). In lateral inhibition a neuron N_i inhibits every other neuron in the set in proportion to its own (N_i's) firing rate. Such a process tends to amplify differences in firing rate, since a fast-firing neuron depresses the firing rate of a slow-firing neuron more than the slow-firing neuron depresses the firing rate of the fast-firing neuron. This is a positive feedback process (small differences produce larger differences) that can push one set of (attended) neurons to the maximum firing rate while depressing all others to the minimum rate. Its strong contrast-enhancing property probably makes lateral inhibition in humans more suited to the higher cognitive levels, where actual choices must be made because thinking and response capacity are limited, than to lower perceptual levels, where no limit need be placed on parallel processing of multiple inputs. In humans and other mammals, the inhibition that helps to define the structure of visual receptive fields for feature detectors is probably mostly forward inhibition. Forward inhibition lacks the mutually interactive (positive feedback) character of lateral inhibition. Thus, forward inhibition has a milder contrast-enhancing effect than lateral inhibition, preserving many levels of activation rather than driving neurons to either zero or maximum firing rate. However, in less intelligent species, choices are made with less central processing, and lateral inhibition may play a larger role nearer the sensory periphery. Indeed, the first discovery of lateral inhibition was made by Hartline —right at the periphery of the visual nervous system in the compound eye of Limulus (the horseshoe crab), where the individual receptor elements laterally inhibit each other in a manner that decreases with increasing distance (Hartline 1949; Hartline, Wagner, and Ratliff 1956). This greatly increases the contrast between adjacent light and dark areas while permitting the eye to perceive several nonadjacent objects.

Attentional Set

Human beings need not always attend to the highest-contrast object in their visual field. They can bias their attention to various portions of the visual field or to various expected objects or sets of objects. This ability to prime one set of neurons centrally at the expense of another may be a purely excitatory process affecting the expected set. It may be an inhibitory process affecting the unexpected set. Or it may be both. To the extent that attentional set is inhibition from more central to more peripheral levels of the sensory nervous system, it constitutes an example of *backward inhibition*.

ADAPTATION

Adaptation means different things in different contexts. There is genetic adaptation of a species to a given environmental niche. There is the adaptation of sensory receptors to the average level of stimulation. Finally, there are several different types of adaptation that result from changes in the nervous system. One example is the light adaptation mechanism discussed in the preceding section. Neural adaptation of various kinds is a genetically constrained, possibly nonassociative form of learning. The mechanisms of neural adaptation probably vary with their functional purpose. However, the present section will discuss all forms of receptor and neural adaptation within a common functional theory. According to this theory, adaptation serves the purpose of centering the dynamic range of activation of receptors and neurons to about the average level of stimulation (adaptation level). This centering of a limited discriminative capacity enhances the discrimination of small differences from the adaptation level.

Light-Dark Adaptation

This problem is particularly acute for visual receptors that have a very limited range of activation levels (generator potentials), but that must somehow be capable of making precise discriminations over a much wider range of illumination levels. Like many electronic measuring instruments, the eye accomplishes this objective by adjusting its sensitivity (gain) to suit the average level of illumination. Thus it is very sensitive in dim light and much less sensitive (that is, it requires more light to evoke any response) in bright light. This permits the receptor elements to concentrate their discriminative capacity at the average intensity level of current illumination (fig. 2.7).

We have already discussed a neural mechanism for light-dark adaptation. There is another mechanism used to help achieve this same objective at the receptor level. We can call this mechanism *receptor adaptation.* Receptor adaptation in rods is rather well understood, so I will use it to illustrate. Rods generate an electrical potential (that activates neurons) when a certain visual pigment molecule, rhodopsin, absorbs a photon of light and changes to a

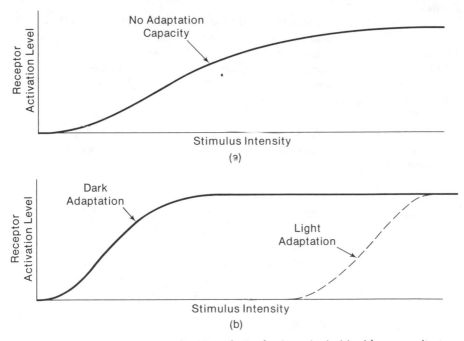

Fig. 2.7 Receptor activation as a function of stimulus intensity in (a) with no capacity to adjust receptor activation level (generator potential) to the average intensity level of illumination, and in (b) with such a capacity. In (b) there is a heightened capacity to make precise discriminations within the more limited range of illuminations expected under given conditions (at night versus midday, for example). At the same time, there is less discriminative capacity outside the expected range.

different molecule (is bleached). The bleached molecule is insensitive to light. The chemistry of the eye gradually converts this bleached molecule back to the unbleached state, so that it is once again capable of being bleached and initiating a generator potential. However, considerably more time is required to unbleach these molecules than to bleach them in the first place. So in bright illumination the proportion of unbleached (sensitive) pigment molecules is greatly reduced. This reduces the percentage of light photons that are absorbed by pigment molecules to initiate generator potentials. In this way the sensitivity of the eye is adjusted to the average illumination level over a period of time.

A minute or two may be required for receptors to reach a sensitivity level appropriate for bright-light adaptation coming out of the dark, as when you emerge from a dark movie theatre into bright sunlight. In the meantime, all the objects are reflecting light at an intensity above the sensitivity range for dark adaptation. See the right-hand asymptotic limb of the dark adaptation curve in figure 2.7(b). When this happens, you cannot discriminate objects very well because they all appear too bright. This condition is called *glare*.

When you leave a brightly-lit environment for a dark one, it takes even more time (20 to 30 minutes) for your eye to adapt completely to the dark. This is because unbleaching takes longer than bleaching. During the adaptation period you are insensitive to contrasts (relative reflected light intensities) that become highly discriminable after dark adaptation. As you well know, when you first enter a dark room from the light, everything looks black, but after a few minutes you see details much more clearly. The faster component of both dark and light adaptation is the neural adjustment of receptive field size discussed in the preceding section. The slower component is receptor adaptation.

Absolute Judgments

In an absolute judgment task, a subject is required to assign numbers to stimuli in proportion to their subjective value along some such dimension as brightness, length, area, or angle of orientation. In performing such an absolute judgment task, the subject adapts to the range of stimuli presented by concentrating his discriminative capacity within the range of values for frequently presented stimuli.

It is easier to discriminate between two similar stimuli when they appear in immediate succession (e.g., by responding "higher" or "lower" rather than "same") than it is to discriminate between two similar stimuli by absolute judgment of each single stimulus in isolation (e.g., by assigning different numbers to them). The first is a comparative judgment task; the second is an absolute judgment task. So long as similar stimuli are perfectly discriminable in an immediate comparative judgment, human beings appear to have a strict capacity to discriminate in absolute judgment about seven unidimensional stimuli (stimuli that differ in only one dimension such as length). This capacity is only slightly affected by the range of stimulus values, so long as the range is big enough for seven stimuli within that range to be perfectly discriminable in immediate successive comparison (Miller 1956, Alluisi 1957). Thus a constant limited capacity to discriminate between stimuli in an absolute judgment task can either be spread out over a wide range with reduced discriminability of nearby stimuli or concentrated on a limited range of nearby stimuli.

The mechanism of adaptation in absolute judgments is quite different from the mechanisms of light and dark adaptation. But there is a common functional consequence of adaptation in both cases, namely, to focus limited discriminative capacity where the action is—in the region where stimuli are occurring. In the case of light-dark adaptation, we probably only have the capacity to change a single mean adaptation level, but for the more central, and probably associative, adaptation in absolute judgments, we can also change the range of discriminative capacity. We do this by setting both ends of the range, or the mean and variance, or whatever (Parducci and Perrett 1971).

Figural Adaptation

Gibson observed that after prolonged viewing, curved lines tend to appear somewhat straighter, and tilted straight lines tend toward the vertical or horizontal, whichever is closer. Prolonged viewing of one contour also tends to repel subsequently presented nearby test contours, so that they appear farther from the adapting contour than they did prior to adaptation. Attneave has also shown that the perceived location of a point in a circular field is systematically displaced from the circular boundary of the field and from both the vertical and horizontal reference axes that were present as an aid to localization (Attneave 1955; Gibson 1933; Gibson and Radner 1937; Held and Shattuck 1971; Kohler and Wallach 1944). The functional purpose of altered perception of the adapting stimulus is unclear, but this effect is weaker and less consistent than adaptation effects on the perception of other nearby (similar) stimuli. These latter effects are often called figural aftereffects because they persist for some time after cessation of the adapting figure.

Although the most appropriate experimental tests have rarely been performed, figural adaptation may well accomplish the same focusing of discriminative capacity in the region of the adapting stimulus that appears to be generally characteristic of adaptation in other realms. Certainly the perceived displacement of nearby contours away from the position of the adapting contour appears to indicate enhanced discriminability of stimuli in the vicinity of the adapting figure.

The focus in figural adaptation research has been on the negative consequences of adaptation. This is consistent with the dominant hypotheses, which view figural adaptation as a fatigue effect—an imperfection in the nervous system. It has been shown that prolonged viewing of a straight line or a straight-line grating increases the threshold for detection of brief or low-contrast test lines or gratings that are oriented like the adapting stimulus (Campbell 1974). These findings might seem to contradict the hypothesis that figural adaptation is a functional focusing of discriminative capacity onto the region of the adapting stimulus. In fact, they do not. Light adaptation also increases the threshold for detecting a dim spot of light, but no one doubts that light adaptation is positively adaptive, as its name suggests. Similarly, under the hypothesis that figural adaptation is designed to enhance the perception of small changes in the adapting stimulus, we ought to expect increased discriminability of *small* changes from the adapting stimulus with increasing adaptation time. Decreased detectability of very dim-line stimuli when the appropriate analyzers have adapted to "expect" a much more intense level of activation is directly analogous to what occurs in light adaptation.

Blakemore, Muncey, and Ridley (1971) have confirmed this hypothesis by demonstrating that while adaptation to a high-contrast grating of a given frequency lowers the apparent contrast of the grating and decreases the absolute sensitivity for detection of low-contrast gratings of that frequency, it *increases* the relative sensitivity to changes in contrast from that of the adapting grating. Blakemore and Sutton (1969) and also Karen DeValois (1977) have found that adaptation to a grating of a particular frequency increases the relative discriminability of the frequency of test gratings in the vicinity of the adapting grating frequency. However, Barlow, Macleod, and van Meeteren (1976) could find no such improvements as a consequence of adaptation to gratings.

McCollough effects may be caused by the same figural adaptation process (McCollough 1965; Skowbo et al. 1975). The most frequently studied example of a McCollough effect is as follows: prolonged viewing of a grating of alternating green and black bands will produce an aftereffect in the perception of a similarly oriented grating of white and black bands such that to most observers the white bands will appear slightly reddish (red is the complementary-inhibitory opposite color to green). McCollough effects and some other perceptual adaptation effects can last a very long time (would you believe 12 weeks!) in the absence of a specific interfering adaptation. This renders the hypothesis that they are caused by neural fatigue implausible, to say the least (Jones and Holding 1975). Perceptual adaptation probably does not happen because neurons and synapses get tired out or run out of transmitters. More likely it is a positive adaptive process.

Movement Adaptation

Prolonged viewing of a pattern (such as a grating) moving in a particular direction produces adaptation to the movement such that a stationary presentation of the same pattern will now appear to move slowly in the opposite direction. One example of movement adaptation is the "waterfall illusion." After staring at a waterfall for a few minutes, shift your gaze to a nearby rock face. You should observe a waterfall-like streaming moving *up* the rock. Movement aftereffects have been reported to last over 20 hours after a 15-minute exposure. The aftereffect of a pattern with a certain velocity is to decrease the perceived velocity of movements that have a slower velocity but the same or similar patterns (Over 1971). Presumably this increases the discriminability of pattern movement in the vicinity of the velocity of the adapting stimulus. This function of movement adaptation is precisely analogous to that hypothesized for all other forms of perceptual adaptation.

Ambiguous Figures

Certain stimuli are ambiguous in that they can be seen as a representing either of two different objects. A classic example is the Necker cube shown in figure 2.8. This diagram can be seen as representing a cube with point A in front or a cube with point B in front. The cube is presented to subjects without the letter labels. Subjects see first one version of this ambiguous figure and then the other. With prolonged viewing, perception of such figures shifts back and forth at a rate that increases over the first three minutes or so to an asymptotic (maximum) rate of perceptual alternation. K. T. Brown (1955, 1962) speculates that this increase in the reversal rate over the first few minutes of viewing a figure is yet another consequence of the figural adaptation process we have been discussing. It is consistent with the hypothesized functional purpose of this adaptation that the observer becomes more likely to perceive changes in the figure over time. The rate of reversal in the percep-

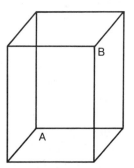

Fig. 2.8 The Necker cube. This reversible figure represents a cube with either point A or point B in front.

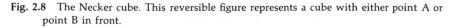

tion of ambiguous figures can be influenced by high-level cognitive processes, such as intent to "hold" onto one percept as long as possible (Pelton and Solley 1968; Rock 1975, pp. 263–70). These facts seem more consistent with the positive view of adaptation than with the negative neural fatigue view.

The figural adaptation responsible for the increase in the rate of reversal for perception of ambiguous figures occurs at some central (cortical) level, after the point where binocular integration has occurred. We know this because there is complete transfer of the adaptation achieved by monocular viewing of an ambiguous figure by one eye to monocular viewing by the other eye. For example, Brown (1962) showed that switching viewing from one eye to the other after three minutes of adaptation produced no decrease in the reversal rate for an ambiguous figure. Large degrees of interocular transfer are found for many other forms of figural adaptation. This also implies a more central cortical loci for at least some of these perceptual adaptation processes.

GROUPING: FIGURES AND GROUNDS

Grouping Principles

One of the most basic principles of perception is that we organize the attributes of a stimulus array into groups. This organization into groups is not random, but follows principles first described by Wertheimer (1923) and thereafter by many others.* The principles can be given the mnemonic labels *proximity, similarity, continuity, smooth continuation, symmetry,* and *familiarity.*

Proximity.   The closer elements are to each other, the more likely they are to be grouped together. For example, figure 2.9(a) is more likely to be seen as four rows than as four columns of dots.

Similarity.   The more similar elements are to each other, the more likely they are to be grouped together. For example, figure 2.9(b) is more likely to be seen as four rows of homogenous colored dots than as four columns of alternating black and white dots. Color, shape, texture, and velocity of movement are some of the dimensions of similarity that affect grouping. Common velocity is a particularly important determinant. Elements that move together tend strongly to be grouped together perceptually (elements that stray together stay together). Proximity can also be subsumed under similarity—as similarity of position in space. Possibly the only aspects of shape similarity that are important for grouping are certain lower-level shape features such as the slopes of component lines. Shape perception is primarily a higher-order process that occurs after grouping. Color and texture

*Also see Rock (1975, pp. 253–83) and Sutherland (1973).

perception may be lower-order processes whose primary function is to sub-serve grouping (Julesz 1965; Beck 1966, 1967; Olson and Attneave 1970.

Continuity. Elements that are enclosed within a single contour tend to be grouped together. They tend to be distinguished from elements that can only be reached by crossing a contour boundary. Thus figure 2.9(c) tends to be grouped into two closed regions.

Smooth continuation. For the mathematically sophisticated reader, smooth continuation means differentiability of a contour (line). We group elements so as to form contours that have as few abrupt changes of direction as possible. Hence we see figure 2.9(d) as a wavy line crossing a zigzag line, not as two contours touching (but not crossing) at one point.

Symmetry. We tend to group elements to form symmetrical shapes. Thus we prefer to see figure 2.9(e) as an object in a window, rather than as two saw blades facing each other.

Familiarity. We tend to group elements so as to form familiar objects or other percepts. Thus we prefer to see figure 2.9(f) as a triangle in (or on) a circle, rather than as a triangle and three segments of a circle. This is a long-term memory familiarity grouping effect. There is also a short-term tendency to persist in seeing whatever grouping we were first induced to impose on a stimulus field. Thus we might continue to see figure 2.9(a) as four rows of dots even when the distance between adjacent dots in a row is increased to equal the distance between adjacent dots in a column.

Figure-Ground Distinction

Whenever we perceptually group those elements that compose a *figure* that we are attending to, the rest of the elements of the stimulus field have been, in some sense, also grouped by exclusion to form the *ground* (background). One basis for the distinction between figure and ground is attentional: the group that we are attending to at any moment is the figure. The elements that are present but which we are not attending to are the ground. According to this distinction, if you are attending only to the circle in figure 2.9(f), the embedded triangle is part of the ground.

A logically different figure-ground distinction is based on form versus texture. Figures have both form and texture, while grounds have only texture (here considered to include color). According to this distinction, both the circle and the triangle in figure 2.9(f) are figures on a common ground, regardless of which figure is at the focus of attention. Furthermore, according to this distinction, one could focus attention on a ground as well as on a figure. This distinction seems preferable to the one that is based on attention. We do tend

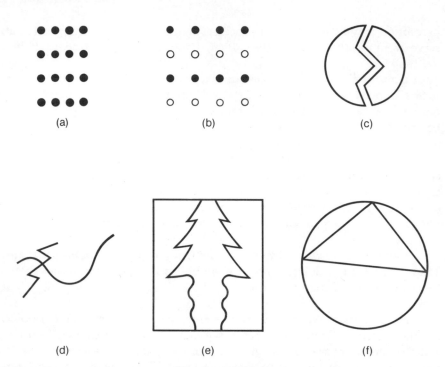

Fig. 2.9 Six grouping principles: proximity (a), similarity (b), continuity (c), smooth continuation (d), symmetry (e), and familiarity (f).

to pay attention to figures and ignore grounds, but it is quite possible to attend to a formless texture.

Does Grouping Impose a Strict Partitioning of a Scene?

Attneave (1971) makes the strong claim that elements that are currently being perceived as members of one group cannot simultaneously be perceived as members of another group. Ambiguous figures such as the Necker cube provide strong support for this claim. There is a clear alternation in the perception of each version of the Necker cube. We do not simultaneously see the cube in both ways, as if each line were simultaneously cross-classified with respect to its position in each perception of the cube.

Not every case is so clear-cut, however. Attneave alleges that if we see a matrix of dots as several rows of dots, we do not simultaneously see it as several columns of dots. This may be true, but we must also admit the perception of a *matrix* of dots—a different, higher-order chunk concept that includes both rows and columns. There are many other examples in which one can integrate seemingly diverse percepts into a common higher-order percept. A single element may be seen as belonging to only one highest-level group at a time, but apparently it can be a constituent of more than one subgroup of the same highest-level group. For example, a dot is a part of both a row and a column within a matrix. A side of square is a part of two right angles. This matter is discussed in more detail in the section concerned with context-sensitive coding.

Innate Grouping
and Perceptual Learning

One known mechanism for grouping visual elements is the convergence of spot detectors to define line and corner detectors and possibly grating and higher-level texture detectors. The specification of at least the line detectors appears to be partly innate, since it is present to some degree in very young kittens with no patterned visual experience (Hubel and Wiesel 1963). However, early visual experience appears to play an important role in specifying the receptive fields of line detectors. First, it increases the acuity (quantitative precision of resolution) of these genetically biased line detectors. Second, it makes (typically small) qualitative changes in the orientation and binocular disparity of the optimum stimulus for a line detector (Barlow 1975). Rearing newborn kittens in a highly abnormal visual environment—for example, one having only vertical lines—can produce a more drastic qualitative change in the population of line detectors. In this example it would produce an excess of vertical line detectors and a paucity of horizontal and oblique line detectors (Blakemore 1974). A young kitten reared with only monocular visual input will lack binocularly activated line detectors. It will consequently be unable to use binocular disparity (difference in the stimulation of the two eyes by a visual stimulus such as a line) to judge depth (Barlow 1975; Pettigrew 1974).

The innately biased grouping of spot detectors to form line detectors does not explain the grouping of many lines to form a unitary but complex figure such as a building or a face. It is worthwhile to question just how unitary the perception of a complex figure is, but it does seem to involve some grouping. This grouping could hardly be by innate specification of complex figure detectors, since we appear capable of grouped perception of any of an infinity of figures. It is an attractive hypothesis that all grouping in perception occurs because several lower-order feature nodes converge onto a single higher-order node representing the entire group. But the specification of this group (chunk) node in the case of complex figures must be by experience (learning). Because there are over ten billion neurons in the brain, it is quite possible to represent each of the figures we attend to by means of a single neuron, but we would run out of neurons if this specification were done entirely genetically. For this coding scheme to work, there must be a pool of genetically unspecified (free) neurons—in the cortex, undoubtedly—that initially represent nothing, but that come via the learning (chunking) process to represent various figures, events, or concepts.

Context-Sensitive Coding: Line and Angle Features

The foregoing hypothesis unifies perceptual grouping at all levels of complexity. However, having a single node represent a complex figure does not explain why we group *unfamiliar* elements in the systematic ways we do. That is, it does not explain any of the grouping principles except the effects of familiarity. The most parsimonious hypothesis at present is that there is a largely innate grouping up to the level of line, corner, color, and texture detectors; but beyond that all grouping results entirely from experience.

If closed figures tend to have an innate unity even prior to visual experience—and this is not definitely established (Sutherland 1973)—it may be because each corner (angle) detector "glues" together its constituent line segments, and each line (segment) detector "glues" together its terminal corners. The result would be a simultaneous activation (grouped perception) of all the line and angle detectors that are the constituents of a closed figure.* Such simultaneous activation is presumably a necessary condition for the specification of a chunk node to represent the entire group of features. This hypothesis is a kind of context-sensitive coding for forms, in that the corner detectors are strongly associated (either innately or as a result of early visual experience) to the intersecting line detectors that specify the corner detector. In the reverse direction the line detectors should be strongly associated to all corner detectors that they help specify. This hypothesis is illustrated in figure 2.10 for a triangle coded redundantly by three line segment detectors and three corner detectors.

The coding is redundant, since we know from plane geometry that three sides (or two sides and an included angle or two angles and an included side) determine a unique triangle. (Three angles determine a set of similar triangles.) As in plane geometry it is reasonable to assume that the angle detector ab does not encode the length of its component sides. This means that angle detector ab could be activated by any of a large variety of line segments (a_i and b_i) with many different lengths and locations, provided that these lie along lines a and b. However, in our mental geometry a 30° angle defined by one pair of lines (of indefinite extent) would probably be represented by a different angle detector at some level of processing than would a 30° angle at a different location or facing in a different direction. Thus in this mental geometry, activation of three (or even two) angle detectors would be sufficient to define a triangle uniquely. Indeed, presentation of two or three angles

---

*Hebb (1949) and Milner (1974) have pointed out some of the theoretical advantages of angle detectors.

without connecting sides (or of three sides without connecting angles—i.e., with the intersections blanked out) is sufficient to give a fairly strong perception of a triangle.

This type of coding is termed context-sensitive because no constituent of the whole (form) is independent of the others (its context). Whenever we have an ab angle constituent, we know that we must have one of the line segment constituents $a_i = a_1, \ldots a_n$, and one of the line segment constituents $b_i = b_1, \ldots b_n$, though we do not know which pair of line segments a_i and b_i from knowing ab alone. That is, we know the direction of the lines, but not their lengths. Similarly, if we know the line segment constituent a_i, we know that we must have two angle constituents, both having line a_i as one side, with one angle located at one end of line segment a_i, and the other located at the other end. But we don't know the size of the angles. Context-sensitive coding is just a fancy name for a special kind of redundant coding of wholes in terms of associated parts. Similar types of context-sensitive coding may underlie many other cognitive coding structures, as we shall see.

At any given level of processing in the visual system (and indeed throughout much of the nervous system), it is reasonable to assume that every node has lateral inhibitory connections to every other node. This tends to focus attention on those nodes that are maximally activated and suppress attention to other nodes. The side-angle context-sensitive coding of forms will tend to make closed figures pop into or out of attention as a group, while lateral inhibition suppresses other forms, especially figures that are less "good" according to the grouping principles. One rather impressive piece of evidence that supports a local excitatory connection between constituents (such as that provided by side-angle context-sensitive coding) is provided by research on images that have been stabilized on the retina, so that they always

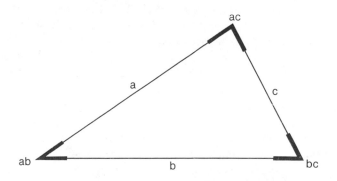

Fig. 2.10   Context-sensitive coding of a triangle in terms of three line segment detectors (a, b, c) and three corner detectors (ab, bc, ac). Because each corner detector (e.g., ab) is strongly associated with its constituent line segment detectors (e.g., a and b) and vice versa, a positive feedback loop is set up. This tends to keep the entire set of line and corner detectors in a closed figure activated simultaneously as a group.

stimulate the same point on the retina regardless of eye movements. Under these conditions the visual system adapts to the stabilized image, so that eventually all of the image disappears. However, the image disappears in connected groups, leaving other connected groups still visible. This is just what it ought to do according to context-sensitive coding theory. Furthermore, lines, and to a lesser extent angles, strongly tend to disappear as entire units. This supplements the neurophysiological evidence for line and corner detectors and buttresses the assumption that sides and angles are basic units of visual form coding (Pritchard, Heron, and Hebb 1960; McFarland 1968).

As a closed figure becomes more complex (has more sides and angles), the lateral inhibition on each constituent increases. This reduces the level of activation of each constituent and therefore reduces its attentional clarity. The context-sensitive coding "glue" is local in its effect. The more parts to the image, the greater the strain placed on each part. To understand this, imagine a complex picture frame glued at its corners. You would place a greater strain on each corner as you increased the number of sides. Lateral inhibition between constituents may also decrease with increasing distance —although presumably not to zero—to make the theory consistent with the apparent fact that image clarity tends to decrease with increasing image complexity.

Constituent Structure

Let us assume that we are familiar with the concept of a triangle inscribed in a circle and can therefore have a unitary perception of an example of this concept such as that shown in figure 2.9(f). It is unlikely that this unitary grouped perception takes place by single-step convergence of (straight and curved) line and corner detectors onto a node representing a triangle inscribed in a circle. It is more likely that this more complex percept has intermediary nodes representing the triangle, the circle, and the relation between them. Thus a whole learned perceptual group may have one or more levels of learned subgroups for constituents, and each subgroup may have one or more levels of innate sub-subgroups (such as corner, line, and spot detectors). In this way every percept or image has a definite hierarchical constituent structure, much like a sentence in language. This structure will be discussed in chapter 3.

There is often one preferred constituent structure for a particular percept. But human beings appear to have the option of defining alternative constituent structures. For example, one can see figure 2.9(f) as having four immediate constituents: a triangle and three circular segments. Sutherland (1968) considers this ability to segment complex visual input in several alternative ways to be a critical competence in form recognition. Certainly it is important in identifying *hidden* figures, such as a 5 embedded in a scrambled mess of lines. The ability to impose alternative segmentation on visual input may also play an important role in the perception of the less dominant interpretation of an ambiguous figure. Finally, ordinary object perception may involve choosing among a set of alternative groupings of the elements of complex visual input.

Imposing a multilevel constituent structure on a complex form provides a long-distance vertical associative "glue" to hold together a complex image. This adds to the horizontal (or short-distance vertical) associative "glue" provided by context-sensitive coding at any given level. Constituents of a group have innate or learned upward and downward associations to the group node. These provide excitatory input that tends to hold the group together and makes it pop into or out of attention as a whole. This explains why the disappearance of stabilized images tends also to preserve meaningful (familiar, learned) groups as well as connected groups. For example, a complex character such as ℬ fades so that what remains is 4, B, or 3 (Pritchard, Heron and Hebb 1960).

Encoding a form by means of a simultaneously activated multilevel constituent structure, made possible through vertical associative chunking, gives the present theory a major advantage over the very important cell assembly theory of Hebb (1949). Hebb used only horizontal associations between already (innately) defined nodes representing the parts of forms. He could only represent the constituent (grouping) structure of complex forms by activation of cell assemblies in a particular sequence (phase sequences).

Integral versus Separable Combinations of Stimulus Dimensions

Following up on related ideas proposed by Torgerson, Attneave, Shepard, and Lockhead, Garner has assembled a variety of evidence to support the distinction between *integral* and *separable* combinations of stimulus dimensions. Examples of the former include combinations of two form dimensions (e.g., height and width) or two quality dimensions (e.g., brightness and color) of the same form. Examples of the latter include just about any combination of dimensions for two separate forms (e.g., the height of one rectangle and the height of another rectangle). Note that any given stimulus dimension is not integral or separable in all combinations. It is each particular combination of two dimensions that is integral or separable. Combinations such as the form and color of the same figure are intermediate in integrality between the most integral or separable combinations. Combinations of stimulus dimensions may have many degrees of integrality. The most integral are those combinations of dimensions that are combined into chunks at the lowest level of the visual system. The most separable are those combined into chunks at the highest level of the visual system—or not at all.*

---

*The evidence supporting the conclusions of this section comes primarily from Teuber (1960); Garner and Felfoldy (1970); Lockhead (1972); Garner (1974); and Garner (1976).

Integrality affects the dynamics of perceptual processing in some interesting ways. First, when the visual system rapidly classifies a multidimensional stimulus according to a single dimension (e.g., according to the height of one form), variation in an irrelevant dimension that is integrally related to the relevant dimension (e.g., the width of the same form) slows down information processing considerably. Thus a subject would be slower to classify a rectangle on a card as "tall" or "short" in height if across trials the rectangle being classified also varied in width than he would be if the width remained constant. Variation in the irrelevant dimension lengthens reaction time for a given degree of accuracy in classifying the relevant dimension. By contrast, variation of a highly separable irrelevant dimension (e.g., the height of a second form—perhaps a triangle—on the same card) may have little or no effect. Intermediate results can be obtained for dimensions of intermediate integrality. Thus selective attention is less effective in suppressing the distracting effects of an irrelevant attribute the more integral the combination of the relevant and irrelevant attributes is. That is, it is less effective the lower down in the constituent structure of a percept chunking occurs.

Second, when the values of the irrelevant dimension are perfectly correlated with the relevant dimension for classification (e.g., when the high form is always narrow and the low form is always wide), classification speed is increased on the relevant dimension. This is termed *redundancy gain.* The greater the degree of integrality of the two dimensions—in our theory, the lower down in the hierarchical constituent structure chunking of the two dimensions occurs—and the greater the redundancy gain.

OBJECT CONCEPTS
AND FORM PERCEPTION

Conjunctive and Disjunctive Aspects

The primary purpose of form, color, and texture perception is to recognize objects. An object does not always present the same "face" to the same locations on our retinas. Sometimes we see it in the center of our visual field; sometimes off to one side. Sometimes we see the front of the object; sometimes the back, side, top, bottom, or various combinations thereof. Sometimes the appearance of the object changes. Sometimes we see not the object, but only its name. There is no subset of stimulus attributes common to all these groups of cues. Yet we can often recognize the same object given any one of this large variety of cues. How do we do it?

Chunking can account for the conjunctive aspect of object recognition. Presumably those features that frequently form part of the same group will become strongly associated to the chunk node representing that group. However, we must also account for the disjunctive aspect of concept recognition.

Somehow all the chunks cueing the same object concept must be associated either to each other or, more probably, to a higher-order (more abstract) concept node representing the object in any of its manifestations.

Object Nodes

According to the primary theoretical framework adopted in this book, there is one unique node that represents any familiar object. When we perceive or think of that object, its node is activated more than any other node. A single node may or may not correspond to a single neuron. Even so simple a stimulus as a single line activates many line detectors to various extents, though perhaps only one neuron or a very small set of equivalent neurons are maximally activated. Should we consider the psychological node representing the line to be the maximally activated neuron? Or should we consider the node to be a small group of neurons, or perhaps all the neurons in the brain weighted in proportion to their rate of activation? We do not know.

The same uncertainty applies even more strongly to the coding of more complex objects. Here we have only a few scraps of evidence to suggest that single neurons respond differentially to particular complex objects or concepts. A few neurons have been found in monkey cortex for which the optimum stimulus appeared to be a hand, a bottle brush, or some other complex object (Gross, Bender and Rocha-Miranda 1974). Single neurons have also been found that appear to encode number concepts, responding selectively to the second, fifth, sixth, or seventh stimulus in a series. For these "number cells" the specific character of the stimulus was unimportant, as was its rate of presentation over a one- to five-second range between successive stimuli (Thompson, Mayers, Robertson, and Patterson 1970). Such reports of neurons encoding complex concepts are not sufficient to establish the specific neuron principle of encoding for complex learned concepts. But this principle is a very plausible extension of the specific neuron encoding used at lower levels of the nervous system.

The most frequently mentioned alternative to specific-neuron encoding of objects is to represent an object by the activation rates of all the neurons in the brain or some large part of the brain (e.g., the visual system). In an abstract psychological theory one can consider this set of activation rates to be a single node. At present we cannot say whether a node is one neuron or an activation function defined over a small or large set of neurons. Regardless of the neural basis of object representation, it is useful to assume that the psychological representative of a familiar object is a unique node in a network of partially associated nodes. This assumption provides a clear way of thinking about what it means to perceive or think of an object (or a concept). Then, too, object perception has a unitary, holistic quality that is well captured by assuming that, however complex the constituent structure of visual attributes, there is at the top of this hierarchy a single node representing the entire object. As we shall see, there is also specific experimental evidence to support the assumption that the perception of a familiar object is a single unitary decision, not the result of several separate decisions regarding component attributes.

Object Constancy

Several sets of cues are typically sufficient to activate an object concept that has no common features. Therefore, a completely arbitrary, learned disjunction of these cue sets must be associated to the common concept node. However, not all of our capacity to recognize an object from diverse sets of cues comes from such an arbitrary learning process. The innate organization of our visual system is such that we can recognize the identity of a particular object despite changes in the *brightness* of illumination of the object, in the *retinal position* of the image, and in our own *distance from the object* (and therefore in its *retinal size*). To some extent we can also recognize objects as equivalent despite changes in their *orientation* with respect to us. This is especially true for rotation in the two depth planes; it is less true for rotation in the frontal plane. Human beings (and other species to varying extents) also frequently treat *filled and outline shapes* as equivalent, as if external contour were a highly salient set of attributes. We can also recognize shapes despite considerable *noise* or *jitter* (e.g., bending the sides of a rectangle or deleting small parts of the contour). The first three of these six invariances for form perception—brightness, retinal position, and retinal size—are known to be largely mediated by innate mechanisms. There may also be some contribution from perceptual learning. The relative importance of innate organization versus perceptual learning is less clear for the last three factors: orientation, filled versus outline shapes, and noise.* We will now discuss in more detail object constancy (or the lack thereof) with respect to changes in brightness, position, distance and size, and orientation.

Brightness. The absolute level of illumination changes drastically from twilight to midday. Therefore, it would be highly functional if our visual system were innately constructed to recognize objects independent of the level of illumination. As we saw in the sections on light and dark adaptation, our visual system is, in fact, constructed in this way—and the mechanisms are surely innate, since they occur in the retina. (One mechanism occurs in the receptors and another in the neurons connected to the receptors.) The visual system responds primarily to the contrasts (relative reflectances) of adjacent areas, not to absolute light intensity. Throughout this discussion of object constancy we will see various examples of the general principle that *the visual system encodes relational features,* not absolute features.

*The evidence supporting the conclusions in this section is taken from Neisser (1967, pp. 52–58); Sutherland (1968, 1973); and Rock (1975, pp. 295–312).

When the *contrasts* of a figure are inverted, as in a photographic negative, our ability to recognize familiar objects is sharply reduced. The effects of less drastic changes in contrast have not been systematically investigated. Presumably they are smaller. However, contrast is basic to form recognition (zero contrast is a blank field), so we hardly expect form recognition to be invariant with changes in contrast.

Retinal position. As you move your eyes, head, and body, the retinal location of stimulation changes for a given object in your environment. It would be highly functional if your visual system were constructed to represent any object in an invariant manner regardless of retinal location—and apparently it is. If a new form is exposed to humans (or to many other species) in one retinal location, it will subsequently be recognized when it is presented in a different retinal location. This transfer of form perception from one location to another is apparently innate. At least, it is apparently innate over a displacement range of 5° of visual angle, because Ganz and Wilson (1967) demonstrated it in infant monkeys who had had no prior experience with pattern vision. Novel context can sometimes disrupt the recognition of familiar objects. But we also have a considerable capacity to recognize the same object in new positions in the world—that is, in novel contexts of accompanying stimuli. This capacity probably involves other mechanisms besides the one that is required to explain invariance over retinal position.

Size and distance. Since the retinal size of a perceived object decreases with increasing distance from the observer, it would be functional if we possessed a mechanism for achieving object constancy (equivalent encoding of a form) with varying size and distance. We do have such a mechanism, and once again Ganz and Wilson have demonstrated that it is innate. Of course, what should be treated as equivalent is encodings of the same form seen at different distances with corresponding changes in retinal size. Objects that are truly different in real size while similar in form are discriminably different objects. We can also, of course, discriminate between two different distances for the same object. The fact that our visual system has object constancy with respect to size changes, position changes, level of illumination, orientation, or any other factor means that we can recognize an invariant object out of a varying set of irrelevant stimulus dimensions. It does not mean that we cannot perceive these irrelevant dimensions and use them to discriminate distance and size, retinal and real position, level of illumination, orientation, and so forth.

Orientation. As we tilt our head or body to the right or left, the retinal position of an object we are viewing changes as if the object were being rotated in the frontal plane. As we bend our head or body forward or backward, the retinal position of an object changes as if the object were being rotated in depth around a horizontal axis. As we twist or turn our heads or bodies to alter our direction of gaze, the retinal position of an object changes as if it were being rotated in depth around a vertical axis. Accordingly, it would be desirable if we had some capacity to recognize objects independent of their rotational orientation—and we do.

However, we often do not perceive an object as having the same form at different orientations. Two of the classic examples are that a square rotated 45° in the frontal plane appears to be a diamond, and that an upside-down face is very hard to recognize. We also distinguish between p and d or between 7 and L on the basis of orientation. On the other hand, you probably would have no trouble recognizing an upside-down telephone, and you can read words upside down, though it takes you longer to do so (turn your book upside down and try it). Rotations of 30° or less in the frontal plane do not greatly impair the accuracy of object recognition. For a rotation in depth around a vertical axis, Massaro found that rotation away from the frontal plane had a very gradually increasing deleterious effect on the speed and accuracy of circle versus ellipse discrimination. This effect increased up to nearly 80°, where accuracy was still well above chance.

Orientation is probably always a relevant form dimension for objects that have a typical (most frequent) orientation. At least, it is relevant in the sense that object recognition is faster in the familiar orientation. The relevance of orientation to the description of objects is confirmed by cases such as that of p versus d. These two different forms (objects) are discriminated primarily (or in some cases exclusively) on the basis of orientation. However, as Attneave and Rock have emphasized, it is not the retinal orientation of a form that is critical. The critical factor is its cognitive orientation with respect to some internally adopted frame of reference that describes objects using coordinate axes and directions—*top* and *bottom, right* and *left, front* and *back.* This cognitive frame of reference is generally strongly determined by external stimulus factors, though it can be altered by a purely cognitive *act of will.* There appear to be at least four important stimulus determinants of cognitive orientation. These are retinal orientation, gravitational ("real-world") orientation, orientation with respect to surrounding stimulus frames (e.g., the outline of a page), and orientation with respect to other stimuli. As an example of the ability to adopt a cognitive reference axis based on relations between nearby stimuli, Attneave points out that the stimuli shown in figure 2.11 are most easily seen as an oblique row of squares tilted at a 45° angle with respect to the page. But each figure in isolation would be seen as a diamond, and the page frame would then provide the coordinate axes for describing the *top* of each form (Attneave 1968; Attneave and Olson 1967; Attneave and Reid 1968). Furthermore, Rock (1973) demonstrated that subjects viewing unfamiliar forms in a particular orientation later show substantially less ability to recognize the previously exposed forms when their orientation is rotated by 90°. In this study subjects adopted a gravitational

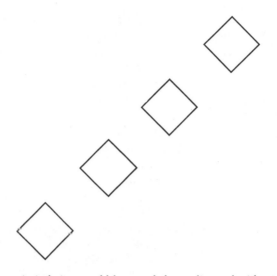

Fig. 2.11 Each figure in isolation would be encoded as a diamond with respect to axes formed by the page frame of reference. However, when the reader views the whole row of figures, the subjectively adopted reference axis shifts. Now these figures are encoded as a row of squares tilted at 45° to the page. (Reprinted from Fred Attneave, Triangles as ambiguous figures, *American Journal of Psychology* 81 (1968): 449, by permission of the University of Illinois Press and the author.)

reference frame. Recognition was primarily affected by changes in gravitational orientation—whether upright or tilted 90° in the external world. It was much less affected by changes in retinal orientation—accomplished by tilting the head 90°.

Relational Features
versus Transformations

There are two general theories of object constancy. The first theory holds that we extract *relational features* of objects that are truly invariant with respect to brightness, position, distance and size, and orientation. The second theory holds that we internally *transform* the stimulus to some prototypical brightness, position, distance and size, and orientation in order to recognize it. As we shall see in chapter 3, there is good evidence that we can perform various mental operations on images such as rotation, translation, and size changes. The issue here is whether such transformations occur as an integral part of the perceptual object recognition process. At present this simply is not known. On the other side, we have already noted evidence for the existence of neural feature detectors that can encode a line of a given orientation over a range of retinal positions. Again, we do not know whether a form can be recognized by a set of abstract feature detectors of this kind.

An experiment relevant to this issue was performed by Attneave and Block (1974) on the comparison of two linear extents—bar length or width as a function of the difference in angular orientation of the bars being compared. They found little or no difference in either speed or accuracy of judging length as the difference in orientation increased. They concluded that the length attribute of a bar was directly comparable for bars independent of orientational discrepancy, and that no mental rotation to achieve a corresponding orientation was required. On the other hand, as we shall see in chapter 3, we know that mental image rotation is required in order to judge the equivalence of two complex forms that are either identical or mirror-image reversed. Ordinary form perception involves perception of more than one dimension but requires less difficult discriminations than that involved in mirror-image reversals. The relative importance of feature extraction and mental transformations in ordinary form perception remains to be determined.

Serial versus Parallel Processing in Object Perception

Imagine that you are to identify as fast as possible which of two possible stimuli is being presented. Could you do it faster if the two stimuli differed in only one dimension (e.g., a large circle versus a small circle) or if they differed in two dimensions (e.g., a large, bright circle versus a small, dim circle)? If humans can only process one stimulus dimension at a time (*serial processing*), we would expect at least one (and possibly both) of the unidimensional discriminations to be faster than the redundant bidimensional discrimination. However, if humans can process both dimensions at the same time without much loss in efficiency (*parallel processing*), we would expect the redundant two-dimensional discrimination to be faster than either one-dimensional discrimination. (This is known as *redundancy gain.*) Biederman and Checkosky (1970) obtained the latter result when they gave subjects the task described above. This shows that human beings are capable of parallel processing in perception.

This parallel processing capacity applies to different types of stimulus dimensions of the same object (e.g., to size and brightness or to frequency and orientation of a grating). We cannot process two different orientations at the same time without a serious loss of efficiency. Wing and Allport (1972) presented stimuli of the type shown in figure 2.12 and limited the time for perception by flashing a patterned visual-noise *masking field* on the screen a fraction of a second after the stimulus. In one set of conditions subjects reported on only one of the three stimulus dimensions (frequency of grating, orientation of grating, orientation of break). In another set they reported on two dimensions (either grating orientation and frequency or grating orientation and break orientation). Reporting on two *different types* of dimensions—

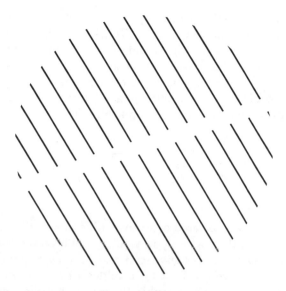

Fig. 2.12 Stimulus of the type used by Wing and Allport differing in three dimensions: grating frequency, grating orientation, and break orientation.

grating orientation and frequency—was as accurate as reporting on either dimension in isolation (perfect parallel processing). However, reporting on two *similar types* of dimensions—grating orientation and break orientation— was substantially inferior to reporting on either dimension in isolation. It may be that performing two orientation analyses requires strictly successive use of the orientation analyzing feature system. Or at least there may be a substantial lateral inhibitory interference when two orientations are being processed in parallel.

How do we perform this parallel processing? Do we process each dimension separately to determine its value and then, if necessary, combine these attribute decisions to determine which object is present? Or do we let the developing perceptual information about each attribute continuously flow through to the object chunk level, differentially activating one object node more than the others? Are the decisions made in parallel at the attribute level? Or is the information processed in parallel at the attribute level, and is a single decision made at the object level regarding what stimulus chunk (or *blob* in Lockhead's terminology) is present? By means of a very clever analysis, Lockhead was able to demonstrate that, at least in some instances, decision making occurs at the object level, not at the attribute level. Only one decision is made regarding what object is present. But information concerning all relevant stimulus dimensions is processed through lower feature-analyzing levels in parallel to provide the input necessary for activating one object node more than another. So long as the stimulus attributes are of different types, there is no interference in the processing of each attribute. We can probably process in parallel stimulus attributes in different sensory modalities—such as the sight of a cat, the sound of its purr, and the touch of its fur —to activate a single object node in an abstract (multisensory) cognitive modality. Presumably, we must acquire an object node for each entity to be discriminated in order to achieve chunk parallel processing. Indeed, Lockhead cites practice effects that support this supposition (Lockhead 1972; Monahan and Lockhead 1977).

EXPECTATION AND FEEDBACK IN PERCEPTION

If you have in the past associated cobwebs with spiders and have stored this fact in your memory, then when you walk through an old building full of cobwebs, you will expect to perceive spiders. In such a context, a light tickle on your leg may cause you to look for a spider when you would not do so in another context. The most plausible theory of the effect of context and memory on perception is that contextual stimuli activate their nodes in memory. These in turn, partially activate (prime) nodes representing associated event concepts. This makes you more likely to perceive an expected event than an unexpected one, because sensory input is summing with central associative input to "expected" nodes. It also makes you more likely to "false alarm" to expected events—to think you saw something that wasn't there (Palmer 1975a).

Expectations may influence perception only at the level of object concepts in semantic memory. Alternatively, partial activation (priming) of an object node in semantic memory may cascade downward toward the sensory periphery, priming its featural constituents, which prime their constituents, and so on. The use of downward as well as upward associations in perception constitutes a *feedback process* in perception. Such a process would help us to make maximum use of context and of our previously established memories.

PERCEPTUAL RESPONSES

Perception of an object under ordinary circumstances often involves a series of eye fixations on different parts of the object. Obviously we integrate these views of separate parts of the object at some high level of processing where *place* is not rigidly determined by retinal location, since the successive eye fixations put interfering visual stimulation on the same (central) region of the retina. We have the capacity to map retinal location in conjunction with eye, head, and body position onto real-world location nodes in one or more cognitive (spatial or image) modalities.

In doing this mapping, we also use information concerning the movement of the stimulus object itself. Rock and Gilchrist (1975) showed that perception of an object is possible even when the object is moved behind a small slit, and the observer fixates the slit so that all stimulation is delivered to the same small region of the retina. In such a case there is no distributed pattern of retinal stimulation whatsoever. The place of any given thing in our cognitive map of the world is determined by far more than retinal location.

SUMMARY

1 The visual nervous system has single neurons that appear to represent (encode) specific features (attributes) such as spots, lines, rays, segments, corners, and miniature gratings at particular locations and with particular orientations, widths, and so on. Presentation of the specific stimulus feature activates the neuron maximally. Presentation of other features is less effective; effectiveness depends on the degree of similarity between the feature presented and the optimum feature. Many neurons may redundantly encode the same feature. The extended representation of a feature may include all of the neurons that respond maximally or submaximally to that feature (the entire generalization gradient of activation induced by the feature).

2 More complex, higher-level, feature neurons, such as line detectors, appear to receive both excitatory and inhibitory input from simpler, lower-level, feature neurons, such as spot detectors. When a chunk node receives inhibitory input from a lower-level, feature node, this means that the absence of that feature is a constituent of the chunk. Higher-level neurons appear to compute approximately logical functions of their constituent features (attributes). Examples are conjunctions (e.g., spot A_1 AND spot A_2 AND ... AND spot A_n AND not spot B_1 AND not spot B_2 AND ... AND not spot B_n) and disjunctions (e.g., line L_1 OR line L_2 OR ... OR line L_n).

3 Instead of, or in addition to, edge and slit detectors, miniature spatial frequency (grating) detectors may serve as the basis of encoding forms, textures, or both.

4 Inhibition makes possible the positive representation of dark spots and lines. It enhances contrast and compensates for blurring by the lens of the eye. It permits the eye to retain its sensitivity over an enormous range of illumination by means of neural light adaptation. Finally, it may play a substantial role in attention.

5 Like any measuring instrument, the visual system has a limited range for representing different values along any feature dimension. This is an especially acute problem when it is necessary to represent relative differences in brightness, since the range of absolute levels of brightness from starlight to midday is enormous. To solve this problem, we have two light-dark adaptation mechanisms (one receptor, one neural) that center our limited light discrimination capacities on the appropriate absolute illumination level to achieve maximum discrimination. Although the mechanisms may differ somewhat, all our sensory adaptation processes, including those involved in absolute judgments, figural adaptation, and movement adaptation, may focus limited discriminative capacity in the region of the adapting stimuli. This will diminish sensitivity for

stimuli far away from the adapting range, but it enhances the ability to discriminate stimuli within that range.

6 Attributes are grouped to form figures (objects). They are distinguished from the attributes grouped to form other figures or backgrounds on the basis of proximity, similarity, continuity, smooth continuation, symmetry, and familiarity. Some grouping of lower-order attribute nodes into higher-order chunks is innate, as in the grouping of dots to form lines. Other grouping is learned, as in the unitary perception of a familiar building or face.

7 Tight coupling (grouping) of the line (segment) and angle constituents of a figure may be achieved by a kind of overlapping, redundant, context-sensitive coding. In this coding each line segment node is strongly associated to the angle (corner) nodes it ends at, and each angle node is strongly associated to the nodes representing each line segment that composes it. Such associations could be either innate or learned. They form a horizontal, context-sensitive "glue" that helps to hold a figure together. In addition, there is a vertical "glue" formed by feedback associations from a higher-level chunk node to its line and angle constituents.

8 From a logical standpoint, the conditions for activating an object concept may be represented as a disjunction of conjunctions of attributes—one set of attributes OR another set of attributes, and so on. We are able to recognize the same object over large changes in brightness of illumination of the object, retinal position of the object, distance from the object (and therefore retinal size), and to some extent orientation (perspective). There are two bases for this object constancy. The first is innate feature extraction of higher-order invariants (as for changes in brightness, position, and distance). The second is learned association of different groups of attributes (as for orientation, especially in the case of objects for which some pairs of views may have no common attributes).

9 We can process several stimulus dimensions in parallel (simultaneously), provided that no two dimensions draw on the same stimulus-analyzing mechanisms. If two dimensions are so highly similar that they compete for attention by the same stimulus-analyzing mechanism, they must be processed serially (sequentially).

10 Downward (feedback or expectation) associations from chunk nodes to their constituents play an important role in perception. They sensitize perception of expected, as compared to unexpected, events.

11 Perception has an active, information-seeking aspect in which we perform perceptual responses (e.g., eye, head, and body movements) to obtain several views of an object. These views may be integrated to form a unified perception of that object.

CHAPTER 3
SPATIAL COGNITION AND IMAGERY

OBJECTIVES

1 To distinguish between the *what* modality and the *where* modality. The what modality is images of the form of objects and operations on images. The where modality is spatial memory for the locations of objects and movement operations on location.

2 To describe how the abstract spatial modality encodes position and movement in motor memory and visual, tactile, and kinesthetic sensory memory.

3 To discuss the following properties of the imagery modality: (a) the constituent structure of images, (b) the nature of a simple image and the synthesis of a complex image by successive imaging of its parts, (c) the relation between image size and image adequacy (clarity), and (d) the relation between imagery and perception.

4 To describe the phenomenon of eidetic imagery.

5 To distinguish between nondestructive image operations (generation, scanning, and zooming)—which add to an image without actively destroying previously established image components—and destructive image operations (deletion, rotation, reflection, translation, magnification, minification, squashing, stretching, and tearing)—which actively inhibit or negate some or all previously established image components.

6 To describe mental rotation of images. To examine the evidence that large-angle rotations are composed of smaller-step rotations, that image rotation speed is faster for two- than for three-dimensional forms, and that image rotation is a destructive operation.

7 To describe mental synthesis of two separate images into a unified whole.

Without looking, reach around and touch something that you know is behind you, but that is not touching your body or stimulating your senses in any other way. If you're too far away from any such object to touch it, estimate how far behind you the nearest wall is. Now turn around and look. How accurate were you? Not perfectly accurate, of course, but vastly more accurate than pure chance would allow.

How were you able to do this? You must carry around a mental map of your immediate spatial environment that does not require constant sensory input to be maintained, though you can localize an object better in space just after or while it is stimulating your senses. You can demonstrate this latter point for yourself. Put a cross on a piece of paper and put the paper on the desk in front of you. Now make dots with your pen on the paper, trying to hit the cross. Close your eyes for 10 seconds and try it again. Try it several more times, closing your eyes a little longer each time. Your localization performance will be best if you make the dots while looking at the cross. It will be very good if you make the dots shortly after closing your eyes. And even after you have kept your eyes closed for a long time, it will still be far more accurate than pure chance would allow. Your ability to touch, grasp, kick, or walk to (but not into) objects in your immediate vicinity is called *spatial localization.* This ability is discussed below.

Now let's examine your mental map of the world beyond your immediate environment. Take a mental walk (or drive) from where you are to someplace else. Presumably you experience a succession of images of various parts of your environment connected by straight-ahead moves, left turns, right turns, steps up, steps down, even a slight sinking feeling in your stomach as you descend in an elevator. The memory structure you must have in your mind to take these mental walks or get from one place to another is called a *cognitive map.* A cognitive map is often considered to be an image like the image of a complex form, scene, or face. Certainly we can form an image of a map as we can of any complex pattern, but are most of our cognitive maps actually images of road maps or building floor plans? Was your mental walk initially present in your mind in its entirety as a schematic trail map? I doubt it. Cognitive maps are typically strongly sequential; in them images are related to one another by movement operations of various kinds. This relating of images by operations is similar in many respects to constructing a complex image by scanning its parts. Furthermore, both cognitive maps and imagery appear to be predominantly right-hemisphere functions. Nevertheless, there is evidence to indicate that the spatial abilities that mediate the learning of complex images in the laboratory or of cognitive maps of our environment are different from the capacity for imagery that mediates the learning of complex forms, scenes, and faces (Newcombe and Russell 1969; Warrington and James 1967). Because there has been no systematic research on cognitive maps, we cannot resolve the exact relation between cognitive maps and images.

In any event, we must somehow distinguish between the form properties of objects, people, and scenes and their locations in the world. We have
all had the experience of forgetting where we put something. We remember
the form properties of the lost object well enough, but we have forgotten its
location in the world. This is because the form and the location of an object
are dissociable types of information. There may also be separate representations in the brain for forms (images) and spatial locations, including movements. As Attneave puts it, there may be separate *what* (image) and *where*
(spatial) systems. Attneave also observes that the what and where systems
must be closely interconnected, since we are capable of perceiving specific
objects in specific locations (Ingle et al. 1967–68; Schneider 1969; Attneave
1974). Furthermore, the what system must include at least the relative locations of the points, lines, and other constituents of a form in relation to each
other. However, it seems reasonable to consider this local relative positional
information (for image representation) to be distinct from the larger-scale
information concerning the position and movement of objects in three-
dimensional space (for spatial representation).

SPATIAL MEMORY

Human beings code and remember the spatial positions of significant objects.
They also appear to encode and remember certain characteristics of the
changes of positions of objects (movement). These characteristics include
speed, acceleration, duration, and extent of movement. Knowledge of position and movement for objects that are not a part of the body or in contact
with parts of the body can only be given by vision or hearing. We derive
information regarding position and movement of our body parts or of objects
in contact with our body from the visual, auditory, tactile, and kinesthetic
sensory systems.

We also derive information concerning the position of body parts from
central motor representatives (motor outflow) that control the position of
these parts. This can happen even in the absence of any sensory feedback.
Take the example of an effector that has a constant load (constant weight to
move), such as the eyeball. Knowledge of the eyeball's position (and therefore
the direction of gaze) can be signaled entirely by the motor representatives
that control the muscles of the eye. Thus it is not surprising that the eye
muscles of various species are thought to lack kinesthetic sensory receptors.
All too often it has been assumed that knowledge of the position of some
effector, such as the arm or the tongue, is given only by sensory feedback.
Such sensory feedback does typically play an important role in knowledge
and control of the position of the various effectors. However, a good deal of
this knowledge and control can be derived independent of sensory feedback,
from central motor commands to the muscles.

Although spatial features must be separate for different sensory and motor modalities at some level of processing, all these sensory and motor systems may converge on some common abstract spatial representation modality that encodes position and movement. Such an abstract spatial modality would perform the useful function of integrating information regarding position or movement gained from any of these sources. Furthermore, as Laabs (1973) has demonstrated, information regarding position acquired through one modality (motor commands and kinesthetic feedback) can be interfered with by a processing task that requires the use of spatial information in a different modality (vision). The integration of spatial information from different sensory and motor modalities, and the fact that interference appears to be specific to the type of information (rather than to the sensory or motor modality from which it was obtained), argue for a common cognitive representation of position and movement independent of the input mode. Nevertheless, most studies have concentrated on a particular sensory or motor modality, and this provides a convenient way to organize the following discussion.

Visual Position and Movement

Kinchla and his colleagues have studied memory for the position of visual dots. Kinchla employed the psychophysical method of delayed comparison. This is a simple generalization of the standard successive comparison procedure used in psychophysics. In delayed comparison a subject is presented with a *standard stimulus,* followed, after a variable delay, by the *comparison stimulus.* The subject is to judge the relation between the standard and comparison stimuli (in all respects or in one or more respects). The subject may be asked to make a *same-different judgment* (again, with respect to all dimensions or only one dimension, such as vertical position). The subject might also be asked to make a *directional judgment*—to judge whether the comparison stimulus was higher or lower, larger or smaller, more or less intense than the standard stimulus.

In delayed comparison of dot position, Kinchla distinguished between knowledge of *absolute position,* which is the position of a dot within some unchanging frame of reference, and *relative position,* which is the position of a dot in relation to some other dot, object, or movable frame of reference (Kinchla and Allan 1969; Kinchla 1971). It is clear that we encode the spatial position of an object in relation to one or more frames of reference. If these frames move with respect to one another, we can to some extent make separate judgments concerning the remembered position of an object with respect to each frame. Furthermore, we can remember a number of different locations for the same object at different times. It is not known whether this encoding of temporally or contextually specific associations between objects and locations occurs strictly within the spatial modality or involves associations between the spatial and the verbal propositional modality.

The tactile sense provides input to the same abstract spatial and image modalities as the visual system. This is suggested by our capacity to recognize both the nature and the location of objects in space beyond the reach of our limbs through the use of a hand-held stick. If you pick up a stick and use it to "feel" an object some distance beyond your reach, you can very frequently identify that object. Furthermore, if you know the approximate length of the stick, you can determine the approximate location of the object. As James Gibson has pointed out, the object "feels" as if it were at the end of the stick, not at the point where the stick touches the hand. Try this little experiment for yourself. Take a stick (a pencil or ruler will do), close your eyes, and open a drawer with several hard objects in it. Use your stick to feel around and identify the objects and their locations within the drawer. Now open your eyes and see how accurate you were. Did the tactile experience feel as if it were taking place on your hand or out in space at the end of the stick? It should be noted that kinesthetic and motor information gained from tracing the object may also play a role in identification, but this only makes the present argument even more general. The spatial and image modalities are abstract and cognitive; they are not tied to particular sensory or motor modalities. The spatial and image modalities provide a model of the real world, not a model of the pattern of sensation on the eye or skin.

Kinesthetic and Motor Memory

The most extensive investigations of memory for position and movement have been those concerned with short-term memory for one-dimensional motor responses. A typical example of a one-dimensional motor memory task consists of having a subject move a lever from one position to another and then asking him to repeat that movement after a given interval.

Performance in this task confounds memory for terminal *position* with memory for the extent of the *movement* if the subject begins both movements from the same starting position. Posner, Keele, and their students have devised experimental designs to test each kind of memory separately. For instance, by using different starting positions for the original movement and the test movement, one can instruct subjects to reproduce either the same extent of movement or the same terminal position. Subjects are able to perform with a fair degree of accuracy on both tasks. This indicates that terminal position and the extent of movement are both encoded and remembered.

Memory for position and memory for movement have been studied under conditions where the subject was able to view his hand while performing the movement rather than performing the movement blind. Accurate performance is possible under both conditions, but the combination of visual with kinesthetic and motor memory produces a better performance than does kinesthetic and motor memory alone (Posner and Konick 1966; Posner 1967; Keele and Ells 1972).

Recognition tests have occasionally been used to assess motor and kinesthetic memory. In a recognition test a subject moves a lever until he encounters a stop. Then he judges whether this movement was terminated at the same position or after the same extent of movement as a prior movement, which was also terminated by a stop (Kantowitz 1974). However, kinesthetic memory and motor memory have more typically been tested by a recall procedure in which the subject attempts to produce a movement or terminal position identical to a prior movement. In this latter case accuracy is judged both by the average extent to which the recalled positions or movements deviate from the original positions or movements (constant error) and by the variability (standard deviation) of the subject's responses around that average recalled position or movement.

Performing movements or exerting forces during a retention interval adversely affects short-term memory for a movement or force, as measured by an increase in constant error or variability or both (Pepper and Herman 1970; Craft and Hinrichs 1971; Kantowitz 1972; Roy and Davenport 1972). Laabs (1974) found that the interference effect of interpolated movements to increase response variability only occurred in memory for movement and not in memory for position. However, interpolated movements produced assimilative constant errors in both cases such that the recalled movement or position changed in the direction of the interfering movement or position.

Another commonly observed difference between memory for position and memory for movement is that the former is more susceptible to verbal interfering tasks such as adding digit pairs, classifying digit pairs as high or low and odd or even, or counting backwards by threes with three-digit numbers during the retention interval. This difference was first observed by Posner and Konick. The reasons for it are not clear, but the backward counting task (and perhaps the other tasks) appears to involve some type of spatial as well as verbal representation. You can demonstrate this for yourself by attempting to write your name (which presumably involves some use of a spatial modality) at the same time as you recite the alphabet (presumably a purely verbal task). Now write your name again—this time while you count backwards by threes starting from 947. The difference is dramatic. It is trivial to write your name accurately while rapidly reciting the alphabet. By contrast, it is extremely hard to do so while counting backwards by threes. Nor will it be much easier even when you have learned to count backwards fluently. Counting backwards with three-digit numbers appears to involve a certain degree of place keeping for digits in the tens and hundreds positions while the digit in the unit position is being decremented, and this place keeping subjectively appears to involve a spatial code. Furthermore, although spatial position concepts appear to be involved in the backward counting task, no spatial movement concept appears to be involved. This may explain why such tasks interfere with position information and not with movement information.

Laabs (1973) has shown that interpolating a spatial relations test during

the retention interval interferes with memory for both location and movement information. Spatial relations tests appear to involve both positional
and movement concepts, since judging the relation between two complex
objects often requires mental translation and rotation operations. Thus when
the interference task contains both positional and movement concepts, there
is interference with memory for both. Since Laabs used blind lever-position-
ing movements, and the spatial relations test was visual rather than kines-
thetic-motor, the experiment also demonstrates the abstract cognitive
character of spatial memory, independent of modality of input.

There is little doubt that visual input is in some sense the most precise
and dominant form of input to the cognitive spatial modality, but a variety
of other sensory and motor channels contribute as well. High-level cognitive
modalities are not specific to the mode of input, but to the type of information
represented.

IMAGERY

Think about your living room. How many windows does it have? Where are
they? What size and shape are they? How many doors to the living room?
Where are they? Do the doors have windows in them or are they solid? What
do the door handles look like? Chances are that you can answer most if not
all of these questions, and that to answer them, you undergo the subjective
experience of recalling visual images and "seeing" the answer to the questions
in those images.

Mental imagery has long been neglected in experimental psychology,
but there has been an upsurge of interest in it during the past decade. Because
some S-R psychologists were at one time reluctant to admit the existence of
mental imagery, numerous cognitive psychologists have engaged in experimental overkill merely to demonstrate the existence of an imagery modality
separate from the verbal modality. Today we have perhaps a hundred alleged
experimental demonstrations of the *existence* of imagery for every study that
purports to say something about the *properties* of imagery. Here we shall
concentrate on the properties of the imagery modality, but because the
amount of evidence is limited, it should be understood that the conclusions
reached here are largely speculative.

Constituent Structure

A simple geometric form such as in figure 3.1 is encoded at the level of
primary visual cortex by nodes representing all of its constituent line segments. Various combinations of these line segments comprise simple forms
that may be represented by single nodes in the image modality. The constit-

uents of an image for a simple form would then be nodes representing all the lines and angles that compose it.

A more complex form, such as in figure 3.1, might be thought to have as its constituents all the lines and simpler forms that are contained in it. But this hypothesis has been demonstrated to be false. Human beings encode a complex form like A by a set of constituents that does not include all the possible simpler forms contained within it. Reed and Palmer investigated the constituent structure of forms by presenting a form like A, removing it after a second or so, and a few seconds later presenting a form like B, C, or D. Subjects were asked whether B was contained in A. Subjects were instructed to respond quickly in order to tap what had been directly encoded in the visual image, rather than to decide by a slower, inferential comparison process. Some of the simple forms were identified as parts of the complex form much more frequently than others. For example, B and C were identified as constituents of A almost two-thirds of the time, but D was identified as a constituent of A only 10% of the time. Figure D is a closed geometric figure like B and C, and it is at least as simple and familiar as C. Finally, there are other images in which D is recognized as a constituent more rapidly than C (Reed 1974; Reed and Johnsen 1975; Palmer 1976).

One can conclude that a complex image like A has a definite constituent structure that does not include all possible features and combinations of features equally, as a simple photograph theory of image representation might suggest. Rather, the constituent structure of an image is selective, and the components selected depend in an as-yet-undetermined way upon the context in which they appear. That is, there is no simple rank ordering of image constituents such that a constituent higher on the rank ordering is more likely to be perceived in any complex image context than a constituent lower in the ordering.

Image Complexity

The more constituents an image contains—the more complex it is. Is the vividness of a visual image independent of its visual complexity? That is, can we imagine all the constituents of a complex image as adequately as we can the constituents of a similar image? We might guess that when an image becomes sufficiently complex, its parts cannot all be simultaneously activated in image memory and must be activated in rapid succession. Hebb and others have put forward this hypothesis with respect to both acquisition and retrieval of complex images. In particular, Hebb (1968) suggests that the parts of a complex image are successively fixated during the initial acquisition (perception) of the image. Fixation of a particular part of a figure establishes a simple image for that part. This simple image is "glued together" with the simple images that result from fixations of other significant parts of the figure.

There is substantial evidence to support the proposition that visual perception of a complex picture involves successive eye fixations on different,

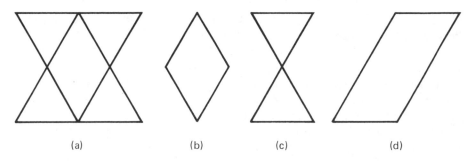

Fig. 3.1 Figures (b), (c), and (d) are all contained in (a). However, subjects appear to encode (a) using constituents (b) and (c), but not using constituent (d).

informationally rich portions of the picture. People do not stare at the center of a picture and build up an image from prolonged fixation focused on a single point (Kolers 1970). In this respect image acquisition differs sharply from acquisition of a visual sensory afterimage, for which a steady fixation is virtually essential. Thus images are undoubtedly associative traces rather than nonassociative activity traces.

This conclusion is also supported by the fact that image memory can persist as long as verbal memory—sometimes for a lifetime. Loftus has demonstrated that recognition memory for pictures increases as a function of the number of fixations on a picture during learning, and that it is independent of exposure time when the number of fixations is held constant. Initial learning of a complex picture generally depends primarily upon the number of fixations, provided study time per fixation is at least a few hundred milliseconds (Loftus 1972).

Retrieval also appears to involve a revival of the image by means of successive generation of the parts. Several investigators have demonstrated that recall of complex visual material is often accompanied by eye movements. Furthermore, Hall showed that image recall is better when eye movements are permitted than when the subject is required to fixate a single point during retrieval of the image. Some studies have failed to obtain a positive relationship between eye movements and image retrieval. These studies do *not* weaken the case for the highly plausible theory that generation of complex images often proceeds in parts via shifts of attentional focus. What they show is that image retrieval need not always be accompanied by eye movements (Marks 1972, 1973; Kahneman 1973; Hall 1974; Bower 1972).

I would like to make four points here. First, if an image is simple enough to be generated all at once with maximum clarity, there is no need to generate it in parts via shifts of attentional focus. Second, shifts of attention across a mental image would not appear logically to require an eye movement, nor is it obvious why eye movements should benefit image retrieval. Miniature or even full-blown eye movements may often occur as an irrelevant "downstream" consequence of mental scanning. Such external indicators of thought are useful to psychologists when they show otherwise sensible regularities. However, the absence of eye movements no more indicates the absence of internal shifts of attention in imagery than the absence of miniature speech muscle potentials indicates the absence of verbal thinking. Third, it is doubtless possible to retrieve part of a scene "on center stage in the mind's eye" directly, rather than first retrieving the entire scene and then focusing on one part. This would explain Marks's failure to find "appropriate" eye movements when subjects were correctly answering questions without explicit positional cues (e.g., "What color was the goose's beak?"). He did find an above-chance frequency of appropriate eye movements when subjects were answering these questions incorrectly, and when they were answering questions with explicit positional cues (e.g., "How many windows were in the house in the upper left-hand corner?"). Fourth, Marks's correlational data—which show that good imagers make fewer eye movements than poor imagers in recall of pictures—seem best interpreted to indicate that good imagers can generate more complex images in a single focus than can poor imagers. These correlational individual difference data do not oppose the hypothesis that retrieval of complex images often involves piecemeal generation of its parts.

Several basic questions remain to be answered. What is the maximum number of image constituents that can be simultaneously activated? What is the maximum size of a *simple* visual image? How complex an image can be visualized without loss of vividness? The maximum complexity of the simple image might depend upon the nature and organization of the constituents rather than on their number. Perhaps we can only attend to one node in image memory at a time, but if that node stands for an entire image, it might simultaneously activate all the constituent nodes with which it is associated. The degree of activation of each constituent node might vary inversely with the number of constituent nodes. That is, vividness of imagery might decrease monotonically with increases in the number of constituents.

Indeed, Reed and Johnsen (1975) found that when a complex figure was presented first, followed by a form that the subject was to recognize as being part of the complex figure, subjects made 72% errors. This held true even when they were given unlimited time to decide. This inability to recognize parts of a complex image was presumably due to some difficulty in maintaining an image of the complex figure while performing whatever mental operations are necessary for part identification, since subjects were highly accurate in drawing the complex figure from memory.

Other experimental demonstrations support the hypothesis that increasing the complexity of the visual image decreases its adequacy, as measured by the speed with which subjects can make decisions regarding image constituents. Weber has invented a task that appears well suited for evaluating the relationship between image complexity and image adequacy. The subject hears a word and is required to form a visual image of it. Several seconds later he hears a probe digit such as "three." This probe digit signals the subject to decide whether the third letter in the word is tall (b, d, f, g, . . . y) or short (a, c, e, . . . z). Since height is a visual property, we know that the subjects must be using image memory to make this decision (though quite conceivably this memory is in the verbal modality, or at least in the same hemisphere as the verbal modality). When subjects have a relatively long time (four seconds) to construct the visual image, the speed with which they decide whether a letter is tall or short is largely independent of its serial position within both three- and five-letter words. Decisions regarding the last three letters of five-letter words tend to be made more slowly than decisions regarding the first two letters. Weber and Harnish also performed the useful control of presenting the words visually and having subjects make the same decisions while they looked at them. Figure 3.2 presents their findings (Weber and Harnish 1974). Hebb (1966) had earlier proposed one good test to determine whether decisions were based on a visual image of a word or on some verbal representation. The test was to see whether the image could be read off equally rapidly backwards or forwards. The Weber and Harnish results demonstrate that this property of word images being equally readable in both directions does indeed hold for visual perception (as Hebb had assumed) and also demonstrate that the same property holds for visual images, provided the image is not too complex.

Three-letter words appear to yield a flat reaction time function across serial position, but five-letter words do not. This suggests that all the constituents of a simple image are activated in parallel, and that the maximum size of a simple image may be three or four letters. It is also interesting to note that for three-letter words decisions based on the image were made slightly faster than decisions based on the percept, but that the reverse held true for five-letter words. Weber and Harnish suggest that the maximum capacity for a simple visual image might be assessed by the maximum-length word for which the image can be processed as rapidly as the percept. By this measure, too, the maximum size of a simple image for words would appear to be on the order of three or four letters.

Another criterion for determining the maximum size of a simple image using the Weber and Harnish paradigm would be the longest word for which decision times regarding each letter are independent of the number of letters in the word up to that maximum length. This criterion also places an upper bound on the size of a simple image at either three- or four-letter words. However, decisions regarding the visual properties of a single letter might be made more rapidly than decisions regarding the properties of a single letter from a three-letter word. If this result were obtained, it would suggest that even "simple" images differ in the adequacy of visualization of their component parts.

Of course, other factors—such as the increase in difficulty of processing the serial position probe—might produce differences as a function of a list

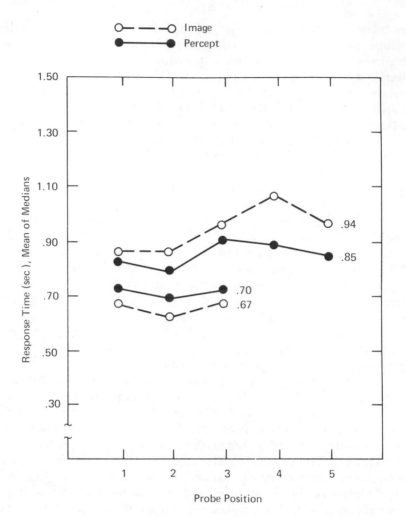

Fig. 3.2 Response time as a function of image-percept representation and letter position. (From R. J. Weber and R. Harnish, Visual imagery for words: the Hebb test, *Journal of Experimental Psychology* 102 (1974): 409–14. Copyright 1974 by the American Psychological Association. Reprinted by permission.)

length independent of the vividness of the visual image. Perhaps, as Weber and Harnish suggest, the effects can best be assessed by means of a percept control condition. This makes the discrepancy between the image condition and the percept condition the best dependent measure of the change in visual-image adequacy with increasing image complexity. However, we have no results for one- and two-letter words. Perhaps the advantage of the image over the percept would be substantially greater for one- and two-letter words than for three-letter words. We do not know. The Weber and Harnish results suggest a maximum size for a simple image—but not a minimum size. Even a simple image consisting of simultaneously activated constituents might show a progressive decrease in the adequacy of imagery with an increase in the number of constituents.

Image Size

Kosslyn also investigated the relationship between image complexity and image adequacy. Basically he was interested in the effects of image size on the speed of verifying the properties of the image. For example, he demonstrated in a number of contexts that the larger the size of the image, the faster its properties were verified.

Kosslyn showed that the smaller characteristics of an imaged animal took longer to verify than its larger characteristics. When a subject was instructed to image a cat, it took longer for him to verify that the cat had claws than that the cat had a head. In a control condition where subjects were not asked to form a visual image and were presumably performing on the basis of verbal memory, subjects could decide whether a cat had claws faster than whether it had a head. Presumably this is because they had a stronger association in verbal memory between cat and claws than between cat and head. That this relationship was reversed in the imagery condition verifies that here subjects were indeed using visual images to make decisions. Kosslyn also showed that it took subjects less time to make decisions about the visual properties of a large animal than a small animal. Finally, he showed that when the same animal was imaged at larger and larger sizes, it took subjects less and less time to make decisions about one of its properties.

Kosslyn (1975) also demonstrated the limited capacity of imagery by showing that when subjects were required to image an animal next to a matrix of numbers, they evaluated its properties faster next to a simple (four-cell) matrix than next to a more complex (sixteen-cell) matrix. Furthermore, even when the number of cells in the matrix was held constant, properties of animals imaged next to a physically large four-cell matrix were verified more slowly than properties of animals imaged next to a small four-cell matrix. It appears that the larger the size of the matrix, the more capacity in image memory is consumed in representing it. As Kosslyn suggests, larger images have a richer grain of representation and are therefore easier to "see." In the same way, blowing up a small section of a photograph makes that section easier to see, despite the fact that no information can be added by the enlarging process.

Alternatively, the effects of size may be subsumed under the effects of image complexity discussed in the previous section. That is, when subjects image a larger object, they may represent it in greater detail, enabling them to verify its components faster. Furthermore, to the extent that one image in the field is represented in greater detail, there is less capacity to represent other images, making the verification of their visual properties more time consuming.

Imagery and Perception

Palmer (1976) and Reed and Johnsen (1975) have done further research on judging parts as constituents of whole figures. They have found the same systematic parsing (subgrouping) tendencies whether the figure and the part are presented simultaneously, or the part is presented before the figure, or the figure is presented before the part. These conditions are equivalent to *hidden-figure* perceptual recognition tests. Recognizing a part embedded in a figure is considerably easier when both are presented simultaneously or when the part is presented before the figure than it is when the more complex figure must be retained in image memory—that is, when the figure is presented before the part. However, the pattern of errors and reaction times in the two perception conditions is highly correlated with the pattern of errors and reaction times in the imagery condition. This indicates that the constituent structure representation (structural description) of a figure is highly similar whether it is a percept (receiving sensory input) or an image (generated or maintained by purely central memory input). Indeed, the minor differences between these conditions are probably due to the contextual biasing of figure perception by prior or simultaneous perception of the part, rather than to any intrinsic difference between the encoding modalities for perception and imagery. The modalities for form perception and imagery are very likely identical at the highest level. Indeed, Palmer found that the same grouping principles (chiefly proximity and continuity, but possibly also similarity) predicted which parts of figures were easiest to identify in both perception and imagery conditions.

Bower and Glass (1976) have studied subjects' ability to recall entire figures, given one part as a cue. They have found that "good" parts yield five times better recall than "bad" parts. All subgroups of a complex figure are not equally strongly encoded into memory any more than they are equally strongly activated in perception. Presumably there are many subgroups of a complex form that we simply do not code as a group. According to the specific node principle of encoding, no node is specified to represent these unperceived subgroups. Thus when such a subgroup is presented as a cue to recall of the entire figure, it has no previously existing node to represent it. Therefore, the subgroup cue as a whole has no previously established associations to the entire figure—though components of the cue may have weak associations to the figure through their participation as constituents of perceived subgroups.

Another line of support for the hypothesis that a single modality serves both visual perception and imagery is the tendency to confuse mental images with low-intensity stimuli. Segal and Fusella have shown that instructions to generate irrelevant visual images impaired visual detection more than instructions to generate irrelevant auditory images. Similar modality-specific interference effects of imagery on visual perception have now been demonstrated in six different sensory modalities (vision, audition, touch, smell, taste, and kinesthesis) (Perky 1910; Segal and Fusella, 1970, 1971; Marks 1977).

All of this supports the general principle that visual form perception and image memory are performed by the same modality. We do not have separate modalities for these functions. Perceptual recognition of a familiar form is the activation of existing nodes in image memory by some combination of (1) appropriate sensory input and (2) central (associative) memory input from nodes previously activated by the context. Perceptual learning of a new form is the acquisition of new nodes in image memory to represent the form by means of vertical associations from nodes representing some of the form's already familiar constituents. As we shall see, precisely the same sort of integration of perception and memory occurs in the verbal modality—and presumably in every other cognitive modality as well.

Eidetic Imagery

Most of us have friends who claim to be able to remember great quantities of material by forming an image of the words or diagrams on a page. There has been little definitive research on individual variations in image capability, but it seems very likely that the differences are as large as differences in any other human capacity. At one extreme are individuals whose visual capacities are so remarkable that their imagery has been called *eidetic.* Although such imagery has a special name, there is no reason to believe that eidetikers—subjects said to have eidetic imagery—possess a qualitatively different capacity for visual imagery than the rest of us. Rather, it seems most parsimonious to assume that they represent one extreme of the normal human distribution in imagery capacity (Gray and Gummerman 1975).

Eidetikers build their visual images by eye movement scanning of complex pictures, just as the rest of us do. Thus eidetic imagery is like ordinary visual imagery and unlike sensory afterimages, which would be blurred by eye movements. Eidetikers apparently retrieve complex visual images by a generative process involving scanning as well, though as Marks has shown, good imagers appear to do less scanning of moderately complex images—presumably because they can generate more complex simple images (Haber and Haber 1964; Marks 1972).

The eidetikers reported throughout history have ranged from idiot savants to people with normal or high general intelligence. There is no reason to associate eidetic imagery with idiocy or the inability to do abstract thinking. Nor is there any reason to believe that eidetic imagery conveys any special intellectual advantage. The most useful memory is associative, and the ability to generate images of all of the pages of hundreds of books, as the

Shass Pollacks were alleged to be able to do, is of little conceptual value (Stratton 1917).

IMAGE OPERATIONS

The image modality does not consist of a passive collection of images arranged like so many paintings on a wall. The range of operations that can be performed on images is an equally important component of the image modality. Image operations can conveniently be classified as *nondestructive* or *destructive*.

Nondestructive operations may include initial *generation* of a mental image from some retrieval cue or cues, subsequent *scanning* of the image (*focusing* attention on some part of the image), and *zooming* (retrieving more detailed constituents of some part of the image to achieve something like a photographic blowup).

Destructive operations include deletion, rotation, reflection, translation, magnification, minification, squashing, stretching, and tearing of visual images. The destructive operations that can be performed on images probably include all of the destructive actions that an individual can take on objects in the physical world, as well as some that can only be imagined. The only destructive operation that has been extensively studied is mental rotation.

We can also distinguish between *basic* (elementary) and *complex* image operations. We know almost nothing about the inventory of basic image operations. Indeed, this classification may turn out to be largely a matter of theoretical convenience. At the neural level there may be only two image operations—excitation and inhibition—but this does not mean that we should take these two operations to be basic at the psychological level, if to do so would make our theories extraordinarily complex and therefore less revealing of psychological principles. At this early stage in our understanding of imagery, all the operations listed above—both nondestructive and destructive—can be considered basic. This list of basic operations will of course be modified as cognitive psychology progresses.

Of the image operations that have been studied experimentally only one would appear to be complex. This is the mental *synthesis* of a whole image from two or more separately stored image parts. In this section we will discuss image operations in four categories: (1) generation, (2) scanning and zooming, (3) rotation, and (4) synthesis.

Generation

The generation of an image is nothing more than the basic act of retrieving an image from memory. Presumably this is done by activating a set of nodes representing the image constituents—from the top node down to some level of detail. The generation of an image may often include the destruction (inhibition) of whatever nodes were activated in the immediately preceding image. However, since one sometimes wishes to retain, but add to, an existing image, it would be desirable if generation did not necessarily entail inhibition of the preceding image.

Perhaps all operations involve some degree of (lateral) inhibition that limits the complexity of simultaneously activated images. If so, the distinction between destructive and nondestructive operations is simply a matter of the degree of inhibition. Such differences could be achieved in a variety of ways. First, they could be achieved through compensating excitation, as in cases where image components are strongly associated to each other directly or indirectly by superordinate chunk nodes. Second, they could be achieved through the presence or absence of selective inhibitory suppression mechanisms. Finally, they could be achieved through quantitative variation in the magnitude of general lateral inhibition relative to excitation, as in light adaptation.

Scanning and Zooming

Scanning operations can be classified according to whether one scans to the front or back, to the left or right, to the top or bottom, or to any diagonal combination of these six directions. Zooming operations can be classified according to whether one zooms at the center, at the lower left corner, at the upper right corner, and so forth. There may be no difference between scanning and zooming operations. Alternatively, scanning could be the mere focusing of attention on a part of an image, while zooming could be adding detail to the representation of that part by retrieving lower-level constituents.

Scanning and zooming should logically be nondestructive, since one is merely focusing attention on or adding to part of the image without destroying the rest. Presumably when an image component is not currently the focus of attention, its vividness decays passively and must be periodically refreshed by scanning or zooming. According to this hypothesis, the more complex the image, the greater the delay between original generation of an image component and returning to refresh it. Successive regeneration of each component would occur much as an image on a TV picture tube is generated by an electron gun scanning over all the points on the screen. At present there is little direct evidence to support this hypothesis, and little is known about the speed of scanning and zooming operations or the activation-decay function for image components.

Simple images are those that we can generate simultaneously without shifting our attention from one part of the image to another. As I remarked earlier, we do not know the capacity limits of simple images in general. However, in the case of images of verbal symbols (letters and words), it appears that a simple image can contain a fairly complete representation of the features of only one letter at a time. This is not to say that we cannot have a simple image of an entire word shape. We well may have unitary word shape images, but apparently they do not suffice to determine all the properties of each individual letter. To determine the more detailed properties of individual letters, some scanning or zooming or both is apparently required. The evidence supporting the assertion that, in general, the capacity of a simple image is the complete representation of a single letter is found in a further experiment by Weber and Harnish.

Weber and Harnish (1974) studied the generation process for the visual image of a word by presenting a probe digit first, followed by either an auditory word to be imaged or a visual word. As shown in figure 3.3, the time it took to decide whether a letter was long or short was still reasonably flat as a function of serial position for both three- and five-letter visual words. The time it took to make a decision regarding the letters of the image—generated by the subject from the auditory word—tended to increase from left to right, although there was a significant reversal between the fourth and fifth position for five-letter words. Thus generation of the visual image from an auditory word is not a simultaneous process in the case of three- and five-letter words. As we noted earlier, however, the components of the image for three-letter words apparently can be simultaneously maintained at equal vividness. Furthermore, generating a visual image for a word does not appear to be a strictly left-to-right process. There appears to be some flexibility in the order with which we generate the image components, although the Weber and Harnish results suggest a fairly strong left-to-right component in generating images of words. It is as if the verbal modality were playing a dominant role in the generation of the visual image for words.

Incidentally, Weber and Castleman (1970) using a completely subjective procedure, assessed the maximum rate at which subjects can generate images of successive letters of the alphabet and compared this to the rate at which they can verbally rehearse successive letters of the alphabet. Verbal rehearsal (speech "imagery") was faster (about six letters per second) than visual imagery (about two letters per second). You can perform this experiment for yourself. First, time yourself reciting the alphabet verbally. Then time yourself while you go through the alphabet again, this time imaging each letter as if it were projected on a screen. It will take you about three times as long to construct the image of each letter mentally as it did to rehearse each letter verbally.

Kosslyn studied the role that attentional focus plays in retrieving information from images by asking subjects to verify whether a particular previously memorized drawing of an object—such as a car—contained some property—such as a headlight. In one condition subjects were given the name of the drawing, then they were asked to generate a visual image and to focus on the whole image. In another condition they were asked to focus on only

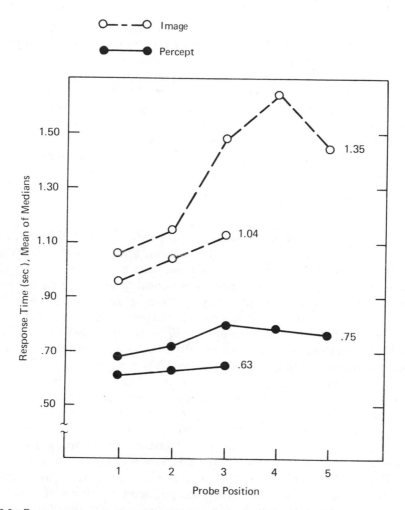

Fig. 3.3 Response time as a function of image-percept representation and letter position. (From Weber and Harnish. Copyright 1974 by the American Psychological Association. Reprinted by permission.)

one end of the image. Kosslyn demonstrated that decision time was shorter in the part condition than in the whole condition for properties within the attentional focus. However, decision time was slower in the part condition than in the whole condition for properties outside the attentional focus. The drawings Kosslyn used were moderately complex, suggesting that they might well be beyond the capacity of a simple image. Kosslyn also found that the time required to change the focus of attention from one position to another in an image increases (linearly in one case) with the distance between the two positions (e.g., between pairs of cities on an imaged map). Distance affects scanning time, even when the number of parts scanned over is held constant. Furthermore, it takes more time to scan over an object imaged large than the same object imaged small (Kosslyn 1973; Kosslyn 1976; Kosslyn and Pomerantz 1976). These results suggest that image representation has many of the properties of an analogue to physical space, though it undoubtedly falls short of the complete isomorphism assumed by some Gestalt psychologists. Another line of support for the hypothesis that imagery representation has some of the properties of physical space derives from the research on mental rotation discussed in the next section.

Rotation

The first study of image rotation was undertaken by Shephard and Metzler (1971). It was a kind of spatial relations test in which subjects were to judge whether pairs of projections of three-dimensional shapes were identical or different (fig. 3.4). The pairs were constructed to be mirror image reflections so as to prevent the subjects from solving the problems by a feature extraction process, without using image rotation.

The results of this study strongly support the hypothesis that subjects actually solved these problems by mentally rotating one shape into the other in order to determine congruence. The basic datum supporting this hypothesis was that the time to reach a "same" judgment increased linearly with the size of the angle through which one object had to be rotated in order to make it congruent with the other. This was true both for rotations within the frontal (picture) plane, as in figure 3.4 (a), and for rotations in depth, as in figure 3.4 (b). The average reaction times of "same" pairs for rotations in both the picture plane and the depth plane are shown in figure 3.5.

The Shephard and Metzler study not only demonstrated the existence of the image rotation operation, it also determined a number of its important characteristics. First, rotation in two dimensions was not significantly faster for three-dimensional images than rotation in three dimensions (in depth). Thus there is probably at least some sense in which mental rotation of a solid-object image is a three-dimensional operation rather than an operation applied to the two-dimensional projection of the object.

Mental rotation also appears to involve transitions through intermediate stages; it is not a single jump from one position to another differing by X degrees. Mental rotation of an object image through 60° may consist of three elementary rotations of 20° each. By this hypothesis, we may have learned associations for how a set of spatial features are transformed to a new set of spatial features for a 20° rotation in a particular direction. To accomplish a 60° rotation, one performs a succession of three 20° rotations in the same direction. In a manner not yet understood, the two views of an object determine the direction of rotation. Then the subject proceeds to carry out

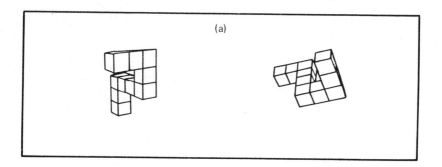

(a)

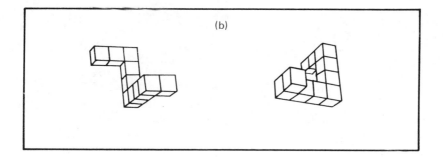

(b)

(c)

Fig. 3.4 Examples of pairs of perspective line drawings presented to subjects by Shepard and Metzler. (a) A "same" pair, which differs by an 80° rotation in the picture plane; (b) a "same" pair, which differs by an 80° rotation in depth; and (c) a "different" pair, which cannot be brought into congruence by *any* rotation. (From R. N. Shepard and J. Metzler, Mental rotation of three-dimensional objects, *Science* 171 (1971): 701–3, by permission. Copyright 1971 by the American Association for the Advancement of Science.)

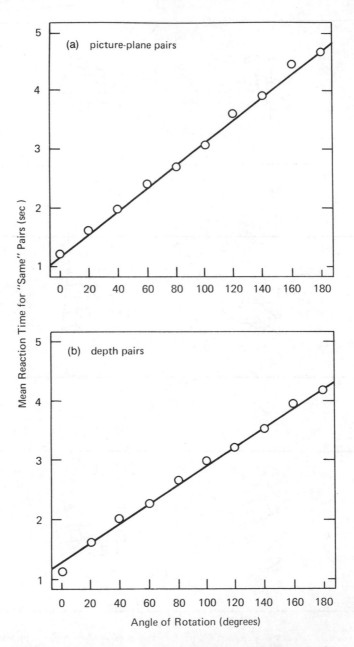

Fig. 3.5 Mean reaction times to two perspective line drawings portraying objects of the same three-dimensional shape. Times are plotted as a function of angular difference in portrayed orientation: (a) for pairs differing by a rotation in the picture plane only; and (b) for pairs differing by a rotation in depth. (From Shepard and Metzler by permission. Copyright 1971 by the American Association for the Advancement of Science.)

rotation in that direction over a series of steps. Thus there is a linear (straight-line) increase in the time required to complete the rotation with an increasing angular disparity (fig. 3.5).

Cooper and Shepard (1973*a*) studied rotation of two-dimensional letter images. The speed of rotation of these images was considerably faster than the speed of rotation of the three-dimensional images studied by Shepard and Metzler. Since Shepard and Metzler had already demonstrated that rotation of three-dimensional images in the picture plane is not intrinsically faster than rotation in depth, the essential difference appears to be whether the image being rotated is itself two- or three-dimensional. Cooper and Shepard had subjects decide whether an original upright letter matched a test character presented at some rotated position (fig. 3.6). Nonmatching test characters were mirror image versions of the original letter. First, the original letter was presented. Then subjects were shown an orientation arrow indicating the angle at which the test character would be presented following a variable delay from 0.1 to 1 second. During this delay they were to rotate the original letter mentally into the test position. When subjects had enough time to rotate the letter to the test orientation, they were able to decide more rapidly whether the original letter and the test character matched. The speed of mental rotation could therefore be determined.

A subsequent experiment by Cooper and Shepard (1973*b*) using a modification of this paradigm also suggested that mental rotation involves passing the image through intermediate angular orientations. Subjects were given a test character and instructed to begin mentally rotating it in the clockwise direction at a rate of 60° per half second, paced by an auditory cue of the form "up," "tip," "tip," "down," "tip," "tip" representing six positions around the face of a clock. When the test stimulus was presented at the orientation coincident with the angle at which the subject was currently imaging the

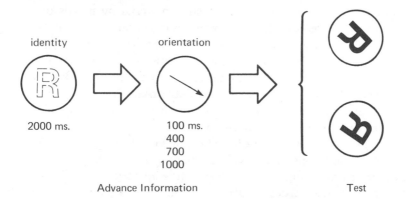

identity   orientation

2000 ms.   100 ms.
                  400
                  700
                  1000

Advance Information   Test

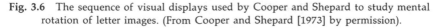

Fig. 3.6   The sequence of visual displays used by Cooper and Shepard to study mental rotation of letter images. (From Cooper and Shepard [1973] by permission).

original character, the matching decision was made much more rapidly than when the test character appeared at one of the other five orientations.

Furthermore, Cooper and Shepard imply that when the test character was presented at the position 60° before the currently imaged position, it was not processed any faster than a test character presented at a position 60° after the imaged position. This is consistent with the hypothesis that mental rotation is a destructive operation. If rotation were nondestructive, one might expect a more rapid match for a test character presented at a more recently imaged position, 60° before the current position, than for a less recently imaged position, 60° after the current position. According to this hypothesis, the creation of an image in a new position is accompanied by the active destruction or negation of the image at a previous position.

The distinction between destructive and nondestructive operations in mental imagery is supported by Coltheart and Glick's (1974) case study of a subject with unusual visual imagery capabilities. The subject came to their attention because of her ability to "talk backwards." Talking backwards consists of pronouncing a word or sequence of words in reverse order. For example, given the word *backwards,* she could immediately pronounce it backwards as *sdrawkcab.* Unlike most human beings, this subject could pass the Hebb test for visual imagery of words in that she could spell a word as rapidly backwards as forwards. She apparently did this by generating a visual image of the word and reading the letters from her visual image. She was also extraordinarily good at tachistoscopic recognition of arrays of letters, being able to report about 7.5 letters from an array of 8, while control subjects averaged fewer than 5.

However remarkable these imagery capabilities, the subject was not an eidetiker. Coltheart and Glick concluded that the subject's principal advantage in visual imagery was that the images she generated were extraordinarily resistant to destruction. Thus she did not appear able to form images of large amounts of material or to remember such material by means of an image. Rather, she appeared to retain text material in verbal memory with no better than normal capacity. However, she could use what she had in verbal memory to generate a visual image and maintain this image with very little disruption while she pronounced the material in either direction. Once her images were generated, they were much more stable than those of normal subjects, so she could generate and use a much larger visual image than is normal and read it off rapidly without interference.

While this resistance to disruption of visual images benefits a nondestructive scanning operation, such as spelling a word backwards, it should impair image processing that uses destructive operations. This was in fact the case with the subject described above. She was very deficient in mental rotation compared to normal subjects.

Synthesis

Mental synthesis is the combination of two separate images into a larger whole. This is not the same as what happens when the parts of a complex image are scanned. In scanning, the higher-order nodes integrating the parts are presumed either to be unnecessary or else already to exist in image memory. In synthesis, these integrative nodes do not already exist, and the experimental task is to form them in order to obtain a unified composite image. For an example of image synthesis see figure 3.7. A subject might be asked mentally to move the two forms in image A together until they touched and then judge whether image B is the composite form.

Synthesis is more creative than scanning. Synthesis is the acquisition of higher-order nodes that combine the constituents of the parts. Synthesis is similar to the acquisition of an image from sensory input, except that now the acquisition of the integrative image constituents must be accomplished purely in image memory without sensory support. As we shall see, acquiring a higher-order node structure to represent the relationships among the parts is considerably harder in image synthesis than in form perception. The two likeliest reasons are first, that images have less detail than percepts, and second, that our capacity for retrieval (generation, scanning and zooming) of the parts of the image is limited.

Palmer (1976) studied synthesis of two three-line image parts. He found substantial differences among the various pairs with respect to the time subjects needed to achieve synthesis and also with respect to the speed and accuracy with which they subsequently judged whether the synthesized image pair was identical to a subsequently presented six-line composite.

On the whole, the part figures easiest to synthesize appeared to be those

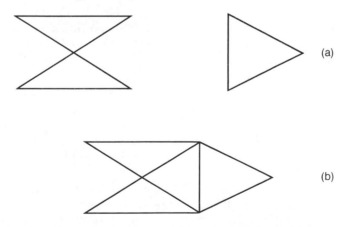

(a)

(b)

Fig. 3.7 Mental synthesis of the two parts of image (a) yields image (b).

that were easiest to analyze out of the composite in the constituent identification task described earlier. This is to be expected, since these are the cases where the node (grouping) structure encoding the parts in isolation is identical to a large subset of the node structure for the composite. The more the node structure for the parts in isolation differs from any subset of the composite, the more difficult both analysis and synthesis are. The biggest surprise in Palmer's study was that parts consisting of disconnected lines were as easy to synthesize as parts consisting of connected lines whose grouping structure was inconsistent with the assumed grouping structure of the whole. Palmer speculates that this reflects a trade-off between the greater ease of mentally translating the connected parts and the greater difficulty of breaking down the old constituent structure to form a new one. Palmer's and Reed's findings regarding the selective constituent structure of images establish one way in which imagery is not isomorphic to physical space. Another finding that indicates that imagery is to some extent abstract-propositional is that it is possible to fail to remember the orientation of an object while remembering its location relative to other objects (Frost and Wolf 1973; Palmer 1975b). How to combine the hierarchical propositional features of imagery with its spatial analogue features is the principal theoretical challenge in this area of cognitive psychology.

SUMMARY

1 There is an image modality, which represents the form of objects—the what system—and a spatial modality, which represents the location of objects—the where system. Both modalities have operations that convert (relate) one form or location to another.

2 One abstract (cognitive) spatial modality represents locations and movements (operations) for all sensory-input and motor output modalities.

3 Movement concepts in the spatial modality are most closely linked to central motor commands, while position concepts are most closely linked to sensory input.

4 An image has a constituent structure just like a verbal proposition. A whole image is analyzed into part images in a manner that can vary with context.

5 Simple images are images whose activation can be maintained as a whole simultaneously, without scanning. Complex images can only be maintained by successive scanning of their simple image constituents. Some more complicated simple images may require successive scanning for generation but not for maintenance.

6 Larger images are clearer or more adequate in a way that makes it easier to retrieve information from them. Simultaneous imagery capacity is limited, so the more detailed the representation of one part of an image is, the less detailed is the representation of other parts.

7 Visual form perception and imagery are performed by the same cognitive modality. Perceptual recognition of a familiar form is the activation of nodes representing the form and its constituents in the image modality by some combination of (a) sensory input and (b) associative memory input from nodes activated by the context (expectation). Pure imagery is the activation of such image nodes from the central associative source alone, without sensory support.

8 Eidetic imagery appears to be qualitatively like ordinary visual imagery and unlike afterimages in that complex eidetic images are acquired by eye movement scanning—which would blur an afterimage. Retrieval of eidetic images also appears to involve scanning.

9 Generation of an image is the basic act of retrieving an image from memory. Scanning is the focusing of attention on a part of an image. It may or may not be identical to zooming, which is to "blow up" a part of an image to retrieve from image memory more detail concerning that part.

10 Generation, scanning, and zooming of images are logically nondestructive image operations. However, there is little evidence to support the notion that they are actually nondestructive in the human mind.

11 Deletion, rotation, reflection, translation, magnification, minification, squashing, stretching, and tearing are logically at least partly destructive operations. There is some psychological evidence to support the actual destructive character of mental image rotation.

12 There are associations from the verbal modality to the image modality that enable us, for example, to visualize the letters of the alphabet or the letters in a word. The generation of images for letters of the alphabet appears to occur strictly one letter at a time. The phonetic level of the verbal modality is involved in pronouncing the letters. The generation of images for the letters in a word may not always occur one letter at a time, does not always proceed in strict left-to-right order, and does not appear to require pronunciation of the word.

13 Mental image rotation through large angles appears to be accomplished in small-angle steps. This leads to a linear increase in the time required to rotate an image as the size of the angle increases.

14 Image rotation of two-dimensional forms is faster than image rotation of three-dimensional forms.

15 We can combine two separate images into a unified whole image by a process of mental synthesis that probably combines more elementary image operations, such as generation and translation. Synthesis involves the acquisition of higher-order nodes that combine constituents from the separate parts. Synthesis is easiest to achieve when the node (grouping) structure encoding the parts is identical to a large subset of the node structure for encoding the composite.

CHAPTER 4
AUDITORY PERCEPTION

OBJECTIVES

1 To explain the elementary mathematical description of sound in terms of sinusoidal (pure-tone) frequency components. These components have three properties: frequency (in cycles per second), intensity (in decibels), and phase (in degrees).

2 To illustrate the principle of specific node encoding of these three auditory features: frequency (pitch), intensity (loudness), and phase difference (localization of sound direction). The auditory modality offers some important examples of the representation of these three features in codes that are not specific neuron codes. However, these violations of the principle of specific neuron encoding occur near the periphery of the auditory nervous system. The information appears to be completely transformed to a specific neuron code at higher levels of the auditory modality.

3 To describe our auditory localization capacity and the two primary cues on which this capacity is based (phase and intensity differences between the two ears). To describe the beneficial effects of head movement. To describe our ability to ignore echoes in determining the direction of a sound source (the precedence effect).

4 To discuss the important roles of inhibition in auditory encoding. Inhibition sharpens the precision of extraction of the frequency components of sound. It represents intensity and direction by a specific neuron code. It suppresses echoes (the precedence effect), and it probably mediates adaptation, habituation, and selective attention.

5 To describe several different forms of auditory adaptation. The first is the acoustic reflex, which tightens the middle-ear muscles to help protect the ear from damage by intense sounds. The second is peripheral and long-term auditory (receptor) fatigue. The third is central and temporary threshold shift. The fourth is frequency adaptation, which increases sensitivity to small changes from the adapting frequency.

6 To describe auditory grouping of sounds on the basis of factors analogous to the grouping principles in vision: similarity, spatial proximity, continuity, and familiarity.

7 To report some striking findings concerning the perception of the temporal order of sounds. These findings clearly indicate that the encoding of temporal order is *not* based on the temporal order of activation of (chunk) nodes representing the component sounds. Rather, we encode temporal order cognitively, the way we encode every other concept. That is, we encode temporal order by activating specific nodes. This indicates the existence of feature nodes that encode transitions and the existence of overlapping context-sensitive coding of individual sounds in a sequence, whether these sounds are notes in a melody or phonemes in a word.

8 To discuss the capacity for parallel processing in the recognition of auditory objects or patterns. To discuss the role of expectation and feedback in auditory perception. To compare the role of perceptual responses in audition and in vision.

9 To discuss the encoding of music at featural and segmental levels, the basic principle of aesthetics, and a wildly speculative idea concerning the functional origin of aesthetics.

Natural selection suggests that we are what we are because at one time our present characteristics had survival value. It's easy to understand the survival value of our auditory modality. Hearing can be used to recognize significant objects or events—an approaching enemy, a nearby friend, prey, or running water—at a distance, when one is not looking at them, or when they are hidden from sight. Audition can help us to recognize not only *what,* but *where* an object is. Auditory localization ability varies considerably over species. It reaches a peak in echo locators such as bats, which have exquisitely precise sonar that enables them to catch insects in flight. It is substantially poorer in animals with a good capacity for visual localization. Audition also serves as a primary medium for intentional verbal communication in humans and to lesser extents in songbirds, dolphins, and some insects (though intentionality in lower species is a murky issue—partly a matter of fact and partly a matter of definition). But of all the functions of audition, the one that puzzles me the most is music.

 Why do we love music? What purpose does music serve that enhances our chances of survival? Survival is all that the principle of natural selection cares about. Enjoyment is only a means to survival, from the standpoint of natural selection. So why do we create music? Why do we delight in listening to it, singing it, playing it, and dancing to it? Of course I don't know for sure, but I do have a couple of ideas. One has to do with audition; the other has to do with aesthetics. Here's the first: the fundamental units of audition in human beings (and in all vertebrates so far as I know) are essentially pure-tone frequency detectors. The original purpose of evolving such auditory analyzers was to permit higher-level combinations that could mediate object recognition, localization, and, in some species, communication. However, such frequency analysis also provides the basis for music. At the end of the chapter, I'll tell you my idea concerning the function of aesthetics. Between now and then you are supposed to learn some principles of audition perception—which you will find beautiful if, and only if, you developed some schematic understanding of perception in chapter 2.

Although the input is qualitatively completely different, most of the principles of auditory perception are either identical or strikingly analogous to the principles of visual perception. Furthermore, auditory and visual input project onto common cognitive modalities at higher (usually cortical) levels. These common cognitive modalities are the nonverbal object concept, verbal concept, spatial localization, and musical modalities. Often one or the other of the sensory input modalities is dominant for any given cognitive modality. For example, most concrete object concepts are more strongly activated by nonverbal visual stimuli than by nonverbal auditory stimuli. Conversely, auditory stimuli are presumably the dominant input for concept nodes in the musical modality, though some people with musical training can presumably activate many of these concept nodes by visual input (musical notes or symbols like C#). The same convergence of visual and auditory sensory input modalities occurs for the verbal modality as well. However, the present chapter focuses on coding and processes at the lower featural levels of the auditory modality, which are presumed to be common to verbal and nonverbal auditory stimuli. It also discusses higher-level cognitive processing of nonverbal auditory input in object concept recognition and music. Higher-level processing of both auditory and visual verbal stimuli is discussed in the chapters on speech, reading, and semantic memory.

SOUND

Sound is the vibration of matter. For humans, the long-distance communication medium for this vibration is chiefly the vibratory motion of air. Sound propagates from a vibrating source (such as a tuning fork or a plucked violin string) through the air to produce air pressure changes on the eardrum. This vibration is then transmitted through a series of tiny bones to induce motion of the fluid and basilar membrane of the inner ear. This motion initiates electrical generator potentials in the auditory receptors along the basilar membrane, and these generator potentials initiate spikes in the auditory neurons connected to them. Auditory receptors transduce sound (energy) into neural firing (electrochemical energy), just as visual receptors transduce light into neural firing.

Pure tones are the easiest sounds to describe. Pure tones are simple sinusoidal variations in the movement of matter—such as a tuning fork, the eardrum, or the molecules in the air. Sinusoidal variation in the position of matter has three basic parameters: frequency, intensity, and phase (fig. 4.1). Frequency is the number of complete cycles (back and forth) that the matter undergoes in a unit of time, such as a second. The modern unit of frequency is *hertz,* abbreviated hz, but meaning simply *cycles per second.* Middle C is about 260 hz or 260 cycles per second. The audible range for humans is 20 to 20,000 hz.

The greater the extent of the vibration of matter, the greater the intensity of the sound. As air (or other matter) vibrates back and forth, the pressure at any given point in space (for instance, on the surface of the eardrum) varies around some average value. The maximum variation in pressure from that average is the intensity of the (pure-tone) sound. Although sound intensity is sometimes represented on an air pressure scale, for human psychophysical purposes intensity is more frequently represented on a decibel (dB) scale. The zero point of the decibel scale is frequently not zero deviation from average pressure, but the pressure change at which a 1,000 hz tone is just barely detectable (at a 75% accuracy level) in absolute quiet. This absolute threshold varies for different individuals and for different frequencies. Therefore, the

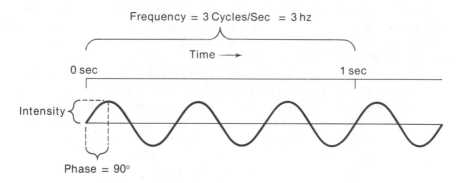

Fig. 4.1 A pure tone is a simple sinusoidal vibration of matter. It can be completely specified by three numbers. That is, a sinusoidal function has three parameters. The first is its *frequency*—the number of complete cycles in a unit of time—3 cycles/sec = 3 hertz = 3 hz in this example. The second is its *intensity*—the magnitude of the vibration from the center point, or the maximum change in (air) pressure at any given point that results from this vibratory movement. The third is its *phase*—temporal deviation of the time of maximum intensity from the zero point on the time scale. Phase is often measured in degrees, with 360° representing one complete pass through a cycle. The phase angle in this example is 90°.

zero point on the decibel scale was set at a value close to the absolute threshold for most subjects for 1,000 hz tones. That zero point is .0002 dynes/cm^2. The decibel scale is a logarithmic scale. In particular, the dB scale is 10 times the log of the ratio of the squares of (1) the measured sound pressure to (2) the zero reference sound pressure level (SPL) of .0002 dynes/cm^2 (dB $= 10 \log P^2/P_o^2 = 20 \log P/P_o$, where $P_o = .0002$ dynes/ cm^2). On the decibel scale, a tenfold increase in P above P_o, $P = 10P_o$, means a 20 dB increase in intensity above threshold, while a hundredfold increase ($P = 100P_o$) means a 40 dB increase (since log 10 = 1 and log 100 =2). This holds at all intensity levels, so that *multiplying* any level of sound pressure by 10 means *adding* 20 dB on the dB scale. The dB scale is convenient for human psychophysical purposes because to a first approximation, constant P_1/P_2 ratios are equally detectable, while constant P_1-P_2 differences become vastly less detectable at higher sound pressure levels (Weber's Law). Thus, a 1 dB increase in sound intensity from a 40 dB level is about as detectable as a 1 dB increase from a 0 dB level. (Actually, a 1 dB increase from the 40 dB level is somewhat more detectable, but we can ignore this for present purposes.) However, the absolute increase in sound pressure necessary to achieve a constant percentage increase is obviously vastly greater from the 40 dB level than from the 0 dB level. The decibel scale is a relative scale, and it makes no sense to speak of the dB level of a sound unless a zero reference level is stated. In this book the dB value of an auditory stimulus will either be (1) in relation to the absolute threshold intensity—the so-called SPL (sound pressure level) scale or (2) in relation to the intensity of some background sound. When we talk of 1 dB increments being equally detectable at varying background intensities, we mean a 1 dB increase from whatever the background intensity is. A 1 dB increase in absolute SPL units added to a background sound level is much less detectable at higher background sound intensity levels (Weber's Law).

The absolute phase of a tone in relation to some arbitrarily set zero point on the time scale is of no interest, but the phase difference between two tones often is. However, the explanation of the phase concept is completely equivalent regardless of whether one is comparing two tones or one tone with an arbitrary zero point on the time scale. As shown in figure 4.1, phase is the difference between the arbitrary zero time and the time at which the pure tone sound reaches maximum amplitude. The phase difference between two tones of equal frequency is the time difference between the points at which they reach maximum amplitude. Phase could be measured in microseconds, but for most purposes it is simpler to measure phase in degrees. A complete pass through one cycle—from maximum positive amplitude to maximum negative amplitude and back to maximum positive amplitude—is considered equal to a complete pass around a circle, which is a 360° cycle. In figure 4.1, the maximum comes one-fourth of the way through the cycle after t = 0 (the zero point on the time scale), so we say that the phase is 90° (one-fourth of 360°).

HIERARCHICAL FEATURES*

Single neurons at different levels of the auditory nervous system appear to encode specific features of auditory input. The auditory system is identical to the visual system in this respect. As in the visual system, the specificity of the range of stimuli that activate a neuron appears generally to increase at higher levels of the nervous system (farther from the sensory periphery). That is, the range narrows, so that one appears to have more particular feature detectors at higher levels of the auditory nervous system. As in the visual system, the first phase of this increasing specificity appears to serve the function of "cleaning up" the rather blurred representation of sound achieved by the sensory receptor organ. Again as in the visual system, the second phase of increasing specificity appears to serve the function of representing more complex combinations (conjunctions, disjunctions, and negations) and sequences of the simpler lower-level features.

There are also several differences between audition and vision. First, the cleanup problem is more severe for audition than for vision. Second, the auditory nervous system appears to make some use, near the periphery only, of information (neural firing frequencies for pitch and phase for localization) that is *not* in a specific neuron code and that must be converted to this code for use by the rest of the brain. Third, coding at the higher cortical levels of the auditory system is not as well understood as cortical coding in the visual system (and you will recall that there is some basic controversy there as well). All descriptions of auditory cortical feature detectors should be considered highly tentative.

Temporal Frequency Analysis

The input to one eye at a given time is inherently multidimensional. Light consists of a spectrum of different colors striking the various retinal locations. Ignoring bone conduction, the primary input to one ear at a given time can be completely described by a single number: the number that expresses the degree of air pressure on the eardrum. However, this unidimensional input at the eardrum is transformed right at the periphery (in the inner ear) into a multidimensional input—the amplitude of vibration of the successive sections of the basilar membrane. This transformation of auditory input provides a short-term temporal integration of the sequential auditory input. This integration is highly similar to that provided by (Fourier) frequency analysis of a time-varying unidimensional function into a weighted sum of pure tone components. It is a remarkable fact that any complex sound can be

---

*Except where additional references are explicitly cited, the evidence supporting the conclusions drawn in this section is to be found in Deutsch and Deutsch (1973, pp. 123–69); Somjen (1972, pp. 99–123 and 265–74); Whitfield (1967, 1969); and the references cited therein.

represented by a weighted sum of pure-tone components (e.g., 3 dB of a 400 hz tone mixed with 6 dB of a 1,000 hz tone, 7 dB of a 1,300 hz tone, 2 dB of a 3,011 hz tone, and so on). In the case of the ear, each peripheral auditory neuron is activated by several receptors at neighboring points along the basilar membrane. This occurs in such a way that the rate of firing of an auditory neuron represents the magnitude of a pure-tone component (auditory frequency) to a crude first approximation. The encoding of the intensity of a component frequency is accomplished in two ways. First, greater intensities induce stronger generator potentials in auditory receptors. Second, auditory receptors have different threshold levels for the initiation of any generator potential at all.

Pitch

The analysis of sound into component (pure-tone) frequencies is not complete at the peripheral auditory neurons. This analysis is completed at several levels further on by neurons whose rate of activation (firing) is maximum for a pure tone of a particular characteristic frequency and is less for pure tones of greater or lesser frequencies. A plot of the firing rate of a neuron as a function of the frequency of pure-tone input is called a *tuning curve*. An example of a tuning curve for an auditory neuron is shown in figure 4.2.

Several conclusions can be drawn concerning the representation of frequency (pitch) at the various levels of the auditory nervous system. First, at

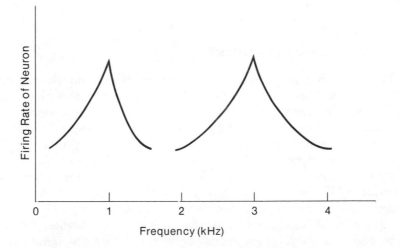

Fig. 4.2 Hypothetical tuning curves for two auditory neurons. For the curve on the left the optimum frequency is 1,000 hz. For the curve on the right it is 3,000 hz. Note that the generalization gradient is broader for the neuron tuned to the higher characteristic frequency.

higher subcortical levels there are neurons with more sharply peaked tuning curves (narrower generalization gradients) around the characteristic (optimum) frequency. This sharpening of the tuning curves is undoubtedly accomplished largely by inhibition, making it possible to discriminate more precisely between different frequencies. Second, while the response of the basilar membrane peaks at a particular location for a particular characteristic frequency, there is a considerable spread of activation, particularly to the part of the membrane that vibrates maximally to higher frequencies. This asymmetry is eliminated by some combination of neural inhibition and the response characteristics of the auditory receptors. Thus the tuning curves of auditory neurons are vastly sharper and more symmetrical than one would expect on the basis of the vibration of the basilar membrane. Third, the extraction of precisely tuned frequency components of sounds is probably completed at levels below the cortex, since cortical neurons appear to represent combinations and sequences of frequencies and thus do not generally have sharply peaked tuning curves to single tones. Furthermore, cortical lesions have little or no effect on pitch discriminations.

The preceding discussion assumes that the primary neural code for pitch is *which* neurons fire most rapidly (specific neuron encoding). There is another encoding of tonal frequency that is not a specific neuron code—namely, neural firing frequency. Single auditory neurons at the periphery can emit spikes at a maximum rate of about one spike every msec. (.001 sec), allowing peripheral auditory neurons to *follow* auditory frequencies up to about 1,000 hz. This is called the *frequency principle* of pitch perception. Of course this frequency code will not work to discriminate tones above 1,000 hz. The *volley principle* is often invoked to *extend* the range of the frequency code by assuming that multiple neurons somehow fire in volleys to represent higher frequencies. However, 4,000–5,000 hz appears to be the upper limit of the frequency code supplemented by the volley mechanism. There is some evidence supporting the hypothesis that the nervous system makes use of the frequency of neural firing as one cue to pitch at lower frequencies.* However, firing frequency is probably not the basic code for pitch—for three reasons. First, specific neuron encoding appears to be the general code used by the nervous system for all types of information. Second, firing frequency probably cannot be used to encode higher auditory frequencies. And finally, the ability of auditory neurons to *follow* stimulus periodicities by firing in phase with the sound vibration is largely lost as one ascends to higher levels of the auditory modality. Whatever use is made of the firing frequency information contained in peripheral auditory neurons, this information is probably transformed to the specific-neuron code (the code that is based on which neuron fires) at higher levels. In the nervous system, *pitch is which* (and so is nearly everything else).

*See a very readable discussion by Lindsay and Norman (1972, pp. 262–72).

Loudness

The intensity of any particular frequency component of a sound is contained in the rate of firing of pitch neurons representing that frequency. This special meaning of loudness is an integral part of the definition of pitch components and requires no separate discussion here. However, there are also neurons that have an optimum level of activation at intermediate intensity levels and fall off in level of activation with increasing auditory intensity. Such neurons encode the loudness, as well as the frequency of sound. Thus even so simple and basic an attribute as intensity probably gets encoded ultimately not by rate of firing but by *which* neurons fire most rapidly. This is the specific neuron principle of encoding. As with pitch, loudness feature analyses seem to be complete at subcortical levels, so that cortical lesions have little or no effect on the capacity to discriminate simple intensity differences.

Localization

It is convenient, and it may be psychologically valid, to consider the location of a (sound) source as being defined by three coordinates. The first is *distance.* The second is angular *height,* ranging from 0° for sounds in the horizontal ear level plane to ±90° for sounds directly below or overhead. The third is angular *direction* in the horizontal plane—0° for the vertical midline plane up to ±90° for sources directly to the right or left.

Distance. Tests of our ability to judge the distance of a sound source when we do not know how loud the sound is indicate that we have little ability to judge distance *per se.* We also have a strong bias to judge loud sounds as close, whether or not they are (Gardner 1969; Scharf 1975, p. 146). To the extent that we know beforehand the expected intensity of a sound, perceived intensity is a good cue to distance. Thus the feature nodes for distance are probably largely or entirely the same as those for loudness at lower levels of the brain. At higher levels distance might be cued by a difference between observed and expected loudnesses.

Height. When the head is not permitted to move, there are no binaural (two-ear) comparison cues to the vertical height of a sound. For example, in the straight-ahead plane the sound reaching the right ear is identical to the sound reaching the left ear, regardless of the height of the sound source. There do appear to be some monaural (single-ear) cues to height in complex (multiple-frequency) sounds with components above 7,000 hz. These cues permit rather accurate vertical height localization for such sounds. The external ear appears to play a critical role in the discrimination of sound height. The ability to determine vertical location without head movement is thus sharply limited, since neither pure tones nor complex sounds without very high frequency components can be vertically localized (Roffler and Butler 1968). The neural feature detectors for vertical height are unknown.

Direction. Virtually all work on auditory localization is concerned with the determination of direction in the horizontal plane. There are two primary cues to direction, both binaural: the differences between the arrival *times* and between the *intensities* of the sound reaching the two ears. The time difference arises because sound approaching from the left must travel a longer distance to reach the right ear than the left ear and vice versa. The maximum time difference occurs for 90° left or right directions and is about 800 μsec (800 microseconds or .0008 sec). Straight-ahead yields zero binaural time difference, and deviations of as little as 3° from straight-ahead are detectable by means of time cues alone, so the nervous system must be preserving the information regarding relative arrival time to an accuracy of 30 μsec or better (Lindsay and Norman 1972, pp. 275–80). At the level of the peripheral auditory nerve these time difference cues are represented by the precise timing pattern of neural firing, but at higher levels of the nervous system this temporal pattern code is transformed into *which* specific neurons fire. Some higher-level auditory neurons will fire optimally to binaural input—with a characteristic time delay between the input from the two ears—and suboptimally to input with greater or lesser time delays (Rose et al. 1966). Thus the nervous system transforms a temporal code into the specific neuron code that appears to be its basic code. Many neurons that encode sound coming from a particular direction appear to encode a particular frequency as well, so that one of these neurons represents a specific frequency component coming from a specific direction.

Each frequency component of a sound is a periodic (sinusoidal) waveform of vibration of air or other matter. The binaural time difference for any frequency component is the time (phase) difference between the peaks of the two waveforms as they reach the two ears, as shown in figure 4.3. A sound

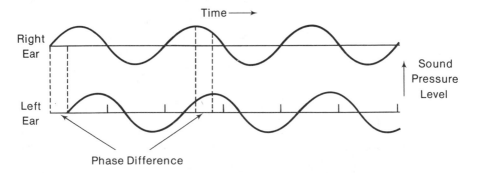

Fig. 4.3 Sinusoidal waveforms for a pure tone reaching the right ear slightly in advance of the left ear (sound source to the right of the straight-ahead direction). The binaural difference in the arrival time of the sound at the two ears is its phase difference.

frequency of 1,000 hz has a time difference between its peaks of 1 msec (.001 sec). If the maximum (directly left or right) binaural time difference could be as great as 1 msec (1,000 μsec), we could not tell the difference between a 1,000 hz tone coming from straight ahead and one coming from the right or left. This is because a 1 msec displacement of the waveforms causes the two waveforms to have the peaks and values in exact coincidence—the same as for a 1,000 hz tone from straight ahead. Because the human head is only about nine inches wide, the maximum binaural time difference is only .8 msec, so we can localize the direction of frequencies up to a bit over 1,000 hz on the basis of the time difference cues.

However, binaural time difference is not a useful cue for higher frequencies. For these higher frequencies (particularly those above 3,000 hz), the primary cue for direction is the binaural intensity difference. This intensity difference is not caused primarily by the greater distance required for sound to reach one ear than the other, although this can be a factor for very close sounds. For sounds originating from more than a few feet away, the primary cause of the binaural loudness difference is the acoustic "shadow" cast by the head. This acoustic shadow occurs primarily for high-frequency sounds, so it is a useful direction cue for precisely those (high) frequencies for which binaural time difference is not useful. At higher levels of the auditory nervous system, neurons have been found that respond to intensity differences between the two ears, rather than responding merely to the absolute level of intensity (Geisler, Rhode, and Haselton 1969). Such neurons can therefore be feature nodes for auditory direction based on binaural intensity cues.

Head movement. The ability to discriminate direction is best in the vicinity of the straight-ahead listening angle, though there are probably also secondary maxima in the 90° right and left listening angles. Under some conditions the average localization error has varied from a minimum of 1° in the straight-ahead angle to about 15° in the 45° left or right angles (Pollack and Rose 1967). For sounds of short duration there is not enough time to move one's head and improve auditory directional acuity by "fixating" the sound in the straight-ahead angle. However, this is possible for sounds of longer duration. In fact, improvement is so substantial that some scientists have suggested that the purpose of many auditory localization neurons may not be to determine auditory location exactly, but rather to drive head movement so as to center the organism in the region of maximum directional sensitivity (Leiman and Hafter 1972). For animals with highly developed visual systems, the same auditory centering mechanism might serve primarily to direct eye, head, and body movements for highly precise visual localization, since sound sources are frequently visible. For such animals auditory localization is far inferior to visual localization, making this a very plausible notion. Indeed, the coordination of auditory direction and eye movements may be at least partly innate in humans, since Butterworth and Castillo have demonstrated that newborn infants can make eye movements that are spatially coordinated with sound location (Harrison and Irving 1966; Butterworth and Castillo 1976).

Auditory localization also demonstrates another important constancy—*location constancy* independent of head movement with respect to the body. That is, the average direction in which an observer points to localize a stationary sound source is almost completely unaffected by rotation of the head up to 80° to the right or left (Day 1968). As I said before, the average error in localizing a sound is greater when the head is not fixating the sound. However, as long as the head fixates the sounds, the position of the body (twisted right or left) is largely irrelevant to localization accuracy (Pollack and Rose 1967).

Precedence effect.   In an open field or an anechoir (echo-free) chamber, sound emitted by a single source comes to the ears from only a single direction. However, wherever there are hard surfaces to reflect sound (the walls of a room, for instance), sound from a single source comes to the ears from many directions. The reflected versions of the same sound take somewhat longer to arrive at the ears than does the unreflected version. Observers nevertheless hear a single sound source and locate it accurately. This phenomenon is known as the *precedence effect* (the first-heard version takes precedence). The probable neuronal basis of the precedence effect is a transient inhibition of frequency analyzers (nodes) similar to the first-activated frequency analyzers but representing different locations. Transient inhibition with such properties has been demonstrated in the auditory nervous system.

Sound movement.   Not only can we determine the location of stationary sounds, we can also detect changes in sound location—that is, auditory movement. Auditory movement detectors have been found in the nervous system; they are single neurons that respond best to sound moving in a particular direction (Altman 1968).

Complex Features: Range, Or, Transition, and Chord Detectors

A variety of more complex feature detectors are being discovered at the level of the auditory cortex. Some of these are described below. However, it must be acknowledged that our understanding of auditory feature analysis at cortical levels is at a rather primitive stage of development, so any description of this analysis is liable to substantial future modification.

Range detectors.   Many neurons in primary auditory cortex appear to be *range* (broad-band frequency) detectors, responding at a high rate to any frequency tone over a very broad range. (Abeles and Goldstein 1972). Such range detectors might be useful in encoding broad-band frequency components in certain fricative sounds (e.g., the hissing or buzzing of s, z, and sh sounds). This would be particularly true if these units responded at a greater rate to broad-band (multiple-frequency) noise in the appropriate range. Whether or not they do so is unknown. However, we do know that such range units are inhibited by sequential (as opposed to simultaneous) presentation of two different tones with frequencies in the appropriate range. This would be a desirable property for a range detector of simultaneous broad-band noise, but the fact that it is true lends no great support to such an interpretation of those units.

Or detectors. Both narrow-band pitch detectors and broad-band range detectors have a single maximum for their tuning curve (fig. 4.2), although the flatness of that maximum is very different for pitch versus range detectors. By contrast, some cortical units appear to represent a disjunction of two different pitches (pitch X or pitch Y). Such units have tuning curves with two distinct maxima. The units represent pitch X or pitch Y, not pitch X and pitch Y (which would make them chord detectors), because presentation of both optimum pitches produces a response either equal to (inclusive-or) or less than (exclusive-or) the response to either tone alone (Abeles and Goldstein 1972).

Transition detectors. Some cortical neurons are specialized to detect frequency changes. Whitfield and Evans (1965) describe three basic types: those that respond to rising frequencies over a range, those that respond to falling frequencies over a range, and those that respond to rising frequencies in the lower part of a range and to falling frequencies in the upper part. The magnitude of the effective frequency transition differs. It may be as little as a quarter tone or semitone or as much as half an octave. Rate of change of frequency is remarkably unimportant. Thus such units could serve as sequential musical-interval (melody) detectors, though their more fundamental purpose must be to distinguish one complex natural sound (e.g., an animal call, a branch cracking) from another. The third type of transition detector might be useful in speech recognition. It might be used to recognize a certain target frequency (characteristic of a particular phoneme) regardless of which direction it was approached from (which varies with the nature of the prior phoneme). However, you should be aware that at present such functional interpretations are pure speculation.

Chord detectors. To my knowledge, chord detectors—neurons encoding a conjunction of two or more different pitches (e.g., pitch A and pitch B)—have not yet been found. This is not to say they won't be.

INHIBITION

Inhibition probably plays an important role in every auditory perceptual phenomenon.* In the representation of pitch, there is a blurring problem in the ear vastly more serious than the blurring of light by the lens of the eye. A pure tone excites a very broad range of auditory receptors, which overlaps extensively with the range of receptors activated by tones of similar frequency. To sharpen the tuning curve of a pitch feature neuron, its central excitatory region of frequencies is typically flanked on both sides by bands of frequencies that inhibit the neuron. This excitatory-center, inhibitory-surround organization of the receptive field apparently holds at all levels of the auditory modality—from the cortex down to the peripheral auditory neurons, which receive input from the receptors (Abeles and Goldstein 1972; Sachs and Kiang 1968). Up to the level of the medial geniculate (the last level of the auditory modality before the cortex), there is an increase in the sharpness of the tuning curves for neurons with a single best (characteristic) frequency (the pitch neurons). This increasing precision in the representation of single pitch components as one ascends in the auditory modality is presumably achieved by the sharpening effects of successive levels of inhibition (forward, lateral, or whatever). The precise analysis of pitch appears to be completed subcortically. The cortex seems to be primarily concerned with more complex simultaneous and sequential relations between different frequencies. This conclusion is based both on the study of the receptive fields of neurons at cortical versus subcortical levels and on the fact that cortical lesions often have little or no effect on simple frequency discrimination (Goldberg, Diamond, and Neff 1958, Goldberg and Neff 1961).

Inhibition also appears to play an important role in the encoding of auditory intensity. Some neurons not only have a low-intensity threshold below which they will not respond, but they also have a high-intensity threshold above which they decrease their firing rate (Goldberg and Greenwood 1966). This decrease in firing with increasing intensity is presumably the result of inhibition by neurons with a higher low-intensity threshold. Such inhibition simplifies the representation of loudness in terms of specific neuron coding. Instead of representing a low loudness by the firing of a set of neurons L_1, and a higher loudness by the firing of a set (L_1 and L_2), we use L_1 for the low loudness and L_2 for the higher one.

Inhibition also appears to play an important role in localization. Some neurons at higher levels of the auditory modality receive excitatory input from one ear and inhibitory input from the other. Others receive excitation or inhibition depending upon the time or intensity difference between the

*Evidence supporting the conclusions in this section is from Deutsch and Deutsch (1973, pp. 123–69); Somjen (1972, pp. 265–74); Whitfield (1969); and Webster and Aitkin (1975).

two ears. Inhibition almost certainly underlies the precedence effect—the suppression of response to delayed echoes of a stimulus. Excitation of a pitch neuron for one location apparently inhibits excitation of neurons representing the same pitch at other locations in auditory space.

The representation of pitch transitions in the cortex probably depends on a neural circuit that uses inhibition in much the same way as the neural circuit that represents movement of a visual stimulus in a particular direction across the retina.*

Other possible roles for inhibition in auditory perception are in adaptation, habituation, and selective attention. The distinctions among these three concepts are not clear at present. To the extent that sensory adaptation is an active, reversible, inhibitory process and not simple receptor or neural fatigue, adaptation may be identical to habituation. To the extent that adaptation-habituation is regulated by higher cognitive levels, it may be an important component of selective attention.

Although adaptation, habituation, and selective attention could be same-level or lower-to-higher-level phenomena, these sensory gating phenomena have often been thought to involve a large centrifugal (higher-to-lower-level) component. Some years ago Hernandez-Peon and others claimed that habituation (to a repeated auditory stimulus) and attentional distraction (to another modality) could reduce the response to an auditory stimulus very near the sensory periphery (Hernandez-Peon and Scherrer 1955; Hernandez-Peon, Scherrer, and Jouvet 1956; Deutsch and Deutsch 1973, pp. 422–28). The presumption was that this peripheral sensory gating was under central control and was mediated by auditory efferent (centrifugal) connections—that is, by higher-to-lower connections. Some better-controlled studies have failed to find these effects at peripheral levels, though reductions in responsiveness in habituation and distraction were found at higher levels of the auditory modality (W. O. Wickelgren 1968*a,b,c*). It has been suggested that peripheral sensory gating may occur only in noisy environments (Somjen 1972, pp. 268–69). Presumably, various types of sensory gating may occur at many levels of the auditory modality, and some of this gating is surely under centrifugal control. There are many auditory efferent neurons, so they must be accomplishing something. Furthermore, electrical stimulation of auditory efferent neurons is known to produce both excitatory and inhibitory effects at lower levels (Deutsch and Deutsch 1973, pp. 167–68).

Such efferents may also play an important role in the ordinary dynamics of auditory perception, to the extent that higher-order chunk neurons have centrifugal excitatory connections to their lower-level constituents and inhibitory connections to negative constituent attribute neurons. (The latter are attributes that are negatively related to the concept represented by the chunk neuron.) Such a feedback process in auditory perception could make maxi-

*See Whitfield (1969) for one such hypothetical neural circuit.

mum use of all the associative information stored in the nervous system at any level to improve the recognition process at any other level.

ADAPTATION

Acoustic Reflex

In a sense there is a type of receptor adaptation in audition analogous to that in vision, but it is relatively insignificant under most circumstances. The middle-ear muscles can be contracted to different extents, reducing the coupling between sound energy and the vibration of the basilar membrane in the inner ear. The contraction of the middle-ear muscles is an efferent control mechanism, initiated by loud sounds, whose primary purpose is to protect the ear from damage by intense sound. This *acoustic reflex* is more analogous to reflexive closing of the eyelid in the presence of bright light than it is to receptor adaptation. However, it also serves to reduce the loudness of sound by as much as 10 dB out of a total auditory range of over 100 dB (Bekesy and Rosenblith 1951, p. 1085). It achieves this reduction in sensitivity with only minor distortion, like visual receptor adaptation and unlike eyelid closure.* Thus the contraction of the middle-ear muscles does serve as a kind of auditory receptor adaptation process, but its maximum effect is very small compared to receptor adaptation in vision.

The acoustic reflex is initiated within about 10 msec (.01 sec) after an intense sound strikes the ear. It achieves maximum ear muscle contraction within 100 to 300 msec, both the initial dead time and the rise time decreasing with increasing sound intensity. The reflex is bilateral (at both ears) and of nearly equal magnitude, even when initiated by a monaural (single-ear) stimulus. After the loud sound terminates, the middle-ear muscles return to normal within about one second (Dallos 1964; Simmons 1965).

Loudness Adaptation, Fatigue, and Temporary Threshold Shift

If you listen to loud music for a while, your sensitivity to soft tones in the same frequency range as the music will be reduced for a time after the music ends—that is, your threshold for detecting such tones will be increased. These *temporary threshold shifts* lasts anywhere from a few seconds to many hours. The magnitude and duration of the loudness aftereffect increase with the intensity and duration of the adapting stimulus (in this case, the music).

---

*Since the inner ear is most susceptible to damage by low-frequency sound, it is not surprising that this acoustic reflex causes a greater reduction in the transmission of low than of high frequencies (see Dallos 1964).

The magnitude of the reduction in sensitivity varies from 0 to 50 dB or more. Loudness aftereffects are in no way due to any persistence of the acoustic reflex. They are confined to the adapted ear (in monaural adaptation) and to test tone frequencies in the vicinity of the frequency of the adapting stimulus, whereas the acoustic reflex is bilateral and affects all frequencies. However, the more intense the adapting stimulus, the broader the range of frequencies experiencing temporary threshold shift (the broader the generalization gradient on the pitch continuum for loudness aftereffect) (Caussé and Chavasse 1947; Selters 1964; Wever 1949).

There appear to be at least two different kinds of loudness aftereffect: long-term fatigue and short-term adaptation. Long-term aftereffect can last minutes, hours, or days, but it requires very intense stimulation—90 dB or more above threshold. The end of the audible range and the beginning of tickle and pain is around 120 dB above threshold (for frequencies near 1,000 hz). Since intensity differences of about .5 dB are discriminable (about 75% of the time), you can see that long-term aftereffect is produced only by very intense sounds—jackhammers, very loud rock music, and the like. Long-term aftereffect is quite peripheral in its locus—being perhaps a fatiguing or damaging of the auditory receptors. The effect is ear- and frequency-specific, but the maximum long-term threshold shift is obtained for frequencies half an octave or more *above* the fatiguing stimulus frequency. If such intense auditory stimulation is repeated over many weeks, without sufficient time to recover from one day to the next (absence of temporary threshold shift is a good index of recovery), auditory sensitivity is often permanently damaged (Selters 1964; Ward 1967).

By contrast, short-term adaptation can be produced by sounds as soft as 5 dB above threshold (about 1 dB reduction in sensitivity), and the maximum short-term sensitivity loss of about 8 dB is obtained with adapting sounds 40 dB or more above threshold. Short-term adaptation is just that—short-term—lasting only about 20 to 30 seconds. Like long-term fatigue, it is ear- and frequency-specific, but now the maximum threshold shift occurs for test tones at the adapting tone frequency. Since adaptation is ear-specific, we know that its locus is peripheral to the level of binaural combination in the auditory modality. However, there is good reason to believe that short-term adaptation is a mechanism distinct from long-term fatigue, since Selters showed that exactly the same amount of short-term adaptation is obtained in a fatigued ear (with 20 dB loss of sensitivity) as in a rested ear. That is, adaptation and fatigue have additive effects on threshold. Furthermore, though adaptation takes place very peripherally to the cortical cognitive levels, there is evidence that the magnitude of loudness adaptation can be increased by about 2 dB if subjects engage in strenuous mental arithmetic while listening to the adapting tone (Selters 1964; Ward 1967; Collins and Capps 1965).

The functional significance of such central cognitive effects on adaptation is unclear. So indeed is the entire process of loudness adaptation. *Both short-term adaptation and long-term fatigue appear to serve a purpose analogous to that of light adaptation in vision—namely, adjusting a limited physiological sensitivity range to a much larger range of acoustic intensity levels.* However, there is no convincing evidence for this functional-adaptation explanation as opposed to a functionless-fatigue explanation. For example, it would be nice to know whether adaptation improves the ability to discriminate small intensity differences in the vicinity of the adapting stimulus, but all that has been demonstrated is that adaptation has a greater negative effect on sensitivity the farther the test stimulus is from the level of the adapting stimulus. For example, the greatest negative effect is at the absolute detection threshold (Parker et al. 1976). To my knowledge, no one has determined whether this trend continues so that adaptation can actually increase sensitivity in the region of the adapting stimulus or above it.

Pitch Adaptation

The functional character of adaptation to tones with respect to pitch was demonstrated over a quarter of a century ago by J. A. Deutsch (1951). Deutsch showed that four minutes of listening to a tone of 1,000 hz reduces the difference threshold by almost 50% for detecting a change in pitch of a 1,000 hz tone. This very large increase in sensitivity to pitch changes in the region of the adapting stimulus was replicated by Clarkson and Deutsch (1966) for a 180 hz tone. They also showed that such pitch adaptation reduced the pitch variability in a subject's singing of a 180 hz tone. Results such as these strongly support the hypothesis that adaptation is a positive, functional process as opposed to the hypothesis that it is a functionless or dysfunctional fatigue process. This pitch adaptation appears to occur at a more central locus than the level of binaural combination, since the same magnitude of pitch adaptation occurs for the ear contralateral to the ear that heard the adapting tone as occurs for binaural adaptation and testing. Thus the relation between this pitch adaptation process and the loudness adaptation process is unclear.

GROUPING IN AUDITORY PERCEPTION

Grouping Principles

There is less interference with the perception of one auditory stimulus by another (less auditory *masking*) the less similar the two stimuli are in quality, localization, and time of occurrence (Massaro 1973, 1975, pp. 238–43; Thurlow 1972; Zwicker and Scharf 1965; Scharf 1975; Thurlow 1972). Susceptibility to masking derives in part from the degree to which the test stimulus attributes are integrated (grouped together) with the mask attributes. Thus there are auditory analogues of the visual Gestalt principles of similarity (quality) and spatial proximity (localization). What assumes somewhat larger significance in audition than in vision is the temporal dimension. As one would expect, grouping of stimulus attributes is facilitated by temporal proximity.

To my knowledge, there are no experimental demonstrations of auditory analogues to continuity, smooth continuation, and symmetry in the spatial domain. It might be a bit easier to obtain a grouped perception of a chorus singing one song when all the spaces between the ends of a chorus line are filled in with singers, but auditory spatial resolution is so inferior to visual spatial resolution that there may be no auditory analogues to these three more detailed visual grouping principles in the spatial domain. In the temporal domain, however, there may well be analogues to continuity, smooth continuation, and symmetry.

Familiarity is a very important grouping principle in auditory perception. Compare your ability to segregate a speech stream into words in a familiar versus an unfamiliar language. Never mind that you do not know the meanings of the words in the unfamiliar language. Just try to say where one word ends and the next begins. Ordinary speech does not have long pauses between words. Often there is no greater (or even less) temporal separation between the last phoneme of one word and the first phoneme of the next word than between adjacent phonemes within a single word. Our ability to break a speech stream into word units depends a lot on our learned familiarity with those word units.

Auditory Stream Segregation

One auditory analogue to the figure-ground distinction in vision is the ability to attend to a verbal or musical signal out of a background of noise. This is somewhat analogous to the distinction between form and texture in vision. In addition, we can attend to one meaningful auditory signal and ignore another, just as we can attend to one form and ignore another. One very striking phenomenon that enables us to do this is auditory stream segregation. It has been known in music for a very long time that a rapidly played sequence of notes that differ widely in frequency will often break up into two separate sequences of high notes and low notes. The temporal ordering of the high notes is perceived, as is the temporal ordering of the low notes, but the temporal relation between the high and low notes is completely lost. This can permit one solo instrument to sound like two instruments playing two melodic lines at the same time. Telemann and Bach, among others, made use of this principle.

Miller and Heise (1950) presented subjects with two rapidly alternated tones of different frequencies. They found that stream splitting could be obtained with only a 15% difference in frequency if the alternation rate was fast enough. In general, the slower the presentation rate, the larger the frequency difference that could be perceptually grouped into a single sequence of high and low tones before the sequence split into two separate streams.

More recently, Norman has realized the general importance of this grouping phenomenon for our understanding of the perception of the temporal order of events, and Bregman and his colleagues have done some important research on the properties of auditory stream segregation. For example, Bregman and Campbell demonstrated that a sequence of six notes (e.g., 2,000, 550, 2,500, 350, 1,600, and 430 hz) will produce much more accurate perception of the temporal order of the high notes (2,000, 2,500, 1,600) and of the low notes (550, 350, 430) than of the temporal relations between notes in the two different streams. This inability to order temporally the notes from different streams occurred even though subjects listened to a repeating cycle of the same six notes in the same order for as long as they wished (Norman 1967; Bregman and Campbell 1971).

Actually, the subjects would probably have done better on the cross-stream ordering by listening to the sequence only once, since we have some ability to identify which tone occurred last (and to a lesser extent, first). Most studies eliminate this confounding factor by using repetitive cycles or by embedding the test stimuli within a context of irrelevant prior and subsequent tones. An elegant experiment of the latter type by Bregman and Rudnicky showed that the discrimination of the temporal order of the A and B tones in an XABX sequence could be made *better* by embedding the XABX sequence into a context consisting of a single C tone—namely, CCCXABXCC —provided that C was close to X in frequency. Tones A and B were slightly higher than X, which in turn was either the same as or higher than C. When C was close to X in frequency, it "pulled" X out of the group with A and B and into the group with C. This reduced the interfering effect X had on the perception of the temporal order of A and B. This study confirms in audition the principle Attneave stated so clearly for vision: that one stimulus element can be a member of only one perceptual group. At least in this case, grouping does appear to induce a strict partitioning of stimulus elements (Bregman and Rudnicky 1975).

Finally, Bregman and Dannenbring (1973) have demonstrated an auditory analogue of continuity or smooth continuation or both in the temporal realm. They showed that a sequence of high and low tones can be kept from splitting into two streams by a ramplike increase or decrease in frequency during the transition from one tone to the next, instead of an abrupt shift.

As Bregman has emphasized, auditory stream segregation is *not* primarily a matter of attending to one stream and ignoring the other; rather, it is a matter of constituent analysis. In the important Bregman and Rudnicky experiment, the A and B elements were, in all conditions, the focus of attention. But perception of the C elements could not have been totally inhibited, else how could the similarity between the C and X elements have been so important for isolating A and B in one group and the Cs and Xs in another? There probably are some attentional differences here. But the primary meaning of grouping is just that—*grouping* (constituent analysis). Grouping permits us to focus more attention on one group than another, but it is primarily a matter of placing elements under some superordinate group chunk node and encoding the relations only among elements within a group, not across different groups. In the musical example this may mean encoding melodic relations between successive notes *within* a group (stream or melodic line), but *not across* groups. An F to F# transition could be said to activate a particular node representing this particular transition. A melodic phrase could then be represented by a set of notes and transitional (relational) elements. The transitional elements are then context-sensitive elements that "glue" the notes together into a melodic group, much as angle nodes may "glue" line nodes together into a visual-form group.

PERCEPTION OF TEMPORAL ORDER

The findings in auditory stream segregation are significant not only for the auditory grouping of temporally distributed elements, but also for the basic issue of how we perceive the temporal order of elements. We must conclude from these studies that we do not automatically encode the temporal order of two elements A and B just because their nodes are activated sequentially. We must group them together so as to encode the relation between them, e.g., a whole-step increase or decrease in pitch, a musical fifth, and so on. It is the existence of nodes representing particular transitions that permits us to encode the temporal order of elements. If we place two elements into different groups, we will not have encoded their temporal order. Temporal succession is not a sufficient cue for encoding temporal order, and once again we see the nervous system using specific node coding to represent concepts—in this case the A→B transition versus the B→A transition. Temporal order, like everything else in the nervous system, is represented by the activation of specific nodes.

If this is so, it should require some learning to list a set of familiar elements in their correct order, if these elements have not been presented as temporally ordered sets in the past. That is, we may have learned names for the elements, and we may be able correctly to name each of the elements in a sequence ABCD, but if we never learned the order (transition) concepts for A→B, B→C, and C→D, we might be totally unable to list these elements in their correct order. Different (transition) elements would be activated by ABCD than by BDAC. But if we had not learned that activation of the A→B node meant that we should say, write, and think, "B comes after A," we would not be able to report the order correctly even though we could report all the elements correctly as an unordered set.

Precisely this effect has been reported by Warren and his colleagues in a brilliant series of experiments. They set up a sequence of 200 msec stimuli, such as a high tone (1,000 hz), a hiss (2,000 hz octave band noise), a low tone (796 hz), and a buzz (40 hz square wave), and showed that unpracticed subjects could listen to such a sequence for as long as they wished, clearly identify every element, and yet operate at chance in reporting the order of the elements! These are not brief stimuli—200 msec per item is far slower than the rate at which we can correctly perceive the order of familiar sequences such as melodies, digit sequences, and phonemes in words. The problem is not that the different orderings are indiscriminable. Same-different recognition tests show that subjects can correctly state that ABCD is the same as ABCD and that ABCD is different from BDAC. They just cannot state what the order is—until they get some feedback. As soon as the experimenter tells them, "that was an ABCD; that was a BDAC," subjects can learn to report the order of hisses, buzzes, and tones. The transition elements are being activated by unfamiliar sequences of stimuli, but we need to learn what orderings they signal. Presumably it was this way with music and speech at one time in our lives (Warren, Obusek, and Farmer 1969; Warren 1974a,b, 1976; Warren and Ackroff 1976).

Temporal order is thus not fundamentally represented in the nervous system by temporal order of activation of nodes (except at the lowest levels). Temporal order is represented by the activation of transitional, or context-sensitive, nodes. This representation of temporal order is probably not fundamentally different from the representation of spatially distributed, simultaneously presented elements in vision. Thus the close analogy between spatial and temporal ordering becomes understandable. Furthermore, this encoding of temporal order by specific nodes has important "time-binding" advantages over the encoding of temporal order by sequential activation. One can perceive or think about a sequence of elements (e.g., a word, a phrase, a melody) as a single unit all of whose constituents are (partially) activated at the same time. Input and output may be serial, and so, therefore, must be the representation at peripheral sensory and motor levels, but thought can be simultaneous. Because of the slower sequential character of input and output, we are primarily cognizant of the sequential aspects of thought. But we probably (unconsciously) plan what we are going to say (and perceive what others say) at a level where the units are propositions and concepts that must be decoded into sequences of words and then into sequences of articulatory gestures. The indications are that the necessary encoding of sequential order is by *which* specific nodes are the constituents of higher-order chunk nodes, and that these constituents may be activated simultaneously without losing the information regarding temporal order. Can you think of another plausible way for your brain to convert the unitary thought "Jingle Bells" into a long sequence of words and notes? We could assume that temporally ordered constituents are automatically associated with their superordinate chunk nodes, and that their temporal order is specified. But this theory and others like it that assume a general capacity for representing temporal order are too powerful to be squared with actual human limitations in the perception of temporal order.

OBJECT CONCEPTS
AND AUDITORY PATTERN PERCEPTION

Although vision is the primary input modality for the perception of objects, we can recognize thousands of entities by means of their sound (a dog barking, a vacuum cleaner humming, a car horn sounding)—aided mightily by our knowledge of the context, of course. This is just the tip of the iceberg, for we also have an enormous capacity to signal both abstract and concrete concepts by means of spoken words. The auditory temporal patterns of these words need have nothing in common with sounds emitted by their referents (if any). Speech recognition will be discussed extensively in the next chapter, and I will say a little about music later in this chapter. Little research has been done on the identification of objects by means of their sounds. There is some evidence for the existence of single neurons in the auditory cortex of squirrel monkeys that are selectively tuned to encode monkey vocalizations (Funkenstein et al. 1971). We obviously have the capacity to activate concept nodes from nonverbal auditory, as well as verbal auditory and visual, patterns. And that's about all there is to say on this topic at present.

Serial versus Parallel Processing

In hearing as in vision there is evidence that humans can process two stimulus dimensions simultaneously (in parallel); we are not restricted to successive (serial) processing. The evidence is again *redundancy gain*—that the discrimination of two auditory stimuli is faster (and more accurate) if they differ in two dimensions at once than if they differ in either dimension alone. This redundancy gain holds for both verbal and nonverbal auditory stimuli (Wood 1974; Blechner, Day, and Cutting 1976).

EXPECTATION AND FEEDBACK
IN PERCEPTION

People make articulatory errors (slips of the tongue) all the time. Most of these errors go completely unnoticed by their listeners, unless those listeners are on the lookout for them. We listen primarily for meaning, and speech is generally so highly redundant that the semantic and phonetic context forces activation of the correct concept nodes even when words are mispronounced or missing. When we have strong expectations, we often hear what we expect to hear and not the auditory stimulus that actually did occur. You might try the following little experiment to demonstrate this for yourself. Try greeting your friends in the morning with "Could borning, Maryann (or whatever)." Talk for ten seconds (to let the echoic memory fade away). Then ask them to repeat your initial greeting. See how many notice anything out of the ordinary, let alone can state accurately what you said. Or answer the telephone with "Bellow," or "Yellow," and see if anyone notices. Be cool and natural, if you want to fool everyone.

Not only can expectations produce misperceptions in the unsuspecting listener, Warren (1970) has demonstrated that, under some circumstances, expectations can prevent even a listener who knows something is wrong with a word from perceiving what is wrong. Warren replaced the "gis" syllable in "legislatures" with a cough, tone, or buzz. Subjects not only recognized the word, they were unable to discriminate the altered word from the normal word. Activation of the correct word or concept node must have fed back activation to the phonetic level so that the phonetic segment nodes for "gis" were as strongly activated as when the "gis" sound was actually presented.

PERCEPTUAL RESPONSES

Human ears do not have mechanisms analogous to the eyelid or eye muscles to control the input of information to the sense organ. However, we can move our heads or bodies, extend our external ear with our hands or something else in order to increase its sound-gathering capacity, or cover our ears to reduce auditory input. In addition, auditory localization may often serve to direct eye, head, and body movements for more precise visual localization and identification of objects.

MUSIC

Most subjects can remember the pitch, loudness, and duration of a presented tone for a few seconds or even tens of seconds following its presentation (Gleitman 1957; Kinchla and Smyzer 1967; Wickelgren 1969e; Deutsch 1970; Massaro 1970; Kinchla 1972). Subjects exhibit this short-term memory by judging a subsequently presented comparison tone to be the same as or different from the previously presented standard tone in pitch, loudness, or duration. Alternatively, they may judge the comparison tone to be higher or lower than the standard tone in any of these features. For most subjects the capacity to perform such successive comparisons of primary auditory features declines rapidly over a period of several seconds or minutes following presentation. A few subjects, who are said to possess *absolute pitch,* can translate the presented tone into a more permanent, possibly verbal, code and remember the pitch of a presented tone indefinitely. But most of us have a poor long-term memory for these primary auditory characteristics.

Hence it is not surprising that musical memory is highly independent of the absolute pitch for the notes in a song. Rather, we remember the relationships (musical intervals) between simultaneously presented notes (chords) and the relationships between successively presented notes in a song. We can sing a song from memory in a large variety of different keys. Indeed, most of us probably have little idea whether we sing a song in the same or a different key from one time to another. However, we do (more or less) preserve the proper musical intervals between successive notes in the melodies we sing, and we can certainly recognize inappropriate chords in music we hear.

Diana Deutsch (1969) has developed a very clever theory of the higher level of the encoding of music. Deutsch assumes the existence of two higher-level encoding systems operating on the lower-level pitch representatives. The two systems may be called the successive system and the simultaneous system. The successive system represents all of the possible musical intervals between successive notes, so that a transition from C to C# would be encoded by a different node than the transition from C# to D or the backwards transition from C# to C. Thus the successive system is concerned with representing all of the *ordered pairs* of successive notes. It might be noted in passing that such a system constitutes a form of context-sensitive coding for the successive notes in a song.

In the simultaneous (chord) system all notes an octave apart are considered as equivalent. In Western music this reduces the entire frequency domain to the 12 fundamental notes. The node representing a chord then encodes a combination (unordered set), typically of 3 component notes from the set of 12. Chords might also be context-sensitively coded. That is, a node might represent a particular sequence of three chords. If this were so, a short song or a passage from a longer song might be encoded by means of an unordered set of such context-sensitive chord representatives in conjunction with the context-sensitively coded interval representatives for the successive notes of the melody. Little is known about higher-level representations of musical compositions, so such suggestions are both imprecise and completely speculative.

One particularly surprising consequence of Deutsch's theory is the so-called "Yankee Doodle" phenomenon, which she predicted and discovered (Deutsch 1972a, b). According to Deutsch's theory, perception of a melody requires perception of the absolute interval between successive notes, before the notes are collapsed by octaves to the 12 fundamental notes of the scale. Thus while it is quite easy to recognize a tune regardless of what octave it is played in, according to Deutsch's theory it should be extremely difficult, if not impossible, to recognize the tune when successive notes are taken from different octaves. That is to say, if instead of consistently transposing by one or two octaves, one randomly transposes by zero, one, or two octaves in either direction from note to note, the melody should be unrecognizable. When Deutsch played a familiar tune, such as Yankee Doodle, randomly transposing by octaves from note to note, subjects found it essentially impossible to recognize. This confirms the hypothesis that the perception of successive musical intervals proceeds independently of the system that achieves octave generalization.

AESTHETICS

All very well, but the question I posed at the beginning of this chapter remains. Why do we like listening to these "functionless" musical chords and sequences? I don't see that music or any other area of aesthetics has any direct survival value, so my guess is that human aesthetic motivation is a delightful byproduct of something that *is* directly beneficial to survival. What could that something be? Whatever it is, it must be consistent with the primary principle of aesthetics, which is that *stimuli with intermediate degrees of predictability are aesthetically pleasing.* In music, art, or caressing the skin, we are bored by completely predictable repetition and floored by completely unpredictable stimuli. My enjoyment of a new song is never as great the first time I hear it as it is after I have heard it a few times, but after I have heard it many times, it becomes too predictable and therefore boring. It also appears that highly complex music requires more listening time to become enjoyable and also more listening time to become boring. A style of music with which one is totally unfamiliar is not enjoyable until one has listened to enough of it to develop appropriate predictive schemata. Even if there is considerable predictive structure in something, we will not enjoy it unless we have the necessary concepts to encode that structure and generate fairly accurate expectations. All of this is equally true of visual aesthetics—and even cutaneous aesthetics for those of us who are blessed with the ability to "tingle." Repetitious caressing is boring, but so is completely random, punctate touching. It's the smooth, continuous caress, where you can anticipate the approximate region, but not the exact point, of the next place touched, that is pleasurable.

What else, besides aesthetic pleasure, thrives on intermediate degrees of expectancy guided by predictive schemata? Learning! We learn best and enjoy it most when we can partially predict what we are going to be told next —when we already possess much of the basic conceptual structure for encoding an experience. We dislike subjects that are too elementary for us (and so boringly familiar) and subjects that are too far over our heads. Pleasurable learning is learning that fits into our existing schemata (conceptual frameworks) and is therefore likely to be related to our existing goals. Human beings choose what they will learn on the basis of this aesthetic pleasure principle to an enormous extent, and it is probably highly functional to control learning in this way. It is highly speculative but rather fun to imagine that the primary purpose of our aesthetic sense is to guide learning in fruitful directions, but that the mechanism is such as to make certain forms of (aesthetic) sensory experience especially suited to turning on that pleasure.

SUMMARY

1 At early levels of the auditory nervous system, sound is represented spectrographically in terms of the magnitude (intensity) of its different sinusoidal frequency components.

2 The decibel scale for intensity is a logarithmic scale, relative to some base intensity. An increase of 1 dB from some background intensity is a fixed *percentage* increase, not a fixed absolute increase from the background intensity. Such a relative decibel scale is especially appropriate for measuring auditory intensities because, to a first approximation, equal percentage increases in intensity are equally detectable for human beings across different background intensities.

3 At the lowest levels of the auditory nervous system, pitch is represented both by a specific neuron code (*which* neurons are maximally activated) and by a pattern code (rate of firing of neurons). Furthermore, near the periphery the specific neuron code is very blurred, and there is substantial generalized activation of many pitch detectors having widely varying center frequencies. However, at higher levels the rate code (precise preservation of auditory frequency in rate of firing) is completely lost. It becomes transformed into a sharply tuned specific-neuron code for pitch.

4 Loudness is also initially represented by rate of firing. Loudness is apparently also transformed into a specific neuron code such that some neurons fire only to sounds of appropriate intensity—that is, within some range of intensities. Such ranges have a maximum as well as a minimum intensity. Different ranges represent different intensities.

5 Information concerning the direction of a sound source is represented initially by relative differences between the two ears in phase and rate of firing (not by specific neuron codes). However, at higher levels of the auditory modality, this information is integrated and transformed into a specific neuron code such that particular neurons are activated by sounds coming from a particular direction, as indicated by the binaural phase and intensity differences.

6 Auditory localization is most precise in the straight-ahead direction. We may use our encoding of other directions in auditory space to make head movements to center both our ears—and more importantly our eyes—on a sound source. We locate objects primarily by vision; our sound localization capacity is primitive compared to that of certain less "visual" animals. Chief among these are the echolocators, such as bats and dolphins, who produce sounds that reflect off distant objects and return to be analyzed, in order to locate objects in space (sonar).

7 Inhibition serves many important known or probable functions in the auditory nervous system. It sharpens the precision of specific neuron encoding of pitch; it permits specific neuron encoding of intensity and direction; and it produces adaptation, habituation, and selective attention.

8 There are several forms of auditory adaptation. The first is tightening the middle-ear muscles to protect the ear from intense sounds. The second is peripheral (probably receptor) fatigue, which is long lasting but is brought on only by very intense sounds. The third is central neural (true) adaptation, which is short lasting and modest in its effect but is produced by even exceedingly soft sounds. Central neural adaptation has not yet been shown to be functional for perceiving small deviations in loudness from the adapting level. It has been shown to be functional for perceiving small deviations in pitch from the adapting pitch.

9 We group sounds together into a single chunk and encode the relations between such constituents of a single chunk on the basis of properties analogous to those used in vision. These are temporal and spatial proximity, qualitative similarity (for instance, similarity in pitch), continuity, and familiarity (previous occurrence together in a group). Grouping is not primarily a matter of attending to some sounds and ignoring others. It is a matter of encoding the relations among constituents in a common group and not encoding the relations among constituents of different groups.

10 Temporal order is not encoded by temporal order of activation of nodes (except at the lowest levels of the nervous system). It is encoded by the activation of specific transitional feature nodes or context-sensitive chunk (e.g., phoneme, tone, complex sound) nodes (specific node encoding of temporal order).

11 We can process the multiple features of an auditory "object" in parallel. Like visual perception, auditory perception is guided by expectations produced jointly by context and prior knowledge. The central associative input to nodes that constitute expectations can sometimes sum with nonspecific acoustic sensory input to activate nodes exactly as the appropriate specific acoustic input would do. This produces a kind of hallucination.

12 At higher cognitive segmental levels, music may be encoded using two systems: the context-sensitive successive system for representing sequences of notes and the simultaneous system for representing chords. The simultaneous system shows complete octave generalization; the successive system does not.

13 The primary principle of aesthetics is that we enjoy stimuli for which we have an intermediate degree of expectation. The same principle applies regarding the material we most enjoy learning and learn best. Aesthetic appreciation may derive from a basic emotional-cognitive control mechanism for learning, so that we are in essence motivated to learn what is beautiful. Or rather, so that what we find beautiful is what we are most highly motivated to learn.

CHAPTER 5
SPEECH AND READING

OBJECTIVES

1 To describe and distinguish several different levels of processing in the verbal modality. These levels are concerned with speech and reading, and they include propositions, concepts, phrases, words, segments (e.g., letters, syllables, phonemes, allophones), and phonetic and graphic features (e.g., voicing, nasality, line segments, corners).

2 To explain briefly the distinction between phonemes (units of speech) and letters (units of writing), and between context-sensitive allophones (overlapping sequences of phonemes) and syllables (nonoverlapping sequences of phonemes).

3 To distinguish among sensory, motor, and cognitive levels of processing in the speech modality. To define one clear dimension of difference between cognitive and S-R theories of speech.

4 To discuss the relation between the phonetic (listening and speaking) and graphic (reading and writing) submodalities of the verbal modality.

5 To discuss the process of speech recognition. The discussion will emphasize four problems of: (a) the segmentation of speech into phonemes, (b) the variation in the acoustic features of the same phoneme in different contexts, (c) the problem of representing order, and (d) the use of phonetic, syntactic, and semantic context to aid recognition.

6 To describe context-sensitive coding of speech segments. To show how this coding appears to solve many of the fundamental problems of speech recognition and articulation that bedevil a context-free phonemic code.

7 To define ballistic versus feedback control systems and to describe the basic functioning of the gamma feedback system in motor control.

8 To discuss some issues in speech articulation. These include the role of sensory feedback; coarticulation (contextual variation in phoneme targets); motor pre-planning several segments ahead of the segment being articulated; and the role of syllables in speech.

9 To discuss the graphic features and segments that appear to play an important role in reading, including the probable role of context-sensitive coding in the encoding of letter order in words.

10 To discuss the process of reading. Topics include the role of the phonetic modality (mental subvocalization); parallel processing of all the letters in a word; chain parallel processing of sensory input at many levels simultaneously; and contextual expectation effects in reading. These effects include feedback from higher word and context levels to lower graphic, segmental and featural levels.

11 To discuss the use and limitations of speed reading. To emphasize that the purpose of reading is to acquire new knowledge in semantic memory (under-standing), not just to activate already existing nodes.

I venture to say that every reader has had the following experience (perhaps while reading this book). You were reading, perhaps had even turned a page, when suddenly you realized that you had been reading words, but not meanings. That is, you were recognizing the words in a manner somewhat equivalent to pronouncing them to yourself, but the higher levels of your mind that are concerned with the extraction of meaning were shut off from these lower structural levels—probably because you were thinking of something else. Indeed, when I read familiar stories to my children, I sometimes discover that I have read several pages aloud without consciously thinking about the meaning of what I was reading. Finally, it is possible to *shadow* the speech of another person—that is, to repeat what the other person is saying without paying attention to its meaning. Even meaningless sequences of nonsense syllables can be adequately shadowed.

Over the course of 20 years and thousands of hours of listening to rock music, I have learned to sing (sort of) substantial portions of hundreds of different songs. Yet I rarely have any conception of the message conveyed by the lyrics (when there is one). This is true even for songs I have heard and sung hundreds of times. Some years ago, when I realized that I was paying no attention to the meaning of rock lyrics, I started to do so for a while, but quickly stopped, realizing the good sense of my former habit. The lyrics definitely contribute something to my appreciation of rock, since I typically prefer songs with words to songs without. However, it is apparently the sound of the words and not their meanings that I find aesthetically appealing.

As these experiences illustrate, there are levels of processing, perhaps unconscious or only semiconscious, that lie below the level of meaningful thought, and that play an important role in listening, speaking, reading, or writing. The number of these levels and the nature of encoding within each level is not completely known. Nevertheless, we can say a great deal about coding at various levels in the verbal system. This chapter will first discuss structural units (nodes) at various levels of the verbal modality and then consider the processes of speech recognition, articulation, and reading.

VERBAL LEVELS AND UNITS

Semantic Memory

Consider the *sentence* "The American struck oil." The entire sentence expresses a complete thought, which we shall call a *proposition*. The sentence is obviously composed of four *words*. However, in thought, the proposition is composed of only three *concepts*, since "the American" refers to a particular individual, and thus the two words refer to a single concept. As you know, the same word often has different meanings in different contexts, so concepts are certainly not identical to words, nor do they bear a one-to-one relation to them.

"The American" could also be called a *phrase*, as is "struck oil." Propositions have conceptual compounds (phrases) for constituents, and phrases have concepts as constituents. Concepts are expressed by words; I will say more about this in chapter 11. For the purpose of the present chapter, we will consider concepts, compounds, and propositions to be part of *semantic memory*, which encodes meanings. In the hierarchy of levels composing the verbal modality, we will consider words as being one step below concepts. For most people the familiar constituents of words are letters and syllables. Letters are units within the graphic (vision-writing) level of the verbal modality and will be discussed in the next section.

Phonetic Segmental Level

Phonemes. The phonetic speech unit most analogous to the letter is the *phoneme*. The word "struck" is composed of six letters but only five phonemes: /s/, /t/, /r/, /u/, /k/. From an articulatory viewpoint, phonemes correspond to target positions of the vocal tract. In pronouncing the /t/ phoneme, the tip of the tongue is placed at the front part of the mouth just back of the teeth, and other parts of the vocal tract must also be in certain positions. Thus the successive phonemes of a word can be considered to represent the successive positions of the vocal tract during articulation. As you know, English is not a simple phonetic language—that is, in English the same letter frequently makes a different sound (phoneme) in different words. In addition, some single phonemes are represented graphically by a combination of two letters, such as /th/, /sh/, /ch/. In other cases, a single letter stands for a sequence of phonemes. For example, the letter x is phonetically /e/, /k/, /s/.

Syllables.   Syllables may be considered to be basic units in and of themselves, or they may be considered to be composed of a sequence of phonemes. Typically a syllable contains exactly one vowel, though liquids such as /l/ or /r/ may occasionally function as syllable nuclei in place of vowels. We shall ignore such complexities and consider the number of syllables in a word to be equal to the number of vowels.

While a phoneme corresponds to a particular target position of the vocal tract, a syllable is much more complex. Essentially, a syllable corresponds to a sequence of target positions of the vocal tract. Thus it is very difficult to imagine the syllable as the most basic *segmental* constituent of words, though it might be a constituent intermediate between words and phonemes.

In words that contain more than one vowel, it is not always obvious where to place the syllable boundaries. Syllable conventions are recorded in dictionaries, but it is by no means clear that the syllable divisions are psychologically real. Indeed, the entire analysis of words into phonemes or syllables, while it is natural to any educated person with phonics training, is of questionable psychological validity. There is actually little evidence to support the hypothesis that syllables are constituents of words at any structural level of the verbal modality.

Context-sensitive allophones.   Phonemes and syllables are non-overlapping constituents of words. That is, words are analyzed into segments that correspond to separate portions of the speech train. These segments do not overlap one another. Recently it has been proposed that the segmental constituents of words are overlapping phoneme triples called context-sensitive allophones (Wickelgren 1969a, 1969b, 1972a, 1976a). For example, the word "struck" would be composed of the following context-sensitive allophones: $_\#s_t$, $_st_r$, $_tr_u$, $_ru_k$, $_uk_\#$.

Context-sensitive coding has some intriguing properties. The most important of these is that it permits representation of very long *ordered sets of phonemes* by means of an *unordered set of context-sensitive allophones.* That is, one could scramble the order of the context-sensitive allophones in a word and uniquely reconstruct the correct order in the following manner. First, in the set of allophone constituents of a word, there will be exactly one allophone whose initial element is the juncture marker #. Select that allophone first; in the case of the word struck it is $_\#s_t$. The first allophone tells you what the first two elements of the second allophone are. In the present example, knowing that the first allophone is $_\#s_t$ tells you that the second allophone starts with the elements $_s$t. There is only one such allophone in the set of allophone constituents for the word "struck," namely $_s$t$_r$. Knowing the second allophone, you have sufficient information to select the third, and so on until the final allophone is selected. This final allophone has the property that its terminal element is once again the juncture symbol #. Reconstructing the correct ordered set from the unordered set in this way is a lot like assembling a linear jigsaw puzzle. As we shall see, the ability to represent an ordered set of segmental constituents by means of an unordered set is extremely useful in speech recognition, articulation, and reading.

If one assumes that accented and unaccented vowels are represented as different segments, then, to my knowledge, the correct ordering of segments in every word in English can be uniquely reconstructed from the unordered set of context-sensitive allophones. Furthermore, one can represent quite long phrases of words by taking an unordered set of context-sensitive allophones and uniquely reconstructing the order of the segments. To represent the sequence of allophones in a phrase, we assume that context-sensitive word-juncture segments connect adjacent words. For example, the segment $_k$#$_r$ connects the allophones in the two words "struck rock."

It is a remarkable fact that we can reconstruct the order of the phonetic segments of individual words and even moderately long phrases if we know the immediate left and right neighbors of each segment. This is by no means mathematically necessary, since it is quite possible to construct ordered sets for which context-sensitive coding would be inadequate to produce a unique reconstruction (e.g., "natanananub," whose context-sensitive coding can be read out as "nanatanaunb"). However, except for extremely long sequences of phonemes, such sets are very rare.

Phonetic Feature Level

The constituents of a segment such as a phoneme or an allophone are a bundle of features (attributes). In speech production (articulation) the features of a segment are the specifications of the positions and movements of movable parts of the vocal tract needed to produce that segment. For example, some segments are voiced—that is, the vocal cords are vibrating during production of the segment. Examples include all vowels, semivowels (w, y), and liquids (l, r), and many consonants (b, d, g, n, m, ng, [as in "sing"], v, zh [as in "azure"], j, and th [as in "the"]). Other consonants are unvoiced—that is, the vocal cords are not vibrating during articulation. An unvoiced consonant is often articulated in other respects very much like some other voiced consonant. The pairs of consonants that are considered to differ only or primarily with respect to voicing are p and b, t and d, k and g, th (in think) and th (in the), f and v, sh and zh, ch and j. Other articulatory features include specification of tongue position, jaw position, lip position, and velar position (nasal versus nonnasal).

We have been discussing the articulatory features of phoneme or allophone segments. As sensory input, phoneme or allophone segments have auditory feature constituents. For example, the voiced segments have a fundamental frequency component like that present in singing. It is somewhere around 130 hz for men, 220 hz for women, and 260 hz for children (Peterson and Barney 1952). People with low voices have a lower fundamental frequency component than people with high voices. This voicing feature is only present during voiced segments—it is absent during unvoiced consonants. Of course, the listener must determine many other features besides voicing in order to identify unambiguously the segmental constituents of words in spoken speech.

Sensory, Motor, and Cognitive Levels

An extremely noncognitive theory of levels might postulate that the analysis of sensory input, from features to segments to words to concepts and propositions, is performed by units entirely separate from the units on the response or motor side. The most extreme of such noncognitive theories would have separate representations for concepts and propositions on both the sensory and motor sides; it would only allow links at the top between the highest level of sensory propositions and the highest level of motor propositions. A somewhat less radical neo S-R theory might admit that concepts and propositions were abstract, in the sense of being neither purely sensory nor purely motor, but it would maintain a separation of sensory and motor representation up to the level of words. Such a theory is diagramed in figure 5.1(a).

In figure 5.1(a) there are separate representations on the sensory and motor sides for features, segments, and words. However, the possibility of direct associations between the auditory and articulatory levels is represented by the double arrows with question marks over them.

A more abstract, cognitive theory is represented in figure 5.1(b). Here only the featural representations are assumed to be separate for audition and speech. Sensory input and motor output are assumed to converge on common segmental units. These segmental units are therefore abstract or cognitive in the sense that the same units receive auditory input in speech recognition and provide motor output in speech production. The possibility of mapping between auditory and articulatory features is represented by the double arrow with the question mark over it in figure 5.1(b). Obviously, the representation in figure 5.1(b) is more parsimonious and less complex than the representation in figure 5.1(a). At present there is no reason to prefer a complex neo S-R representation to a simpler cognitive representation. Therefore, I will use the more abstract cognitive representation in figure 5.1(b) as a working model.

Of course one might extend the cognitive theory so as to postulate a common set of feature representatives. The position taken by some linguists

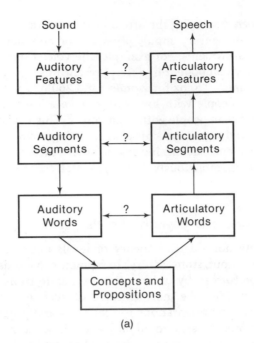

(a)

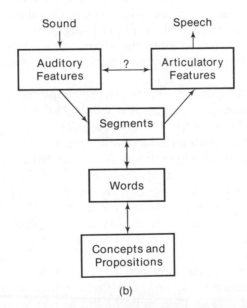

(b)

Fig. 5.1 Two flowchart theories of the levels of representation for speech recognition and articulation. (a) is a rather extreme S-R theory that separates sensory and motor levels through the word level. (b) is a highly cognitive theory that separates sensory and motor levels only through the feature level but assumes that they converge on common cognitive segment nodes.

—such as Jakobson, Fant, Chomsky, and Halle—might be interpreted as assuming common abstract feature representatives for audition and speech (Jakobson, Fant, and Halle 1963; Chomsky and Halle 1968). However, the research of Liberman and his associates on speech perception has amply demonstrated that there is no simple one-to-one correspondence for many auditory and articulatory features (Liberman et al. 1967). Hence it seems best to retain separate sensory and motor feature units at present. A diagram like figure 5.1(b) that represents the features of audition and speech as separate, but allows for some possible direct mapping between them, appears to be the best way to describe the system at present.

Graphic Levels

Although the phonetic (audition-speech) system is the most universal medium for linguistic communication, educated human beings also make extensive use of the graphic (vision-writing) system. The graphic system is composed of the same kinds of units as the phonetic system—namely, features, segments, words, concepts, phrases, and propositions.

Features.   The graphic features of written language are probably much the same as the visual features involved in the analysis of nonlinguistic stimuli. Though this has not been clearly established, it would appear that letters and words are not qualitatively different from nonverbal visual forms. They probably do differ quantitatively in that they have a higher degree of similarity among items. Speech sounds are a much more distinguished class of auditory stimuli—one for which we undoubtedly have specialized feature detectors. Visual linguistic stimuli are not so distinguished, and there is no reason to think that we have evolved specialized feature detectors for verbal visual material. Hence the visual sensory features for letters and words—like the visual sensory features for diagrams and scenes—probably include line detectors and corner detectors. The graphic features involved in the production of handwritten (printed) language are ultimately the features that specify the position and movement control of the muscles in the fingers, hand, and arm that control writing behavior.

Segments.   The most obvious choice for the segments of alphabetical written language characters would be the letters. Of course the lines (more generally marks) that make up a letter might be considered segments. Alternatively, one could assume that combinations of letters are segments. These combinations of letters might be nonoverlapping, as in syllabic coding, or overlapping, as in context-sensitive coding. Perhaps there are several graphic segmental levels that are functional in reading and writing. Once again we shall assume that, while vision and writing are distinct at the feature level, they coincide at the graphic segmental level. That is, the segmental units, be they letters, lines, syllables, or context-sensitive letter sequences, are the same for reading and for writing.

Relation Between Phonetic and Graphic Systems

Of course the phonetic system and the graphic system for language are closely related. But exactly what is the nature of this relationship? Once again, one might assume that the two systems communicate only at the highest propositional level of semantic memory. However, at present it seems most reasonable to assume that the union of the two systems occurs at the word level, just below the level of meaningful semantic memory. This relationship of the two principal subsystems of the verbal modality is diagramed in figure 5.2.

According to figure 5.2, the same word representatives are used in both the phonetic and the graphic systems. However, the segments are assumed to be distinct for the phonetic and graphic subsystems. Because most children are capable of learning phonetics before they learn to read each word as a

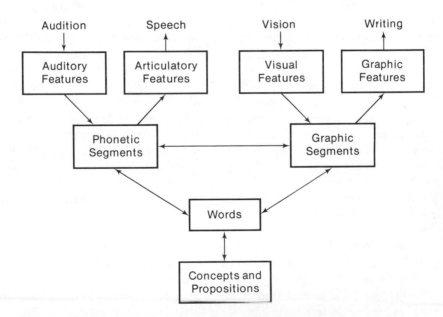

Fig. 5.2 Flowchart theory of the integration of the auditory and visual sensory and motor modalities into the multilevel verbal modality. Note that the phonetic and graphic segment modalities are assumed in this theory to converge on common abstract word nodes, which are therefore neither purely phonetic (auditory-articulatory) words nor purely graphic (visual-writing) words.

whole, it is assumed that a more or less direct mapping can exist between the graphic segments and the phonetic segments (fig. 5.2).

In terms of figure 5.2, learning to read phonetically means going indirectly from graphic segments to phonetic segments and then making use of the existing links from phonetic segments to words. Learning to read by the whole-word method means attempting to establish the associations directly from graphic segments to words. Presumably most children can learn to read using either method, though one might imagine that some children would find it easier to learn phonetically, while other children would find it easier to learn by the whole-word method. Hence the seemingly endless debate in education. In any event, it is very likely that even when a child learns to read phonetically, direct connections will eventually be established from graphic segments to words. Whatever assistance the indirect phonetic method may provide in early reading, highly skilled reading probably uses a direct connection from graphic segments to words.

SPEECH RECOGNITION

A significant labor-saving invention that may be made before the end of this century is the voice typewriter. This machine would convert spoken language into printed language. Creating a voice typewriter is essentially equivalent to creating an automatic speech recognition device, and this has proved to be considerably harder than many people first imagined. In this section you will see why.

Segmentation and Contextual Variation in Features

One misconception regarding speech is that a word consists of a succession of acoustic feature packages, that each feature package represents one phoneme, and that all feature packages are clearly distinguished by silence breaks or other distinctive cues to segment the speech stream. According to this naive theory, the acoustic features for a particular phoneme (the feature package) would be the same regardless of the adjacent phonemes, the speaker, or any other variable. This naive theory of speech is based on the phoneme theory of the constituents of words, which in turn is heavily influenced by the alphabetic mode of expression for written words. Written words, particularly printed words, do consist of a succession of symbols whose boundaries are generally adequately marked. And in these written symbols the features characteristic of the same letter in different contexts are substantially invariant.

However, in the area of speech perception, the naive theory falls apart. We can record speech and transform it into a visible record known as a speech spectrogram. It is roughly possible to point to a portion of the speech stream on the spectrogram and identify it with a particular phoneme. However, in general there are no sharp breaks between phonemes in the form either of silence or of other distinguishing cues to indicate the end of one phoneme and the beginning of the next. To be sure, there are some sharp breaks in a speech stream, but these are almost as likely to occur inside a phoneme as between adjacent phonemes (Fant 1962). More important, the cues for a given phoneme are scattered in time and intermixed with the cues for adjacent phonemes, particularly the immediate left and right neighbors (Liberman et al. 1967). Thus an automatic speech recognition device that attempted first to segment the speech stream into nonoverlapping regions and then to decide what phoneme had occurred within each region would face insurmountable difficulties.

Not only are the features for a given phoneme mixed with the features for adjacent phonemes, but the set of features characteristic of a phoneme is not constant across different immediate left and right phonemic contexts. Features that are characteristic in one context are often not even present in other contexts. For some phonemes the set of features that is found in all contexts appears to be inadequate to distinguish one phoneme from many others. Thus it does not even seem logically possible to specify a set of features characteristic of a phoneme in all contexts and to use that set of features to build an automatic speech recognition device. Even if it were possible, such an approach would ignore a great deal of useful information concerning the features characteristic of a phoneme in particular contexts. Considering the noise usually present in the speech recognition situation, it is quite impractical to discard relevant information, even if it is redundant under noise-free conditions. As Cole and Scott have emphasized, there are some invariant features characteristic of certain phonemes in all or a wide variety of phonemic contexts. However, these invariant features are only a subset of the total set of relevant features. They appear insufficient to produce as high an accuracy level as is characteristic of human speech recognition (Liberman et al. 1967; Cole and Scott 1974).

Because speech does not consist of a set of segmental phoneme-sized packages of invariant acoustic features, the phoneme is an unsatisfactory unit for speech recognition. On the other hand, the context-sensitive allophone seems ideally suited to the characteristics of human speech. Context-sensitive allophones are overlapping, spanning a range of approximately three phonemes. This is probably sufficient to include almost all of the relevant acoustic information for the identification of a particular allophone. Furthermore, since there are as many allophone representatives as there are phoneme triples, the variation in the acoustic cues for a phoneme contingent upon its immediate left and right phonemic context offers no difficulty. There are some more remote contextual dependencies beyond the immediate left and right phonemic context, but these are very minor effects comparatively speaking. One needs on the order of several thousand context-sensitive allophone detectors, instead of approximately 40 or 50 phoneme detectors. This number of allophone detectors is negligible for the human nervous system, considering that there are $3 \cdot 10^9$ neurons in the cortex. However, it does increase the difficulties of building an artificial speech recognition device.

Reduction and Speaker Variability

Besides the variation induced by the immediate phonemic context, there are other sources of variation in the acoustic features of both phonemes and allophones. First, there is the *reduction* in the acoustic features that occurs in informal dialects or with increased speech rates (Kozhevnikov and Chistovich 1965; Shockey 1973). Reduction often compresses the features in the time domain, sometimes to the point of completely eliminating features and even entire segments. Accurate speech recognition under conditions of extreme reduction (at very fast rates or in informal dialects) undoubtedly depends upon considerable use of syntactic and semantic contextual information. I will discuss this in more detail later.

Second, the acoustic cues for a phoneme or allophone vary across different speakers. The vocal tract is shaped differently in men, women, and children, and this produces corresponding differences in the acoustic cues characteristic of the speech segments of each group. Furthermore, within each group there is substantial individual variation (Peterson and Barney 1952).

Very little is known about how we handle the problem of speaker variability in speech recognition. The sensory features characteristic of a particular allophone may be defined in a sufficiently abstract way so as actually to be invariant across different speakers. Alternatively, we may have a variety of different allophone detectors suitable for the variety of different dialects we encounter in our normal listening environment. Ladefoged and Broadbent conducted a study that supports the existence of multiple allophone detectors. They found that subjects who were listening to one speaker tended to identify a particular set of acoustic features as the vowel phoneme /i/ (as in "bit"), while after listening to a different speaker, they identified the same set of features as /e/ (as in "bet") (Ladefoged and Broadbent 1957). That is, contextual adaptation to the dialects of different speakers substantially influenced identification of a particular speech segment. This sort of contextual speaker adaptation requires an extension of either the phonemic or the allophonic coding theory.

Parallel Processing
and the Representation of Order

A naive theory of the representation of the order of events might state: we know that A preceded B whenever the A node was activated before the B node. Extending this naive theory to the order of words, we might say: we can distinguish phonemic anagrams (the same phonemes in different orders), such as "struck" and "crust," because the phoneme representatives were activated in a different temporal order in each case. Even if this were true, it would still be very hard to specify the exact mechanism by which the nervous system could activate the word node for "struck" contingent upon one temporal order of activation of its phonemic constituents, and the node for "crust" contingent upon a different order.

However, there is reason to believe that the nervous system does not, in fact, possess any general mechanism for distinguishing different temporal orders of rapidly presented events. As we saw in chapter 4, Richard Warren and his colleagues have demonstrated that human beings are very poor at recognizing the order of even a short series of arbitrary sounds, such as a hiss, a high tone, a low tone, and a buzz. Even when each hiss, tone, or buzz is 200 msec long (as long or longer than the duration of most phonemes), subjects could not accurately recognize the order of a fixed sequence of three or four such stimuli, and they did no better even when the sequence was repeated over and over again. Obviously, people have no difficulty in recognizing the order of much longer sequences of verbal segments, each lasting 100 to 200 msec. So Warren's demonstration was quite amazing. Warren has subsequently demonstrated that, with greater experience in listening to sequences of hisses, buzzes, and tones, subjects can accurately perceive the correct temporal order of such stimuli even when these are very rapidly presented. Thus the ability to identify sequential order depends upon prior exposure to such sequences (Warren et al. 1969; Warren and Obusek 1972; Warren 1974a, 1974b).

This is precisely what one would expect on the basis of context-sensitive coding, since the representation of order is derived from which context-sensitive (transition) elements are activated. Prior exposure to sequences of different events permits the establishment of units that represent overlapping event triples—that is, context-sensitive coding. We recognize the order of a sequence of events because of the particular event transition representatives that are activated by this sequence. It is important to note that since context-sensitive coding represents the order of a long sequence of events by means of an unordered set, the allophone representatives need not be activated in the correct temporal order for there to be correct encoding of the temporal order of the events themselves.

It is fortunate that we recognize segmental order by *which* context-sensitive segment nodes are activated and not by the *temporal order* of (context-free) segment node activation. For this specific node coding makes possible the parallel processing of several successive phonemes. Using a backward masking method to terminate the speech recognition process for consonant-vowel (CV) syllables after a variable silent interval, both Pisoni and Massaro have demonstrated that the accuracy of identification for the initial consonant increases with up to 250 msec of silent (unmasked) processing time following presentation of a 40 msec CV syllable. Their findings show that the speech recognition process for each phoneme is slow in relation to the rates at which phonemes are spoken in normal speech (about 12 phonemes per second). Our speech recognition process is such that much more accurate phoneme identification occurs if we have 250 msec to process a phoneme than if processing is confined to the 80 msec that it takes to articulate the average phoneme at an average speech rate. In normal speech, subsequent phonemes presumably interfere with processing (that is, they mask) prior phonemes to some extent. But if this masking is incomplete, recognition accuracy can be much improved by permitting the recognition processes for several phonemes to go on simultaneously (parallel processing). This substantially lengthens the time allowed to recognize each phoneme (Miller 1962; Efron 1963; Pisoni 1972; Massaro 1974, 1975 [pp. 128–43]).

A study by Remington (1977) indicates that in CVC syllables recognition of all three phonemes does indeed occur in parallel. Instead of using the masking design employed by Pisoni and Massaro, Remington limited processing time directly by signalling subjects to respond at various times following the onset of a CVC syllable. The response-signal method shows how recognition accuracy increases with processing time without requiring the assumption that a given masking stimulus is completely effective in terminating processing. In this case the results of both methods agree almost perfectly concerning the dynamics of speech recognition. Both show that speech recognition reaches maximum performance over about a 250 msec period (not including peripheral sensory and motor response time). Furthermore, the increases in accuracy as a function of processing time (speed-accuracy trade-off functions) were completely overlapping for all three phonemes—allowing for the obvious difference in starting times for the articulation of each phoneme. The results indicated that each phoneme began to be processed as soon as relevant acoustic information was available and continued to be processed for about 250 msec, while other acoustic features were being processed for the recognition of other phonemes. Most surprising of all, the middle vowel was actually recognized as fast as or faster than the initial consonant, so that their times of recognition must have been nearly the same. Sometimes the consonant and sometimes the vowel was presumably leading. Yet regardless of the temporal order of recognition, subjects heard a CVC syllable, not a VCC syllable. Speech recognition is a limited-capacity parallel process (like human perceptual recognition in general). In such a process sequential order is represented by *which* (context-sensitive) nodes are activated, not by the temporal order of activation of (context-free) nodes.

Chain Parallel Processing

The distinction between serial and parallel processing depends upon whether two information-processing activities are performed sequentially or simultaneously. The hierarchical organization of the verbal modality diagramed in figure 5.1 has often been assumed to require a degree of serial processing in speech recognition such that features are recognized first, then segments, then words, and so forth. If the activation of a set of features is a necessary and sufficient condition for the activation of a segment representative, then almost everyone assumed that feature information must be processed before segment information. Similarly, processing at the segmental level was supposed to precede processing at the word level, and so forth.

It was therefore extremely puzzling when Savin and Bever, Warren, and later a number of other investigators demonstrated that, under some circumstances, subjects can detect a word in an utterance more quickly than they can detect a syllable, which in turn can be detected more quickly than a phoneme (Savin and Bever 1970; Warren 1971; Foss and Swinney 1973; McNeill and Lindig 1973). How can such results be obtained if the levels are ordered as in figure 5.1? One resolution of this problem adopted by some investigators is to assume that the levels of processing are not ordered as in figure 5.1; rather, these levels are essentially independent channels through which sensory input is processed. This resolution is extremely unsatisfactory. For what, then, are the constituents of higher-order units, if they are not any of these plausible lower-order units?

Fortunately, there is a much more elegant resolution of this apparent paradox. This resolution assumes that while the levels are ordered, and information reaches the feature level before the segmental level and the segmental level before the word level, the activation is passed on very quickly—much more quickly than we can decide which units are maximally activated at each level. According to this theory it takes a relatively long time to process information at a given level and decide which units are maximally activated at that level—on the order of tens or hundreds of msec—while the nodal delay times between nodes at each level are on the order of a few msec. Thus the time required for information to pass from the feature level to the word level is much less important than the time required to process information and reach a decision at each level. Hence the processing of verbal information is occurring at all levels of the verbal modality at essentially the same time. It could therefore easily happen that (due to convergence from many lower-level units or higher-level expectations) a higher-level unit could reach the recognition threshold more quickly than any lower-level unit (Wickelgren 1976d).

Context Effects and Feedback

Early attempts to build automatic speech recognition devices failed partly because most of them made no provision for using the context of a particular segment or word to aid in its recognition. That is, these models assumed that the set of acoustic features within a particular interval of time was sufficient to determine one, and only one, segment. Such a procedure is likely to be more successful when allophones are used than when phonemes are used. Even so, it is much less efficient than human speech recognition, which probably uses a variety of contextual restrictions to assist in the identification of any given segment. No fewer than seven different types of context effects are thought to function in speech recognition.

Segmental sequence restrictions. There are restrictions on the allowable sequences of segments that can occur within syllables in English. For example, the phoneme sequence /vk/ never appears within an English syllable. Furthermore, there are substantial differences in transition probabilities, even between phonemes that can occur in an English syllable. As we shall see later on, context-sensitive coding assumes only those allophones that can occur within a syllable. Hence the theory incorporates such contextual information in the speech recognition process by having only those allophones available to be activated that actually can occur in English.

Segmental context. As I mentioned before, there is context-conditioned variation in acoustic cues for a phoneme contingent upon its immediate left and right context. Since the span of a context-sensitive allophone is equivalent to approximately three phoneme units, some of this information is directly incorporated into the activation of a given allophone unit. In addition, if an allophone unit $_x y_z$ is activated, it provides the information that the preceding allophone had the form $_x y$ and the succeeding allophone had the form $_y z_$, which could activate these sets of allophone nodes by simple association. Since allophone units represent order by which specific allophone nodes are activated, rather than by temporal order of activation, both right-to-left and left-to-right segmental context effects can be used in speech recognition. That is, a particular allophone unit could be activated after receiving feedback from the unit representing the subsequent allophone, with no adverse effect on the recognition process.

Speech rate. Many of the acoustic features characteristic of any particular phoneme (or allophone) change to varying extents with changes in speech rate. To be maximally efficient (and possibly to function at all), our speech recognition processes must be able to adapt to variations in rate of talking. Here we will consider just one acoustic feature that is profoundly affected by speech rate—namely, segment (phoneme or allophone) duration. We know that segment duration is often used to identify a particular segment and distinguish it from other segments that are similar except for duration. For example, the vowels in the words "shut" and "shirt" are highly similar except in duration ("shut" is shorter). If one takes a recording of "shirt" and electronically shortens the vowel portion without otherwise changing the acoustic features of the word, one can radically increase the proportion of times that subjects will identify the word as "shut" (Bennett 1968). Since changes in speech rate have disproportionately large effects on the more prolongable segments, such as vowels, it is especially important to determine segment duration—not absolutely, but relative to speech rate as inferred from the duration of prior segments in the speech context. Ainsworth (1972) showed that when a fixed speech sound is preceded by vowels of varying duration, a shift occurs in the proportion of times subjects will identify the fixed speech sound as containing a short vowel versus a long vowel. A longer preceding vowel makes the subsequent vowel sound seem short by comparison.

Dialect. As we have seen, Ladefoged and Broadbent (1957) showed that subjects adapted to the dialect of the speaker they were listening to, identifying a given set of acoustic features as one segment after listening to speaker A and as a different segment after listening to speaker B. It is conceivable that such dialect contextual adaptation could be achieved simply by selective priming of certain sets of feature and segment nodes. But the simplest interpretation is that what have been primed are the links (associations) from feature nodes to specific segment nodes. However, link priming is far more sophisticated than node priming, and the assumption of the capacity for link priming is a major theoretical decision in our efforts to develop a comprehensive theory of the human mind. Such a decision should not be based on a single phenomenon.

Lexical constraints. The listener ordinarily assumes that the sets of segments he recognizes form words rather than nonwords. Feedback from the higher word level to the lower segmental level is considerably easier according to the theory that the functioning segmental units are allophones rather than phonemes or syllables. This is because the temporal order of activation of the segmental units is irrelevant to the correct representation of the order of the segments within a word. This makes it easy for a few segment units to activate partially a set of word units. These word units feed back to activate partially their other segmental constituents. This top-down feedback, together with bottom-up sensory feature input to segment units, maximally activates more of the correct segment units and therefore selects the one correct word unit.

Syntactic constraints. The syntactic contextual constraints operate at the word, concept, phrase, and propositional levels in that the word must fit into a grammatical utterance. Such syntactic constraints could feed back to operate at the segmental level by priming words, which prime some segments, as I just explained. Whatever the mechanism, we know that grammatical utterances are perceived more accurately than random word strings (Miller and Isard 1963; Martin 1968; Morton and Long 1976).

Semantic constraints. There are likewise semantic contextual constraints. These occur because the subject already knows a lot about what is
being said. He can use this knowledge in semantic memory to prime differentially some concept, phrase, and propositional units. These, again, can feed
back to the word level and ultimately to the segmental level. As a result,
meaningful and grammatical utterances are more accurately perceived than
grammatical but meaningless utterances (Miller and Isard 1963; Martin 1968;
Morton and Long 1976). In all these cases, the representation of segmental
order by *which* segmental elements are activated, rather than by the temporal
order of activation, allows us to use contextual information in speech recognition by means of a simple feedback activation process.

Indeed, the effects of downward lexical feedback and horizontal segmental anticipation and feedback are so strong that under some conditions
subjects cannot distinguish a word that possesses all of its segmental constituents from the same word with some segment missing. Once again, Richard
Warren is responsible for the discovery of this important phenomenon in
speech perception (Warren 1970; Warren and Obusek 1971). Warren deleted
the entire syllable "gis" from the word "legislatures," replacing it with a
cough, tone, or buzz. Not only were subjects still able to recognize the word,
but they filled in the missing segment to such an extent that they could not
discriminate the word with the deleted syllable from the same word with no
deletions. Of course if the deleted syllable is not replaced by some extraneous
acoustic stimulation, subjects can still recognize the word, but in this case
they can also detect the deleted segment. Presumably this is because there is
a difference in stimulation at the segmental level. Thus some peripheral
acoustic input (e.g., a cough) must be combined with the downward and
horizontal feedback to make the deleted syllable undetectable at the segmental level. However, the effect of the contextual feedback is so strong that the
acoustic input in this case need not be very similar to the acoustic features
of the deleted syllable.

ARTICULATION

Constructing artificial talkers, technically known as speech synthesizers, is
considerably easier than constructing automatic speech recognizers. This is
partly because the articulatory features of a phoneme are far more invariant
across left and right phonemic contexts than its acoustic features are. To a first
approximation, the articulatory features of a given phoneme are those features characteristic of a particular target position for the vocal tract (tongue,
lips, jaw, pharynx, velum, larynx, and lungs). The target position is not
always reached when the subject is talking fast, and the targets are not always
exactly the same for a particular phoneme in different contexts, but there is
a much greater degree of invariance in the motor target position for a pho-

neme than in the resulting acoustic features (Liberman et al. 1967; Lindblom 1963; Ohman 1966; MacNeilage 1970; Sussman 1972; Kent and Moll 1972).

Feedback
versus Ballistic Motor Control Systems

If there were no error variability in the operation of the motor neurons, the muscles they control, and the coupling between motor neurons and muscles, and if there were no variation in the load on the muscles (the weight and other forces on the body part being controlled by the muscles), then a specific pattern of activation of the relevant motor neurons would place the body parts in a unique, specifiable target position. Such a purely central, no-feedback control of the position of body parts is called a *ballistic control system*. It is so called because with such a system the brain could fire off a set of motor neurons at specified rates in order to strike a particular target. It would need no guidance that depended on feedback regarding the progress of the body parts in achieving the target position. However, as you may imagine, the operation of any system is subject to error variability. Therefore, a *feedback control system* is usually more accurate, and that is what we have. The feedback control system changes the motor neuron firing rate in response to sensory feedback regarding the body's current state of progress towards achieving the target position. Just as a continuously guided missile can achieve greater accuracy than an unguided, ballistic missile by continually recomputing its position in relation to the target, so the brain can achieve greater accuracy by continually recomputing the deviation of body parts from desired target positions. To do so, it uses sensory feedback. Feedback control may be somewhat slower than ballistic control, but the gain in accuracy is often worth the cost in speed. Moreover, feedback control is not always slower; it may sometimes produce faster movements than would be possible with ballistic control, given the other limitations of the nervous system. In any case, it is the enhanced accuracy of feedback control that we are primarily concerned with here.

Perhaps the greatest source of variability for many skeletal muscles is variability in load—the external forces acting to restrain movement of the body parts. For example, when you want to raise your right hand above your head, the amount of muscular force you must exert depends on how heavy an object you are holding in your hand. The nervous system may use an elegant kinesthetic feedback control system to achieve a specific target position by means of a single neural go-to command, regardless of the load on the muscle. The system is called the *gamma feedback loop*, and it works as follows: there is a little muscle inside the big muscle. The ends of the little muscle are attached not to bones (like the big muscle), but to the ends of the big muscle. The *gamma motor neurons* control the contraction of the little muscle. The *gamma* (kinesthetic) *sensory neurons* register any discrepancy between the degree of contraction of the little muscle and the big muscle. The *alpha motor neurons* control the contraction of the big muscle. Contractions of the little muscle cannot directly move the limbs. Only the big muscle can move the limbs. But the little muscle, in a sense, may control the big muscle. It does this when the gamma motor neurons cause the little muscle to achieve a specific target state of contraction independent of the position of the bones to which the big muscle is attached and independent of the load on the big muscle. (Because the little muscle is attached to elastic muscle fiber, not to bone, you may assume for present purposes that there is negligible variation in the load on the little muscle.) The gamma sensory neurons now start to fire rapidly. This registers a large discrepancy between the current degrees of contraction of the big muscle and of the little muscle inside it. This firing of the gamma sensory neurons causes the alpha motor neurons to fire (by way of a low-level reflex arc through the central nervous system). The alpha motor neurons contract the big muscle until its state of contraction corresponds to the state of contraction of the little muscle. Gamma, and therefore alpha, motor neurons fire faster the greater the discrepancy between the contraction of the big muscle and that of the little muscle (which is essentially setting the target state of contraction for the big muscle). If there is a heavy resistive load on the big muscle, the gamma feedback system will continue to fire rapidly until the big muscle exerts enough contractile force to overcome the load and achieve the target position. As the target position is reached, the gamma control system gradually reduces its rate of firing, though it is still there to maintain that target position against perturbations.

Although the foregoing description of how the gamma feedback loop functions is accurate, it is not established that this feedback loop is used to issue *load-invariant go-to* commands (which do not require prior determination of load). The brain could use various sensory systems (kinesthetic, cutaneous, and visual) to estimate load. This would allow the brain to issue *load-dependent go-to* commands to alpha motor neurons directly. This would constitute a ballistic control system.

The most generally accepted use of the gamma feedback system is to *maintain* a fixed position of the body against minor perturbations—for example, in maintaining one's balance.

Perhaps the brain issues movement commands simultaneously to both alpha and gamma motor neurons, and the gamma feedback loop merely adds some fine-grain control to the ballistic control system, especially near the end of the movement. In addition, the gamma system might produce greater positive acceleration in the beginning of the movement, when there was a relatively long distance to go. Finally, other sensory systems besides the kinesthetic system may be used to provide feedback control of the movement (or maintenance) of body parts to (or in) various positions.

Ordinarily, speech muscles do not have to operate in the face of highly variable external loads. However, Folkins and Abbs added resistive loads to the jaw and discovered that humans could compensate for this by using added alpha muscular force to speak adequately. This demonstrates the possibility of feedback control of the articulatory muscles, though it does not prove that such feedback control is ordinarily used in speech. Another way to determine whether sensory feedback loops play a role in speech production is to anesthetize the sensory neurons that provide feedback regarding the positions of the articulators and see how this affects speech (when the motor neurons are not anesthetized). Such oral anesthesia is similar to, but more extensive than, the type of anesthesia the dentist uses when he is working on your teeth. Deprivation of sensory feedback does interfere markedly with speech fluency, indicating that sensory feedback plays a role in ordinary speech production. However, speech does not break down completely, so there would also appear to be some purely central, ballistic, control of speech production that does not depend on the operation of the gamma or cutaneous sensory feedback systems (Scott and Ringel 1971; Horii et al. 1973; Folkins and Abbs 1975, 1976).

Coarticulation

In normal rapid speech we often do not reach our articulatory targets, and in any case we often spend a lot of time in moving toward targets, rather than in maintaining articulatory positions. Since the movement toward a phoneme target position necessarily differs depending on the preceding phoneme, and the movement away from a phoneme target necessarily differs depending on the succeeding phoneme, you can see why the acoustic cues deriving from these articulatory movements are so highly sensitive to the immediately adjacent context. Such acoustic context-sensitivities would result even if articulation could be characterized by a simple sequence of context-free phoneme targets that were absolutely independent of prior and succeeding context. At present it is unclear just how far articulation differs from a simple sequence of context-free phoneme targets. We do know that there are *some* clear differences in the target positions for a single phoneme in different phonemic contexts (articulatory context-sensitive allophones). One example is the front and back /k/ in "kit" versus "caught." The phoneme /k/ is made by lifting the back of the tongue to the roof of the mouth, but the position of this closure of the vocal tract differs consistently depending on the immediately prior and succeeding phonemes. Variation in the articulatory target positions that depends upon phonemic context is true *coarticulation*—the modification of articulatory targets to facilitate transitions to and from adjacent targets. For example, if an adjacent vowel is articulated with constriction of the vocal tract near the front of the mouth, the target closure of the vocal tract for /k/ will be nearer the front of the mouth and vice versa. True coarticulation should not be inferred from the demonstration that muscle potentials are different for a given phoneme in different contexts.

An invariant go-to command to a gamma motor neuron to achieve a constant target position will produce different time sequences of alpha motor activity (and therefore of muscle potential) from different articulatory starting positions. However, since there is also evidence for context sensitivities in articulatory targets, true coarticulation may be considered to be securely established (Wickelgren 1969a; MacNeilage 1970).

The context-sensitive allophone nodes already postulated for speech recognition could also function in articulation to activate a distinct target position for a given phoneme in different left and right phonemic contexts. Since the acoustic cues for speech are automatically context-sensitive, even if articulation consisted of a sequence of context-free phoneme targets, no greater complexity in speech perception would be introduced by coarticulation on the motor side. Indeed, coarticulation enhances the distinctive cues for each allophone, facilitating precise discrimination of these redundant overlapping speech segments, and permitting parallel processing and the encoding of segmental order by which context-sensitive segment nodes are activated. Besides, coarticulation produces easier transitions between segment (allophone) targets and thereby allows us to speak more rapidly.

Planning and the Representation of Order

Some years ago Karl Lashley wrote a very thought-provoking paper on the problems of serial order in behavior. In one part of this paper Lashley argued that associative chain theories were inadequate to explain articulation of the ordered sequence of phonemes in a word. The alternatives proposed by Lashley and others have generally been rather vague references to schemas, determining tendencies, motor programs, and the like. No attractive nonassociative theory has ever emerged in any precise form. Lashley's objections to the associative chain theory for the representation of segmental order made the implicit assumption that the functioning segmental units of words in speech articulation are phonemes. If context-sensitive allophones are assumed to be the functioning segmental units, an associative chain theory provides a very elegant mechanism for producing the correct ordering of the allophones in a word (Lashley 1951; Wickelgren 1969a, 1969b, 1972a, 1976a).

The basic theory is as follows: the node representing the word we wish to speak is activated at the word level. This word node primes the set of allophonic constituents at the segmental level. When we wish to speak the word, the initial allophone of the word is activated first, and there is only one allophone in the word set of the form $_{\#}x_y$. This will in turn activate the second allophone, because the second allophone will have the strongest association to the first allophone out of all the allophones in the set primed by the word representative. The second allophone will be most strongly associated to the third allophone, and so on. As a specific example, consider the word "struck," which has some alternative orderings that also form words, and is therefore a particularly crucial test of any theory of serial order in articulation. By long-term, downward association, the word node for "struck" primes the set of context-sensitive allophones. From this point on, previously established, long-term, horizontal associations between the members of the set of allophone representatives will suffice to produce the correct order. There is only one element in the unordered set whose initial element is #, namely, $_{\#}s_t$. Hence this allophone unit will be spoken first. The $_{\#}s_t$ allophone unit will be most strongly associated to some $_st_-$ unit, of which there is only one in the present set, so the correct second allophone—namely, $_st_r$—will be articulated, and so on to the end of the word. Thus the same mechanism for the representation of serial order that is so useful in speech recognition also proves useful in speech articulation.

Furthermore, it is possible to plan a long utterance consisting of many words by activating the unordered set of allophonic constituents at the segmental level, and then turning control over to the segmental level for articulation of the utterance, without the need for further intervention from higher word and conceptual levels. Thus one can be planning the next utterance at the lexical and conceptual levels of semantic memory while one is controlling the articulation of the last utterance at the segmental level. This is possible with context-sensitive allophonic coding because extremely long sequences of allophones can be stored at the segmental level with a very low probability of generating ambiguities when these sequences are decoded into a temporally ordered activation of the allophone units.

The above theory asserts that speech production has two phases, planning and articulation; that the planning phase consists of a priming of the segments to be spoken in an utterance; and that the segments are context-sensitive allophones. The context-sensitive coding hypothesis is supported by a considerable amount of evidence discussed throughout this chapter. The other two parts of the priming theory of speech planning also have considerable empirical support. Lashley (1951) supported the hypothesis of priming by noting that speech errors often anticipate later words in an utterance—for instance, "asnaid of frakes" for "afraid of snakes." Donald MacKay (1969, 1970, 1971) has extensively investigated speech errors; his work provides more evidence for the advance priming of segments to be articulated later.

Ladefoged, Silverstein, and Papcun (1971) provide additional evidence in support of a speech planning phase. In their experiments subjects were asked to stop saying something they intended to say and to start saying something else, upon being given a cue. They found no differences in the speed with which subjects could stop one utterance and begin another when the cue was delivered during the actual articulation of a phrase. However, when the cue was given just before a subject began articulation, the subject responded much more slowly. Ladefoged, Silverstein, and Papcun interpreted their results as indicating that just before he begins to speak, the speaker is planning the utterance. Therefore he cannot readily switch to planning another utterance.

Yet another phenomenon supports the existence of a planning process with a scope larger than a single segment. This is the fact that the reaction time to begin pronunciation of a word following visual presentation increases with the number of syllables in the word. Although the time to pronounce the word itself would naturally increase with the number of syllables, the reaction time to begin pronunciation would not—if there is no planning phase. Indeed, if the subject knows in advance which word is to be pronounced and upon being given a cue merely performs the simple reaction time task of pronouncing that word, there is no relationship between the reaction time and the number of syllables in the word. Under these circumstances the subject can preprogram his utterance before he gets the cue to respond, and so he needs no time for planning following the cue (Ericksen, Pollack, and Montague 1970; Klapp, Anderson, and Berrian 1973; Klapp 1974, 1976).*

Finally, there are remote coarticulatory effects that also support the existence of a priming type of planning process in speech production. As I have already mentioned, the vocal tract configuration for a phoneme is to some extent influenced by its immediate left and right neighbors. However, there are also more remote coarticulatory effects whereby a phoneme to be pronounced later in an utterance influences articulation of up to four phonemes in advance of itself. These more remote effects do not occur in the other direction. That is, the remote coarticulatory effects appear to be strictly anticipatory. This supports the assumption that a set of segments in an utterance have been primed in advance of their articulation, and that the degree of priming exhibits a gradient such that the currently articulated allophone representative is most highly activated, the next allophone is second most highly activated, and so on. Incidentally, this priming gradient is also easily explained in terms of the associative chain theory of segmental activation (Daniloff and Moll 1968; Wickelgren 1972a).

Syllable Juncture

The assumption that the phoneme is the functional segmental unit in speech perception and production poses many problems. Recognizing these problems, many researchers have proposed the syllable as an alternative. Although the syllable does not pose all of the problems posed by the phonemes, it poses some of them, and it introduces at least one new problem of its own. Since syllables are nonoverlapping segments, they do not represent order information as elegantly as do context-sensitive allophones. Thus it is necessary to specify some additional mechanism for the representation of the

*Further RT evidence in support of planning—of entire phrases—is provided by Lindsley (1975).

order of syllables. This has never been done satisfactorily. Furthermore, the syllable has the defect that it does not represent a single target position for the vocal tract. Rather, it represents a sequence of such targets. Thus the internal ordering of vocal tract positions within a syllable is in no way specified. Hence the syllable is deficient compared to the context-sensitive allophone in that it encodes neither the external ordering of syllables in a multisyllabic utterance nor the internal ordering of target positions (phonemes or allophones) within the syllable.

The only convincing evidence for the psychological reality of syllables comes from studies of errors in speech articulation. Consider a speech error like "tips of the slung" for "slips of the tongue." Here the /t/ segment is transposed with the /sl/ segment. Such transpositions of segments in speech tend to preserve syllable position. That is, initial segments in one syllable replace initial segments in another syllable, medial segments replace medial segments, and final segments replace final segments. Boomer and Laver (1968) originally formulated this law, and it has been repeatedly confirmed by others, such as Fromkin (1968), MacKay (1970b), and Nooteboom (1967, 1968). In addition, MacKay has noted that transpositions of initial phonemes are much more frequent than transpositions of phonemes at other positions within the syllable. This indicates that the transition from the terminal consonant of one syllable to the initial consonant of the next is the weakest link in the ordering of segments in an utterance.

These findings demonstrate that *syllable boundaries* (or junctures) must be included in the phonetic encoding of words and phrases. They do not demonstrate that the syllable is a functioning segmental unit in speech production. The context-sensitive coding theory can be elegantly modified to incorporate *syllable juncture* as a segmental element. This is done by introducing a new segment that stands for syllable juncture, namely $/+/$. A word like "segment" that contains two syllables would be encoded at the segmental level as follows: $_\#s_e, {}_se_g, {}_eg+, {}_g+_m, {}_+m_e, {}_me_n, {}_en_t, {}_nt_\#$, where $\#$ represents word juncture. It is not clear whether word juncture and syllable juncture should be distinguished; indeed, they may be identical concepts. Introducing syllable juncture into segments somewhat reduces the redundancy of the encoding of order across syllable boundaries. However, MacKay's evidence from speech errors indicates that this probably agrees with human speech production.

The hypothesis that syllable juncture is a segment has two other advantages. First, it drastically reduces the number of context-sensitive allophone units that must be assumed to function at the segmental level. This is because there are substantial restrictions on what consonant phonemes can follow what other consonant phonemes within a syllable, but few, if any, restrictions across syllable or word juncture boundaries. Introducing syllable juncture segments eliminates the need for tens of thousands of allophones.

Second, one can assume that syllable juncture is an *optional* segmental component of words containing more than one vowel. That is, one need not assume that words containing two or more vowels have a corresponding number of syllable junctures. Since words like "syllabic" can be divided into syllables in a large variety of almost equally plausible ways, it is highly desirable that words should have the capacity for optional insertion of syllable juncture segments. It is not at all obvious how one would make syllable units optional. Furthermore, syllable juncture should be obligatory at precisely those places where consonant transitions occur across syllable boundaries that are not allowable within syllables. It should be optional everywhere else. In fact, this seems to be how it works. There is no ambiguity regarding the positioning of syllable juncture between the /g/ and the /m/ in a word like "segment." And there would appear to be no need for syllable juncture markers at all in a word like "syllabic."

READING

Reading is one of the most important cognitive capacities an educated human being has. Indeed, the terms "literate" and "illiterate" are often taken to be synonymous with "educated" and "uneducated," though technically literacy refers only to reading and writing capacity. It is quite likely that many educated people acquire far more information by reading than by listening to spoken speech. This is true even though reading alphabetic verbal material is more difficult and less natural than recognizing speech (Liberman et al. 1967). However, it should be noted that most individuals have no difficulty in attaching words to their visually presented referents or to pictorial (ideographic) representatives of these referents. What is difficult and relatively less natural for the nervous system is to associate visual *alphabetic* constituents to word and concept representatives. Indeed, some children with reading disorders (dyslexia) who have great difficulty learning to read an alphabetic language such as English can sometimes rather easily be taught to read an ideographic language such as Chinese (Rozin, Poritsky, and Sotsky 1971). In an ideographic language the segmental constituents of words are equivalent to little pictures related to the referents of the word.

What are the cognitive processes involved in reading? At what point does visual verbal input converge with auditory verbal input? Should children be taught to read using phonics or by the "look and say" whole-word method? What are the graphic segmental units of reading? Should you take a speed reading course? The present section addresses itself to certain theoretical issues underlying these questions.

Graphic Features and Segments

Letter features. The letters c, o, and s have only curved lines, while the letters v, w, and x have only straight lines in many (but not all) type fonts. Most letters have both straight and curved lines. Some letters (such as a, c, and e) are called *small letters* because they have no lines that extend above the central part of the writing line (like b, d, and f) or below the line (like g, j, and p). Some letters contain vertical lines (such as b, h, and p); some contain oblique lines (such as k, v, and y). These are but a few of the many graphic features that distinguish one letter from another. A particular letter in a particular case (capital versus lowercase), mode (print or script), and style (there are many different type fonts for printing and many individual differences in handwriting) can be defined by the simple presence or absence of each of several features. If a feature system has enough different feature dimensions, each letter can be distinguished from every other letter by its own unique combination of features. Many different graphic feature systems have been proposed to distinguish among letters in a particular set (e.g., printed capitals or printed lowercase letters in a particular type font). Some of these feature systems employ only binary feature dimensions (e.g., vertical straight lines are present in M and absent in Q). Others employ multivalued feature dimensions (e.g., number of vertical straight lines: zero in Q, one in P, and two in H). There are typically no more than a dozen feature dimensions in a feature system. Thus there is not much redundancy in such a system, and if a perceiver lacks information concerning the value on just one feature dimension, the perceiver often cannot distinguish between alternative letters. Even when all feature information is correctly perceived, there are many artificial characters that would be classified as particular letters by such feature systems, but that are perfectly distinguishable from those letters by the human visual system. The actual feature system we use to perceive letters cannot be any of these. Rather, it must be a large subset of all the visual feature dimensions we use to discriminate objects in general. If so, it is considerably larger than the number of dimensions characteristic of extant graphic feature systems.

We can evaluate a proposed theory of graphic features with respect to its *capacity* for distinguishing among the forms humans can distinguish. We can also evaluate it with respect to the degrees of similarity predicted of pairs of forms. Two letters (more generally, two forms or objects) that are coded similarly by a feature system should be judged similar by humans. Thus they should be more frequently confused in visual recognition than letters that are more distinct in their feature code. A number of graphic feature systems have been evaluated in this way by presenting sets of alternatives to subjects. The success of these evaluations has varied. There is no general agreement regarding the correct graphic feature system.*

Word features.   The simplest hierarchical theory of word recognition has sets of letter feature nodes activating letter nodes and sets of letter nodes activating a word node. However, the ordered set of letters comprising a word

---

*For a more extensive discussion of letter feature systems, see Gibson and Levin (1975, pp. 15–20) and Massaro and Schmuller (1975).

generates higher-level word shape features (e.g., s̲t̲a̲m̲p̲). These features are characteristic of a word but not of any of its letters. Existing evidence on the role of word shape features in reading is mixed. Some studies indicate that the word shape feature plays little if any role in word recognition, perhaps because so many words have identical or highly similar word shapes. However, a recent study indicates that word length and word shape information can enhance word recognition in a text that constrains the possibilities (Gibson and Levin 1975, pp. 195–200; Groff 1975; Haber and Haber 1977).

Context-sensitive letter features. Unlike spoken words, graphic words often do consist of a sequence of symbols (letters) whose physical features (on the printed page) are invariant with changes in adjacent letter context. That is, an o is printed (though not written) the same way regardless of what letters come before and after it. However, this only refers to a nuclear core of invariant features. Whenever two letters are placed next to each other, one automatically creates emergent, interactional features characteristic of the ordered *pair* of letters, but not of either letter individually. There are many ways to define these context-sensitive letter features: as the shapes of the spaces between letters, as the outline shape of (overlapping or nonoverlapping) letter pairs or triples, or as geometric relations (parallel, perpendicular) between the line segments of adjacent letters. However these context-sensitive letter features are defined, an FR letter pair will have different interactional features than an RF letter pair. As with context-sensitive coding in speech, this may be the basis of the perception of order. There is a very neat demonstration of the importance of context-sensitive graphic features in the recognition of mixed-case words (e.g., "fAdE" or "FaDe") versus same-case words ("fade" or "FADE"). Although we are surprisingly efficient in reading these unfamiliar mixed-case words, we are clearly better at reading same-case words. This would not be true if we used only the invariant, nuclear (core) features to identify each letter and then identified the word from the letter set. Context-sensitive letter features must ordinarily play an important role in word recognition (Smith, Lott, and Cronnell 1969; Coltheart and Freeman 1974; Fisher 1975; McClelland 1976).

Context-sensitive letter segments. McClelland (1976) has demonstrated that we also read same-case pseudowords (e.g., "gade" or "GADE") better than mixed-case pseudowords (e.g., "gAdE" or "GaDe"), and that the degree of superiority is the same for pseudowords as for true words. This rules out an explanation that has context-sensitive feature nodes directly associated to word nodes. Pseudowords have presumably never been experienced before, so for them there could be no such associations. If context-sensitive features help us to recognize pseudowords, as they clearly appear to do, they must be associated to some unit smaller than the word. Letter dyads, triads, and syllables are the likely candidates. Because of its remarkable order-representing properties, my personal favorite graphic segmental unit is the context-sensitive letter. An example would be $_\#f_a$—the particular f that is preceded by a space, #, and followed by an a. Context-sensitive letter coding assumes that the context-sensitive features of each adjacent letter pair, along with the invariant core features of all three letters, are associated to each (overlapping) letter triple node in a word or pseudoword. Such letter triples in pseudowords are familiar, even though the entire pseudoword is not. Incidentally, McClelland (1976) found no significant superiority of same-case over mixed-case letter strings where the letter strings contained phonologically unfamiliar letter sequences (e.g. efdt). This rules out some uninteresting interpretations of the same- versus mixed-case effect and agrees completely with the hypothesis advanced in this section. The reason for assuming *overlapping* letter triple encoding is that the overlap provides associations to encode the order of the letters. Patently $_\#f_a$ is the initial letter of a word, and this will be strongly associated to every member of the set of $_fa\_$ nodes that can occur in English. Of these nodes only one is present in the word "fade"—namely, $_fa_d$—and so on.

Phonetics and Graphic Processing

There has been considerable debate as to whether skilled reading involves a direct mapping from visual features or segment nodes onto words and concept nodes, or an indirect mapping from graphic nodes through phonetic (feature or segment) nodes to word and concept nodes, or both. The evidence is not completely definitive, but it suggests that many human beings use both (fig. 5.2).*

Apparently, *all* readers subvocalize to some extent while they read. This subvocalization can be suppressed to a considerable extent by training, but comprehension will suffer as a result. Children just learning to read subvocalize more than skilled readers, but the more difficult the reading, the greater the degree of subvocalization for both skilled and unskilled readers. The following interpretation appears to be well supported by current evidence. Subvocalization is beneficial, rather than detrimental, to reading. But the higher the level of skill or the easier the reading task, the less subvocalization occurs (Hardyck and Petrinovich 1970; McGuigan 1973). Thus the decrease in subvocalization with increasing reading skill is a *result* of increased reading proficiency, not a *cause*. It is probably detrimental to attempt to teach people to read better or faster by suppressing subvocalization. Some investigators have concluded that the kinesthetic feedback from subvocalization facilitates

---

*I believe this is the only reasonable conclusion based on all the evidence, but you are invited to explore the matter further by reading Gibson and Levin (1975, pp. 201–7); Massaro (1975, pp. 260–73); Bradshaw (1975); Green and Shallice (1976); Rubenstein, Richter, and Kay (1975).

the reading process, but this is not established. It is at least as likely that subvocalization is a downstream epiphenomenon of the functionally important central connection from graphic segments to phonetic segments to words. According to the latter view, suppression of subvocalization is detrimental not because it interferes with kinesthetic feedback, but because the suppression is inhibiting processing at the central phonetic level.

There is also evidence to support the simultaneous existence of direct associations from graphic segments to word nodes (Meyer and Ruddy 1973; Gibson and Levin 1975, pp. 201–7; Massaro 1975, pp. 260–73; Bradshaw 1975; Green and Shallice 1976). First, Meyer and Ruddy have shown that subjects can decide more rapidly that the word "tail" is not spelled like the name of a fruit than that the word "tail" is not pronounced like the name of a fruit. Results such as this would appear to be possible only if there exists a direct linkage from graphic segments to words and concepts that does not involve phonetic mediation. Second, it is possible to read silently, understand, and remember words and text presented visually while one is simultaneously engaged in rapid, irrelevant vocalizations. Demonstrate this for yourself by reading a paragraph of this text while saying, "da, da, da. . . ." Now read it while saying, "1, 2, 3, 4, 5, 6, 7, 8, 9, 10, 1, 2,. . . ." The second task is more difficult than the first, and both are more difficult than normal reading, but both tasks are quite possible. Third, although profoundly deaf children are greatly impaired in learning to read (which provides support for the importance of the indirect phonetic channel in reading), most of them do learn to read, which indicates that the indirect channel is not necessary.

In light of these findings, should a child be taught to read phonetically or by the whole-word method? Apparently both methods are useful. Children learn to speak long before they learn to read, and there does typically appear to be a period of several years during which a child can be taught how to pronounce single letters and pairs or even triples of letters. This permits him to read slowly by the phonic method. During this period the child evidently cannot read an entire word as a whole without sounding it out.

My own children existed in this neverland of intermediate reading competence, or incompetence, for a period of over two years. During this time, despite extensive training in phonics, including pronunciation of blends of two or more letters, they did not come to pronounce even highly familiar words as a whole. Rather, they continued to sound out each word before they pronounced it, no matter how many times they had practiced sounding that same word out before. Only when they had reached a particular stage of reading readiness, at about the age of 5-½, were they able to begin reading words as units. Thus while phonics training produced the ability to "read" whole words by first sounding them out, this training, in the case of my children, did not lead them to learn to pronounce words immediately as wholes. By contrast, after they had reached the stage of reading readiness, they rapidly acquired a large vocabulary of words that they were able to read as wholes. When they encountered a new word, they would often use their prior phonics training to sound it out and thus learn how it was to be pronounced, but they learned lots of words by the look-and-say method as well. Before they achieved reading readiness, they made almost no use of their ability to acquire information by phonic reading. That is, they did not read stories or any other material on their own volition. The reason for this is clear. Phonic reading is simply too slow. Only when a child is able to read whole words does reading have any significant practical value.

The look-and-say method should not carelessly be identified with establishing a direct link from graphic nodes to word nodes. This may be the additional factor that leads to reading readiness. However, it is at least equally likely, since the indirect phonetic stage is heavily involved in reading even for skilled adult readers, that the capacity to read whole words develops as large chunks of graphic segments (e.g., letter triples) are associated to large chunks of phonetic segments (e.g., context-sensitive allophones) via the indirect pathway. In any event, phonics training seems to be extremely useful in learning to read, but all reading training should be aimed at developing the capacity to read whole words, or even larger units, as single chunks.

Most of this section has been concerned with the role of phonetic codes in the recognition of single words. However, one of the main functions of phonetic encoding may be to enhance short-term memory for sets of words. This would permit activation of larger-scale syntactic and semantic units, which is a critical process in sentence comprehension. Memory for sentences is impaired by having subjects count while they read (presumably because this interferes with the phonetic encoding of the sentences), and there is some evidence to suggest that this is not entirely a general attentional deficit. However, nothing definite has been established on this issue (Kleiman 1975; Levy 1975).

Parallel Processing and Fixation Span

In chapters 6 and 7, we will see that up to the fixation span of four or five random letters, even unrelated letters are processed in parallel rather than serially. If four or five unrelated letters can be processed simultaneously, one would certainly expect the letters that form short words to be processed simultaneously in reading, and indeed they are. The fixation span, measured in number of letters that can be processed in parallel, would appear to be at least seven when the letters form a familiar word. Perhaps all the component letters of a single word are processed in parallel irrespective of length, though due to the substantial redundancy of English, not all the letters need be recognized in order to recognize a long word. Kolers and Lewis have data strongly implicating the word as the basic unit of parallel processing in reading. They have found that two three-letter words are much less frequently identified than a single six-letter word under comparable conditions. Thus although we clearly have the capacity to process six or more letters in parallel when they form a single word, recognizing one (three-letter) word appears to inhibit the recognition of another (three-letter) word. Jacobson showed that the inhibition of one word node by another is counteracted to some extent when the two words are strongly associated. This could permit the parallel processing of words in short phrases. Associations among the (context-sensitive) letter components of a single word may also partially counteract lateral inhibition among letter nodes. This would account for the greater fixation span for letters that form a word. It is also interesting to note that good readers apparently have longer fixation spans than poor readers— *both* for letters that form words and for unrelated letter strings (Kolers and Lewis 1972; Jacobson 1973; Jackson and McClelland 1975).

The data supporting parallel processing of the letters in a word are many and various. The first study on this subject was undertaken by Cattell in 1886. Cattell showed that the time needed to recognize a word was nearly as short as the time needed to recognize a single letter, and that it did not increase appreciably with the number of letters in the word. Recently, Johnson replicated these results, obtaining no significant difference in the times needed to recognize words and letters. Sloboda even found word recognition to be substantially faster (and slightly more accurate) than letter recognition under the conditions of his well-controlled and well-analyzed experiment. In view of such findings it would appear impossible for word recognition to occur as a serial, letter-by-letter recognition process (Cattell 1886; Huey 1908; Johnson 1975; Henderson 1975; Theios and Muise 1976; Sloboda 1976a).

Another convincing line of evidence supporting parallel processing of letters in word recognition is Travers's demonstration that a single 50 msec exposure to a seven-letter word produces better recognition of the word than sequential presentation of the seven letters over a period of 350 msec, when each letter is presented for 50 msec. If word recognition were a serial, letter-by-letter process, we would certainly expect superior performance with an unhurried sequential presentation. Instead, we get the reverse. We know that reading consists of a series of eye fixations of approximately a quarter of a second each, each encompassing about one word. Clearly, all the letters in a single fixation span are processed in parallel (Travers 1973, 1974, 1975; Smith 1971; Gibson 1965; Gibson and Levin 1975).

Letter Order
and Context-Sensitive Coding

Encoding the order of letters in a written word is as important to word recognition as encoding the order of phonemes in a spoken word. I have already presented evidence indicating that the representation of order information in speech (and auditory information processing in general) is not accomplished by means of the temporal order of activation of segment nodes. If this is so for the phonemes of speech, which are physically sequential in time, temporal order of letter-node activation is not likely to be the basis for encoding the order of letters in words. Furthermore, I have just presented evidence demonstrating that all the letters of a word are recognized in parallel. This makes temporal order of letter activation an even less likely vehicle for representing the order of letters in words.

The most obvious hypothesis is that the order of letters is encoded by their spatial order in the visual field. This is surely true in some sense. But it is pretty clearly not the *absolute* spatial positions of letters on the retina that are encoding letter order in words, since the absolute retinal positions of letters can and do vary substantially, and yet we are highly accurate in word recognition. *Relative* left-right position is more important than absolute position and the spacing of letters (Kolers 1968; Terry, Samuels, and LaBerge 1976). However, what may be most important is the context-sensitive features derived from two adjacent letters, discussed above. Asso and Wyke (1967) performed a fascinating experiment in which they investigated the perception of briefly presented words whose letters had been right-left mirror image reversed—for example, "WOꟼ." In all cases these stimuli formed words in both the left-to-right and the right-to-left order. That is, the preceding example could be read as "WOLF" or as "FLOW." If spatial order were dominant in the representation of letter order in reading, one would expect subjects to see the word "WOLF." However, subjects overwhelmingly saw the word in the right-to-left order as "FLOW." This indicates that the features for the representation of order are in some way derived from the letter-to-letter transitional features, much as they are in context-sensitive allophonic coding for speech. Other findings with mirror image reversed words support this conclusion (Kolers 1968; Krueger 1976). That is, the letter dyads FL, LO, or OW, or the letter triads FLO or LOW, form overlapping context-sensitive letter pattern nodes that represent the order information by means of an unordered set, much as context-sensitive allophones represent order information in speech. According to this hypothesis, the appropriate context-sensitive letter analyzers are activated virtually simultaneously during a given fixation. The unordered set of such context-sensitive letter nodes activates word nodes via the direct-channel and activates context-sensitive allophone nodes and word nodes via the indirect channel.

Another beautiful finding by Travers (1974) really wraps this story up. In one of his experiments Travers compared word recognition under four conditions: (1) sequential presentation of one letter at a time, (2) presentation of two adjacent letters at a time, (3) presentation of three adjacent letters at a time, and (4) presentation of the whole word at once. In the pair and triple conditions, the sequential pairs and triples were *overlapping* (e.g., me, et, th, ho, od, or met, eth, tho, hod). Overlapping letter triples are precisely the ideal stimuli for context-sensitive letter nodes. Word recognition increased sharply from the single-letter to the pair sequential condition and again to the over-lapping triple condition, but it was essentially equivalent for overlapping letter triples and entire words. Travers's experiment supports the importance of the context-sensitive features that arise when two letters are simulta-neously adjacent. It also indicates that the critical segmental unit immediately below words may be the (overlapping) letter triple, which gets context-sensitive features from the interaction between a central letter and both of its neighbors.

Levels of Coding
and Chain Parallel Processing

Not only can entire words be recognized as fast as or faster than single letters, but when letters or words are followed by masking fields, recognition of single letters in words is often significantly more accurate than recognition of letters in equally long, unrelated letter strings, or even than recognition of isolated letters. Reicher discovered this word superiority effect in 1969. Since then it has been demonstrated that subjects are less accurate in discriminating which of two isolated letters occurred (e.g., K versus T) than in discriminating between the same two letters in a pronounceable letter string (e.g., "GARK" versus "GART") or a word (e.g., "PARK" versus "PART"). To get this word superiority effect, it is important to follow presentation of the test stimulus with a masking field containing letter fragments. This will destroy informa-tion at the feature level and to a lesser extent at the letter level, but it will not destroy very much information at the context-sensitive letter triple or word levels. It is also important to induce subjects to attend to the entire word in the word condition and not to a single letter position—otherwise the word superiority effect will not occur. This can be accomplished by cuing the subject regarding the two alternatives only after the test stimulus has been presented. However, this form of cuing admits more explanations of the word superiority effect. Reicher did get the word superiority effect by precuing the two alternatives at a single position, but others have not. However, Carr and his colleagues have shown that precuing the two alternatives still yields a word superiority effect, provided the subject does not know which of three positions the critical letter will appear in. Altogether, the word superiority effect undoubtedly indicates the presence of higher-level nodes than the letter node. These may be context-sensitive letter triple nodes or word nodes. Most or all of the word superiority effect is apparently obtained with pro-nounceable nonwords or unpronounceable but familiar letter sequences. This too supports the existence of a unit between letters and words, such as the context-sensitive letter triple. In further support of such a unit, Pollatsek, Well, and Schindler found that the magnitude of the word superiority effect decreases with an increasing number of case transitions (e.g., "CITE" to "cITE" to "CItE" to "cItE"). Capital to lowercase transitions (e.g., Ci) are familiar, since they often occur at the beginning of words, but lowercase to capital transitions (e.g., cI) should be fairly unfamiliar (Reicher 1969; Wheeler 1970; Smith and Haviland 1972; Baron and Thurston 1973; Massaro 1973; Thompson and Massaro 1973; Johnson and McClelland 1974; Manelis 1974; Estes 1975; Pollatsek, Well, and Schindler 1975; Carr et al. 1976; McClelland 1976).

Given that there are several different size units in reading—features, letters, letter triples, words, and probably phrases and propositions as well—the obvious assumption is that these units are organized in a hierarchy of levels in the mind. Thus feature nodes would activate letter nodes, letter nodes would activate letter triple nodes, triple nodes would activate word nodes, and so on. The fact that we find superior perceptual accuracy for words over letters, and especially the fact that we find as fast or faster recognition of words than of letters, would superficially seem to contradict this simple ordering of levels. However, like the analogous findings concerning speech, what these findings actually demonstrate is chain parallel processing. Activation is passed from lower to higher levels (and back again in a feedback loop) immediately; spread of activation does not wait for processing and recognition to be completed at the lower level. Due to the redundancy and convergence of activation from several letter or letter triple nodes, word nodes may often reach the recognition threshold of activation faster than letter nodes, even though letters are constituents of words and so come earlier in the hierarchy of levels.

Context Effects and Feedback

As in speech recognition, there are context effects that help us to read by creating generally appropriate expectations. When we have understood the material we have read, the nodes activated by this context will generally have some weak association to at least some of the nodes needed to encode the next word or phrase we are reading. This associative priming of expected nodes makes these partially activated nodes more easily activated by appropriate sensory input. In addition, primed nodes may pass on this heightened degree of activation to their lower-level constituents. That is, priming a concept node may prime appropriate word nodes, which in turn prime their segmental (letter triple) constituents, and so on. In a system with chain parallel processing, preliminary activation of word and concept nodes would then feed back to facilitate activation of the appropriate segmental constituent nodes, and so on.

The superior identifiability of letters in graphically familiar combinations (e.g., "com" versus "cmo") is a segmental-level context effect. According to context-sensitive coding theory, we have all three of the letter triple nodes used to encode "com," namely, $_\#c_o$, $_co_m$, and $_om_\#$. However, we do not have two of the three letter triple nodes needed to encode "cmo," namely

$_\#c_m$ and $_cm_o$, since these two letter triples do not occur in English syllables. Thus, feedback activation from letter triple nodes to letter nodes will aid perception of "com" more than "cmo." In addition, such letter triple nodes would provide lateral (same-level) associative activation of sets of adjacent letter triple nodes. For example, $_\#c_o$ will prime the entire set of $_co_-$ nodes, and $_om_\#$ will prime the entire set of $_-o_m$ nodes. The combined effect of activating the initial and terminal letter triple nodes of "com" is to prime doubly exactly one medial letter triple node—the correct one, $_co_m$. This is one way overlapping, redundant, letter triple nodes could enhance recognition, particularly of letters in the interior of words. Sloboda (1976b) has shown that the interior of words is precisely where segmental contextual inference appears to be greatest, though word-to-segment feedback activation probably occurs as well as lateral segmental interactions. Sloboda drew this conclusion from the fact that subjects failed oftenest to detect spelling errors while reading when the errors occurred in the interior of words.

Syntactic and semantic expectations surely influence reading as well, though there is less evidence on such effects than we might wish. Kolers had subjects read various types of geometrically transformed text (letters inverted or right-left mirror image reversed). He found that substitution errors were often the same part of speech (noun, verb, adjective, and so on) as the correct word. This occurred far oftener than chance would allow. Even when an error was not the same part of speech as the correct word, it almost always maintained a grammatical syntactic structure. A number of studies of oral reading also show that errors tend to be semantically similar to the correct word. They are particularly likely to be consistent with the preceding clause. There are also several studies that indicate lower perceptual thresholds and faster recognition for words semantically associated to prior context (Kolers 1970; Massaro 1975, pp. 225–59; Morton and Long 1976; Schuberth and Eimas 1977).

Skimming and Scanning

In addition to normal careful reading, which ostensibly aims to extract all or most of the information in a passage, we possess two more rapid reading modes: skimming and scanning. Scanning is rapid reading for particular information, ignoring everything else. Skimming is rapid reading, but with the less specific purpose of acquiring some general idea of the content of the passage. Probably these are not discrete modes but merely points in a continuum of reading modes varying in speed and specificity of purpose.

It is now quite well established that so-called "speed reading" courses teach mostly skimming. That is, increases in speed beyond a certain point are invariably followed by decreases in comprehension, despite the unscientific claims of many promoters of speed reading courses. Reading rate is limited primarily by comprehension rate. This is why we read more slowly when we are processing conceptually difficult material. To the extent that you are reading a passage more slowly than you are capable of understanding it, you can increase your reading speed without drastic losses in comprehension, though if you spend more time studying the material, you will generally learn more and retain it better. You should vary your reading rate substantially depending upon the material and your objectives. In particular, you can read faster when you only need a general idea of what is being said, or when you only need to remember the material for a very short time. Thus it is certainly worthwhile to develop the capacity to skim and scan, but remember that, in general, comprehension and retention do decrease the faster you read. Furthermore, in many instances what you ought to do is to think about the material you are reading, getting ideas of your own and fitting these ideas into your own cognitive framework. The faster you read, the less time you will have for this extremely important cognitive activity (Carver 1972; Graf 1973; Smith 1971).

Finally, there is little evidence to support the hypothesis that slow readers are slow because they make inefficient eye fixations, including many regressions. It is at least as likely that more fixations per line of print and more frequent regressions are the *result* of comprehension difficulties, not the cause of them (Poulton 1962; Carver 1972; Graf 1973). Forcing a slow reader to take in more information per fixation and make fewer regressions may simply make him read faster and understand less.

Reading Is Understanding

One of the popularly debated nonissues in cognitive psychology is: What is *the basic unit* in speech perception or reading? In speech recognition one researcher will argue for features, another for phonemes, another for phoneme strings (syllables or allophones), another for words, and so on. In reading, the most popular alternatives are letters, familiar letter strings, words, concepts, and propositions. A good deal of evidence exists for nearly all of these basic units, which is why I call this a nonissue. If speech recognition and reading make use of all these units at many different levels, then none of them is *the basic unit*—or they all are, whichever way you want to look at it.

However, if I had to choose, I would probably argue that the *final decision unit* is the most basic. All the preceding (and succeeding) units are means to the end of making some decision. This decision appears to be made only at the relevant level; activation (and probably inhibition) simply flow continuously through to that level. The decision level changes according to whether the task is monitoring for a particular letter, word, concept, or proposition.

Adults are not ordinarily reading to identify letters, letter strings, words, or even familiar concepts and propositions. We are reading to identify new concepts and propositions—that is, expressions of fairly complex thoughts. We read to learn new concepts and propositions in our semantic memory. We want newly learned propositions to be true and useful (whether or not they are identical to the propositions the writer was trying to communicate). These new concepts and propositions we learn must be built upon (related to) the concepts and propositions we have already learned. In short, reading is understanding. The more you already know about a topic, the faster you can read about it, because you have already learned many of the concepts and propositions you need in order to understand what you are reading. And what is understanding? That is the extended topic of the last three chapters in this text, which are concerned with coding and processes in semantic memory.

SUMMARY

1 Several levels of processing in the verbal modality mediate speech recognition, articulation, and reading. These levels are auditory features, articulatory features, visual features, graphic (writing-motor) features, phonetic segments (phonemes and context-sensitive allophones), graphic segments (letters and letter triples), words, concepts, and propositions.

2 Context-sensitive coding in the form of redundant, overlapping-triple encoding of phonemes and letters permits a specific-node encoding of the order of the segmental constituents of words.

3 Phonetic segments (such as context-sensitive allophones) may well be encoded by abstract cognitive nodes that are activated by sets of sensory features and that activate the sets of speech motor features in articulation. In much the same way graphic segments (such as letter triples) may represent both visual sensory units and writing motor units. In a cognitive theory of speech and reading, S meets R not at the top level of brain, but several levels below the top. Higher levels are neither purely sensory nor purely motor in function, but a mixture of both. The segmental and word levels are actually an abstract cognitive representation of language, and the conceptual and propositional levels are a cognitive representation of the real world. As an example of how such a system might work, we conjectured that S meets R at the segmental level, that the phonetic modality meets the graphic modality at the word level, and that the verbal modality meets the spatial-image modality at the level of semantic memory (concepts and propositions).

4 The acoustic features used to identify a phoneme occur simultaneously with the features used to identify the immediately adjacent phonemes on both sides. This produces a segmentation problem. Furthermore, the nature of these features varies with different prior and succeeding phonemes. Such contextual variation in acoustic features creates a problem for speech recognition devices based on phonemes. Using context-sensitive allophones instead of phonemes as segmental recognition units solves both problems.

5 The order of phonemes is not represented by temporal order of activation, but by simultaneous activation of context-sensitive nodes that contain the order information by means of *which* nodes are activated. This permits the recognition of several speech segments to occur in parallel. It extends the time allowed for

recognizing each. And it allows extensive opportunity for contextual feedback activation laterally from prior and subsequent segments and downward from word and concept units that have been primed by other segmental input or semantic and syntactic expectations.

6 Speech recognition and reading use a form of chain parallel processing in which processing occurs at all levels simultaneously, from features to concepts.

7 A ballistic motor control system imposes a particular activation pattern on the motor neurons. This activation pattern would achieve a specific movement and terminal position if there were no variation in the load on the muscle or other sources of error variability. A feedback control system (such as the gamma feedback loop) sets a certain target position, uses sensory feedback to monitor disparity from the target position, and activates motor neurons in proportion to this disparity. The gamma feedback system is known to play an important role in maintaining bodily position (e.g., in balancing against the force of gravity). It may also play a role in moving body parts to new target positions (e.g., in speech).

8 The motor target positions for the articulators (tongue, lips, jaw, larynx, and pharynx) are much more context invariant for each phoneme than are the acoustic features for each phoneme. Nevertheless, there is some coarticulatory variation in phoneme target positions. This variation depends upon prior and succeeding phonemes.

9 Context-sensitive coding permits us to plan an entire phrase in semantic memory, input that phrase more rapidly than we can speak it to the phonetic segmental level, and then automatically have the segments (context-sensitive allophones) output to the articulatory muscles in the correct order.

10 There is no evidence to support the syllable as a functioning phonetic unit in speech recognition or articulation. There is evidence to support context-sensitive syllable juncture (boundary) segments as optional segments separating phonemes that we do not coarticulate into context-sensitive allophones.

11 The most important segmental units in reading are probably also context-sensitive (overlapping) letter triples. These segmental units represent order by *which* nodes are activated (specific node encoding) and permit parallel processing of all the letters in a word.

12 There are clearly two associative paths connecting graphic segments to words —a direct path and an indirect path by way of phonetic segmental units. Phonics training and subvocalization help one to learn to read, but eventually the shorter, direct path probably takes precedence. Certainly there is no doubt that one must learn to read words whole, not letter by letter, if reading is to be a useful skill.

13 Chain parallel processing also takes place in reading, and higher-level semantic and syntactic expectations feed back onto lower-level phonetic nodes to help activate them.

14 Slow and steady does not always win the race. Skimming and scanning (speed reading) are very useful skills. However, the primary purpose of reading is comprehension, in particular the learning of new concepts and propositions. This kind of new learning is definitely reduced by speed reading.

CHAPTER 6
ATTENTION

OBJECTIVES

1 To discuss some practical issues in the control of attention and distraction in studying. For instance, should you study with a friend, or with the radio on?

2 To distinguish between *attention* and *attentional set*.

3 To discuss our limited capacity for simultaneously attending to more than one stimulus, performing more than one response, or making more than one decision. To discuss the role of automatization in permitting parallel processing.

4 To discuss our capacity for rapid visual search—scanning an array of stimuli in search of some target stimulus or looking for any stimulus in some set of target stimuli.

5 To discuss our attentional set capacity for selectively listening to or looking for messages that come from a particular direction, or that have particular physical or semantic characteristics.

6 To discuss the effects of attentional set on both speed and accuracy of response.

Where are you reading this book? Wherever you are, you know that there are factors that may distract your attention from the material you are trying to learn. If you can choose where you study, your choice may well have been influenced by the relative likelihood of being distracted. Sometimes the distractions are so compelling that you cannot study at all—for example, when friends are talking to you, or when you are watching an interesting program on television. A library is a pretty good place to study from an attentional point of view, unless you are too interested in looking at the other people. Studying alone in a quiet room is supposed to be ideal for avoiding distraction. And yet if it is your own room, and there are a lot of alternative things to do in that room, it may be more distracting than a library. Perhaps an isolated study carrel in a library is ideal, since there is little you can do in such an environment except study the material you brought along. But there are always your own affairs to think about, something perhaps a bit more personally relevant than the book in front of you. Putting yourself into an environment with no external distractions is ideal so long as you have enough intrinsic interest in the task at hand to keep you from woolgathering.

Many students like to study with the radio on, or with another person, as on a study date, or in a semisocial setting such as a library or courtyard. This tendency can be functional from an attentional standpoint. If the distractors are not too powerful, they can make the difference between some studying and no studying at all. After all, if you cannot make studying at least minimally interesting, you are very likely not to do it at all (which might be thought of as complete distraction). Not enjoying what you are doing constitutes an extremely distracting internal stimulus, and if having the radio on suppresses that source of distraction, you may actually be less distracted with the radio on than with it off. Managing distraction is a tricky business. The ideal approach is to find some way to increase your interest in material you must attend to. One way to accomplish this is to be continually on the lookout for ways to make use of the knowledge you are gaining. It is a good thing for teachers to point out the potential uses of knowledge, but as a student you do not need other people to show you the relevance of what you are studying to your own life. In certain respects no one is better able than you to see the potential use to you of knowledge. If you set out aggressively to think how you might use the knowledge you are acquiring, you will quite frequently succeed. To the extent that you do succeed, your interest in the material will be increased, and consequently it will be easier to attend to it and learn it.

Motivation is a strong determinant of attention, but other factors are important as well. For example, intense or unexpected stimuli will attract your attention, even though you are deeply engaged in some other activity quite unrelated to the unexpected event. However, intense stimulation that is repetitive and irrelevant loses its capacity to attract attention and is generally ignored. For example, there was a rather noisy fan immediately above the ceiling of my former office. When I first moved into this office, I was very much aware of the noise, and I found it very annoying. However, after a couple months I became so habituated to this constant sound that I rarely paid any attention to it. Except for the times when I thought of the fan as an example of habituation, the only time I attended to it was when it went off

—that is, when there was an unexpected decrease in its intensity. We habituate to many repetitive stimuli that require no reaction, and we preferentially attend to unexpected stimuli. The principal component of the reaction to unexpected stimuli is attentional. Thus a rustling of leaves in the forest causes a deer to prick up its ears, look in the direction of the sound, and prepare to run. All higher organisms show this *orienting reaction* to unexpected stimuli of at least moderate intensity. The orienting reaction has a number of externally observable components. One is an increase in general arousal (as measured by, say, the EEG). Another is observing responses directed to the source of the stimulation in order to obtain more specific information. A third is selective mobilization of response systems, such as running. And a fourth is selective priming of nodes associated to the unexpected stimulus.

Not only can irrelevant unexpected stimuli preferentially capture attention, so can relevant expected stimuli. We make substantial use of verbal context in speech recognition and reading. That is, we hear and see what we expect to hear and see, based both on the topic of the conversation and on the semantic, syntactic, and phonetic constraints of the individual sentences we are attending to. The more we are biased to expect a particular event to occur, the more likely we are to perceive that event, if it is relevant to our goals. That is, our attention tends to be captured by that to which we are *set*. There is no conflict between this fact and the material in the preceding paragraph. The logical distinction between the expected stimuli to which we habituate and the expected stimuli that preferentially attract attention is that the former are irrelevant to what we are currently thinking about and doing, while the latter are highly relevant. Thus we can have either positive or negative *attentional set* for expected stimuli, depending upon whether the stimuli are relevant or irrelevant to our goals and the decisions we must make.

Psychologists have used the word *attention* in at least as many different ways as it is used in ordinary conversation. For instance, attention in the sense of "paying attention" is often used to refer to general arousal or alertness factors, as well as to specific attention paid to a given concept or stimulus. Attention is also used to refer both to the processing of external stimuli and to the internal direction of thinking. More generally, we may ask what role attention plays in perception, responding, and thinking, including retrieval from memory and decision making. Finally, we are concerned with the span of attention in perception, responding, and thinking. So, for example, we ask how many stimuli a subject can see at once when an array of letters or digits is briefly exposed to him on a tachistoscope. How many decisions can be made at the same time? How many responses can be executed simultaneously? What are the limits of attentional set? How do we control our attention? Are there general attentional strategies? What is the role of learning in attention? Can we learn to pay attention? These questions will be explored in the present chapter.

THEORETICAL ANALYSIS
OF ATTENTION AND SET

The most fundamental distinction in the area of attention is that between attention and attentional set. *Attention per se* refers to a decision process by which we think of one or a few things, as opposed to others, at any given moment. *Attentional set* refers to our capacity selectively to prepare our nervous system to process one set of stimuli, think about a certain topic, or make certain responses as opposed to others.

Limited Capacity

Many people think that they can attend to only one thing at a time. As we shall see, they are probably wrong. Existing evidence clearly indicates that we can attend to more than one event, decision process, or response at a time, especially if the information-processing activities are in different modalities or levels. Apparently we can sometimes attend to more than one thing within a single modality as well, though this is generally more difficult. We may think that we can attend to only one thing at a time because we narrowly identify attention with a kind of "inner speech." In speech the physical impossibility of pronouncing two phonemes at the same time necessarily produces sequential motor output and sensory input. More cognitive levels of speech articulation and recognition probably involve substantial parallel processing.

However, our capacity for simultaneous attention is definitely limited. For example, when an array of 16 letters is flashed briefly on a screen, we can perceive (attend to) 4 or 5 letters simultaneously after about 50 msec of perceptual processing (the span of apprehension). However, we cannot attend to all 16 of them. It is true that we may be processing the other 11 or 12 letters to some extent at the same time as the 4 or 5 we recognize (Sperling et al. 1971). In any case, while I shall be at some pains to demonstrate that attention is not limited to one thing at a time, you must nonetheless remember that it is sharply limited.

At present we do not know to what extent attention can be distributed across different modalities, if at all; some people have assumed totally separate processing limits within each modality. Existing evidence indicates that it is easier to attend to two things in different modalities than to two things in the same modality. Thus our attentional capacity is not completely free-floating. That is, the attentional capacity limit across all modalities is probably greater than the maximum attentional capacity possible within a single modality. However, processing in each modality may not be completely independent of processing in the other modalities. We may, for example, be able to allocate from a common resource pool more attention to the auditory modality than to the visual modality in one case and to reverse this allocation in another case. On the other hand, if we are careful to distinguish between attention and attentional set, it is not at all clear that there is any differential allocation of attention across different modalities—though there is clearly differential allocation of attentional set. Here we shall assume that attention is a decision process that operates in precisely the same way at all levels of all modalities at all times, and that the internally induced fluctuation in attention results entirely from different attentional sets.

Activation and Lateral Inhibition

According to the theory originally advanced by Deutsch and Deutsch (1963) attention is the process of selecting the node or nodes that are maximally activated by a combination of external stimuli and prior associations from previously activated nodes in memory. In order to account for the parallel processing capabilities that have recently been demonstrated, it is necessary to generalize this *maximum decision rule* for attention along the lines suggested by Walley and Weiden (1973). They propose that the process of attention consists of an amplification of the difference between more strongly activated and less strongly activated nodes. That is, suppose that nodes A and B are approximately equally activated, and that they are more strongly activated than any other nodes in that modality. The process of attention will amplify the difference in degree of activation between nodes A and B, on the one hand, and all of the remaining nodes, on the other hand. If we further assume that some absolute level of activation for a node A or node B or both is necessary to initiate an observable response or to lay down a memory trace, then the attentional process will function as a gate to determine whether and when the response or the memory trace will be realized. Walley and Weiden also state that this amplification of differences of level of activation proceeds by means of lateral inhibition, which was discussed in chapter 2. That is, each node has an inhibitory connection to every other node at that level of that modality, and the amount of inhibition is proportional to the activation of the node exerting the inhibition. The lateral inhibition process of attention could act to boost the nodes that are maximally activated above some threshold necessary for conscious perception, decision making, action, memory acquisition, or retrieval from memory. Since this maximum rule is identical to the rule I will propose for recall from memory in chapter 9, and since it is also the most plausible decision rule for perceptual choice between a number of alternatives, I have made no new assumption here regarding attention.

Attentional Set and Priming

Thus far we have a device that will choose the node or nodes that are maximally activated under some conditions. Thus far in this chapter we have not specified a way to bias internally the system so that one set of nodes would be more likely than another to have the maximum degree of activation. However, an associative memory can easily have varied attentional set due to the priming effects of prior activation, as discussed before. It is therefore unneccessary to specify any additional mechanism. In the first place, previously activated nodes may remain partially activated (primed) for a time following maximum activation. In the second place, previously activated nodes will provide input to other nodes to which they are associated, the input being proportionate to the strength of association. Thus if we have been listening to "Mary had a little—," the propositional memory structure activated by this input will very strongly prime the perception of the word "lamb." Thus we would be more likely to report hearing the word "lamb" in this context (even if the word were not presented at all or were presented in very noisy background) than we would in a completely neutral context. Similarly, in an experiment in visual recognition, if we are told that only digits will be presented, we are much more likely to report a digit than if we are told that either a letter or a digit may be presented. Such obvious examples of attentional set are sometimes downgraded as being merely "response biases." Those who study attentional set are often primarily interested in such questions as whether attentional set can influence perception as well as response, and whether it can increase the discriminability of stimuli within the attentional set. We shall consider these matters later on. For the present, note that regardless of where such biases act, they are of substantial functional importance.

Attentional set involves differentially biasing (priming) either nodes or links (the connections between nodes). This bias may be excitatory, inhibitory, or both. An associative memory with excitatory and inhibitory connections between nodes would appear to have the capacity for both positive attentional sets (of which "Mary had a little—" is one example) and negative attentional sets (for example, habituation to repetitive stimuli). However, we do not know for sure whether both excitation and inhibition play a role in attentional set. Nor do we know whether excitatory and inhibitory priming apply to an entire node or only to certain connections into a node. Node priming makes a node easier (or harder) to activate by any input link. Link priming makes a node easier (or harder) to activate only by input through the primed link. Link priming is really more powerful than node priming because it can be more selective, but we don't know whether human associative memory has link priming. Nevertheless, whether attentional sets are placed on the nodes or the links, the result is to make certain nodes more likely to be maximally activated than other nodes. Once again it should be pointed out that these assumptions regarding attentional set are actually consequences of the type of associative memory assumed throughout this book. Thus this theory of both attention and set is about as parsimonious as possible, involving as it does few or no additional assumptions beyond those already made to account for other cognitive phenomena.

ATTENTION

Serial Processing
and the Psychological Refractory Period

In a simple reaction time task, the subject must make a response, such as pressing a key, as soon as possible after the presentation of a stimulus, such as a tone or a flash of light. In a choice reaction time task, there are two or more stimuli and two or more associated responses. One elementary two-choice paradigm involves two lights, one on the right side of the subject and one on the left side, and two responses, a key on the right side and a key on the left side. Typically, the subject's task is to press the right key when the right light comes on, and the left key when the left light comes on. Under ideal conditions, with stimuli of moderately high intensity, simple reaction time to an auditory or visual stimulus is on the order of 150 msec. It is somewhat faster for auditory than for visual stimuli, and the reaction time to each varies with the intensity of the stimulus. The fastest two-choice responses are around 220 msec, and reaction time continues to increase with the number of alternative stimuli and responses.

The foregoing results refer to reaction times to single stimuli processed in isolation. When two stimuli are presented simultaneously or in rapid succession, the reaction time to either or both may be prolonged compared to the reaction time to a single stimulus. When the stimuli are presented in rapid succession, the reaction time to the second stimulus is typically substantially delayed. The period following the onset of the first stimulus during which processing of the second stimulus is delayed is known as the *psychological refractory period.*

The psychological refractory period is well illustrated in an experiment by Karlin and Kestenbaum (1968). Subjects were first presented with a visual stimulus (a luminous digit), to which they responded by pressing a button with the left hand. This was followed by a tone, to which subjects responded by pushing a button with the right hand. When the second stimulus followed the first within half a second, the response to the second stimulus was substantially delayed. The actual reaction times for both the first and the second stimulus are illustrated in figure 6.1. Note that the reaction time to the first stimulus was essentially unaffected by the presence of the second stimulus at any interstimulus interval (delay between the onset of the first and second stimulus). At long interstimulus intervals, the simple reaction time to the second stimulus approaches a limit of about 190 msec. This limit is characteristic of the reaction time to the auditory stimulus when it is presented alone. The fact that the asymptotic level of the second (auditory) stimulus is below that of the first (visual) stimulus is of no theoretical importance. It merely illustrates the generally obtained difference in simple reaction time to auditory versus visual signals. What is important is that subjects appear to be

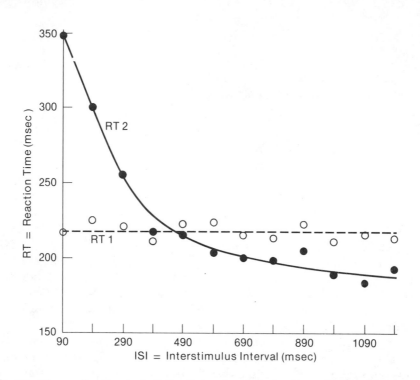

Fig. 6.1 The reaction time to both the first and second stimuli as a function of the time interval between the onsets of the two stimuli (ISI = interstimulus interval). Note that the reaction to the second stimulus is delayed at short ISIs when the first stimulus is still being processed (and even for a short time after RT1).

unable to complete processing of the second stimulus during the processing of the first stimulus—and even for some time thereafter. The fact that reaction time to the second stimulus can be delayed even when it is presented after completion of the response to the first stimulus may indicate not only that subjects cannot attend to both reaction time tasks at once, but also that time is required to shift attention from processing the first stimulus to processing the second.

The dominant theory of the psychological refractory period is that *under these conditions* subjects can attend to only one decision process at a time, and attention to the second stimulus has to be delayed until the first stimulus is processed. There are two major alternative theories. One is that the nervous system is made somewhat less sensitive by processing the first stimulus. This is the *refractory theory*. The other is that the reaction to the second stimulus is delayed because subjects do not expect it to follow the first stimulus so rapidly. This is the *expectancy theory*. Although prior stimuli can exert a masking effect on subsequent stimuli, and expectancies (attentional sets) certainly do affect reaction times, it is now quite clear that under many conditions the psychological refractory period cannot be explained in terms of such mechanisms.

Apparently we must assume that there is a phase in the processing of each stimulus that must be carried out successively rather than simultaneously, so that the second stimulus has to wait until the first stimulus has been processed. This attentional theory is often referred to as a *single-channel theory*. According to the single-channel theory there is a channel of limited capacity at some place in the information processing that cannot attend to both stimuli simultaneously. In my opinion, this terminology is somewhat misleading, because it suggests that at some point both stimuli pass through the same physical location in the brain. This is not likely to be the case. More probably the signals are processed by quite separate nodes, each competing for a limited-capacity attentional boosting mechanism. Under the conditions of these experiments this competition causes the first signal to be amplified and temporarily inhibits the second signal until the first signal has been processed.

According to the serial processing theory of the psychological refractory period, the longer it takes to process the first stimulus, the longer the delay in processing the second stimulus. This prediction has been verified in a couple of different ways. First, one can increase the information-processing difficulty of the first task, to increase RT1 (e.g., by using a two- or four-alternative choice reaction time task rather than a simple reaction time task). This produces a correspondingly longer delay in processing the second stimulus (Karlin and Kestenbaum 1968). Second, more intense stimuli activate their cognitive representations more rapidly than less intense stimuli and so have shorter RT1s. This also reduces the psychological refractory period by the same amount. For example, Smith (1967a) showed that a bright first stimulus that can be responded to approximately 30 msec faster than a dim first stimulus produces a psychological refractory period that is approximately 30 msec shorter than that produced by the dim first stimulus. This agrees with the serial processing theory in that the sooner the first stimulus can be processed, the sooner the attentional boosting process can be directed to the second stimulus. The results of this experiment also contradict the refractory theory. If the first stimulus reduces the sensitivity of the nervous system to the processing of the second stimulus, one would expect a bright first stimulus to produce a greater loss of sensitivity, and thus delay the processing of the second stimulus, more than a dim first stimulus would do. Precisely the opposite result was obtained.

We can break down the processing of a stimulus into three stages: (1) perceptual encoding *(recognition)*, (2) association of the stimulus to response *(decision making)*, and (3) execution of the motor *response*. In which of these three stages does the limited-capacity attentional mechanism occur? This question is not definitely settled, but it seems to occur primarily in the central decision-making component—that is, in the association of the encoded stimulus to the central motor node controlling the response. There is considerable evidence to suggest that the perceptual recognition of several familiar stimuli can occur in parallel, at least up to the span of apprehension. An attentional boosting process may take place in this perceptual encoding phase, but if so, it is not typically limited to one stimulus at a time (Sperling et al. 1971; Schneider and Shiffrin 1977). One of the simplest and most convincing of the phenomena supporting the hypothesis of parallel processing in perception is the so-called *Stroop effect.* In studies of the Stroop effect, words are written in different-colored ink, and subjects are required to name the color of the ink in which the word is written. In controlled conditions, subjects name the color of a spot of ink. In general, it makes little difference whether the colored stimuli are words or colored spots; the reaction time to name the color of the ink is about the same. That is, the subjects can selectively attend to the color attribute of the stimulus and ignore its other properties. However, the other properties of the stimulus are clearly being processed in parallel with color information, since if words are used that are themselves the names of colors, reaction time to name the color is shortened if the word "green" is written in green ink, and so on. However, there is interference (a slowing down of the reaction time or an increase in the error rate) if the color represented by the word and the color of the ink disagree (Keele 1972; Hintzman et al. 1972). Thus both the verbal information and the nonverbal color information must be encoded in parallel up to the level of semantic memory, at which point the verbal and nonverbal cues for color concepts converge.

The limitation in attentional capacity is not typically located in motor performance either—at least, not in the case of simple or highly practiced *responses.* For example, we are perfectly capable of pushing two buttons simultaneously in response to a single stimulus. This demonstrates that there is no intrinsic incompatibility between the right hand and the left, though there may be some degree of mutual inhibition. Furthermore, in a psychological refractory task Smith (1967b) found a substantial delay in the response to the second stimulus even when no response is required to the first stimulus. In Smith's experiment the first stimulus was a light on the left or the right. Subjects pressed a key if the first stimulus was on the left and made no response if the stimulus was on the right. In the second half of the experiment this rule was reversed. The second stimulus was a bar that could appear either above or below a fixation light. Subjects said "boo" if the bar was above the light and "bun" if it was below it. Substantial delays in responding to the second stimulus were obtained whether or not subjects had responded to the first stimulus, though a slightly larger delay was obtained on trials where a response was required. Most of the delay in processing the second stimulus appears to result from limited attentional capacity in the decision stage, but execution of responses may produce some additional delay.

Thus although attention may play some role in the encoding and responding stages of these tasks, it is primarily in the association of stimuli and responses that attentional capacity is strained to the point of requiring serial processing. However, it should also be noted that in most experiments concerned with the psychological refractory period, the stimuli and responses have been familiar. Only the association between the stimuli and the responses is unfamiliar and has, therefore, a lower memory strength. There is reason to think that it is low-strength associations, wherever they may be in the chain from stimulus to response, that place the greatest demand on attentional capacity, sometimes to the extent of forcing serial processing. It has long been thought that perceptual-motor skills (typing, driving, playing tennis) require considerable attention in the early stages of learning but become highly automated with practice, so that these skills can be performed faster and also simultaneously with other information-processing activities. Thus I can carry on a conversation and simultaneously draw five-pointed stars (★), but I cannot carry on a conversation and simultaneously draw some unfamiliar figure composed of five lines. Coding a familiar form, such as the outline of a bird or a car, probably requires little attentional capacity. Recognizing the same form as a hidden figure embedded in a complex visual display requires more attention.

Parallel Processing

Doing two things at once.   By the same token, complete parallel processing in reaction time tasks can be obtained, provided the stimulus node is strongly associated to the response node. In one such task Smith (1967c) obtained completely parallel processing of successive stimuli. The task employed four lights (two on the left and two on the right) and two toggle switches (one on the left and one on the right). The toggle switches were placed between the lights on the left and right, as illustrated in figure 6.2. When one of the two lights on the right came on, subjects were to move the right switch towards that light. If one of the lights on the left came on, subjects were to move the left switch towards that light. Moving towards a nearby stimulus is a familiar, highly practiced association (often called a *compatible* S-R association). When both lights came on at the same time, subjects were able to move *both* right and left switches *simultaneously* as quickly as they could move one switch to the first of two successive stimuli. For successive stimuli at short interstimulus intervals, there was no delay in processing the second stimulus, since its reaction time was no longer than the reaction time to the first stimulus. When subjects knew in advance of the trial that they would only be required to make a single response, reaction times were about 30 msec shorter than reaction times to either stimulus on trials when subjects were set to make two responses. Thus there is a 30 msec difference depending upon the breadth of attentional set (one versus two

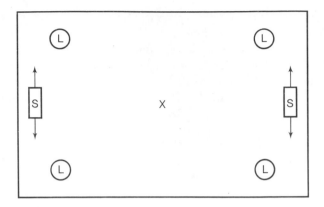

Figure 6.2 Diagram of Smith's apparatus for a reaction time task with high S-R compatibility. S = switch, L = light, X = fixation point. Subjects were instructed to move the left switch towards whichever light (above or below the switch) flashed on the left, and to move the right switch towards whichever light flashed on the right. (From M. C. Smith, Stimulus-response compatibility and parallel response selection, *Canadian Journal of Psychology*, 21 (1967): 496–503. Copyright 1967, Canadian Psychological Association; reprinted by permission.)

responses). Furthermore, in the task requiring two responses with long inter-stimulus intervals, the reaction time to the second stimulus declined by approximately 30 msec to the level characteristic of responses to a single stimulus. After performing the first response, subjects were apparently able to narrow their set, resulting in a 30 msec advantage in processing time. Thus the broader attentional set required to process two stimuli simultaneously does produce somewhat slower processing in this case, but the difference is too small to be consistent with a serial processing assumption. Under these conditions, subjects appear to be able to attend to two tasks at once, and indeed when the two stimuli came on simultaneously, the two responses were made virtually simultaneously (mean of zero, average deviation of 12 msec).

Even in tasks where the S-R compatibility is initially so low that a substantial psychological refractory period is observed, Gottsdanker and Stelmach (1971) have demonstrated that extensive practice will eliminate all or almost all of the delay in processing the second stimulus. After practice there was still a slightly faster reaction to the second stimulus at long interstimulus intervals, but this is probably due to narrowing of attentional set after the first stimulus occurs. Thus there is every reason to believe that extended practice of any associations produces the capacity to process these associations in parallel, provided they do not make contradictory demands (e.g., move the right index finger up and down at the same time).

Even two rather complex skills can be performed at the same time, provided they are both highly practiced and do not place contradictory demands on the muscles. Skilled pianists can sight-read music (play it on the piano) while simultaneously shadowing prose (repeating passages spoken to them). Professional typists can type from copy and simultaneously recite familiar nursery rhymes with only a slight reduction in typing performance. Typing from (auditory) dictation is much more seriously impeded by shadowing, reciting, or reading aloud. It is easier to perform multiple information processing tasks when the parts of the mind employed in each are dissimilar. Finally, Spelke, Hirst, and Neisser showed that after extended practice people can read stories at a normal rate and with normal comprehension while simultaneously copying random words from dictation, or even while writing down the categories the words belong to. Neural incompatibility (e.g., excitation and inhibition of the same nodes), as well as muscular incompatibility, must limit the number of cognitive processes that can go on simultaneously. But we are certainly not limited to doing one thing at a time—provided both "things" are highly practiced to a level of automatization (Allport, Antonis, and Reynolds 1972; Shaffer 1975; Spelke, Hirst, and Neisser 1976).

Visual Search

Because we can close our eyes and make eye and head movements, we can voluntarily control our exposure to visual input much better than we can control our exposure to auditory input. One of the components of learning to read consists of developing a control structure for the systematic shifting of eye fixation from left to right within a line of print and then from the end of one line to the beginning of the next. This eye movement scanning is serial; but within a single fixation several letters are processed in parallel. Reading rates can vary enormously—from slow, careful reading to a rapid visual search for information related to a particular topic. Studies of rapid visual search by Neisser and his colleagues have demonstrated some of the characteristics of the attentional process in visual perception. In one of his experiments Neisser presented subjects with 50-line lists, each line consisting of several letters. Subjects visually searched these lists for a target letter, starting at the top and flipping a switch when the target letter was discovered. Subjects searched lines containing four to six letters extremely rapidly, obtaining speeds of 10 or more lines per second. The maximum rate depended on a number of factors. For example, lines containing more letters were searched less rapidly, but the decrease in speed was not proportionate to the increase in letters. This suggests that subjects do not process one letter at a time in a strictly sequential manner but instead process several letters in parallel. Subjects claim that they do not "see" individual letters at all, and that everything is more or less a blur until the target pops out at them. One of the most striking findings in this series of studies was that under some conditions highly practiced subjects can search for multiple targets (as many as 10) as rapidly as for a single target. Whether or not they can always search for multiple targets as rapidly and accurately as for a single target, it is clear that they do search for multiple targets extremely efficiently. Neisser points out that we should not be too surprised at this finding, considering that readers in newsclip agencies search through newspaper articles at over a thousand words a minute looking for any reference to the agency's clients (of whom there are typically several hundred) (Neisser 1963, 1966, [p. 68–71]; Neisser, Novick, and Lazar 1963; Neisser and Lazar 1964).

Clearly, we can rapidly shift attention from one visual location to another until the input from visual perception activates a node on which we have placed a short-term or long-term bias. At that point attentional set will stop being shifted so rapidly, giving us more time to process the material we are interested in. Even though this rapid shifting of attentional set undoubtedly results in some omission errors, its enormous speed makes it very useful in selecting information relevant to our goals. Over-compulsive individuals who believe that slow and steady always wins the race are making a mistake if they always read carefully and never skim.

Further evidence in support of a limited-capacity parallel search for a target in a single fixation derives once again from the finding of redundancy gain. Recognition of a given target letter is faster and more accurate if the target letter is redundantly presented two or three times than if it is presented once on an otherwise blank field. The three-target condition also appears to give better results than the two-target condition (van der Heijden 1975).

Sperling et al. (1971) developed a way to measure perceptual recognition time in visual search without including the motor response time. The technique involves presenting a sequence of frames, each of which contains an array of one, two, three, four, or more characters. Subjects search either for a particular target character or for any one of a set of target characters. The results of this study, and a very extensive and well-controlled series of experiments by Schneider and Shiffrin (1977) using a variant of the same technique, indicate that subjects require about 50 msec to process a set of four or five letters or digits in parallel for the purpose of detecting either a single target or one of a set of targets, provided the single target or target set is a member of a well-learned category, and provided the targets on one trial are not the distractors (nontarget characters) on another trial. In particular, if the targets are always digits and the distractors are always letters (or vice versa), subjects can process four or five items in each frame at the same time. Furthermore, they show little or no reduction in efficiency when searching for a set of up to 10 (and possibly more) alternative targets. Schneider and Shiffrin call this procedure of keeping targets distinct from distractors a *consistent mapping*. Consistent mapping appears to produce a rapid automatic parallel processing of about four or five items. This is the same as the visual memory span—the number of items that can be "seen" (and reported) from a single brief presentation of an array of items. To obtain such automatic parallel processing, not only must the target set be a familiar category, but the roles of the target and distractor sets must not be switched. A large slowdown in search rate occurs if, after searching for digits in letters, the subject is switched to searching for letters in digits.

The automatic detection of targets is not a conscious cognitive process where the role of a set as target or distractor can be instantly shifted by a verbal instruction. It is more like a perceptual-motor skill that develops after long practice and will interfere with the learning of any contradictory skill. Results like these suggest that there may be some truth in the idea that it's bad to play golf for fun if one wants to play professional baseball. Automated skills are not very cognitive, which means that they cannot easily be altered by instruction from one context to another.

Schneider and Shiffrin also studied visual search under conditions of *variable mapping.* Here the target set was changed from trial to trial and consisted of items that were distractors on other trials. Variable mapping produces far slower visual search 100 msec or more per item in the frame. Furthermore, the search appears to be serial through the frame and also through the target set. That is, each item in the frame is compared serially with each item in the target set until the subject finds a match. Visual search under variable mapping would appear to be a much more conscious, attention-demanding process than visual search under consistent mapping. Once again we see that it is the strength of association that determines the attentional capacity for parallel processing.

Chain Parallel Processing

When two cognitive processes A and B are logically independent of each other—that is, when A consists of recognizing an F and B consists of recognizing a K presented at two different locations in the visual field—it seems natural to ask whether the two processes are psychologically independent. If they are, they can go on simultaneously; if not, they must occur sequentially. However, when two cognitive processes are obviously logically dependent— when output from process A appears to provide the necessary input for the initiation of process B—then serial ordering of the two processes would seem to be implied. For example, it would appear that visual recognition of some structural components of a word (letters, syllables, or whatever) should precede recognition of the entire word. Wrongo! Of course, process A must begin before process B. However, process A may provide fast preliminary output to start process B, and then process A may continue to provide ever more refined (more accurate, higher strength) output to B (Norman and Bobrow 1975). Both processes can go on simultaneously with perhaps only a small difference in starting time. If several logically prior (lower) cognitive processes $A_1, \ldots, A_n$ provide partially redundant input to a logically subsequent (higher) cognitive process B, then B may actually achieve a high level of accuracy faster than any of the logically prior A processes. That is, B may terminate before any of the logically prior A processes that provide input to

B. Furthermore, since B integrates information from several lower-order (constituent) A's, it would be desirable if B provided feedback to its constituent A's to assist them in reaching more accurate decisions that take advantage of previously learned dependencies among the A's. Such a system has what may be called *chain parallel processing* capability (Wickelgren 1976d).

There is considerable neurophysiological and psychological evidence supporting chain parallel processing in the nervous system. At a neural level, activation of neurons at one level produces activation of neurons at the next level after transmission and synaptic delay times on the order of a few msec. Activation in many neurons continues for substantial periods of time at any given level, overlapping extensively in time with the activation of neurons at prior and subsequent levels.

At a psychological level the evidence is also clear-cut. There are many conditions under which higher-order units can be recognized faster than lower-order units. For example, in visual search through meaningful prose, semantic targets (e.g., a single word or any word belonging to a semantic category such as "fish") can be recognized faster than simpler visual graphic targets (e.g., a single letter) (Cohen 1970; Ball, Wood, and Smith 1975). Similar findings have been obtained in speech perception. Here phrase targets can be recognized faster than word targets, which in turn are recognized faster than syllable or phoneme targets (Savin and Bever 1970; Warren 1971; Foss and Swinney 1973; McNeill and Lindig 1973). Such results are possible because prose and speech are redundant, and convergence of lower-order units on higher-level units sometimes produces strong activation of a higher unit before any of its constituents can reach that level of activation, provided the system has chain parallel processing capacity. Evidence that the higher units feed back to assist in the strong activation of their constituents was obtained by Krueger (1970) and by Krueger and Weiss (1976). Their studies showed that subjects recognized a letter target faster when they searched through words than when they searched through nonwords composed of the same letters as the words, but in scrambled order. If letter processing were completed before word processing began, this would be impossible.

ATTENTIONAL SET

Selective Listening

You are standing listening to a group of friends at a crowded, noisy party. The conversation begins to bore you, and you shift your attention to another group of friends who are standing nearby. You want to find out if they are discussing something more interesting to you. Suddenly, some distance away, you hear your name mentioned. Immediately your attention is riveted on the conversation where they are talking about you. How are you able to listen to one message out of so many when all the messages are reaching your ears at once? You could account for your ability to listen to the first conversation on the basis of relative intensity—you were standing closer to this sound source than to any other. If someone shouted your name from across the room, your shift of attention could also be accounted for on the basis of relative intensity. However, since we can attend to the less intense of two messages, our auditory attention is obviously not the passive slave of physical intensity. Furthermore, even "involuntary" shifts of attention can be affected as much by the personal importance of the new message as by its relative intensity. The present section is concerned with the characteristics of our auditory selective attention capacity and with the mechanisms that make it selective.

The earliest experiments on selective attention were conducted by Cherry (1953) and Broadbent (1954, 1958). They presented subjects with two simultaneous messages, one to each ear. Subjects were often instructed to attend primarily to one ear. Selective listening instructions are frequently accompanied by instructions to repeat one of the messages verbally while listening to it (a shadowing task), or to monitor one or both of the message channels for the presence of some target item such as a digit or a tone (a monitoring task). As Cherry originally demonstrated, and as many others have since confirmed, it is far easier to listen selectively to one of two simultaneous messages when one message is presented to one ear and the other message to the other ear than when both messages are presented to the same ear or both messages to both ears. It is not that subjects are listening to auditory input from one *ear* or the other. The selective attention takes place at a higher level of the nervous system that can represent independently messages coming from different directions in auditory space. Treisman (1964*a*) demonstrated this by presenting three messages—one to the left ear, one to the right ear, and one equally divided between the two ears. The message presented to both ears had a subjective localization in the middle of the head. Subjects were perfectly able to listen to the midline message and ignore the messages to each ear, despite the fact that this could not possibly be accomplished by shutting off or attenuating the input from either ear. Thus one of the cues we use to listen selectively to one conversation or another at a party is the difference in the localization of the sound source.

Other physical cues besides auditory localization can be used as well. For example, Egan, Carterette, and Thwing demonstrated that we can listen selectively to one of two monaurally presented messages if the messages differ in pitch. Relative intensity of the two messages can also serve as a physical basis for selective listening. Thus even when the target message was softer than the interfering message, the advantage gained by the differential intensity cue offset the disadvantage of the lower intensity, and selective listening was easier than when both messages were equally intense. Of course, listening to the louder of two messages is considerably easier than listening to the softer of two messages or to one of two equally loud messages. Finally, voice quality can serve as a basis for selective listening. Subjects find it easier to attend to one message and ignore the other when the two messages are articulated by different speakers. In most cases two cues differentiating the two messages—such as different voice quality combined with a different direction in auditory space—facilitate selective listening more than either cue alone would do (Egan, Carterette, and Thwing 1954; Treisman 1964b; Moray 1970, pp. 39–73).

Physical acoustic cues are by no means the only basis of attentional set in selective listening. One can also make use of higher-level syntactic and semantic cues. It is possible to achieve some degree of success in listening to one of two messages spoken by the same speaker from the same location in auditory space, provided the message being listened to is an integrated prose passage rather than a list of random words. The contextual prediction process is discussed at many points in this text. This process provides the basis for selective priming of words that are likely to follow currently perceived words in the message one is following. This enables a selective attentional set to distinguish the message to be shadowed from the message to be ignored. Treisman compared selective listening for lists of words that differed in their degree of approximation to English prose (measured by the sequential probabilities of one word following another in English). The higher the transition probabilities between words, the easier it was to keep attention focused on the target message and avoid crossing over to the interfering message. Treisman also demonstrated that the points at which subjects crossed over to the interfering message tended to be those where the transition probabilities were lowest in the target message. In another experiment, subjects were instructed to listen to the (prose) message presented on one ear, and the prose passage was switched to the other ear somewhere in the middle. This produced a significant tendency for subjects to cross over to the other channel for one or two words at exactly the point where the message switched, though subjects always crossed back to the correct ear very quickly. Thus selective listening is influenced by attentional sets based on both physical acoustic features and learned cognitive associations (Treisman 1960, 1964b; Moray 1970, pp. 39–73).

Selective Looking

One form of selective attention in vision consists of making eye and head movements to center the stimulus being attended to on the fovea. The fovea is the central, most sensitive region of the retina. However, the focus of attention in visual perception is not always centered on the fovea, though this is undoubtedly the most frequent focus. One experimental paradigm used to study selective looking has been to present an array of 8 to 20 characters, typically letters or digits or both. Before or after the array is presented, the subject is instructed which character or characters to report. When subjects are instructed to report as much of the array as possible, 4 or 5 characters are the most that they can usually report correctly. This is the visual memory span or span of apprehension. The span is somewhat lower if responses are scored as correct only when they are placed in the proper positions in the array. It is somewhat higher under a free recall procedure (Sperling 1960).

In 1960, Sperling initiated the modern research on selective attention in vision by developing a partial-report procedure. Instead of having subjects attempt to recall as many of the items in the array as possible, Sperling cued them to report either the first, the second, or the third row of an array containing three rows of three items each. Averbach and Coriell extended the technique by using a visual indicator (a bar above the position) to cue recall of a single item from an array. These studies demonstrated that if the partial report cue is delivered before or within a few milliseconds after presentation of the array, subjects can report any character from the array with close to 100% probability. Of course for a whole report of large arrays, the probability of correctly reporting any particular item is far below 100%. So advance cuing of the location of the item to be reported can substantially enhance the probability of perceiving that item. Attentional sets based on physical location are as effective in biasing visual perception in the presence of a number of competing inputs as they are in biasing auditory perception under similar conditions. Furthermore, since a locational cue is effective in biasing visual perception even after the array is turned off, or when eye fixation is otherwise controlled (e.g., by instructions to fixate a particular point), we know that this visual selective attention can occur within the brain—not just as a result of eye movements. That is, we can bias our attention to either the top row or the bottom row of an array of characters while our eye remains fixated in between the two rows, or after the array has been turned off and all we can see is the persisting afterimage. An afterimage is "pasted" on the retina and moves when the eye moves, so there is no way to fixate on the center of the retina the afterimage of an item that was not originally presented there. However, we can selectively attend to any part of an afterimage that we wish to attend to and ignore other parts, at least within a region of 10° from the fovea. The peripheral limits (if any) of such location-selective attention have not yet been determined (Sperling 1960, 1963; Averbach and Coriell 1961; Averbach and Sperling 1961).

Another physical cue—namely, color—has been shown to yield some partial-report advantage. Subjects are presented with an array of red and black items. They use a cue, delivered either before or just after the array is presented, to report only the red items or only the black items. Subjects can achieve a level of performance on these target items higher than the level they achieve on the same items using a whole-report (nonselective attention) method. Location excepted, the physical dimensions of selective visual attention have not been extensively investigated. It appears likely that subjects can achieve some selective visual attention on the basis of other physical cues besides color, such as brightness, size, shape, and orientation. But location is the best cue for selective looking, as it is for selective listening (von Wright 1968, 1970, 1972; Keren 1976; Bongartz and Scheerer 1976).

Selective visual perception of multiple-item arrays on the basis of semantic cues is also possible (though in some cases it has produced only small differences). When subjects are instructed in advance to report only the digits from a briefly presented mixed array of letters and digits, they are more likely to report any given digit *correctly* than when they are instructed to report both letters and digits, or when they are given the partial-report cue after the array has been presented. Semantic (learned categorical) cuing of this type appears mainly to benefit the free recall of the items for which one is set. It may not benefit recall of the correct position of these items in the array, whereas physical attribute cuing benefits both. This difference agrees with the hypothesis that semantic attentional sets place biases on nodes in semantic memory that are activated by appropriate input from anywhere on the retina and thus contain no position information. By definition, locational cuing places biases on nodes that retain positional information. The results on color cuing suggest that color-specific nodes are also location specific, whereas semantic nodes are not (von Wright 1968, 1970, 1972; Keren 1976; Bongartz and Scheerer 1976).

Why is the selective attention advantage of semantic cuing in these mixed-array studies so small? We know that semantic expectations play an important role in reading, as they do in speech recognition. Selective listening on the basis of semantic cues is a robust effect, albeit smaller than selective listening on the basis of physical-attribute, particularly locational, cues. Furthermore, we know from studies of visual search that we can selectively scan (skim) an array for one set of targets faster than we can recognize every character in the array. Finally, when we detect the target, we can report its location in the array rather accurately (Sperling et al. 1971). This is selective looking based on a semantic attentional set that benefits both item and position recognition.

So what's going on to produce such a small semantic cuing advantage in the mixed-array, multiple-item recognition paradigm? Frankly, I don't know. At any given time, visual attentional set can probably be spread out over a larger or smaller, compact connected region of visual space, but it probably cannot be divided among several unconnected regions of visual space. Imagine a locational set not for four positions in a row, but for position two in row one, position four in row two, position one in row three, and position three in row four. Performance under this kind of locational attentional set might be as poor as performance under other types of physical-attribute sets. Conversely, performance under either semantic or physical-attribute attentional sets should be much improved if the cued items were in a locationally compact clump, even if the locations were not cued in advance. And so it is (Bongartz and Scheerer 1976). This explains why locational sets have been superior to other physical-attribute sets and semantic sets, but it does not explain why these other physical attribute sets are superior to semantic sets in the mixed-array paradigm. That remains a mystery. However, it is clear that both semantic and physical-attribute attentional sets operate to guide attention in both vision and audition.

Set and Reaction Time

The conclusion here is clear: for S-R associations of low to moderate strength (that is, all low to moderate levels of practice or S-R compatibility), the narrower the attentional set, the faster the reaction time. As I mentioned earlier in the chapter, increasing the number of S-R associations for which a subject must be set increases the average reaction time to any given stimulus (Merkel 1885; Hick 1952; Hyman 1953). For example, if one associates each of one's 10 fingers with a different light, reaction time will be slower when one must be set for all 10 lights than when one can be set for 6. Six in turn is slower than 2, and so on. However, well-learned associations (such as can be achieved by extensive practice on key-pressing tasks or such as pronouncing a familiar word given auditory or visual presentation of it) result in virtually the same reaction times regardless of the number of alternatives. Thus strong associations appear to be best facilitated by a general set to perform the task. They cannot be facilitated by a further narrowing of the set of alternative stimuli or responses, though prior knowledge of stimulus location does decrease stimulus-naming time (Mowbray and Rhoades 1959; Mowbray 1960; Davis, Moray, and Treisman 1961; Eriksen and Hoffman 1974).

For low- to moderate-strength associations, anything that increases the subject's attentional set towards a particular association will facilitate reaction time. Thus increasing the probability of presenting one signal as opposed to another decreases the reaction time for the more probable signal and increases reaction time for less probable signals. Similarly, if the same signal is repeated from the previous trial, reaction time to that signal is reduced. This so-called *repetition effect* in reaction time often decreases somewhat with increasing intertrial intervals up to 10 seconds. This decrease may be due to passive decay of the priming effects of prior activation of an S-R pathway. Or it may occur because the focus of attentional set has a greater opportunity to shift actively from the previous S-R association. The repetition effect is to some extent a special case of anticipation effects in general, since when sequences are devised that minimize the frequency of repetitions (so that nonrepetitions are much more probable than repetitions), the magnitude of the repetition effect is substantially reduced. Furthermore, when subjects definitely expect some event other than a repetition, reactions to a repetition of the prior trial are not especially fast, while reactions to the anticipated stimuli are (Hyman 1953; Bertelson and Renkin 1966; Smith 1968; Keele 1969; Keele and Boies 1972).

Perceptual Tuning

Simple unitary stimuli. Appropriate attentional set almost always improves reaction time. It has been much more difficult to demonstrate that it improves the accuracy of perception for a briefly presented stimulus when the subject has unlimited time to respond. Of course, the probability of choosing the correct alternative in a perceptual recognition task is increased by restricting the number of alternatives to two. However, this increased probability of correct choice may simply be due to the narrower range of alternatives. In a number of studies that have presented a single, unitary stimulus at a time, narrower attentional set has had no beneficial effect when the data have been corrected for chance guessing (Holloway 1970; Haggard 1974). Another method used to investigate the perceptual tuning hypothesis has been to see if presenting the alternatives before the stimulus facilitates perceptual recognition more than presenting them afterwards. The consensus seems to be that it does not (Lawrence and Coles 1954; Lawrence and La Berge 1956; Long, Reid, and Henneman 1960; Egeth 1967; Allport 1971; Smith et al. 1976).

Moore and Massaro demonstrated that subjects can judge two attributes of a test tone simultaneously as well as they can judge either attribute in isolation. Allport got similar results in studies of visual perception using the attributes of color and form. He found that subjects could perceive color and form simultaneously as well as they could perceive either attribute alone. However, subjects did not perceive two form attributes together as well as they perceived them separately. Allport interprets these results as indicating that parallel processing of form and color occurs without loss of efficiency, while the processing of two form dimensions may result in some mutual inhibition and possibly force serial processing of each form. Obviously, if (as I have argued at several points in this text) we can often process two or more different dimensions in parallel without reduction in quality, narrowing the task to the processing of only one dimension at a time will not produce a beneficial set effect (Moore and Massaro 1973; Allport 1971).

If a narrowing of attentional set in terms of relevant (qualitative) stimulus dimensions often fails to improve the perception of simple single stimuli, so does restriction on "irrelevant" dimensions, such as location and modality. Shiffrin and Grantham demonstrated that subjects could detect the occurrence of a simple stimulus in any of three different modalities (vision, audition, and touch) simultaneously as well as they could detect the occurrence of a stimulus in only one of these modalities at a time. The target stimuli were a dot, a tone, and a vibrotactile stimulus. In another condition, subjects monitored all three modalities simultaneously for the absence of a particular stimulus in one of the modalities. They monitored for absence in all three modalities as accurately as they monitored any single modality for the absence of a stimulus. Shiffrin, Pisoni, and Casteneda-Mendez found no beneficial effect on recognition of one of four stop-consonants ("ba," "pa," "da," "ga") when subjects knew which ear the stimulus was to be presented to. This was true even when a distracting speech sound was presented to the other ear. However, the distracting sound (wa) was quite unlike any of the targets. This probably would have prevented it from exerting a strong distracting effect under any conditions. Furthermore, when subjects knew which ear the stimulus would be presented to, there were two intervals during which the presentation could occur, and subjects had to shift their attention rapidly from the right ear to the left ear in order to have an appropriate attentional set regarding the ear of presentation. Subjects may have been unable to shift their attention as rapidly as the circumstances required, or they may not have considered it worthwhile to perform this shift and so may merely have maintained a constant set to attend to both ears throughout. Finally, there is reason to believe that it may require several seconds of selective listening for attention to become fully focused on the attended-to ear. Thus experiments involving presentation of a single stimulus may be far from ideal for demonstrating the positive effects of attentional set (Shiffrin and Grantham 1974; Shiffrin, Pisoni, and Casteneda-Mendez 1974; Treisman, Squire, and Green 1974).

The following generalization emerges from these studies of perceptual tuning: when simple unitary stimuli are presented with no competing stimuli, or when the distracting stimuli are very unlike the target stimulus—either because they are presented in different stimulus modalities or because they are grossly dissimilar within a modality—attentional set has little or no beneficial effect on accuracy (though it often improves response speed). Attentional set does bias subjects to perceive items appropriate to the set. But it need not improve the accuracy of discriminating among items within the set, when the alternative stimuli are simple unitary stimuli.

Complex stimuli. In contrast to these findings a substantial beneficial effect of attentional set has been demonstrated for more complex stimuli, such as photographs of real objects. Even here the beneficial effect of appropriate attentional set is obtained only if the actual target picture is presented before the stimulus. The effect is not obtained if the name of the object—but not its picture—is presented before the stimulus (Egeth and Smith 1967; Pachella 1975).

Multiple stimuli. Complex "single" stimuli are probably essentially equivalent to multiple stimuli in the sense that not all the incoming information can be processed in parallel without some loss of accuracy. As long as the capacity limit for simultaneous attention is not exceeded, a broader attentional set will not substantially impair performance accuracy. However, when more stimuli are impinging on an organism than it can process at one time, an appropriate attentional set will allow selection among competing inputs for processing and improve perceptual accuracy. I have already discussed a good deal of evidence in support of just such a perceptual tuning effect with multiple competing inputs in the cases of two-channel selective listening and partial report from large visual arrays. I have also mentioned that Allport found a divided attentional deficit when the subject was processing two forms, as opposed to one form, at a time, though not when the subject was processing a single form and its color. Long found that subjects discriminated between two similar tone frequencies and two similar light intensities less well when both the tone and light stimuli were presented together than when they were presented separately (Allport 1971; Long 1975, 1976).

A new method of data analysis in a recent series of experiments by Sorkin, Moray, and their colleagues has clarified considerably those conditions that do and do not produce impaired accuracy with broader attentional set. If one is attempting to detect targets (e.g., tones in noise, letters in streams of digits) in two or more channels (e.g., the two ears) simultaneously, detection of targets in any one channel will be less accurate than when one's attention is set to detect targets on only one channel. However, that *divided attention deficit* occurs almost exclusively on trials where a target also occurred on the other channel, or where the subject imagined that one had occurred (false alarm). When no target occurs on the other channel and the subject does not think one did occur (a correct rejection), there is little or no decrement due to the divided attentional set. It is the process of attending to a second channel when the subject thinks a stimulus is occurring there that produces the biggest divided attention deficit. This deficit is not caused by the fact that there is less attentional set for each channel before the stimulus is presented. Missed targets on the other channel produce results intermediate between detections (correct or false) on that channel and correct rejections, also on that channel. This is probably because missed targets do succeed in attracting some attention, although they do not reach the threshold for detection (Sorkin, Pohlmann, and Gilliom 1973; Sorkin, Pohlmann, and Woods 1976; Pohlmann and Sorkin 1976; Moray, Fitter, Ostry, Favreau, and Nagy 1976; Ostry, Moray, and Marks 1976).

Selective attention deficit.   Even under a set to attend to a particular channel, events occurring on an "unattended" channel can lower the detectability of events on the attended channel, as compared to a single-channel condition. This is the so-called *selective attentional deficit* as opposed to the previously discussed *divided attentional deficit* (Moray et al. 1976; Ostry et al. 1976; Holloway 1972). Imperfect selective attention probably occurs for the same reason as imperfect divided attention—namely, because even subthreshold stimuli often succeed in attracting some attention, and this can lower the detectability of targets on a channel for which one is attentionally set. Some of the previously discussed studies by Treisman show that an attentional set to listen to one ear only attenuates, but does not completely block, central processing of the input from the other ear. If the strength of contextual association from prior words in the attended ear is greater to a word in the unattended ear than it is to the simultaneously presented word in the attended ear, the word from the unattended ear may be the one that captures the subject's attention (Treisman 1960). Several studies have shown that associatively related words on an unattended channel can affect the processing of words on an attended channel—speeding up or slowing down recognition, or biasing the perceived meaning of ambiguous words (Lewis 1970, 1972; Treisman, Squire, and Green 1974; Bradshaw 1974; Dallas and Merikle 1976). Thus there will frequently be a selective attention deficit in single-channel attention due to the presence of a distracting channel, because attentional set does not completely block processing of stimuli presented on the unattended channel. Selective attention only gives an advantage to stimuli on the attended channel; it does not completely block stimuli on the unattended channel. This has the functional advantage of permitting you to perceive an event on the unattended channel if it is especially relevant to your interests (for example, if somebody speaks your name)—while you continue to perceive events on the attended channel (Moray 1959; Loftus 1974; Treisman 1960).

Overview of Attentional Set

The purpose of attentional set appears to be to produce selective processing of a subset of information when the total incoming information exceeds our capacity for efficient simultaneous (parallel) processing. There would appear to be little reason to inhibit the processing of information coming in over a channel to which we are not attending, provided there is no simultaneously presented information to be processed on an attended channel (perceptual or cognitive). Except for a slight slowing of reaction time, there is no evidence to suggest that we cannot see and hear stimuli presented on unattended channels with normal accuracy, provided no competing stimuli are presented on an attended channel. Neither does a narrower attentional set produce more accurate perception in the absence of competing stimuli, though it does appear to shorten recognition time. Attentional set appears to give stimuli that fall within its bounds a slight head start in the perceptual activation process—a partial activation *(priming)*—without necessarily altering the ultimate level of activation and the detectability or discriminability of stimuli. (An exception occurs when there are competing stimuli that exceed the capacity for simultaneous processing.)

Although the evidence is far from conclusive, Neisser believes that attentional set is primarily positive—priming of the processing of certain information—rather than negative—attentuation of the processing of information outside the informational set (Neisser 1976; Neisser and Becklen 1975). This positive priming of some nodes may have the secondary effect of inhibiting nodes outside the attentional set. However, the inhibition comes later than the positive priming and may be a secondary consequence of priming some nodes (which then inhibit other nodes) rather than a basic mechanism of attentional set (Posner and Snyder 1975). The task of specifying the exact roles of excitation and inhibition in attentional set is still in the future.

SUMMARY

1 There are internal as well as external sources of attentional distraction. Improving one's motivation to study may be worth the price of some increased external distraction from a radio or a friend. The best way to focus your attention on a subject is to think of ways in which knowing that subject will help you to accomplish some of your life goals. And if you don't have any life goals . . . you're in a heap of trouble.

2 We habituate (do not pay attention) to expected stimuli that are irrelevant to our goals, but our attention is attracted to expected stimuli that are relevant to our goals.

3 Attention is a decision process that limits the number of ideas we can think about (nodes we can activate) at one time. This limit is roughly four items in visual perception, but it probably varies for different tasks.

4 Attentional set is priming (partial activation) of a target set of nodes; it gives these nodes a head start toward full activation and thus facilitates the perception of the stimuli they represent.

5 The lower the strength of the relevant associations, the more severe the attentional limit. Several high-strength decisions can be made in parallel, but only one low-strength decision can be made at one time. Conscious attention appears to be necessary for those relatively new and unpracticed decisions that require sequential processing.

6 We have the capacity to engage in very rapid visual search, processing about four items in parallel every 50 msec as we look for a target item from a particular set. However, this association from target stimulus to the required detection response must have high-strength, with no interference, as when the target and distractor sets are different and held constant (consistent mapping). When the target set changes from trial to trial (variable mapping), visual search becomes much slower—about 100 msec per item.

7 Contextual feedback from higher nodes facilitates the activation of their lower-level constituent nodes. For example, we perceive a target letter faster when it occurs in a word than when it occurs in a nonword.

8 We can selectively listen to or look at one of several competing messages by biasing our attentional set to messages that come from a particular direction or

that have other physical or semantic properties. Attentional set probably results from the advance priming of nodes that encode messages in the attentional set.

9 Attentional set (priming) speeds perceptual activation of nodes in the attended (expected) set and may retard activation of nodes in the unattended (unexpected) set.

10 Attentional set helps the subject to perceive stimuli more accurately within the attended set when there are potentially distracting stimuli, or when the subject thinks there are distracting stimuli, but not otherwise. Attention to (full activation of) one node appears to interfere with the activation of another node, but attentional set (priming or partial activation) only gives a slight temporary advantage to stimuli in the attended-to set. This advantage *speeds* activation of expected stimuli without necessarily improving the asymptotic *accuracy* of perception when there are no distracting stimuli. Unexpected stimuli can easily overcome this slight bias and be perceived, provided there is no competition from expected stimuli. However, the slight bias is critical in determing what is perceived when there are two or more competing stimuli. This selection between competing messages is probably the primary purpose of attentional set.

CHAPTER 7
SHORT-TERM MEMORY

OBJECTIVES

1 To define short-term activational (primary) memory as a persistence of activation in a set of recently activated nodes.

2 To discuss visual-sensory (iconic) memory, including persistence of vision and afterimages. The discussion will consider (a) the storage capacity of iconic memory, (b) the role played by perceptual scanning of iconic memory in establishing a longer-lasting visual memory, (c) the location in the brain of iconic memory, and (d) its nonassociative character.

3 To present the evidence for preattentional auditory-sensory (echoic) memory. To discuss whether it is a nonassociative activity trace analogous to iconic memory, and whether it is different from the trace underlying phonetic short-term memory for attended material.

4 To discuss the somewhat higher-level graphic (visual) short-term memory for verbal material. This is the longer-lasting memory derived from the visual scanning process.

5 To discuss phonetic short-term memory. This is the type of memory that you use to dial a telephone number that you have just heard. It appears to involve nodes at least at the featural, segmental, word, and phrase levels.

6 To discuss some associative properties of phonetic short-term memory, but to explain how this type of memory could result from a nonassociative activational memory within an associative memory, using a context-sensitive code.

7 To discuss briefly the concept of working memory—short-term memory as it functions in chunking (learning), retrieval and thinking.

Well, here we go again—beginning another chapter. But this one is different from all the others. In keeping with the spirit of our topic, all the concepts and principles taught in this chapter have been especially designed to self-destruct in your mind in less than a minute! So you'd better enjoy them while you can. Seriously, what were you thinking about just before you started reading this chapter? Chances are you can remember fairly accurately. However, you probably have little or no idea what you were thinking about just before you began reading chapter 3 (unless you always think the same thing before you begin any chapter). This ability to remember very recent events is called *short-term memory,* or sometimes *primary memory.*

Presumably you do not store associations from the node "recent event" to the node activated by a current event. Or if you do, such associations have a rather distinctive status, since they must always be rapidly forgotten as subsequent events interfere with these associations. More likely, recently activated nodes have some degree of activation that persists to a diminishing extent for a short period during which the mind is concentrating attention on other thoughts. For example, after you read one word or phrase and go on to read the next word or phrase, the nodes representing the first word or phrase probably remain activated for a time. Otherwise it would be hard for you to understand and encode the sentence as a whole. Short-term memory allows us to integrate information distributed over a period of time and encode it as a single chunk. If we didn't have some temporal integration capacity of this kind, information transmission by speech, which uses an inherently sequential code, would probably be impossible.

The main purpose of short-term memory is not to give us high scores on visual or auditory memory span tests, or even to allow us to remember a telephone number as we dial it. The main purpose is presumably to encode meaningful event sequences into higher-order chunks (concepts). However, most cognitive research on short-term memory capacity has used random arrays and sequences of letters, digits, or forms, so we must base our theoretical conclusions on such evidence. There is no reason to believe that this restriction in scope is misleading, and there are some substantial advantages to using these materials over more complex ones, but our theories are surely incomplete as a consequence. The first four sections of the present chapter will be concerned with short-term memory for random arrays and sequences. The fifth section will attempt to integrate all types of short-term memory into the larger category of active memory. The sixth and last section will briefly consider the role of short-term memory in thinking (retrieval and inference) and in long-term memory acquisition. Both fall under the heading of *working memory* (memory that works for us to accomplish other objectives, rather than being an end in itself).

The first two sections are concerned with iconic and echoic memory. I consider these to be largely peripheral, preattentive, sensory memories. For example, retinal receptors (especially rods) remain in an activated state for a short time after the light stimulus ceases, like the decaying phosphors on your TV screen after you turn the set off. This persistence of sensation is called *iconic memory* because it so completely mimics the persistence of the stimulus itself (it is an *icon*). There may be an analogue in the auditory realm —persistence of auditory sensation or *echoic memory*. Both iconic and echoic memory are considered preattentional because the memory traces are established by the stimulus without its being necessary for the subject to attend to the stimulus.

The next two sections are concerned with short-term memory for visual and auditory material that was attended to at the time of presentation. Such short-term memory is generally longer lasting than iconic and echoic memory. It is also less susceptible to disruption by subsequent stimuli, unless these subsequent stimuli are also attended to (processed in some way). Furthermore, postattentional short-term memory is more sensitive to interference by conceptually similar material, but less sensitive to interference by sensorily similar material, than either preattentional iconic or echoic memory. That is, flashes of light disrupt iconic memory for letters, while noise has no effect on it. Postattentional visual short-term memory for alphanumeric characters (letters and digits) is little affected by either flashes of light or noise. However, it can be strongly disrupted by subsequent processing of other alphanumeric material, especially but not exclusively in the same sensory modality. To reflect the presumably higher, more conceptual, less sensory level of this type of memory, we refer to it as *graphic short-term memory* or as *phonetic short-term memory*, depending on whether the input was visual or auditory.

ICONIC MEMORY

Afterimages

Stare at some form fixedly (without moving your body, head, or eyes) for 30 seconds or so. Now look away at a blank wall. If you maintained a fairly constant fixation, and if the wall is brightly lit and the contrast between the form and the wall is high, you should see an afterimage—a faint image having the same form as the thing you stared at. Visual persistence and afterimages have long been studied by perceptual psychologists, but George Sperling's classic work in 1960 was very influential in producing systematic consideration of these phenomena as examples of sensory memory.

There are both positive and negative afterimages. If you stare at a light square on a dark background, the positive afterimage will be a light square on a dark background. This will be followed by the negative afterimage—a dark square on a light background. The initial visual sensation persists for a very brief period (usually less than a second) following the termination of a stimulus. This is what produces the positive afterimage, which thereafter can change to a negative (reversed contrast) afterimage. Sometimes there is more than one cycle of positive and negative afterimages.

Persistence of Vision

The initial persistence of vision is often sharply distinguished from subsequent negative or positive afterimages. The physiological mechanism of the initial persistence of vision is presumed to produce a persistence of activation of the neurons originally activated by the stimulus at one or more levels of the nervous system. Subsequent negative afterimages are presumed to result from fatigue of the elements previously activated. It is not known whether subsequent positive afterimages have a different physiological mechanism than the original persistence of vision. It seems parsimonious to assume that both persistence of vision and positive afterimages are produced by the continuing activation of neurons first activated by the original stimulus, while negative afterimages are produced by a depression in the activation of these neurons.

Many memory psychologists who study visual sensory memory and persistence of vision do not refer to these phenomena as afterimages. I shall use Ulric Neisser's term—*iconic memory*—to refer to them, but remember that we do not know whether iconic memory differs from what perceptual psychologists mean by the term "positive afterimage." Furthermore, studies of iconic memory have typically concentrated on memory for form information independent of whether the phenomenal contrast of the forms is dark on light or light on dark. Thus most experimental studies of iconic memory have not rigorously excluded the possibility of contributions from negative afterimages. Under the conditions of many experiments, iconic memory may consist of an unknown mixture of persistence of vision and negative afterimages.

The study of iconic memory after Sperling differs in one potentially important respect from earlier perceptual studies of afterimages. In studies of iconic memory the original vision stimulus is presented for a very short period, whereas in studies of afterimages it is fixated for many seconds or tens of seconds. A long fixation produces a strong negative afterimage, whereas the brief fixation characteristic of iconic memory experiments is presumed to produce persistence of the original positive image with little or no negative afterimage. If this is true, then studies of iconic memory are concerned strictly with persistence of vision and not with the fatigue or adaptational mechanisms that produce negative afterimages.

Capacity of Iconic Memory

Iconic memory has a substantial information storage capacity for a brief period after the visual stimulus is terminated. For example, Averbach and Sperling presented an array of 18 letters, as illustrated in figure 7–1, for 50

```
        K   D   Z              B   J   L

        N   S   P              W   G   X

        T   M   R              C   V   D
```

Fig. 7.1   Letter array of the type used by Averbach and Sperling to study iconic memory.
At various delays following a 50 msec presentation of such an array, subjects were
cued to report the letter that had been presented in the cued location.

msec at a very high level of intensity and contrast with the background.
Either immediately upon termination of the stimulus array or at delays of 0.1,
0.2, 0.3, 0.5, 1.2, or 5 sec following the array, they cued the subjects to report
which letter occurred in one of the 18 possible positions. (Subjects were cued
using combinations of tones, so as not to disrupt the icon, but it is also
possible under some conditions to use visual cues, such as faint little arrows
pointing to the positions to be recalled.)

   If the probability of correctly recalling the cued letter is multiplied by
the number of letters in the array (18), one obtains an estimate of the number
of letters available in iconic memory at various delays following presentation
of the array. The results of the experiment are illustrated in figure 7–2 for two
conditions: where the fields preceding and following the stimulus array were

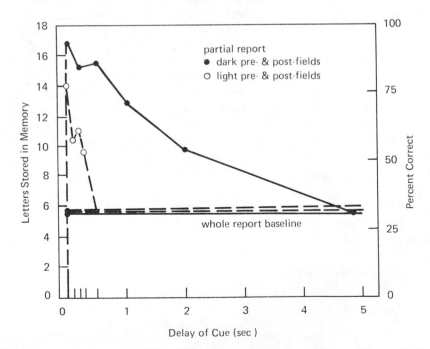

Fig. 7.2   Decay of iconic memory to the whole-report baseline under conditions of light
versus dark pre- and postfields. (From Averbach and Sperling [1961] by permission.)

light and where they were dark. Figure 7–2 also demonstrates the number of letters that are available when subjects attempt to recall as many letters as possible from the array using the method of *whole report* rather than the *partial report* procedure developed by Sperling.

The results are striking. Immediately following presentation, from 14 to 17 of the 18 letters appear to be available in iconic storage. However, the partial report procedure demonstrates that visual iconic memory decays precipitously, especially with light pre- and postexposure fields, which presumably create more interference with the icon than do dark pre- and postexposure fields. When light pre- and postfields are used, the iconic memory decays within half a second to an asymptotic level of approximately five items. This is precisely the number of items that can be reported using the whole-report procedure characteristic of earlier visual memory span (span of apprehension) studies. Visual memory span, as assessed by the whole-report procedure, is not much affected by a delay in instruction to report. Presumably this is because a subject begins scanning iconic memory immediately, and this scanning transfers the memory to some longer-lasting form. If by means of the partial report procedure the subject's attention is directed to a particular item in the array shortly after exposure, he can scan it (read it out of iconic memory) with a high degree of accuracy. However, the number of items that can be scanned from iconic memory and retained in the longer-lasting memory seems to be limited to about five. This limit appears to be the same regardless of the rate of decay of iconic memory, since the same limit was approached under the conditions of either light or dark pre- and postfields (Averbach and Sperling 1961).

Iconic memory is defined as the rapidly decaying memory component in excess of the visual memory span (amounting to approximately 10 or 12 items in the Averbach and Sperling experiment). The duration of this iconic memory can be anywhere from a few milliseconds (for arrays with low intensity and low contrast from the ground, short exposure duration, and light pre- and postfields) to several seconds (for characters presented at high intensity and high contrast, long durations, and dark pre- and postfields). Interestingly enough, the persistence of iconic memory beyond stimulus offset is largely invariant with changes in the duration of the stimulus that created it, provided the original stimulus was well above the threshold for clear visibility (Sperling 1960, 1967; Haber and Standing 1969).

Scanning Iconic Memory: Perception

The rapid visual scanning process that converts fragile iconic memory for about five characters into a longer-lasting memory is apparently not silent verbal rehearsal (prouncing the letter names to oneself). They are thought to be different for two reasons. First, visual scanning appears to be much faster than verbal rehearsal—five characters per 50 msec versus one character per

100 msec for verbal rehearsal of familiar sequences. Verbal rehearsal is even slower when the task consists of pronouncing from a new visual array. Second, visual scanning is apparently a limited-capacity parallel process, while verbal rehearsal certainly seems to be serial (Sperling 1963; Sperling et al. 1971; Shiffrin 1976). Furthermore, the longer-lasting memory created by scanning is apparently (visual) graphic short-term memory not (auditory) phonetic short-term memory, since the graphic memory span of 5 alphanumerical items is well below the phonetic memory span of 6.5 alphanumeric characters, and since intrusion errors made in recall tend to be graphically, not phonetically, similar to the correct item, unless the subject has deliberately rehearsed the material (Steinheiser 1971; Wolford and Hollingsworth 1974).

The limited-capacity attentional process in visual scanning should not be considered all-or-none. Probably all the characters in an array get processed to some extent. The capacity limit of about five characters refers to the number that are activated to the point of accurate identification with respect to both form and position. When position can be ignored (as in tasks that score for items perceived without regard to position or tasks that only require the subject to decide which of two target characters was in an array), then estimates of the number of characters scanned in a single brief exposure are about double the ordinary visual memory span (Estes and Taylor 1964; Graves 1976).

The perceptibility of any single character in an array is affected by all of the variables one might expect to affect visual perception: size, contrast, intensity of illumination, delay of report and order of report (for arrays containing more than five characters), distance of a character from the fixation point (retinal position), and the number of other characters in the array and their distance from the target character (Sperling 1963; Estes and Wolford 1971; Sakitt 1976). End characters and characters next to blank spaces are particularly likely to be perceived. This suggests the presence of some kind of mutually inhibitory interaction between the nodes representing nearby characters, with the extent of inhibition decreasing as distance between characters increases. Presumably it is this mutually inhibitory interaction among the nodes representing characters in the array that often places the upper limit of around five characters in the visual memory span. Under many conditions five simultaneously activated chunk nodes for characters may be all that can be sustained against the inhibition these nodes generate on each other and on other nodes. Some factor such as this must be limiting visual memory span to account for the fact that the large differences in longevity of iconic memory produced by light versus dark pre- and postfields have so little effect on whole report. On the other hand, Sakitt obtained large differences in visual memory span (0 to 7.5 characters!) with very large changes in level of illumination (from about absolute threshold to 7 log units above threshold). So visual factors can have a major effect on span as well (Averbach and Sperling 1961; Sakitt 1976).

These physical sensory characteristics of visual arrays are not the only important variables that influence visual perception. What we see can be strongly influenced by attentional set—especially when there is more to be seen than can be seen at once. This is demonstrated by the fact that subjects can use the partial report cue (e.g., "report only the second row") to achieve far better performance on the cued characters than they can achieve on those same characters in whole report. The same capacity for attentional control of perception produces poorer performance on characters outside the focus of attention.

Furthermore, requiring subjects to perform some secondary task at or just before presentation of an array can reduce the efficiency of visual scanning. Secondary tasks have not always reduced the accuracy of reporting characters from briefly exposed arrays, but they have done so often enough to demonstrate that visual scanning does draw on some of the same limited attentional capacities as other tasks. For example, requiring a subject to retain a string of (auditory or visual) letters or digits in short term memory at the time an array is presented will reduce visual memory span for the characters in the array. This holds true even when the requirement to report the string first is lifted just before the subject is asked to report the array. Just having a short-term memory load (a set of activated nodes) at the time the array is presented reduces the subject's visual memory span. (This may be due to inhibition from the previously activated nodes.) Presentation of a simple tone at the time of the array does not interfere with perception of the characters in the array, but the requirement to respond to that tone (a monitoring task) does (Scarborough 1972; Chow and Murdock 1975, 1976).

Location of Iconic Memory

Where is iconic memory located? A number of findings indicate that long-lasting afterimages are localized in the retina, and it would be parsimonious to assume a retinal location for iconic storage as well, since a known physiological mechanism exists that could produce such iconic memory. The mechanism is as follows: light bleaches the pigment molecules in the visual receptors (rods and cones) of the eye, and this activates the peripheral neurons of the visual system. This activation in the retina is known to persist for some time following termination of the stimulus, possibly because the rods and cones require time to become unbleached (Julesz 1971, p. 34). On the basis of our physiological knowledge concerning pigment bleaching and generator potentials in rods and cones, one would expect that most, if not all, of iconic memory is located in the rods and cones themselves.

Sakitt verified this expectation by studying the vision of a person whose eyes had rods but no cones. Rods are used primarily in night vision, while cones are used primarily in daylight. Since rods reach maximum activation level at a much lower level of illumination than cones, this person had considerable difficulty seeing in ordinary daylight, much as you have difficulty seeing in glare. When stimuli were presented in ordinary daylight, she did not see them; but if she closed her eyes after the stimulus was presented, she could then see an icon of the presented stimulus! In fact, she used this technique in normal seeing by going around blinking (Sakitt 1976).

Actually, there is no mystery about why this takes place. At moderate daylight levels of background illumination, rods are at a maximum level for activation of visual neurons. At this level there is still plenty of unbleached pigment that will be differentially bleached by presentation of a stimulus. Since the chemical process that converts bleached pigment back into unbleached pigment takes time, after the eyes are closed, the rods that have received the extra bleaching will maintain their potential to activate visual neurons somewhat better than the other rods. This allows the icon to emerge from the background. These results indicate that the iconic storage—at least in this case—is entirely retinal, since the visual stimulus was not registered by the higher levels of the nervous system at the time it was presented. A closely related demonstration was previously made in normal subjects. A form that is below recognition threshold when presented against a masking field can be made visible by terminating the masking field within 100 msec of the test flash (which presented the form) (Standing and Dodwell 1972; Turvey, Michaels, and Port 1974). Again, since the form was not visible at the time it was presented, we know that the location of the icon was peripheral to the level of the nervous system where activation of nodes produces form recognition—and a retinal location is most plausible.

Some researchers have claimed that iconic memory cannot be retinal because the icon for an array presented to one eye can be masked by interfering input to the other eye. This reasoning is invalid because input from both eyes is combined at a more central level in the brain before it is "read." Hence, our ability to read an icon in the left eye would be interfered with by a masking stimulus delivered to the right eye (Schiller 1965; Turvey 1973; Sakitt 1976, pp. 271–72).

One final piece of evidence consistent with a retinal location for iconic memory is that the image moves when the eye moves, instead of remaining in the location where it was presented. This shows that the icon is stored in a level of the visual system that has a moving, retina-based coordinate system, rather than the more stationary, real-world coordinate system characteristic of visual perception (where images do not change perceived location just because the eye moves). This and other more complex and more convincing evidence supports a retinal location for much or all of iconic storage (Sakitt 1976).

Iconic Memory Is Nonassociative

A retinal location for iconic storage strongly suggests that iconic memory is nonassociative. If an A is presented to two different locations, presumably two different but equivalent pattern representatives will be activated at these locations. Furthermore, there are presumably no associations from the character representative in one position to character representatives in adjacent positions. Somehow we know which locations are adjacent to each other, but the character representatives within the locations have no associations one to another.

The hypothesis that iconic memory is nonassociative has been tested directly. Under conditions fostering iconic memory, subjects were presented with two rows of alternating letters and digits (fig. 7.3). Recall of a character was cued in two ways. Both ways involved presenting a cue character in one location and instructing the subject to recall the character to its immediate right. In one condition the cue was the correct character for the location it was in. For example, in figure 7.3 the cue might be "3 in the second position from the left in the first row." In the other condition a dummy character (either the letter A or the number 8) was presented, which subjects knew had not been in any location. For example, in figure 7.3, 8 might be presented as the number in the second position of the first row. If all the cue character does is signal the location to be reported from iconic memory, and if there are no associations between character representatives in adjacent positions, there is no reason why a correct cue character should produce better recall than a dummy character—and in fact it did not (Wickelgren and Whitman 1970). No associations were formed between the adjacent characters in iconic memory. The memory is nonassociative; the pattern for an item is impressed upon a memory location.

The foregoing experiment studied visual memory at delays ranging from 200 msec, where most of the memory was iconic, to 2 sec, where iconic memory was essentially gone. The same equivalence of the two cuing conditions was obtained at all delays. This suggests that, at least under these conditions, even the more stable component of visual memory does not involve associations between character representatives. However, it would be premature, and probably erroneous, to generalize from this result to the hypothesis that all longer-lasting visual image memory is nonassociative. Some aspects of image memory may be nonassociative, but other aspects are likely to be associative.

Fig. 7.3 Alternating letter and digit array for testing the nonassociative nature of iconic memory. In all conditions subjects were tested by presenting a cue character in a particular position of the array (e.g., F in position three of the first row) and were asked to recall the character that had been presented in the adjacent position to the right (e.g., 9). Subjects recalled the character in the adjacent position equally accurately whether they were given the correct cue character for the cue position (e.g., F in position three, top row) or an incorrect dummy character for that position (e.g., A in position three top row).

Central Iconic Memory

Most of the iconic memory extensively studied since Sperling's classic research is probably located in the retinal receptors, especially where the storage lasts for 200 msec or more. However, this does not disprove the existence of a more central, neural activational memory for images.

Some demonstrations of central iconic memory establish the central locus of the memory by testing properties of images that could not be stored in the retinal receptors. One of these properties is depth perception induced by the disparity between the locations of stimulation of the two eyes. The depth of an image can only be determined in the brain, where information from the two retinas is combined. Another property is motion perception, which is no better encoded in a retinal receptor image than it is in a single photograph. Central iconic storage lasting 50 to about 100 msec has been demonstrated using these and other properties (Ross and Hogben 1974; Hogben, Julesz, and Ross 1976; Treisman, Russell, and Green 1975).

ECHOIC MEMORY

Like many people, I seldom pay much attention to someone's name unless I think I will need to know it later. People's other characteristics are simply more important and more interesting to me than their names. So it happens fairly often that when I am introduced to someone, I realize a split second *after* I hear the name that I should have been paying more attention to the name at the time it was spoken. If I realize this soon enough, I can sometimes "hear" the name in my mind almost as if it were being spoken again. This may be a persistence of audition analogous to that persistence of vision that we call iconic memory.

I shall use Neisser's term, *echoic memory,* to refer to persistence of audition, and I shall consider echoic memory to be equivalent to what Crowder and Morton call *precategorical acoustic storage* and what Massaro calls *preperceptual auditory storage* (Neisser 1967; Crowder and Morton 1969; Massaro 1976). The basic hypothesis is that there is an auditory, or perhaps a phonetic, analogue of visual iconic memory such that the nodes activated by an auditory stimulus remain activated for some time after the stimulus is over.

Four basic types of experiments have been employed to demonstrate the existence of echoic memory and to measure its duration. These are probe, modality, interference, and repetition studies.

Probe

Probe studies are analogous to the probe experiments Sperling used to investigate iconic memory. Moray, Bates, and Barnett presented as many as four letters in sequence at each of four different locations in auditory space.

(We can't discriminate different locations in auditory space nearly so well as we can discriminate locations in visual space, but we can discriminate four different locations adequately.) They showed that immediate probe recall of the sequence at any particular location was substantially more accurate than attempted whole recall of the entire "array." Darwin, Turvey, and Crowder showed that this superiority of probe recall declined with increasing delay of the probe, until at a probe delay of somewhere between 2 and 4 sec, probe recall was at the same accuracy level as whole recall (Moray, Bates, and Barnett 1965; Darwin, Turvey, and Crowder 1972).

Modality

In immediate memory span, where subjects recall a list of about seven items (such as letters or digits) Corballis, Murdock, and others have repeatedly demonstrated that the last two or three items in a list are remembered better when the list is presented auditorially than when it is presented visually. The items in the earlier positions on the list are remembered equally well or better when the list is presented visually. Thus the only consistently observed advantage of auditory presentation is at the terminal list positions. This has been interpreted to indicate a significant contribution from echoic memory for auditory presentation (and none from iconic memory for visual presentation under these conditions). This contribution from echoic memory is thought to last for one or two subsequent interfering items (typically anywhere from half a second to a couple of seconds, depending on the rate of presentation) (Corballis 1966; Murdock 1967).

Interference

The ability to recognize and subsequently to remember an auditory stimulus increases with the amount of time the subject has to attend to the stimulus, up to some limit. This is true when the stimulus is on during the entire study time, but it is also true when the stimulus is on for only a very short time at the beginning. Massaro presented a tone for 20 msec, varied the blank time following it, and then presented an interfering (masking) tone. Subsequent ability to recognize the original tone increased with increasing blank time up to about 200 or 300 msec. During this poststimulus interval, Massaro contends, there must be been an echoic memory trace being processed in order for memory to improve (Massaro 1970). (Massaro used a nonverbal stimulus, but there is no reason at present to believe that either echoic or iconic memory is different for verbal than for nonverbal material.)

Crowder and his colleagues have done a large number of experiments using a similar interference technique to study verbal echoic memory. At a constant retention interval memory for a list of items is compared to memory for a list of the same length that is followed after a variable delay by a suffix item. The suffix item is known to the subject in advance and is not to be reported; hence it is considered an interference with the supposedly preattentional, echoic components of memory for prior list items. Findings are consistent with this interpretation: it is primarily memory of the last one or two items that is impaired by the suffix. And the greater the physical acoustic similarity of the suffix to the last few items (in modality, location, pitch, and so on), the greater the interference, while the semantic similarity has little or no effect. Memory for the last few items improves with suffix delay out to anywhere from 2 to 6.4 sec in different experiments (Crowder and Morton 1969; Crowder and Raeburn 1970; Morton and Holloway 1970; Crowder and Prussin 1971; Routh and Mayes 1974).

Repetition

Treisman presented two separate messages to the right and left ears (dichotic listening), instructing subjects to shadow (repeat back) one message and ignore the other. The messages were identical but displaced in time, with either the attended or the nonattended message being presented first. Subjects recognized the identity of the two messages at a maximum lag of about 4 sec when the attended message led, but at a maximum lag of only about 1.5 sec when the nonattended message led. This suggests a duration of 1.5 sec for echoic memory under these conditions (Treisman 1964).

In a somewhat similar single-channel experiment, Guttman and Julesz tested the ability to detect repeating segments of random (white) noise. The longest segment that could be recognized was slightly less than 1 sec. Here the involvement of higher conceptual levels of memory was presumably excluded by the absence of any conceptual codes for random noise (Guttman and Julesz 1963).

Note that estimates of the duration of echoic memory have varied from 200 msec to 6.4 sec. This variation is not surprising. There is no reason to expect a constant duration for echoic memory any more than for any other kind of memory. The conditions that presumably affect the duration of echoic memory—the intensity and duration of the stimulus to be remembered and the intensity, duration, and physical similarity of subsequently presented stimuli—are analogous to those that affect the duration of iconic memory.

The juxtaposition of the Guttman and Julesz experiment with the Treisman experiment points up the tendency among many cognitive psychologists to identify preattentional or nonattended memory with lower-level featural or even nonverbal memory. Whether this is a reasonable identification is debatable. It is also debatable whether nonattended echoic memory is basically anything other than a lower-strength or less consolidated version of the same type of trace that operates in phonetic short-term memory for attended material (Crowder 1975). Finally, it is certainly not established that echoic memory is partly or entirely a nonassociative activity trace rather than an associative memory trace. The next two sections consider somewhat longer-lasting graphic and phonetic short-term memory for material that was attended to during initial presentation.

GRAPHIC SHORT-TERM MEMORY

There is some evidence for higher-level, short-term storage of verbal material in the visual-structural levels of the verbal modality. Using a reaction time task, Posner and Keele have demonstrated a visual short-term memory for single letters that lasts for at least 1.5 sec following presentation of the letter. Subjects were run under two conditions. In the *physical match* condition they had to decide whether two successively presented visual letters were physically identical (saying "yes" to A-A and "no" to A-a, A-B, or A-b). In the *name match* condition they had to decide whether two successively presented letters had identical names (saying "yes" to A-A or A-a and "no" to A-B or A-b). If memory for the first letter was strictly phonetic, the time to say "yes" to A-A in the name match condition should be identical to the time to say "yes" to A-a. This was found for delays between the two letters of more than 1.5 sec; however, for delays of less than 1.5 sec the physically identical pair (A-A) yielded a shorter name match reaction time than the physically differ-ent pair with the same name (A-a). This suggests that subjects retain a short-term memory trace for the initial item in some visual modality for about 1 sec under these conditions. This graphic short term memory does not appear to be iconic memory, since the contrast and illumination levels used by Posner and Keele were inadequate to sustain a persistence of vision for as long as 1.5 sec. Phillips and Baddeley argued that the Posner-Keele tech-nique underestimates the duration of visual-graphic short-term memory. They presented data to show that visual short-term memory can last for at least 10 sec (Posner and Keele 1967; Phillips and Baddeley 1971).

Kroll, Parks, Parkinson, Bieber, and Johnson found comparable short-term visual storage of verbal material. Many previous studies had found a preponderance of phonetic encoding in short-term memory for verbal mate-rial, even when the material was presented visually. To prevent such phonetic recoding of visually presented verbal material, Kroll and his associates used a technique similar to that previously employed by Munsterberg and Murray. The subject's verbal pronunciation and rehearsal systems were kept busy by the requirement to shadow (repeat back) auditory letters presented at a rate of two per second. While they were shadowing, a letter that they were to remember would be presented either visually or auditorially (in a different voice). After a retention interval of 1, 10, or 25 sec, filled with shadowing, subjects attempted to recall the letter. At the 1-sec retention interval, recall was very accurate and almost equally good for visual (96.5%) or auditory (96%) presentation. This suggests that there is little difference in initial perception, though auditory letters were forgotten much faster than visual letters (40% versus 69% correct retention at the 25-sec retention interval) (Kroll et al. 1970; Munsterberg 1890; Murray 1967). This differential susceptibility to the phonetic shadowing task suggests that there is some modality of storage for the visual letters other than the phonetic storage presumed for the auditory letters. This idea is reinforced by the finding that intrusion errors for the visual letters did not tend to be phonetically similar to the correct item.

The presumably visual or graphic character of the memory for the visual letters was more directly indicated by a recognition memory study modeled after the Posner and Keele name-matching technique. Errors were lower and reaction time to recognize a test item as having been in a previous list was faster for test items that were physically identical to the previous list item (e.g., A-A) than for test items that were physically different, but identical in name to the previous list item (e.g., A-a). A variety of other evidence supports the conclusion that visual or graphic short-term memory often mediates retention of verbal material under these conditions (Parks et al. 1972; Kroll 1975). Furthermore, there is every reason to believe that the visual-graphic short-term memory discussed in this section is the same kind of memory trace as that which produces asymptotic performance at longer delays of the partial report cue in tachistoscopic memory experiments. That is, visual scanning of (attention to) the iconic memory of an array of characters produces longer-lasting visual-graphic memory for these characters. Whether this visual-graphic short-term memory is a qualitatively distinct trace from both activational, nonassociative, iconic memory on the one hand and associative, long-term image memory on the other is an open question. It could be a distinct trace, or a stronger or more central version of iconic memory, or a weaker (and therefore shorter-lasting) long-term image memory.

PHONETIC SHORT-TERM MEMORY

When you learned to understand speech, you learned to associate various sequences of phonemes, such as /c/, /a/, /t/, to word or concept nodes, such as "cat," (and to the visual images of the referents for concrete words). When you learned to speak, you developed strong associations in the other direction —from words or concepts such as "cat" to the sequence of phonemes (/c/, /a/, /t/) that must be pronounced to utter the word. Barring serious insult to the relevant part of the brain, these phonetic associations are long-term memories that last for a lifetime. In addition to long-term phonetic associations, there appear to be phonetic memory traces that last for only a few seconds or tens of seconds. These are the short-term memory traces that mediate performance in memory span tasks and allow you to remember a telephone number long enough to dial it after hearing it or looking it up in the telephone book.

Chunking

The average college student can recall about seven digits in order on an immediate memory span test. As an experiment, have a friend read lists of five, six, seven, eight, or nine digits at about one digit per second. Find out how long a list you can repeat back correctly about 50% of the time. This is your immediate memory span for random digits. Now find a friend who knows the names of the digits in a language you do not know, and do the same experiment (preferably using different lists of digits). Your memory span will now be much lower—perhaps only three or four digits, even making generous allowances for your mispronunciations in recall. Why this enormous difference in immediate memory? One plausible explanation is pro vided by the *chunking* mechanism. As a result of past experience you have formed a unitary chunk node to represent the mass of phonetic information comprising each familiar digit name. If immediate memory span is limited to a constant number of chunks and is roughly independent of the amount of information in each chunk, as George Miller (1956) proposed, then you will remember more total information when you have previously formed chunk nodes representing combinations of stimulus attributes. The chunk nodes you use in the familiar language are usually entire digit names, but in the unfamiliar language they may be a mixture of phonemes and syllables (and that's allowing subjects to mispronounce by using the closest English approximations).

Would you like to increase your immediate memory span for digits? You can probably do it, if you are willing to learn 100 associations. Form an association from every two-digit number to a single word. Use already familiar associations to help you: 65 is "quit" (for retirement age), 00 is "start," 99 is "end," 49 is "gold" (I associate 1849 with the California gold rush), 50 is "half," 76 is "spirit," 98 is "beer" (you already have a good mnemonic for 99, so think of starting with 98 bottles of beer on the wall), and so on. It is a bit of work to think up 100 such mnemonics for two-digit numbers, and then to practice with them until you have the associations well learned, but if you form the new chunks you might almost double your memory span for digits. It will not do you much good, except to show off, but it does serve to illustrate the very important chunking capacity of human memory.

A less trivial example is that while the memory span for random words is about five, the memory span for words in a sentence is about triple that (Marks and Jack 1952). This can be explained by the hypothesis that we are familiar with many of the phrases in sentences and have unitary chunk nodes for them. It is probably very important to ordinary understanding of speech and writing that we are able to chunk phrases into units and thereby encompass longer passages in our span of immediate memory. Similarly, our ability to speak integrated longer utterances may depend on our being able to plan utterances using entire phrases as units.

The role of chunking in short-term memory has several practical applications in the area of man-machine communications. The most familiar one has to do with telephone numbers. After you live in a place for a while, you become pretty familiar with most of the prefix codes for your area. Even though the prefixes are all digits (342, 345, 686), many of them become single chunks for you. Accordingly, Shepard and Sheenan (1963) reasoned, people should dial the last four digits of an unfamiliar telephone number *first* and *then* dial the familiar prefix. This way the most easily forgotten four chunks get dialed when the memory trace for them is the strongest, and retrieval of the fifth chunk takes place after the fourth digit has been dialed. Shepard and Sheenan found that there was a 20% reduction in dialing time and a 50% reduction in dialing errors with this prefix-last method. (This research was done at the Bell Telephone Laboratories; unfortunately we are not likely to see this method adopted in the near future because of the great expense involved in switching equipment. But we can hope that human engineers will keep these findings in mind when they are designing new systems for man-machine communication.)

Phonetic Coding

The importance of chunking in short-term memory indicates that short-term memory traces often involve units at the word, concept, and phrase levels. However, traces at lower phonetic levels also appear to play a role in verbal short-term memory. A classic study by Conrad demonstrated that intrusion errors in memory span tasks tended to be phonetically similar to the correct items. For example, if in recalling a letter sequence, such as TMBFSP, one substitutes another letter for B, the substitution is likely to be another letter containing the /ē/ sound (as CPT). But if one makes an intrusion error for the F, it is likely to be another containing the /ĕ/ sound (as MNS). Similarly, memory for /ē/ letters is impeded more by processing other /ē/ letters than by processing letters that are phonetically less similar. The phonetic nature of errors in short-term memory and the importance of phonetic similarity to the magnitude of retroactive interference have been demonstrated repeatedly for a wide variety of verbal materials including letters, numbers, nonsense syllables and words (Conrad 1964; Wickelgren 1965a).

Most demonstrations of phonetic encoding in short-term memory have focused on the segmental level, as in the demonstration that intrusion errors tend to share phonemes with the correct items. But a number of demonstrations have shown that intrusions for single vowel or consonant segments tend to share the same phonetic features (voicing, nasality, openness of vocal tract) as well. In a sequence of consonants paired with a common vowel, such as KA, TA, BA, SA, DA, LA, an intrusion error at a particular consonant position will tend to have the same phonetic features as the correct consonant at that position. There has been considerable debate as to whether phonetic short-term memory is auditory, articulatory, or abstract-cognitive (having common phonetic nodes for speech recognition and articulation). At present the matter remains unresolved (Wickelgren 1965*b*, 1966*a*, 1969*d*).

Phonetic Short-Term Memory
Is Partly Associative

The memory span test has been around for a very long time, but psychologists did not begin to study short-term memory extensively until the middle 1950s. It was probably no coincidence that this research accompanied the introduction of high-speed digital computers. In addition to large-capacity long-term storage, computer systems use small-capacity buffer storage for short-term information that must be kept readily accessible. Such buffer storage is nonassociative; it consists of a small, ordered set of locations in which information can be stored. When they began studying short-term memory in the 1950s, most psychologists appeared to assume, explicitly or implicitly, that human short-term memory was a nonassociative buffer store. Many psychologists still accept this assumption, which holds that we have the capacity to repeat about seven digits on a memory span test because we have a buffer store with seven locations, each of which can hold one chunk of information.

The fact that verbal short-term memory has a small capacity certainly permits us to use a nonassociative memory, since a serial search of up to seven locations would not take an inordinate amount of time. However, there is much data to support the idea that verbal short-term memory has a strong associative component.

Item versus order memory. In short-term memory for a list of consonant-vowel (CV) bigrams, such as NA, FO, JI, there is an experimental demonstration of a dissociation of item and order memory that holds good under certain conditions. This is exactly what one would expect with an associative memory. The task is to remember only the initial consonants from a list of CV bigrams, and the two conditions being compared are a homogeneous vowel condition (NA, FA, JA, . . .) and a heterogeneous vowel condition (NA, FO, JI, . . .). When we consider the associative encoding at a segmental phonetic level, the encoding of each CV item consists of two parts—one corresponding to the consonant and one to the vowel. When we consider only the intraitem associations between the consonant and the vowel parts and the direct forward interitem associations between the consonant and vowel parts of adjacent CV items, we obtain the structure shown in figure 7.4. Adding

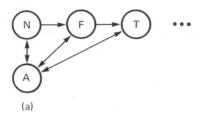 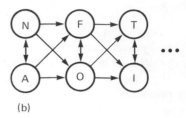

(a)   (b)

Fig. 7.4   Intraitem and direct forward item-to-item associations for (a) a homogeneous
            vowel CV list and (b) a heterogeneous vowel list. Note that many more associations
            encode order information in the heterogeneous vowel condition than in the
            homogeneous vowel condition.

backward or remote associations in no way changes the argument; it simply
makes the diagram more complicated.

If you examine the connection structures for the letters in figure 7.4, you
will see that memory is better replicated for the correct order in the heterogeneous than in the homogeneous vowel condition, since there are four
associations connecting each adjacent CV item. In the homogeneous vowel
condition, only one association—that between adjacent consonants—encodes
the order of the items in the list. To the extent that item-to-item associations
play a role in short-term memory for such material, one would expect the
order of consonants to be far better remembered in the heterogeneous than
in the homogeneous vowel condition, and indeed it is (Wickelgren 1965c).

In an associative memory, recall of the individual consonant items irrespective of order might well be superior in the homogeneous vowel condition,
since the vowel is sure to be remembered, and since it has strong intraitem
associations with each of the consonants in the list. This fact was demonstrated in the same experiment that showed superior retention of order information in the heterogeneous condition. In this case the retention of order
information was tested independently of item information. This was done by
scoring for correct order only those items that had been recalled correctly
irrespective of order. (I might note in passing that item-to-item associations
appear to play a substantially greater role in short-term memory for rapidly
presented lists than they do in longer-term serial learning, where the list is
repeated many times at a generally slower rate.) Since item memory and order
memory are generally positively correlated, predicting the dissociation of
item and order information is a considerable tour de force for the associative
memory theory. It is very difficult to imagine how a nonassociative memory
could predict this.

Repeated items.   In an associative memory the connection structure of
associations between item representatives will be rather different for lists
with repeated items than for lists without repeated items. A nonassociative

memory predicts no difference between the connection structure of the two lists. Figure 7.5 shows how a list with a repeated item is encoded in the associative and in the nonassociative theory.

Experiments comparing short-term memory for lists with and without repeated items have demonstrated many differences that are entirely consistent with the associative memory theory. The easiest of these findings to describe and interpret is the associative intrusion phenomenon. In lists having the form . . . A, B, . . ., A, D, . . ., B intrudes in the place of D or D in the place of B far more frequently than in lists having the form . . . A, B, . . ., C, D, . . . (Wickelgren 1965d, 1966b). Of course, serial position is an important cue in short-term memory for such lists; it provides a means for reducing the frequency of such intrusions far below the 50% level that might be expected on the basis of item-to-item associations alone. However, the prior item does appear to be an important cue in verbal short-term memory, and there would seem to be no parsimonious way in which a purely nonassociative memory could account for repeated-item phenomena, such as associative intrusions.

Grouping. The serial position cues that subjects use to encode a list do not appear to be the numbers 1, 2, 3, 4, 5, . . ., N. Rather, subjects typically break a list into groups and encode it by using such concepts as the beginning, middle, and end group and the beginning, middle and end position within a group. That is, they use a cross-classification of serial position concepts corresponding to two levels of encoding: the order of groups and the order of positions within a group (Wickelgren 1964, 1967a).

It is not at all obvious with a nonassociative memory why a subject should resort to such elaborate grouping schemes, if the serial order of items could be easily encoded by stuffing adjacent items into adjacent locations. However, this use of grouping is very functional for an associative memory. If we assume that the number of serial position concepts is sharply limited for most subjects (mnemonists may possess more than the rest of us), then multilayered usage of these position concepts is necessary to encode the

(a) Nonassociative Memory   (b) Associative Memory

Fig. 7.5 The connection structure for a list with a repeated item (F) in an associative and a nonassociative memory. Note the greater potential for associative interference between items that follow repeated items in an associative memory.

positions of the different items in the list uniquely. It is not at all clear why that number should be on the order of three, as it appears to be, since we clearly have many more number concepts than that. But this is not really relevant to the present discussion.

It is important to distinguish a cross-classification scheme from a hierarchy. In a *hierarchical* encoding of serial position, the classification into groups is primary, and the classification by position within a group is secondary. The order of items within any group must be preserved by an adequate hierarchical memory, but this memory for the order or relative position within a group is not directly accessible by itself. One must first have access to the group. With such a hierarchical memory one could not know that an item had been in the first position within its group unless one first knew what group it was in. With a *cross-classification* memory, information concerning either the group membership of an item or its position within a group could be retrieved independently. These are extreme definitions. Intermediate types of memory are possible, but the extremes serve to illustrate the basic distinction. The basic connection structures of a hierarchical and a cross-classification memory are shown in figures 7.6 and 7.7.

Many psychologists have assumed that grouping three items is equivalent to combining them into a single chunk. In a nonassociative memory this permits the subject to economize on the number of memory locations by stuffing three items into one location. If the associative encoding of grouped lists were achieved by means of a simple hierarchy, it might be rather difficult to distinguish such a theory from the nonassociative theory with chunking. However, when grouping has been explicitly manipulated by instructing the subject to rehearse in groups of different sizes, some interesting error results have been observed. Not too surprisingly, items are transposed within a group more often than items are transposed between the same positions when the grouping method causes these positions to fall into different groups. What

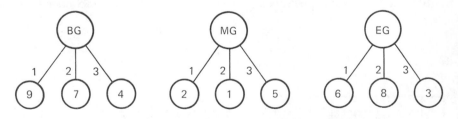

Fig. 7.6   A hierarchical memory for the group list 974, 215, 683. Note that the links from the group nodes to the digit nodes might be labeled in some way to help encode all the order information (though note that item-to-item links also encode order information). However, in an extreme version of a hierarchical memory, this information concerning the secondary dimension of position-within-a-group is not retrievable unless the group membership links are intact.

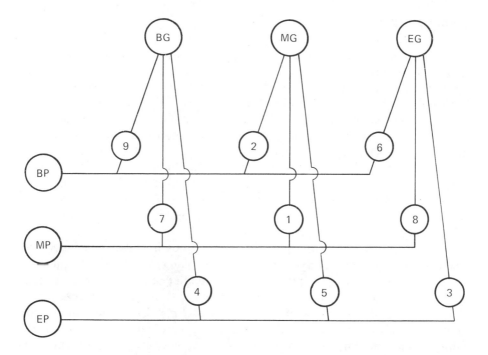

Fig. 7.7 A cross-classification memory for the group list 974, 215, 683. The group and the position information about an item can be retrieved independently of each other.

is much more difficult for a nonassociative chunking theory or for a simple hierarchical associative theory to explain is the fact that intrusion frequencies are also elevated for comparable positions in different groups. That is, when an error is made in a certain position, it is much more likely than chance would allow to be an item from the same position in a different group. Such findings suggest a cross-classification scheme for associative memory in which both the group serial-position concepts and the within-group serial-position concepts are at least semiindependently associated to each item in the list (Wickelgren 1964, 1967a).

These results simultaneously contradict the nonassociative theory and provide evidence that grouping should not always be considered equivalent to chunking. Sometimes grouping is simply a multilayered (in this case a cross-classification) system of serial-position concepts to aid in the associative encoding of a list. Chunking is the formation of a new node to stand for a conjunction of other nodes. In some cases grouping may be accompanied by chunking, but these concepts are not equivalent, and grouping does not always imply chunking.

ACTIVE MEMORY

It would be parsimonious if all four types of short-term memory discussed in this chapter (iconic, echoic, graphic, and phonetic), as well as every other type of short-term memory, could be considered to be a persistence of the activation of nodes at different levels or modalities of processing in the mind. Such activational memory (or *active memory*, for short) is, in a fundamental sense, nonassociative, while human long-term memory is associative. In this elegant view, short-term memory is a change in the state of the nodes—initiated by activation in perception or thinking, but persisting for a short time after the focus of attention shifts to other nodes. Long-term memory is a change in the state of the links between nodes—initiated by contiguous activation of a pair of nodes, but persisting for a longer time after the focus of attention shifts to other nodes.

Iconic memory is fairly well established to be nonassociative memory, and one study has indicated that post-attentional graphic short-term memory is nonassociative as well. We do not know whether echoic memory is nonassociative, but this hypothesis seems consistent with the views of many psychologists who have studied it. It is particularly consistent with the notion that order information is poorly represented in echoic memory. The trouble spot for unifying all short-term memory phenomena as active memory is phonetic short-term memory, where considerable evidence exists to indicate associativity. One plausible resolution of this problem preserves the assumption that phonetic short-term memory is nonassociative active (primary) memory, but that it exists within an associative network and uses a special code that gives it many of the properties of an associative memory.

The question that we must answer is this: Why is the prior item a useful cue for recall or recognition of an item in phonetic short-term memory for lists? If phonetic short-term memory is merely a persistence of activation of nodes representing each item in the list, and not a short-term facilitation of the association between nodes for adjacent items, how could further activation of one item node activate the next-item node more strongly than the nodes for other items? Here is one possible answer:

Imagine that code for a list of digits $(3, 1, 7)$ is not an activation of the 3, 1, and 7 nodes but an activation of more specific, context-sensitive nodes—namely, $_\#3_1$, $_31_7$, and $_17_\#$. The node $_\#3_1$ represents the particular 3 that begins a list and is followed by 1; $_31_7$ represents the particular 1 that is preceded by 3 and followed by 7; and, $_17_\#$ represents the particular 7 that is preceded by 1 and ends a list. When, for example, 3 is presented as a recall cue, all 3 nodes are activated equally, but the persistence of primary memory for the $_\#3_1$ node gives this node an activational advantage over all other context-sensitive 3 nodes. Long-term associations are obviously greater from $_\#3_1$ to $_31_7$ than to $_17_\#$, so the second item will be correctly recalled by virtue both of the primary (activational) memory for the context-sensitive item nodes used to encode the list and of the long-term memory for associations between context sensitive item nodes. Thus it is possible to maintain the elegant hypothesis that all short-term memory is active memory. This hypothesis has certainly not been established, though there is a wide range of evidence supporting context-sensitive coding in perception in general, and speech perception and reading in particular (see chapters 2, 4, and 5).

This theory of active memory also gives an interesting perspective on the relations among short-term and long-term memory, the processes of learning and retrieval, and the phenomenon of priming in retrieval. We can consider learning to be a transformation from active (nonassociative short-term) memory to passive (associative long-term) memory. *Retrieval* is the reverse transformation from passive to active memory. The *priming* effect in retrieval is the facilitation of the later retrieval of a particular association for a short time following its initial retrieval. Presumably this facilitation results from the fact that the activation persists for a short time following retrieval (even while attention is shifted to other nodes), so that a subsequent identical act of retrieval will be faster for the duration of the activational memory produced by the prior act of retrieval. Retrieval is faster because part of the trace is already in the active state.

WORKING MEMORY

Presumably the capacities to (1) chunk several sequentially activated concept nodes into a single new node in acquisition and (2) use several sequentially activated nodes as cues in retrieval (and thinking in general) both depend upon short-term (active) memory capacity. This seems to be virtually a logical necessity, and many psychologists have used this hypothesis to claim that short-term memory is the focal point of all cognition. Nonetheless, there is surprisingly little direct research on the functioning of short-term memory in either acquisition or retrieval. The failure of unattended material to establish much, if any, long-term memory suggests that activation is a necessary precondition for the learning of long-term memories, and that longer durations of activation in conscious study produce higher levels of learning, at least up to some point (Peterson and Kroener 1964; Norman 1969; Wickens, Moody, and Shearer 1976; Wardlaw and Kroll 1976; Nelson 1977). However, it is not at all established that greater persistence of activation (short-term memory after attention has shifted to other thoughts) benefits long-term learning.

We have already mentioned that recent retrieval of a memory trace primes subsequent retrieval of the same or similar traces. We interpreted this as being due to a persistence of active memory, but this is only a reasonable conjecture, not an established truth. Baddeley and Hitch have studied the role of short-term memory in a truth verification type of perception-retrieval thinking task. In a typical task subjects were shown a visual display of two letters, such as "AB." Then they were given a sentence, such as "A does not follow B," and were instructed to press a "true" or "false" key. On memory load trials subjects performed the verification task while holding one to six letters in short-term memory for subsequent recall after performing the verification task. Short-term memory load (especially when it was heavy at six items and the memory task was emphasized) did appear to have a deleterious effect on the verification task. It was as if a limited-capacity short-term memory played an important role in the verification task, and the memory preload inhibited this role to some extent. However, the magnitude of the effect was less than Baddeley and Hitch had expected. They interpreted this to indicate that the short-term memory load was primarily at a phonetic coding level peripheral to the more central semantic-image coding level that played the primary role in the visual-reasoning task (Baddeley and Hitch 1974; Hitch and Baddeley 1976).

The hypothesis that short-term memory capacity is closely related to general intelligence has had its ups and downs over the years. There is no question that there is a positive correlation between IQ and short-term memory span. The question is how to interpret this relationship. Does high IQ merely lead to more efficient rehearsal strategies in short-term memory tasks? A number of researchers have reached this conclusion, but recently the hypothesis that high IQ is associated with a more basic difference in short-term memory encoding or persistence capacity has received a boost. Cohen and Sandberg (1977) found that the highest positive correlations between IQ and short-term memory performance were obtained for the last three items in a list and for the fastest rates of presentation (four digits per second versus one digit per second), where any differences in rehearsal strategy should have the *least* effect. (Indeed, it is highly unlikely that subjects can rehearse at all at four digits per second.) Lyon (1977) also presents evidence that individual differences between adults in short-term memory span are not due entirely to coding and rehearsal strategies. Huttenlocher and Burke (1976) argue convincingly that the increase in short-term memory performance as a child grows older is largely due to a basic increase in short-term memory capacity, not just to increasingly efficient memorizing strategies. It is attractive to speculate that higher intelligence is associated with greater chunking capacity, which produces a richer, more differentiated set of concepts for encoding material in either short-term or long-term memory. But this has most definitely not been proven.

SUMMARY

1 Short-term (primary) memory is a persistence of activation in recently activated nodes.

2 Iconic memory is a persistence of activation of nodes in the visual modality—that is, a persistence of vision or afterimages.

3 Iconic memory can fade within a tenth of a second under ordinary light adapted conditions, but it can last for several seconds under dark adapted conditions. Negative afterimages following intense and prolonged visual stimulation can last for tens of seconds.

4 The capacity of iconic memory is at least 14 letters. Of these about 5 can be scanned simultaneously before the iconic memory is destroyed, possibly by the inhibition present in the scanning process itself.

5 Much of iconic memory is due to a persistence of activation in retinal receptor units, but there may also be some central iconic memory.

6 Iconic memory is nonassociative. A pattern of stimulation is impressed upon each storage location in a two- or three-dimensional array, and this pattern persists for a time after the stimulus ceases.

7 Echoic memory is a persistence of activation in the auditory modality. Like iconic memory it lasts anywhere from a tenth of a second to several seconds.

8 Graphic (visual) short-term memory is the type of post-attentional memory produced by scanning iconic memory. It is longer-lasting than iconic memory.

9 Phonetic short-term memory, which can last many seconds, permits us to repeat back sequences of about seven items, dial telephone numbers, and so on. We know that part of this memory uses a phonetic code because it produces errors that are phonetically similar to the correct items.

10 Verbal short-term memory is not limited to the phonetic level but extends to the word, concept, and phrase levels. We know this because short-term memory span can include many more phonetic attributes when these phonetic attributes form familiar chunks. Memory span is limited to an approximately constant number of chunks, independent of the number of attributes in each chunk.

11 Phonetic short-term memory has some associative properties, and item-to-item associations and position-to-item associations both play important roles in immediate memory for serial lists.

12 Grouping often refers to the use of a cross-classification by two levels of serial position cues. These are beginning, middle, and end groups and beginning, middle, and end positions within a group. Grouping is therefore a distinct concept from chunking, which refers to defining a new node to represent a combination of old nodes.

13 Phonetic short-term memory may be nonassociative active memory with certain associative properties that result from the activation of context-sensitive nodes that have differential long-term associations.

14 Short-term memory probably plays an important role in chunking, retrieval, and thinking.

CHAPTER 8
ASSOCIATIVE
LONG-TERM MEMORY

OBJECTIVES

1 To define and explain more precisely the concepts of *associative* and *nonassociative* memory. To point out that the most characteristic property of an associative memory is the *specific node encoding* of events. This property was described in chapters 2 and 4 as the basis of representation at featural and segmental levels of perceptual analysis. Network models of long-term memory may be either associative or nonassociative, but the basic network model discussed in this book is associative.

2 To define and explain the two alternative conceptions of retrieval: *direct access* to memory traces without search (which is made possible by an associative memory) and *serial search* of memory locations (which is possible in both associative and nonassociative memory, but which is required by a nonassociative memory). The activation process discussed throughout this book is a direct-access retrieval process.

3 To describe several basic learning and memory phenomena that support the hypothesis that long-term conceptual memory is associative. These phenomena are rapid access to a memory of very large capacity, limited accuracy of recency and spacing judgments, and similarity effects in interference.

4 To describe several learning and memory phenomena that illustrate chunking. Chunking may be an essential component of concept learning. Chunking points up the probable importance of vertical associations as opposed to the older conception of horizontal associations in memory.

214

5 To define and distinguish the three phases of memory traces: learning, storage, and retrieval.

6 To discuss the effects on learning efficiency of a number of conditions during learning. These are attention, motivation, intentional versus incidental learning, arousal, semantic versus phonetic levels of processing, amount of repetition, and similar prior learning that produces proactive interference or facilitation of learning.

7 To define and distinguish three processes that occur during storage: consolidation, decay, and interference.

8 To describe retrograde amnesia due to head injury, electroconvulsive shock, and drugs, and to discuss its significance for theories of memory consolidation.

The term *memory* has many different meanings. In common parlance memory usually refers to a conscious recollection of some prior experience, but psychologists use the term more broadly to refer to a wide variety of changes in the nervous system that result from experience and that can affect behavior. Conscious awareness is not considered a critical defining attribute of memory.

Many other kinds of records besides psychological memory are often referred to as memories. There are *physical memories,* such as those produced on magnetic recording tape, a record disc, a calculator or computer memory storage cell, a computer card, a table of numbers, a page from a book, a knife scar on a tree, a scar or scab or bruise on one's body, and so on. There are more uniquely *biological memories,* such as changes in motivation that result from deprivation or stimulation, changes in the muscles or circulatory system that result from exercise, and immunological memories that result from exposure to germs and nonreproductive allergens.

What changes inside us when we learn things? Something must change if there is to be a systematic change in performance. The term *memory trace* refers to the change that occurs as a result of learning. The terms *association* and *habit* are also sometimes used to refer to the change established by learning, but these terms make some assumptions concerning the nature of the memory trace and so are not theoretically neutral. Use of the term *trace* assumes nothing more than that learning produces some change in an organism. It should not be taken to mean that memory is like a groove that becomes deeper in learning and fades away in forgetting. Nor should we assume that a particular memory trace is located in a specific part of the brain. One of the fundamental issues in the physiological basis of memory concerns whether a specific memory trace is produced by a change in a specific part of the nervous system or by changes that are widely dispersed throughout the nervous system.

ASSOCIATIVE
AND NONASSOCIATIVE MEMORY

Memory traces can be classified as associative and nonassociative. The idea of associative memory has been around since Aristotle. In this section we shall define associative and nonassociative memory and provide several examples of each.

Nonassociative memories are records of events that are encoded and stored in locations (cells, registers, boxes, and the like) in the order in which they occur. There are one-dimensional nonassociative memories—for example, the columns of an IBM card, the successive sections of magnetic recording tape, or the successive character positions in the lines of print in a book. There are also two-dimensional nonassociative memories—for example, a table, a chart, or a picture.

Associative memories are records of events that are encoded and stored by networks of nodes that are connected with each other by means of associations. These associations may vary in strength and perhaps in other ways as well. Virtually every theory of associative memory has assumed that associative strengths are increased by the activation of two nodes close together in time. As we shall see, however, the strength of association between two nodes can represent more than the frequency with which one event follows another.

Associative memories are found almost exclusively in the nervous systems of living organisms. It is hard to find other examples, but here is one. Imagine that you are studying the interactions of four people in a small group. The individuals are supposed to interact only in pairs, and you are recording how often various pairs interact. You could use a nonassociative memory for this interaction pattern. To do so, you would record all the events as they occurred, in successive lines of your notebook, using a conceptual notation such as CD, AC (meaning C and D interacted, then A and C interacted), and so on. But you could also use an associative memory like the one shown in figure 8.1. In the associative memory you represent each individual only once. You record the frequency of interaction for each pair by adding to the strength of association between each node (represented by the tally on the line between each pair of nodes).

If all you ever want to know about this small group experiment is how often each pair of individuals interacted, this associative memory is very efficient. To learn (record), you just add another mark on the appropriate line every time an interaction occurs. Storage is very economical; it requires only part of one sheet of paper. In retrieval it is easy to see how many times each pair interacted. But if you want to know things that depend upon the exact sequence of events—for example, whether D's interactions with C tended to precede or follow C's interactions with A—the associative memory shown in figure 8.1 will not help. The basic purpose of an associative memory is to

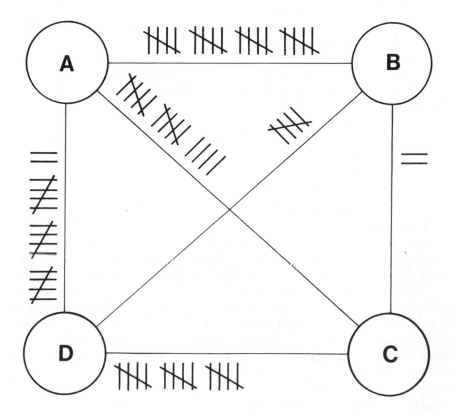

Fig. 8.1 An associative memory for recording the number of times each pair of individuals (A, B, C, and D) interacted in a small-group experiment. The four nodes represent the four individuals, and the tally on the lines (association) between each pair is the number of times those two individuals interacted.

increase the efficiency of learning, storage, and particularly retrieval. In doing so, it ignores many aspects of the temporal sequence of events.

The basic purpose of many nonassociative memories is to record the exact temporal sequence of events. However, one must process nonassociative memories extensively at the time of retrieval to answer any question. For example, to find out how often A and B interacted, one must *search* for the AB pair representatives through all the memory storage locations in succession. With the associative memory shown in figure 8.1, we have what is called *direct access* to how often A and B interacted. We just have to look at the number of marks on the line between A and B.

Almost all of our external memories—books, articles, lecture notes, tape recordings, and the like—are nonassociative memories. The integration of all the separate associations that go with each concept discussed in a book is not done in the book itself but in the mind of the reader. A book would be an associative memory if every concept that was used in it was printed only once, and connections (associations) were made in some way between these concepts so as to represent all of the sentences in the book.

The index is actually the only associative memory component of a book. The index lists many (but far from all) of the concepts in the book and records the page numbers where these concepts are related to other concepts. However, the memory for the exact relations between concepts is expressed by the sentences printed on a page. These sentences are stored in a purely nonassociative manner by means of a sequence of letter patterns impressed on an ordered set of locations on the page.

Event Representation

In a nonassociative memory the representation of an event is defined as a particular set of patterns impressed upon any location in memory. The patterns represent the concepts used to encode the event. It is rather like a computer card, where each letter of the alphabet is represented by two holes punched in any column of the card. For example, T is a punch in the 0 row and a punch in the 3 row. Just as the same T pattern can be punched into several different columns of a computer card, so there can be many identical pattern representatives encoded in different locations in the memory (many *tokens* of the same *type*), as when the "same" event occurs at different times. If the same word occurs repeatedly in a tape recorder memory, each occurrence will impose approximately the same pattern on physically different sections of tape. If human memory were like a tape recording, one might imagine the pattern representation of an event being impressed on the "next" location, and so on. As we shall see, human conceptual memory is nothing like a tape recording.

In an associative memory an event is represented by a particular node or set of nodes. The nodes represent the concepts used to encode the event. The most important property of an associative memory is that when the "same" event occurs at a later time, precisely the same node or node set is activated. This contrasts sharply with a nonassociative memory, in which multiple token representations are impressed in different locations when the same event occurs at different times. An associative memory thus achieves an important economy in the representation (encoding) of an event. Of course, two events are never exactly the same, so "same" events are those that are classified as equivalent by an organism.

This property of *specific node encoding* in an associative memory is, of course, precisely the same principle that played such an important role in our analysis of visual and auditory perception.

Retrieval: Search versus Direct Access

In computer terminology the representation of events in a nonassociative memory is said to be *location addressable*, because one can go directly to a particular location. One cannot go directly to a particular event representation. To locate a particular event representation in order to learn, for example, whether that event ever occurred before, or what the next event was, one must serially *search* through all the memory storage locations. Searching for one representation in a large location-addressable memory can be very time consuming. Digital computers typically use nonassociative, location-address-able memories, though associative memories can also be programmed to some extent.

In an associative memory, it is thought that presentation of an event *directly accesses* (activates) its internal representation (node). When the same event occurs again, the same nodes are activated (directly accessed). It is not necessary to do any serial searching of locations for the internal representa-tion of that event, as one must with a location-addressable memory. In the brain, a neuron that represents a line segment of a certain length and angular orientation located at a specific place in the visual field will be directly activated by the appropriate stimulus. The connections from the appropriate combination of lower-level visual spot nodes to this line segment node are already wired into the nervous system.

In computer terminology an associative memory is often referred to as *content addressable,* because one can employ a program using the same loca-tion-addressable hardware to permit direct access to a location with a particu-lar content. Even with the high search speeds characteristic of modern digital computers, it is clear that to apply computers to information storage and retrieval on any large scale, it is essential to develop associative memory systems.

It is interesting to compare human and computer memory systems. The terms of such comparisons will change, of course, as we continue to improve computer hardware and software (programs). The human nervous system has two big advantages over present computers. It has a very large number of elements (about 10^{10} neurons) and connections (about 10^4 per neuron in the cortex). And it has a substantial degree of parallel (simultaneous) information processing. Computer systems have fewer elements and a very limited degree of connectivity between the elements, and they rely almost exclusively on serial processing. However, they can operate very much faster than the hu-man nervous system.

Hybrid Memories

Computer memories that are fully associative in the way that the ner-vous system is are not likely to be developed soon. What does appear to be feasible is a sort of hybrid, a combination of associative and nonassociative memories in the following form. Information (say in a document) will still be stored in some nonassociative manner (probably some form of graphic storage similar to a photograph or microfilm). However, each document will be in-dexed by a large number of terms. Any of various combinations of indexing terms will provide relatively direct access to the document through a sorting tree that is a functional analogue of associative memory. But because the documents will not be fully indexed by the associative memory, there will always be some types of search that cannot be carried out by means of the direct-access, associative component of this hybrid memory system. These types of search will have to be done serially.

Some memory psychologists talk as if human conceptual memory had this sort of hybrid character when they compare it to a file cabinet, or when they distinguish between *available* information and *accessible* information. The indexing cues yield the directly accessible information, but other information is potentially available by virtue of having been stored somewhere in the system. However, a considerable serial search of terminal locations of the sorting tree might be required in order to retrieve this available, but not accessible, information.

For example, let's assume that you want to buy a house and have gone to a real estate agent who has stored the photographs, floor plans, and descriptions of some 50,000 homes in such a hybrid computer memory. Naturally you can't take the time to scan the descriptions of these 50,000 homes to find the one best suited to your needs. Fortunately each of the homes is classified according to various attributes (indexing or retrieval cues): geographical region, amount of land, number of bedrooms, price, and so on. By choosing the proper retrieval cues, you can have direct access to exactly the set of homes that meets your specifications: three bedrooms, 50-foot lot, $40,000–$50,000 price range, in any of three geographical regions. However, not all the attributes that are important to you (wooded lot as opposed to a lawn, acoustic separation of the bedrooms from the rest of the house) have been used to index the descriptions. To determine which house meets *all* your specifications, you have to look at the entire set of homes that the computer said met your other specifications. Of course, in this day of skyrocketing inflation the list of homes that meets your price specifications may be rather short. All of which reminds me of a cartoon I saw of a real estate agent discussing houses with a young couple, who was saying something like, "I do have a couple of homes in your price range—unfortunately, one is in Mexico and the other was torn down this morning."

LONG-TERM CONCEPTUAL MEMORY IS ASSOCIATIVE

You are walking to your final exam in sociology, and you ask yourself, "What do I know about sociology?" For what seems like an eternity, nothing comes to mind (or at least nothing you'd care to write in a blue book), and then gradually you recall a few scattered bits of knowledge. You panic! You think to yourself, "I have studied hard for this course. My mind should be filled with knowledge of sociology. How come so little comes to mind?" Relax. You have merely demonstrated that conceptual memory is associative. The little test you gave yourself is virtually irrelevant to assessing your knowledge of sociology, because your knowledge of sociology is not in a set of file folders, each neatly headed, that you can open and scan over. Such a memory would be of much less value than the associative memory you actually have.

Your memory stores associations to specific cues. You just gave your associative memory the wrong sort of cue, a cue so nonspecific to a large body of knowledge that little in particular emerged in response to that cue (like the wrong sort of bees that Winnie-the-Pooh supposed would make the wrong sort of honey). Of course in time you can generate specific concepts and propositions in sociology that will serve as cues for further retrieval, but there is nothing surprising in your getting off to such a slow start.

Now let's consider specific arguments for the associative character of long-term conceptual memory. The purposes of this section are to provide you with a more detailed understanding of the theory of associative memory, and to present some interesting phenomena that you can remember in an organized way within the framework provided by this theory.

Capacity

How many concepts and propositions are both stored in our long-term memory and retrievable via the proper cues? No one has a very accurate estimate, but there must be tens of millions or more. Many people have vocabularies that are estimated at hundreds of thousands of words. Now consider the combinations of concepts associated with these words that compose the various propositions (facts and principles) that these people have stored in their memories. You can see that the capacity of long-term conceptual memory is staggering. To retrieve a proposition from a nonassociative storage system for such a large body of material using a serial search process would require an enormous amount of time. Long-term conceptual memory must rely on some direct-access retrieval system that entails little or no searching.

Recency Judgments

Perhaps the principal advantage a tape recorder memory has over associative memory is its capacity for extremely precise temporal resolution. Once one has located an event on a tape, one ought to be able to make very precise recency judgments, and one certainly should be able to judge the relative recency of two events, assuming that each event is still stored on the tape. In fact, there is little reason to expect that temporal order judgments for two well-remembered events will ever be inaccurate in a tape recorder memory. It is true that with a tape recorder memory the representatives of events can decay, or be erased, or be covered over with noise, but we would not expect such a memory to interchange the order of event representatives.

Human beings do have some capacity for making relative recency judgments, but it is abysmally small compared to what could be achieved by someone with a tape recorder memory. We can frequently remember two facts, but not know which fact we learned first. What capacity we do have for making temporal judgments of the order of events seems likelier to be a function of direct or indirect associations to time concepts. Possibly these associations are supplemented by some sort of intermediate-term biological clock that allows us to judge about how long ago we experienced an event, up to a limit of an hour or so.

Spacing Judgments

Hintzman and Block (1973) tested subjects with a list of 19 words presented on a screen at a rate of one every five seconds. Some words appeared twice on the list, others only once. After the list was presented, subjects were given pairs of words from the prior list, some of which were the same word repeated (A . . . A) while others were two different words (A . . . B). Subjects were to estimate the number of words that had intervened either between the two occurrences of the same word or between the two different words. The results are shown in figure 8.2. Subjects showed some

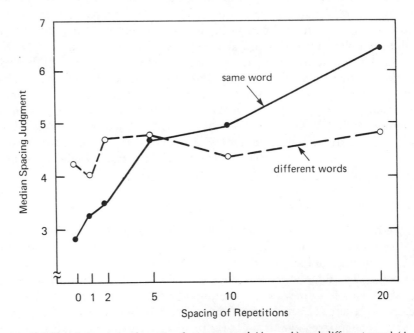

Fig. 8.2   Median judgments of spacing for same word (A . . . A) and different word (A . . . B) test pairs. (From D. L. Hintzman and R. A. Block, Memory for spacing of repetitions, *Journal of Experimental Psychology* 99 (1973): 70–74. Copyright 1973 by the American Psychological Association. Reprinted by permission.)

ability to judge the prior spacing between repetitions of the same item (A . . . A) but no ability to judge the prior spacing between two different items (A . . . B). If the memory of a list of words consisted of a sequence of pattern representatives for the words stored in successive locations, as in a tape recording, spacing judgments for two different words ought to be equivalent to spacing judgments for two occurrences of the same word. Therefore the significant difference in spacing judgments under these conditions contradicts the nonassociative tape recording theory of memory.

An associative theory holds that the second time A is presented, it activates the same A node as it did the first time. If the associations to the A node that were strengthened by the first presentation have not been forgotten, then the second activation of A can be recognized as a repetition. There also appears to be a second property of a memory trace, besides strength, that allows us to judge about how long it had been since A was first presented. For example, the second time A is presented, the subject may think to himself, "There's A again. I saw it before about 10 items back." In such cases a subject will acquire a new associative trace that encodes the spacing information for A . . . A, but there will be no such trace for A . . . B.

Similarity Effects in Interference

One of the best-established and most fundamental facts concerning human memory is that it is susceptible to interference from subsequent (and sometimes prior) learning of similar material. Learning many associations to a common stimulus reduces your ability to recall or recognize any of these associations (except sometimes the last one you learned). Anderson (1974) has shown that this applies to memory for meaningful (propositional) material as well as for the paired-associate material so frequently studied in the laboratory.

Since it is easier to describe interference phenomena for paired associates, I will use paired associate learning as an example. When a subject learns an AB pair and then an AD pair, he almost always finds it harder to recall either the first or the second associate of the A item than he would if he had learned an AB pair and than a CD pair.

The negative effect of subsequent learning on the storage or retrieval of prior learning is termed *retroactive interference* (RI). The negative effect of prior learning on the learning, storage, or retrieval of subsequent learning is here termed *proactive interference* (PI). The term *negative transfer* is often used to refer to the negative effects of prior learning on subsequent learning. The term *proactive inhibition* is used to refer to the negative effects of prior learning on storage (retention). However, this terminology leaves the negative effects of prior learning on the retrieval of subsequent learning without a word to refer to it. For some purposes it is convenient to have a term like proactive interference, which is neutral with respect to the phase locus of the negative effect.

Since repeated presentation of the same event often directly accesses the same internal representatives in an associative memory, AB-AD paradigms often result in the establishment of two associations with the A representative. Clearly such memories might interfere with each other (like two men living with the same woman). In particular, unless it stores auxiliary information concerning the relative time of occurrence of each association, an associative memory can forget which pair occurred first. Hence, one would expect it to be harder at the time of retrieval for an associative memory to recall the first associate of A in the AB-AD paradigm than in the AB-CD paradigm. And so it is. A tape recorder memory need not have this problem.

Subjects given recognition tests to determine whether AB was previously presented as a pair also exhibit similarity-dependent retroactive interference. Learning of a subsequent AD association appears to weaken the strength in storage of a previously stored AB association. That is, learning AD produces some unlearning of AB. Learning of a subsequent CD association produces no greater forgetting than is found in a nonlearning control condition that prevents rehearsal.* Since human associative memory must be limited in its capacity to connect one node to other nodes, such similarity-dependent unlearning is very reasonable. In a tape recorder memory, the ability to retrieve an AB pair might decline with an increase in the intervening material learned, but there is no reason why either storage or retrieval interference should depend on the nature of the material learned in the retention interval. That is, the AB-AD and AB-CD conditions might both produce poorer recognition of AB than the (nonlearning) AB, Rest (with rehearsal control) condition. However, the pattern of results is that AB-AD produces interference in recognition memory for AB, while AB-CD produces no interference at all (that is, AB-CD produces a level of AB recognition equal to the nonlearning control condition).

Of the many studies of recognition memory that demonstrate similarity-dependent unlearning as an associative interference mechanism, let us examine the first such demonstration by McGovern (1964). McGovern had all subjects learn two lists of paired associates, the stimuli consisting of eight nonsense syllables and the responses being eight adjectives—for example, CED-joyful, MUZ-great. All subjects learned the same first list of paired associates, using the method of serial anticipation with a 2:2 second rate on a memory drum. That is, the stimulus item of a pair was presented for two seconds, during which the subject was to attempt to recall the response member of the pair, followed by two seconds in which the correct response member was presented simultaneously with the stimulus member. Then there would be a new stimulus item. A learning trial consisted of anticipation testing and feedback regarding the correct response for each of the pairs. Four

---

*For a review and listing of 22 experimental studies that support these conclusions, see Wickelgren (1976b, pp. 321–61).

seconds elapsed between trials, and stimuli were randomly reordered for each trial so that serial position could not serve as a cue to the correct response. All subjects learned the first list to a criterion of one errorless trial—that is, they correctly anticipated all eight responses to the stimuli on a given trial. An average of 9.5 trials were required to reach the criterion on the first list. Following this, subjects were divided into four groups, and each group learned a second list that differed in its relation to the first list. One group learned a list consisting of the same stimuli used in the first list, but these stimuli were paired with new responses (the AB-AD paradigm). Another group had the same responses but new stimuli (the AB-CB paradigm). A third group received the same stimuli and the same responses but with the pairings changed (the AB rearranged or ABr paradigm). All groups had 15 learning trials on the second list followed by a recognition-matching test for the associations learned on the first list. In this test subjects were presented with all eight stimuli and all eight responses from the first list and were instructed to match them together.

McGovern did not have a Rest control group that performed some nonlearning rehearsal-controlling task during the retention interval while other groups were learning the second list. However, AB recognition matching was so close to perfect in the AB-CD paradigm (7.83 out of 8 pairs correctly matched) that this Rest control group would have been largely superfluous anyway, since its performance could not have significantly exceeded that of the AB-CD group. In any event, other studies indicate no difference between the AB-CD paradigm and the nonlearning (Rest) control condition. However, all of the other conditions demonstrate that learning a second list of similar pairs produces unlearning of the first list of pairs. An average of 6.5 pairs were correctly matched in the AB-AD paradigm, 6.9 pairs in the AB-CB paradigm, and 5.6 pairs in the ABr paradigm. McGovern interpreted these results as indicating that subsequent AD learning produces partial unlearning of the forward association from A to B, while subsequent CB learning produces partial unlearning of the backward association from B to A, and subsequent ABr learning produces unlearning of both forward and backward associations between A and B. She made the further reasonable assumption that a recognition memory test taps the strength of both forward and backward associations so that weakening either association will produce a reduction in correct performance. McGovern's results and those of over 20 other studies support the conclusion that approximately equal unlearning of the bidirectional AB association is produced by subsequent AD or CB learning, and that subsequent ABr learning produces the greatest unlearning, as assessed by a recognition matching test.

Anderson (1974) obtained a rather different demonstration of associative interference, this time in semantic memory for meaningful sentences. First, he had subjects learn a data base of 26 sentences of the form "A person is in the location." For example, subjects learned sentences such as "A hippie is in the church" and "A policeman is in the park." In the data base of 26 sentences some persons were paired with only one location and some locations were paired with only one person. Other persons were paired with two or three locations (in different sentences), while other locations were paired with two or three persons. Following learning, Anderson performed a reaction time experiment to determine how rapidly subjects could verify the truth or falsity of a test proposition of the form "A person is in the location." Some of the test propositions were correct pairings of previously presented persons and locations, while others were incorrect pairings. The error rate and the subject's reaction time were measured for all conditions. Reaction time was measured from the projection of the test sentence on the screen to the depression of one or two response buttons corresponding to the judgments that the test sentence was true or false (based on the preceding data base of 26 sentences). There were 18 different conditions in the experiment, representing all possible combinations of three different factors: the number of pairings of the test person with different locations in the data base (one, two, or three); the number of pairings of the test location with different persons in the data base (one, two, or three); and whether the pairings were true or false.

Error rate was low in all conditions, averaging around 4 or 5%. In the case of the false test sentences the error rate tended to increase with associative interference (more locations associated with the test person or more persons associated with the test location). However, Anderson was primarily interested in reaction time, and reaction time for both true and false sentences increased systematically and significantly with the amount of associative interference. The results are shown in table 8.1. This associative interference effect might occur in the storage or in the retrieval phase of memory or in both. Furthermore, Lewis and Anderson (1976) have shown that learning fantasy facts about famous people (e.g. George Washington wrote *Unwed Father of His Country*) produces associative interference in memory for actual facts about the same people (e.g. George Washington crossed the Delaware). These results demonstrate that semantic recognition memory has the same

		True Sentences Locations Per Person				False Sentences Locations Per Person			
		1	2	3	Aver.	1	2	3	Aver.
Persons Per Location	1	1.18	1.24	1.27	1.23	1.26	1.27	1.32	1.28
	2	1.28	1.25	1.32	1.28	1.34	1.32	1.32	1.33
	3	1.19	1.24	1.51	1.32	1.36	1.39	1.41	1.39
	Average	1.22	1.24	1.37	1.28	1.32	1.33	1.35	1.33

Table 8.1   Average reaction time (sec) in Anderson's study. (From J. R. Anderson, Retrieval of propositional information from long-term memory, *Cognitive Psychology* 6 (1974):451–74. By permission of the author and Academic Press.)

associative interference effects as were previously found in studies of rote paired-associate learning.

CHUNKING
AND VERTICAL ASSOCIATION

Associations between concept nodes that already have well-specified meanings are *horizontal associations.* For example, the concept nodes in figure 8.1 have an established meaning. They represent the individuals in the small group. The horizontal associations provide additional information about these individuals—who they interact with and how frequently—but the referential meaning of each node (that is, what each node represents) has been specified independent of the strength or nature of these horizontal associations.

Instead of, or in addition to, horizontal associations, human beings and other higher vertebrates can form powerful vertical or chunking associations. In one of the most influential papers written so far in cognitive psychology, George Miller (1956) described the process by which human beings recode several elements (attributes or concepts) into a single new element called a *chunk.* Miller's clearest example of chunking concerns the recoding of binary numbers into decimal numbers. The binary system uses only the digits 0 and 1, and recoding from binary into decimal (or octal) works as follows: 000 = 0, 001 = 1, 010 = 2, 011 = 3, 100 = 4, 101 = 5, 110 = 6, 111 = 7. This system recodes three symbols (chunks) into one symbol, thereby reducing the number of chunks but preserving all the information. Subjects in a memory span test were required to recall a sequence of binary numbers. Those who knew how to use the binary-to-decimal recoding scheme nearly tripled their memory spans. Miller pointed out that we can recall an approximately constant number of chunks, regardless of the amount of information contained in each chunk. This constant number of chunks constitutes our memory span.

Concept Learning

We use the chunking process whenever we attach labels to new events, concepts, or sets of concepts. The dictionary contains hundreds of thousands of words whose meanings can be expressed in phrases or sentences, but the single-word designation is more efficient. Mathematicians and scientists frequently invent new concepts to stand for long sequences of previously defined concepts. This practice is essential to the codification and manipulation of complex subject matter.

The ability to define a new concept to stand for a combination of previously defined concepts appears to require an extension of associative memory. One possible theory assumes that associative memory contains a large pool of previously unspecified elements (nodes), each of which has weak connections to other elements. When we attempt to chunk a set of these nodes, one unspecified node will be most strongly connected directly or indirectly to this set of already defined nodes. This new node will be maximally activated by the simultaneous activation of its constituents, and the strength of association from these constituents to the new *chunk node* will be strengthened by this simultaneous activation, In this way a new element of the system can come to stand for some combination of old elements.

This association of component nodes to a superordinate chunk node is called a *vertical association.* Do not confuse it with the more commonly assumed *horizontal association,* in which already defined nodes are associated to each other by contiguous activation. An example of vertical versus horizontal associative encoding is shown in figure 8.3 for the word "cat."

A chunk node also serves as an intervening node in that it indirectly connects the nodes being chunked. Human memory probably has an enormous number of nodes that represent all the concepts and principles we learn. It seems unlikely that every pair of nodes is *directly* connected; more probably they are generally *indirectly* connected through at least one intervening node. Chunk nodes make these indirect connections and have other useful properties as well.

Genetically specified vertical associations are an important part of associative memory. As we saw in chapter 2, the simple line detectors in the visual cortex appear to be specified by associations from a linear set of lower-level spot detectors. The more of these spot detectors that are activated by visual stimulation, the greater the activation of the higher-order line detector via the vertical associations. The assumption of *learned* vertical associations established by the chunking process simply extends this notion.

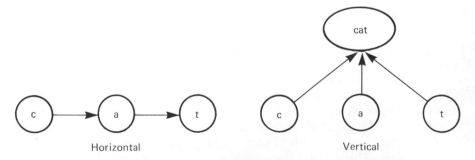

Fig. 8.3 Horizontal versus vertical associative memory for the word "cat." In the horizontal associative memory the associations encode the ordering of the letter constituents. In the vertical associative memory the associations encode the constituency (part-whole) relation between the word and its component letters. This chunking in effect defines the word node as the combination of its letter constituents.

Since the number of concepts (chunks) we are capable of learning appears to be infinite, it is clear that we cannot have innate specification of every node. However, since the number of concepts we do learn is finite, we may assume specification of nodes by learning, and the chunking process is one plausible way to accomplish it.

Semantic Memory

Chunking and vertical association explain an important part of elementary concept learning. They also permit the specific-element encoding of higher-order conceptual compounds and propositions (Anderson and Bower 1973; Wickelgren 1976c). Elementary concepts, which are often signaled by single words ("dog," "he," "run," "blue," "in") or short phrases ("the girl," "a boat"), form the basic nodes of semantic (meaningful) memory. To represent our knowledge of the world requires the encoding of these elementary concepts into higher-order combinations or conceptual *compounds* (signaled by phrases such as "in Amazon Park" or "hit the ball") and *propositions* (signaled by clauses and sentences such as "Ingrid often plays in Amazon Park," "Abe hit the ball"). In this section we shall compare a horizonal associative minimemory with a vertical associative minimemory for two propositions.

A simple horizontal associative memory for two propositions ("Sharks live in seas," "Sunfish live in lakes") is illustrated in figure 8.4. The memory in figure 8.4 is associative because every concept is represented by one specific element. It is horizontal because the contiguous concepts in each sentence have horizontal associations between them (represented by arrows). Such a horizontal associative memory is inadequate because it is subject to associative interference. For example, we could just as easily retrieve the false statements "Sunfish live in seas," "Sharks live in lakes" as the correct ones.

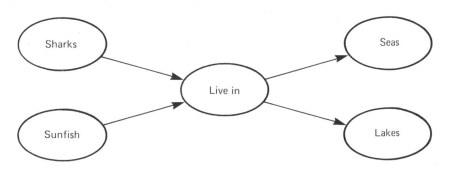

Fig. 8.4   A simple (and inadequate) example of a horizontal associative memory for two propositions. Concepts are represented by specific elements, and the sequence of concepts is represented by unidirectional associations (arrows).

The vertical associative memory illustrated in figure 8.5 uses specific nodes to represent (1) elementary concepts, (2) significant conceptual compounds (phrases) in both propositions, and (3) the propositions themselves. Associations are used to encode the constituents of higher-order nodes, rather than to encode temporal sequence. To retrieve a proposition from this network, one starts at a propositional node (one that has only incoming arrows) and retrieves its subject and predicate constituents, then retrieves their constituents, and so on, until one reaches the elementary concepts. (One also needs some simple grammatical rules to achieve the desired sequential ordering of the concepts, but this is a secondary problem and one beyond the scope of this text.) The important thing to note is the way this vertical associative memory reduces associative interference in retrieval and thus permits only correct propositions to be retrieved from memory. The concepts of chunking and of associative versus nonassociative memory are central to an understanding of many learning and memory phenomena.

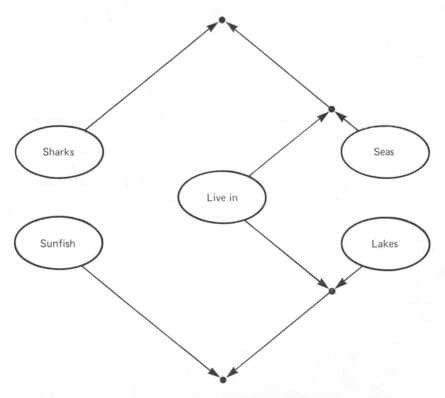

Fig. 8.5   A vertical associative memory for two propositions. Elementary concepts and higher-order concepts (phrases and propositions) are both represented by specific elements. Vertical associations are used primarily to encode the constituents of a higher-order concept rather than to encode temporal sequence.

Chunking in Verbal and Image Learning

Chunking plays an important role in verbal and image learning. Indeed the support for chunking is so widespread that the principle has already penetrated to the broader culture in the form of a rather well-known joke. In the final examination of a psychology of learning course, one student is sitting with his head in his hands, apparently deep in thought. The professor, observing that the student has not written a word for 20 minutes, walks over and asks what is wrong. The student answers, "Well, I did just what you said to do—I chunked the material. First, I read over the text and my lecture notes and condensed all the ideas into a 10-page outline. Then I reduced that to three file cards, then to three sentences, and finally to a single word. But now I can't remember the word." "Bullshit," said the professor. "That's it!" said the student.

Underwood and Schultz (1960) did a series of studies to explore the notion that when a subject learns a serial or paired-associate list, there are at least two different phases of the list-learning process: learning the responses and learning the associations between stimuli and responses. If the response elements are nonsense syllables or other nonunitary, poorly integrated verbal material, subjects first learn to associate the parts of the responses to form single units. In terms of the current theory, they form chunk nodes. After they form chunk nodes for the responses, they can more easily associate the stimulus nodes to the response nodes. If the stimuli are poorly integrated verbal units, subjects may sometimes chunk stimulus elements as well, though this is not usually so essential to correct performance.

Material that has been chunked together to form a familiar single unit appears for most purposes to function as a single unit in learning and memory. For example, Glanzer and Razel (1974) found that free recall of words containing two syllables ("donkey," "chestnut," "earthquake") was at least as good as free recall of monosyllabic words ("elm," "yawn," "scrap"). At a somewhat higher level Bower (1969) demonstrated that familiar three-word phrases ("ballpoint pen," "birth control pill," "turtleneck sweater," "good old days") can function as single units in lists of items to be recalled, but that unfamiliar three-noun compounds ("couch flag sun") function as if they were three separate units. The familiar three-word phrases were recalled in a perfect all-or-none manner—that is, there were no partial recalls—but partial recall of the three-noun compounds was common. (Words of a feather chunk together.) Furthermore, the familiar three-word phrases were recalled virtually as often as single words. Finally, Neal Johnson (1968, 1970) showed that syntactically defined units (e.g., "of my father") were learned more rapidly than equally probable and acceptable word strings that are not syntactic units (e.g., "father of my").

It is now clear that the process of associating two words in a paired-associate learning experiment is not a matter of forming a horizontal association from one word to the other. Paivio (1971), Bower (1972), and many others have demonstrated that learning paired associates is greatly facilitated by generating a unitary visual image that contains the concepts represented by two words and relates them in some way. For example, Bower studied paired-associate learning for 100 pairs of unrelated concrete nouns, such as "dog-bicycle." Subjects were given five seconds to learn each pair, and a cued recall test was given after every 20 pairs for the preceding 20 pairs. (In cued recall the stimulus is presented and the subject attempts to recall the response.) After all 100 pairs had been presented and tested once each, a final cued recall test was administered. One group of subjects was instructed to associate the nouns by imaging a visual scene in which the two objects were interacting in some way (a dog riding a bicycle, a dog jumping over a bicycle). The other group received typical, neutral, paired-associate learning instructions to "learn the pairs so the stimulus (left member) could cue recall of the response (right member)." On the final recall test the imagery group recalled about 80% of the responses to stimuli, while the control group recalled about 50%. This enormous difference is typical and illustrates the effectiveness of learning by interactive imagery.

Rohwer (1966) and others, following the lead of Epstein, Rock, and Zuckerman (1960) demonstrated that memory for paired associates can be greatly facilitated by embedding the two words into a meaningful sentence that unites them into some common idea. For example, the pair "boy-turtle" might be learned by embedding it into the sentence "The boy looked for his lost turtle." As Asch, Ceraso, and Heimer (1960) and Epstein, Rock, and Zuckerman demonstrated, associations between pairs of visual forms are also greatly facilitated by learning them as parts of a unitary visual image (fig. 8.6). The beneficial effects of chunking obtained even though the recall test involved decomposing the picture into parts, which produced a condition similar to that in which the pairs are learned as separate parts. The effects of chunking are so strong that they overcome any such negative factor.

The beneficial effects of semantic chunking also obtain with material more complex than pairs of words. Kintsch, Crothers, and Jorgensen (1971) studied short-term memory for word triples using a distractor paradigm over

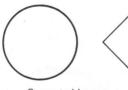   

Separated Images   Unitary Image

Fig. 8.6   Presentation of a visual paired associate as two separated images and as a unitary image. Memory is far superior for the unitary image.

retention intervals ranging from 3 to 24 seconds. Subjects were prevented from rehearsing during the retention interval by being required to start from a three-digit number and count backwards by threes as fast as possible until the experimenter gave the signal to recall the three words. They found that memory performance was greatly improved when subjects were instructed to form a phrase or sentence that in some way connected the three words into a single unit. A variety of control conditions demonstrated that this improvement occurred because the subjects formed a single chunk that integrated all three words into a single unit—not because the instructions induced a higher semantic level of processing of the three words. For example, in one control condition subjects were instructed to form an appropriate separate phrase or sentence for each word (the phrase "the ferocious dog" or the sentence "The dog barks" for the word "dog"). Even when subjects were allowed more time for this type of separate semantic processing and elaboration, memory for the three words was substantially poorer than when the three words were integrated into a single chunk.

Horowitz and Prytulak (1969) studied *redintegrative memory*. A subject is presented with a picture story, sentence, or phrase composed of several parts, is later given (or recalls) some of the parts, and then must remember the rest—that is, must reinstate the whole from some of the parts. It now appears that much human conceptual memory is redintegrative. Most conceptual memory probably involves the formation of propositions and images that unite several constituents into a single higher-level chunk. The psychologists who emphasized the importance of structure and organization in human memory were clearly correct, though it should also be clear that there is no conflict between a vertical network organization and the assumption of associative memory.

Why do our associative memories have the chunking property of defining new nodes to stand for a set of old nodes? The chunk could be represented by the set of nodes representing its constituents. The association of two chunks could proceed by associating every node in one set to every node in the other set. However, since the same constituent nodes would appear in many different chunks, there would soon be a large number of interfering associations. Defining a new node to stand for a particular combination of old nodes greatly reduces the memory's susceptibility to associative interference.

Let me make one final point concerning the relation between vertical and horizontal associations. A vertical associative memory has all the capacities of a purely horizontal associative memory and more. Any chunk node for A + B must have upward associations from the individual A and B nodes to the chunk node and downward associations from the chunk node to its A and B constituents (fig. 8.7). Thus a chain of two links, upward from A to A + B and downward from A + B to B, can be the equivalent in a vertical associative memory of a single direct link from A to B in a horizontal associative memory. For many purposes, therefore, it is still reasonable to discuss

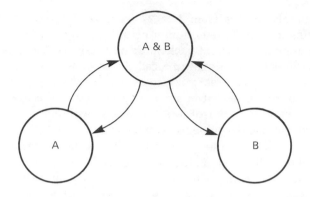

Fig. 8.7 Upward and downward associations from the constituent nodes A and B to the chunk node A + B. A forward association from A to B is mediated by a chain of two associations: upward from A to the A + B chunk node and downward from the A + B chunk node to B. A backward association from B to A uses a chain composed of the other two associations.

forward associations from A to B and backward associations from B to A without considering the need for mediation by an intermediary chunk node.

THREE PHASES OF MEMORY

As you know, "Many a truth is spoken in jest," and so it is with the Lazy Student Paradox, which goes as follows: "The more we study, the more we learn (first law of learning). The more we learn, the more we forget (second law of learning). The more we forget, the less we know (obvious truism). So why study?" Setting aside its important practical value as a justification for play instead of work, this piece of logic is useful because it illustrates the theoretical analysis of the memory process into three phases: learning, storage, and retrieval. First, a trace is learned as a result of some experience. *Learning* is the cognitive process that produces a memory trace. *Retrieval* is at the other end of the memory process; it is the cognitive process that uses memory traces to know things and affect behavior. For example, retrieval allows you to answer correctly on a recall or recognition memory test. To retrieve a memory means to use it. Everything that happens in between learning and retrieval happens during the *storage* phase (retention interval), and the processes that affect memory during the retention interval are called *storage processes.*

The principal storage processes are consolidation, interference, and decay. *Consolidation* is an unconscious process that makes a memory trace more resistant to decay. *Interference* is an active decrease in the strength of a trace or a decrease in its retrievability due to the learning of a similar memory trace. *Decay* is a passive decrease in trace strength or retrievability due simply to the passage of time. (Actually it is due to spontaneous activity of the nervous system, which is independent of specific experience.) *Forgetting* is a loss of memory for any reason: interference, decay, or whatever. Learning and retrieval are at least partly conscious processes. Storage processes are completely unconscious—except, of course, that we are conscious of the learning experiences that produce interference. Learning and storage of associative long-term memory will be discussed in this chapter. Retrieval will be discussed in chapter 9.

The classification of memory into learning, storage, and retrieval leaves the cognitive process of rehearsal somewhat in limbo. *Rehearsal* has aspects of all three phases of memory. It is, in a sense, a continuous retrieval process. It can serve to maintain a memory trace in an active (retrieved) state from learning to retrieval and could therefore be considered a storage process. Finally, rehearsal is an active repetition or practice, which tends to increase the strength of a memory trace and is therefore a learning process.

Learning

Learning begins with the activation of some nodes in the nervous system. It is a plausible working assumption that the learning of an association (vertical or horizontal) between A and B nodes requires the contiguous *activation* of these nodes. The activation might result from perception or thought —it probably makes little difference as far as learning is concerned. That is, we probably learn new memory traces from our own thoughts as well as from the perception of external events. However, while the activation of two nodes appears to be *necessary* for the learning of an association between them, it may not be *sufficient*. We do not know.

Attention. Just because you are exposed to stimuli it does not follow that nodes representing those stimuli will be activated. If you do not attend to the stimuli in question because your attention is focused on other stimuli, or on internally generated thoughts, you will not learn much. This has been demonstrated in two-channel listening studies where a subject is presented with two streams of material, one to each ear. Material presented to whichever ear the subject attends to will establish a relatively normal level of long-term memory. Material presented to the other ear produces a zero, or close to zero, level of learning. (Norman 1969).

Motivation, intent to learn, and arousal. As you might suspect, motivation to learn is important. Indeed, in practical terms it is critical for learning. If you're not motivated, you don't read the book; you don't go to class; you don't pay attention if you do go to class; you don't do the assignments—in short, you don't think the thoughts (activate the nodes) that need to be associated. So you don't learn. But however potent the practical effect of motivation on learning, it is an *indirect* effect mediated by the more basic activation factor (no activation implies no learning). The important theoretical question is this: Is there any *direct* effect such that the more highly motivated you are to learn an association between A and B, the greater the increase in trace strength with each repetition of contiguous activation of the nodes representing A and B? So far as we can tell, the answer is "no." No such direct effect has been demonstrated.

Some studies have manipulated *payoffs* for right answers. The results of such studies are inconclusive. Often they have controlled poorly for the indirect effects of motivation on learning behavior. And, surprisingly enough, many of these studies have found that payoffs have little or no effect—direct or indirect. This may be because human subjects are already very highly motivated just to get the right answers (Sidowski and Nuthmann 1961; Weiner 1966).

The best-controlled studies of the direct effects of motivation on learning are those that examined the *intent to learn.* In an intentional learning paradigm subjects know while they are being exposed to the material that their memory for that material will be tested later. In an incidental learning paradigm subjects must process the material in some manner, but they do not know while they are doing so that their retention of the material is going to be tested. Psychologists who have compared incidental and intentional learning have concluded that the intent to learn is unimportant to level of acquisition and subsequent forgetting. Intentional learning instructions facilitate learning only to the extent that they cause subjects to process material differently than they would process it in the incidental condition, and this difference establishes stronger or longer-lasting memory traces (Postman 1964; Jenkins 1974). It is the type and duration of processing that determines the type of memory traces established, and it does so more or less automatically, whether or not the subject is trying to learn the material being processed. The conclusion that intent to learn is unimportant should be regarded as tentative, but it appears to be a reasonable working hypothesis that memory traces are established automatically during mental processing. The type of memory trace acquired depends upon the type of mental processing. In particular, meaningful (semantic) memory traces will not be formed if processing occurs entirely at a rote (phonetic) level.

Arousal at the time of learning is another quasi-motivational factor often alleged to affect learning and even subsequent retention. Once again the evidence is frequently contradictory, and no serious effort has been made to control indirect effects on level of activation.* Sleep and anaesthetic drugs depress the response of the nervous system to sensory input, and less extreme

---

*See discussion in Weiner (1966); Wickelgren (1977b, pp. 355–60); and the references contained therein.

states of low arousal probably do too, albeit to a lesser extent. From a practical standpoint a bored, sleepy student is a poor learner, but again this is easily explained by the activation factor (low activation implies low learning).

Encoding: levels of processing. The most important factor affecting learning (besides contiguous activation) appears to be the nature of the encoding. That is, what nodes are being activated and between which nodes is one attempting to form associations? Some encodings (activated node sets) are rapidly associated; others are associated much more slowly, if at all.

Tresselt and Mayzner (1960) studied free recall of a list of words in an incidental learning paradigm as a function of three different orienting tasks: crossing out vowels, copying the words, and judging the extent to which each word was an example of the concept "economic." Recall of the words following the semantic orienting task was twice as high as recall following the word-copying task, which, in turn, was twice as high as recall following the letter-processing task. This is consistent with the hypothesis that the higher the level of processing of the material, the greater the degree of learning or the slower the rate of forgetting or both. Many other studies support the same conclusion—that the processing of verbal material at lower phonetic levels leads to weaker or less persistent traces than the processing of material at higher semantic levels (Hyde and Jenkins 1969; Johnston and Jenkins 1971; Chabot, Miller, and Juola 1976; Nelson 1977).

Bower and Karlin (1974) have shown that the more extensively a picture of a face is processed, the greater the subsequent recognition memory of the face. If subjects were required to make a relatively superficial judgment during initial learning—if they were required, for example, to judge the person's sex—subsequent recognition memory was poorer than if they were required to make a more complex judgment—for example, to judge the person's likeableness or honesty. The same relationship held true under both intentional and incidental learning instructions. Also, there was no significant difference between intentional and incidental learning instructions. (This finding agrees with the results of many other studies.) It is the mode of processing of input that is important. When this is controlled, intent to learn is either much less important or totally unimportant.

Of course level of processing not only determines how much we remember, but also what properties of the input we remember. In chapter 10 I shall discuss several studies that show that processing of connected discourse largely at the semantic level produces long-lasting memory for the meaning of a sentence but virtually no memory for the particular words or syntactic structure. Under other conditions, where the subject's attention is focused on the lexical and syntactic properties of a sentence, he can remember these properties for a long time—although not as long as he can remember semantic information, which is intrinsically less susceptible to interference (Sachs 1967; Anderson and Bower 1973, pp. 224–28).

Repetition. The first law of learning, as confirmed by thousands of learning studies, is that memory improves with practice. That is, the more times we repeat a learning experience, the better we remember. Since we lack a satisfactory quantitative formulation of this obvious truism, there would be relatively little to say about it were it not for the temerity of some levels of processing enthusiasts who claim that if learning improves with increased study time, this is solely because the subject is achieving progressively higher levels of encoding. On the face of it there would appear to be some correlation between study time and level of processing. Manifestly the sensory-feature levels must precede the phonetic-segmental level, which in turn must precede the word and concept levels, which in turn must precede the phrase and propositional levels. Surprisingly enough, as we saw in chapter 5, structural priority in the nervous system does not necessarily imply temporal priority. Letters and phonemes are sometimes recognized more slowly than words and concepts—which makes some sense functionally, since the purpose of reading and listening to language is to extract meaning, not letters and phonemes (which are the structural vehicles of meaning).

In an incidental learning paradigm, Nelson (1977) held processing at a phonetic level by means of a phonetic classification task (e.g., "Does the word contain an 'r' sound?"). He found that two phonetic classifications of a word led to significantly better memory for the word than a single classification (on an unexpected recall or recognition test). Exposure to the words in a semantic classification task (e.g. "Does the word represent an object that you could carry in your hand?") produced better memory for the words than the phonetic classification task, but several repetitions of an identical phonetic classification also produced better memory. Nelson and Dark and Loftus (1976) argue cogently that we can conclude nothing from those few studies that have found increased study time (or the number of repetitions) has no beneficial effect on memory. Of course, there are a mountain of prior studies that contradict these findings and support the beneficial effect of repetition. Dark and Loftus also find that repetition improves memory when they use precisely the same paradigm that some other investigators had used to prove the opposite—but include certain important controls. Clearly, repetition is beneficial to memory. The results of Nelson's study indicate that even repetition at the same phonetic level of coding with the same question each time (e.g., "Does the word have an r sound?") increases the strength of the trace at that level.*

Proactive interference and facilitation. When the same stimulus words must be associated with two different sets of response words in paired-associate learning (AB, AC paradigm), many (though not all) studies obtain negative transfer or proactive interference effects on the learning of the sec-

*See also Chabot, Miller, and Juola 1976.

ond (AC) list (Osgood 1949; Dallett 1965; Tulving and Watkins 1974). There would appear to be some limit on the total number or strength (or both) of associations to a single node in memory. Once we have used up some of that capacity in learning one (AB) association, it is somewhat more difficult to learn another (AC) association. In life, when we have a large category, such as "animals," we generally recall its members in terms of subcategories, such as "cat family," "dog family," "tame," "wild," "African," "aquatic," and so on. It seems likely that a single node has a limited associative capacity, though at present we have no idea what that limit may be.

Proactive interference does not mean that the more you learn about a subject, the harder it is to learn more about that subject. On the contrary. The first law of child development is: "Children get better at most tasks with age." (The second law is: "Girls do it sooner.") All of us know from personal experience that the more you know about some subject, the easier it is to learn new information about that subject. We do not fully understand why this is so, or how this overall proactive facilitation from prior learning relates to the proactive interference just discussed. However, there are probably two facilitating factors. First, prior acquisition of new concept nodes (chunks) for A and B definitely facilitates the forming of associations between them (Underwood and Schulz 1960; Martin 1967; Wickelgren 1977b, pp. 244, 334. Second, much new associative learning builds on—rather than competing with—prior associative learning. For example, the chunk node for the AB pair—rather than the node for A alone—may be what is to be associated to C. This second facilitating factor is really identical to the first, except that in the second factor the prior chunking is raised to a higher level. Thus establishing a new chunk node A greatly facilitates later associative learning involving A; but establishing an association with A (AB) interferes slightly with the later formation of other associations with A alone.

Consolidation

Like rehearsal, consolidation takes place during the retention interval and is beneficial to memory. Unlike rehearsal, consolidation is an unconscious process that is assumed to be largely beyond voluntary control. Consolidation is often assumed to proceed at the same rate whether or not the subject simultaneously performs other tasks. The hypothesis that memory traces become more firmly fixated after formal practice ends has been debated ever since Müller and Pilzecher (1900) advanced their theory of perseveration and consolidation in 1900.

Associative memory traces appear to have two important dynamic properties: strength and fragility (Wickelgren 1974a). Strength affects the probability of recall and recognition, but reductions in trace fragility decrease susceptibility to time decay and retrograde amnesia. Interestingly enough, this theory assumes that a reduction in fragility does not affect the susceptibility of the trace to associative interference, such as that produced by learning a subsequent AC association on the strength of a previously learned AB association. According to this theory, susceptibility to interference remains constant with increasing trace age, but susceptibility to temporal decay decreases.

Temporal decay decreases as the trace ages because the consolidation process has made the trace less fragile. This reduction in fragility as a consequence of consolidation continues throughout the lifetime of the memory trace, which accounts for the progressive reduction in both forgetting rate and susceptibility to retrograde amnesia. Consolidation is assumed to go on for years, but it slows down as the trace age increases. That is, the highest rate of consolidation (the greatest reduction in trace fragility) occurs during the first few minutes following learning. Thereafter the rate of consolidation decreases progressively over the life of the memory trace. Considerable evidence supports the hypothesis that consolidation is a reduction in trace fragility.

Retention functions.   As we have seen, the rate of forgetting for all types of verbal and nonverbal material appears to decrease gradually with increasing trace age over retention intervals that range from seconds to months and even years. This fact is consistent with the fragility hypothesis. Mathematical formulation of this hypothesis provides a good fit to the retention functions obtained for a wide variety of verbal and nonverbal material over retention intervals ranging from seconds to over two years (Wickelgren 1974a, 1975a).

Retrograde amnesia.   Following severe head injuries that produce concussion, human beings frequently experience a loss of memory known as retrograde amnesia. This loss can last for anywhere from a few seconds to several years. The more serious the concussion, the longer the period of retrograde amnesia. As Russell (1959) noted, this fact appears to require the assumption of a consolidation process that extends for virtually the lifetime of the memory trace. It is important to note that the consolidation process cannot be acting on the strength of memory traces, since it is not the strongest or weakest traces that are lost, but the last traces established prior to the concussion. Thus we must assume that consolidation acts on some second parameter of the memory trace, which I call *fragility,* and that concussion destroys or renders irretrievable the most fragile traces irrespective of strength.

Occasionally retrograde amnesia from concussion is permanent, but usually the patient recovers most of the lost memories. In these cases retrograde amnesia can be considered a temporary irretrievability of memory rather than a complete destruction. Recovery from retrograde amnesia is also temporally specific—that is, the first memories recovered are the oldest memories, and the retrograde amnesia gradually shrinks toward the present (Russell 1959). Thus the initial loss and the recovery both appear to require the assumption of a property such as fragility that is continually being reduced as a result of an ongoing consolidation process. The ability to recover from retrograde amnesia demonstrates that the disruption of the most fragile traces is often only temporary. Predicting the temporary or permanent character of retrograde amnesia is beyond the scope of any current consolidation hypothesis.

Electroconvulsive shock.   Squire, Slater, and Chace (1975) have demonstrated that patients undergoing electroconvulsive shock treatments for mental disorders also experience retrograde amnesia that appears to be temporally specific, much like the retrograde amnesia produced by concussions. Many experiments on animals also show that electroconvulsive shock can disrupt memory traces. These animal experiments were undertaken on the hypothesis that consolidation involved an increase in the strength of the long-term memory trace that would be completed in anywhere from a few seconds to four or five hours. However, the results indicated no particular time after which consolidation is complete. Various conditions, particularly the severity of the electroconvulsive shock, can produce disruptions of memory at varying delays following original learning (Weiskrantz 1966).

Recency judgments.   The decreasing fragility of a memory trace could also serve as a kind of biological clock measuring its age. If fragility were a retrievable attribute, recency judgments could be based on trace fragility. Of course many of our recency judgments, especially those for events that occurred a very long time ago, are based directly or indirectly on associations with time concepts. I remember how long ago I graduated from high school because I remember the month and year by association. I know the current month and year, and so I can figure out the difference.

However, my judgment for the time that has elapsed since I entered my office cannot be based on association, because I have not looked at any watch or clock in the interim. Human beings deprived of clocks can nevertheless make recency judgments that are accurate far beyond chance. One of the advantages of the fragility theory is that it provides an automatic mechanism for determining the recency of events for which we have established memory traces. A mathematical version of this hypothesis has been found to provide an excellent fit to human abilities to judge recencies of words presented in a continuous recognition memory paradigm where subjects had no access to clocks of any kind (Wickelgren 1974a). Interestingly enough, the mediation of recency judgments via trace fragility should be useful primarily for intervals of less than an hour, and in this experiment subjects showed little ability to discriminate the recencies of events that occurred one hour, as opposed to two hours, ago.

The data from this time discrimination experiment also indicate that the property subjects are judging is recency rather than "oldness." That is, the internal memory property subjects use to judge recency has a high value at short retention intervals, but it decreases progressively at longer retention intervals—not vice versa. This is why we describe consolidation as a reduction in trace fragility rather than as an increase in trace resistance.

Note that the biological clock provided by the fragility consolidation mechanism cannot be the same as the circadian rhythm that enables some people to choose to wake up at a particular time. To a first approximation this latter clock measures the time since the sun set and not the time since *any* arbitrary prior event such as going to bed.

Interference

A young child must learn hundreds of new associations every day. So why do you suppose it often takes months or years of diligent practice for a child to learn the basic addition and multiplication tables? Taking into account the fact that addition and multiplication are commutative ($X + Y = Y + X$ and $X \cdot Y = Y \cdot X$), and that $X + 0$, $X + 1$, $X \cdot 0$ and $X \cdot 1$ are rather easy to learn, there are fewer than 100 associations to be learned that are not derived from simple rules. So why should they be so difficult to learn?

The reason is interference. One is forming an association between a stimulus consisting of 2 digits and an operator symbol ($+$ or $\cdot$) on the one hand and a number response on the other. The same 10 digits and the same two operator symbols appear over and over again in different compound stimuli associated to different responses. If you give a child a single addition problem, such as $5 + 8 = 13$, you can teach this association very quickly, and the child will remember it very well—so long as you do not attempt to teach a lot of other addition problems. But as soon as you begin teaching that $5 + 6 = 11$ and $9 + 8 = 17$, you are beginning to establish competing associations to each of the elements of the original compound stimulus. The formation of these associations to the same stimulus produces a variety of interfering effects on both the strength of the original association between $8 + 5$ and 13 in storage and the ability to retrieve an answer correctly using the association between $8 + 5$ and 13.

The hypothesis that interference from prior and subsequent learning is the cause of forgetting is as old as the scientific study of human learning and memory. Sometimes one hears it referred to as *the* interference theory of forgetting, but there are many different interference theories. For one thing, the hypothesis that interference plays a major role in forgetting does not preclude the possibility that other factors also play a role. One such factor is passive temporal decay, which is independent of the nature of prior or subsequent learning. There is considerable evidence to support both interference and temporal decay as contributors to storage loss. For another thing, there are several different interference mechanisms, each of which has empirical support. We shall discuss two: *competition* and *unlearning*. Finally, we will discuss the effects of *proactive interference,* which appear to be due entirely to competition.

Competition. Do you know how to spell the five-letter word that begins with w, ends with rd, and means "mysteriously strange?" Doubtless you know that it is either "weird" or "wierd," but which? This is an example of competition, an interference factor that occurs at the time of retrieval. The definition and structural information concerning the first and last letters of the word is strongly associated to both the "ie" form and the "ei" form. (Incidentally, the correct spelling is "weird"—a violation of the "i-before-e" rule. A simple mnemonic will permit you to remember the spelling: "Weird is weird.")

Competition has been studied in the laboratory setting with conventional paired-associate recall experiments by having subjects first learn an AB list and then an AC list (AB-AC paradigm). After subjects have learned both lists, they are asked to recall the B associate of A from the first list. They can sometimes recall both B and C, but not remember which was the correct associate for the first list and which for the second. List differentiation—the ability to distinguish between the responses from the first list and responses from the second—is typically over 95% accurate immediately after learning the second list. But a week later it may have declined to perhaps only 80% accuracy. This decline is not due to competition between a correct and an incorrect association with the same stimulus, but rather to competition between associations with two highly similar compound stimuli: "A + first list" and "A + second list" (Koppenaal 1963; Birnbaum 1965). As long as the association of the compound stimulus "A + first list" with the correct B item is much stronger than the association of the compound stimulus with the incorrect C item, competition need not markedly reduce the percentage of correct recall. However, as the associations grow weaker during the retention interval, competition may emerge as a more significant factor. Chunking compound cues to form new nodes (e.g., the "first A" node) probably reduces competition interference at the time of retrieval. But clearly chunking does not eliminate competition.

Competition arises because a common stimulus element A has two associations B and C. Learning the second AC association need not weaken the stored strength of the AB memory trace in order for competition to lower recall of AB at the time of retrieval. For this reason, competition can be called a retrieval interference factor, because the interfering effect occurs primarily at the time of retrieval, even though it was caused by the learning of a competing AC association during the storage phase for the AB association.

Unlearning. Melton and Irwin (1940) proposed that the subsequent learning of an AC pair also reduces the strength of the originally learned AB pair. They called this phenomenon *unlearning.* For many years there was no convincing experimental evidence to support the unlearning hypothesis, because memory was tested largely by recall, and recall is subject to retrieval interference factors such as competition. As discussed previously in this chapter, it has now been conclusively demonstrated that AC interpolated learning produces retroactive interference on recognition tests of memory for the originally learned AB pair. Although recognition tests are not completely immune to retrieval interference factors, they can be made substantially freer of such interference at the time of retrieval than any kind of recall test.

Recognition tests probably tap the combined strength of association both forward from A to B and backward from B to A. Consistent with this hypothesis, unlearning can be produced in both directions. That is, a backward unlearning design AB-CB produces approximately the same unlearning —as measured by recognition tests—as a forward unlearning design AB-AC. Furthermore, when the interfering learning consists of the same stimuli and responses, but with the pairings rearranged so that both the forward and backward associations are unlearned (AB-ABr paradigm), the unlearning effect on recognition memory is greatest (McGovern 1964; Wickelgren 1976b).

Proactive interference.   Prior learning of an AB pair has no effect on the rate of forgetting for a subsequently learned AC pair as measured by recognition tests. That is, there is no proactive interference effect on the rate of reduction in trace strength in storage. Furthermore, while the learning of AC causes a one-time reduction in the strength of the previously acquired AB association (unlearning) *at the time of AC learning,* there is no increase in the forgetting rate for the AB trace *after* AC learning. Thus two associations to the same node decay at the same rate as a single association to that node (Postman, Stark, and Fraser 1968; Wickelgren 1974a).

Recall tests of AC retention following prior AB learning do show a proactive interference effect on retention. The reduction in recall accuracy in the retention interval for AC is more rapid if there was prior AB learning than if there was prior dissimilar—DB—learning or no list learning at all (Underwood 1957). Competition is one likely reason for the proactive interference effect on recall. For example, when a subject attempts to recall the associate of A on the second list, there may be competition between the B and C items. Such competition is known to increase with the retention interval, as the subject gradually forgets which item, B or C, was in the first list and which in the second. Subjects also appear to develop a set to produce the responses in the list that they are currently learning, and to suppress any previously established response sets for the same stimuli. During the retention interval following second-list learning, the set for the second-list responses diminishes, and the set for the first-list responses recovers (Postman, Stark, and Fraser 1968; Earhard 1976; Wickelgren 1976b). Such changes in response set and decreases in list differentiation with increasing retention interval apparently cause subjects to forget (as measured by recall tests) the AC list faster when it is preceded by a similar AB list than when it is learned in isolation or preceded by a dissimilar—DB—list. Thus the faster forgetting of a target list preceded by a similar list is a phenomenon limited to recall tests of memory and is not found on recognition tests. (This phenomenon is also known as the proactive interference effect on retention.) Hence there is no reason to believe that the basic storage dynamics for AC associations is in any way affected by the presence of previously learned AB associations.

On the whole, the evidence at present indicates relatively little interaction between learning and subsequent retention. Theoretically the nature of encoding ought to have an effect on the susceptibility of a trace to interference, and consistent effects of this type will probably be demonstrated eventually. However, stimuli must be highly similar (near identity) before interference can affect long-term memory. Most long-term forgetting is due to temporal decay, the rate of which does not appear to be affected by the encoding level, or by the nature of encoding within a level.

Decay

In the years of research on memory that followed the classic work of Ebbinghaus, the passive decay in time of memory traces, independent of subsequent experience, was considered a possible mechanism of forgetting. Then, Jenkins and Dallenbach (1924) published a study that demonstrated far more rapid forgetting during a period of wakefulness than during a comparable period of sleep. This sleep effect was interpreted as providing strong support for the interference theory of forgetting, because passive temporal decay was presumed to go on as rapidly during sleep as during waking. McGeoch (1932) further assaulted the idea of passive temporal decay as a forgetting mechanism on what he called logical grounds: nothing occurs solely as a function of time; something has to make it occur. If time does not cause anything, something else must cause forgetting.

Almost everyone accepts McGeoch's philosophical position that time itself does not produce temporal decay, but rather a process or processes within the nervous system. The distinguishing feature of a decay process is that it is not influenced by the nature of the material learned or processed during the retention interval. Rather, it depends upon activity of the nervous system that is relatively independent of the specific material being processed. However, it is perfectly reasonable to imagine that temporal decay may vary as a function of such factors as level of arousal, activity rhythms, and the like. For example, it now appears likely that the slower forgetting during sleep is due largely to a reduction in decay or to an increase in consolidation during sleep, rather than to a reduction in interference during sleep (Ekstrand 1972; Ekstrand et al. 1977).

In the consolidation section I discussed evidence derived from rate-of-forgetting and retrograde-amnesia studies that memory trace becomes less susceptible to storage loss the older it gets. If the only mechanism that produced storage loss were interference, then the shorter the delay between original and similar interfering learning, the greater the interference should be. However, both recall and recognition of AB associations have been studied as a function of the delay between AB learning and subsequent AC interfering learning; and these studies are virtually unanimous in rejecting the hypothesis that interference is greater the shorter the delay between original learning and subsequent interfering learning (Archer and Underwood 1951; Newton and Wickens 1956; Houston 1967; Howe 1969; Postman and Warren 1972; Wickelgren 1974*a*, 1976*b*). Subsequent learning produces interference that is greater the more similar it is to original learning, so there is no doubt that interference produces storage loss. At the same time, there is also no doubt that another factor that produces storage loss becomes less effective as the trace grows older. Experimental findings on delay of interfering learning clearly indicate that this factor is not interference. Therefore, by exclusion, it is the susceptibility to some noninterference (decay) factor producing forgetting that is reduced as the trace becomes consolidated.

SUMMARY

1 Memory trace refers to any change in the nervous system that results from a learning experience.

2 A nonassociative memory consists of a set of locations that contain the patterns representing the concepts used to encode an event. Temporal order is represented by storing the events in a fixed order of locations. Locations are directly accessible, but to find event or concept representations, one must generally search a set of locations.

3 An associative memory consists of a set of nodes, each of which is the unique representation of a concept. An event is represented by the activation of a set of nodes. Event representations are directly accessible, obviating the need for search in most cases.

4 The enormous capacity of rapidly accessible human conceptual memory indicates that our memory traces are directly accessible, obviating the need for search in most cases.

5 Our capacity to judge the recency and ordering of events falls far short of what a nonassociative (tape recorder) memory could accomplish.

6 We can judge the temporal spacing between two occurrences of the same word (A . . . A) substantially better than we can judge the spacing between occurrences of two different words (A . . . B). This difference appears to be inexplicable if memory is nonassociative.

7 Proactive interference is the negative effect of prior learning on learning, storage, or retrieval of subsequently learned material.

8 Retroactive interference is the negative effect of subsequent learning on the storage or retrieval of previously learned material.

9 Proactive and retroactive interference increase sharply with increases in the similarity between the interfering material and the material to be remembered.

10 Human associative memory appears capable of forming vertical associations to specify a new chunk node to represent a combination of elements. The chunking process may play an important role in concept learning, in the response-integration phase of paired-associate learning, and in the learning of associations between elements by incorporating these elements into higher-order propositional or image units.

11 Memory traces have two important dynamic properties: strength and fragility. Strength determines the probability of correct recall and recognition. Fragility determines the susceptibility of the trace to decay.

12 Learning is the acquisition of a memory trace—here described simply as an increase in the strength of that trace.

13 Consolidation is an unconscious process that occurs during storage (the retention interval). Consolidation progressively reduces the susceptibility (fragility) of the trace to passive temporal decay.

14 Forgetting is produced both by active interference from similar subsequent learning and by passive temporal decay of memory traces. The latter depends on the overall activity level of the nervous system (degree of arousal) but is independent of specific experiences.

15 Attention is necessary for learning. We do not learn what we do not attend to. Lesser degrees of attention produce lower degrees of learning, but apparently not faster subsequent forgetting.

16 Motivation and intent to learn indirectly affect learning by affecting exposure to learning experiences, attention, and the level of processing (and therefore the level of encoding). However, when such factors are controlled, motivation and intent to learn have no effect on speed of learning or on the rate of subsequent forgetting.

17 Level of processing (encoding) has a substantial effect on speed of learning. Semantic processing produces much faster learning than phonetic processing. However, mere repetition also produces better learning.

18 Prior learning can either facilitate or interfere with subsequent similar learning. Prior similar learning has no theoretical effect on forgetting rate for associations in storage (as measured by recognition memory tests). It does often increase the rate of forgetting, in a practical sense, on recall tests because competition between the similar memory traces increases over time.

19 Retrograde amnesia appears to be temporally selective, in that the memories most likely to be lost are those most recently established, independent of strength. The same temporal selectivity applies to recovery from retrograde amnesia—the first memories to return tend to be the oldest memories.

20 Nonassociative recency judgments of events occuring within the last hour may be based on the fragility (degree of consolidation) of the memory traces for these events. The results of the consolidation process may thus provide a kind of intermediate-term biological clock that time tags events for recency.   .

21 Associative interference is the strengthening of at least two associations to the same node (AB and AC). Interference can operate during learning, storage, or retrieval.

22 Retroactive associative interference has three negative effects on memory for the previously learned association. First, the subsequently learned association competes with the previously learned AB association at the time of retrieval in a recall test (retrieval interference). Second, the learning of the subsequent AC association reduces the strength in storage of the prior AB association (unlearning or storage interference). Third, the learning of the C response may temporarily reduce the subject's set to produce the B response to any stimulus in a recall test.

23 Temporal decay is the forgetting factor that slows down owing to decreasing trace fragility with increasing trace age. The susceptibility of an AB association to storage interference (unlearning) that results from learning an AC association remains constant regardless of trace age and consolidation.

CHAPTER 9
RETRIEVAL:
RECALL
AND RECOGNITION

OBJECTIVES

1 To distinguish elementary retrieval tasks from more complex retrieval tasks.

2 To discuss the relation between perceptual recognition and recognition memory.

3 To make the point that even item-recognition memory must be considered a type of associative recognition memory—that the familiarity of an item is based on the strength of some association.

4 To describe a two-stage model of recall and recognition: a memory retrieval process followed by a decision process.

5 To discuss the decision processes for several different recognition and recall tasks and the measurement of memory strengths in these tasks.

6 To compare the direct-access and search hypotheses of memory retrieval and to present the evidence favoring a direct-access process for both recognition and recall.

7 To discuss whether recognition is better (easier) than recall.

8 To compare the storage, retrieval, and decision aspects of recognition and recall.

9 To discuss the fact that in recognition memory (and perhaps also in recall), we can trade off decreased response accuracy for increased response speed apparently continuously over a period that ranges from 200 to 1,500 msec depending on the task.

10 To use these speed-accuracy trade-off functions to explore the dynamics of the retrieval process. The discussion will focus on three issues that involve serial versus parallel processing.

11 To discuss the process of automatization: how repeated retrieval of the same association sometimes converts retrieval into a faster (perhaps unconscious) process.

12 To discuss priming (facilitation) of the retrieval of an association due to (a) recent activation of that association and (b) persistence of part of this activation as a kind of short-term (primary) memory trace.

13 To discuss the possible role of inhibition in memory retrieval.

How often have you failed to *recall* the name of someone you know rather well? It is an embarrassing but all too common experience. Usually you would recognize the name immediately if you heard it, and often you can recall it later, given more time, new cues, and less anxiety. This memory problem is not primarily one of learning or storage. The trace for the name is in your memory; you just cannot retrieve it at the moment.

It is even more disorienting to meet someone you are certain you know (and who comes over and starts talking to you like an old friend), but about whom you cannot recall a single fact. Usually it will turn out to be someone you met in a very different context from the one you are in at present. Apparently the context is an important cue for retrieving information about a person. Here again the primary problem is likely to be one of retrieval. No doubt your mind contains at least some memories about this person—if only you could get to them.

The retrieval process in *recognition* memory can also be unreliable, as illustrated by the déjà vu experience. In déjà vu you suddenly feel that what is happening has all happened before, even though you know perfectly well that it hasn't. We get this strong feeling of false familiarity for places and for events. Déjà vu experiences are particularly powerful and frequent in some types of neurological disorders, but most normal people have also experienced them. One plausible explanation for normal déjà vu is that the event that triggers the déjà vu experience resembles some previously stored event (or dream).

ELEMENTARY
AND COMPLEX RETRIEVAL TASKS

Retrieval is the process by which we use our memories to *recognize* something as familiar, *recall* something we previously learned, or judge the *recency* of some event we experienced in the last hour. Among the three Rs of retrieval, recency has received the least systematic attention. In fact, recency has not been established as a discrete form of retrieval, on a par with recognition and recall. Therefore I shall not discuss it here. Nor shall I discuss the more complex memory retrieval processes that frequently occur in our daily lives and that have sometimes been studied in the laboratory. Instead we shall confine our attention to elementary recognition and recall.

Recognition can be subdivided into yes-no and multiple-choice recognition. A *yes-no recognition memory* task is one in which the subject is given a small amount of material and required to make a single mental decision as to whether that material was presented before. This decision seems to be based on the strength of the subject's overall feeling of familiarity for the material. A *multiple-choice recognition memory* task is one in which several alternatives are presented and the subject chooses the one that was presented before. Multiple-choice recognition seems to be based on the comparative familiarity of each alternative. An elementary *recall* task is one in which a subject reports the first thought that comes to mind after he has attended to some cue.

Complex retrieval tasks presumably involve a sequence of elementary recognition and recall processes. Ordinary memory retrieval frequently involves a complex sequence of recognition and recall judgments. For example, in trying to recall someone's name, I first attempt to generate it directly from my concept or image of the person. If that fails, I try to recall specific information concerning the person in an attempt to provide additional retrieval cues to increase the probability of recall from associative memory. During this process a number of alternative names usually pop into my mind, and I test these for correctness using recognition memory. Finally, I have sometimes resorted to going through the alphabet generating common first names—Ann, Amy, Alice, Betty, Barbara, and so forth—testing each name by recognition memory.

It is difficult to control an experimental recognition or recall task so as to insure that it is confined to a single elementary recognition or recall process. In this respect most experimental tasks probably fall short of the ideal. Nevertheless it seems worthwhile to keep the ideal definition in mind and to concentrate on studies that appear to come closest to achieving it.

It is generally good scientific strategy to break a complex process into parts and study these parts one at a time. For example, in the *free-recall* paradigm the subject is presented with a list of perhaps 20 words. Then he is instructed to recall as many of the words as possible. Free recall is a complex process—it requires repeated recall, and subjects can, and probably do, check their generated responses by using recognition memory. Most important, the cues the subject uses to recall each member of the list are not under experimental control. In free-recall situations, retrieval strategies differ enormously, and this makes precise analysis of the process difficult if not impossible. It is often argued that free-recall situations are useful to study because they resemble the more complex recall tasks that occur in real life. However, one of the principal advantages of scientific experimentation is that processes can be studied in the laboratory under much more carefully controlled conditions than occur in real life. Free-recall tasks simply lack this advantage. In analyzing recall, I shall concentrate on studies of *probe recall,* where subjects produce a single response to a specific cue, as in a paired-associate recall paradigm.

It is harder to find examples of complex recognition tasks. Of course a multiple-choice recognition task is more complex than a yes-no recognition task, and the more alternatives it offers the subject, the more complicated it becomes. Complexity can also be introduced into a simple yes-no recognition task if subjects can recognize an item more easily by recalling some mnemonic that they used at the time of acquisition. For example, a subject may have learned the pair "B-eggs" by learning the mediated association "B-bacon-eggs." In principle it might be possible to study such examples of recall-mediated recognition separately from elementary recognition by strictly controlling the time permitted the subject to make a recognition decision. However, recall can be very rapid, and there are no studies available today that allow us to distinguish between elementary recognition memory and recall-mediated recognition memory.

Nor do many studies of paired-associate recall restrict the time for recall enough to prevent the subject from using a recognition check on the first thought that pops into his mind after the stimulus is presented. We know so little about the temporal dynamics of the recall and recognition retrieval processes that we do not know how little time to allot to recall in order to exclude recognition checking. Thus many of the elementary recognition and recall tests I discuss in this chapter are probably not so elementary as we might wish.

PERCEPTUAL RECOGNITION AND RECOGNITION MEMORY

Please pronounce the following list of consonant-vowel-consonant (CVC) syllables as rapidly as possible: GIP, FIP, MIP, SIP, KIP, WIP. Now without looking back, cover the list of CVC syllables and answer the following questions: Were any of the CVC syllables words? If so, which one? Did you recognize some CVC syllable as a word at the time you read it or only later, after you had used your phonetic short-term memory? Many people fail to recognize a word like SIP when it is embedded in a set of nonsense syllables. This demonstrates that it is possible to perceive and pronounce a word at some phonetic level without recognizing that it is a word and getting the associated feeling of familiarity. The word "recognition" is often used to describe both perceptual recognition and recognition memory. However, there is at least some sense in which one can perceive a whole stimulus (presumably you pronounced each CVC syllable as a single integrated verbal unit, not as a sequence of letter names) without recognizing it in the sense of retrieving its familiarity in memory as a unit.

Of course in this case what you perceived was presumably not an integrated word unit but a syllable unit or a set of phoneme units. Presumably you had a feeling of familiarity for the letter constituents of each CVC syllable, and this feeling may have been completely coincident with your perceptual recognition of each syllable. Had you received a sequence of stimuli like GLAP, PLAP, TLAP, you might have recognized immediately upon perceiving TLAP that it contains an unfamiliar phoneme transition /TL/. Had you activated the chunk representative for SIP at the word or concept level, you might well have simultaneously retrieved its familiarity value.

The relationship between the perception of a stimulus and the retrieval of a feeling of familiarity for that stimulus—that is, between perception and recognition memory—is still a mystery. When the same word appears in an associative memory on different occasions and signals the same concept, it should activate the same internal representative in memory. There may be some degree of independence, or some time delay, between the time the stimulus activates its appropriate internal representation (perception) and the growth of a feeling of familiarity for that stimulus (recognition memory). However, it is at least as plausible to assume that these two processes occur at precisely the same time in a manner that is so totally interdependent that the processes cannot and should not be distinguished. At present we simply do not know how these two processes interact.

ITEM MEMORY
AND ASSOCIATIVE MEMORY

Asking subjects whether they have ever been exposed to an item before is a relatively pure test of what might be called recognition memory for a single item. By contrast, when subjects are asked whether two familiar words have been presented before as a pair in a paired-associate learning task, the question refers not to the familiarity of the individual words, but to their pairing. In this case the decision is presumably based on the strength of association between the two words, which may be indirectly mediated by the strength of associations from each word to some higher-level proposition or image of which these two words are constituents.

Most so-called item-recognition tests involve presenting a list of words followed by a recognition test in which the presented words are mixed with a number of distractors, and subjects have to decide whether each word was presented in the preceding list. Under these conditions the decision is not whether any word is absolutely familiar—they all are, since the subject has generally experienced them all tens of thousands of times before. Rather, the decision concerns some type of association between each word and the experimental context. Thus such relative item-recognition memory tests are actually special cases of associative recognition memory tests.

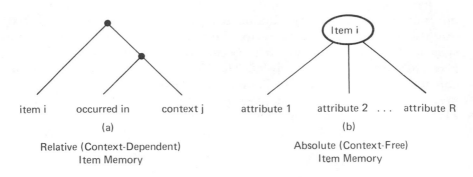

item i   occurred in   context j   attribute 1   attribute 2 ... attribute R

(a)   (b)

Relative (Context-Dependent)   Absolute (Context-Free)
Item Memory   Item Memory

Fig. 9.1 Two associative interpretations of item memory. In (a) the meaning of item memory is that item i has been associated to context j, possibly by means of a proposition such as "item i occurred in context j." In (b) the meaning of item memory is that a chunk node has been formed for the attributes of item i at some time in the past.

Furthermore, even the supposedly absolute recognition memory tests for completely novel stimuli may well tap the strength of association between the familiar constituents of the novel stimulus and some higher-level chunk node created to represent the entire set. Since this is probably how many word-word paired associates are learned, precisely the same type of associative strength may constitute the familiarity dimension judged in all cases of recognition memory. There is really no need to assume two types of strength —item strength and associative strength. Associative strength alone would appear to suffice. It is sometimes convenient to talk about item strength in the context of "item" recognition memory tests. There is no harm in this, so long as it is understood that "item" strength probably refers either (1) to the strength of association between an item node and a node representing the context or (2) to the intraitem associative strength—that is, to associations of the attributes of the item to each other or to their chunk node. A diagram representing an associative coding of item memory is shown in figure 9.1.

Throughout this chapter I shall discuss memory retrieval using examples from either paired-associate or item-recognition memory more or less interchangeably. So far as we can now determine, item memory is a kind of associative memory, so there is little reason to distinguish between them.

TWO MEMORY OUTPUT STAGES:
RETRIEVAL AND DECISION

There are two stages in output from memory. The first stage is the *retrieval* of relevant memory traces. The second stage is a *decision* as to what response to make based on the traces retrieved. The retrieval process is assumed to operate on memory storage, using the retrieval cues (stimuli) as input to retrieve (access) the relevant memory traces. In the strength formulation, what is retrieved is the strengths of one or more memory traces, which then become input to a decision process that selects a response. The response is "yes" or "no" on a yes-no recognition test, or one of several responses on a recall or multiple-choice recognition test.

Let's consider AB paired-associate memory as an example. In the usual forward recall test, the retrieval cue is stimulus item A. This initiates retrieval of the memory traces to item A. When the AB association is in storage and when the recall retrieval process retrieves the AB memory trace (as the only trace retrieved or as the trace with the greatest strength), the decision process selects and outputs B as the response. It is reasonable to assume that the decision rule used by the recall decision process is to output the response that has the greatest retrieved strength of association with the stimulus (retrieval cue). Perhaps there is also a recall threshold such that no response is emitted unless an association with A has a strength greater than some threshold level. A pure *threshold decision rule* is that a response is emitted if, and only if, its strength of association with A exceeds the threshold. If more than one associative strength exceeds the threshold but only one response is permitted, subjects might then also employ a *maximum decision rule* and select the alternative with the greatest strength.

Obviously recall can be aided by introducing additional *retrieval cues*. For example, in paired-associate recall, if one supplies not only the stimulus word but also the first letter of the response word, the probability of correct recall will increase. Besides such structural retrieval cues, one can also provide a synonym or a strong associate of the response words as a retrieval cue. All these cues will increase the probability of correct recall. This is perfectly reasonable under the assumption that the strengths of association from various cues accumulate in some way, increasing the probability that the strength of the correct alternative will exceed the threshold.

In paired-associate recognition memory the retrieval cues for the AB association consist of both the A and B items of the pair. The recognition retrieval process takes these retrieval cues as input and produces the strength of association between A and B as output. This strength serves as the input to the decision process, which may then follow the *criterion decision rule:* respond "yes" (the pair is familiar) if the retrieved strength of the AB association (its familiarity) exceeds some criterion; respond "no" if the retrieved strength is less than the criterion. A recognition criterion differs from a recall threshold in one respect. The recognition criterion is assumed to be highly variable depending on the subject's bias to say "yes." The recall threshold is assumed to be a constant, high level of strength of the AB association below which one simply cannot think of (retrieve) the B response to the A stimulus.

DECISION RULES
AND STRENGTH MEASUREMENT

Yes-No Recognition: Criterion Rule

The most plausible hypothesis about the decision stage of recognition memory is the *criterion rule,* whereby strength (familiarity) is compared to a criterion. If memory strength is above the criterion, the subject responds "yes" (the pair is old or familiar). If it lies below the criterion, the subject responds "no" (the pair is new or unfamiliar). Even under constant conditions there is assumed to be substantial variability in the amount of memory strength acquired by pairs during learning, and there may be variation at the time of retrieval as well. There may also be variation in the storage phase as a result of different rates of consolidation, decay, or interference for previously presented (old) items. Furthermore, there is variation in the strength of new pairs owing to their similarity or association to old items and to noise in the retrieval process. All this produces a distribution in the memory strength for both old and new items (fig. 9.2).

A rather elegant way to measure the strength of the memory trace for

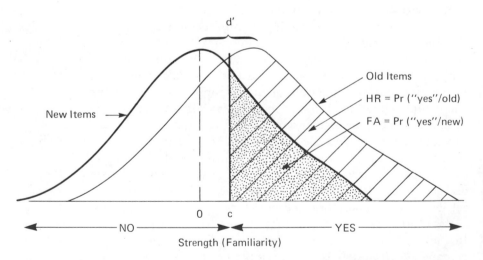

Fig. 9.2 Hypothetical strength distribution for old and new items. According to the criterion decision rule, whenever the strength of an item is above the criterion (c), the subject responds "yes," and whenever the strength is below the criterion, the subject responds "no." The hit rate, HR, is the probability of correctly recognizing an old item. The false-alarm rate, FA, is the probability of incorrectly recognizing a new item. From the hit and false-alarm rates, d' can be calculated. This is the difference between the average memory strength of the old and new items. It is measured in units of the standard deviation of the distributions (here assumed to be equal for old and new items).

old items under any condition is provided by statistical decision theory. This theory was introduced into psychology by Thurstone and greatly extended by Tanner, Swets, and Green. The methods of statistical decision theory and its application to memory are discussed in detail elsewhere, and a detailed analysis is beyond the scope of this book (Thurstone 1927a,b; Tanner and Swets 1954; Egan 1958; Green and Swets 1966; Wickelgren and Norman 1966). The statistical decision analysis of recognition memory converts the empirical probabilities of correct and false recognition (hit rate and false-alarm rate) into a measure of the strength of the memory trace for the old pairs. This measure of memory strength (often given the symbol "d'") takes the average strength of new pairs to be the zero point on the strength scale, and the standard deviation of the strength distribution for new pairs is the unit of measurement. The strength measure d' is thus an *interval scale*—that is, a scale that measures the difference between the strength of correct and incorrect pairs, rather than absolute strength.

Statistical decision analysis of yes-no recognition memory solves the problem of differences in criterion across subjects and across different conditions for the same subject. That is, both correct and false recognition rates will increase, the lower the subject places his criterion on the strength scale. It is desirable to obtain a measure of recognition memory accuracy (strength) that is independent of criterion placement. Such a measure is provided by the d' score, since the same d' value will be obtained using the methods of statistical decision theory no matter where the subject places his criterion on the strength scale.

Multiple-Choice Recognition: Maximum Rule

The statistical decision analysis of recognition memory can be extended to multiple-choice recognition rather plausibly by means of the *maximum rule,* suggested by Thurstone. According to this rule the subject chooses the alternative that has the maximum strength of familiarity (Thurstone 1927a; Wickelgren 1968). Tables exist that translate from the probability of correct choice for various numbers of alternatives to the measure of d', using simplifying assumptions such as the equality of the standard deviations of all of the strength distributions for each alternative.

The probability of correct choice on a multiple-choice recognition task decreases as the incorrect alternatives become more similar to the correct alternatives. For example, if one has learned the paired associate "ball-pink," the probability of correct recognition is lower when the choice is among "pink," "red," "blue," and "maroon" than when the choice is among "pink," "sad," "ant," and "democracy," because in the former case one must remember the exact response, whereas in the latter case one need only remember that it was a color. Most of you know that the difficulty of a multiple-choice test depends greatly on the nature of the incorrect alternatives (the distractors). Whenever you can rule out an absurd alternative answer, your probability of guessing correctly will be greater than chance, even if you have little specific knowledge. In strength-theoretic terms, the difficult distractors are those most strongly associated to the cues in the question. The greater the average strength of the distractors, the smaller the difference in strength (d') between the distractors and the correct alternative.

The fact that multiple-choice recognition memory depends on the similarity of the incorrect alternatives to the target alternative has important implications for the police lineup, the procedure by which witnesses identify criminal suspects. If the criminal is known to be a young, red-haired male, it is obviously no protection whatsoever to a young red-haired male to see if an eyewitness can pick him out of a lineup composed of blonds, brunets, women, and an aged derelict. I feel sure that this extreme is not typical of police lineups, but the similarity of the distractor subjects to the actual suspect depends on thousands of variables, and the more closely the distractors resemble the suspect, the more protection the suspect receives. Where do we draw the line? It is an important legal question, and it needs a precise answer if we are to provide more nearly equal (if not perfect) justice for everyone.

Small Recall: The Maximum Rule

When one is testing recall with the alternative responses selected from a small population (such as the set of binary digits 0 and 1), there may be little difference between what is nominally called a recall test and what is nominally called a multiple-choice recognition test, provided the subject is highly familiar with the response set. However, when there were only four possible alternatives, one study found substantially shorter latencies in paired-associate recall than in four-alternative multiple-choice recognition for the same pairs (Norman and Wickelgren 1969). Thus while it may be reasonable to apply the maximum-decision rule to recall from a small population of alternatives, even in this case recall and recognition may be fundamentally different mechanisms. For example, multiple-choice recognition may be *sequential* retrieval of familiarity for each alternative, followed by choice of the strongest alternative. Recall may be a *simultaneous* comparison of alternative strengths: parallel retrieval of all the associations with the stimulus item, followed by choice of the strongest alternative.

Large Recall: The High-Threshold Rule

When the number of response alternatives is extremely large, as in a word-word paired-associate recall task with hundreds or thousands of different words, the subject's ability to recall a response word, given a stimulus word, probably depends virtually entirely on a specific association between the stimulus word and the response word. Response sets are largely eliminated as a factor. Under such conditions it is not reasonable to assume the maximum-decision rule, since the number of alternatives is not well defined. When the number of response alternatives is extremely large, it seems more reasonable to assume the *high-threshold rule,* suggested by Bahrick. According to this rule the subject responds only if the strength of association between the stimulus and a response exceeds some high threshold (Bahrick 1965; Wickelgren 1974*b*). If the recall threshold is very high, an incorrect alternative will have little or no chance of exceeding the threshold, and errors will consist largely of omissions, as often appears to be the case in such situations. Intrusions (incorrect guesses) may result either because an incorrect item occasionally exceeds threshold strength, or more often because the subject resorts to random guessing when no alternative exceeds the threshold.

RETRIEVAL:
DIRECT ACCESS OR SEARCH?

Retrieval is the process of accessing a memory trace to convert it from the passive stored state into the active state, so that you are consciously thinking of it. Retrieval makes a stored memory usable. There are two basic types of retrieval processes: direct access and search. With a *direct-access process* the cues presented at the time of retrieval *(retrieval cues)* directly activate the associated memories; there is no need to search alternative memory locations. The associated memories just pop into mind automatically. With a *search process* one must look for the desired memories in a number of possible memory locations. In a pure search process the retrieval cues serve as checks to identify the desired memories as one searches each location. As we saw in chapter 8, hybrid retrieval processes are also possible. In a hybrid retrieval process one uses some retrieval cues to access directly a subset of all the possible memory traces. Then one performs a serial search through this subset, using the remainder of the retrieval cues as a check.

A familiar analogy may help. Instead of retrieving a memory from your mind, imagine that you want to retrieve a flashlight to help you see in your tent in the middle of the night. Direct access is when the retrieval cue "flashlight" causes your hand to go straight to the top right side of your sleeping bag, where you remember leaving it. Search is when you grope all over the tent with no idea where it is, but with sufficient knowledge checks to recognize the flashlight when you grasp it and to reject items that are not flashlights. A hybrid (mixed direct-acess and search) process is when you know it's in your pack, but you have to search through the whole pack to find it.

As we saw in chapter 8, a nonassociative memory requires search in retrieval. An associative memory makes it possible to have direct-access retrieval, though search can still play an important role in making full use of the knowledge stored in an associative memory. Since human long-term memory is associative, and even nonassociative short-term memory is the priming of nodes (and possibly links) in an associative network, I shall argue that the basic memory retrieval process in both recognition and recall is direct access. To retrieve the familiarity of an A-B pair in recognition, or to retrieve the strongest associate of A in a recall test, we do not need to search any alternative memory traces. The retrieved strength (familiarity) of an A-B pair comes to mind automatically. Similarly, activation of an A node automatically activates all nodes associated to it, and if the strength of the (forward) association from A to B is great enough (that is, if it exceeds the recall threshold and is greater than the strength of association from A to any other C node), then the B node will be activated automatically.

However, the search process may play an important role in retrieval from associative memory. What if the forward association from A to B were too weak to produce B, given retrieval cue A, but the backward association from B to A were strong enough to serve as a good check that B was indeed the desired associate of A? Since forward and backward associations are separate, can have different strengths as a result of learning, can be unlearned separately to different extents, and can be subject to substantial differences in competition, this situation will occur fairly often. Hence if one could generate a reasonably small set of possible Bs in memory, one could retrieve additional information from associative memory by using a search procedure that checked each possible B for a strong (backward) association from B to A. It's not always possible to limit the subset of memory traces enough to make this search process practical—but sometimes it is. An example of such a search process was given earlier in the chapter when we discussed trying to recall a person's name by generating A-names (Amy, Abby, etc.), B-names (Barbara, Betty, etc.), and so on. I don't know how often we engage in such complex search processes in retrieval from long-term memory. In any case, the generation of alternatives is a direct-access recall process using general retrieval cues. Hence the two basic components of this complex memory search process are the direct-access retrieval processes of recall and recognition checking.

The next two sections will describe the direct-access theory and the search theory in more detail. In the four subsequent sections we will consider a variety of evidence that favors direct access as the basic retrieval process for both recall and recognition at short and long retention intervals.*

The Direct-Access Theory

When a test item or pair of items is presented in a recognition test, the strength of the relevant associations either between the pair of items or

*For further discussion of this issue, see McCormack (1972); Corballis (1975); Wickelgren (1975b).

between the item and the context (list cues) is assumed to be directly retrieved. Although the retrieval of trace strength is assumed to be a direct-access process, it is still assumed to require time. Thus the retrieval of trace strength grows over a period of time following presentation of the test items. A period of one or two seconds yields relatively complete retrieval of trace strength in a variety of tasks (Reed 1973, 1975; Dosher 1976; Corbett and Wickelgren 1978). At any time during the retrieval process the subject can make a decision regarding the test items based on the strength retrieved thus far. He does so by comparing that strength to some criterion. If the strength lies above the criterion, the subject decides "yes," if not, he decides "no."

The simplest direct-access hypothesis for recognition memory is that the retrieval process for one association is unaffected by the strength of any other associations in memory. In particular, if one is retrieving the strength of an AB test association, the strengths of AC or DB associations are assumed to be irrelevant to the retrieval process for the AB association. There is some evidence to support this hypothesis with respect to the ultimate asymptotic retrieved strength of the AB association (after two seconds or more of retrieval time) (Wickelgren 1967b; Postman, Stark, and Fraser 1968), though the rate of retrieving an AB association appears to be slowed very slightly by the presence of a strong AC association. Existing data on retrieval dynamics are consistent with the direct-access theory, in which the rate of retrieving an AB association is somewhat slower in the presence of an AC interfering association (Wickelgren and Corbett 1977; Dosher 1978).

Any theory of recall must almost necessarily assume the possibility of competition between AB and AC associations under some conditions. In the usual recall procedure a choice is required among all the possible responses to the A stimulus. Thus a comparison of the relative strengths of associations between A and all possible responses is logically required in the recall task, although if omissions are permitted, the competition may only be among those associations that exceed the recall threshold. In recall as in recognition there is evidence that the presence of a strong AC association retards the rate of retrieval of strength for an AB association; and the magnitude of this association interference effect on retrieval appears to be exactly the same in recall as in recognition (Houston 1968; Wickelgren and Corbett 1977). This suggests that the same retrieval process is used in both cases. I shall argue that in both cases this retrieval process is direct access.

The Search Theory

Even when the direct-access process logically involves the retrieval of more than one associative strength, as in recall, this retrieval is assumed to proceed in parallel—that is, simultaneously for all associations. By contrast, a search theory assumes that memory retrieval for even a single association requires sequential accessing of several different memory traces. Sternberg

(1966, 1969), for example, assumes that a subject, in recognizing whether an item came from some previously presented list, sequentially searches every memory location used to store items from the previous list, looking for a match between the test item and an item in memory.*

Sternberg distinguishes two types of search: self-terminating and exhaustive. The self-terminating search is assumed to end whenever a match is made between the test item and an item in memory. The exhaustive search compares the test item with *every* item stored in some set of memory locations, whether or not a match occurs part way through the set. The self-terminating search appears a priori to be more functional, but Sternberg felt that certain evidence compelled the assumption that recognition memory search was exhaustive rather than self-terminating.

Even the most extreme search theories have always implicitly or explicitly assumed that the subject need not search all the millions of locations or associations in memory, but instead can directly access a relatively small population of alternatives (small set) through which the sequential search takes place. Clearly it would be more parsimonious if a direct-access theory could be made to fit all the facts of memory retrieval, since both the search and the direct-access hypotheses assume that direct access is a large component of retrieval.

Let's consider two recall tasks that illustrate the assumptions of the typical search theory. In a test by probe recall of verbal short-term memory for a list of digits, the subject is instructed to produce the item that followed the probe digit in the preceding list. For this task Sternberg (1967) assumed the following retrieval process: (1) the subject has direct access to the memory locations corresponding to the successive list items, (2) the subject begins to search sequentially through the list (typically from the beginning) until he matches the probe item, and (3) the subject retrieves the item in the next memory location and produces it as a response. Note that Sternberg assumed that the search process in recall was self-terminating. It is, of course, logically possible that recall involves a self-terminating search while recognition involves an exhaustive search, but such an assumption is less elegant than assuming the same type of search for both.

Another type of recall task involves presenting subjects with a category, such as "animals," and a letter, such as H. Subjects are instructed to recall a member of the category whose name starts with the letter, in this case an animal whose name begins with H. A typical search theory of this type of recall assumes that the subject first directly accesses all storage locations that correspond to members of the category and begins to search sequentially for one whose name begins with H (Freedman and Loftus 1971). Here the recall search process is usually assumed to be self-terminating.

---

*Note that Sternberg formulated his search theories of memory retrieval *only* for a very limited-capacity short-term memory. Others extended the search theory to long-term memory.

Recognition Memory

Short-term retention. In a study of enormous influence, Sternberg (1966) asked subjects to memorize a target list of anywhere from one to six digits. Then he presented a probe digit and measured the reaction time subjects took to decide whether or not this digit had been on the list. The time it took to make this decision appeared to increase linearly with the length of the target list. That is, the reaction time function was a straight line. Furthermore, the same rate of increase obtained both for probe items in the list (old items) and for probe items not in the list (new items). Finally, Sternberg found no significant differences in the reaction time for old items chosen from different serial positions within lists of any given length. These results led Sternberg to conclude that recognition memory involved an exhaustive serial search of the target list. If the search proceeded from the beginning of the list and was self-terminating, one might expect a primacy effect: faster reaction times for probe items from the initial positions in the list. Alternatively, one might expect a recency effect if subjects began scanning from the end of the list. Furthermore, if the search were self-terminating, subjects would encounter the old items, on the average, after searching only half of the items in the target set, while in order to say "no" to new items they would have to search the entire set. This leads to the prediction that the rate of increase in the reaction time as a function of set size (list length) for old items would be a half the rate for new items. This prediction is contrary to what was obtained. The predicted functions for both exhaustive and self-terminating search are shown in figure 9.3.

Under other conditions one typically obtains primacy and recency effects in the strength of items in lists. In particular, the probabilities of correct recognition are greater for the first and last items than for the middle items. Therefore one might expect a direct-access strength theory to predict primacy and recency effects in decision latencies for recognition memory as well. Furthermore, while a direct-access strength theory should predict that the reaction times will increase with the length of the list, because items in longer lists should have a lower average strength in memory, it is harder to make a direct-access strength theory predict that reaction time will increase as a linear function of target set size—though this has been done (Anderson 1973; Cavanagh 1976). Accordingly, Sternberg's results were taken as strong evidence for an exhaustive-search process in recognition retrieval from short-term verbal memory.

Sternberg's findings have been replicated in studies that adhere strictly to critical aspects of his procedure. They have not generally been replicated in studies that use other experimental procedures. The results of these studies strongly favor the direct-access theory over the search theory. Furthermore, the conditions required to obtain Sternberg's results suggest a very plausible reason why Sternberg obtained no primacy or recency effects.

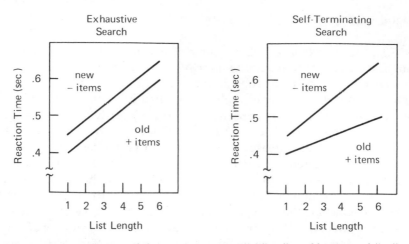

Fig. 9.3 Example predictions of the reaction time to say "yes" to old items and "no" to new items, according to a serial exhaustive search theory and a serial self-terminating search theory. Sternberg's experimental findings agreed with the exhaustive search theory, where the rate of increase in reaction time as a function of list length is the same for old and new items. If the search were self-terminating, the rate for old items should be half the rate for new items.

To obtain Sternberg's results, the presentation rate must be relatively slow (no faster than one item per second), and there must be a relatively long (two-second) interval between the end of the list and the presentation of the probe item. These conditions allow ample opportunity for rehearsal. And rehearsal could easily eliminate those differences in degree of learning that typically account for primacy effects and those differences in retention interval that account for recency effects. Strong primacy and recency effects *are* obtained when presentation rates are faster and testing is immediate, precisely as one would expect under the direct-access strength theory (Morin, DeRosa, and Stultz 1967; Morin, DeRosa, and Ulm 1967; Corballis 1967; Kirsner and Craik 1971; Burrows and Okada 1971; Corballis, Kirby, and Miller 1972).

If the linear increase in recognition latency with increasing set size were established as a valid indicator of retrieval time in recognition memory, it would still be strong evidence for the search hypothesis. However, the linear increase has been established only for relatively small variations in set sizes (from one to six in Sternberg's study). It is a fact that any steadily increasing function will be reasonably well fit by a linear function over a small range of variation in the independent or dependent variable. The range of variation in the independent (set size) variable and the dependent (reaction time) variable in these studies has been very small. Therefore it is not surprising that they are well fit by linear functions.

264

But the significance of the supposedly linear increase in reaction time is seriously compromised, under even these limited conditions, by Sternberg's failure to deal with an important confounding factor—namely, speed-accuracy trade-off. Subjects can trade off speed for accuracy in any known reaction time task, including recognition memory retrieval (Reed 1973, 1975; Dosher 1976; Wickelgren 1977*a*). Thus there appears to be some sort of time or accuracy criterion that subjects are capable of varying. This produces corresponding variation in the actual reaction times and associated error rates in any given condition. In every study that I have seen in which error rates have been reported, error rates have increased substantially with increasing list length in the Sternberg paradigm (Wickelgren 1975*b*). Such results suggest that the recognition times for long lists are underestimated, perhaps seriously. The form of the speed-accuracy trade-off is such that, at the very high levels of accuracy that subjects are typically instructed to obtain, small differences in error rate translate into extremely large differences in reaction time. Thus the actual reaction times obtained in these studies at varying error rates for different set sizes may not be very meaningful.

Finally, even under the standard Sternberg conditions, Baddeley and Ecob (1973) have found that presenting a digit more than once in a target list reduces the reaction time for that digit compared to the reaction time for nonrepeated digits in the same list and for digits in comparable lists without repeats. These results are precisely what one would expect under the direct-access strength theory, but they appear inconsistent with an exhaustive-search theory. Baddeley and Ecob obtained a linear increase in reaction time with increasing list length and an absence of serial position effects, just as Sternberg did. This demonstrates that the findings that are said to support an exhaustive theory can be obtained under conditions where another finding clearly contradicts it.

Long-term retention. As I have pointed out, it was never very reasonable to assume that a serial search process operated as a general model of long-term recognition. One must assume, at a minimum, that subjects can directly access some relevant subset of memory locations to search. It would simply require too much time to search all the contents of long-term memory, even at the high-speed scanning rates Sternberg proposed.

One of the most promising paradigms for evaluating a search theory of long-term recognition memory is the category-exemplar recognition task: deciding whether a given word is a member of a given category. Some studies have found that recognition memory reaction time increases with the number of examples in a category, and these studies tend to support the search theory, but other studies have failed to obtain this finding. It seems likely that such category-membership recognition decisions are mediated by the strength of the association between an example and a category concept (Landauer and Freedman 1968; Meyer 1970; Juola and Atkinson 1971; Wilkens 1971; Collins and Quillian 1970; Egeth, Marcus, and Bevan 1972). As with short-term recognition memory, the recognition time for an item in long-term memory is reduced by increasing the frequency of past exposure to that item or by increasing its saliency in other ways (Atkinson and Juola 1973). At present there is no evidence that requires us to reject the parsimonious direct-access retrieval hypothesis in favor of a more complex hypothesis.

Recall

Short-term retention.   In Sternberg's (1967) probe digit experiment recall times increased monotonically and approximately linearly with serial position. Recall time was fastest for the first item and slowest for the last item on the list. However, Sternberg clearly could not assume that all his subjects were beginning their search at the beginning of the list, since the time to recall the second item, given the first item as the cue, increased as a function of list length. There were some more complex discrepancies as well. To resolve these discrepancies, Sternberg proposed that subjects begin their search at various positions in the list. However, it is equally plausible to assume that under Sternberg's conditions, which encouraged rehearsal, the strength of associations decreased systematically with increasing serial position. Since recall time should decrease with increasing associative strength, Sternberg's results are easily accounted for by a direct-access strength theory. Once again we must question the significance of the linear increase in recall time with either list length or serial position, considering the probability of a speed-accuracy trade-off. Furthermore, even the monotonic increase in recall reaction times as a function of serial position (pure primacy effect) is very rarely observed in either short-term or long-term recall studies. For example, under conditions that minimize rehearsal of prior items, Norman found a simple recency effect, wherein the fastest probe reaction times were for the last items in the list. Other investigators have found both primacy and recency effects in probe recall studies (Norman 1966; Waugh 1970; DeRosa and Baumgarte 1971).

Long-term retention.   The oftener a pair of items is presented, the more the probe recall latency of the response to the stimulus decreases for a very large number of trials beyond the last error in paired associate-learning.* Freedman and Loftus (1971) tested long-term recall of a category member beginning with a given letter. They found that the number of examples in a category has no necessary effect on reaction times when the category cues are strongly associated to the response items—for example, in recalling an animal whose name starts with the letter Z, to which a correct response is Zebra. Thus the strength of association between the cues and the response—not the

---

*See the long list of studies in Wickelgren (1975*b*, p. 241).

number of items in the relevant categories—appears to be the variable that significantly influences recall reaction time.

RECOGNITION AND RECALL COMPARED

Is Recognition Better Than Recall?

In general, subjects score higher on recognition than on recall. One reason for this, as Davis, Sutherland, and Judd emphasized, is that the number of alternatives is typically much higher in a recall test than in a recognition test. This leads to differences that are the result of chance guessing alone. When such differences are eliminated by using a correction procedure, or by having the number of alternatives on the recognition test equal the number on the recall test, the difference between recognition and recall scores is partly or wholly eliminated (Davis, Sutherland, and Judd 1961; Green and Moses 1966; Kintsch 1968; Norman and Wickelgren 1969).

Up to now, the greatest problem in comparing recall and recognition scores has been the tendency to confound the differences in the retrieval process with differences in the memories being tested. This confusion has created flagrant errors. For example, there have been numerous studies in which recognition of words from some previously presented list was compared with free recall of the words on the list. Under such circumstances recognition may be nearly perfect while free recall is less than 50% accurate. The comparison has little meaning. Recognition tests tap associations in both directions—from the words to the context (or list-name concepts) and from the context to the words. Free recall depends primarily on associations from the context to the words. Since direct associations in this direction are typically very weak, free recall often uses a much more complex process of subjective organization of the list. In this process subjects recall words in clusters, using associations between related words in the list or between superordinate category labels (for example, "vehicle") that are associated with various words in the list (for example, "car," "truck," "bus") (Jenkins and Russell 1952; Deese 1961; Rothkopf and Coke 1961; Bousfield 1953; Cohen 1966; Tulving and Pearlstone 1966; Mandler 1967). Because the associations that mediate free-recall performance are almost completely different from the associations that mediate item recognition for words in the same list, any differences between recognition and free recall are more plausibly attributed to differences between the associations tapped by the two retrieval processes than to differences between the retrieval processes themselves. This interpretation is consistent with the fact that using lists with a high level of interitem associative strength, or lists that are highly organized into categories, facilitates free recall far more than it facilitates item recognition (Cofer 1967; Kintsch 1968).

In reaction to some of these inconclusive comparisons of recognition and free recall, the incomparable Endel Tulving (1968), who likes to poke holes in other people's theories, performed an "inappropriate" recall and recognition experiment in which recall performance was actually superior to recognition. Watkins (1974) used the same idea to produce spectacularly higher performance in recall than in recognition. He gave subjects paired associates of the form "spani-el," "amnes-ic," and "explo-re." In the recall condition subjects were given the first five letters and asked to produce the last two letters. In the recognition test they were given only the last two letters mixed with distractor letter pairs and were asked to identify those pairs that had occurred in the preceding list. Subjects clearly recognized that the two parts of the items on the original paired-associate list combined to form English words. They had no idea that they were going to be tested later for recognition of the last two letters in isolation. After a retention interval of a little over half an hour, performance on the recognition test (for the last two letters) was only slightly above chance, while on the recall test it was extremely high. Once again completely different associations were being tapped by the recognition and recall tests, which totally confounds the tests as comparisons of the recognition and recall retrieval processes.*

A Theoretical Comparison of Recall and Recognition

There are three primary issues in a theoretical comparison of recall and recognition: Is the same memory store used in both recall and recognition? Is the same retrieval process used in both recall and recognition? Is the same decision process used in both recall and recognition? Whenever the answer to one of these questions is "no," one wants to know the nature of the difference.

Storage.   It is widely believed that recall and recognition tap the same basic memory storage system. There is no reason to doubt this assumption. The same information is used to answer either type of question, and it would be dysfunctional for humans to store the same information in two different storage systems.

However, it does not follow that any comparison of recall and recognition tests retrieval of exactly the same associations. As we have just seen, most comparisons of recall and recognition have probably confounded the comparison of output processes by tapping very different memory traces in recall and recognition.

---

*One variable is confounded by another when differences in the first variable are accompanied by differences in the second variable; thus we do not know which variable is responsible for the effects observed.

In recognition and free recall of items, Tulving has pointed out that recall and recognition can be considered end points on a continuum defined by the number of *retrieval cues* (and therefore the number of memory traces) used in the retention test. Tulving and Watkins (1973) performed an experiment that, as they admit, demonstrated the obvious: that recall of the words in a list increases as you provide the subject with an increasing number of letters from the words to be recalled. Recognition—in which one provides all of the letters in a word—represents the most extreme form of such a test. It certainly makes sense to consider the retrieval cues operative in any retention test. This is simply another way of discussing the associations that are tapped by any retention test.

An ideal comparison of output processes in recall and recognition probably occurs for AB paired associates. Even here two recall tests—forward recall from A and backward recall from B—may be necessary in order to tap the same memory traces as are tapped by a single AB pair recognition test (Wolford 1971; Wickelgren and Corbett 1977).

Retrieval.   As we have seen, the existing evidence supports a direct-access retrieval hypothesis for both recall and recognition. Furthermore, the rate of retrieval in AB paired-associate recognition memory appears to be precisely the same as it is in forward recall of B, given A as a cue. (The retrieval rate for backward recall has not yet been determined [Wickelgren and Corbett 1977].) Hence there is reason to believe that the same basic retrieval process may be employed in recall and recognition.

Decision.   In the decision stage conventional recall and yes-no recognition memory necessarily differ, because recall is a comparative judgment of many possible B responses, while yes-no recognition is an absolute judgment with respect to a single B response. Both the motor responses and the logical character of the decision are different.

Multiple-choice recognition can provide essentially the same decision problem as small recall (recall from a small population of alternatives). However, as we have seen, multiple-choice recognition may not be a single elementary retrieval task. Rather, it may be a task in which a succession of recognition retrievals are performed and the alternative with the greatest retrieved strength is then chosen.

Finally, a yes-no decision task has been invented for recall of paired associates. One presents the A item to which the subject is to recall the B item. After a variable lag one presents either the correct B item or an incorrect D item, and the subject must respond "yes" or "no" within 0.4 sec. Since it has been established that 0.4 sec is too little time to perform above chance on a test of AB paired-associate recognition memory, we know that the high level of performance subjects achieved in this task was the result of recalling B to the A cue (Wickelgren and Corbett 1977).

Overview.   The retrieval process appears to be identical in recall and recognition, and the same memory system is used in both tasks. There are two principal differences between recall and recognition. First, typically (although not necessarily) they differ in the decision stage. Second, there are typically differences in the associations tapped by recall and recognition, because recognition has more retrieval cues than recall.

RETRIEVAL DYNAMICS

Suppose you were asked to decide "yes" or "no" by pressing one of two buttons whether a loud auditory stimulus was presented to your right (as opposed to your left) ear within 250 msec of its onset. You could accomplish this task with a high level of accuracy. Now suppose you were asked to decide within 250 msec whether that auditory stimulus was an English word, or whether it had been presented earlier in the experiment. This time you would be highly inaccurate. Indeed, you would perform at chance. The memory retrieval processes required by the latter two tasks have not progressed far enough to influence choice responding 250 msec after stimulus onset. One can monitor the time course of these memory retrieval processes by varying the time subjects are given to respond and measuring accuracy as a function of response time. This means of measuring the dynamics (time course) of the retrieval process is called a speed-accuracy trade-off (SAT) function.

Response time can be manipulated in a variety of ways. Subjects can be instructed to respond within a certain time interval (e.g., between 400 and 500 msec following stimulus onset) and can be given trial-to-trial feedback regarding their actual response time. Subjects can be given differential payoffs for speed versus accuracy of response. Finally, an auxilliary response signal telling the subject to respond now can be presented at a varying time after the primary stimulus. ("Now" in this case means a fixed 200 msec after the onset of the response signal.) Standard reaction time instructions ("respond as fast and accurately as possible") yield a single point on such an SAT function. Generally this point is fairly near the asymptote of the SAT function (the highest accuracy level that is reached at long processing times). Reaction time (RT) studies thus yield a much less complete characterization than SAT studies of the memory retrieval process in any one condition. However, RT studies are much easier to perform. They permit one to study several conditions for what it would cost to obtain the entire SAT function for a single condition. So it becomes a matter of scientific judgment which approach is best to answer a particular question concerning the dynamics of cognitive processes, such as memory retrieval. In discussing the issue of search versus direct access, I relied primarily on evidence from RT studies. In the present section I shall rely primarily (but not exclusively) on evidence from SAT studies.

An example SAT function for word-word paired-associate recognition memory is shown in figure 9.4. In this experiment subjects answered "yes" or "no" when asked whether a test pair of words had been presented as a pair earlier in the experiment (Wickelgren and Corbett 1977). SAT functions have three basic parameters. The first is the *intercept*—I—the time below which performance is at a chance level of accuracy. The second is the *asymptote*— A—the maximum level of accuracy achieved with unlimited retrieval time. Presumably A is determined by the strength of the memory trace in storage. The third is the *rate*—R—at which accuracy increases as a function of retrieval time after the intercept. The dynamics of memory retrieval are measured by the nature of the SAT function and its intercept and rate parameters. Across a variety of conditions and types of materials, SAT functions for memory retrieval have been found to be approximately exponential in their approach to asymptotic accuracy with increasing retrieval time (Corbett 1975, 1977; Dosher 1976, 1978; Wickelgren and Corbett 1977), namely:

Retrieved Memory Strength (d') = A $(1-e^{-R(T-I)})$

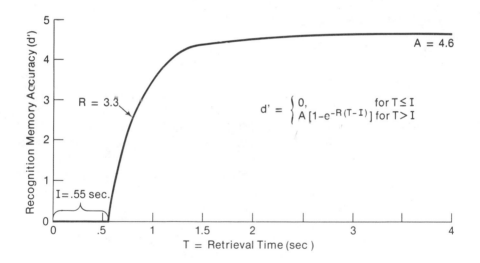

$$d' = \begin{cases} 0, & \text{for } T \leq I \\ A[1-e^{-R(T-I)}] & \text{for } T > I \end{cases}$$

Fig. 9.4 Speed-accuracy tradeoff (SAT) function showing how accuracy in recognition memory for a pair of words increases as a function of the time the subject has to decide whether the pair is old (previously presented) or new (not previously presented). Accuracy is here measured in d' (memory strength) units, with d' = 0 representing chance accuracy and d' = 4.6 representing about 99% accuracy in classifying pairs as old or new. I (intercept of the SAT function) is the retrieval time below which recognition performance is at chance. A (asymptote of the SAT function) is the maximum level of accuracy achievable with essentially unlimited retrieval time. Presumably A is limited by the level of trace strength in storage. R is the rate at which recognition accuracy increases from the intercept to the asymptote.

All-or-None
versus Incremental Retrieval

In recognition memory for word-word pairs, the intercept is about 400 msec, and to achieve near asymptotic performance requires another 600 msec of retrieval time (Wickelgren and Corbett 1977; Corbett 1977; Dosher 1978). This is a very substantial time interval over which slower speed of responding can be traded off for increased accuracy. If memory retrieval were an all-or-none process that always finished after a fixed 700 msec, the SAT function would be a step function that went along at chance accuracy ($d' = 0$) until 700 msec, when it would increase abruptly to whatever the asymptotic accuracy level was for the retrieval process. It is clear from figure 9.4 that memory retrieval is not an all-or-none process with a fixed (invariant) finishing time. It is still possible that memory retrieval is an all-or-none process, but the retrieval time is enormously variable (over a 600 msec range for simple paired associates and even longer for more complex material). However, the most natural interpretation is that memory retrieval is a continuous, incremental activation of memory strength over a period of 600 msec or so.

Parallel Processing of Retrieval Cues

As we have seen, the basic retrieval process appears to be the same for recall and recognition prior to the output or decision phase. Even the dynamics of retrieval (the form of the SAT function, rate, and intercept) appear to be identical for recognition of an AB pair and yes-no recall of B to the A retrieval cue. In addition to providing support for the hypothesis that recall and recognition use identical retrieval processes, this result shows that retrieval can proceed in parallel from two memory nodes (two retrieval cues) as fast as from a single memory node (Wickelgren and Corbett 1977).

A more direct demonstration of parallel processing of retrieval cues was obtained in a study of recognition memory for sentences consisting of five parts: subject, verb, object, location, and time (e.g., "The dog bit a boy in the park yesterday"). Subjects were asked to decide whether all the parts of a test probe came from the same sentence. Retrieval dynamics were identical regardless of whether the test probe had two or three parts (e.g., SVO versus SV, VO, or SO). When the test probe consisted of an entire sentence (all five parts), retrieval dynamics were slower than when the test probe consisted of two or three parts. This indicates that somewhere between three and five such parts (chunks) is the limit for parallel memory retrieval (Dosher 1976). This limited-capacity parallel process for memory retrieval is so close to the limited span of apprehension in visual perception that one is tempted to assume that the limitation is the same in both cases.* Reading is a limited-capacity,

*See the discussion in chapter 6.

272

parallel process that is capable of recognizing about four chunks simultaneously with little or no loss in efficiency. Beyond this span we process material serially in groups of four or fewer chunks each.

Associative Interference

In the last section I pointed out that it is possible to process in parallel a limited number of cues converging on the same higher-level (propositional) chunk node. At several points in earlier chapters I have discussed the somewhat similarly limited capacities of the mind for parallel processing of several independent stimuli, which may or may not converge on any higher-order node that integrates them into a single unified percept. In this section I discuss the simultaneous retrieval of two divergent associations to the same node (AB and AC).

Perhaps because we can only pronounce one word at a time, many people have the impression that they can only think of one word at a time. As I have been at some pains to point out, we have a substantial capacity to think of several ideas—including words—at once. (I will discuss this capacity in the following sections.) Retrieving two divergent associations to the same node is just another example of this parallel processing capacity. True, we cannot simultaneously recall out loud two words ((B and C) associated to the same stimulus word (A). However, when this output limitation is avoided by means of the yes-no recall technique, it appears that subjects can in some sense think of two associates to a stimulus at the same time. Subjects can make a yes-no response that matches a test item (B, C, or D) against both of the correct (B and C) associates almost as fast as they can match a test item with a single associate (e.g., B). Retrieval of two associates to a common stimulus is slightly slower than retrieval of a unique association, but not so much slower as to suggest serial retrieval of each association. Furthermore, the existence of an interfering AC association slows *recognition* retrieval dynamics for an AB pair as much as it slows *recall* dynamics for B, given retrieval cue A. Once again we see support for a common retrieval process in both recall and recognition (Wickelgren and Corbett 1977).

Coding Level
and Chain Parallel Processing

Posner and his colleagues have shown that subjects can classify two same-case forms of the same letter (e.g., AA or aa) as belonging to the same letter name class faster and more accurately than they can classify two different-case forms of the same letter (e.g., Aa or aA). Subjects can classify different-sized letters (e.g., AA or aa) faster than different-case forms but more slowly than same-case forms. Classifying two letters as belonging to the same higher-order class (e.g., vowel versus consonant) is the slowest of all of the previously mentioned memory retrieval tasks. Although the interpretation is complicated by a variety of factors, these results have been interpreted to mean that the higher the coding level at which the classification (convergence on a common memory node) takes place, the slower the dynamics of memory retrieval (Posner and Mitchell 1967; Posner et al. 1969; Posner and Taylor 1969; Corcoran and Besner 1975; Besner and Coltheart 1975; Allard and Henderson 1976).

I have already noted that higher-level decisions are not necessarily made faster than lower-level decisions, and I have taken this fact as evidence for the existence of chain parallel processing. When a stimulus activates memory nodes at some peripheral feature level, the wave of activation is passed on to the next higher level before processing is complete at the earlier level, and so on. Processing occurs at all levels virtually simultaneously. There is only a small difference in the onset of processing at each level; the information (differential activation) reaching higher levels from lower levels is continually updated; and there is probably feedback (activation) from higher to lower levels as well. Nevertheless, when the nature of the decision and the decision criteria are carefully controlled, differences in reaction time may indicate differences in coding level. Lower-level nodes (codes) may in fact be activated at least a few milliseconds or tens of milliseconds earlier than higher-level nodes.

SAT functions provide a way to eliminate complicating factors such as differential response biases, differential speed-accuracy criteria, and differential asymptotic (stored) strength for different decisions. Comparisons of the dynamics parameters (rate and intercept) for different decisions provide perhaps the most convincing evidence for the existence of a hierarchy of coding levels such that memory retrieval at lower levels begins sooner than at higher levels. In this instance, SAT studies overwhelmingly confirm the general conclusion drawn by Posner and his colleagues from RT studies. They concluded that we can retrieve information stored at the visual feature level faster than information stored at the letter name level, which in turn is retrieved faster than information stored in semantic memory. Directly analogous SAT studies have not been performed. However, the lowest-level psychophysical reactions (e.g., to light on the left versus the right) have intercepts of around 170 msec. Recognition memory for a single letter in short-term memory has an intercept of around 250 msec. Intercepts for paired-associate recognition of pairs or triples of words from five-element propositions are on the order of 600 msec. Rate of retrieval is also correspondingly slower with higher levels of encoding; it ranges from 200–1,500 msec for reasonably complete retrieval (Schouten and Bekker 1967; Reed 1973, 1975; Dosher 1976; Wickelgren and Corbett 1977).

Polf (1976) made an SAT study of the dynamics of letter versus word recognition. Her findings dramatically demonstrate how much faster the recognition process really is at the lower, letter level of processing, even when conditions are such that the accuracy of perceptual information is much greater at the higher, word level of processing. In the letter-processing condition subjects were presented with a single letter (e.g., K). This was followed very quickly by a patterned masking field superimposed on the location where the letter had been presented. Along with the masking field subjects were given two alternative test letters (e.g., K and T) to choose between. The two test letters appeared immediately above and below the place where the masked letter had been. The word-processing condition was similar. Subjects were presented with a word (e.g., "PARK") followed by a mask and two alternative words (e.g., "PARK" and "PART") that differed in only a single letter. In both conditions subjects were signaled to choose at various delays following onset of the originally presented stimulus. A plot of choice accuracy as a function of processing time for both single letters and words is shown in figure 9.5. The pattern masking field is clearly much more effective

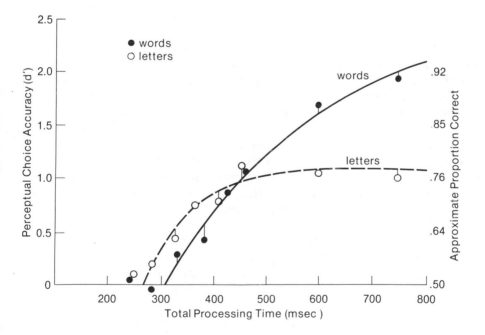

Fig. 9.5 Speed-accuracy trade-off functions representing the temporal dynamics of the recognition processes at the letter and word levels in Polf's experiment. Note that processing begins sooner at the letter level (the SAT function for letters has lower chance intercept) and proceeds faster than processing at the word level, but the time course of processing at the two levels overlaps heavily. This is an example of chain parallel processing. The pattern-masking conditions of Polf's experiment were much more effective in interfering with perceptual information at the letter level than at the word level. That is why the asymptotic accuracy level is much higher for the word condition than for the letter condition. (From Polf [1976] by permission.)

in destroying information at the letter level than at the word level, since asymptotic accuracy of performance in identifying single letters is substantially below that for words. Nevertheless, at shorter processing times letter identification is clearly superior to word identification. This demonstrates that processing at the letter level does indeed begin before processing at the higher, word level of coding.

If anything, RT studies may have underestimated the importance of encoding level for the dynamics of memory retrieval. The higher the coding level, the longer the associative chain that must be activated to get from the stimulus to the correct response; and the longer the chain, the slower the dynamics of retrieval. Strengthening the association along each link of the chain can partly compensate for the slowing effect that increasing the number of links has on reaction time, achieving fast responses at high accuracy levels. But the early dynamics of SAT functions remain sensitive to differences in coding level.

Automatization

When you first learned to drive a car, everything seemed terribly complicated. You were consciously aware of every aspect of the skill, and you reacted slowly and awkwardly to each stimulus situation. Now you drive automatically. You have had repeated opportunities to react to each class of stimulus situation. Gradually you have learned to react more appropriately in less time and with less conscious effort. The same sort of automatization with repeated memory retrieval apparently occurs in a wide variety of perceptual-motor and cognitive areas. For example, one reason why we know that learning is not an all-or-none process is that recall reaction times continue to decrease over many, many trials after 100% correct performance has been reached in a paired-associate learning task.*

There are two major hypotheses regarding automatization. According to the *increasing-strength* hypothesis, retrieval becomes less conscious because it gets faster, and it gets faster simply because the original chain of associations gets stronger. Even with no change in the rate and intercept of the SAT function, an increase in the asymptotic strength of an association will permit a faster and more accurate responding.

According to the *short-circuiting* hypothesis, automatization occurs because the subject acquires a second shorter chain of associations that links stimulus to response through a somewhat lower (and perhaps less conscious) level of coding in the mind. The original chain may have used one or more preexisting relational concepts to create a more quickly learned, but less direct, association than could be acquired. With repeated retrieval, the more direct associative chain eventually gets strong enough to parallel (and in part

---

*See long list of studies in Wickelgren (1975b, p. 241).

to supersede) the original indirect association. Not only would the second path produce higher total asymptotic strength of association between stimulus and response, but it should also decrease the intercept or increase the rate of retrieval or both. This happens because the additional path is shorter (at a lower coding level).

Memory response times will be shorter if asymptotic strength is greater, regardless of whether intercept and rate are affected by automatization. That is why reaction-time studies have not resolved this issue. There is only one relevant SAT study, and it indicates that both hypotheses may be correct under different conditions. Corbett (1977) found that when word-word paired associates are learned by rote repetition, repeated retrieval produces increased asymptotic strength but no change in retrieval dynamics (rate and intercept). However, when the pairs are originally learned by forming visual image mnemonics, repeated retrieval apparently produces acquisition of a shorter, more direct association in parallel with the original, mediated association. This occurs because the intercept of the SAT function is reduced after repeated retrieval. Indeed, the results are very pretty. Initially, image-mediated paired associates have a higher asymptotic strength, but slightly lower retrieval dynamics (a larger intercept), than rote-learned pairs. With repeated retrieval both asymptotes increase, and the intercept of the SAT function for image pairs is reduced to coincide with that for rote pairs, while the intercept for rote pairs remains unchanged with practice. The asymptotic strength difference strongly favors higher-level image learning over lower-level rote learning in both the short and long run, but rote learning enjoys a small initial advantage in retrieval dynamics. This advantage disappears with repeated retrieval. Corbett's study indicates that the fastest way to establish a strong direct connection between two concepts is first to form an indirect mediated connection, which, with repeated use, will produce a strong direct connection. It is generally much less efficient to try to form the direct connection in the beginning by rote repetition.

These results are highly relevant to teaching. For example, everyone eventually needs to learn spelling words and basic arithmetic facts at an automatic rote level. It's simply too inefficient to have to run through some complex mnemonic every time you want to remember what $7 \cdot 9$ is. And anything short of strong rote knowledge makes it very difficult to learn more complex mathematical procedures, such as long division. However, Corbett's findings clearly indicate that the fastest way to achieve a strong direct association is first to learn a strong indirect (mnemonically mediated) association and then to retrieve (use) the association repeatedly. It takes longer to try to learn a generally weaker (rote) association from the beginning. Thus indirect meaningful associations are highly important tools for the achievement of rote knowledge as well as for understanding, in mathematics, language, and so forth. However, some mnemonics are undoubtedly much more useful than others. For automatization the best mnemonic should probably require as little thinking time as possible. By this logic, counting on one's fingers is *not* a good mnemonic for establishing rote learning of elementary addition facts.

Priming and Spread of Activation

In the previous section I discussed the long-lasting facilitative effects of repeated retrieval on both asymptote and retrieval dynamics. In the present section we consider the short-term effects on asymptote and retrieval dynamics of a single act of retrieval. We will examine two questions: First, is retrieval of an association facilitated by the *priming effect*? That is, is an association retrieved more easily when it has been retrieved recently? Second, is an association retrieved more easily when a related association has been retrieved recently? Such an effect would presumably be due to the *spread of activation*. The answer to both questions is apparently "yes." However, the details of the priming effect and the spread of activation are not yet established.

When you think about it, recent retrieval of exactly the same association just about has to have a priming effect. The only issue is how long the priming effect lasts. Retrieval is the cognitive process that converts passive, stored associations into the activated state that can produce responses. When attention is shifted to another association, it is unlikely that the formerly retrieved (activated) association returns instantly to the passive (unactivated) state. Retrieval is the transition of a memory trace from the passive stored state to the activated state. When attention shifts, this activation decays. However, so long as some activation remains, retrieval of that association ought to be facilitated, since the trace is already partially activated. The decay of the priming effect on retrieval presumably corresponds to the decay of trace activation. Such partially activated thoughts are still on one's mind to some extent, and the entire set of such (fully or partially) activated thoughts constitutes the *span of consciousness*—or what William James (1890, ch. 16) and more recently Waugh and Norman (1965) have termed *primary memory*. To the extent that short-term memory is anything other than rapidly decaying long-term memory, it may be identical to primary memory—that is, to the persistence of activation.

There is considerable evidence for some type of priming effect in many reaction time tasks where repetitions of recently performed reactions are faster than baseline performance (Hyman 1953; Bertelson and Renkin 1966; Smith 1968; Smith, Chase, and Smith 1973; Winkelman 1974). This *repetition effect* appears to last for a few seconds, though control of relevant variables in these tasks has been less than ideal. For one thing, conscious attention (expectation) has not generally been adequately controlled during the "retention interval" between repetitions. For another thing, reaction time studies do not distinguish between short-term boosts in asymptotic trace strengths and short-term facilitation of retrieval dynamics (increases in retrieval rate or reductions in intercept). An SAT study of priming effects on recognition of word-word paired associates found a small but reliable facilitation of both asymptote and retrieval dynamics after three seconds of backward counting, as compared to a minute or so of interpolated activity (Dosher 1978). A larger repetition effect on retrieval dynamics was found in an SAT study of mental addition of two single-digit numbers when *both* addends were repeated, but not when only a single addend was repeated from the preceding trial (Winkelman 1974).

When one node is activated, the activation appears to spread out via the links connecting that node to other nodes. That is, there is an *activation halo* surrounding a fully activated node. One source of evidence for the spread of activation is the higher false recognition rates for words that are associated in various ways to previously presented words (Underwood 1965; Davis 1967; Anisfeld and Knapp 1968; Fillenbaum 1969; Grossman and Eagle 1973; Kausler and Settle 1973). Again, these studies have not controlled conscious attention sufficiently to determine whether such elevated false recognition rates derive only from a tendency to generate consciously the associated words at the time of encoding, or from the unconscious spread of activation as well.

In the foregoing studies the associative priming followed acquisition of new memory traces, but it can also result from the activation accompanying retrieval of well-established memory traces. For example, Loftus (1973) showed that recall of one example of a category (e.g., Fruit—A→Apple) primed recall of other examples of the same category (e.g., Fruit—P→Pear), producing shorter recall reaction times. Collins and Quillian (1970) showed that recognition of one category example association primed recognition of other examples of the same category. Once again it's not clear how much of this retrieval priming results from the unconscious spread of activation. Nor do we know whether the associative priming is affecting stored strength or retrieval dynamics or both. Nevertheless, it seems likely that activation can spread to associated nodes and can prime retrieval of related associations (Collins and Loftus 1975).

Inhibition, Negation, and Contradiction

In addition to the excitatory activation halo, is there also an inhibitory halo? Given the neural and perceptual evidence for inhibition, it seems likely that inhibition plays an important role in higher cognitive processes. Negation and contradiction are the most intuitively plausible examples. There are numerous examples of cognitive inhibition, negation, and contradiction, but the relation between these behavioral phenomena and neural inhibition is strictly conjectural at present.

Posner and Snyder (1975) studied the costs and benefits of advance cuing in a letter-matching task. Subjects were asked to decide whether two test letters were identical. When the advance cue matched two identical test letters, subjects responded "same" more quickly and more accurately than they did in the no-cue control condition. When the advance cue did not match the two identical test letters, subjects responded "same" less quickly than they did in the control condition. In this case the costs and benefits of advance cuing may have been largely due to shifts in bias to respond "same" versus "different." However, the choice between contradictory responses as well as any shift in response bias are virtually paradigm examples of cognitive inhibition.

Another example of cognitive inhibition is found in the Stroop (1938) task and its variants. In the Stroop task subjects are asked to name the color of the ink in which an item is printed while attempting to ignore the item itself. If the item is a word, it is harder to ignore than if it is a row of Xs. Subjects will be slower to name the color of the ink, and often they will make more errors as well. If the item is the name of a color—but not the name of the color in which the item is printed—reaction time is even slower and errors are even more frequent. The response set to produce color names primes all color name nodes, making items that are color names more potent competitors than other words (Klein 1964; Jensen and Rohwer 1966). However, Warren (1972, 1974) showed that the potency of any word could be increased by the priming that results from holding an associated word in short-term memory during the color-naming task. The most plausible interpretation of these findings is as follows. Both the letter-word form cues and the ink color cue tend to activate word nodes that at some level are mutually inhibitory, since we cannot pronounce two different words at once. The set to produce color names primes the color word nodes and especially the color feature detectors, so that subjects almost always respond correctly. However, competing word nodes inhibit full activation of the correct word node. This inhibition increases the more strongly the competing word node is activated by concurrent or prior (priming) stimulation.

Finally, MacLeod and Nelson (1976) showed that the enhanced false-recognition rate for new words strongly associated to previously presented words does not hold at a zero retention interval following presentation of the associated word. In fact, there was a slightly lower false recognition for strong associates of the immediately prior word than for random new words. Similarly, at long retention intervals paraphrases of presented sentences tend to be falsely accepted as having been presented. But at very short retention intervals they are rejected as different more often than random new sentences are (Begg and Wickelgren 1974). One plausible interpretation of these findings is that at short delays the persisting activation of the correct word (or sentence) inhibits the activation of closely associated words (or sentences), but at longer delays this inhibition disappears.

SUMMARY

1 Elementary recognition memory is based on the feeling of familiarity aroused by the material in question. Elementary recall is the generation of a new thought in response to one's prior thoughts. Experiments attempt to control prior thoughts by stimulus cues.

2 Complex retrieval tasks are composed of a sequence of elementary recognitions and recalls.

3 Perceptual recognition is the activation of the node that represents a stimulus. Recognition memory is the feeling of familiarity that is generated by this process. The two processes are probably closely linked. They may be inseparable under normal conditions.

4 Item memory is almost certainly a form of associative memory. It may be based on the strength of association between the item node and one or more context nodes. Or it may be based on the associations of the constituents of the item to each other or to the chunk node for the item.

5 There are two stages in output from memory. The first stage is retrieval of associations. The second stage is decision based on the strengths of the associations retrieved.

6 Yes-no recognition memory probably follows the criterion decision rule. The subject responds "yes" only if the strength of the retrieved association exceeds some criterion. Multiple-choice recognition and small recall probably follow the maximum-decision rule. The subject chooses the alternative with maximum associative strength. Large recall probably follows the high-threshold decision rule. The subject recalls the correct alternative only if it exceeds some high-threshold strength of association to the retrieval cues.

7 Retrieval for both recognition and recall is accomplished by a direct-access process. No search of memory is required in elementary retrieval tasks. Memory search is a complex retrieval process that involves a sequence of elementary recalls and recognitions—for example, trying to remember someone's name by giving oneself a succession of cues.

8 Recognition and recall appear to use the same (associative) memory system and the same retrieval process. Sometimes they even use the same decision rules, though typically they use different ones. Generally there are more retrieval cues —and therefore more associations being tapped—in recognition than in recall.

9 We can trade off speed for accuracy in memory retrieval apparently continuously over a retrieval time that ranges from 200 to 1,500 msec. Current evidence is not definite, but memory retrieval appears to be a continuous incremental accrual of strength, not an all-or-none process.

10 In memory retrieval we can process about four items (chunks) simultaneously with little or no loss in efficiency. This is an example of parallel processing within the span of apprehension.

11 We can activate two divergent associations to the same node in parallel with only a very small loss in efficiency.

12 We have a substantial capacity for chain parallel processing—for retrieving nearly simultaneously many associations in chain (AB, BC, CD, . . .). However,

there is a slight lag in the onset of retrieval at each link in the chain. And the longer the chain, the slower the rate of retrieval. Thus associations that involve higher levels of coding (longer chains) have slower retrieval dynamics.

13 Associations formed at high coding levels (that is, associations involving long chains) can sometimes be short-circuited at lower coding levels as a result of repeated retrieval. This reduces the length of the chain and speeds retrieval. The process is called automatization of retrieval.

14 Recently retrieved (fully activated) associations persist for a short time in a partially activated (retrieved) state. During this time retrieval of that association is primed (facilitated). Primary (short-term) memory is the persistence of an association in a partially activated state. Priming of retrieval can also spread from activated nodes to all of their strong associations, whether or not the latter are consciously retrieved.

15 Inhibition probably plays an important role in retrieval and priming, but this issue has not been adequately explored.

CHAPTER 10
SEMANTIC MEMORY CODING: CONCEPTS, PROPOSITIONS, AND SCHEMATA

OBJECTIVES

1 To explain the relation between words and concepts, including the fact that many different concepts can be referred to by a single word, and that many different words (or phrases) can refer to a single concept.

2 To discuss the meaning of meaning. To distinguish between constituent and propositional meaning, between extensional and intensional meaning, and between characteristic and defining features.

3 To point out that most human concepts are *fuzzy*, in the sense that events have several *degrees of membership* in the concept. Natural human concepts are not strictly logical functions of relevant attributes.

4 To discuss the prototype and family resemblance theory of concept constituent structure. To discuss how concepts are learned by abstraction from memory for instances.

5 To distinguish between two types of concept learning: inference and abstraction.

6 To explain Rosch's hypothesis of basic concepts, which are the most inclusive concepts characterized by a single prototype.

7 To discuss the syntactic analysis of phrase structure and the relation between phrases and concepts in semantic memory.

8 To discuss the relation between sentences and propositions. To present a variety of evidence supporting the hypothesis that propositions are important units (nodes) in semantic memory.

9 To discuss three theories regarding the constituent structure of propositions: predicate theory, case theory, and fuzzy-case theory.

10 To provide one fairly precise description of schemata in semantic memory. A schema is a set of knowledge associated to some topic, which can serve as an attentional set in comprehension.

When I was a student, a lot of my professors talked about *concepts* and told us we needed to learn the important ones in their courses. At that time and for many years afterwards, I was puzzled by what that term *concepts* meant exactly. Virtually none of the people who used the term ever defined it, and I became convinced that they didn't know any more about what concepts were than I did—which, at that time, wasn't much. Worse, they did not appear to realize just how little they understood this basic term. Lots of pseudosophisticates went around using the term as if they knew what it meant, and you had to risk looking like an ignorant clod to say, "What do you mean by *learning concepts?* Does that just mean to learn the meanings of the *terms* used in this field? What's the difference between learning terminology or jargon and learning concepts?" Learning concepts seems so grand, learning terminology so boring, and learning jargon positively vulgar.

Unfortunately, practically no one could give decent answers to such questions and I doubt if it's much different today. Intellectual pretense still reigns supreme concerning the difference between learning concepts and learning terminology. The former is good and the latter is bad—but practically no teachers or students know the difference, though many pretend to. In actual practice, there is *no* qualitative difference between what you do when you learn terminology (or even jargon!) and what you do when you learn concepts. There would be a qualitative difference if learning terminology meant just learning how to pronounce and spell new words without learning anything about their meanings—but how many of you think that's what *learning terminology* means? If one searches for a sensible distinction between learning terminology and learning concepts, the most reasonable one is probably purely quantitative. *Learning a concept* means to learn a lot about the meaning of a term, including a lot about its relations to other concepts. Merely *learning terminology* means to learn only a little about the meaning of a term, perhaps just one short definition. As we shall see in this chapter, the definition of a concept is a pretty small part of its total meaning. So all of you *do* want to learn concepts, not just terminology, and now you understand the distinction better than most people. After you read this chapter, you should know a great deal more about it.

This is a very exciting time in the understanding of language and thinking. Before the mid-1960s only a few people trained in linguistic philosophy even remotely understood concepts (the basic units of thought) and how concepts differ from words, from definitions, and from the set of events the concepts represent. And philosophical knowledge is so turgid as to be the next thing to no knowledge at all. This should *not* be taken as an insult to philosophy. Philosophy is where all fields of knowledge begin—by taking that first big step away from the abyss of total ignorance. In any case, since the mid-1960s, under the influence of developments in artificial intelligence, cognitive psychology, and neo- and post-Chomskian linguistics, a new field has been born. This new field—called *semantic memory*—promises to unlock many basic secrets concerning how we think and understand.

Higher-order syntactic and semantic influences on speech and reading were discussed briefly in chapter 5. I have deferred detailed consideration of syntax and semantics to this chapter and to the two chapters that follow. In these last three chapters the processes of understanding and thinking will be analyzed in a variety of cognitive tasks—reading, speaking, recognizing speech, reasoning, and so on. The modern term for the level of the mind where these processes take place is *semantic memory*. Most psychologists assume that semantic memory codes knowledge in an abstract way that is independent of the modality of input. The current explosion of research on semantic memory has focused primarily on the higher mental processing of *verbal* materials. However, there are notable exceptions in both psychology and artificial intelligence research on *nonverbal* concept formation, (visual) spatial imagery, and scene and movement analysis.

We are faced with a problem when we seek to relate verbal and nonverbal (largely spatial) modalities of thought. Should we consider these as two parallel modalities on a par with each other? In this case we would identify semantic memory as the highest level of the verbal modality (located primarily in the left hemisphere). The spatial imagery modality (located primarily in the right hemisphere) would be organized according to different principles. Alternatively, should we consider semantic memory as the single highest level of thinking into which lower-level verbal and nonverbal processing modalities feed? Psychologists do not agree on this matter, so we shall ignore it. In either case, verbal and nonverbal modalities must communicate with each other in semantic memory, and it is the nature of coding in semantic memory that concerns us here.

One thing is clear: the nodes (units) of semantic memory are not in one-to-one correspondence with the linguistic units of words, phrases, sentences, paragraphs, stories, and so on. However, there is a corresponding hierarchical structure of increasing complexity in the units of semantic memory. This structure consists of *concepts* (signaled by words or phrases); *propositions* (signaled by phrases, clauses, and sentences); and *schemata* (signaled by sentences and larger units of text). Actually, if you understand the relationship between words and concepts, between sentences and propositions, and between text and schemata, you understand a lot about semantic memory.

The discussion in this chapter is designed to take you from the word, sentence, and text units with which you are familiar to the concept, proposition, and schema units with which you are, presumably, less familiar.

CONCEPTS

Words and Concepts

It is important to distinguish *words,* which are high-level structural nodes, from *concepts,* which are basic-level semantic nodes. Many single words have multiple meanings. Some meanings of the same word are closely related; others are distantly related or even unrelated. Words with more than one frequently used dictionary definition are said to be *ambiguous,* but all words are ambiguous in the sense that they can refer to different concepts in different circumstances. Even a single dictionary definition of a word refers to many different concepts in different contexts. In one context "bear" may refer to bears in general, in another context to a particular species of bear or to a particular bear. It might even refer to a child's teddy bear, or to a fictitious cartoon character that can talk and think like a human being. All of these concepts are different and must be distinguished in semantic memory if we want to avoid getting hopelessly confused. Thus when people understand and encode into memory a sentence such as "The fish attacked the swimmer," they appear to instantiate the general term "fish" with the concept "shark." This is evidenced by the fact that, subsequently, "shark" is actually a better cue for recall of the last word of the sentence than is "fish," the word that appeared in the sentence. On the other hand, the general term ("fish") must also be encoded in memory (perhaps as a word node). We know this because in 90% of such sentences that are recalled at all on a free-recall test, the general term ("fish") is used, and in only 10% is the instantiation ("shark") used (Anderson et al. 1976). Besides using general terms to refer to specific examples, we also use example names to refer to entire classes—for which I think it is appropriate to offer in evidence a single example: "Where Bambi goes, nothing grows."

Not only does the same word refer to many different concepts in different contexts, but often different words or phrases can be used to refer to the same concept. Synonyms and pronouns are the most obvious examples. Class and superordinate names preceded by definite articles or demonstrative pronouns (e.g., "the apple," "that fruit") are also used to refer to some particular entity in the class (e.g., "the half-eaten apple on the floor"). Proper names versus definite descriptions of the same concepts, such as "George Washington" versus "the first president of the United States," are another example. Definite descriptions are sometimes used in a way that makes distinct concepts from the entities they refer to, but under other conditions they are used as another way of referring to an entity that can be referred to by name (Anderson and Hastie 1974; Ortony 1976). Thus on both logical and linguistic grounds it seems necessary to distinguish between concepts and words and probably to have separate nodes for each.

There is also experimental evidence for the existence of concept nodes. Perfetti and Goodman (1970) tested recognition memory for words that had previously been presented in sentence contexts that biased one meaning of a word with multiple meanings. For example, subjects in one group might have heard the word "top" in a sentence such as "The man set up a ladder and climbed to the *top* of the house," while subjects in another group heard it used in a sentence that biased its meaning as a toy, such as "Jim's father bought him a *top*, but Jim was too young to be able to spin it." After hearing a number of such sentences, subjects were given a list of words and asked to select those they recognized as having occurred in the preceding sentences. Some of the words in the recognition test had been presented in the preceding sentences (old words). Some were new words that were semantically related to old words with the meaning that had been used in the prior sentence context (for example, "bottom" for "top" in one group, or "toy" for "top" in the other group). Some were new words related to an old word with a meaning different from that used in the prior sentence. And some (the control group) were new words that were not specifically related to any old words. Perfetti and Goodman found that the frequency of false recognition was increased for new words that were semantically related to the correct meanings of old words, but not for new words that were related to the other meanings of old words.

Light and Carter-Sobell (1970) and Tulving and Thomson (1971) have demonstrated that recognition memory for a word is decreased by changing the verbal context in which it is first learned in such a way as to change its meaning. For example, if subjects are originally presented with the phrase "raspberry jam" and subsequently tested for recognition of "jam," performance is much poorer when "jam" is presented in the phrase "traffic jam" than when it is presented again in the phrase "raspberry jam." By contrast, little decrement in recognition memory for nouns occurs when the adjectives bias the same meaning of the noun—as, for example, when "raspberry jam" is followed by "strawberry jam."

MacKay has found that associations to ambiguous words (in the traditional sense) take longer than associations to unambiguous words. He controlled for a number of possibly confounding factors and concluded that so-called "word associations" are actually associations between concept representatives rather than between word representatives. The association of multiple concepts to ambiguous words interferes with the generation of a word associated to one of the concepts. However, it makes it easier for subjects to decide that the word is a legitimate English word as opposed to a nonword. Word-nonword decision times are significantly faster for words with many meanings than for words with few meanings (Mackay 1977 [personal communication]; Jastrzembski and Stanners 1975).

There is also evidence that subjects have word nodes as well as concept nodes. However, this evidence is less compelling. In the "raspberry jam" experiments, the subjects' ability to recognize the noun "jam" was still substantial even when an entirely different meaning of the word was contextually biased. In addition, there appear to be several advantages to interpolating something like word nodes between phonetic or graphic nodes and concept nodes. Concept nodes must be activated by a large variety of different conjunctions of attributes. Word nodes appear to chunk the phonetic attributes that characterize the name of a concept.

There is also evidence to support the existence of direct associations between phonetic and graphic nodes and concept nodes. For example, consider the *tip-of-the-tongue* phenomenon. All of you have had the experience of not being able to recall a name. You know that the name is familiar, and that under other circumstances you have recalled it. You may feel that you are on the verge of recalling it, and you can even recall some of its attributes. A well-known experiment by Brown and McNeill (1966) created the tip-of-the-tongue state experimentally and demonstrated that subjects were able to recall beyond chance many of the segmental constituents (letters, phonemes, syllables) of words they could not recall. They could guess better than chance the number of syllables in the word, its initial letter, and words with similar sounds. In the tip-of-the-tongue state, subjects know the concept that they are thinking of, since they can define it using other words. This ability to recall segmental constituents of a word but not the entire word suggests the existence of direct associations from concept nodes to segmental nodes.

Constituent and Propositional Meaning

Concepts occupy an intermediate position in the verbal modality. On the one hand, a concept is the top unit of structural representation for the set of constituent attributes that activate that concept. On the other hand, a concept is the lowest unit of representation in meaningful semantic memory. The meaning of a concept is a combination of these sets of constituent attributes that activate it from below and the propositions in which the concept is incorporated that can activate it from above. For example, the visual-perceptual referential constituents of the "cat" concept presumably include features such as fur, four legs, long furry tail, and pointed ears. The auditory referential constituents include purring, hissing, scratching, and howling. The visual verbal constituents are the letters composing the word "cat," those composing the word "feline," and so on. The auditory verbal constituents are the phonemes or allophones in "cat," "feline," and so on. The propositional meaning of the "cat" concept includes stored propositions such as "cats are pets," "cats are mammals," "cats drink milk," "cats kill small animals," "dogs chase cats," "Ingrid had a pet cat named Triangle, but it ran away," "Abe got a cat when he was 2–1/2 years old, and he agreed with his dad's suggestion that the cat be named Actually, the cutest, most complex word Abe was able to use appropriately at that time." You get the point. The propositional meaning of concepts is enormous and varied.

Concrete and *abstract concepts* differ in the relative emphasis they place upon constituent versus propositional determinants of the meaning of a concept. Concrete concepts ("triangle," "boat," "running," "red") can be directly activated by one or more sets of lower-level constituent attributes. Very abstract concepts ("coding," "derive," "relevant") can only be indirectly activated from sensory input by the prior activation of phrase or propositional representatives that in turn activate the abstract concept representative. That is, we can image a referent of a concrete concept (usually we can image many different referents of the same concrete concept), but we cannot image a referent of an abstract concept. Of course an abstract verbal concept can be activated by the sensory attributes of its name, but it cannot be activated by perceptual referential stimuli. By contrast, a more concrete concept, such as "dog," can be activated by both auditory and visual verbal input (the name "dog") and by referential stimuli, such as the sight of a dog or the sound of barking.

Until recently psychologists who discussed concepts have tended to emphasize the chunking of lower-level sensory constituents to form a concept representative. A balanced treatment of concepts would undoubtedly place at least as much emphasis upon the meaning concepts acquire by being incorporated into relevant propositions. Children probably learn the meanings of many words simply from hearing or seeing them used in a variety of different sentences. In such cases the concept does chunk the lower-level sensory attributes in the name, but the referential meaning of the concept may be encoded largely indirectly by memory for the propositions in which the concept is embedded. After I learned to read and began reading one book after another, my mother would frequently chastise me for not looking up in the dictionary words that I did not understand. Despite her repeated admonitions to look up new words in the dictionary, I almost never did so. Nevertheless, I acquired a large vocabulary—undoubtedly much faster than I could have acquired it by following her advice or by asking her what words meant.

Much of the meaning of both concrete and abstract concepts probably comes from above by way of the propositions of which the concept is a part. Concept learning is really never complete. After we have chunked one or more sets of attributes together to define a new concept node, we begin to associate (chunk) that concept into higher-order propositions. As you learn more propositions that use a particular concept as a constituent, the meaning of the concept is increasing and changing, and its usefulness to you is increasing. It is being integrated or assimilated into the rest of your semantic memory

(Ausubel 1966). As a new concept becomes increasingly strongly related to other concepts in semantic memory, it becomes more useful in making inferences and generating new thoughts, and it also seems to become more familiar —less strange and intimidating. I remember how strange the concepts of calculus seemed to me when I first encountered them, even though I could correctly state definitions of "limit," "derivative," and "integral." Two months later I had used the concepts in theorems and problem solving and now they seemed like old friends. At the time I found this puzzling because I naively thought that to understand the meaning of concept meant to know its definition. Now I realize that a definition is just one of the many propositions concerning a concept that give it meaning (and familiarity and usefulness) in semantic memory. However, most psychologists have emphasized the notion of concepts as logical functions of their lower-level constituents. Keep in mind that this notion of concepts probably tells no more than half the story.

Extensional and Intensional Meaning

The distinction between constituent and propositional meaning may be the closest psychological analogue of the philosophical distinction between the extensional and intensional meaning of a concept.* The *extensional meaning* of a concept is the set of entities in the world to which it refers (the set of examples of the concept). That is, extensional meaning is *referential meaning.* The complete *intensional meaning (relational meaning)* of a concept includes all the relationships the concept has to other concepts, but specific contexts emphasize particular aspects of a concept's intensional meaning over other aspects.

To understand the importance of intensional meaning, consider concepts that are useful in thinking but that currently have *no* existing referent. Let's skip examples such as unicorns and consider instead a goal you have not achieved yet but are working toward, such as the dream house you plan to build, the dinner you plan to cook tomorrow evening, and so on. None of these goal concepts has a referent at present; yet they are real and important concepts. Abstract concepts are another example. The referents of abstract concepts are very difficult to specify. In part, this is a practical problem caused by the enormous variety of situations that evoke the use of abstract concepts. But I also feel that the relative importance of intensional, as opposed to extensional, meaning is greater for abstract than for concrete concepts. Certainly the balance must be heavily weighted in favor of intensional meaning for grammatical function words (articles and prepositions). Such words have virtually indescribable referential meaning in isolation, but they play an important role in determining the meaning (extensional and intensional) of phrases and sentences.

---

*For an interesting discussion of this issue see Woods (1975).

As I use the terms, the psychological distinction between constituent and propositional meaning is not quite the same as the philosophical distinction between extensional and intensional meaning. The constituents of, say, a concrete object concept refer to all sets of lower-level attributes that activate a concept node, including spoken and written words and pictures as well as perception of the object itself. I doubt that all linguistic philosophers would accept pictures and words as a part of the referential meaning of a concept, nor do I necessarily think they should. The philosophical analysis of meaning has overlapping, but somewhat different, objectives than the psychological analysis of meaning. However, from a psychological standpoint, the constituents of a concept are attributes (verbal or nonverbal) that activate it from below, while the propositions of which it is a constituent activate it from above. There is at least some reason to believe that this may prove to be an important distinction.

Characteristic and Defining Features

Another distinction that may be considered a level difference and may be subsumed under the distinction between constituent and propositional meaning is that between characteristic and defining features (Lakoff 1972; Rips, Shoben, and Smith 1973; Smith, Rips, and Shoben 1974; Smith, Shoben, and Rips 1974). Characteristic features include all those attributes that examples of a category tend to have. Defining features are those that one has decided will be strictly necessary to define an example of some particular concept. For instance, breathing air by means of lungs is often considered a defining feature of mammals. Absorbing air dissolved in water by means of gills is often considered a defining feature of fish. By this and other defining criteria, a whale is a mammal, though on the basis of numerous characteristic features (large water animal, swims, tail, no legs, streamlined shape) a whale appears to be a fish. The distinction between characteristic and defining features is not absolute; it is a matter of the degree of definitional relevance. If by some genetic miracle a creature were born to a mother whale that was in every sense a whale, except that it had gills instead of lungs, would we consider it a variety of whale or a new species? Would it be a mammal or a fish? If a rabbit grew leaves on its tail and could produce its own food from air, water, and sunshine, would it be a plant or an animal? If a bird loses its wings, is it still a bird? If you were killed and a split second later an exact duplicate of you were created in your place, would *you* still exist? This discussion is a tad on the silly side, but it's intended to get you to think about your own personal defining features for various concepts. If you conclude that you're not so sure what your defining features are for most concepts, that your defining features for a concept sometimes differ from other people's and from those of science, and that both individuals and science can change the defining features of concepts—you are right! Most of us would be willing to accept scientific definitions for concepts when they exist and when we know them. Scientific definitions tend to be more precise and to partition features into exactly two classes: relevant (defining) and irrelevant. However, almost all human thinking uses concepts for which the distinction between defining and characteristic features is blurred at best. Frequently it is nonexistent—at least in an individual mind, for many concepts. Think how hard it is to define many of the concepts you use every day. You know how to use the concepts and you know many features of instances of the concept. But can you provide a dictionarylike (Aristotelian) definition that puts the concept into a more general class and distinguishes it from all other members of that class?

When one can define a concept, the definition is almost certainly a higher-level proposition about the concept; it is not a partitioning of the concept's constituent features into defining and characteristic features. All constituent features should probably be considered characteristic features. "Animal" is not a (lower-level) constituent feature of "fish," "mammal," or "dog." "Has lungs" is not a (lower-level) constituent feature of "mammal." These class membership and property features are probably attributed to concepts by means of propositions generally learned in a fairly formal way (in school, from books). The class membership propositions, such as "horses are mammals," are learned without necessarily considering those features of horses that make them mammals. Thus we may have nothing more than the rotelike proposition "horses are mammals" stored in memory, though if we know some properties of mammals, we can attribute them to horses by means of an inference ("all horses are mammals," "all mammals have lungs," therefore "horses have lungs"). The rest of the "horse" definition, consisting of a set of properties to distinguish "horse" from other mammals, is probably a concatenation (stringing together) into one sentence of a set of separately learned propositions about horses, though constituent features are probably often mentioned as well. However, definitions are primarily higher-level propositions about concepts, not lower-level constituents of concepts.

Activation and Reference

A concept node represents the set of events that are referents (examples) of that concept. However, we can think about a concept when none of its referents is perceptually present. Many different perceptual and cognitive events will cause us to think about a concept. The nodes activated or their degree of activation or both must differ according to whether we (1) see a cow, (2) see a picture of a cow, (3) see the word "cow," or (4) think of "cow" after seeing "Hey, diddle diddle, the cat and the fiddle, the _____." We know that this is so because we can discriminate among all these "cow" thoughts. However, they must also have a common conceptual core. One of the principal puzzles in understanding the coding of human concepts is to decide in what sense a concept node can represent its referents when what a concept node most directly represents is *whatever turns it on,* and this apparently includes a rich variety of perceptual and cognitive events that are directly or indirectly associated with the most obvious referential events (e.g., a real cow standing before your very eyes). This distinction between reference and activation is not quite the same as the distinction between constituent and propositional meaning, since a picture of a cow is not a real cow, and yet it surely activates the "cow" node via some (but not all) of the same constituent attribute associations as a real cow would do. Probably there are separate but overlapping patterns of nodal activation for real cows, pictures of cows, and so on. However, there is as yet no precise theory of how they work. Maybe you can figure it out. In any case, throughout this chapter I will vacillate between discussing concepts as if they represented their narrowest referent sets and discussing them as if they represented their broader referent (activation) sets. I make no apologies for this; I'm just warning you to be on the lookout. It's the state of the art, and there are useful points to be made from both perspectives.

Concepts as Logical Functions

Attributes. Until recently much of the research on concepts and concept learning was dominated by notions derived from symbolic logic. A concept was said to partition the universe of events into two classes: examples (instances or positive instances) and nonexamples (noninstances or negative instances). Events were analyzed in terms of relevant and irrelevant attributes (e.g., shape, color, size). Relevant attributes are those that are involved in the rule classifying an event as an example or nonexample of the concept. Irrelevant attributes are not involved in this rule. Sets of mutually exclusive attributes (e.g., 1 foot long, 2 feet long . . .) form *dimensions* such that an object (event) could have one and only one *value* on that dimension. A specific value on a specific dimension is an *attribute.*

Types of concept rules (functions). The simplest concepts are *conjunctive.* That is, examples of the concept possess a combination of attributes, and nonexamples lack one or more of these attributes. For example, if the concept were "red squares," a "blue square" would be a nonexample, a "red circle" would be a nonexample, and so on. Color and shape would be relevant dimensions, while size and location, say, would be irrelevant dimensions. Conjunctive concepts are what most people think of when they think of the term "concept" or "category" or "class." That is, they think of the sort of concept in which all the members have some attributes in common.

There are also *disjunctive* concepts. Examples of a disjunctive concept possess one attribute or another attribute or another attribute. . . . Disjunctive concepts can use either the *inclusive-or* (A or B or both) or the *exclusive-or* (A or B but not both). One real-life example of a disjunctive concept would be "citizen of the U.S.," when this term is taken to mean "a person who is either born in the U.S. or born to a U.S. citizen or naturalized." However, "citizen of the U.S." could also be a conjunctive concept when it is taken to mean "a person who is a member of the U.S." or if more detail is desired, "a person who is subject to all the rights and obligations of membership in the U.S." (where, of course, these rights and obligations could be spelled out in even greater detail). When you first acquired the concept "U.S. citizen" you probably didn't learn the disjunctive requirements for admission to the "club." More likely you learned a few of the more obvious conjunctive requirements. Offhand, I cannot think of any real-life concepts people use that cannot be given a conjunctive definition. Furthermore, the proper conjunctive definition would always appear to express the functional purpose of the concept better than any disjunctive definition could do. However, this does not mean that disjunction does not play an important role in the constituent and propositional meaning of concepts. It certainly does—probably for every concept we use at all frequently. Such concepts can be activated by any one of several conjunctions of attributes. Which is to say that, in general, what turns on any concept node is a disjunction of conjunctions of attributes. The definition of a concept's referents is a very small part of the total meaning of a concept.

This raises three serious general criticisms of the view that concepts are logical functions of attributes. First, this view emphasizes only the referential meaning of concepts and completely neglects their intensional (propositional) meaning. Second, this view emphasizes only the attributes of referents of concepts and completely neglects the attributes of linguistic symbols (pictures) or other signs (cues) that may also activate a concept node from below as a part of its constituent meaning. Third, this view does not adequately represent the extraordinary redundancy of attributes characteristic of examples of concepts. Examples of the concept "bird" have many defining (necessary) attributes besides the feet. Yet for most adults, viewing the feet alone would be sufficient to activate the concept "bird." For some limited philosophical purposes, understanding a concept might be considered equivalent to knowing its set of referents (examples) and their attributes, but this is inadequate for cognitive psychology. We need to know the conditions under which a concept is activated, and these conditions extend far beyond the physical presence of an example of that concept.

Negation

The role of negation in concept learning has been studied in two different senses. In investigations that have studied how much subjects can learn from examples as opposed to nonexamples of a concept, the results have generally shown that they learn more from examples than from nonexamples (Hovland and Weiss 1953; Schvaneveldt 1966). With most real-life concepts, nonexamples generally provide less information than examples. However, when the information in nonexamples is controlled so as to equal the information in examples, subjects learn less from nonexamples at first but with practice can learn from them as efficiently as from examples (Freibergs and Tulving 1961). In natural concept learning, nonexamples probably play the role of preventing overgeneralization. The hypothetical child who calls every man "Daddy" has presumably acquired a concept with too few relevant attributes. Misclassifications of this type are generally corrected, so that the differentiating characteristics of other men are associated with the negation of the concept "Daddy."

Negation can also play a different (though probably a closely related) role in concept formation, in that concepts can be defined in terms of the absence—as well as the presence—of certain attributes. Under at least some conditions, it appears that concepts requiring the absence of an attribute can be learned as quickly as concepts requiring the presence of an attribute (Neisser and Weene 1962). To obtain this result, the subject must initially have reason to expect the absent attribute to be present. This happens when the number of attributes is small and the prohibited attribute occurs in nonexamples of the concept. The negation of something is probably only represented in the human mind when there is reason to expect its presence and that expectation is not satisfied. Negative attributes can only be learned when there is some reason to expect them.

The role of negation in concept learning suggests that concept learning may depend as much upon associating similar nonexamples to the negation of the concept (for instance "not Daddy") as upon associating examples to the concept representative ("Daddy"). In addition, the attributes associated to a concept or to its negation may be negations of attributes (negative attributes) as well as positive attributes.

Classes and Collections

The examples of a concept (e.g., "dogs") form a set or class. The members of a family (e.g., "the Wayne Wickelgren family") also form a set. However, this type of set is sufficiently different from first type that Markman and Seibert (1976) give it a different name—*collection*. For example, Lassie is an example of the concept "dog," but my daughter, Ingrid, is not an example of the concept "Wayne Wickelgren family." This latter concept is a set with only one example—namely, the entire set of us (my son, Abe, my daughter, Ingrid, and myself). A collection (e.g., team, bunch, pile, forest) is essentially a kind of object. Both *collections* and *objects* have parts, and the parts must have certain relations to each other (such as spatial proximity) in order to make up the collection or object. The property that makes a block part of a particular pile of blocks is its proximity to the other blocks. Its defining property for membership in the collection is its relation to other members of the collection and not its attributes in isolation. By contrast,

Lassie's membership in the "dog" class is based on Lassie's attributes in isolation, independent of her relations to other dogs and regardless of whether any other dogs even exist. So collections and classes are different kinds of sets, just as ordered and unordered sets are different kinds of sets. Furthermore, this difference points to a difference between types of concepts —essentially between the concept "a dog" (meaning any member of the "dog" set) and the concept "the set of all dogs." Lassie is "a dog," but Lassie is not "the set of all dogs" (that is, Lassie is not an example of the *set* of all dogs). Abe is an example of the concept "member of the Wayne Wickelgren family," but Abe is not an example of "the Wayne Wickelgren family." The difference here between the "family" concept and the "dog" concept is mostly in whether the *set concept* has the simplest name (as is the case for a collection like "family") or whether the *member concept* has the simplest name (as is the case for a class like "dog"). For all concepts, humans have the capacity to distinguish between the *entire set* and *any single member of the set* (more briefly, to distinguish the *set* from its *members*).

Quantification and Qualification

And this is but the tip of the iceberg. All noun concepts are members of a set of related concepts (a *concept family,* if you will) because they can be *quantified* and *qualified.* We can form the concepts "a plum," "two plums," "some plums," "many plums," "the average plum," "all plums" (here meaning the set of all plums), "no plums," to say nothing of particular plum concepts and plum subset concepts such as "the plum Abe is eating" or "Farmer Brown's plums." All of these concepts are different, and humans must have the capacity to encode them differently in the mind. Otherwise we could not tell them apart. Achieving an adequate theory of quantification and qualification is currently one of the major challenges in the area of semantic memory (Woods 1975, pp. 71–79).

Fuzzy Sets:
Concepts with Fuzzy Boundaries
and Degrees of Membership

If we accept the notion that concepts are logical functions of relevant attributes, any item (object, event) that satisfies the rule (e.g., by possessing all of the relevant attributes) is as good an example of the concept as any other example. And any item that fails to satisfy the rule is as good a nonexample as any other nonexample. Once the all-or-nothing, binary character of such logical concepts is pointed out, it is also clear that many (if not all) human concepts are not so all-or-none. As Zadeh observes, concepts often have fuzzy boundaries such that it is more accurate to consider items as exhibiting various degrees of membership in a concept. The degree of membership may be expressed on a multivalued, or even continuous, scale from 0 (most extreme nonexample) to 1 (best example). Zadeh cites numerous examples of very fuzzy concepts—"bald men," "young women," "narrow streets," "small cars," "funny jokes," to name a few. Zadeh has also pioneered the development of fuzzy logic for inference with fuzzy sets. This development may be profoundly significant to an understanding of semantic memory (Zadeh 1965, 1976; Zadeh et al. 1975; Gaines 1976; Gaines and Kohout 1977).

As Zadeh points out, people in specialized fields often provide precise, two-valued definitions for concepts that are fuzzy in general usage. For example, a recession is when GNP goes down for two consecutive quarters; a small car is one that weighs less than 2,000 pounds; and an adult is a person who is 18 or over. However, there is nothing imprecise about fuzzy concepts or about the notion of *degree of set membership*. Indeed, since natural events do vary from other events by degree, and since this variation is only crudely approximated by binary concepts, it is certainly open to question in any given case whether we gain from forcing a multivalued, graduated world into the two-valued logic of law, science, and government. It is absurd to go around shouting, "Down with two-valued thinking!" One need look no further than the digital computer to see what practical and theoretical benefits can be derived from the simplification provided by two-valued logic. However, the human mind is still a more remarkable thinker in many respects than any programmed computer, and it appears to use a lot of fuzzy concepts in its thinking.

Prototypes:
Concepts with Ideal Members

Using a variety of experimental techniques, Rosch has demonstrated that many natural (real-life) concepts—as opposed to artificial concepts learned in the laboratory—have fuzzy boundaries but ideal examples. These ideal examples, or centerpoints, of a concept are termed its prototypes. For example, there are no precise boundaries between colors adjacent in the spectrum. As we move from red to orange in the wavelength of light, the light gradually becomes a poorer red and a better orange. There are, however, ideal, best, or prototypical examples of various colors. Rosch has shown that prototypical red, yellow, green, blue, pink, orange, brown, and purple are in some way innately specified in human beings, so that they are identical for all of us regardless of what language we speak. Certain focal colors are more salient in some way, and these tend to serve as the prototypes for the most basic (simplest, shortest) color names in every language. The universal genetic basis for focal color concepts is not important to the present discussion. My point here is that the constituent structure of color concepts is *not* an all-or-none association of certain sets of color attributes to one color concept, another set to another color concept, and so on. Rather, the strength of association of any particular wavelength of the spectrum to two or more color concepts varies continuously. Thus a sample color could be .7 of the ideal red, .4 of the ideal orange, .3 of the ideal pink, and maybe even .05 of the ideal yellow. It is the prototype of the concept that is the most precisely specified, along with some function that indicates how rapidly the belongingness to that concept falls off as one moves away from the prototype (fig. 10.1) (Heider 1971, 1972; Heider and Olivier 1972; Rosch 1973, 1975*a*, 1975*b*, 1975*c*, 1977; Rosch and Mervis 1975; Rosch et al. 1976; Rosch, Simpson, and Miller 1976).*

A study by Rosch shows how the goodness of examples can vary within a color category. Rosch (1975*a*) demonstrated that cuing a subject with a focal color concept such as "red" produced an attentional focus that was limited to reds fairly close to the prototypical red. The task was to decide whether two colors were identical. Sometimes subjects were given no advance cuing regarding the nature of the color pairs to be matched. Sometimes they were given a focal color name, such as "red," 2 sec before presentation of the pair of colors to be matched. Advance cuing facilitated "same" decisions for colors near the prototype (e.g., good reds). It actually interfered with "same" decisions for colors farther from the prototype of the cued color (e.g., muddy reds). This was true even though in a separate classification experiment the poor examples of focal color names were nevertheless classified as belonging to the correct focal color class over 90% of the time.

The hypothesis that human concepts have ideal centerpoints with fuzzy boundaries can easily be extended to concepts defined over two or more attribute dimensions. It is difficult to represent graphically functions of three or more variables. However, we can represent a function of two variables by

*Eleanor Heider and Eleanor Rosch are the same person.

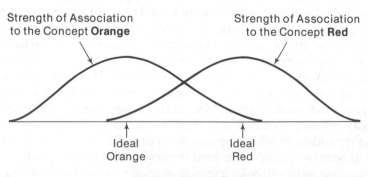

Strength of Association to the Concept **Orange**

Strength of Association to the Concept **Red**

Ideal Orange

Ideal Red

Wavelength of Light

Fig. 10.1 Human color concepts do not divide the wavelengths of light into discrete categories with sharply defined boundaries. Rather, there is a central, ideal example of each color concept (its prototype), and there is a function that defines the degree to which neighboring wavelengths are examples of that color concept.

contour lines representing different strengths of association to the concept for each combination of values of the two dimensions. The result resembles a topographic map showing the elevation of different regions around a mountain. The mountain peak is analogous to the prototype of the concept.* The decreasing elevation away from the peak is analogous to the decreasing strength of association to the concept of different points in the two-dimensional attribute space. This is illustrated in figure 10.2. Concept (a) has a single ideal example (one peak). Concept (b) has two different ideal examples (two peaks). The hypothesis that human concepts have fuzzy boundaries is compatible with any number of peaks in the function that defines how good an example of the concept each point in the attribute space is. However, the hypothesis that concepts have a prototype structure further specifies that this function has only one peak—that is, one ideal combination of attributes.

*For the mathematically sophisticated reader, a concept with a prototype constituent structure is one whose function representing the strength of association to the concept node from each point in the attribute space has a single maximum.

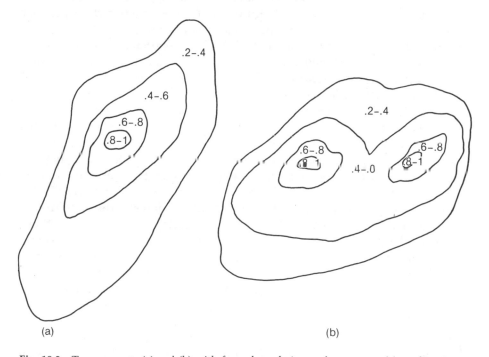

(a)   (b)

Fig. 10.2   Two concepts (a) and (b) with fuzzy boundaries, each represented by a function
defined over a two-dimensional attribute space. The contour lines represent strengths
of association to the concept of .2, .4, .6, and .8, where the peak strength is defined as
1.0. Both concepts are fuzzy, that is, are defined by graded functions in the attribute
space. Only concept (a) has prototype structure—that is, it has a single ideal example
(single peak). Concept (b) has two different ideal examples and therefore, by
definition, does not have a prototype structure.

Rosch cites evidence that natural concepts, such as geometric forms (circle, square, equilateral triangle) and the facial expressions of six basic human emotions (happiness, sadness, anger, fear, surprise, and disgust), also have a prototype constituent structure.* Thus Rosch is asserting that there is only one ideal facial expression to communicate surprise, and the farther one goes away from that ideal facial expression along any relevant attribute dimension (facial size is an irrelevant dimension, for example), the less the facial expression is perceived to express surprise. This assumption could be disproved by demonstrating that two very different facial expressions could communicate a given emotion better than any expression that fell "in between" them in our attribute space for analyzing human facial expressions.

The hypothesis that geometrical concepts have a prototype structure raises a question about the boundaries of these concepts. In terms of the usual mathematical definitions, the boundaries between squares and nonsquares, for example, are sharp. A form either is a square or it is not. If an otherwise square form has one rounded corner, one small gap, or two angles very slightly off 90°, the form is a nonsquare. In ordinary geometry there is no notion of "degree of squareness." But psychologically there certainly is such a notion. Not only does the concept "square" have a prototype structure with an ideal center class of examples, it also has fuzzy boundaries. Intuitively we all know that humans have limited discriminative capacities, which produces some fuzziness in the perceptual encoding of geometric concepts, but the fuzziness I am discussing goes far beyond that. Our repertoire of concepts is not unlimited. When we see a form that clearly deviates from a form for which we have a prototypical concept, but which is nonetheless closer to that concept than to any other concept in our repertoire, we encode it in terms of the *prototype plus a correction*. Or so Woodworth (1938) concluded many years ago, after considering several form memory experiments. Thus a square with a small gap in one side is coded as a "square with a gap." Attneave (1957) showed that learning a new prototype for either a novel letter pattern or a novel geometric form facilitated later paired-associate learning in which minor perturbations of these prototypes were the stimuli. Even a recently learned prototype facilitates coding and differentiation of stimuli in its vicinity. Although a prototype is essentially a stereotype of a group of entities, it does not inhibit differentiation of small differences among individuals in the group. On the contrary, prototypes can actually be used to enhance differentiation, as Hebb (1949) and Attneave have emphasized. The "all Chinese look alike" phenomenon is limited precisely to people who have not seen enough Chinese to build up a good prototype of the "average" Chinese features from which to perceive variations.

---

*The term *schema* is often used in this context instead of *prototype*, but I, and others, use the term *schema* to refer to a higher-order system of interrelated propositions, rather than to the ideal set of constituent features for a concept.

Family Resemblance:
Concepts with No Common Attributes

Most concepts devised in the laboratory have been logical functions of a small number of nonredundant relevant attributes (e.g., green squares). But Rosch points out that most natural concepts take advantage of the many redundant attributes that characterize real-world objects. Wings are more likely to be found with feathers than with fur; scales, fins, and gills tend to go together; and so on. Forming a prototype of many examples of a concept tends to preserve all the attributes common to a lot of the examples, whether or not these attributes are redundant.

Furthermore, while all examples of a prototypical concept are more or less close together in the sense that they have many similar attributes, there need be no set of attributes—or even one attribute—that is common to all real examples of a concept. Following Wittgenstein (1953), Rosch (1975c) refers to prototypical concepts with no common attributes as *family resemblances.* She gives a nice symbolic example of a set of instances that could form a *family resemblance* prototype concept (which I have modified just a bit). Let capital letters stand for attributes. Consider this set of instances of a family resemblance concept: ABCD, BCDE, CDEF, DEFG, EFGH, FGHA, GHAB, HABC, DEAB, EFAB. Not one single attribute is common to all these instances, and yet each attribute occurs frequently in instances of the concept and cooccurs often with other attributes in the prototype. Instances tend to be highly similar to other instances of the concept and to the prototype (ABCDEFGH), which contains all the attributes frequently found in instances of this concept. Wittgenstein and Rosch's assertion, which I tend to support (though it hasn't been proven), is that most human concepts are family resemblances rather than conjunctions of a set of attributes common to all examples of a concept.

CONCEPT LEARNING

Concept learning includes everything from what children do when they learn the meaning of a new word to what college students do when they learn the definition of a new concept. Unfortunately, some psychologists have also used the term *concept learning* to refer to the sophisticated inferential problem solving used to figure out a rule that classifies complex objects into one concept or another. Different psychological processes are involved in the various tasks referred to as concept learning. Accordingly, we distinguish three methods of concept learning: abstraction, propositional learning, and inferential learning.

The primary distinction among methods of concept learning is probably closely related to the distinction between constituent and propositional levels of concept meaning. The most basic method of concept learning is unconscious *abstraction* based on observation of instances and noninstances. This is the method young children use to learn the most basic concepts. Presumably adults retain the capacity to use this method when necessary. Abstraction is presumed to be a basic process that does not require high-level thinking based on previously learned concepts and propositions. That is, it does not entail generating hypotheses, inferences, and problem solving. I shall claim that abstraction establishes a strength-of-association function from a subset of attribute nodes to a new concept node. Abstraction is thus a process that establishes the constituent meaning of a concept.

The other basic method of concept learning is *propositional learning:* incorporating a new concept node into higher-level propositional nodes. Presumably a new concept node does not exist unless it has some lower-level constituents, but these might only be the verbal constituents of its spoken or written name. When we learn concepts from their verbal context in text, we are learning by incorporating the concept into propositions. If I tell you that X eats ants, you will then know quite a lot about concept "X." (Indeed, many people may know little more than this about anteaters.) For instance, you know that X is alive, that it does not live exclusively in water, that it is (presumably) bigger than an ant, and so on. As we have seen, the definition of a concept is one or more propositions about the concept. Thus learning a concept from its definition is included in the propositional learning of concepts. However, the definitional learning of concepts (especially concrete concepts) may also strengthen constituent-attribute associations to the concept node. It would do so by activating attribute nodes vis-à-vis our capacity for imagination. Literally, imagination is the generation of images for concrete concepts.

Developmental studies of the conceptual growth of children, and some appropriate experimental studies of artificial concept learning by adults, allow us to draw some important conclusions about the abstraction of constituent structure for concepts. However, many other studies of artificial concept learning are artificial in ways that make them essentially problem-solving tasks. These tasks consist of a varying mixture of (1) abstraction from instances and (2) inferences based on previously learned propositions concerning the concept and the rules of logical inference. Probably most natural concept learning does not occur in this way. Furthermore, as Rosch (1977) has emphasized, the concepts learned in these studies are nonfuzzy, logical functions of a small number of relevant attributes. These artificial concepts do not appear to resemble natural concepts. Nevertheless, there is no body of literature devoted strictly to propositional learning of concepts, so we shall briefly review the findings concerning what might be called *inferential learning* of concepts. Inferential learning is one higher-level conceptual-learning alternative to abstraction.

Inferential Learning of Concepts

Inferential learning experiments have used examples of a concept that differ on only a few dimensions. These dimensions are clearly explained to the subject. The type of concept rule is also clearly explained. This makes it possible for subjects to draw logical conclusions about the nature of the concept from a small number of examples or nonexamples. For inferential concept learning, subjects should have sufficient time to do the kind of logical thinking required to draw inferences concerning the concept. Inferential concept learning depends heavily upon the use of propositions already stored in semantic memory that encode the rules of logical reasoning.

One of the classic investigations of inferential concept attainment was undertaken by Bruner, Goodnow, and Austin (1956). Subjects were given artificial geometric stimuli that differed in several dimensions, such as shape, color, number of borders, and number of figures. The possible values of a stimulus on each dimension were specified, and subjects were told explicitly what rules they should follow in defining an instance as an example or a nonexample of a concept. For example, subjects might be told that the concept was a simple conjunction of one or more relevant attributes, where an attribute was a particular value of a dimension. A typical concept might be all stimuli containing two red squares. Such a concept has three relevant dimensions: the number, shape, and color of the figures. Bruner, Goodnow, and Austin used Harvard students as subjects.

Given all of these characteristics, it should come as no surprise that the methods the subjects used were highly inferential. They were also completely different from the methods used by children or by adults under other conditions. Bruner, Goodnow, and Austin classified their subjects' methods of inferential concept attainment into two categories: *scanning* and *focusing.* In scanning, subjects formed a hypothesis about the concept (usually from one example). Then they tested that hypothesis against subsequent examples and nonexamples. When it failed, they rejected it and selected a new one. This process continued until the subjects had arrived at a hypothesis that seemed to fit all the examples and nonexamples.

In focusing, subjects made inferences about relevant and irrelevant dimensions. This method is logically more efficient. In the simplest case subjects might compare two examples of a conjunctive concept and infer that all the attributes that differed in the two examples must be irrelevant to the concept. Using the focusing method for conjunctive concept attainment, subjects could also compare an example and a nonexample of the concept that differed in only one attribute and infer that the differing attribute must be relevant to the concept. The more intelligent subjects favored focusing over scanning. Focusing was also favored by subjects who had had more practice in concept attainment tasks.

In inferential concept learning, subjects are frequently generating and testing hypotheses about concepts or inferring relevant and irrelevant attribute dimensions. In either case they are selectively processing the attributes of examples and nonexamples, paying more attention to some attributes than to others at any given time. Studies by Bourne and his associates have demonstrated that increasing the number of either relevant or irrelevant attributes increases the difficulty of concept learning. Such findings are predictable on a number of hypotheses; for example, they may be explained by limitations on attentional capacity. The more irrelevant dimensions there are, the more likely the subject is to pay attention to an irrelevant dimension rather than to a relevant one. The more relevant dimensions there are, the more dimensions the subject must pay attention to in order to learn the concept (Bourne 1957; Bulgarella and Archer 1962; Kepros and Bourne 1966; Haygood and Stevenson 1967).

Subjects in Bower and Trabasso's inferential concept learning experiments apparently used scanning exclusively. In early trials subjects typically performed at chance in classifying items as examples or nonexamples of the concept to be learned. In later trials their classifications suddenly became nearly 100% correct. Furthermore, if the correct values of the relevant attributes were shifted during the presolution period, subjects learned the new shifted concept as rapidly as subjects who had never been exposed to shifted values. These results suggest that under these conditions subjects learn nothing about the correct attributes before they direct their attention to the correct hypothesis. This is not gradual abstraction of a concept from accumulated memory for instances, the most basic concept-learning process. Rather, the college students who performed in these experiments were engaged in a highly inferential problem-solving process—generating and testing hypotheses concerning the concept. Other studies with elementary and junior-high students showed that the more intelligent subjects engaged in hypothesis testing, while the less intelligent subjects learned by a more gradual, incremental abstraction of concepts from examples. The evidence for this is that the students with high IQs classified items at chance during the presolution period and then suddenly jumped to 100% correct performance. The performance of students with low IQs improved gradually (Bower and Trabasso 1963, 1964; Trabasso and Bower 1964, 1968; Osler and Fivel 1961; Osler and Trautman 1961).

At any given time, subjects who are testing hypotheses are paying selective attention to certain stimulus dimensions rather than others. Accordingly, after learning one concept, they might learn a new concept with the same relevant dimensions, but different correct values of those dimensions, faster than they would learn a new concept with different relevant dimensions. This is always the case for adults and older children, but reverse results are sometimes obtained for younger children and animals. This finding also supports the distinction between inferential concept learning and abstraction

(Brookshire, Warren, and Ball 1961; Kendler and Kendler 1962;Johnson 1967; Mackintosh 1974, pp. 597–98). However, note that while animals and very young children are probably not testing hypotheses when they learn concepts, they are capable of selective attention, as a function of the salience of different attributes, in concept learning by abstraction. This point will be discussed later.

There is also evidence for hypothesis testing and all-or-none selective attention in studies of inferential concept attainment by adults, using concepts that have redundant relevant attributes. Two attributes are redundant if they are perfectly correlated—if one never appears without the other. For instance, the examples of a concept might all be blue circles. If circles are never presented in any other color but blue, and if blue is not used as the color of any other form, the two dimensions—blue and circles—are redundant. Thus the subject need only learn the correct value of one of them in order to solve the concept-learning task. If subjects are testing hypotheses, that is probably just what they would do. Indeed, Trabasso and Bower (1968) found that most subjects base their response on only one attribute and are typically unaware of the other relevant attribute in such cases.

The *salience* (attention-getting value) of particular attributes differs for different individuals. The salience of a given attribute for a given individual can also be changed by various means. One way, which I have already discussed, is to make the attribute dimension relevant in some earlier task. Another way is to increase the intensity of the relevant attribute or its degree of contrast with the background. For example, Hull (1920) painted the relevant attributes red and the irrelevant attributes black to facilitate concept learning. Still another way to increase dimensional salience is to increase the range of values on that dimension. Archer (1962) facilitated concept learning by increasing the range of possible values for a relevant dimension and inhibited concept learning by increasing the range of values for an irrelevant dimension. For inferential concept learning by humans, the most effective method of increasing salience is simply to tell the subject in words what to pay attention to. Of course, if you're going to tell the subject what type of concept rule to follow and what the relevant dimensions are, you might just as well communicate the entire concept in words. And that, I think, is what we really should be contrasting with the method of learning concepts by abstraction—that is, learning concepts from propositional descriptions.

Abstraction of Concepts:
Prototypes and Instance Memory

The simplest type of concept is one in which all the examples contain common attributes. Hull (1920) classified a large number of Chinese-language characters into different categories (concepts) such that each character in a particular category contained a specific set of visual attributes. The subject's task was to learn the classification and to respond with a particular nonsense syllable to each Chinese character in each class. Figure 10.3 illustrates the material used in Hull's experiment. The task was presented as rote learning; subjects were not taught that it was possible to learn the correct response on the basis of attributes common to all the examples of each category. Neither were subjects told what type of concept was involved, and there were a great many potentially relevant dimensions that were not specified to the subjects. In short, subjects had virtually no opportunity to acquire concepts by a logical reasoning or problem-solving process. Nevertheless, after a large number of trials subjects could correctly classify characters that they had seen before and new characters as well. Thus the subjects did learn the concepts by observation and abstraction—much, perhaps, as young children learn concepts in the natural world. Indeed, many subjects who could correctly classify characters could not point out the common attributes. Even when subjects were pretrained on a task that involved copying the common attributes out of context, they performed no better in the subsequent concept-learning task than subjects given no pretraining on the common attributes. But if the common attributes were presented in the context of the remainder of the characters and painted red to attract attention, concept learning was facilitated. Finally, subjects who were exposed to a wide variety of different characters containing the common attribute did better than subjects who were only exposed to a few characters. Presumably a larger set of characters conveys more information concerning the components of each character that are irrelevant to the concept. In so doing, it focuses attention on the relevant common component.

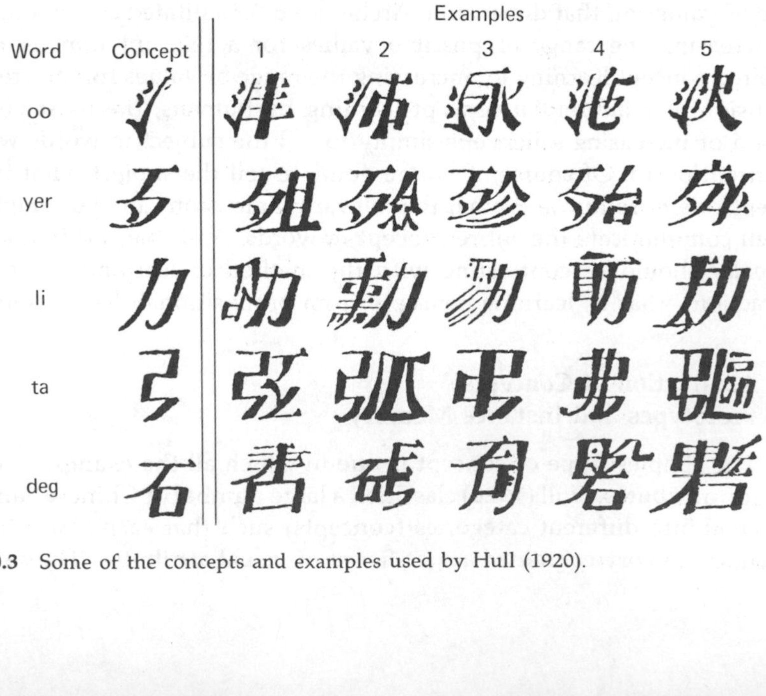

Fig. 10.3 Some of the concepts and examples used by Hull (1920).

In Hull's study all examples of a concept contained a common attribute. Variations among examples were created merely by the addition or deletion of *irrelevant* attributes. Researchers have recently shown great interest in the learning of family resemblance concepts where the variant examples are derived by deleting and substituting *relevant* attributes from an ideal, central, prototypical example. Evans is one of the initiators of this research. According to Evans, prototype concepts are statistical (probabilistic) in the sense that the relevant attributes tend to occur (and occur together) in examples of the concept, but no one of the relevant attributes will necessarily be found in all examples of the concept. Examples of such concepts are not recognized by a few infallible attributes, but by a large number of fallible attributes that tend to be highly associated with each other and highly predictive of membership in a category (Evans and Edmonds 1966; Evans 1967).

Posner and Keele (1968, 1970) used nine dots to construct several different prototype patterns. Then they produced distortions of each pattern by randomly moving the component dots various distances from their original position in the prototype. In one critical condition subjects were given only distorted versions of each prototype. They learned to classify these versions with a single name, without ever seeing the original prototype. Subjects were then given new patterns to classify that included the previous examples as well as new distortions and the prototype itself. Subjects who had rote learned the characteristics of each example separately should classify the original examples more accurately than the new distortions or the prototype itself. In fact, subjects sometimes classified prototypes as accurately as the original examples. In all cases they classified prototypes more accurately than the new distortions, which were constructed to be as similar to any single originally learned example as the prototype was. Thus it would appear that subjects can extract a central prototypical definition of a concept solely on the basis of various distortions of the prototype, provided the distortions are not too great.

Posner and Keele also found that concepts learned in this way were defined not only by their central prototype but also by some knowledge of the degree of variability consistent with classification as an example of the concept. Evidence for this is that subjects who had been exposed to a set of example patterns that varied only slightly from the prototype were less likely to classify highly distorted new patterns as examples than were subjects who had been exposed to patterns that varied greatly from the prototype.

Evidence for the abstraction of prototypes in artificial concept learning has been obtained using a variety of stimulus material. This material includes schematic faces, configurations of simple forms, configurations of stick figures, letter strings, descriptions of facts regarding individuals in some group, and different views of flexible plastic shapes (Reed 1972; Reed and Friedman 1973; Franks and Bransford 1971; Lasky 1974; Posnansky and Neumann 1976; Rosch, Simpson, and Miller 1976; Charness and Bregman 1973; Hyman and

Frost 1974). There is evidence that both children and adults abstract proto-types. Four measured (dependent) variables have been used to determine what has been learned about a concept from a series of examples. The first is classification of new items. The second is confidence judgments. The third is reaction time for such classification. The fourth is judgments of the ideal example of a concept, and more generally of the *goodness* of an example. Let me explain these variables. Suppose that the central example of a concept is rated as the ideal example. Now suppose that goodness judgments, classifica-tion frequency, and confidence of classification drop monotonically with distance from the prototype. Finally, suppose that classification reaction time increases with increasing distance from the prototype. From this we may infer a concept with a prototype constituent structure. Finally, Rosch, Simpson, and Miller found that advance priming with a concept name in an item-matching task facilitates matching good examples of the concept and inhibits matching poor examples.

The statements in the preceding paragraph apply most directly to the case where subjects are asked to judge (yes or no) whether an item belongs in a single given category (concept). More frequently subjects are asked to classify an item into one of two or more categories. In such cases prototype constituent structure for concepts has been inferred when classification, goodness judgments, confidence judgments, and reaction time appear to be a function of the *relative* differences between an item and the prototypes for the different concepts. Most such studies also claim support for a prototype model of concept constituent structure (Reed 1972; Reed and Friedman 1973; Franks and Bransford 1971; Lasky 1974; Posnansky and Neumann 1976; Rosch, Simpson, and Miller 1976; Charness and Bregman 1973; Hyman and Frost 1974).

Several studies have examined differences in prototype abstraction as a function of type of training—specifically of the number of training examples and their dispersion (degree of distortion) from the prototype. The results are entirely reasonable: prototype abstraction and the ability to classify new examples correctly are increased by increasing the number of examples. Nar-row dispersion of examples facilitates prototype abstraction (provided the examples are dispersed so as to be centered on the true prototype), because in this case all the examples strongly resemble each other and the prototype. However, if we want to generalize the concept broadly to more broadly dispersed examples, then the best training is with broadly dispersed exam-ples. Note that this does require more training examples to cover the desired larger region of the attribute space adequately (Posner and Keele 1968, 1970; Charness and Bregman 1973; Peterson et al. 1973; Homa et al. 1973; Homa and Vosburgh 1976; Goldman and Homa 1977).

To some people the term *prototype abstraction* from examples means consciously recognizing the similarity between one example and another. To others it means imaging a center point among a set of examples and learning just that prototype pattern of attributes, perhaps while encoding the type and magnitude of allowable transformations. The most obvious objection to this view of prototype abstraction is that it is excessively conscious and intellectual. This objection applies especially to natural concept learning or even to laboratory concept learning by children. However, there is an even more convincing objection. The prototype and its allowable transformations logically cannot be determined unless the examples have already been encoded more or less faithfully into memory. This is so because concepts can be (and typically are) learned from examples that are not all perceptually present simultaneously. Rather, these examples are presented serially. In fact, considerable time and many other events sometimes intervene between successive examples of the same concept (particularly in natural concept learning) (Reitman and Bower 1973). At least during the period of concept learning, learning prototypes is not an *alternative* to learning examples. Either prototypes are learned in additon to examples, or else the nature of the mind is such that learning examples of concepts naturally produces a prototype constituent structure for many concepts. The latter hypothesis would clearly be more parsimonious of cognitive processes, since rote learning of example-concept associations would automatically result in prototype constituent structure; there would be no need to assume any separate process of abstraction at all. I shall argue that this is indeed the case. Concept constituent structure is learned bit by bit, by associating different specific examples to the same concept node.

This means that somehow we must identify each example as belonging to the same concept. In the laboratory the experimenter does this, and people do similar verbal labeling when they teach natural concepts. However, there is probably also considerable nonverbal classing together of events based on the similarity of their attributes or functional consequences. For example, anything that supports you when you try to sit on it is, in this respect, functionally equivalent, so a child could learn the "chair" concept nonverbally.

Regardless of how a common concept node is activated, the basic paradigm for concept learning is the paired occurrence of a large number of different examples with the activation of the same concept node. By ordinary associative learning, this results in strengthened associations from the nodes for the attributes in the examples to the concept node. The attributes that occur oftenest will have the strongest associations to the concept, so an example composed of *all* these attributes (namely, the prototype) will have the greatest strength of association to the concept. A new item can be classified as an example of the concept if it has enough of the relevant attributes or very similar attributes. As Brooks has emphasized, we can (and do) classify a new entity as a dog because it looks a lot like Lassie, provided we know that Lassie is a dog (Brooks 1977; Levy and Heshka 1973).* Memory for particular examples will permit considerable conceptual generalization. This is so because pairing any point in human attribute space with a concept does more than just strengthen the association from that point to the concept. Directly or indirectly, such pairing generalizes to nearby points in the attribute space (similar events), associating these points to the concept as well. If there are enough examples, their generalization gradients will cover the entire region of attribute space that is to be classed together into the same concept. Imagine that attribute space has only two dimensions, and that associating a point in that space to a particular concept is like dumping a load of dirt on that point. When you dump the dirt on that point, it will form a peak in the center, but a lot of dirt will also fall to the sides. If you dumped dirt on enough spots in an area, it would pretty well fill in the entire space. Actually human concept learning doesn't work quite this way. A center point (the prototype) that is not directly "dumped on" can nonetheless acquire enough generalization from all sides to have a higher peak (strength of association to the concept) than any of the points that are actually associated to the concept (the surrounding points that were dumped on). This can't happen with dirt dumping, but what the heck, I can't always think up perfect analogies.

A closely related way to view the relation between instance memory and concept abstraction is to assert that the attribute nodes of presented instances become associated to the concept node (Reitman and Bower 1973; Neumann 1974; Barresi, Robbins, and Shain 1975; Goldman and Homa 1977). A new combination of strongly associated attributes will itself be strongly associated to the concept. For example, if a subject has previously learned that items with attributes ABC, CDE, and EFG are instances of the concept, he will treat new item ADG as an instance of the concept. This is an extremely context-independent attribute theory; in which the presence or absence of a particular attribute has no effect on the encoding of other attributes. We have seen repeatedly that coding is highly relational—that is, highly context-dependent. This dependency can be represented in many ways. For example, a set of three context-free attributes, ABC, might be encoded as having three context-free and three context-dependent attributes, A, B, C, AB, BC, and AC. Now suppose we apply this context-dependent attribute learning theory to the example where ABC, CDE, and EFG were learned as instances of a concept. The new item ADG would have all three of its nonrelational attributes (A, D, and G) associated to the concept. But all three of its relational

---

*Also see Brooks (1976, 1978). After my obvious debt throughout this chapter to the insights of Eleanor Rosch, my next greatest obligation is to Lee Brooks. His writings and his conversation with me reoriented my thinking to emphasize the importance of memory for instances in concept learning. The usual disclaimers apply—you're not to assume that my position is exactly the same as anyone else's and the blame for any mistakes rests entirely with me, not with the people whose work I cite.

(context-sensitive) attributes (AD, DG, and AG) would be new and not associated to the concept. Presumably this would give substantial, but not complete, generalization, in accord with both intuition and certain facts. Although an unpresented prototype may often have a greater total number of relational and nonrelational attributes strongly associated to the concept than any presented example, it must also have some relational attributes that are not associated to the concept at all, if it is to be discriminably different from any presented instance. That is, an unpresented prototype, like any new item, must at least be a new combination of old attributes. This means that higher-order, context-sensitive, relational coding will produce some attributes that have never been associated to the concept, if the analysis is sufficiently detailed to discriminate new instances from old instances. In most prototype learning studies, new items have been discriminable from old items. The proof is that new items are misclassified more often than old items. Furthermore, although the total strength of association of an unpresented prototype to a concept is often greater than that for presented (old) instances, the dynamics of classification suggests that subjects often do recognize the prototype as an instance that has not been presented before. Posner and Keele (1968) observed that subjects' classification reaction time is greater for previously unpresented prototypes than for previously presented examples. Thus subjects can recognize that the prototype is a new instance, but one that is, in many ways, a super-good instance of the concept.

Concept Discrimination

Obviously, categorizing an item as an example of some concept is not usually a yes-or-no decision. It is a choice among two or more concepts or, in natural situations, a choice among all the concepts in one's repertoire (plus the alternative of defining a new concept). The prototypical example, which will be most consistently and rapidly classified as belonging to a particular concept, is not necessarily any simple average or mode of the attributes that occur in examples of the concept.* The relevant attributes are those that are *criterial* for discriminating examples of the concept from examples of other concepts. As Rosch and Mervis (1975) have demonstrated, the items that are learned and classified most easily as examples of a concept have not only the greatest family resemblance to other examples of the concept, but also the fewest attributes characteristic of other concepts.

We may speculate that attributes that are strongly associated to one concept exert some direct or indirect inhibition on contrasting concepts. Within a single attribute dimension, the association of one set of values of that dimension to one concept could affect the net strength of association of

*The modal example of a concept is the example with the attributes that occur most frequently in examples of the concept.

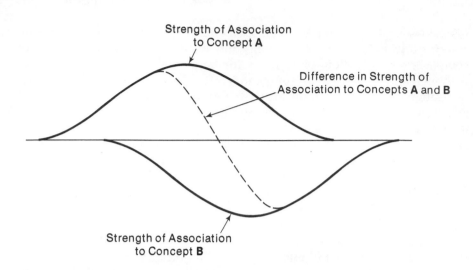

Strength of Association
to Concept **A**

Difference in Strength of
Association to Concepts **A** and **B**

Strength of Association
to Concept **B**

Fig. 10.4 Associating two different sets of attributes of a single dimension to two different concepts can shift the attribute validity of different values of the dimension for classification of examples. When we use a measure of relative strength, such as the difference in strength of association to the two concepts, the optimum value of the dimension for classification as an example of the concept shifts from the average value (found in examples of the concept) in the direction away from the other set of values.

another set of values of that dimension to a contrasting concept (fig. 10.4). Note that values of an attribute dimension that are equally strongly associated to two different concepts are useless as a criterion for discriminating between those concepts. The attribute values that best discriminate between two concepts are those with the greatest *difference* in strength of association to one concept versus the other. These are not necessarily the average values of either concept alone or the values most frequently found in examples of either one of the concepts. The values that are most valid for discriminating between two concepts will often differ slightly from the average or modal values characteristic of examples of a concept. Rosch and Mervis argue that the prototype of a concept is the most valid set of attributes—which is not necessarily the set of attributes that is found most frequently in examples of a concept.

Conceptual Development
and Basic Concepts

As Piaget (1954) has emphasized, the first concepts that children learn appear to be concrete objects and the actions that apply to concrete objects. Children use words like "Mama," "milk," "apple," "drink," and "eat" before they use property adjectives or adverbs like "white," "round," "quickly," or "red" or superordinate noun and verb concepts like "person," "fruit," or "consume." Furthermore, children tend to acquire concepts that have to do with concrete objects, actions, or the properties of concrete objects or actions before they acquire more abstract concepts, which are not so closely linked to observable referents. There are many apparent exceptions to this rule. For example, three-year-olds use the words "good" and "bad" with reasonable propriety, although children's concepts of morality undergo many changes with age.

This raises the methodological point that conceptual development is very inadequately assessed by an inventory of the words in a child's vocabulary. When a child "overgeneralizes" the use of a word, as for example, when he calls all men "Daddy," this does not necessarily indicate an overgeneralized concept. Perhaps the child has developed a reasonably appropriate concept of "Daddy" but knows no other name to attach to another man. So he chooses to use the most appropriate word in his present vocabulary. The sight of a man may activate the concept "Daddy" more than it activates any other concept to which the child has learned a name—hence the verbalization "Daddy." Young children, especially preverbal ones, have presumably learned many concepts for which they have not yet learned any reasonably appropriate word.

We know that a child often does not have exactly the same meaning for words that an adult has. Hence it is dangerous to use adult standards to classify words children use. A word that represents a very abstract concept for an adult may represent a much more concrete concept for a child. Only extensive testing of a child's use and comprehension of concepts can establish what concepts he has formed at any age. Nevertheless, it is possible to make a few tentative statements concerning conceptual development that are relevant to the theory of concept representation.

First, as Anglin has demonstrated, children both overgeneralize (overextend) and undergeneralize (underextend) in their use of concepts. That is, they apply concepts to inappropriate instances (overgeneralization) and fail to apply concepts to appropriate instances (undergeneralization). Overgeneralization is more noticeable in spontaneous speech than undergeneralization, but comprehension tests show that both occur frequently, and there is no reason to assume any instrinsic bias toward overgeneralization. Calling all men "Daddy" is an example of overgeneralization. Reich (1976) has described an example of undergeneralization where his son's behavior in response to the question, "Where's the shoes?" indicated that his "shoes" concept applied only to a subset of all shoes, namely, Mommy's shoes in the closet. It did not apply to other people's shoes or even to Mommy's shoes out of the closet. Children have learned only a little about the extension and intension of adult concepts, and this is reflected in their tendency to over- and underextend (Anglin 1977).

Second, the statement that children's concepts are more concrete than adult concepts does not mean that children's concepts include only those adult concepts with the narrowest range of referential generality. That is, children do not acquire the concept "Jonathan apple" before they acquire the concept "apple," although they usually do acquire the concept "apple" before they acquire the concept "fruit." Theories often assume that conceptual development in children is a process of either (1) beginning with the most specific concepts and later developing the more general concept, or (2) beginning with the most general concept and differentiating it into progressively finer concepts. Both assumptions must be wrong. From the standpoint of referential generality, children usually seem to enter conceptual hierarchies somewhere in the middle; they learn "table" before they learn either "end table" or "furniture." There was no satisfactory explanation for the particular level at which children begin to learn concepts until very recently, when Rosch generated the idea of basic concepts. *Basic concepts* are the most general concepts that can be characterized by a single prototype (Rosch et al. 1976; Rosch 1977). According to this hypothesis, "apple" is a basic concept that a child learns early because apples are characterized by a single prototype, while superordinates of apples, such as "fruit," are not. The concept "apple" may be learned before the concept "Jonathan apple" precisely because "apple" has greater referential generality (and therefore comes up more frequently), though both concepts may be characterizable by prototypes.

This is a plausible hypothesis. It is largely consistent with the hypothesis that the concepts the child learns first tend to be those concepts that adults use most frequently in their interactions with children. If adults tend to talk more about apples and less about fruits and Jonathan apples, there will be selective environmental pressure on a child to learn the concept "apple." Such environmental explanations do not tell us why adults prefer to communicate in terms of such basic concepts. Rosch's hypothesis provides an attractive explanation, and it also explains why it is functional for a child to begin by learning the basic concepts that are intermediate in referential generality.

Further support for distinguishing basic concepts from both superordinates and subordinates is provided in a study of American Sign Language (ASL) for the deaf by Newport and Bellugi (1977). They found that ASL had single signs for basic concepts and used compound signs for superordinates (e.g., "apple-orange-banana" for "fruit") or subordinates (e.g., "purple grapes" for "Concord grapes").

Third, the statement that children learn concrete concepts before they learn more abstract concepts does not mean that children learn all the sensory attribute constituents of a concept before they learn any propositions in which the concept plays a part. As Piaget and many other cognitive development psychologists have emphasized, children tend to learn early the functions of objects in their environment and the actions that are relevant to those objects. A chair is something to sit on, a ball is something to throw, and juice is something to drink. It may be that these functional meanings of words are somehow encoded as sensory constituents of the concept, but this seems unlikely. It seems more plausible that very young children are forming many propositions that embody concepts, and that the meaning of a concept for a child is already determined as much by the learned higher-level propositions in which it is included as by learned connections to lower-level attribute constituents. There is another reason for emphasizing the propositional level of meaning at an early stage of cognitive development. Words that stand for property concepts such as color and shape appear to be acquired substantially later than object and action concepts, which in some logical systems are composed of property constituents (Ervin-Tripp 1973). Anglin (1977) has emphasized that, on occasion, functional considerations can cause a child to acquire concepts first that are either more specific or more general than the basic level. For instance, terms like "Mummy" and "Daddy" are among the first to be learned, and yet these terms in adult usage refer to individuals and are more specific than the most inclusive set of entities similar in form to the child's parents. Even when a basic concept term is learned first, comprehension studies may show that it has a highly specific meaning, as in Reich's example, where "shoes" meant just "Mommy's shoes in the closet." On the other hand, terms superordinate to the basic level may be learned first. Here Anglin cites the superordinate "money" as being often learned before the basic concept "coin" or the subordinate concept "dime" (Ervin-Tripp 1973). Money, which includes both paper money and coins, would not appear to be characterizable by a single visual-form prototype. However, all money has a similar function in the acquisition of goods, and perhaps this could be considered to be a single prototype based on emotional or motivational attributes that we are not yet in a position to describe. In any case, functional importance to the child plays a critical role in determining which concepts the child learns first. This role is in addition to the role played by greater ease of learning concepts that have (single) prototype constituent structure.

Fourth, concepts that are more complex in the sense of taking several other concepts as constituents tend to be acquired later. Gentner (1975) demonstrated that simpler verbs, such as "give" or "take," are understood at an earlier age than more complex verbs, such as "buy," "sell," or "trade," which include all the meaning components of "give" and "take" and more besides.

Fifth, Anglin concludes that a child's knowledge of concepts is often "instance-oriented . . . based on the recall of specific encounters with particular instances." This conclusion agrees with the position Brooks takes on the primacy of instance memory in concept learning.

PHRASES

Syntax and Parsing

In grammar (syntax) the next higher unit beyond the word is the phrase. A phrase is a group of words that forms a constituent of a sentence, and the phrase structure of a sentence is an analysis of the sentence into phrases. The human mind must perform some sort of phrase structure analysis in order to understand a sentence. Consider the now classic sentence "They are eating apples." This sentence has an ambiguous phrase structure. It can be interpreted as (They) (are eating) (apples) or as (They) (are) (eating apples), as opposed to "cooking apples" or the like. The larger context of the sentence would normally resolve this kind of ambiguity, but examples like this point up the need for phrase structure analysis in any sentence of reasonable length. Phrase structure analysis is often called *parsing* a sentence. Speakers of the same language generally agree on how to parse most sentences. For example, how would you parse "The old man down the street gave the red-headed boy a piece of candy for his birthday"? Linguists often do highly elaborate analyses of sentences, breaking them down into phrase constituents that include other phrases as subconstituents. You may do such an embedded-phrase analysis if you wish (and if you've had some practice diagraming sentences), but all I am asking you to do is to partition the sentence into nonoverlapping groups. After you have decided how you would do this, check your phrase structure analysis with the one in the footnote.* Presumably your analysis closely agreed with either the simple nonoverlapping parse (possibly you broke the subject phrase into two groups—"the old man" and "down the street"), or the more elaborate analysis. Laymen, and even linguists, disagree about the more elaborate embedded analyses. This renders suspect the psychological validity of some aspects of these more elaborate analyses. However, almost everyone agrees about the simpler, nonembedded phrase analysis, and these highly reliable linguistic data, combined with the fact that we must perform a phrase analysis in order to understand a sentence, argue strongly for the psychological reality of phrases as units in semantic memory.

Reference and Instantiation

Just as there is a difference between words and concepts, there is a difference between phrases defined as strings of words and the conceptual units these phrases activate in semantic memory. In different contexts, the same phrase will have different referents and will activate different concept nodes. Take the phrase "the old man down the street," for example. This entire phrase will, in normal use, be instantiated by a *single* concept node in semantic memory despite its fairly elaborate internal phrase structure: (the [old man]) (down [the street]). Presumably the processing required to activate the proper concept node is more difficult for such a complex *definite description* than for a simple unique name for the concept, such as "Ivan Stephanopolis." Nevertheless, the ultimate representation of both may be the same concept

---

*(The old man down the street) (gave) (the red-headed boy) (a piece of candy) (for his birthday). A more elaborate analysis would be ([The (old man)] [down (the street)]) (gave) (the [red-headed boy]) ([a piece] [of candy]) (for [his birthday]).

node. Hence the encoding of nominal phrases in semantic memory may be only temporarily more complex (during the recognition process) than the encoding of single words or proper names. Even a prepositional phrase like "for his birthday" can be thought of as a single concept, albeit one that has simpler concept constituents ("for" and "his birthday"), and which is therefore a higher-level concept than the concept "birthday."

Although most phrases are composed of adjacent words in a sentence, we have some capacity to parse sentences with *discontinuous constituents.* An example would be "He called the girl up," which should be parsed into phrases the same way as (he) (called up) (the girl). Thus phrase structure analysis is not totally dominated by adjacency in the word order, though this is a very important factor.

PROPOSITIONS

Propositions as Units of Semantic Memory

The next higher linguistic level beyond the phrase is the *clause.* After that comes the *sentence.* Clauses and sentences in English must have a subject and a predicate. The predicate always includes a verb and often includes various other constituents, such as a direct object, an indirect object, a time, a location, and so on. A simple sentence has a single main clause. A complex sentence has one or more main clauses and one or more dependent clauses. A compound sentence has two or more main clauses. The constituent structure of a clause or sentence probably includes more than just the unordered set of phrases that compose it, but linguists disagree on what additional constituent structure is needed. One principle that everyone agrees on— philosophers, linguists, psychologists, and artificial intelligence researchers — is that the *proposition* is an important unit of semantic memory. A proposition is the semantic memory analogue of a clause, just as a concept is the semantic memory analogue of a word or phrase. A proposition must have a relational term and one or more arguments. The relational term is often a verb, but it may be a preposition or even an adjective. Arguments are nouns or noun phrases that function as subjects or objects of the relation. The sentence "Jim bought a car that cost $4,000" contains two propositions, "Jim bought a car," and "the car cost $4,000." Obviously, exactly the same meaning is conveyed whether one uses the complex sentence with two clauses or the appropriate compound sentence or two simple sentences. Furthermore, the same meaning is conveyed by using a prepositional phrase in conjunction with one clause, as in "Jim bought a car for $4,000," or by using a simple adjective, as in "Jim bought a $4,000 car." (One could argue that there are subtle differences especially in the last case, but let's not—many listeners would encode all these sentences in precisely the same way.)

It would make sense if human semantic memory encoded all these different sentences, and any other meaningfully equivalent sets of sentences, by means of the same set of nodes in semantic memory. This is believed to be the case. Semantic memory researchers believe that we analyze sentences into the same constituent propositions whether these propositions are conveyed by separate sentences, spearate clauses, prepositional phrases, or adjective modifiers of nouns. There are several lines of support for this position, which I shall call the *propositional unit hypothesis.*

First, there is the fact that we can recognize a paraphrase as being meaningfully equivalent to a previously presented sentence, even though they differ in wording and syntax. More impressive support derives from the finding that the time subjects take to verify a paraphrase as true, assuming the truth of the originally learned sentence, is often no greater than the time they take to verify a test sentence that is identical to the original sentence. This equivalence of verification times has been tested primarily in the domain of active-passive transformations. An example of this kind of transformation would occur when "the train hit the bus" becomes "the bus was hit by the train." If the subject is tested immediately after learning the sentence, he will verify identicals faster than paraphrases. This is presumably because we have some memory for wording that operates below the level of semantic memory. For if some time elapses between the learning and the test, and during this time the subject processes other sentences, the difference in verification time disappears. This indicates that long-term semantic memory is for propositions, and that it is independent of surface form (Garrod and Trabasso 1973; Anderson 1974).

Second, sometimes longer-term memory for isolated sentences or integrated text retrieves only the meaning of these sentences, but not the exact words or syntax. In the first study to explore this phenomenon, Sachs (1967) presented subjects with a prose passage to read. Then she immediately asked them to judge whether a test sentence was structurally identical—that is, identical in every respect including meaning, syntax, and words—to a particular sentence in the passage. In some cases the test sentences were identical. In other cases they were identical in meaning but different in syntax or wording. For example, they might exhibit conversion from active to passive voice, or changes in words or word order that did not alter the meaning. Still other test sentences were altered semantically so as to change the meaning. For example, they might interchange subject and object, or contain a word that had occurred elsewhere in the passage. The semantic changes were constructed so as to prevent subjects from identifying changes caused by the introduction of words that had not occurred in passage. There were three retention intervals (the time between the test sentence and the relevant prior sentence). The retention interval was 0 when the relevant prior sentence occurred at the end of the passage. The other two retention intervals were 27 seconds and 46 seconds—representing these two respective amounts of intervening material. When the test sentence was presented immediately after the relevant prior sentence, recognition of both semantic and structural changes was extremely good. At the longer retention intervals recognition of changes in meaning was still extremely high, but recognition of purely structural changes dropped to nearly chance levels.

Sachs's study indicates that structural information concerning the form of a sentence is often stored for a very short time—just long enough for comprehension. What is stored for a long time is meaning—that is, concepts and propositions, independent of original form. Subsequent studies have indicated that there are conditions under which people can remember the words and syntax of a sentence for longer than a few seconds. Even under these conditions the degree of initial learning appears to be greater for meaning. Furthermore, the rate of forgetting is faster for syntax and words (60% faster in one study). Forgetting is probably faster because memory for syntax and words is more susceptible to interference in this case. Furthermore, Begg found that memory for wording was statistically independent of memory for meaning. This indicates that memory for propositions is mediated by different traces from those that encode the specific word strings used to convey meaning (Begg 1971; Begg and Wickelgren 1974; James and Abrahamson 1977).

Third, in a study on memory for sentences composed of two propositons, Anderson and Bower (1973) showed that subjects can recall one proposition better when they are provided with a cue word from that same proposition than when they are provided with a cue word from the other proposition. Kintsch and Glass (1974) showed that subjects exhibit a much greater tendency towards all-or-none recall of sentences containing a single proposition than of sentences containing three propositions. This held true even though both types of sentences contained the same number of content words. These findings indicate that propositions are important units in semantic memory. They indicate that our intuition regarding the analysis of sentences into component propositions is correct. And they indicate that concepts within a propositional unit are more strongly associated to each other than they are to concepts in other propositional units.

Fourth, it apparently makes no difference for long-term semantic memory whether propositions are presented together in the same sentence or in separate sentences. In either case the same traces are established in semantic memory. Semantic memory for compound or complex sentences appears to involve the formation of separate propositional node structures for each of the component propositions. Apparently these structures intersect at the concept or phrase nodes that the two propositions have in common (Bransford and Franks 1971; Wang 1977). See figure 10.5 for an example. Similarly information presented in two separate sentences that involve common co•

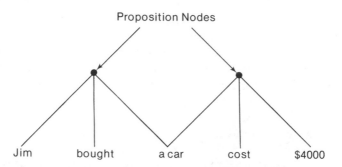

Proposition Nodes

Jim   bought   a car   cost $4000

Fig. 10.5 Diagram of a tiny network in semantic memory consisting of two proposition
nodes, each with three concept node constituents—one of which is common to both
propositions. Many semantic memory researchers allege that the same propositional
node structures intersecting at a common constituent are formed regardless of the
exact syntax and words used to convey the same ideas. These may vary considerably,
e.g., "Jim bought a $4,000 car" OR "Jim bought a car. It cost $4,000" OR "Jim
purchased an automobile for four big ones" (assuming that the listener instantiates
"four big ones" with the same concept as "$4,000").

cepts often creates a semantic memory structure that is indistinguishable
from the structure created by the same information presented in a single
compound or complex sentence. This is called the *semantic integration* phenomenon. A very important experiment by Bransford and Franks (1971)
showed that subjects frequently cannot remember whether several closely
related pieces of information in a test sentence had previously been presented
in the same sentence or in separate sentences. Bransford and Franks constructed sentences composed of anywhere from one to four related component propositions—for example, "The ants in the kitchen ate the sweet jelly
that was on the table." This complex sentence has four component propositions: "the ants were in the kitchen," "the jelly was on the table," "the jelly
was sweet," "the ants ate the jelly." Subjects listened to sentences that contained one, two, or three related component propositions. They were told that
their task was to listen to the sentences in order to answer questions about
them later. This gave them a set to recall the meaning and not the exact form
of the sentences. Under this set the results were analogous to those in the
Sachs experiment. Subjects remembered the component propositions but did
not remember the exact sentences they had heard. Thus when subjects were
asked to state whether a test sentence was exactly identical to one they had
heard, many falsely recognized sentences that included all four related propositions, even though they had never heard a sentence that included all four
propositions during the acquisition period. Subjects certainly can, and under
some conditions do, learn and remember something about the way the propositions were constructed into sentences. But this finding is much less important than the finding that this kind of memory is absent under other

conditions (Bransford, Barclay, and Franks 1972; Flagg 1976; Flagg and Reynolds 1977). Under these latter conditions, subjects apparently establish the same network structure of propositional components intersecting at common phrase and concept units, regardless of how the component propositions were combined into sentences.

Fifth, Kintsch and Keenan found that when the number of words in a paragraph of text is held constant, the study time required to learn the meaning of a text (not its exact wording) increases with the number of propositions in the text. Thus it is not primarily the number of words in a text that makes it more or less difficult to comprehend and acquire traces for in semantic memory. Rather, it is the number of propositions that must be learned (Kintsch and Keenan 1973; Kintsch 1974, pp. 123–36).

Sixth, the structure of propositional coding in semantic memory is such that there is often a high false recognition of sentences that are not complete paraphrases of an originally learned sentence, but only inferences from some previously learned sentence. This goes beyond the very important fact that human beings can draw true inferences from learned propositions. It means that sometimes we do not discriminate between sentences that have an asymmetrical implication relation—that is, a relation in which sentence A implies sentence B, but sentence B does not imply sentence A. Our failure to discriminate sentences of this kind is more surprising than our identical encoding of sentences that are true paraphrases, so that the implication is mutual—that is, A implies B and B implies A. For example, Bransford, Barclay, and Franks (1972) had subjects learn the sentence "Three turtles rested on a floating log and a fish swam beneath them." This produced a very high false recognition of the sentence "Three turtles rested on a floating log and a fish swam beneath it." This test sentence is a correct inference from the presented sentence, but it is not a paraphrase—nor, of course, is it exactly the same in wording. Equivalent coding of asymmetrical, inferentially related sentences is by no means the general rule. There is no doubt that in all known cases such sentences could be encoded differently in semantic memory so as to permit discrimination on a recognition test or whatever. However, they do illustrate both the independence of wording that characterizes semantic memory and the susceptibility of semantic memory to errors in the precise encoding of meaning.

Constituent Structure of Propositions

Perhaps the most important and certainly the most frustrating unsolved problem in the field of semantic memory concerns the constituent structure of a proposition. There are two extant theories, neither of which is completely satisfactory. The first is the *predicate theory,* which is used by many logicians, linguistic philosophers, traditional linguists, Chomsky (1957, 1965) and ma post-Chomskian linguists, and some semantic memory researchers, suc'

Anderson and Bower (1973). The second is the *case theory*. Current interest in this theory derives largely from a famous paper by the linguist Fillmore (1968), which is intriguingly titled *The Case for Case*, but case theory has since been adopted by other linguists and researchers in artificial intelligence and semantic memory. These include Norman and Rumelhart (1975), Kintsch (1974), and Schank (1975).

According to the predicate theory, a proposition has two immediate constituents—the subject and the predicate. The predicate may consist of a verb alone or a verb plus various combinations of direct object, indirect object, instrument, and in some systems time and location. Since the predicate may contain a large number of constituents, it may have an elaborate structure itself. A relatively simple example is illustrated in figure 10.6(a).

Case theory is different in several respects. For one thing, the verb (relational term) is considered to be the central concept constituent. The verb takes a number of cases (arguments). These include its *agent* (often, but not always, the subject of the sentence); its *object* (often the direct object); its *recipient* (often the indirect object); and its *instrument*. An example of case structure is illustrated in figure 10.6(b). The concepts represented by words in diagrams like figure 10.6 should be interpreted as particular instantiations (highly specific concepts) of these words in a given context. However, in a case system like the one used by Norman and Rumelhart the verb concept node must be absolutely unique for each new proposition. The case nodes for a proposition may be constituents of numerous other propositions, but the verb node cannot be, because it is both the verb node and the proposition node for that proposition. So new verb *token nodes* must be created for each new proposition to serve as the focal point for all the constituents of that proposition. The various token nodes for the same verb are also presumed to be associated to one generic *type node* for that verb.

Case theory agrees with our intuition that the verb is more closely related to each of its cases than any of these cases is to another. There is some experimental evidence that supports this (Kempen 1974; Levelt and Kempen 1975, pp. 209–12). Predicate theory places the verb much closer to the object and other such predicate constituents than to the subject. This closer association of verb and object is neither intuitively clear nor experimentally valid (Anderson and Bower 1973; Dosher 1976; Wickelgren 1976c). However, neither predicate nor case theory has had consistent success in predicting error patterns and latencies in memory for constituents of a single proposition.

An alternative theory is needed, and the following criteria seem reasonable. First, we should express all the verb-case relations as they are expressed in case theory. Second, we should have a node uniquely for the proposition, as in predicate theory, rather than a node that serves two functions at very different levels—concept and proposition. Third, we should have nodes for he various verb-case combinations, so that if the same combination occurs another proposition, we do not have to create another duplicate node link

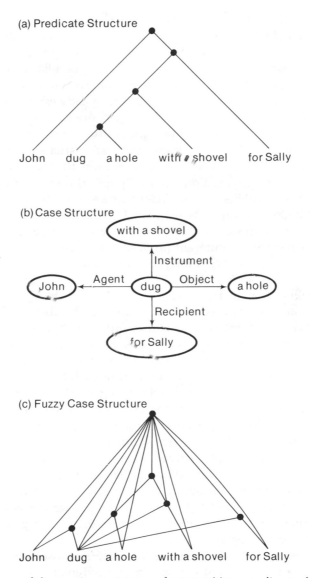

(a) Predicate Structure

John   dug   a hole   with a shovel   for Sally

(b) Case Structure

with a shovel

Instrument

John ← Agent   dug   Object → a hole

Recipient

for Sally

(c) Fuzzy Case Structure

John   dug   a hole   with a shovel   for Sally

Fig. 10.6   Diagram of the constituent structure of a proposition according to three theories. In the *predicate theory* the two immediate constituents of a proposition are the subject and the predicate (composed of the verb and often one or more objects or modifiers). In the *case theory* the proposition is represented by a verb token node, which has various types of relational links to its cases (agent, object, instrument, recipient, and so on). *Fuzzy-case theory* is an attempt to combine the best features of both theories. It specifies a unique proposition node (which is not doing double duty as a verb token node). It eliminates labeled links (for which there is no empirical support). It creates nodes for the various verb-case combinations (which could be used again to encode the same verb-case combinations in other sentences). And it gives proposi the type of fuzzy constituent structure that is characteristic of concepts.

network structure de novo to represent the same subset of concepts all over again. For example, "dig a hole with a shovel" is a familiar compound concept, and it would be absurd for semantic memory to have to create an entirely new node link structure to represent this familiar compound every time it appears with a different agent, or whatever, in a new proposition. Semantic memory ought to be able to build on already established encodings of familiar phrases. There is experimental evidence to support the ability to use established nodes in encoding new propositions. Sentences with familiar verb-case combinations (e.g., "pupil studies," "studies book," "pitcher throws," "throws ball") are much easier to learn than sentences with less familiar verb-case combinations (e.g., "pupil throws," "throws book," "pitcher studies," "studies ball").* Indeed, there ought to be nodes for even larger combinations of concepts than single verb-case constituents, such as "dig a hole with a shovel" (which has two verb-case constituents), when these occur repeatedly in different propositions. Fourth, it would be elegant if propositions had a fuzzy, prototype constituent structure like concepts.

Considerations such as these are incorporated into *fuzzy-case theory* (fig. 10.6[c]). Imagine that in learning, associations are strengthened to nodes representing all verb-case combinations in a proposition and, to a lesser extent, to nodes representing even higher-order combinations of such verb-case pairs. In addition to these associations, there may be associations direct from constituent concepts to the proposition node and from any verb-case node to the proposition node. The strength of each association will depend on two variables. The first of these is the degree of attention the learner pays to each constituent concept, including the verb-case (relational or context-sensitive) concepts. The second is the amount of prior learning experience the learner has had with each verb-case (or other higher-order, relational) concept. As with fuzzy concepts, activation of a proposition would not require a strict conjunction of all the constituents. We know this is true from studies that cue recall of entire propositions from single concept constituents. However, the longer the retention interval and the greater the interference, the more constituents may be required to activate the correct proposition node and recall the remaining constituents.

Prior learning will affect the relative strength of association to the proposition from any constituent concept in two different ways. First, familiar phrases (e.g., "dug a hole with a shovel") will already have a strong set of associations linking the component concepts together via higher-order component nodes. The effect of this will be to facilitate learning, because part of the necessary learning has already been done. Second, the nodes for familiar compounds will usually be associated to other proposition nodes; these latter

---

*The experiment most directly suggested by these examples has not, to my knowledge, ~n performed, but a closely similar experiment was performed by Engelkamp, Meridian, and ~nan (1972). I read about this experiment in Levelt and Kempen (1975, p. 203).

nodes represent the propositions in which they themselves have frequently occurred in the past. Anderson has repeatedly demonstrated that incorporating the same concepts into several propositions produces interference in semantic memory, just as it does in any other modality of human associative memory (Anderson, 1974, 1975, 1976 [pp. 252–319]; Lewis and Anderson, 1976). Thus the potency of any particular constituent as a retrieval cue for a given proposition will depend not only on how strongly it is associated (directly and indirectly through higher-order compound nodes) to the given propositional node, but also on how strongly it is associated to other proposition nodes. This may explain why the subject is typically the best cue for recall of a sentence, while the object constituent is less effective and the verb is generally the worst of all (Blumenthal 1967; Blumenthal and Boakes 1967; Horowitz and Prytulak 1969; Thios 1975). Considering the centrality of the verb in case constituent structure, this was certainly a puzzling result—one that was more consistent with predicate constituent structure. However, it would appear that anything can be a subject; that there are more restrictions on what can be an object; and that there are far fewer verbs than either subjects or objects. This means that verbs and objects tend to occur in many more propositions than subjects, and so the subject constituent has less interference in its association to a particular proposition than the verb and object constituents. No theory of the constituent structure of propositions can in any way be considered established at present, but the fuzzy-case theory seems to be the most plausible (partly because it is so flexible that it is hard to refute).

SCHEMATA AND NETWORKS

Semantic memory is not a forest of separate propositional trees. It is more like a spiderweb or *network* of richly interconnected concepts and propositions. When the same concept (or compound concept) is involved as a constituent in two or more propositions, it creates an associative link connecting the two propositions at (or near) their bases. The capacity to integrate (recall at the same time) separately stored propositions involving a common concept, the greater ease of learning new propositions that results from their having familiar phrasal constituents, and associative interference phenomena in semantic memory are all evidence for this interconnection of propositions into a *network* by means of their common concepts.* Not only are propositions interconnected at their bases by intersection at common concept nodes, they are also interconnected at their tops by the embedding of propositions as constituents of higher-order propositions. Consider the following examples: "Jill knows that Frank is seeing another woman." "After Mary left, everyone

*See Kintsch et al. (1975) and Manelis and Yekovich (1976) for additional evidenc

jumped for joy." "Because the earth rotates on its axis, we experience an alternation of day and night."

Currently, one of the most important, but variously defined, concepts in semantic memory is the *schema* (or *frame* or *script*) (Selz 1922; Bartlett 1932; Minsky 1975; Palmer 1975; and papers by Bobrow and Norman, Kuipers, Winograd, Rumelhart, Schank, and Abelson in Bobrow and Collins 1975). A schema can be thought of as an attentional set that includes every node more or less directly associated to what is currently consciously on your mind. Formally, we might partition the nodes of semantic memory into three sub-sets: *focus, halo,* and *quiet.* The *focus* is what you are (or very recently have been) thinking about. Nodes in the focus are fully activated. The *halo* is nodes more or less directly associated to the focus. Nodes in the associative halo are primed (partially activated). The rest of the nodes in semantic memory are *quiet* (not activated at all). Not every subset of nodes can be a focus. A possible focus is any closed subset of nodes that is dominated by fewer than five top nodes (five top nodes are the span of apprehension). A closed subset is any set of nodes that includes all of its own constituents (down to the basic atomic concepts). A schema is a focus plus its associative halo. This is just one of many semiprecise definitions of a schema. Formal definitions aside, the schema concept is best explored by example. The simplest schema is a small set of concepts associated to a single concept. The most frequently cited examples are verb schemata, such as the "give" schema, which primes the expectation of a "giver," a "receiver," and a "gift." In context it may also prime more specific givers, receivers, and gifts. Such a set of primed nodes, all associated to the generic and specific "give" concepts, constitutes the "give" verb concept schema. There are also noun concept schemata. Paradox-ically these often appear to be much broader than verb schemata. Commonly cited examples include the "restaurant" schema (choosing one, getting there, reservations, ordering, and so on) and the "story" schema (setting, characters, goals, plot, resolution). The "restaurant" schema can contain an enormous number of concept and proposition nodes embodying a great deal of general and specific knowledge about restaurants. In principle verb schema could be equally broad. But because the instantiations of verbs are so diverse (context-dependent and not closely interrelated), interference (possibly inhibition) seems to confine the spread of activation of verb schemata to a relatively small set of nodes. At least this is what most semantic memory theorists assume, though the reason for the difference in size is not at all established.

Schemata are thought to play an important role in the comprehension of speech and text and in the acquisition and retrieval of information. When words are recognized, they prime the schemata associated to them, which amounts to establishing an attentional set for the concepts and propositions included in these schemata. Each of us probably possesses an enormous number of schemata—perhaps on the order of millions or hundreds of mil-ns. One thing is certain—schemata are *overlapping.* For example, the "restaurant" schema includes the "eating" schema, and therefore the "restaurant" schema overlaps the "eating at home" schema because they both contain the "eating" schema. It won't do to think of schemata as a moderate number of large, nonoverlapping, general frames or contexts in which specific knowledge is stored. Schemata include every possible pattern of attentional expectations and inferences from presented information. These patterns range from the highly specific to the very general, and the schemata expand, contract, and merge continually into different schemata, which in turn overlap their predecessors to varying degrees (Anderson 1976, pp. 444–46). This description is perhaps more aesthetic than scientific, but nothing less does justice to the capacity of the human mind.*

SUMMARY

1 The most basic unit of coding in semantic memory is the concept. A single concept node can generally be activated by many different words and phrases, and each word or phrase node is generally associated to many different concepts.

2 Concepts have both constituent and propositional meaning. (This distinction roughly, but not exactly, corresponds to the philosophical distinction between extensional and intensional meaning). The constituent meaning of a concept is given by the sets of constituent attributes that can activate the concept node from below. The propositional meaning of a concept is given by the higher-order propositions in which the concept is embedded and which can activate the concept node from above. Concept learning is never complete, since we can add to both constituent and propositional meaning at any time. The definition of a concept is just one (or more) propositions in which the concept is embedded that happen to differentiate it from all other concepts in semantic memory. The definition of a concept is a very tiny (and often dispensable) part of its meaning.

3 Most human concepts are not strictly logical functions of their constituents. Rather, they exhibit fuzzy constituent structure such that any sufficiently potent set of characteristic features will activate a concept node. Any given event will have various degrees of membership in various concepts—not just two degrees (member or nonmember).

4 Since concept nodes can be activated from above by association to other concepts and propositions, and from below by words and nonverbal referential stimuli, it is clear that the events that activate a concept have no common attributes. Even the set of nonverbal referential stimuli that activate concepts may actually be a family resemblance. In a family resemblance, stimuli in the set share many attributes with other stimuli, but no set of attributes is common to all members in the set.

---

*Word for word, the most sophisticated and yet clear paper I have ever read on semantic memory (as of 24 July 1977) is by William Woods (1975). It is primarily critical and well beyond the scope of this text, but if you want to pursue the study of semantic memory in depth, read it!

5 Natural human concepts appear to have a prototype constituent structure such that the ideal examples of the concept are those that contain attributes that possess the maximum possible strength of association to the concept node. Natural concepts appear to have fuzzy boundaries, but many (the basic concepts) have ideal centerpoints.

6 The two basic methods of concept learning are *abstraction* from examples and nonexamples and *propositional learning* from incorporating the concept into higher-level propositions. Inferential concept learning is a problem-solving task that consists of abstraction, propositional learning, and reasoning in various proportions.

7 Abstraction of prototypes is the natural result of learning associations to the concept node from the attribute nodes in the examples. The attributes that occur most frequently acquire the greatest strength of association, but three other important factors determine the constituent structure of concepts. These are generalization to similar attributes, the importance of context-sensitive relational attributes, and the criteriality (cue validity) of an attribute. The latter is determined by how strongly any attribute node is associated to other concepts.

8 The basic concepts children learn first are neither those with the greatest nor those with the least degree of referential generality. They tend strongly to be the most general concepts, whose referential stimuli can be characterized by a *single* prototype (such as "apple") rather than by many prototypes (such as "fruit").

9 Children both overgeneralize and undergeneralize concepts. Children have learned only a little bit of the adult meaning for most concepts, and so they use nearly every concept somewhat differently than an adult would do. Their use of a concept is much more heavily dominated by instance memory for the few "close encounters" they have had so far with that concept.

10 We analyze sentences into phrases. Phrases refer to simple concepts, compound concepts, or entire propositions.

11 A proposition contains a relational concept (such as a verb) and one or more arguments (nouns or noun phrases that serve as cases of the relation). There is overwhelming evidence to support the hypothesis that propositions are important units of knowledge in semantic memory. The constituents of propositions are concepts, not words. Meaningfully equivalent wordings (paraphrases) are encoded by the same proposition in semantic memory.

12 Propositions that involve common concepts intersect at their common concept nodes, and this provides semantic integration of related knowledge at the base of semantic memory. The packaging of propositions into sentences need not affect the resulting encoding in semantic memory, provided the same concepts are activated in both cases. Related knowledge is also integrated at higher levels by embedding propositions into higher-order propositions (e.g., "Sam's felling the tree caused it to serve as a bridge over the river").

13 At present the most plausible theory for propositional constituent structure is the fuzzy-case theory. In the fuzzy-case theory the immediate constituents of a proposition are relation-case compounds, and possibly also the simpler nonre-

lational concepts in the proposition. Each constituent has a variable strength of association to the proposition node.

14 At any given time the nodes in the mind can be crudely subdivided into three sets: activated, primed, and quiet. In this crude trichotomy a schema is equivalent to an attentional set and consists of a focus with its associative halo. Schemata in semantic memory overlap and vary enormously in breadth, depending on how much knowledge is associated to a given focus.

CHAPTER 11
SEMANTIC MEMORY PROCESSES: RETRIEVAL, LEARNING, AND UNDERSTANDING

OBJECTIVES

1 To describe how recognition and recall use information stored in semantic memory.

2 To discuss the role semantic parsing and syntactic parsing plans play in grouping words into phrases.

3 To discuss three parallel processing issues in retrieval from semantic memory. The first is multiple access (simultaneous activation of several separate concept nodes). The second is divergence (simultaneous activation of several associations to a single node). The third is chain parallel processing (simultaneous activation of several associations in a chain).

4 To discuss whether the links between nodes in semantic memory differ qualitatively to represent different logical relations between concepts.

5 To discuss the role contextual schemata play in recognizing the correct concept nodes to activate in response to the words of an input sentence.

6 To discuss the role inferences and presuppositions play in question answering.

7 To point out that recognizing the familiar concepts and propositions in a sentence is an important part of learning the new associations necessary to encode the sentence. The part of a sentence that is presumed to be already familiar to the learner is the *given* part. The rest is the *new* part. I shall discuss how different syntactic devices signal this partitioning of sentences into *given* and *new* parts. *Given* (in long-term memory) and *new* (not in long-term memory) will be distinguished from *topic* (in short-term memory) and *comment* (not in short-term memory). Syntactic devices that distinguish the topic and the comment of a sentence will also be discussed.

8 To discuss the semantic integration of sentences that are concerned with the same concepts. The discussion will consider the reference problem (how we determine that the same concept should be associated to words or phrases in separate sentences). It will also consider how learning sentences that contain common concepts affects comprehension and memory.

9 To discuss the important role schemata play in the comprehension of text.

10 To discuss the extent to which inferences from presented information are drawn at learning or retrieval. To discuss why it is unlikely that sentences are decomposed into semantic atoms in learning and stored in a unique (canonical) form for all semantically equivalent texts.

11 To discuss the functions of metaphor in language. Metaphor provides a compact expression of ideas that would be difficult or impossible to express in any other way.

12 To discuss one reason why asking questions is an aid to semantic learning.

Like every other modality of the mind, semantic memory has both a structural coding aspect and a dynamic cognitive-processes aspect. The structural coding analysis of semantic memory was presented in the last chapter. The discussion began with basic concepts, which are the atoms of semantic memory, and proceeded through compound concepts, propositions, and schemata. This chapter and the next one consider the cognitive processes that operate on semantic memory to *recognize* (comprehend) familiar concepts and propositions in sentences, to *recall* associated material, to *learn* new material, to *infer* new propositions from stored propositions, to *generate* sentences for speech or writing, to *solve problems,* and to *create* new ideas.

This chapter deals with understanding. In previous chapters you were expected to read about reading, attend to attention, learn about learning, remember memory, and conceptualize concepts. In the next chapter you are to think about thinking. Here you are to understand understanding, a difficult task—but not paradoxically so. You might begin by asking yourself what you mean when you say you understand something. But don't spend too much time trying to define understanding. Not many people can define it adequately, for it is only in the last decade or two that we have begun to understand understanding at all well.

Look at the word itself. You might conclude that understanding means to stand under something. Under what? Under knowledge, perhaps. How do we represent knowledge? By a network of concepts linked together in various combinations to form propositions. So when we understand a sentence or a set of sentences, it means that we are able to represent that material by a knowledge structure of the type discussed in the last chapter (and stand under it—ho, ho). Understanding is not an all-or-none process—there are many degrees of understanding. These degrees depend upon how extensive the network of relations is between concepts used to represent the material, and upon how accurate this network is as a model of the real world. One can also judge adequacy of understanding from a communicative standpoint by the extent to which the reader (or listener) achieves the same network representation of the concepts and principles (propositions) in some topic area as the writer (or speaker).

Let's see how to apply this explanation of understanding to various situations. When we don't understand someone who is speaking an unfamiliar language, our failure to understand is at the word level. We do not have the necessary word nodes to represent (encode) each of the words in the utterance. The failure to understand might even occur at lower segmental and feature levels, if the language includes speech sounds not found in the languages with which we are familiar. On a smaller scale, you experience a failure to understand at the word level whenever you encounter an unfamiliar word in English. For readers of this text, such encounters with unfamiliar words are rare. For you, the failure to understand generally begins at the concept level. Words represent many different concepts. If you activate the wrong concept node (wrong meaning) for a word in a particular context, you have a misunderstanding.

So far I have discussed understanding as if it were completely equivalent to recognition—the activation of the correct, already existing nodes in semantic memory. Recognizing *old* concepts and propositions is an important part of understanding, but what about understanding *new* concepts and propositions? That, after all, is the primary purpose of communication. True, we must recognize the familiar parts of a communication, but we must also *learn* new concepts and propositions to encode the new, unfamiliar parts. Understanding includes both recognition and learning. To the extent that we both activate the appropriate existing nodes in our semantic memory (recognition) and build onto these nodes the required new associated node structure (learning), we have understood the communication.

Communication rarely states everything in nauseating detail. Much is left understood, to be filled in by inference on the part of the listener or reader. If I say, "I had steak for dinner last night," you can infer that I ate the steak, used a knife and fork, cooked the steak first, placed it on a plate on a table, sat in a chair while I ate it, and so on. It is unclear just how many such inferences occur in the process of understanding text, but some inference is essential to understanding. Some or all of this inferencing may be *recall* of information associated in our semantic memories to the presented information. Some of the inferencing in understanding may require more complex inference plans. In this chapter I shall discuss the recall process as it is involved in question answering, and I shall discuss inferencing in comprehension very briefly. Inference will be treated at length in the next chapter, which is concerned with thinking in general. In this chapter I shall concentrate on the memory retrieval and learning processes that are involved in understanding text and answering questions. But keep in mind that understanding involves all three processes: retrieval, learning, and inference.

RETRIEVAL: RECOGNITION AND RECALL

The memory retrieval processes involved in understanding a statement are not ordinarily accompanied by any measurable behavior. This makes them difficult to study. However, there is one exception—namely, answering questions. Much of our knowledge of the memory retrieval processes involved in understanding has been derived from studies of question answering. Presumably the processes that are involved in understanding questions are the same processes that are involved in understanding statements. At present, at least, there is no reason to think otherwise. Our discussion of retrieval processes in semantic memory begins with an analysis of question answering.

Question Answering

There are two types of questions: *yes-no questions* ("Does Jane play bridge?") and *wh-questions* ("*Wh*o plays bridge?" "*Wh*at did Steve do last night?" "*Wh*ere is my bat?"). Elementary questions like these can be answered with a single word or short phrase. Thus they create few problems with respect to the generation of grammatical speech. The wide use of objective testing illustrates the extraordinary degree to which one can test virtually any aspect of the contents of semantic memory by means of elementary yes-no and *wh*-questions.

Although there are some differences, yes-no questions correspond roughly to tests of recognition memory, while *wh*-questions are tests of recall. To answer a yes-no question, one determines whether all of the propositions in the input sentence match propositions stored in one's semantic memory. If they do, one says "yes" to the question. If one or more of the propositions in the input sentence is contradicted by a proposition stored in semantic memory, one says "no." If any of the input propositions can neither be found in semantic memory nor contradicted, one might guess either "yes" or "no" or answer "don't know" (if such a response is permitted).

A *wh*-question asks whether the components of the input sentence already exist in semantic memory together with an additional component that constitutes the answer to the question. To answer the question "When did Lincoln write the Gettysburg address?" one first attempts to find all the components of the input question in semantic memory. That is, one attempts to find an existing node structure that contains the fact "Lincoln wrote the Gettysburg Address." This is the recognition part of the recall process. Then one attempts to fill in the blank represented by the question word—*when*—by retrieving one or more time concepts, phrases, or propositions associated with the recognized node structure.

If I ask you whether 714–8295 is your home telephone number, your yes-no answer to this recognition memory question will reflect the degree of match between the input proposition and a single relevant stored proposition. If I ask you to recall your telephone number, the same stored proposition will

333

be activated by the input *wh*-question, and the strength of association to the phone number constituent will determine whether your recall is successful or not. However, Norman (1973) points out that there is often more involved in answering questions than this simple activation of a single most relevant stored proposition. First, the answer to some questions may require you to combine the information in two or more stored propositions. For instance, suppose you are asked whether there are people living in Canton, China. You can answer "yes" to such a question, even though you probably never stored this proposition, because you know two related propositions: (1) that Canton is a city and (2) that people live in cities. This kind of inference process will be discussed in the next chapter.

Second, questions about one proposition often contain presuppositions (assumptions) about other propositions, which we also evaluate, often without knowing it. We recognize that a presupposition exists when we are asked an unusual question for which the presupposition is false. Norman (1973) supplies a nice example: "What is the famous author Charles Dickens's telephone number?" People do not just say, "I don't know," as they might if you asked them the telephone number of a friend whose number they had never learned. They regard the question as absurd because it violates at least two presuppositions: (1) that the person in question has a telephone number and (2) that there is some possibility that they themselves would know it. Such presuppositions also underlie reasonable questions about people's phone numbers. It's just that since the presuppositions are correct, we are not consciously aware of them.

Third, our answers to questions often depend on our stored knowledge concerning the person asking the question and the context in which the question is asked. Norman cites this question: "Where is the Empire State Building?" If you are in Europe talking to a foreigner, you might well answer "in New York City." If you are talking to a tourist on a New York City street, you would give more detailed directions (if you knew them). Questions specify short-term goals to be achieved by thinking (that is, by mental operations such as recognition, recall, and inference). However, our longer-term goals, instructions, and the more general context (as embodied in our currently active *schema*) are at least equally important in determining question-answering behavior.

Syntax and Parsing

Recognizing a sentence involves more than just recognizing each word in the sentence. At a minimum we must activate the correct concepts to which the words refer—and as we saw in the last chapter, the same word or phrase may be associated to hundreds of different concepts. Furthermore, to recognize a proposition, we must activate the correct compound concepts that represent various relations between the concepts that are the constituents of the proposition. To activate the nodes that represent the basic concepts cued by phrases (e.g., "the old man down the street") or the compound concepts cued by phrases (e.g., "dug a hole," "dug with a shovel," "gardener dug"), we must obviously attend to all of the words that compose the phrase as a group. We can do this in parallel, or to some extent serially, but however it is done, a phrase must be processed as a *group*. Note also that the phrase constituents of sentences are overlapping groups—that is, words may participate in more than one *phrase*. Not all of the tens of combinations of two or more words from a sentence form meaningful groups (phrases), and we wish to process for recognition only the meaningful combinations—namely, the syntactic constituents of a sentence. The meaningful groups tend to occur close together, but the constituents of a sentence are often discontinuous. For instance, when a verb has more than two cases, it cannot be directly adjacent to all of them.

How does the mind group words into phrases? Honestly, we don't know. In artificial intelligence research on natural language processing by computer and in semantic memory models, there is often a special parsing program that analyzes an input sentence into overlapping or hierarchically embedded groups of words (Woods 1970; Kaplan 1972, 1975; Winograd 1972, 1973 [p. 176–86]; Anderson and Bower 1973; Norman and Rumelhart 1975, pp. 159–78; Stevens and Rumelhart 1975; Anderson 1976, pp. 438–89). This parsing plan may operate prior to, or simultaneously with, the association of words, phrases, and clauses with basic concepts, compound concepts, and propositions in semantic memory. Some sentences have ambiguous *phrase structure* (e.g., "The stout major's wife stayed home." Is it (stout major's) wife or stout (major's wife)?). Such sentences can be parsed into groupings only on the basis of knowledge stored in semantic memory. Thus parsing cannot always precede access to semantic memory.

It is possible that much syntactic parsing is accomplished simply by the prior existence of nodes in semantic memory that represent familiar phrases. Familiar combinations of words may directly activate those nodes that were created to represent them in the past. In such cases there is no need for a separate parsing process. However, such a semantic parse of familiar phrases and sentences will not explain how we parse unfamiliar phrases and sentences. Since all phrases and sentences are initially unfamiliar, this is a very serious problem. Some more general parsing process (which may be considered to be either a part of semantic memory or separate from it) would appear to be essential for the learning of node structures that represent propositions in semantic memory. Such a parsing process may therefore also play a role in the recognition of familiar propositions.

Parsing is often considered to include more than grouping into phrases. It is sometimes also expected to yield a labeling (classification) of phrases into types. If this expectation is justified, there are sentences with *phrase-label* ambiguities that are only resolvable using knowledge about the context stored in semantic memory. Riesbeck and Schank provide a good example: "John went to the store for mother." Is the verb-case phrase "went for mother" to be labeled as a *verb-benefactor* relation (as in "John went to get bread for mother")? Or is it a *verb-object* relation (as in "John went to get mother")? Riesbeck and Schank (1977) believe that parsing should always be considered to occur in parallel with (rather than prior to) access to concepts and propositions in semantic memory. There is considerable merit in this position.

Contextual Schemata and Ambiguity

"Today was the day the builders were to begin preparing the site for the house to be built next door. Sure enough, when Kathy stepped outside, she saw a crane on the lot next to her house." Do you think the crane Kathy saw was a bird or a vehicle? Now suppose you read, "Her mother had said that if she wanted to see unusual birds she had to get up early in the morning. Sure 'nough, when Kathy stepped outside, she saw a crane on the lot next to her house." What did Kathy see this time? Sentences that are ambiguous in isolation are rarely ambiguous in context. In this case the ambiguity in the second sentence was *lexical*—that is, one word had two alternative meanings. However, ambiguities can arise at higher linguistic levels, as you have just seen.

Ambiguities on different linguistic levels may differ in important qualitative ways, but the primary difference observed so far is that with phrase ambiguities it takes a little longer to comprehend both meanings, or even to comprehend a single meaning than it does with lexical ambiguities (MacKay 1966; MacKay and Bever 1967; Foss 1970; Mistler-Lachman 1975). Contextual schemata usually permit us to activate a single meaning for sentences that would be ambiguous in isolation. Lackner and Garrett (1972) showed that even presentation of disambiguating context to the unattended ear in a dichotic listening task will strongly bias perception of otherwise ambiguous sentences presented to the attended ear. The priming effect of contextual schemata was found at all linguistic levels of ambiguity. The results of numerous studies of lexical ambiguity indicate that ambiguous words initially activate *both* meanings (concept nodes). However, the concept nodes that have been primed by prior or simultaneous (or probably even subsequent) context have a greater total degree of activation. Thus the meaning that is correct in context becomes dominant and may subsequently suppress the other meaning to some extent (MacKay 1970a; Bever, Garrett, and Hurtig 1973; Foss and Jenkins 1973; Olson and MacKay 1974; Conrad 1974; Cairns and Kamerman 1975; Warren and Warren 1976; Swinney and Hakes 1976; Swinney 1976).

Parallel Processing
and Spreading Activation

When we understand a written sentence, do we recognize each word serially, or can we process several words at a time? When we recall concepts associated to the words in the sentence, can we simultaneously retrieve several associations to a single word or concept node? Or must we search out each link serially? When we recognize a sentence, is processing at the verbal levels strictly serial? That is, do we first recognize the letters in a word; then begin the recognition process for the word; then, after we have recognized the word, begin the recognition process for the concept associated to the word in this context; and finally, after we have recognized the concepts, begin the recognition process for phrases and propositions? The answer to all three questions is that recognition and recall occur in parallel both within and across levels. They do not occur serially. Many nodes can be activated simultaneously, and activation spreads down multiple links in parallel.

The study of parallel processing raises three separate issues. The first is the issue of *multiple access.* Are we able to process several words or phrases at the same time? The second is the issue of *divergence.* Are we able to process several associations that fan out from a common node at the same time? The third is the issue of *chain parallel processing.* Are we able to process at several different encoding levels in a hierarchy at the same time? All three issues were discussed in some detail in previous chapters, where I gave examples of parallel processing. They were derived from experiments on semantic memory, so I shall treat them very briefly in this chapter. The general conclusion is that parallel processing occurs in all three ways, though there is a limit to the number of thoughts that can be activated simultaneously. This conclusion appears to have growing empirical support. Anderson has done several studies of recognition memory in which subjects were required to remember whether two, three, or four context words came from the same previously learned sentence. He interprets the results of these studies as supporting both multiple access and divergence in parallel processing. In both cases he finds evidence for limits on the capacity for parallel processing in that reaction time does increase slightly the more words (retrieval cues) must be processed, and the more (divergent) associations there are to each cue word in semantic memory. There is a slight conflict between Anderson's reaction time studies of retrieval dynamics in semantic memory and Dosher's speed-accuracy tradeoff study, which found no decrease in efficiency when subjects processed three cues from a sentence instead of two. However, both studies support limited-capacity parallel processing. The only issue is just how large a set of cues can be processed simultaneously before there is some loss in efficiency. Dosher found a sharp drop from three to five cues, so the discrepancy between the studies is not large (Anderson 1976, pp. 252–319; Dosher 1976; Thorndyke and Bower 1974).

Chain parallel processing is also supported in both studies by the fact that there is no difference in retrieval dynamics for pairs of words from the same sentence whether they have a direct syntactic-semantic relation (e.g., verb-agent, verb-object) or an indirect relation through more intervening nodes (e.g., agent-object, location-object). There may sometimes be substantial differences in the strength of association between different constituents of a proposition. But the rate of retrieval of direct associations and chains of associations appears to be at least approximately equal for short chains. As we saw in chapter 9, retrieval slows down as the level of complexity of encoding (chain length) increases. This indicates that retrieval of a chain of associations is also a limited-capacity parallel process. However, it appears that activation spreads rapidly through the links of a semantic network, initiating larger-scale and slower activation retrieval processes along each link that it passes through. The nodal delay time in the *initiation* of retrieval at each link appears to be fairly small in relation to the time it takes to retrieve the full associative strength of each link. Thus several associations in a serial chain can be retrieved simultaneously with delays in onset that become significant only for a fairly large number of intervening nodes (Anderson 1976, p. 295; Dosher 1976; Wickelgren 1976d).

Further support for chain parallel processing derives from studies of verification speed for hierarchical category-property associations. Some properties seem to be specifically associated directly to a category node—e.g., "A mink has fur." Others are much more general properties of superordinates of a category—e.g., "A mink has a nose" because "An animal has a nose." Such general properties are indirectly associated to any subordinate category of animal, in this case minks. Indirect associations are said to have greater hierarchical distance than direct associations. Verification of category-property associations is faster the greater the rated strength of association between the category and the property. Speed accuracy tradeoff studies will probably eventually demonstrate slightly slower retrieval dynamics with increasing hierarchical distance. But reaction time is not consistently faster for direct than indirect associations, presumably because a chain of several strong associations can reach a criterion-level of retrieved strength faster than a weak direct association. Finally, from speed-accuracy tradeoff studies it appears that all associations to a node are retrieved in parallel, regardless of strength (Collins and Quillian 1969; Conrad 1972; Nelson and Kosslyn 1975; Ashcraft 1976; Wickelgren and Corbett 1977; Corbett and Wickelgren 1978).

The theory that appears to be emerging from many studies is that activation of a node spreads automatically in parallel to all associated nodes. Nodes or links or both may remain in a state of partial activation (primed) for a few seconds following initial activation. This theory was proposed in various forms by many neural net theorists, starting with Rashevsky (1938) and McCulloch and Pitts (1943). Quillian (1967, 1968, 1969) was one of the earliest semantic memory theorists to embrace the activation theory. Recent extensive statements of the theory are given by Collins and Loftus (1975) and Anderson (1976). Empirical support for the spread of activation to associated nodes is massively documented in these last two references, in chapter 9 of this book, and elsewhere (Meyer and Schwaneveldt 1971; Davelaar and Colt-heart 1975; Ashcraft 1976; Fischler 1977).

Relation Specific Retrieval and Labeled Links

In the sentence "Nixon kicked the lawyer," "Nixon" is the subject of the verb (or the subject of the proposition, as you choose to look at it). In the sentence "The milkman cheated Nixon," "Nixon" is the object of the verb (or proposition). Many semantic-memory models have assumed that there are different types of associations between nodes in semantic memory to encode the different logical relations between concepts. These are called labeled links. The usual alternative is the traditional assumption that there is one type of association (unlabeled link) connecting concepts, and that the nature of logical relations is encoded simply by *which* nodes are associated (and which nodes these nodes are associated to). As Norman and Rumelhart and Anderson and Bower put it, a suitably chosen unlabeled-link associative memory has equal representational power to a labeled-link associative mem-ory (Anderson and Bower 1973, pp. 88–90). So there are two issues. What theory is simplest? And is there any evidence to suggest that excitatory links truly are different? Theoretical simplicity remains an open question. How-ever, Anderson has performed several experiments to test whether subjects can avoid associative interference to a concept common to two propositions when that common concept has a different logical relation to the other con-cepts in the two propositions. He found that they could not. Associative interference was equal whether the common concept played the same or a different logical role in two propositions (Anderson 1975, 1976 [pp. 278–83]). Another experiment by King and Anderson (1976) also supports the un-differentiated (nonlogical) character of associative links. It would be prema-ture to conclude in favor of the single excitatory-link theory. (We know from neurophysiology that there are inhibitory links.) However, at present there is little support for differentiating between types of excitatory links, with the possible exception of upward (is-a-constituent-of) and downward (has-as-a-constituent) links in a local hierarchy.

Associative Asymmetry

We do not know whether the association from node A to node B in semantic memory differs in type from the reverse association—from node B to node A. We do know that these associations may differ greatly in strength. In semantic memory for propositions, the probability of recalling element B of a proposition, given element A as a cue, frequently differs from the probability of recalling element A, given element B (Anderson and Bower 1973; Anderson 1976). In semantic memory for category-example associations, reaction time to verify such an association often differs depending on whether the category or the example is presented first (Loftus 1973). Finally, in some experiments on memory for propositions subjects tend strongly to exhibit wholistic (all-or-none) recall of the entire proposition, given one or more cue words (R. C. Anderson 1974; Foss and Harwood 1975; J. R. Anderson 1976, pp. 406–23). This may be interpreted as indicating that the weak links in recall of a proposition are the associations from the constituent concepts to the proposition node, and that the associations in the reverse direction, from the proposition to the constituents, are much stronger. This is reasonable both on logical and on psychological grounds. Logically, a proposition *implies* each of its constituents, but each constituent only *coimplies* the proposition in conjunction with all the other constituents. Psychologically, a concept constituent is often associated to many other concepts and propositions, producing substantial associative interference for such constituent-to-proposition associations. By contrast, except for some embedding in higher-order propositions, each proposition may only be directly associated to its own constituent concepts, producing less associative interference.

LEARNING

Given-New Distinction

Recognition is an important basic process in both learning and retrieval from semantic memory. In an associative semantic memory of the type human beings appear to possess, recognition involves associating an input sentence or some portion of that sentence with some subset of the existing node structure in semantic memory. When nodes already exist to represent an entire input sentence, we say that we have already learned the propositions expressed by that sentence—that such propositions are familiar to us. When only a portion of the input sentence can be mapped onto an existing node structure in semantic memory, we say that that portion is familiar, but that the rest constitutes new knowledge. Recognition is an important process in the learning of new knowledge, since to be as useful as possible, new knowledge should be associated to old knowledge. When we are learning new material, we recognize as much of it as is familiar. Then we add on new associations and nodes to represent the remainder. Recognition is an important part of learning, because human semantic memory is associative. If we stored every input sentence intact, regardless of whether parts of that sentence were identical to already existing knowledge, there would be a tremendous duplication of memory storage. Furthermore, memory retrieval would be much more difficult, because related information would be stored at many different places in the memory system. The recognition process would then have to take place during retrieval in order to unite information concerned with the same concepts but stored at different times.

Both linguists and psycholinguists have been sensitive to the distinction between (1) the part of a sentence that is already encoded in long-term semantic memory (the *given* information) and (2) the part that is not already encoded in semantic memory (the *new* information) (Halliday 1967; Chafe 1970, 1974; Clark and Haviland 1974, 1975). Many other terms besides "given" and "new" have been used to refer to this and related distinctions. Not all of these distinctions are equivalent. Indeed, in the next section I will sharply distinguish between the concept of a *topic* (material already in short-term memory) and the concept of *given* information (material in long-term memory). I will also distinguish between *comment* (material not already in short-term memory) and *new* information (material not already in long-term memory). However, the term *presupposition* will be used to mean information presented in a sentence as *given* information.

When we communicate with other people, the syntactic structure of our sentences systematically distinguishes between *given* and *new* information. Indeed, making clear the distinction between given and new in communication is probably one of the purposes of the variety of syntactic forms we have in language to communicate the same propositions. Let us consider some of the syntactic cues that distinguish what the speaker considers will be given versus new information for his listeners. First, *main clauses* are generally supposed to convey new information. Second, *definite descriptions* convey given information. For example, in the sentence "Polly gave a $5 reward to the little boy who returned her wallet," the given propositions in the definite description are "boy X was little" and "boy X returned Polly's wallet." The new proposition in the main clause is "Polly gave a $5 reward to boy X." In logical terminology this sentence presupposes that there was a boy who was little and who returned Polly's wallet. Third, *cleft sentences*, such as "It was Jim who ate the cookies," allow one to express that the proposition "someone X ate the cookies" is given information shared by both speaker and listener, while the proposition "someone X is Jim" is new information. A fourth syntactic device available in speech to distinguish given and new information is *stress* (sometimes represented by italics, underlining, or capitalizing in writing). If I say, "JIM ate the cookies" (with stress on JIM), I am presupposing that you know "someone ate the cookies," and now I am telling you that that "someone is Jim."

One type of sloppy thinking to be avoided is the notion that one part of a sentence conveys only new information, while the other part conveys only old information. Unless a new concept is being introduced for the first time, all the lowest-level words and phrases of a sentence refer to previously established concept nodes in long-term semantic memory. That is, they refer to already learned, or given, concepts. Many of the verb-case and preposi-tional-phrase compound concepts will be given as well. For example, one could argue that what was previously learned in "JIM ate the cookies" was an agentless proposition identical to the compound (verb-object case) concept "ate the cookies." Finally, given propositions are already contained in definite descriptions. The new information is often not any specific part of sentence. Rather, it is the higher-order *associations* (into new compound concept and proposition nodes) that must be added to memory in order to encode the sentence.

It is important to choose syntactic forms of communication that distin-guish between given and new information in a way that is appropriate for your listener or reader. If you choose information for your definite descrip-tions that is not given information for your listener, he will not know what you are talking about. Furthermore, human beings apparently tend to concen-trate their attention, in both perception and learning, on the information that the syntax says is new rather than given (Hornby 1974; Singer 1976).

For example, Singer (1976) showed that in memory for cleft sentences such as "It was the king who led the troops," "king" was recognized more frequently than "troops" and was also a better cue for recall of the entire proposition. In the cleft sentence "It was the troops that the king led," "troops" was better recognized and was the better cue. In the pseudocleft sentence "The one who led the troops was the king," "king" was better recognized than "troops," and in the pseudocleft sentence "What the king led was the troops," "troops" was better recognized than "king." The rule that summarizes all these results is: The better cue is the noun that the syntax says is now for the first time to be associated to the rest of the concepts in the sentence; the poorer cue is the noun that the syntax says is already associated to the verb. Presumably what is occurring here is that the noun whose case relation to the verb is presented as given is getting less attention during learning than is the noun whose case relation to the verb is presented as new.

Singer (1976) also showed that the use of a definite article ("the") in front of a noun in a sentence produced poorer subsequent recognition mem-ory for that noun than the use of an indefinite article ("a," "an") or an indefinite adjective ("some"). For example, in "The king led the troops," "troops" was remembered better, while in "A king led the troops," "king" was remembered better. Definite articles say that the noun phrase they begin is already stored in memory (given). Indefinite articles are used to introduce new concepts that must be given a new (token) node in semantic memory that is specific to this context. Subjects in recognition memory tasks such as these are not being asked if the words "king" and "troops" are familiar, or if *any* concept these words can refer to is in memory. They are being asked if they have encountered the word in the experimental context. Thus it is under-standable why a syntactic device (the indefinite article) that draws attention to the introduction of a new concept (for which new concept learning is required) should facilitate subsequent recognition memory for that concept better than a syntactic device (the definite article), that portrays its noun as referring to an already given concept (for which no new concept learning is required).

Topic-Comment Distinction

This distinction is frequently confused with the distinction between given and new. Actually *topic and comment* are an entirely different pair of concepts.* The distinction between *given* and *new* is concerned with whether concepts or propositions or both are in long-term memory. The distinction between *topic* and *comment* is concerned with whether concepts or propositions or both are in short-term memory—that is, with whether they have recently been activated so as to be currently primed and therefore a part of the listener's current schema. Topics (concepts or propositions) are in the current schema. Comments are not. Along these lines, Haviland and Clark (1974) showed that a sentence is understood faster when it is preceded by a context that primes some of its concepts.

A number of syntactic choices depend upon whether a concept (or proposition) in the current utterance is assumed to be in the listener's present schema. The choice of reference words for a concept is a prime example. We use a highly economical pronoun to refer to a recently activated noun concept in the set of noun concepts to which the pronoun is applicable—provided that there is only one such noun concept. For example, it's good English to say, "Sam came over to visit Mary today. He gave her a hat." It is not good English to say, "Sam and Frank came over to visit Mary today. He gave her a hat." If there are two or more recently activated noun concepts in a pronoun class, one must use a sufficiently detailed reference description to activate the correct concept. Note that definite descriptions may exhibit a vast range of detail. A definite description may be a pronoun such as "it," or a short noun phrase such as "the house," or a longer noun phrase such as "the red house," or a still longer phrase such as "the house that used to be on the corner of 4th and Elm until Trichinosis Meats tore it down to put in a packing plant." The longer and more detailed noun phrases are required when the desired noun concept is associatively far removed from the listener's currently active schema. The closer the concept is to the focus of the schema, the shorter the

---

*Of course, it is I who, like Humpty Dumpty, have chosen to make these words "mean just what I choose them to mean—neither more nor less." Others deserve the credit for pointing out all the relevant phenomena and developing most of the basic theoretical concepts. They just missed one important differentiating feature: the distinction between long-term and short-term memory.

necessary description, on the whole (Olson 1970; Osgood 1971; Norman and Rumelhart 1975, pp. 66–67).*

A second example of how syntax reflects the topic-comment distinction is that the subject of a sentence is typically a topic, if there are any topic concepts in the sentence. The major purpose of passive voice is to permit logical objects, recipients, and benefactors to serve as subjects when they are topics and the agent is not (Olson and Filby 1972). Active voice is used if the agent is a topic, or if there are no topic concepts in the current sentence. If a verb-object compound concept is a topic, it may be used as a subject by making it into a gerundive noun phrase, as in "Judging fly balls is a difficult skill." If instead one had previously been discussing difficult skills, one would be likely to say, "Another difficult skill is judging fly balls." There are many communicative benefits to be derived from distinguishing words and phrases that refer to concepts presumed to be in the listener's active schema (topics) from words and phrases that refer to concepts presumed to be outside the reader's schema (comments). The need to distinguish topic and comment, given and new, and the various semantic relationships within a sentence necessitates a wide variety of syntactic forms.

Reference and Semantic Integration

In the last chapter I discussed the fact that subjects tend to learn a set of related sentences in the same way as they learn a single, more complex sentence. Some psychologists explain this *semantic integration* effect with semimystical ideas about wholistic, Gestalt-like encoding. One can just as well argue that this phenomenon shows that we analyze and store complex sentences in terms of their component propositions. Since there is a lot of other evidence for this propositional-unit hypothesis, it is clearly the more plausible, as well as the more precise, explanation of semantic integration. This being the case, one might argue that the effect is misnamed—that it should be termed the *semantic analysis* effect. But the term *integration* is accurate because there is a vitally important semantic integration mechanism underlying the effect. This is noun phrase *reference* integration. In the last chapter I discussed at length the fact that subjects remember primarily concepts rather than words, and that a single word (even with a single dictionary meaning) may be used to *refer* to hundreds or thousands of different concepts over a lifetime. (How many *different* specific occurrences of *table* can you recall? Stop! Please don't waste your time.) When several propositions are presented in the same sentence, we know that a given word refers to the same concept in each proposition. We know this because the word that refers to each concept occurs only once, if for no other reason. However, when separate sentences are used to convey the same propositions, a *reference problem*

---

*See also Woods (1975, pp. 60–68) for a discussion of issues I have swept under the rug.

arises. How are we to associate the same concept to each occurrence of the same word in order to achieve semantic integration? What must be integrated into a single concept node are the words (or phrases) in separate sentences that refer to the same concepts.

As I explained in the topic-comment section, if two words (or phrases) that refer to the same concept occur sufficiently close together in time so that the appropriate concept is still primed, it is likely that they will both be associated to the same concept by passive associative priming. In this case semantic integration will occur. Moeser (1977) has demonstrated experimentally the importance of presenting sentences with common concepts close together in time, if semantic integration is to be obtained. When she separated related sentences with unrelated sentences or with questions that focused the subject's attention on processing one sentence at a time, she produced a decrement in semantic integration. Moeser has demonstrated two kinds of decrements in semantic integration. The first is poorer recall of the sentence actually presented. Such recall is enhanced by semantic integration. The second is a decreased ability to draw inferences that result from semantic integration. (E.g., "The jelly was under the tree" + "The ants ate the jelly" IMPLIES "The ants were under the tree.")

In these experiments, Moeser did not systematically manipulate the similarity of the material separating the related sentences to the words in the related sentences. However, the most severe disruption of semantic integration should occur when the interpolated sentences contain words that are identical to those that are to be referentially integrated, but that have different meanings in the interpolated sentence. For instance, consider the following sequence: "The jelly was under the tree." "Frank rubbed petroleum jelly on his ant bites." "The ants ate the jelly." This sequence poses word-to-concept associative interference problems that will reduce the level of semantic integration of the first and last sentences below the level it would attain in a sequence where the middle sentence had no words in common with the first and last sentences. Moeser has not quite done this experiment, but she has provided evidence that associative interference with semantic integration results from using the same words in the interpolated sentences as in the sentences to be integrated. From a practical communicative standpoint, I always try to avoid using the same words too close together to refer to different concepts. From a theoretical standpoint, this must certainly cause problems of associative interference.

One of the importance variables that affect the difficulty of learning a text is the number of different concepts that appear in it. Texts with many different concepts require more time to learn to a given level of comprehension than texts with few concepts. This is true even when the number of words and the number of propositions in the text are held constant (Kintsch et al. 1975; Manelis and Yekovich 1976). Repeated use of the same concept in several different propositions places much less strain on comprehension and learning than does the continual introduction of new concepts. It is important to note that in these text learning experiments (by and large) no unfamiliar words were being introduced in either the texts with many concepts or the texts with few concepts. Texts with many concepts were harder to learn. Presumably this was due to a combination of two factors. The first is that texts with many concepts may entail a greater frequency of new concept learning. The second is that in such texts it is harder to activate concepts that are already established in long-term semantic memory by prior learning, but that have not recently been primed by comprehension of earlier sentences in the same text. In texts that use the same concepts over and over again, activation of these concepts is faster because they have recently been activated and remain primed in the developing schema for the current text.

When concepts are repeated in various propositions in a text, it is easier to activate the repeated concepts in comprehension. But this repetition also establishes a very different structure of associations in memory for the text. Manelis and Yekovich (1976) performed a rather amazing experiment that demonstrated that repetition of concepts can aid memory even when it increases the number of words to be processed and the number of associations to be learned in a fixed time period for learning. In each condition subjects learned a minitext of three sentences. In the nonrepetition condition one such minitext was "Arnold lunged." "Norman called." "The doctor arrived." In the comparable repetition condition, the minitext was "Arnold lunged at Norman." "Norman called the doctor." "The doctor arrived." The surprising result was that short-term recall of the three propositions was significantly superior in the condition where the sentences had overlapping concepts, even though there was more to be processed and learned in this case. The minitext in the foregoing example forms a reasonably integrated episode in the repetition condition, but Manelis and Yekovich showed that beneficial effects of concept repetition are obtained even for less well-integrated minitexts. For example, the sequence "Ellen pushed Judith." "Judith obeyed the nurse." "The nurse coughed." was recalled better than the sequence "Ellen pushed." "Judith obeyed." "The nurse coughed." These findings may be explained by the structure of associations formed in the two conditions (fig. 11.1). In the no-repetition condition we have three isolated propositions stored in memory with no connections between them. In the repetition condition the extra associations that must be learned are bridging associations that connect (integrate) the three propositions in semantic memory. Though the learning of such bridging associations unquestionably takes time and mental effort, and so reduces our limited capacity for learning the other associations, it pays dividends in the form of more highly integrated knowledge. In this case the greater degree of integration enhanced the subjects' ability to recall the entire text. Similar memory benefits have been found for much longer texts and for single complex sentences (Thorndyke 1977; Bower 1976; Wanner 1974).

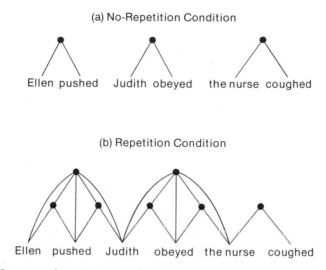

(a) No-Repetition Condition

Ellen pushed   Judith obeyed   the nurse coughed

(b) Repetition Condition

Ellen   pushed   Judith   obeyed   the nurse   coughed

Fig. 11.1 Structure of associations produced by a minitext of three propositions with no concept overlap in (a) and by a minitext with concept overlap in (b). Note that the three propositions are interconnected in (b) and isolated in (a).

Furthermore, as we shall see in the next chapter, semantic integration also enhances the memory's inferential and creative power. On the other hand, storing unconnected propositions limits the memory to rote recall and recognition of just those directly stored propositions.

Finally, one might predict that there would be differences in the level of recall of different propositions in a text, based on how extensively the propositions are associated to other propositions in the text (and probably outside the text as well). Propositions that are richly associated to other propositions have many potential retrieval cues, and so—all other factors being equal—they should be easier to recall. Indeed, in the Manelis and Yekovich (1976) study the advantage of the integrated (repetition) condition over the separated (no-repetition) condition was greatest for the middle proposition, which had two direct connecting links to other propositions in the integrated condition. Several other studies have found evidence that propositions that are considered central to a text are more likely to be recalled. These would include the main topic or high-ranking subtopic in an essay or a principal goal or event in a story (Johnson 1970; Kintsch and Keenan 1973; Kintsch et al. 1975; Meyer 1975; Neisser and Hupcey 1972; Thorndyke 1977; Bower 1976). However, centrality has been defined in innumerable ways (no two studies use the same criterion), and these definitions have been applied imprecisely to real texts. We must improve our theoretical understanding of the propositional structure of complex texts before we can do any definitive experiments on this issue.

Learning by the Socratic Method

Asking and answering questions is an extremely good way to learn. When you read a book or listen to a lecture, you will learn a lot more if you will actively think of questions you want the book or the lecturer to answer. What makes learning from a personal tutor so terrific is that you can ask a tutor just what you do not know and want most to learn. No one knows for sure why asking questions is so beneficial for learning, but the theoretical analysis of *wh*-question answering suggests one plausible answer. To ask (or answer) a *wh*-question, one must have built a semantic memory node structure that includes a large part of what is necessary to encode (or retrieve) the answer. If we ask the question "What constituent provides the best cue for recall of a proposition?" we need to establish a node structure like the one shown in figure 11.2. Note that after we have asked this question, we have already established six of the eight higher-order nodes and 12 of the 16 vertical associations necessary to encode the answer—which is "The subject constituent provides the best cue for recall of a proposition." Asking questions tends to insure that we will store the complete answer in semantic memory rather than just part of the answer, because by the time we have asked the question, so much of the learning process has already occurred.

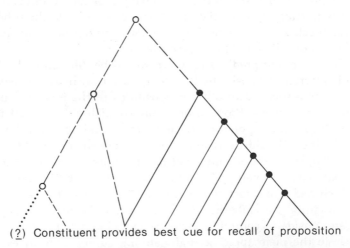

(?) Constituent provides best cue for recall of proposition

Fig. 11.2 The black dots and the solid lines represent the immediate-constituent node structure that *must* be established in semantic memory by asking the question "What constituent provides the best cue for recall of a proposition?" The open circles and dashed lines represent additional nodes and immediate-constituent links that *may* (or may not) be established by asking this question. The dotted line represents the only link that we know is not present in the question and must therefore be supplied by the answer. Note that asking a question provides a large part of the associative node structure necessary for encoding the answer in semantic memory.

UNDERSTANDING

Schemata

We do not simply learn the propositions as presented in a text, paying equal attention to each one. Rather, we recall and prime related material already stored in our semantic memory—that is, we generate schemata. We use these schemata to decide what parts of the text are most important to learn, to draw inferences beyond what is presented in the text, and to attach text propositions onto previously existing memory structures. Until we know more about the nature of these learning schemata and can control them better, we cannot really understand the structure of nodes and associations that we use to learn texts containing familiar concepts.

The facilitative effects of such memory schemata on learning are easy to demonstrate. The funniest and most dramatic demonstration I know is the following paragraph, taken from Bransford and Johnson (1973). Read it and try to make sense of it. When you have read it, I will tell you the schema (a two-word title that describes what the paragraph is about). Read it again then and see how easy it is to comprehend.

The procedure is actually quite simple. First you arrange things into different groups. Of course, one pile may be sufficient depending on how much there is to do. If you have to go somewhere else due to lack of facilities, that is the next step; otherwise you are pretty well set. It is important not to overdo things. That is, it is better to do too few things at once than too many. In the short run this may not seem important, but complications can easily arise. A mistake can be expensive as well. At first the whole procedure will seem complicated. Soon, however, it will become just another facet of life. It is difficult to see any end to the necessity for this task in the immediate future, but then one can never tell. After the procedure is completed, one arranges the materials into different groups again. Then they can be put into their proper places. Eventually they will be used once more and the whole cycle will then have to be repeated. However, that is a part of life. *

Without the appropriate interpretive schema, this passage is almost hopelessly obscure and the subjects in Bransford and Johnson's experiment could remember very little of it after they had read it. However, a group that was told in advance that the paragraph was about washing clothes found the text quite easy to understand and remembered much more of it. Now read the passage again for yourself and enjoy the difference. Providing short titles that described the theme or main idea of a text produced similar benefits in a study by Dooling and Lachman (1971).

Many semantic memory theorists believe that both writers and readers in our Western culture employ a general story schema in the generation and comprehension of stories (Van Dijk 1972; Rumelhart 1975; Kintsch 1975, pp. 105–12; Kintsch and van Dijk 1975; Thorndyke 1977; Bower 1976). Opinions

*Text quoted by permission.

vary as to the exact structure of this general story schema, but its major constituents usually include two or more of the following: setting, theme or goals, plot (which contains episodes), and final outcome. There is some evidence that subjects remember propositions that are ranked by the story schema as most significant better than they remember lower-ranking details, and that subjects are more likely to include these significant propositions in summaries of the stories (Kintsch and van Dijk 1975; Kintsch 1975, pp. 105–12; Thorndyke 1977; Bower 1976). You probably feel that your grandmother knew this, but precise work on schema theory is in its infancy and more impressive results are expected in the future. Finally, Gentner (1976) studied recall of a short history passage after each of several repeated auditory presentations. He observed that recall was based both on the serial order of the propositions in the passage and on the structure dictated by Rumelhart's story schema. However, over trials the story schema became dominant in the organization of recall.

Semantic Decomposition and Canonical Form

If you hear the sentence "John bought a book from Mary," you can conclude from the meaning of the verb "bought" that "John transferred ownership of some money from himself to Jane, which caused Mary to transfer ownership of a book from herself to John." Some theories assume that all verbs and other relational elements (e.g., "is" + a preposition, for example, "is on," "is beside") are encoded in semantic memory in terms of a small set of basic verbs (relations), such as "do," "cause," "transfer ownership," and "transfer location" (Schank 1975a; Norman and Rumelhart 1975). Nouns, adjectives, and adverbs can also be decomposed into a set of basic component features for storage in semantic memory, and some theorists have proposed doing so. For example, "bachelor" is "male," "human," "animate," "not married," and so on (Katz and Fodor 1963). However, the main emphasis of late has been on the semantic decomposition of verbs (relations).

Taken to the extreme, the goal of semantic decomposition is a common encoding in semantic memory unique to all paraphrases of a single sentence or phrase. Such a unique encoding is said to have *canonical form*. To judge whether two phrases or sentences are paraphrases, one simply transforms each one to canonical form. If they have the same canonical form, they are paraphrases; otherwise they are not. The hooker in this is that it requires a procedure that will guarantee the transformation of all paraphrases to a single canonical form. As Woods (1975) points out, there is good reason to believe that it is impossible to define a completely adequate canonical form procedure for natural language, since this impossibility has been proved mathematically for some computer programming languages that are a good deal simpler than natural language. It seems likely that the transformation of paraphrases to equivalent form occurs to a certain extent at the time of initial learning. This explains why we can sometimes decide equally fast that a test sentence was previously stored in memory whether the originally learned sentence was in the active or the passive form, for example (Garrod and Trabasso 1973; Anderson 1974). However, it is extremely doubtful that we transform *all* meaningfully equivalent phrases and sentences to a single canonical form.

As Woods points out, determining the meaningful equivalence of two propositions is only one of the things our semantic memory can do. Two propositions, A and B, are equivalent if, and only if, A implies B and B implies A. However, the implication is usually not symmetric. More often A implies B but B does not imply A—or vice versa. The more general theoretical problem is how semantic memory achieves inferences, from which equivalence (symmetric implication) is achieved as a special case. However, it can be claimed that semantic decomposition aids in solving the inference problem. For example, the decomposition of "John bought a book from Mary" automatically tells us that "ownership of a book was transferred at some point in past time." This is the sort of elementary inference that semantic decomposition accomplishes at the time of learning. However, it is not clear whether one ever reaches irreducible meaning primitives that cannot themselves be used to derive more inferences. That is, semantic memory need not have a truly basic set of meaning atoms. Even the most basic concepts appear to have inferential relations to other concepts in a circular manner that is incompatible with the assumption of semantic decomposition. There is an even bigger problem. The inferential power of a proposition may not be fully contained in itself and the meanings of its constituents by themselves. These are analytic inferences. The inferential power of a proposition may be contained partly in its power to combine with separately stored, logically independent propositions to yield inferences from the *set* of two or more propositions that cannot be derived from any of these propositions individually. These are synthetic inferences. In principle one could combine each newly stored proposition with every set of previously stored propositions to determine all the possible inferences at the time of learning, but from a practical standpoint this is impossible. So we can show that some inferences are achieved at the time of learning, but it is clear that initial storage in semantic memory of any input proposition cannot contain all of these potential inferences. Most of these inferences must be made when they are needed—and most of them never will be needed. So we probably acquire semantic memories for propositions that have undergone some inferential expansion and some transformation to an underlying form less varied than the surface syntactical form of sentences. But we almost certainly do not perform a complete semantic decomposition.

Experimental evidence supports this theoretical reasoning. While Gentner (1975) has shown that children tend to acquire verb concepts in the order of increasing logical complexity ("give" and "take" before "pay," and "trade" before "buy" and "sell"), Kintsch (1974, pp. 219–42) found no evidence that logically more complex concepts lead to any greater processing difficulties or are any harder to learn and remember than logically simpler concepts. Apparently subjects learn propositions in terms of their immediate constituent concepts, which are already learned chunks (nodes) in their own right. They defer most of the further analysis of these constituents until this analysis becomes necessary—if it ever does. That is, most inferences, analytic or synthetic, are probably performed in retrieval, not in learning.*

This raises the question of *which* inferences are made at the time of learning. Johnson-Laird has suggested the intuitively plausible answer that this depends on the current schema, which in turn depends on the context. Johnson-Laird (1975) cites the very different properties of tomatoes that are likely to be activated in different sentence contexts—e.g., "He peeled a tomato" (tomatoes have skins); "He sat on a tomato" (tomatoes are squishy); "He likes tomatoes" (tomatoes are edible.)

Metaphor

Metaphors are verbal supermarkets in which the thrifty shopper finds only what he needs, the creative shopper finds something he always needed without realizing it, and the impulsive shopper finds too much.† That is, of course, a metaphor about metaphors—in this case, a metaphorical expression of what Ortony (1975) calls the *compactness thesis* of metaphor. To a lesser extent this metaphor about metaphors also expresses Ortony's *inexpressibility thesis* of metaphor (check that philosophical paradox: expressing inexpressibility). Finally, in an appropriately frivolous vein (or artery), it expresses Wickelgren's *watch-your-step-as-you-walk-down-the-garden-path thesis* of metaphor. These three theses will be discussed in order of importance.

The *compactness thesis* sees metaphors as highly efficient communicative vehicles (there goes another metaphor—this time a dead one) that transfer many properties at once from the already established (so-called *literal*) domain to the new *(figurative)* domain. I say "so-called" literal because although metaphorical transfer usually moves from more concrete physical to more abstract intellectual domains, it can sometimes go the other way. What is necessary in metaphor is this: semantic properties that were previously stored in one part of semantic memory must be duplicated in the part of one's semantic net that is currently being woven (sorry, can't help it—my metaphor node is out of control). Of course, many of the properties of the metaphor in its old (literal) meaning are inappropriate in its new (figurative) meaning. The selection of relevant properties is presumably accomplished by one's

---

*See also Anderson (1976, pp. 54–55, 73–74, 334) for arguments that reach the same conclusion.

†The literary distinction between simile and metaphor has little apparent psychological significance, so I am ignoring it throughout this discussion.

currently operative schema. It's like our thrifty shopper, who matches items in a supermarket to items on a list.

The *inexpressibility thesis* of metaphor starts off with the plausible notion that there are many combinations of semantic properties for which we have no name, and often no concept node either. If we had a name for each individual property in a set we wished to communicate, we might name them all individually and give the set a new name. This would be a nonmetaphorical definition of a new set of properties—inefficient perhaps—but possible. However, in some cases we will not have previously analyzed and named all of the properties in the set we now wish to transfer to a new domain. In this case metaphor may be our only practical vehicle for expressing what we wish to express—a not-yet-fully-analyzed set of properties. Indeed, such metaphorical extensions may cause us to discover some new and useful concept we never abstracted before—like our creative shopper, who is always on the lookout for something truly new and useful that isn't on the list.

Now for our third thesis: a metaphor can be a dangerous maze for impulsively fuzzy thinkers. If you can't separate the wheat from the chaff, you'd better not be a miller (and I wouldn't care to eat your bread either). Judging from the lack of metaphorical restraint in this section, I think you would be ill-advised to send me to the store with your life savings to get a loaf of bread.

SUMMARY

1 To answer a question, we must recognize its components—for example, by identifying these components with existing nodes in semantic memory. A yes-no question asks whether there is a network of nodes in semantic memory that matches the input statement. A *wh*-question asks us to fill in a missing constituent by its association to the recognized set of nodes that represent the information in the question.

2 To encode a sentence in semantic memory, we must parse the sentence into phrases. (A phrase is a group of words that will refer to a single concept or proposition node in semantic memory.) We may use only semantic parsing to deal with familiar phrases (which refer to previously established nodes in semantic memory). We must use more general syntactic parsing processes to deal with novel phrases.

3 Multiple-access, divergence, and chain parallel processing all occur in semantic memory, but parallel processing capacity is limited in all three cases.

4 Apparently the same type of association connects the relational constituent (e.g., verb) of a proposition to *each* of its cases (e.g., agent and object). There is no evidence to support the hypothesis that there are differently labeled links between nodes, but there is some reason to distinguish upward (is-a-constituent-of, coimplies) links from downward (has-as-a-constituent, implies) links.

5 Sentence comprehension and question answering are guided by two factors. The first is contextually activated schemata, which play a critical role in resolving

the highly ambiguous relation between words and concepts. The second is inferences based on knowledge previously stored in semantic memory. These inferences include, in particular, our presuppositions concerning a speaker's or listener's (or a writer's or reader's) knowledge and goals.

6 To learn new propositions in semantic memory, we must first recognize the *given* (familiar) portions of the input sentence (familiar concepts, phrases, and propositions) and then form *new* vertical associations and chunk nodes that link these familiar nodes in new ways. One of the uses of syntax is to distinguish between *given* and *new* information. For example, main clauses convey new information. Definite descriptions refer to given information (they do so to locate accurately the proper concept nodes already established in semantic memory). And stress is often placed so as to differentiate between given and new information.

7 Another function of syntax is to distinguish between *topic* (in short-term memory) and *comment* (not in short-term memory). For example, pronouns and other brief definite descriptions of concepts are used for topics. Subjects of sentences are also typically topics, which may be why language has both an active and a passive voice.

8 Semantic integration of propositions with overlapping concepts is the major function of an associative semantic memory. To communicate well, we must make proper use of what's in short-term memory (topics), so as not to use the same words too close together to refer to different concepts. Texts that are well integrated by having extensive concept overlap are easier to understand and remember than texts that have less concept overlap.

9 We draw some inferences at the time of learning, but we draw most inferences only when we need them. Complete semantic decomposition of sentences into elementary semantic features that are invariant over all paraphrases is probably impossible. Even if it were possible, it wouldn't solve the more basic inference problem.

10 Metaphor greatly extends the capacity of a limited vocabulary of words and phrases to represent a large number of concepts and propositions. Even when a more literal expression of ideas is possible, metaphor often permits a more compact expression.

11 When we encode a question in semantic memory, we encode a considerable part of the answer. This facilitates learning by breaking down the job into simpler parts.

CHAPTER 12
THINKING: PLANS, INFERENCE, PROBLEM SOLVING, AND CREATIVITY

OBJECTIVES

1 To point out that most of the questions we can answer, most of the sentences we generate and recognize, and most of the thoughts we can think are novel. Accounting for the creative capacity of human thinking is the main theme of this chapter.

2 To distinguish between declarative knowledge, as embodied in propositions, and procedural knowledge, as embodied in plans. To describe a context-sensitive coding of plans that permits their representation in semantic memory side by side with propositions. To illustrate how the branching and looping characteristics of such plans allow them to control thinking in sophisticated ways.

3 To discuss the human capacity for inferring the truth or falsity of new propositions that are based on propositions stored in semantic memory. To provide examples of seven types of inferences: equivalence, implication, coimplication, contradiction, disjunction, quantification, and linear ordering.

4 To describe briefly a theory of problems and problem-solving methods that divides the latter into two classes. The first class consists of search reduction methods. These include recognizing equivalence, evaluating progress towards the goal, working backward, and setting subgoals. The second class consists of representation methods. These include encoding givens, operations, and goals; contradiction; analogy; simpler problems; and special cases.

5 To discuss how set affects problem solving.

6 To discuss some possible roles that incubation may play in problem solving.

355

7 To discuss creativity. The discussion will emphasize (a) chance; (b) how a mind filled with novel integrative schemata evaluates ideas; (c) asking questions; (d) creative versus scholarly reading and listening; (e) general creative plans that can enable you to force out creative ideas; and (f) why you shouldn't believe most reports on how ideas are generated.

Chomsky (1957) points out that one of the most significant aspects of language at the syntactic and semantic level is its creativity. We can speak and understand an infinite number of sentences, and most of these sentences are new in that we have never been exposed to them or thought of them before. Nor are the sentences we speak mere paraphrases of familiar propositions—we also state propositions that we never learned directly. We are forever drawing inferences from the information stored in semantic memory that allow us to generate novel propositions and to judge whether they are true or false. Sometimes we put a sequence of basic inferences together to solve a problem or create a new idea. Indeed, most of the questions we can answer require more than the retrieval of information from a single proposition. Rather, they require the combined (inferential) use of two or more propositions stored in semantic memory. Accounting for the inferential—or creative—capacity of human semantic reasoning is probably the most important task in the area of semantic memory. We have not yet developed a theory of semantic memory that has the complete inferential capacity humans possess. But we do know some things about human inferential capacity. In this chapter I begin by discussing cognitive plans for the control of thinking in any associative memory. Next I discuss some basic types of inferences. Finally I analyze problem solving and creative thinking.

PLANS AND PROCEDURAL KNOWLEDGE

At several points in this chapter I will indicate that some more organized control than simple stimulus-induced activation is probably necessary to account for our information-processing capacities. This is especially true in the case of inference and the syntactic analysis of sentences. Such control processes are called *plans,* and the purpose of this section is to describe how mental plans might operate. I will use a plan for a simple motor skill as an example. Plans that use similar principles may direct our thinking as well. I use the term "plan" to refer to the basic unit of *procedural knowledge* (*how* to do things). The *proposition* or *image* is the basic unit of *declarative knowledge* (*what* is true). However, I intend no specific commitment to Miller, Galanter, and Pribram's (1960) notion of plans; to Newell's (1973) or Anderson's (1976) production systems; or to Woods's (1970) and Kaplan's (1972) transition networks. Instead I will concentrate on those branching and looping properties that are common to all formulations of procedural knowledge and then describe how context-sensitive coding permits the representation of plans in an associative semantic memory.

Plans are something like little computer programs that program the mind to perform certain cognitive tasks, such as long division, brushing your teeth, or generating a sentence.* Like propositions, simple plans can be embedded in more complex plans to produce a hierarchical control system. For example, the plan of making pancakes includes the plan of preparing the batter, which includes the plan of measuring out a precise quantity of milk, which requires getting a measuring cup from the drawer, placing the cup on a surface, getting the milk from the refrigerator, pouring it into the cup until it reaches a certain mark, and so on. The most basic plans have as constituents a partially ordered set of elementary actions and their consequences. The complete inventory of basic actions is unclear, but presumably it includes such acts as attending to particular visual locations, moving limbs to particular locations, and recalling associations. The consequence of attending to a particular visual location is the activation of the nodes that represent whatever stimulus is there. The consequences of moving a limb to a location are also certain visual, cutaneous, kinesthetic, and other feedback stimuli. The consequence of recalling associations to, say, "7 + 2" is thinking "9." A plan must have variables that are bound by these consequences to have specific values. And a plan must be specified in a sufficiently general way to be able to handle many or all of the probable consequences of its actions at all phases of its operation.

There are probably many important differences between the encoding of plans and the encoding of propositions in semantic memory. Certainly there are important differences between their respective roles in thinking. For one thing, the encoding of the order of actions and possible consequences is critical in plans, while the ordering of constituent concepts in propositions is probably completely irrelevant and therefore is not encoded. Plans must be concerned with performance in real time; propositions are "timeless" knowledge. Despite the important structural and functional differences between declarative and procedural knowledge, there is every reason to believe that both kinds of knowledge are stored in an associative memory—perhaps side by side and intermixed. In declarative knowledge, associations encode the constituency relation. In procedural knowledge, associations encode the temporal order of activation.

In chapter 5 I discussed one simple class of plans—namely, plans for articulating phonemes in the correct order in words. This is a simple linear order with no branching or looping. Thus, assuming a context-sensitive code for the phoneme constituents of a word such as "struck," articulation begins

*For a remarkable article on the arithmetic plans used by a lightning calculator, see Hunter (1962).

with $_\#s_t$, then proceeds to $_st_r$, $_tr_u$, $_ru_k$, and ends with $_uk_\#$. Note that there are no branch points where the choice depends upon external stimuli or the results of prior internal processing. The same basic idea of context-sensitive coding can be extended to encode *branching* (partially ordered, hierarchical) and even *looping* action control systems. For example, consider the motor control program for hammering a nail. Miller, Galanter, and Pribram (1960, pp. 33–37) provide a simple plan for this skill in the form of a flow chart whose elements are of two types: *actions* (operations) and *tests*. By changing *tests* to *states* (which depend on both the external world and the consequences of prior actions), and by using a context-sensitive code, we can eliminate the *homunculus** residing in the *tests* and still retain all the feedback control power inherent in Miler, Galanter, and Pribram's plans. Consider the context-sensitive control process for hammering shown in figure 12.1.

When one activates the higher-order node that represents the macroaction of hammering a nail, it primes all the state and action nodes that are its constituents (fig. 12.1). At the beginning of any action sequence the node that has the form $_\#x_y$ is activated, and at the end the node having the form $_wz_\#$ is activated. So first we grasp the hammer (which is presumed to be down on the workbench). This produces the *down* state in the prior context of grasping. This activates the state node $_{grasp}down_{lift}$, which activates the action node $_{down}lift_{up}$, producing the *up* state, and therefore activating the state node $_{lift}up_{check}$. This state node is associated to two action nodes, both of which produce the same action—namely, *checking* the nail to see if it is *flush*. Thus both *check* nodes may be activated simultaneously at first, but as we perceive the consequences of the check, one node or the other will become more activated. This determines which branch we take. Assuming that the nail is not flush, we enter the branch that strikes the nail. This branch eventually loops back to the $_{down}lift_{up}$ state and continues looping around until the nail is flush. At that point we take the branch that stops the macroaction by entering the terminal state $_{check}flush_\#$. This diagram does not represent the full plan for hammering nails. In reality we must be able to grasp a hammer that is lying in any position and move it to the correct position in the horizontal plane over the nail. We must also be able to change its vertical position in the act of hammering. Furthermore, Miller, Galanter, and Pribram assumed that the acts of lifting and striking were feedback controlled—not ballistic, as I have represented them. Feedback control could be added to the plan, if one wished. However, the essential branching and looping characteristics of feedback control systems are present in the plan shown in figure 12.1, so there is no theoretical problem in extending the adequacy and complexity of such plans in any of these ways.

This discussion of context-sensitive plans demonstrates that all plans (control programs, mental operation sequences, and so on) can be encoded in

---

*A *homunculus* is a hypothetical "little man in the head" who makes decisions.

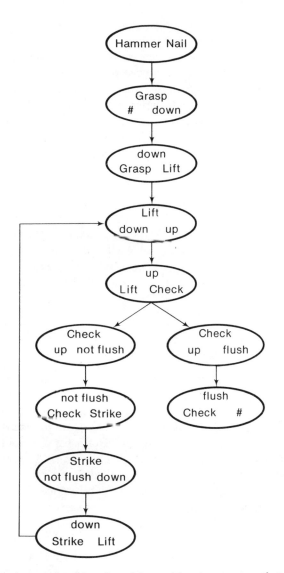

Fig. 12.1 Set of nodes associated in a branching and looping structure that could constitute a plan for hammering a nail. When the macronode that represents the entire plan of hammering a nail gets activated, it primes all of the nodes that constitute the plan. When one chooses to initiate the plan, one activates the *beginning* node, which is always of the form $_{\#}x_y$—in this case $_{\#}grasp_{down}$. This initiates full activation of the beginning node in the partially ordered set of nodes. The flow of control (full activation) follows the associations between nodes. Choices between branch points are determined by external or internal stimulus events, which may be consequences of one's prior actions.

an associative memory, just like propositions. This does not mean that the old S-R conceptions of language and thinking were correct. The structure and functioning of plans and propositions, and the chunking capacity to define new nodes that associative memory must possess to learn plans and propositions, provide just the kind of contextually dependent, wholistic, feedback-controlled, and looping characteristics that cognitive psychologists have insisted are necessary to account for mental functioning. Semantic memory research appears to be bringing about a synthesis of the useful elements from both the cognitive and associative approaches to the mind.

INFERENCE

In this section I will discuss seven semantic inferences that people can make. In each case I will try to indicate, as best I can, the role that associative activation may play in these inferences and the need to assume cognitive control processes—*plans*—that guide the associative activation process (Miller, Galanter, and Pribram 1960).

Equivalence and Reference: Synonyms and Definite Descriptions

"If Abraham Lincoln was born in Kentucky and the sixteenth president of the United States was Abraham Lincoln, then the sixteenth president of the United States was born in Kentucky." Whenever two concepts are synonyms, or whenever a concept is equivalent to some phrase that is a definite description of it, we can conclude that what holds for one holds for the other. Such *equivalence inferences* are presumably achieved by the reference mechanism discussed earlier, in which meaningfully equivalent words and phrases are associated to the same concept node. This reference mechanism probably consists of more than just passive (stimulus-driven) activation and priming. Any propositions that concern a concept may be used to reference (activate) it. After the proposition node has been activated, the reference mechanism must focus activation on the desired concept constituent and probably inhibit the very constituents that were used initially to activate the desired concept. This would apper to require a cognitive control process—a reference subroutine of a *recognition plan.* Among other things, this recognition plan also parses sentences into phrases and may label phrases as to syntactic function.

Implication: Set Inclusion and Expansion

"Finches are birds, birds can fly, therefore finches can fly." This is a noun *set inclusion inference.* We are assuming that propositions true of a super-ordinate concept are true of all examples of that concept. Since concepts are fuzzy, and since we store propositions that are true of many, but not necessarily all, examples of a concept, such set inclusion inferences have a high probability of being valid. However, they are not infallible—e.g., ostriches are birds, but ostriches cannot fly. When we know these special-case contradictions to generalizations, we store them as propositions that are true of the special case, and we follow the rule that whenever more directly associated information contradicts less directly associated information, the more directly associated information is correct. However, the existence of contradictory special cases should not detract from the main point. This point is that a semantic memory that can perform such set inclusion inferences has far more cognitive power than one that cannot. As Quillian (1968, 1969) and others have demonstrated, set inclusion inferences provide us with a far greater number of inferable propositions than the number of directly stored propositions.

There are also verb (relational) inclusion inferences. "Amy bought a book from the Coop" implies that "Amy acquired a book," and that "Amy paid money to the Coop," and so on. "Bought" implies "acquired" and "paid money."

More generally, compound concept (e.g., predicate or noun phrase) and propositional nodes imply other concepts and propositions. "Caught a fish" implies "being on or beside a body of water," which is not implied by either "caught" or "fish" alone. "The lawyer presented his closing arguments" implies "the lawyer was in a courtroom" and "the lawyer was talking to a jury." These propositions are not implied by any of the concepts individually or in any combination short of the entire proposition. Schank and Rieger have identified and explored relational, predicate, and propositional *expansion inferences* of this type (Schank and Rieger 1973; Rieger 1975; Schank 1975a, 1975b) Many expansion inferences occur automatically during comprehension, though as I argued earlier, it seems inconceivable that we draw all possible inferences during comprehension in a complete semantic decomposition of input concepts and propositions.

Noun and verb set inclusion inferences and predicate and propositional expansion inferences can all be subsumed under the general notion of *constituent implication inferences.* That is, a chunk node implies its direct and indirect constituents. Constituent implication is downward associative activation—an analytic inference process. As long as enough of the constituents of a concept or proposition are presented to activate it, the activated concept or proposition node can activate any of its other lower-level constituent concepts and propositions. In reality it does not generally activate all of them, being prevented from doing so by attentional limitations and competing demands to process other information. This unification of inclusion and expansion inferences under constituent implication is consistent with the hypothesis that both concept and proposition nodes have a fuzzy constituent structure such that only a subset of a node's constituents is sufficient to activate the node.

Thus it is reasonable to presume that a word constituent of a concept can activate the concept node (e.g., "finch"), and that by downward constituent activation, the concept node can then activate a category constituent ("bird"), which in turn can activate some of its property constituents ("flies," "has feathers," and so on). Similarly, "the lawyer presented his closing arguments" is sufficient to activate a propositional node previously stored in semantic memory that has many other constituents, such as "to a jury," and "in a courtroom."

Constituent implication ($\rightarrow$) is closely related to the concept of logical implication ($\supset$).* However, the two concepts are not identical.

Constituent implication is like logical implication in two ways. First, "finch$\rightarrow$bird" is true when both "X is a finch" (the antecedent) is true and "X is a bird" (the consequent) is true. Second, "finch$\rightarrow$fish" is false when "X is a finch" is true and "X is a fish" is false. Constituent implication is unlike conventional logical implication in many ways. Three of these are discussed below.

First, in conventional logic, "X is a finch $\supset$ X is a fish" is true if the antecedent ("X is a finch") is false, whether or not the consequent ("X is a fish") is true. Thus in logic "a spider is a finch $\supset$ a spider is a fish" is true, because a spider is not a finch. In constituent implication, such implication propositions with false antecedents are simply not defined. Human beings clearly interpret the notion of implication as constituent implication and not as logical implication (Wason 1966; Johnson-Laird and Tagart 1969; Wason and Johnson-Laird 1972, pp. 90–92; Evans 1972).

Second, in logical implication, "p $\supset$ q" is true does not permit an occasional case where proposition "p" is true but proposition "q" is false. In constituent implication, because concepts and propositions have a fuzzy constituent structure, "X is a bird$\rightarrow$X can fly" is true because it is usually true, despite the existence of exceptions like "an ostrich is a bird but an ostrich cannot fly." In logic, one may say "some birds can fly" or "all birds can fly," but humans say "birds can fly" meaning essentially "most birds can fly." Probably what is stored in memory is that "bird$\rightarrow$can fly," and exceptions and qualifications (or quantifications) on such implicational generalizations are not considered unless it becomes necessary.† The qualifiers "all" and "some" are basic in predicate logic, but unqualified thinking appears to be basic to human semantic memory. Qualified thinking appears to be possible but con-

---

*There are many different systems of logic, but I shall use the term "logic" to refer to the most familiar, symbolic logic. The symbols "$\rightarrow$" and "$\supset$" should be read as implies, although two different "implies" concepts are being referred to.

†I will use the term *qualification* to include the narrower term *quantification* from predicate logic because the logical quantifiers "some" and "all" are probably just two out of many qualifiers in human semantic memory.

siderably more difficult. Perhaps the most convincing proof of this assertion is the enormous difficulty humans have with even elementary qualified inferences (e.g., a syllogism such as "all B are A" and "some C are B," therefore "some A are C"). By comparison, humans find it easy to make accurate unqualified inferences (e.g., "A is a B," "Bs can C," therefore "A can C"). Constituent implication is basic to human thinking. Probably it mostly consists of simple associative activation. Qualification is complex and must certainly involve inference plans (control processes).*

The third and perhaps the most basic difference between constituent implication and logical implication is that logical implication applies only to propositions, while constituent implication is a relation between two nodes of any kind. The concept "bird" implies the predicate "can fly" in the constituent sense. This is rather different from the propositional version of this implication relation—namely, "X is a bird→X can fly." In support of constituent implication among concepts as a basic inference process, Rowe (1964) found that logical reasoning was faster and more accurate with implicational syntax ("A implies B") than with quantified syntax ("all As are Bs"). This, in turn, was easier than conditional propositional syntax ("if X is A, then X is B"). We have a semantic network in which concepts have constituent implicational relations to each other (e.g., "cat→has fur") and possibly to propositions (e.g., "mice→cats catch mice," though this could be stored as "mice→caught by cats"). Of course, as previously discussed, propositions imply their concept and propositional constituents. A semantic memory network of the type I have described automatically has constituent implication, and it is striking just how much of what is easy and natural in human reasoning appears to be constituent implication and how few and fairly elementary are the required attentional control processes.

Coimplication

There is another phenomenon supporting the hypothesis that implication in semantic memory is association rather than logical implication. This is the frequent human error of making *backward implication inferences.* Such inferences assume that "p→q" also means that "q→p." That is, they interpret unidirectional implication as bidirectional implication (equivalence). This has been found to be a major source of error in numerous studies of logical reasoning in both children and adults. It is far more likely to occur with unfamiliar or abstract material than with familiar material. Thus, for example, humans do not usually interpret "all sharks are fish" to mean "all fish are

---

*For a review of the enormous difficulties human beings have with symbolic logic reasoning, especially reasoning that involves quantifiers, see the outstanding book by Wason and Johnson-Laird (1972, especially pp. 129–70). It is not surprising that network models of semantic memory have had so much difficulty with quantifiers (Woods 1975).

sharks."* Such results are to be expected if implication in semantic memory is association of nodes. When "shark" is associated in a downward implication relation to "fish," "fish" is also associated in an upward coimplication relation to "shark."† However, "fish" is also associated to concept nodes for "bluegill," "bass," "perch," and so on. These nodes contradict (perhaps inhibit) "shark" and contradict each other (Holyoak and Glass 1975). Unless other constituents of "shark" besides "fish" are activated, the "shark" node will not be activated any more than many other nodes that represent other species of fish. Thus when we deal with familiar implications, the existence of other associations in the network protects us from interpreting the weaker coimplication relation as the stronger implication relation. The fact that subjects make such errors for unfamiliar material, where the other contradictory associations have not been formed, argues that implication and coimplication may not be structurally different types of links. Rather, they may be the same type of link, which functions differently depending upon larger network characteristics. The fact that subjects do not always interpret unfamiliar (including abstract) material as if "p→q" also means "q→p" indicates that we may have logic plans that lay down auxiliary associations upon seeing "p→q" to provide the same sort of protection against implication-reversal errors as inhibition from competing associations provides in semantic memory for familiar material.

Coimplication produces an important kind of inference, as well. It activates the chunk whenever one has activated more constituents of that chunk than of any other competing chunk. This is essentially what happens in perceptual recognition, and similar (upward) coimplication must occur in thinking as well. Associative activation is probably guided by plans in both cases.‡

Negation and Contradiction

"If John is tall, John is not short." "If Chicago is located in Illinois, Chicago is not in Florida." Within the theory of semantic memory described earlier in this chapter, one could hypothesize that the node representing "tall" is associated with the node representing "not short," and the representative "short" is associated with the node "not tall." Similarly, one can assume that "Illinois" is associated with the negation of "Florida." This may be how such

---

*A good review of evidence on this issue is provided by Wason and Johnson-Laird (1972, pp. 54–85). Other relevant studies are listed by Revlis (1975, p. 128), and a further relevant study is in Neimark and Chapman (1975, pp. 138–39).

†Coimplication is the joint association of several constituents in an upward direction to their chunk node.

‡See Anderson (1976, pp. 320–77) for examples of associative inference guided by plans, which in this case are in the form of production systems.

inferences are accomplished in semantic memory, but it is difficult to explain how all these associations got formed in the first place. Clearly we have not consciously learned each of the $50 \cdot 49$ ordered pairs of associations required by this hypothesis to represent the fact that the 50 states are mutually exclusive. We cannot solve this puzzle until we understand more about the role of negation in inference.

We are primarily interested in storing positive implications—what properties a thing has, rather than what properties it does not have. The reason is simple. Positive statements typically contain much more information than negative statements. Negation functions to deny incorrect expectations. We must have some positive preconceptions of "A" before we can process and encode "not A" in memory. When the positive preconception has not previously been established in the mind, negative sentences are harder to process than positive sentences. However, when the positive preconception has previously been established, negative sentences may actually be easier to understand than positive ones (Wason 1965; Greene 1970a, 1970b; Johnson-Laird and Tridgell 1972; Wason and Johnson-Laird 1972, pp. 30–53; Clark 1974).

The notorious difficulty of *double negatives* appears to derive from a breakdown in the process of keeping track of the preconception for each one. For example, note how difficult it is to comprehend the following sentence containing the two negatives "not" and "deny": I do not wish to deny that negative statements are typically harder than positive statements (Wason and Johnson-Laird 1972, pp. 30–53). This difficulty is probably not due to the slowness of mental processing, but rather to the fact that the negation operator typically precedes the constituent to be negated in English syntax. Our recognition plan is such that this causes no serious problem for single negatives, but when we get a double negative, we have *embedded* one negative in another. We must skip over two negatives to get the first positive preconception, negate it, and then negate it again. If double negatives simply cancelled each other out and were always equivalent to an assertion of the preconception (as they are in two-valued logic), then we could always use this simple plan to process them. However, in natural language, double negatives are usually not meant to be meaningfully equivalent to the simple positive preconception. If they were, writers or speakers would make the simple positive statement in the first place (your cynical opinion of their pedantry notwithstanding). If negatives in natural language are informationally weaker statements than positives, double negatives are doubly weaker (or is it weaker squared?). For example, saying that one doesn't wish to deny A is not to say that one wishes to affirm A. One might wish to assert nothing at all about A. One might well question whether such statements have any value. The value, if any, lies in the encoding of expression "A." The encoding of its truth or falsity is deferred to some future time.

Double negatives (e.g., "not not A") are only one special case of the class of embedded negatives (e.g., "not [A→not B])." Even in two-valued logic this class cannot be processed simply by canceling the two negatives. In human sentence understanding, all embedded negatives are probably difficult because they must be processed from the *inside out,* starting with the most deeply embedded positive constituents and negating them as a second encoding operation, if necessary. Again, encoding an embedded negative sentence such as "not (A→not B)" would probably be quite easy if the preconception "A→not B" were already encoded in semantic memory and would become more difficult the more unfamiliar constituents there were. However, the main point is that "not B" is not as simple a constituent as "B." One cannot directly encode the constituent "not B" unless one has already encoded the constituent "B."

What kinds of constituents can be negated in natural language? In propositional logic and some formulations of predicate logic, only propositions can be negated—not concepts. If we accept the assumption that concepts can be involved in constituent implication relations, then both concepts and propositions should be negatable in semantic memory; this appears to be true (Engelkamp and Hörmann 1974).

Holyoak and Glass (1975) suggest an inference plan whereby contradiction can be used indirectly to falsify erroneous *backward implication* inferences. They assume that humans falsify a statement like "all robins are hawks" because they have directly stored the fact that "robin" and "hawks" are contradictory: "robin→not hawk" and "hawk→not robin," in present terminology. This assumption agrees with the theory of negation and contradiction presented here. Holyoak and Glass specify a *counterexample* inference plan for falsifying a backward implication like "all birds are robins" in which subjects generate (by upward coimplication links) examples of birds, getting "hawk," for example. Then they falsify the generalization "all birds are robins" by the counterexample "hawk," since "hawk→not robin." We end with the mystery with which we began. How did we acquire all these "A node" to "not B node" associations in the first place?

Disjunction

"Lila can come over either Wednesday or Thursday (as far as I'm concerned). She can't come over on Wednesday (because she has other plans). Therefore, she should come over on Thursday." I have deliberately varied this disjunctive inference from its purely logical form "p or q" and "not p" implies "q," to give a better feeling for the range of natural *disjunctive inference.* Sometimes we use disjunctive inference when we are playing the role of scientists—first determining that one of several alternatives holds, then falsifying all but one of these alternatives, and therefore concluding that the remaining alternative is true. (This is called the *method of contradiction* or *indirect proof* in mathematics.) More often, we may formulate a disjunction of alternatives on the basis of one constraint (e.g., "when I am free") and then "contradict" some of these alternatives on the basis of other constraints (e.g., "when Lila is free"). The nature of our plans for disjunctive inference are such that it is easiest to make the appropriate inference when we have two positive propositions (e.g., "I am free on Wednesday or Thursday") and an explicit negation (denial) of one of these alternatives (e.g., "Lila is not free on Wednesday"). Implicit negation of one alternative by a positive proposition (e.g., "Lila has to study Wednesday") is more difficult to use to make disjunctive inferences (Johnson-Laird and Tridgell 1972). This finding might superficially appear to be in conflict with the results Clark (1974) obtained for a different inference task, in which implicit negatives (negatives stated in a positive form like "absent") were easier to understand than explicit negatives (like "is not present"). There is no conflict, however. The proper conclusion is not that positives are always easier to understand than negatives. This depends on the task. For the initial assertion of a proposition, positives (e.g., "the red dot is present") or implicit negatives (e.g., "the red dot is absent") are easier to understand than explicit negatives (e.g., "the red dot is not present"). In denying a previously stated proposition, however, explicit negatives are easier to understand than implicit negatives or positives. The most difficult condition for disjunctive inference occurs when one of the alternatives of the disjunction is negative, and this negative alternative is then contradicted (e.g., "Lila will go to the fair or she will not come over on Thursday. She will come over on Thursday. Therefore, she will go to the fair") (Johnson-Laird and Tridgell 1972; Roberge 1976).

In ordinary mathematical logic, disjunction is inclusive ("p or q" allows the possibility that both "p" and "q" are true). Occasionally humans use inclusive disjunction in natural semantic reasoning. More often they use *exclusive disjunction* ("p" or "q" but not both). Both inclusive and exclusive disjunction permit the *disjunctive inference* previously discussed: ("p or q" and "not p") implies "q." Exclusive disjunction permits another kind of inference: ("p or q" and "p") implies "not q." People appear to be at least as efficient at drawing such *exclusive disjunctive inferences* as they are at drawing the more general *disjunctive inferences* (Roberge 1976).

Quantifiers

I noted previously that when the proposition "birds can fly" is stored in semantic memory, it means something logically equivalent to "most birds can fly." Similarly, when "fish can swim" is directly stored in semantic memory, it does not mean "all fish can swim" (though I believe this is true). Verifying an unquantified statement like "fish can swim" is a simple direct-access recognition process. Verifying a quantified statement like "all fish can swim" requires an inference plan in which one coimplies (associates) from "fish" and from "can't swim" to see if any example of "fish" exists in one's semantic memory with the property "can't swim." If no counterexample emerges, one responds "true" (as far as one's knowledge goes). To verify that "some fish can swim," one might just rely on direct access to the proposition "fish can swim." Or one might use the general *"some" inference plan* in which one coimplies from "fish" and "can swim" to determine if there is an example of "fish" that has the property "can swim" (e.g., a node representing "sharks can swim"). The inference plans for "some" and "all" are identical except that for "some X are P" one coimplies from "X" and "P," and for "all X are P" one coimplies from "X" and "not P." The yes-no decisions are also reversed if an intersecting node is found. Most theories of the verification of quantified statements have assumed some type of serial search of semantic memory, and this assumption is still tenable (Meyer 1970; Glass, Holyoak, and O'Dell 1974; Holyoak and Glass 1975; Rips 1975). However, as illustrated here, a plan-guided direct-access theory is also tenable. And as I have already noted, a direct-access theory is more parsimonious because considerable direct access to concepts in semantic memory is necessary to be consistent with the observed speed of retrieval, verification, and thought generation.

Quantifier inferences produce yet another example of the difference between ordinary mathematical logic and human logic. In mathematical logic, "some" includes "all" as a possibility. In most cases when humans say "some," they mean to exclude "all" as a possibility. In natural language, "some birds can fly" is virtually always taken to mean also that "some birds cannot fly"—otherwise the person would have made the unquantified statement "birds can fly" or the stronger quantified statement "all birds can fly." If we do not instruct subjects on the mathematically "correct" meaning for "some," they will make errors in logical reasoning tasks for this reason (Wason and Johnson-Laird 1972, pp. 143–44; Revlis 1975).

Linear Orderings: Transitive Relations

If "John is taller than Bill" and "Bill is taller than Sam," then "John is taller than Sam." It is still an open question whether inferences that involve transitive relations are performed in verbal semantic memory or in a nonverbal image memory. In image memory each item in a linear ordering may have a certain absolute size, and we may compare these sizes in the same way as we compare perceptual images to determine which is taller, wider, and so on. One piece of evidence that initially appeared to support some type of processing of this sort is the *semantic distance effect:* we make decisions regarding remote pairs in a linear ordering (e.g., "Is a tiger bigger than a flea?") faster than we make decisions regarding close pairs (e.g., "Is a tiger bigger than a lion?"). However, the semantic distance effect is also obtained for comparisons on dimensions that are not ordinarily considered imageable, such as intelligence or ferocity. Thus the semantic distance effect does not provide a basis for deciding whether the locus of such linear-order judgments is verbal or nonverbal. Whatever the modality, it appears that linear-ordering decisions are based on direct retrieval of the relevant attributes (length, intelligence, ferocity, and so on), followed by a comparison that is highly similar, if not identical, to perceptual psychophysical comparisons. Another intriguing (but unexplained) finding for linear-order judgments is the *semantic congruity effect:* we choose the larger of two large objects or the smaller of two small objects faster than we choose the smaller of two large objects or the larger of two small objects. The same holds true for other dimensions (Potts 1972, 1974; Moyer 1973; Paivio 1975; Moyer and Bayer 1976; Holyoak and Walker 1976; Riley 1976; Banks and Flora 1977; Kerst and Howard 1977; Lawson 1977).

The cognitive efficiency of a *property abstraction and comparison* process for linear-order judgments is easy to demonstrate. See if you can generate a rank ordering of 30 or more different entities of decreasing size, from "the universe," "our galaxy," . . . down to "electrons" and "neutrinos." If you had to store directly the propositions "X_i is larger than X_j" or "X_i is smaller than X_j" for all i $\neq$ j, you would have to store $30 \cdot 29 = 870$ propositions to be able to answer every paired-comparison question just for these 30 entities. (It would be 435 propositions if you could infer "X_i is larger than X_j" from "X_j is smaller than X_i.") If you store the size of each entity in some way and then make relative size judgments by a psychophysical comparison process (property abstraction and comparison), you need store only 30 propositions. A similar efficiency is obtained by storing the 29 adjacent paired comparisons, "X_i is larger than X_{i-1}" (for all i) then inferring that X_i is larger than X_j (and for all j $<$ i), by means of the transitive property of the relation "is larger than" (if "A is larger than B" and "B is larger than C," then "A is larger than C"). At first glance the semantic distance effect suggests that we should use the property abstraction and comparison process for paired comparisons, because a *transitive inference process* would seem likely to give either an inverse distance effect, if the combination of adjacent relations was performed serially, or no distance effect, if the combination was performed in parallel. Indeed, Hayes-Roth and Hayes-Roth (1975) taught subjects a complex partial ordering of items (B $>$ J $>$ H $>$ F $>$ Z $>$ P $>$ C; K $>$ H $>$ D $>$ S, F $>$ T, and Z $>$ V) by means of adjacent relations only. Then subjects were required to combine adjacent pair relations to answer questions concerning remote pairs. An inverse distance effect was obtained—namely, verifying "J $>$ H" was faster than verifying "J $>$ F," and so on. This indicates that under these conditions subjects used a transitive inference process, and that there was some degree of seriality to the processing.

However, a theoretical transitive inference process can probably be devised that would yield the more common semantic distance effect. One such process is parallel retrieval of all of the indirect associative chains and direct links between remote items. Such a scheme would give remote items a higher asymptotic strength. This higher strength corresponds to the fact that remote items are, by definition, more discriminable on the ordering dimension than adjacent items. With parallel processing of divergent links and chain parallel processing, there might be only slightly slower dynamics for remote versus adjacent paired comparisons. Speed-accuracy trade-off functions would then show slightly slower processing dynamics for remote versus adjacent pairs. But with the much higher asymptote, reaction time to remote pairs could be much faster than to adjacent pairs, with comparable or even superior accuracy for remote pairs. Thus it is not possible at present to conclude that the ordinary semantic distance effect supports a property abstraction and comparison process, as opposed to a transitive inference process, for linear-order judgments.

PROBLEM SOLVING

There's problem solving and then there's problem solving. If I solve an elementary algebra problem, such as $4x - 3 = 2x + 9$, for the value of x, I am engaged in more than a single elementary act of inference, so the task is more complex than either rote retrieval or verifying that "raccoons have hearts." A conscious sequence of at least three (and probably more) steps is required (get the x terms on one side, get the number terms on the other side, divide by the coefficient of x). Such elementary equation solving is for me a skilled act for which I follow a well-learned plan. It is what Wertheimer (1945) calls *reproductive thinking,* not *productive thinking.* It is not *problem solving* in the sense in which I shall use the term here. Any problem that falls into a class for which one has already learned a solution method (algorithm) requires *computational plans* but not *problem-solving plans.* Solving a new type of problem the first time may use problem-solving plans, if one figures out the solution method for oneself to some extent. However, the adequacy of problem-solving plans differs enormously for different individuals. Young children's problem-solving plans are the least adequate, and teachers cannot take the time to have every child re-create the solution for every type of problem that he must learn to solve if he is to receive an adequate education. Thus we are often taught the plans for solving large classes of problems without ever having to use any general problem-solving plan (metaplan) to figure out such computational plans for ourselves.

So long as we are given instruction on general problem-solving plans and enough problems to figure out for ourselves, unaided or guided only by hints, our mental development is not damaged by being told directly how to solve a lot of problems. Indeed, the purpose of education is to transmit knowledge so that each individual won't have to rediscover it all over again for himself, and this applies to both procedural and declarative knowledge (plans and principles). Unfortunately, despite much wailing and gnashing of teeth over the desirability of teaching problem solving and letting students discover methods and principles for themselves, many students never develop their problem-solving skills. In part I blame the wailers. They are often unrealistic in expecting *all* education to be self-discovery. Pure self-discovery is much too slow, and it has been repeatedly shown to fail when it is used to the exclusion of direct instruction (hints and other guidance are direct instruction on one part of a problem). Furthermore, there is every reason to believe that problem-solving plans can be directly taught, just like other plans, and we have hundreds of millions of walking examples of the ineffectiveness of letting them just grow, like weeds.

However, the main reason we have not provided decent instruction and guided experience in problem solving is that until very recently we have not understood the nature of problems and the nature of problem-solving plans. Now, thanks to the insights of the mathematician Polya (1957, 1962), and to research in artificial intelligence and computer simulation of human thinking, especially research by Newell and Simon (1972), we are beginning to remedy this situation. Insights concerning semantic memory will increasingly be combined with insights concerning problem solving to provide a unified theory of thinking. The ultimate educational consequences of this theory will be profound. Such expectations have been voiced before without the expected results. This time it is true—we really have acquired useful knowledge about how the mind works—but I wouldn't blame you for being skeptical. However, it is unrealistic to expect any kind of engineering to produce great new inventions overnight. Practical applications of science require creative problem solving. They do not follow automatically from the development of a scientific base.

Let us examine the scientific base that has been developed so far in the area of problem solving. It has three parts: a theory of problems; a theory of search reduction methods (plans) for problem solving; and a theory of the representation (coding) of information in problems and problem solving. This last is part of the general theory of semantic memory.

Problem Theory

As initially presented, a problem has three components: *givens, operations,* and a *goal.* The *givens* are the declarative (propositional) knowledge you use in attempting to attain the goal. The *operations* are the procedural knowledge you use. The *goal* is some additional proposition (or propositions) that you add to the given declarative knowledge by using the allowable operations. For example, consider this algebra story problem: "John is twice as old as Harry was five years ago. Nineteen years from now Harry will be twice as old as John is now. How old is John now?" The givens are the two statements that relate John's and Harry's ages plus all of your knowledge concerning the mathematics of integers. The operations must be supplied from your semantic memory. They include representing sentences as equations, adding the same quantity to both sides of an equation, dividing both sides by the same (nonzero) quantity, and so on. The goal is to complete the proposition "John is _____ years old." This is a degenerate (trivial) problem for anyone who has mastered the calculative plans of elementary algebra (including those for translating sentences into equations). However, because it is simple and familiar, it makes a good example problem to illustrate the basics of problem theory.

A *solution* of a problem is a sequence of propositions, each of which is derived by allowable operations from given or previously derived propositions and which terminates with the goal proposition. Here is one solution to the example problem:

(1) $J = 2(H - 5)$ where J is John's age now and H is Harry's age now.
(2) $H + 19 = 2J$.
(3) $H = 2J - 19$.
(4) $J = 2(2J - 19) - 10$.
(5) $J = 4J - 48$.
(6) $48 = 3J$.
(7) $J = 16$.

A *problem state* is a set of propositions obtained by applying allowable operations to given or previously derived propositions. Any problem state that includes the goal proposition is a terminal state. The problem state achieved in each of the seven steps shown above is the set of *all* of the propositions derived up to and including that step. So a description of the problem state achieved by step 3 would be: the problem as given plus $J = 2(H - 5)$, $H + 19 = 2J$, and $H = 2J - 19$.

We can represent all of the possible sequences of operations one might perform in attempting to solve a problem in the form of a *problem tree*. A problem tree starts from a single node representing one's state of knowledge at the beginning of the problem. This is called the given state. Each branch from that beginning node represents an allowable operation one might perform to change one's state. This gives rise to a new set of state nodes from each of which a new set of branches arises representing all the allowable operations that could be performed on that state, and so on. See figure 12.2 for a hypothetical problem with four alternative operations that could be applied at each state. In virtually any real problem there are many more possible operations than this—often an infinite number. The number of possible operations sometimes differs for different states. Often this number increases the farther along one has proceeded in solving a problem, because there is more information to which to apply the operations. One of the basic difficulties in problem solving is posed by the enormous number of possible operations sequences. In most problems only a tiny fraction of these operations sequences will lead to the goal in any reasonable time. But how to find

Beginning State

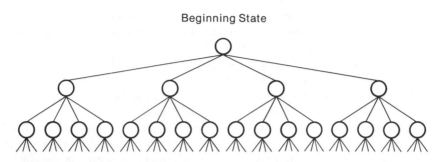

Fig. 12.2 Problem tree representing all the possible alternative sequences of operations, starting from the given state, that might be searched in order to find the goal state. In this case there were just four alternative operations at each state, but in most problems there are many more. Note that the number of paths (operation sequences) grows enormously (geometrically or exponentially) as the sequence lengthens.

this tiny fraction? We must use intelligent problem-solving methods that entail trying out the likelier possibilities first, even if such *heuristic methods* do not always work. This, of course, is what intelligent human or computer problem solvers do. They guide search by using either *search reduction methods* —which prune large problem trees in clever ways—or *representation methods* —which code (or recode) problems so as to replace large problem trees with small ones that are nevertheless equivalent to the large trees with respect to solving the given problem.

Search Reduction Methods

Equivalent operation sequences. In many problems there are operations that can be performed in more than one order and still produce the same state. In other problems there are inverse operations, which wipe out the effect of having applied a previous operation. And in many problems more than one sequence of operations may well produce the same problem state. If you can classify operation sequences into equivalence classes, you need only investigate one member from each class. If you cannot recognize the equivalence of certain operation sequences in the beginning, try to recognize when you have reached the same state you were in before. You can then heuristically terminate that line of attack on the problem on the grounds that it did not lead to a solution the last time. That is, if you can recognize equivalent states, you can avoid *going around in circles* and get out of the loop by attempting to do something different (Wickelgren 1974c, pp. 46–66).

State evaluation. This is perhaps the most frequently used problem-solving method. It works as follows. Start from the state you are at. Evaluate the alternative states you could reach in one step by performing different operations. This evaluation is a measure of how close (similar) each state is to the goal state. Now choose to perform an operation that brings you closer to the goal. This choice is based on the dimensions you used to evaluate the similarity of each state to the goal state. For example, if I'm trying to drive to some highly visible landmark and I don't know how to get there, I will probably choose roads that head most directly toward that landmark from my present location. This is the fastest way to reduce my distance from the goal. Of course, my choices may well prove erroneous. They may lead to dead ends or go off in wrong directions later on. However, the state evaluation method does order search in an intelligent way. Its adequacy depends on the dimensions one chooses to evaluate the states.

State evaluation is helpful in the early stages of learning a new computational algorithm. An example is the algorithm used to solve elementary algebra problems (e.g., $9x - 8 = 4x + 12$). Since the goal is of the form $x = N$, where N is some number, one should choose an operation that reduces the difference between the given equation ($9x - 8 = 4x + 12$) and the partially specified goal equation ($x = N$). This means that one should do the addition ($+ 8$ to both sides) or subtraction ($- 4x$ from both sides) before the division, for example, since dividing both sides by any number will still produce an equation of the form $N_1x + N_2 = N_3x + N_4$. This is just as dissimilar from the goal as the given equation (two x-terms instead of one, two number-terms instead of one). When one has mastered elementary algebra, one can rip off the operations in the calculative plan automatically without using any general problem-solving plan. But when you are still somewhat unfamiliar with specific calculative plans, general problem-solving methods can help you to learn how to solve a class of problems (Wickelgren 1974c, pp. 67–90).

Working backward.   In some problems it is easier to start at the goal and work back toward the given state than it is to start at the given state and work forward. Nim games provide a good example.

Consider a Nim game in which two players take turns removing either 1, 2, or 3 coins from a pile of 11 coins. The winner is the one who takes the last coin. How many coins should the first player take from the original pile of 11 coins, and how should he play thereafter so as to guarantee a win?

Go to the goal, which is to be the player whose turn it is and to be faced with one, two, or three coins on the table. Now work backward. How many coins would you want to leave your opponent on his prior turn to guarantee that, no matter whether he took one, two, or three coins, you would still have one, two, or three coins left on the table on your turn? Clearly you want to leave him with exactly four coins. Then, no matter what he does, you will still have one, two, or three coins left to take. (If he takes one, you take three and win; if he takes two, you take two and win; if he takes three, you take one and win.) Now work backward again from this subgoal. How many coins should you leave your opponent on his next to last turn to guarantee that you will be able to leave him exactly four coins on his last turn? Clearly, you want to leave him with exactly eight coins. Then if he takes one coin, you take three and leave him four coins. If he takes two coins, you take two, and if he takes three coins, you take one. Now you can achieve this second subgoal of leaving your opponent eight coins by taking three coins from the original eleven on your first turn.

Note that for most problems it is probably best to work forward (though no matter which direction you work in, it is almost always important to analyze the goal in some way). However, whenever the goal seems to have much more information in it than the givens, and when the allowable operations are reversible (work equally well in either direction), working backward will probably produce the answer faster (Wickelgren 1974c, pp. 137–51).

Subgoals. Probably the most powerful search reduction method is defining the subgoals that break up a problem into subproblems, each of which is much simpler to solve than the original whole problem. Defining one subgoal along the solution path to the goal breaks the original problem into two subproblems. These subproblems consist of getting from the givens to the subgoal and then from the subgoal to the goal. If one defines subgoals that have a high probability of being on a solution path in the problem tree, the search is greatly reduced. The reasons are explained by Newell, Shaw, and Simon (1962) in one of the finest papers ever written on problem solving (also see Wickelgren 1974c, pp. 91–108).

We use the subgoal method all the time (though many people would use it oftener and more effectively if they understood it better). For example, if you want to wax your hardwood floor, what do you do? First, you acquire the floor cleaner and wax and any necessary tools (mop, sponge, polisher). Second, you remove the furniture from the part of the floor you're going to do first. Third, you clean the floor and let it dry. Fourth, you apply the wax and polish it. Each of these four steps is a subgoal. Many tasks seem difficult until we think how to break them up into parts. Then they seem easy.

The subgoal method can be used to solve a system of two equations with two variables (e.g., $x + y = 12$, $2x - y = 9$). We set the subgoal of determining the value of one of the variables (e.g., x). Then we look for a way to solve that subproblem (e.g., by adding the two equations to each other to get rid of one variable (y) and obtain $3x = 21$, from which we get $x = 7$). Having achieved the subgoal, we set about solving for the value of the other variable to achieve the final goal (e.g., by substituting into the first equation to get $7 + y = 12$, therefore $y = 5$).

Representation and Understanding

One of my favorite puzzle problems is the notched checkerboard whose diagonally opposite corner squares have been removed (fig. 12.3). You start with a supply of dominoes, each of which covers exactly two squares. The problem is to decide whether or not 31 such dominoes can be placed so as to cover the 62 remaining squares of the checkerboard, and to prove your answer one way or the other. This problem is fun, so you might stop for awhile and try to solve it.

This is an insight problem, which means that once you get the key idea, you've essentially solved it. In other words, the problem can be solved in a very few steps once you have represented the relevant information in the correct way. Actually I've already helped you to solve the problem by presenting the notched board of 62 squares in a checkerboard coloring pattern. The problem has the same answer whether or not you color the squares in this way, but the checkerboard coloring makes it much easier to get the relevant insight, which is that a domino must always cover exactly one white square and one black square. Thus 31 dominoes cover 31 white squares and 31 black squares. But the notched checkerboard in figure 12.3 has 32 white

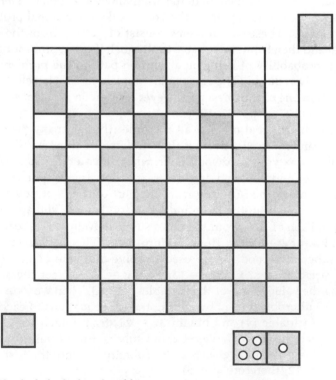

Fig. 12.3 Notched-checkerboard problem.

squares and only 30 black squares (since both of the removed squares were black). Thus it is impossible to cover the remainder of the board with 31 dominoes.

Any problem requires the problem solver to represent the information in some way in his head (possibly using auxiliary memory devices such as a pencil and paper to draw diagrams or write equations). Some representations are clumsy to work with in the sense that they generate problem trees that are much larger than necessary, and the principles for ordering search through these trees are obscure. Some representations leave out information that is essential or nearly essential to a solution. This often happens when people try to solve the notched-checkerboard problem. They totally ignore the fact that each domino must cover two squares, one of odd and one of even "parity" with respect to some origin square.

As Greeno (1973, 1977) and Hayes and Simon (1974, 1976) have emphasized, representing the information in a problem is a process of understanding the problem in much the same way as we understand any other paragraph-sized chunk of text in semantic memory (also Simon and Hayes 1976). We want to represent all of the relevant concepts in the problem and all of the relevant relationships (among concepts) in propositions (such as equations) or in diagrams (images). The richer and more accurate the representation of the concepts and relations in the problem, the greater the understanding of the problem. Problems usually also contain concepts and relations that are irrelevant to their solution, and we are forever making judgments of relevance. The first place in problem solving is to represent (understand) the givens and the goal. Sometimes it's best to focus first on the givens, sometimes on the goal, sometimes on both. In any case, some representation of the problem is logically necessary in order to generate the problem tree of alternative operation sequences in the first place. Hence some representation must precede the use of search reduction methods.

Understanding the givens and operations.   Representing the given information (including both givens and operations) is not an all-or-nothing process. Indeed, the entire problem-solving process consists of expanding your understanding of the relations inherent in the given information by means of perceptual recognition and inference. So before you rush off to try to achieve the goal, it sometimes pays just to think about what you can say based on the given information, whether or not what you say is relevant to the goal. Noticing that a domino covers one black square and one white square in the notched-checkerboard problem is a good example of the useful insights that this method sometimes (but not always) affords (Duncker 1945; Wickelgren 1974c, pp. 21–36).

Understanding the goal.   Sometimes you should focus first on enriching your understanding of the goal. Whenever you use the method of working backward, you are doing this. In other cases you don't actually work backward from the goal towards the givens—you just think about what the goal means and try to generate a richer representation of it. One good example of this is provided by the solution to the following problem: Can two triangles be noncongruent if five of their six parts (three angles and three sides) are equal? This is one of those problems where there are no givens specific to the problem. The givens are all the axioms and the theorems of plane geometry. The specifics are all in the goal, so you just about have to focus on it. Assume that you have two triangles like the ones the problem specifies. What could you infer? First, their three sides cannot all be equal. If they were, the triangles would be congruent by a theorem of plane geometry. Therefore, they must have three equal angles and two equal sides. The equal sides must be noncorresponding—opposite different angles—otherwise the triangles would again be congruent. The rest of the solution to this problem is a little involved, so we'll skip it, but my point is that a problem like this can be solved entirely by drawing inferences from the goal (Wickelgren 1974c, pp. 36–45).

Another good example of the importance of understanding the goal occurs in design problems. An architect designing a house, for example, must first generate detailed specifications of the properties the customer wants the finished house to have. A house with these specifications is the goal. In many mathematical problems the goal is, in one sense, completely specified, though our understanding of the implications of this goal may be incomplete as we begin work on the problem. In most practical (e.g., design or engineering) problems the goal is *not* completely specified beforehand. We have a general idea of some of the properties we want the final product to have, but as we work on the problem, we must specify many more properties if we want to be at all sure that the final product will be satisfactory. As you know very well, many of life's problems consist largely of specifying what you want to achieve.

Contradiction.   The method of contradiction is used on problems that have a small set of alternative answers, only one of which can be correct. The most important use of this method is *indirect proof* of theorems in mathematics. In indirect proof you assume that the theorem is false and derive a contradiction from this assumption. Indirect proof is also used to answer multiple-choice tests. Often it's faster to see if you can contradict all but one of the alternatives in a multiple-choice problem than it is to derive the answer from the information in the problem and only then look to see which alternative answer (if any) matches your own answer (Wickelgren 1974c, pp. 109–36).

Understanding a problem.   There is often much more to be learned from a problem than the minimum necessary to get a solution. As Duncker (1945) and Greeno (1977) point out, one may understand why each step of a solution is correct without having represented the higher-order relations that chunk steps into larger groups (which achieve various subgoals). Without such higher-order chunking, solutions that consist of a long series of individual steps seem terribly complex, convey little understanding, are almost impossible to remember, and have little beneficial transfer to the solution of related problems. My favorite characterization of such narrow individual-step understanding is the *uh-huh mathematician,* who says *uh-huh* as he verifies each line in a proof without understanding the subgoal structure of the proof. It is all too common for students to achieve only *uh-huh* understanding of mathematical proofs, for unfortunately that is often all that mathematics books, courses, and teachers attempt to convey. You're supposed to develop mathematical intuition (read that as "understanding") on your own—by osmosis or something.

Analogy. Whenever possible, we look for some similarity between the problem we are currently attempting to solve and some problem we have solved before. Recognizing that problems are similar is part of the process of understanding a problem. When we analyze a problem as being similar (partly analogous) to some prior problem, we think of using search reduction methods similar to those we used before. When the objects in the current problem are similar or identical to those in a prior problem (as in two linear-equation-solving problems or two compound-interest problems), there is a high probability that we will make reasonably successful use of analogy in problem solving. Analogy can also be used when the objects in two problems are completely different, but the relations between them are identical or similar. However, we are far less likely to recognize analogies in this case (Reed, Ernst, and Banerji 1974; Wickelgren 1974c, pp. 152–57).

Similar problems and special case. Often it helps to pose a simpler related problem or a special case of the more general problem. Many of the ideas one gets for representing information in the simpler problem will generally apply to the more complex problem, and often some of the search reduction methods will apply as well. For example, consider the problem of determining which player can force a win in the following game:

Two players take turns placing one of a set of poker chips anywhere on a circular table in such a way that the chip doesn't stick out over the edge and doesn't overlap another chip. The one who is last able to place a chip on the table is the winner. Assuming that the table is big enough to hold one or more chips, which player is the winner—the one who plays first or the one who plays second?

Consider the special case of a table so small that it will hold only one chip. Clearly, the first player is the winner. Now consider a slightly larger table. A chip played in the exact center of this table may prevent other chips from being played anywhere around it. If the table is just large enough to put one circle of chips around the center chip, then for every place the second player can put his chip, there must be a symmetrically opposite spot for the first player to put a chip. Hence the first player can force a win. The understanding of a general problem that is achieved by understanding a special case is much like the understanding of a general principle that is achieved by understanding a single example (Wickelgren 1974c, pp. 157–80).

Functional fixedness and set. Experimental studies of problem solving have served primarily to tell us some of the methods people use to represent information and reduce search in seeking solutions to problems. Virtually all of this information has been gained by observation and logical analysis of problems and problem solving. Most of these methods are as applicable to artificial intelligence as to human problem solving. We know very little that is uniquely human about human problem solving. One exception is the work on functional fixedness and mental set in problem solving by Duncker (1945), Luchins (1942), and others. The basic idea is that knowledge gained from past experience—which can be very helpful, as in the method of analogy—can also be dysfunctional if it directs our thinking in an inappropriate way. For example, Duncker gave subjects some candles, some tacks, some matches, and three boxes. The goal was somehow to mount three candles vertically on the face of a door to serve as lamps. The solution was to use the tacks to mount the boxes on the door and use the matches to melt some wax to attach the candles to the boxes. In the functional fixedness condition the normal function of the boxes as containers was emphasized by putting the candles in the first box, the matches in the second box, and the tacks in the third box. In the control condition the boxes were empty, and the candles, matches, and tacks were lying loose on the table. Subjects were less likely to think of the unusual use for the box when its normal use was emphasized. A variety of other practical problems have demonstrated the same human vulnerability to functional fixedness. Functional fixedness is more generally a *mental set* to persist in using a representation of the givens and operations in a problem, even though this representation is inadequate. Finally, as one might expect, such mental sets have less effect on problem solving the more time elapses between the experience that established the set and the problem-solving activity in question (Birch and Rabinowitz 1951; Adamson 1952; Adamson and Taylor 1954; Glucksberg 1964; Glucksberg and Weisburg 1966; Glucksberg and Danks 1968).

Incubation. In the alleged phenomenon of incubation the solution to a problem comes to light after an interpolated period of time during which no conscious work is done on the problem. There are countless anecdotal reports of incubation, many by highly creative thinkers. Unfortunately, as Olton points out, there is no consistent experimental support for incubation. Failures to replicate are the rule, not the exception, in incubation research.

When conscious time spent working on a problem is held constant, interpolated delays have not consistently benefited problem solving. As Olton so cleverly puts it, it is still very questionable whether incubation is the *pause that refreshes.* Incubation anecdotes may be only chance occurrences. After all, who is going to report (or even take note of) all the times when he failed to solve a problem after a period of incubation? However, as Olton also emphasizes, it would be premature (and probably wrong) to assert that incubation does not occur. If incubation is a real phenomenon, there are a number of plausible cognitive mechanisms: dissipation of fatigue, dissipation of deleterious mental sets, beneficial new learning that occurs during the delay, and the presence of new cues that may cause new ideas to be retrieved from memory. The most exotic possibility is unconscious problem solving during the incubation period, but there isn't a shred of evidence to support it (Olton and Johnson 1976; Olton 1976; Posner 1973, pp. 169–75; Wickelgren 1974*c,* pp. 65–66).

CREATIVITY

The jumping-off point for discussing creativity, in my opinion, is Campbell's (1960) thesis that the basis of all creative accomplishment is a *blind variation and selective retention process* analogous to random mutation and natural selection in biological evolution. Virtually everyone acknowledges that chance plays an important role in creativity, though as Pasteur noted, "In the field of observation, chance favors only the prepared mind." In any case, there appear to be two critical phases to the creative process: *generation of ideas* and *evaluation of ideas.* Chance plays a role in both, through environmental variation beyond our control. By accident you may be exposed to two ideas in close proximity that together produce a new idea. Partly due to chance variation in your past experience, you possess the knowledge in your semantic memory to recognize the value of that new idea. In some ultimate sense, as Campbell asserts, perhaps your creativity (and everything else about you) can be attributed to chance variation in your heredity and environment. However, there is also a *here and now* perspective in which one can say that your getting a creative idea depends both on chance variation in current stimuli and on the nature of your mind (in particular, of your semantic memory).

Evaluation of Ideas

As Pasteur's remark suggests, the ability to recognize a valuable new idea is as important as, or perhaps more important than, the ability to generate new ideas. A creative idea either in art or in science is much more than just the visual or verbal vehicle that may be the first bare expression of that idea. Ideas obtain much, if not all, of their value from their relations to other ideas. Consider the following example. Lucky Jack generates some sentence or produces some work of art for a mundane, narrow reason. Jill is, by chance, exposed to this original product. She recognizes its relation to all sorts of other ideas—perceiving its value to an extent far beyond Jack's meager perception. Jill discusses the idea extensively, communicating its profound ramifications to the world and charitably giving credit to Jack for originally generating a physical expression of the idea that may still seem ideal to convey the central meaning. Who deserves the greater credit for creativity, Jack or Jill? I'd give it to Jill, if I could know that Jack had little conception of the significance of his product when he generated it. In fact, since not everyone is equally articulate, we rarely know for sure what was in someone's mind when he said something. Assignment of intellectual credit aside, the point is that evaluation of an idea is perhaps the most important component of creativity. The present view of evaluation is that it is a generative process—the generation of lots of associations to other ideas.

The ability to evaluate (develop) an idea is obviously enhanced by the possession of related knowledge. However, the scholarly approach of amassing a great deal of knowledge in close to its original form does not seem to encourage creativity. Good scholarship demands that we record fairly faithfully exactly what each person thought at any given time—the wheat and the chaff. Furthermore, this knowledge must be heavily contextualized by propositional modifiers, such as "In 1900, Thorndike thought that. . . ." Our semantic memory capacity is limited in learning, storage, and retrieval. The more we concentrate on such heavily contextualized (specific) concepts and propositions, the less capacity we will have available to learn general principles and questions that crosscut different areas and perspectives. These principles and questions relate knowledge from different areas; they are the sine qua non of the creative evaluation of ideas. The more your knowledge is integrated (organized) into one or a few schemata, the better you can recognize a valuable idea by generating its relations to previously stored ideas (generating its intensional meaning). Scholarly knowledge tends to be highly compartmentalized into many separate schemata for different areas, thinkers, and time periods. The existence of such a multiplicity of scholarly schemata does not *logically* preclude the existence of integrative creative schemata, but I suspect that it tends *psychologically* to preclude them. This effect must be due to limited capacity, as well as to differences in what scholars and creators attend to in learning and retrieval.

The tendency to *ask questions* is equally important to creativity. Asking a good specific question (that you cannot now get an answer to) formulates explicitly what you have already learned about a problem and directs your attention towards relevant additional knowledge. A good question also describes properties by which you can in the future recognize the answer to the question. Storing such questions in your semantic memory alerts you to relevant knowledge that may become available to you in the future and records your prior thinking about the problem in a way that permits you to combine separately experienced but related propositions into a creative new idea. Suppose that you store a proposition like "What thing with properties a, b, and c would explain x, y, and z?" Later on, if you encounter something with properties a, b, and c, you can activate this previously stored proposition by association to the a, b, and c nodes. This permits you to generate an idea from the combination of the two separated experiences that would never have occurred to you if you had not stored your partial knowledge and asked a question about the relevant unknown knowledge. This example also suggests some of the properties of a good question. A good question specifies the properties of the desired answer (e.g., Is there an entity with properties a, b, and c?). A good question is related to some prior knowledge base in a fairly specific way, so that the answer to the question will have a rich set of relations to preexisting concepts and propositions in semantic memory (e.g., will explain x, y, and z). In the last chapter we saw how much of the structure of the propositional answer to a question is already established in our semantic memory by encoding a question. Here we note that a question has the important capacity to integrate partial knowledge obtained at different times. Asking questions *now* is the basis for obtaining creative answers in the *future*— often in the form of insight (aha!) experiences.

Generation of Ideas

You can get ideas in either of two ways. You can read or listen to other people's ideas and let them combine with your ideas and especially with your previously stored questions. Or you can just dredge up several ideas from your own semantic memory and play with them in your mind and on paper to see what new combinations of thoughts you can generate this time that you never generated before. The former method usually works better. However, it's probably best to combine both methods—working on a problem in your own mind and giving yourself extra stimulating input whenever you find the flow of ideas slowing to a trickle. The essential thing in generating ideas is to spend time at it—thousands of hours of creating your own little ideas, questions, and integrative schemata. Campbell (1960, p. 393) emphasizes ". . . the tremendous number of nonproductive thought trials" that precede genuine accomplishment. I believe that the thousands of little ideas and inadequate ideas we generate do help prepare the way for the occasional major creative idea. Edison is supposed to have evaluated his progress on some invention by saying that he now knew a hundred ways that wouldn't work. I think (as did Edison) that this constitutes important intellectual progress. It helps us to understand the constraints on our problem and to recognize a solution when we encounter it. To generate and evaluate hundreds of possibilities takes time. If you don't put in that time, it is unlikely (though not impossible) that you will ever create an important idea.

Since reading and listening to other people's ideas are important sources of creative stimulation, it is critical to distinguish between creative and scholarly reading and listening. If you read and listen just to remember someone else's ideas, rather than to create your own ideas (by asking and answering your own questions), then you are *not* putting in creative work time. Active, idiosyncratic processing of input according to your own integrative schemata —not just other people's schemata—is necessary for creative accomplishment. This is so because other people's schemata have usually already been mined for most of the ideas in them.

All thinking, creative or scholarly, requires selectivity in processing. The selectivity is determined by the nature of the schemata being used. Selectivity is necessary to avoid what Crutchfield (1961) so aptly calls *mental dazzle,* the confusion that results from trying to generate ideas from too much information at one time. Good ideas will eventually relate to many other ideas, but because we have only a limited capacity for simultaneous activation of thoughts, we can only use a very small number of old ideas to generate new ideas at any given moment.

Some seemingly perpetual students delay their entry into creative thinking out of the mistaken belief that one must know a lot to create a new idea. They are partly right, but they are unlikely to become creative following the *learn first, create later* philosophy. First, as I have just said, a single act of idea generation does not require a large knowledge base. Indeed, only a few (often just one or two) prior thoughts *can* be used to generate from at any one time. Second, the advantages (and they are substantial) of knowing a lot lie (1) in the number of different combinations of ideas you can generate from; (2) in your critical capacity to evaluate ideas; and probably (3)in the fact that you have learned plans for selecting combinations that are likely to generate valuable new ideas. However, if you defer creative idea generation until you know a lot, you build a semantic memory filled only with old ideas. And most of the combinatorial potential of old ideas has been used up by others. Only if you strike out on your own and begin mixing your new ideas with other people's ideas will you have much chance of eventually creating a big new idea.

Many creative ideas are generated via the question-asking and answering process described above. You will recall that in this process a current thought is recognized as answering a slightly novel question you formulated earlier—perhaps much earlier. Every question you ask yourself is a finger into the unknown. The more fingers, the greater the probability of grasping something new. You often make some progress on a problem while you are in one state of mind (mental set). If you formulate a question regarding what you've learned in relation to what you still want to learn, you set the stage for later combining these thoughts with thoughts, generated in a different state of mind, that are associated to some of the nodes in the question. Of course two propositions can overlap (have concepts in common) or be more indirectly associated to each other, and by their simultaneous activation generate a new thought. But there is something open-ended about a question that enhances its ability to combine creatively with subsequently activated concepts and propositions. So to be creative, be active, but be patient. Ask questions now; the answers will usually come later. And remember Campbell's thesis— creativity is partly a statistical matter. You may have to ask a hundred questions for every exciting answer.

Can you force it? Can you sit down at your desk (or in your easy chair, your shop, your studio, your lab,), say, "Today I'm going to try to create such and such," and hope to succeed? Many highly creative thinkers and virtually all less creative thinkers say "no," but I say "yes." That is, you can force it *sometimes.* Four conditions are necessary. You must have prepared your mind with a critical mass of long-term knowledge, ideas, and questions on a particular topic. You must deliberately warm up (prime or set) your mind at the beginning of your thinking time by going over some of your previous thoughts and other people's thoughts on the matter. You must be in a suitable mood—task oriented and not distracted by other problems or worries. And you must employ creative plans for the combination of ideas. This is called *playing with ideas* or *mental gymnastics.* To some extent, creativity is natural for an associative memory. For example, if a→b and b→c, you can put these two facts together and get a→c. However, the probability of generating new worthwhile combinations of ideas can be increased substantially if the generative capacity of associative memory is guided by creative plans.

Many of these plans are essentially specific ideas about what might be related to what in a particular area. Or the idea may be about some new concept or proposition that you want to juxtapose with all the concepts and propositions you have stored as relevant to some topic. However, more general creative plans can also be profitable. In trying to generate potentially useful new concepts, you may begin with old concepts and try stripping away (*deleting*) one or more attributes that you have analyzed to obtain a more general concept. Or you may try *adding* one or more attributes to make a more specific concept. Or you may try *modifying* some attribute. Or you may try any combination of these things. To guide your concept redefinition process, it is useful to analyze the deficiencies of the old concept—its vagueness or other undesirable attributes. This will often suggest more precise definitions, or more desirable attributes, or both.

The concept of context-sensitive coding was generated in precisely this way. Lashley (1951) had pointed out that associations between phonemes could not account for our capacity to articulate the sequence of phonemes composing a word in the correct temporal order. Because each phoneme is associated to many different phonemes in long-term memory, Lashley concluded that what was deficient was the assumption that memory is associative. Because there is a mass of evidence favoring associative memory, Lashley's conclusion seemed to me to be questionable. So I asked myself an attribute-analytic question: "What other assumptions did Lashley make in the associative theory of word articulation?" One important other assumption (implicit in Lashley's formulation of the associative theory) was that phonemes were the immediate segmental constituents of words that constituted the basic units of articulation. So I analyzed the properties of phonemes to see if I could modify them to obtain a new segmental concept. This concept had to retain the desirable property of specifying one particular target position for the vocal tract (not a sequence of positions as is the case for a syllable). At the same time it must not have the undesirable associative interference property that Lashley had identified. The answer seemed to be to make the segmental units more distinctive, increasing their properties and therefore the number of different units so as to yield the correct unique association from one segmental unit to the next in a word. How could this be done? One way would be to assume that a particular phoneme had a different token node representing it in every different word in which it appeared. This seemed inelegant and ad hoc—an expensive solution with no other obvious useful properties. Was there a more elegant segmental code for words? Well, a phoneme is completely context-free—the same phoneme node is supposed to be a constituent of every word in which that phoneme appears. In the radical-token theory, a different specific token node is defined for a phoneme in every word in which it appears. The coding of that phoneme depends on its phonemic context. How about taking a less extreme degree of context-sensitivity? I knew that the acoustic (and to a lesser extent the articulatory) characteristics of many phonemes were strongly influenced by the nature of the immediately adjacent phonemes. Aha! Maybe the functional segmental units of speech were overlapping phoneme triples, for example, struck $\rightarrow$ $_\#s_t$, $_st_r$, $_tr_u$, $_ru_k$, $_uk_\#$. Such phoneme triples are sensitive to local context, but not to more remote context. The context-free phoneme concept had been modified to form the context-sensitive allophone concept. This solved the Lashley serial-order problem with an associative memory and later proved to have an enormous number of other uses.

This historical account of the generation of the context-sensitive allophone concept is probably largely fictional. I wasn't paying that much attention at the time to what I was doing before I got the insight. But I have even less faith in many similar accounts by other people. Such accounts are usually given long after the fact, and they are often given by thinkers with little or no relevant training in cognitive psychology. To describe and understand any phenomenon, one must have adequate concepts for encoding what one observes. This is equally true when it is one's own higher mental processes that one is observing. A biologist's account of his mental processes, say, is about as useful as my account of what I see when I look in a microscope—and I'll give you five guesses how useful that is.

Reports of *where* and *when* ideas came—in the tub, while asleep, etc.—probably have substantial accuracy, but they are highly selective in the direction of emphasizing the bizarre and romantic conception of creativity as a mysterious force normally buried deep in the unconscious mind, which after worrying over a problem for some time, springs forth into consciousness with the solution. What a lot of balderdash! Storing a question at one time and having a subsequent event simultaneously activate the question and provide its answer is a marvelous property of an associative memory, and this process is not understood as precisely today as it will be later. But such an insight experience is not a mystery to modern cognitive psychology that requires exotic assumptions such as unconscious mental processing. Furthermore, one can sketch quite plausible conscious thought processes (which could surely occur in a tub and possibly in a dream) that will account for the creation of new ideas. Finally, new ideas may often be generated by force through the operation of general creative plans without waiting for chance exposure to a stimulus to provide the answer and certainly without unconscious thinking. Creativity is almost certainly a learnable skill, like playing the piano. You can sit down to create ideas just as you can sit down to play a piece on the piano. But you have to know how to play. And you either have to have memorized the piece or else know how to read the sheet music.

SUMMARY

1 Most of the questions we can answer are not based on retrieval of a single stored proposition that is equivalent to the proposition partially or completely contained in the question. Rather, they require deductions from a single stored proposition or from two or more stored propositions.

2 It is worthwhile to distinguish between declarative knowledge, stored as propositions in semantic memory, and procedural knowledge, stored as plans. Plans that have a branching and looping capacity to control thinking can be encoded into associative semantic memory side by side with propositions, using a context-sensitive code that alternates action nodes and state nodes.

3 Basic semantic inferences use the automatic associative activation process, negation, and some elementary inference plans to achieve inferences. There are seven types of inferences, as follows:

Equivalence (That man is the registrar. The registrar can answer your question. Therefore, that man can answer your question.)

Implication (A pelican is a bird. A bird has wings. Therefore, a pelican has wings.)

Coimplication (A chair that tilts back is a recliner. That is a chair that tilts back. Therefore, that is a recliner.)

Contradiction (Indiana is not Illinois. Munster is in Indiana. Therefore, Munster is not in Illinois.)

Disjunction (I will either visit Maryann or I will go to Ingrid's gymnastics meet. I will not visit Maryann. Therefore, I will go to Ingrid's gymnastic meet.)

Quantification (Canaries are birds. Canaries can fly. Therefore, some birds can fly.) (X_i is a fish and X_i can swim, for all X_i. Therefore, all fish can swim.) (An ostrich is a bird. An ostrich can't fly. Therefore, not all birds can fly.)

(X_i is a fish and X_i does not have feathers, for all X_i. Therefore, no fish have feathers.)

Linear ordering (John is older than Bill. Bill is older than Sam. Therefore, John is older than Sam.)

4 Coimplication associations may be qualitatively identical to implication associations, but the existence of other excitatory and inhibitory associations in the network causes them to function differently in natural semantic inference. When these other associations do not exist in artificial inference problems, the equivalence of implies and coimplies links shows up in the form of implication reversal errors. In this kind of error, "A implies B" is interpreted to mean also "B implies A."

5 The function of negation is to deny incorrect expectations. When the positive expectation (preconception) has previously been established, negative sentences are no harder to process than affirmative sentences.

6 The simplest and most basic semantic inferences are unqualified (unquantified). Qualified inferences (for example, those in syllogistic reasoning or other predicate logic problems) require more complex inference plans.

7 Problems have three components: givens, operations, and goals. A solution to a problem is a sequence of propositions, each of which either is a given or can be derived from previous propositions by the allowable operations, terminating with the goal proposition. A problem state is the set of propositions derived up to some point in problem solving. A problem tree represents all the possible operations that might be applied to any problem state, starting from the given state.

8 The basic difficulty in problem solving is the enormously large number of alternative operation sequences to be searched for a solution. There are two types of problem-solving methods. Search reduction methods prune large problem trees in clever ways. Representation methods code (or recode) problems so as to replace large problem trees with equivalent smaller ones.

9 Search reduction methods include (a) recognizing equivalent operation sequences and equivalent states; (b) evaluating problem states and choosing operations that make maximum progress towards the goal; (c) working backward when the tree is smaller in that direction; and (d) setting subgoals that break up problems into parts.

10 Representation methods include (a) enriching your encoding of the givens, operations, and goals by drawing inferences; (b) contradiction; (c) analogy; and (d) solving simpler problems and special cases.

11 Mental sets (schemata) can sometimes be harmful as well as helpful, as when they produce functional fixedness.

12 There is no consistent experimental evidence for the value of incubation in problem solving, but if it is a real phenomenon, there are several plausible explanations. These include the dissipation of fatigue or deleterious mental sets, beneficial new learning in the interim, and the presence of new retrieval cues. There is no evidence for unconscious problem solving.

13 Chance plays a large role in creativity. So does time. It takes time to think of thousands of possibilities. If you don't put in the time, your chances are slim. As Linus Pauling put it, "The best way to have a good idea is to have lots of ideas."

14 "Chance favors the prepared mind." The ability to recognize a good idea is fundamental to creativity. This ability derives from a semantic memory with a rich store of novel integrative schemata and unanswered questions, most of them posed much earlier.

15 The scholarly approach to the acquisition of knowledge does not encourage creativity because it uses familiar schemata, and it tends to store knowledge in a highly compartmentalized manner. You can generate new ideas from very little stored knowledge. Indeed, you cannot generate ideas from more than a few stored thoughts at a time. The best way to build a creative semantic memory is to be creating new ideas and new questions while you learn. Don't wait to create until you are "ready." Waiting builds uncreative thinking habits—and that's all.

16 If you have a rich store of novel integrative schemata and unanswered questions in your semantic memory, and if you have good cognitive plans for playing with ideas, you can create ideas on demand much as you can perform any other skill.

REFERENCES

ABELES, M., AND GOLDSTEIN, M. H. 1972. Responses of single units in the primary auditory cortex of the cat to tones and to tone pairs. *Brain Research* 42:337–52.

ADAMSON, R. E. 1952. Functional fixedness as related to problem solving: a repetition of three experiments. *Journal of Experimental Psychology* 44:288–91.

ADAMSON, R. E., AND TAYLOR, D. W. 1954. Functional fixedness as related to elapsed time and set. *Journal of Experimental Psychology* 47:122–216.

AINSWORTH, W. A. 1972. Duration as a cue in the recognition of synthetic vowels. *Journal of the Acoustical Society of America* 51:648–51.

ALLARD, F., AND HENDERSON, L. 1976. Physical and name codes in auditory memory: the pursuit of an analogy. *Quarterly Journal of Experimental Psychology* 28:475–82.

ALLPORT, D. A. 1971. Parallel encoding within and between elementary stimulus dimensions. *Perception & Psychophysics* 10:104–8.

ALLPORT, D. A.; ANTONIS, B.; AND REYNOLDS, P. 1972. On the division of attention; a disproof of the single channel hypothesis. *Quarterly Journal of Experimental Psychology* 24:225–35.

ALLUISI, E. A. 1957. Conditions affecting the amount of information in absolute judgments. *Psychological Review* 64:97–103.

ALTMAN, Y. A. 1968. Are there neurons detecting direction of sound source motion? *Experimental Neurology* 22:13–25.

ANDERSON, J. A. 1973. A theory for the recognition of items from short memorized lists. *Psychological Review* 80:417–38.

ANDERSON, J. R. 1974. Retrieval of propositional information from long-term memory. *Cognitive Psychology* 6:451–74.

———. 1974. Verbatim and propositional representation of sentences in immediate and long-term memory. *Journal of Verbal Learning and Verbal Behavior* 13:149–62.

———. 1975. Item-specific and relation-specific interference in sentence memory. *Journal of Experimental Psychology: Human Learning and Memory.* 1:249–60.

———. 1976. *Language, memory, and thought.* Hillsdale, N.J.: Erlbaum.

ANDERSON, J. R., AND BOWER, G. H. 1973. *Human associative memory.* Washington, D.C.: Winston.

ANDERSON, J. R., AND HASTIE, R. 1974. Individuation and reference in memory: proper names and definite descriptions. *Cognitive Psychology* 6:495–514.

ANDERSON, R. C. 1974. Substance recall of sentences. *Quarterly Journal of Experimental Psychology* 26:530–41.

ANDERSON, R. C., AND ORION, A. 1975. On putting apples into bottles—a problem of polysemy. *Cognitive Psychology* 7:167–80.

ANDERSON, R. C.; PICHERT, J. W.; GOETZ, E. T.; SCHALLERT, D.; STEVENS, K. V.; AND TROLLIP, S. R. 1976. Instantiation of general terms. *Journal of Verbal Learning and Verbal Behavior* 15:667.

ANGLIN, J. M. 1977. *Word, object, and conceptual development.* New York: Norton.

ANISFELD, M., AND KNAPP, M. 1968. Association, synonymity, and directionality in false recognition. *Journal of Experimental Psychology* 77:171–79.

ARCHER, E. J. 1962. Concept identification as a function of obviousness of relevant and irrelevant information. *Journal of Experimental Psychology* 63:616–20.

ARCHER, E. J., AND UNDERWOOD, B. J. 1951. Retroactive inhibition of verbal associations as a multiple function of temporal point of interpolation and degree of interpolated learning. *Journal of Experimental Psychology* 42:283–90.

ASCH, S. E.; CERASO, J.; AND HEIMER, W. 1960. Perceptual conditions of association. *Psychological Monographs* 74 (whole no. 490):1–48.

ASHCRAFT, M. H. 1976. Priming and property dominance effects in semantic memory. *Memory and Cognition* 4:490–500.

ASSO, D., AND WYKE, M. 1967. Experimental study of the effect of letter reversals on reading. *British Journal of Psychology* 58:413–19.

ATKINSON, R. C., AND JUOLA, J. F. 1973. Factors influencing speed and accuracy of word recognition. In *Attention and performance IV,* ed. S. Kornblum. New York: Academic Press.

ATTNEAVE, F. 1955. Perception of place in a circular field. *American Journal of Psychology* 68:69–82.

———. 1957. Transfer of experience with a class-schema to identification learning of patterns and shapes. *Journal of Experimental Psychology* 54:81–88.

———. 1968. Triangles as ambiguous figures. *American Journal of Psychology* 81:447–53.

———. 1971. Multistability in perception. *Scientific American* December:63–71.

———. 1974. Apparent movement and the what-where connection. *Psychologia* 17:108–20.

ATTNEAVE, F., AND BLOCK, G. 1974. The time required to compare extents in various orientations. *Perception and Psychophysics* 16:431–36.

ATTNEAVE, F., AND OLSON, R. K. 1967. Discriminability of stimuli varying in physical and retinal orientation. *Journal of Experimental Psychology* 74:149–57.

ATTNEAVE, F., AND REID, K. W. 1968. Voluntary control of frame of reference and slope equivalence under head rotation. *Journal of Experimental Psychology* 78:153–59.

AUSUBEL, D. P. 1966. Meaningful reception learning and the acquisition of concepts. In *Analyses of concept learning,* ed. M. J. Klausmeier and C. W. Harris. New York: Academic Press.

AVERBACH, E., AND CORIELL, A. S. 1961. Short term memory in vision. *The Bell System Technical Journal* 40:309–28.

AVERBACH, E., AND SPERLING, G. 1961. Short term storage of information in vision. In *Information theory,* ed. C. Cherry. London: Butterworths.

BADDELEY, A. D., AND ECOB, J. R. 1973. Reaction time and short term memory: implications of repetition effects for the high speed exhaustive scan hypothesis. *Quarterly Journal of Experimental Psychology* 25:229–40.

BADDELEY, A. D., AND HITCH, G. 1974. Working memory. In *The psychology of learning and memory,* vol. 8, ed. G. H. Bower. New York: Academic Press.

BAHRICK, H. P. 1965. The ebb of retention. *Psychological Review* 72:60–73.

BALL, F.; WOOD, C.; AND SMITH, E. E. 1975. When are semantic targets faster than visual or acoustic ones? *Perception and Psychophysics* 17:1–8.

BANKS, W. P., AND FLORA, J. 1977. Semantic and perceptual processes in symbolic comparisons. *Journal of Experimental Psychology* 3:278–90.

BARCLAY, J. R.; BRANSFORD, J. D.; FRANKS, J. J.; McCARRELL, N. S.; AND NITSCH, K. 1974. Comprehension and semantic flexibility. *Journal of Verbal Learning and Verbal Behavior* 13:471–81.

BARLOW, H. B. 1975. Visual experience and cortical development. *Nature* 258:199–204.

BARLOW, H. B.; FITZHUGH, R.; AND KUFFLER, S. W. 1957. Change of organization in the receptive fields of the cat's retina during darkness adaptation. *Journal of Physiology* 137:338–54.

BARLOW, H. B., AND LEVICK, W. R. 1969. Changes in the maintained discharge with adaptation level in the cat's retina. *Journal of Physiology* 202:699–718.

BARLOW, H. B.; MACLEOD, D. I. A.; AND VAN MEETEREN, A. 1976. Adaptation of gratings: no compensatory advantages found. *Vision Research* 16:1043–45.

BARON, J., AND THURSTON, I. 1973. An analysis of the word superiority effect. *Cognitive Psychology* 4:207–28.

BARRESI, J.; ROBBINS, D.; AND SHAIN, K. 1975. Role of distinctive features in the abstraction of related concepts. *Journal of Experimental Psychology: Human Learning and Memory* 104:360–68.

BARTLETT, F. C. 1932. *Remembering: a study in experimental and social psychology.* Cambridge: Cambridge University Press.

BECK, J. 1967. Perceptual grouping produced by line figures. *Perception and Psychophysics* 2:491–95
———. 1976. Perceptual grouping produced by changes in orientation and shape. *Science* 154:538–40.

BEGG, I. 1971. Recognition memory for sentence meaning and wording. *Journal of Verbal Learning and Verbal Behavior* 10:176–81.

BEGG, I., AND WICKELGREN, W. A. 1974. Retention functions for syntactic and lexical vs. semantic information in sentence recognition memory. *Memory and Cognition* 2:353–59.

BEKESY, G. VON, AND ROSENBLITH, W. A. 1951. The mechanical properties of the ear. In *Handbook of experimental psychology*, ed. S. S. Stevens. New York: Wiley.

BENNETT, D. C. 1968. Spectral form and duration as cues in the recognition of English and German vowels. *Language and Speech* 11:65–85.

BENSON, D. F., AND GESCHWIND, N. 1967. Shrinking retrograde amnesia. *Journal of Neurology, Neurosurgery, and Psychiatry* 30:539–44.

BERTELSON, P., AND RENKIN, A. 1966. Reaction times to new versus repeated signals in a serial task as a function of response-signal time interval. *Acta Psychologica* 25:132–36.

BESNER, D., AND COLTHEART, M. 1975. Same-different judgements with words and non-words: the differential effects of relative size. *Memory and Cognition* 3:673–77.

BEVER, T. G.; GARRETT, M. F.; AND HURTIG, R. 1973. The interaction of perceptual processes and ambiguous sentences. *Memory and Cognition* 3:277–86.

BIEDERMAN, I., AND CHECKOSKY, S. F. 1970. Processing redundant information. *Journal of Experimental Psychology* 83:486–90.

BIRCH, H. G., AND RABINOWITZ, H. S. 1951. The negative effect of previous experience on productive thinking. *Journal of Experimental Psychology* 41:121–25.

BIRNBAUM, I. M. 1965. Long-term retention of first-list associations in the AB-AC paradigm. *Journal of Verbal Learning and Verbal Behavior* 4:515–20.

BITTERMAN, M. E.; KRAUSKOPF, J.; AND HOCHBERG, J. E. 1954. Threshold for visual form: a diffusion model. *The American Journal of Psychology* 57:205–19.

BLAKEMORE, C. 1974. Developmental factors in the formation of feature extracting neurons. In *The neurosciences: third study program*, ed. F. O. Schmitt and F. G. Worden. Cambridge, Mass.: M.I.T. Press.

BLAKEMORE, C.; MUNCEY, J. P. J.; AND RIDLEY, R. M. 1971. Perceptual fading of a stabilized cortical image. *Nature* 233:204–5.

BLAKEMORE, C., AND SUTTON, P. 1969. Size adaptation: a new aftereffect. *Science* 166:245–47.

BLECHNER, M. J.; DAY, R. S.; AND CUTTING, J. E. 1976. Processing two dimensions of nonspeech stimuli: the auditory-phonetic distinction reconsidered. *Journal of Experimental Psychology: Human Perception and Performance* 2:257–66.

Bliss, J. C.; Crane, H. D.; Mansfield, P. K., and Townsend, J. T. 1966. Information available in brief tactile presentations. *Perception and Psychophysics* 1:273–83.

Blumenthal, A. L. 1967. Prompted recall of sentences. *Journal of Verbal Learning and Verbal Behavior* 6:203–6.

Blumenthal, A. L., and Boakes, R. 1967. Prompted recall of sentences. *Journal of Verbal Learning and Verbal Behavior* 6:674–76.

Bobrow, D. G., and Collins, A., eds. 1975. *Representation and understanding.* New York: Academic Press.

Bongartz, W., and Scheerer, E. 1976. Two visual stores and two processing operations in tachistoscopic partial report. *Quarterly Journal of Experimental Psychology* 28:203–19.

Boomer, D. S., and Laver, J. D. M. 1968. Slips of the tongue. *British Journal of Psychology* 3:2–12.

Bourne, L. E. Jr. 1957. Effects of delay of information feedback and task complexity on the identification of concepts. *Journal of Experimental Psychology* 54:201–7.

———. 1967. Learning and utilization of conceptual rules. In *Memory and the structure of concepts,* ed. B. Kleinmuntz. New York: Wiley.

Bousfield, W. A. 1953. The occurrence of clustering in the recall of randomly arranged associates. *Journal of General Psychology* 49:229–40.

Bower, G. H. 1969. Chunks as interference units in free recall. *Journal of Verbal Learning and Verbal Behavior* 8:610–13.

———. 1972. Mental imagery and associative learning. In *Cognition in learning and memory,* ed. L. Gregg. New York: Wiley.

———. 1976. Experiments on story understanding and recall. *Quarterly Journal of Experimental Psychology* 28:511–34.

Bower, G. H., and Glass, A. L. 1976. Structural units and the redintegrative power of picture fragments. *Journal of Experimental Psychology: Human Learning and Memory* 2:456–66.

Bower, G. H., and Karlin, M. B. 1974. Depth of processing pictures of faces and recognition memory. *Journal of Experimental Psychology* 103:751–57.

Bower, G. H., and Trabasso, T. 1963. Reversals prior to solution in concept identification. *Journal of Experimental Psychology* 66:409–18.

———. 1964. Concept identification. In *Studies in mathematical psychology,* ed. R. C. Atkinson. Stanford, Calif.: Stanford University Press.

Bower, T. G. R.; Broughton, J. M.; and Moore, M. K. 1970. Demonstration of intention in the reaching behavior of neonate humans. *Nature* 288:679–81.

Bradshaw, J. L. 1974. Peripherally presented and unreported words may bias the perceived meaning of a centrally fixated homograph. *Journal of Experimental Psychology* 103:1200–202.

———. 1975. Three interrelated problems in reading: a review. *Memory and Cognition* 3:123–34.

Bransford, J. D.; Barclay, J. R.; and Franks, J. J. 1972. Sentence memory: a constructive versus interpretive approach. *Cognitive Psychology* 3:193–209.

Bransford, J. D., and Franks, J. J. 1971. The abstraction of linguistic ideas. *Cognitive Psychology* 2:331–50.

Bransford, J. D., and Johnson, M. K. 1973. Considerations of some problems of comprehension. In *Visual information processing,* ed. W. G. Chase. New York: Academic Press.

Bregman, A. S., and Campbell, J. 1971. Primary auditory stream segregation and perception of order in rapid sequences of tones. *Journal of Experimental Psychology* 89:244–49.

Bregman, A. S., and Dannenbring, G. L. 1973. The effect of continuity on auditory stream segregation. *Perception and Psychophysics* 13:308–12.

Bregman, A. S., and Rudnicky, A. I. 1975. Auditory segregation: stream or streams? *Journal of Experimental Psychology: Human Perception and Performance* 1:263–67.

Breitmeyer, B. G., and Ganz, L. 1976. Implications of sustained and transient channels for theories of visual pattern masking, saccadic suppression, and information processing. *Psychological Review* 83:1–36.

BROADBENT, D. E. 1954. The role of auditory localization in attention and memory span. *Journal of Experimental Psychology* 47:191–96.

———. 1958. *Perception and communication.* New York: Pergamon Press.

BROOKS, L. R. 1967. The suppression of visualization by reading. *The Quarterly Journal of Experimental Psychology* 14:289–99.

———. 1968. Spatial and verbal components of the act of recall. *Canadian Journal of Psychology* 22:349–68.

———. 1976. Visual pattern in fluent word identification. In *Toward a psychology of reading,* ed. A. Reber and D. Scarborough. Hillsdale, N.J.: Erlbaum.

———. 1977. Non-analytic concept formation and memory for instances. In *Cognition and concepts,* ed. E. Rosch. Hillsdale, N.J.: Erlbaum.

———. In press. Non-analytic correspondence and pattern in word identification. In *Attention and performance VIII.*

BROOKSHIRE, K. H.; WARREN, J. M.; AND BALL, G. G. 1961. Reversal and transfer learning following overtraining in rats and chickens. *Journal of Comparative Psychology* 54:98–102.

BROWN, K. T. 1955. Rate of apparent change in a dynamic ambiguous figure as a function of observation-time. *American Journal of Psychology* 68:358–71.

———. 1962. Complete interocular transfer of an adaptation process responsible for perceptual fluctuations with an ambiguous visual figure. *Vision Research* 2:469–75.

BROWN, R., AND McNEILL, D. 1966. The "tip of the tongue" phenomenon. *Journal of Verbal Learning and Verbal Behavior* 5:325–37.

BRUNER, J. S.; GOODNOW, J. J.; AND AUSTIN, G. A. 1956. *A study of thinking.* New York: Wiley.

BULGARELLA, R., AND ARCHER, E. J. 1962. Concept identification of auditory stimuli as a function of amount of relevant and irrelevant information. *Journal of Experimental Psychology* 63:254–57.

BURROWS, D., AND OKADA, R. 1971. Serial position effect in high-speed memory search. *Perception and Psychophysics* 10:305–8.

BUTTERWORTH, G., AND CASTILLO, M. 1976. Coordination of auditory and visual space in newborn human infants. *Perception* 5:155–60.

CAIRNS, H. S., AND KAMERMAN, J. 1975. Lexical information processing during sentence comprehension. *Journal of Verbal Learning and Verbal Behavior* 14:170–79.

CAMPBELL, D. T. 1960. Blind variation and selective retention in creative thought as in other knowledge processes. *Psychological Review* 67:380–400.

CAMPBELL, F. W. 1974. The transmission of spatial information through the visual system. In *The neurosciences: third study program,* ed. F. O. Schmitt and F. G. Worden. Cambridge, Mass.: M.I.T. Press.

CAPPS, M. J., AND COLLINS, W. E. 1965. Auditory fatigue: influence of mental factors. *The Journal of the Acoustical Society of America* 37:167–68.

CARR, T. H.; LEHMKUHLE, S. W.; KOTTAS, B.; ASTOR-STETSON, E. C.; AND ARNOLD, D. 1976. Target position and practice in the identification of letters in varying contexts: a word superiority effect. *Perception and Psychophysics* 19:412–16.

CARVER, R. P. 1972. Speed readers don't read; they skim. *Psychology Today* August: 23–30.

CATTELL, J. M. 1886. The time it takes to see and name objects. *Mind* 11:63–65.

CAUSSE, R., AND CHAVASSE, P. 1947. Etudes sur la fatigue auditive. *Année Psychologie* 42–3:265–98.

CAVANAGH, P. 1976. Holographic and trace strength models of rehearsal effects in the item recognition task. *Memory and Cognition* 4:186–99.

CHABOT, R. J., MILLER, T. J., AND JUOLA, J. F. 1976. The relationship between repetition and depth of processing. *Memory and Cognition* 4:677–82.

CHAFE, W. L. 1970. *Meaning and the structure of language.* Chicago: University of Chicago Press.

———. 1974. Language and consciousness. *Language* 50:111–33.

CHARNESS, N., AND BREGMAN, A. S. 1973. Transformations in the recognition of visual forms. *Canadian Journal of Psychology* 27:367–80.

CHERRY, E. C. 1953. Some experiments on the recognition of speech with one and with two ears. *Journal of the Acoustical Society of America* 25:975–79.

CHOMSKY, N. 1957. *Syntactic structures.* The Hague: Mouton.

————. 1965. *Aspects of the theory of syntax.* Cambridge, Mass.: M.I.T. Press.

CHOMSKY, N., AND HALLE, M. 1968. *The sound pattern of English.* New York: Harper and Row.

CHOW, S. L., AND MURDOCK, B. B. 1975. The effect of a subsidiary task on iconic memory. *Memory and Cognition* 3:678–88.

————. 1976. Concurrent memory load and the rate of readout from iconic memory. *Journal of Experimental Psychology: Human Perception and Performance* 2:179–90.

CLARK, H. H. 1974. The power of positive speaking. *Psychology Today* 102:108–11.

CLARK, H. H., AND HAVILAND, S. E. 1974. Psychological processes as linguistic explanation. In *Explaining linguistic phenomena,* ed. D. Cohen. Washington, D.C.: Hemisphere Publishing Corp.

————. 1975. Comprehension and the given-new contract. *Social Sciences Working Paper 67,* School of Social Sciences, University of California, Irvine.

CLARKSON, J. K., AND DEUTSCH, J. A. 1966. Effect of threshold reduction on the vibrato. *Journal of Experimental Psychology* 71:706–10.

CLELAND, B. G., AND LEVICK, W. R. 1974. Properties of rarely encountered types of ganglion cells in the cat's retina and an overall classification. *Journal of Physiology* 240:457–92.

COFER, C. N. 1967. Does conceptual organization influence the amount retained in immediate free recall? In *Concepts and the structure of memory,* ed. B. J. Kleinmuntz. New York: Wiley.

COHEN, B. D.; NOBLIN, C. D.; SILVERMAN, A. J.; AND PENICK, S. B. 1968. Functional asymmetry of the human brain. *Science* 162:475–77.

COHEN, B. H. 1966. Some-or-none characteristics of coding behavior. *Journal of Verbal Learning and Verbal Behavior* 5:182–87.

COHEN, G. 1970. Search times for combinations of visual, phonemic, and semantic targets in reading prose. *Perception and Psychophysics* 8:370–72.

————. 1973. Hemispheric differences in serial versus parallel processing. *Journal of Experimental Psychology* 97:349–56.

COHEN, R. L., AND GRANSTROM, K. 1970. Reproduction and recognition in short-term memory. *Quarterly Journal of Experimental Psychology* 22:450–57.

COHEN, R. L., AND SANDBERG, R. L. 1977. Relation between intelligence and short-term memory. *Cognitive Psychology* 9:534–54.

COLE, R. A., AND SCOTT, B. 1974. Toward a theory of speech perception. *Psychological Review* 81:348–74.

COLLINS, A. M., AND LOFTUS, E. F. 1975. A spreading-activation theory of semantic processing. *Psychological Review* 82:407–28.

COLLINS, A. M., AND QUILLIAN, M. R. 1969. Retrieval time from semantic memory. *Journal of Verbal Learning and Verbal Behavior.* 8:240–47.

————. 1970a. Does category size affect categorization time? *Journal of Verbal Learning and Verbal Behavior* 9:432–38.

————. 1970b. Facilitating retrieval from semantic memory: the effect of repeating part of an inference. *Acta Psychologica* 33:304–14.

COLLINS, W. E., AND CAPPS, M. J. 1965. Effects of several mental tasks on auditory fatigue. *The Journal of the Acoustical Society of America* 37:793–96.

COLTHEART, M., AND FREEMAN, R. 1974. Case alternation impairs word identification. *Bulletin of the Psychonomic Society* 3:102–4.

COLTHEART, M., AND GLICK, M. J. 1974. Visual imagery: a case study. *Quarterly Journal of Experimental Psychology* 26:438–53.

CONRAD, C. 1972. Cognitive economy in semantic memory. *Journal of Experimental Psychology* 92:149–54.

————. 1974. Context effects in sentence comprehension: a study of the subjective lexicon. *Memory and Cognition* 2:130–38.

CONRAD, R. 1964. Acoustic confusions in immediate memory. *British Journal of Psychology* 55:75–84.

COOPER, L. A., AND SHEPARD, R. N. 1973a. The time required to prepare for a rotated stimulus. *Memory and Cognition* 1:246–50.

————. 1973b. Chronometric studies of the rotation of mental images. In *Visual information processing*, ed. W. G. Chase. New York: Academic Press.

CORBALLIS, M. C. 1966. Rehearsal and decay in immediate recall of visually and aurally presented items. *Canadian Journal of Psychology* 20:43–51.

————. 1967. Serial order in recognition and recall. *Journal of Experimental Psychology* 74:99–105.

————. 1975. Access to memory: an analysis of recognition times. In *Attention and performance V*, ed. P. M. A. Rabbitt and S. Dornic. New York: Academic Press.

CORBALLIS, M. C.; KIRBY, J.; AND MILLER, A. 1972. Access to elements of a memorized list. *Journal of Experimental Psychology* 94:185–90.

CORBETT, A. T. 1975. Artificial categories and semantic distance in a categorization task. Master's thesis, University of Oregon.

————. 1977. Retrieval dynamics for rote and visual image mnemonics. *Journal of Verbal Learning and Verbal Behavior* 16:233–46.

CORBETT, A. T., AND WICKELGREN, W. A. 1978. Semantic memory retrieval: analysis by speed accuracy tradeoff functions. *Quarterly Journal of Experimental Psychology* 30:1–15.

CORCORAN, D. W. J., AND BESNER, D. 1975. Application of the Posner technique to the study of size and brightness irrelevancies in letter pairs. In *Attention and performance V*, ed. P. M. A. Rabbitt and S. Dornic. New York: Academic Press.

CRAFT, J. L., AND HINRICHS, J. V. 1971. Short-term retention of simple motor responses: similarity of prior and succeeding responses. *Journal of Experimental Psychology* 3:297–302.

CREELMAN, C. D. 1967. Empirical detectability scales without the *JND*. *Perceptual and Motor Skills* 24:1079–84.

CROWDER, R. G. 1975. Inferential problems in echoic memory. In *Attention and performance V*, ed. P. M. A. Rabbitt and S. Dornic. New York: Academic Press.

CROWDER, R. G., AND MORTON, J. 1969. Precategorical acoustic storage (PAS). *Perception and Psychophysics* 5:365–73.

CROWDER, R. G., AND PRUSSIN, H. A. 1971. Experiments with the stimulus suffix effect. *Journal of Experimental Psychology Monographs* 91:169–90.

CROWDER, R. G., AND RAEBURN, V. P. 1970. The stimulus suffix effect with reversed speech. *Journal of Verbal Learning and Verbal Behavior* 9:342–45.

CRUTCHFIELD, R. S. 1961. The creative process. Paper presented at the Conference on the Creative Person, Lake Tahoe Alumni Center, University of California, Berkeley, California, 13–17 October 1961.

DALLAS, M., AND MERIKLE, P. M. 1976. Semantic processing of non-attended visual information. *Canadian Journal of Psychology* 30:15–21.

DALLETT, K. M. 1965. A transfer surface for paradigms in which second-list S-R pairings do not correspond to first-list pairings. *Journal of Verbal Learning and Verbal Behavior* 4:528–34.

DALLOS, P. J. 1964. Dynamics of the acoustic reflex: phenomenological aspects. *The Journal of the Acoustical Society of America* 36:2175–83.

DANILOFF, R., AND MOLL, K. 1968. Coarticulation of lip rounding. *Journal of Speech and Hearing Research* 11:707–21.

DARK, V. J., AND LOFTUS, G. R. 1976. The role of rehearsal in long-term memory performance. *Journal of Verbal Learning and Verbal Behavior* 15:479–90.

DARWIN, C. J.; TURVEY, M. T.; AND CROWDER, R. G. 1972. An auditory analogue of the Sperling partial report procedure: evidence for brief auditory storage. *Cognitive Psychology* 3:255–67.

DAVELAAR, E., AND COLTHEART, M. 1975. Effects of interpolated items on the association effect in lexical decision tasks. *Bulletin of the Psychonomic Society* 6:269–72.

DAVIES, G. M. 1969. Recognition memory for pictured and named objects. *Journal of Experimental Child Psychology* 7:448–58.

DAVIS, G. A. 1967. Recognition memory for visual presented homophones. *Psychological Reports* 20:227–33.

DAVIS, R.; MORAY, N.; AND TREISMAN, A. 1961. Imitative responses and the rate of gain of information. *Quarterly Journal of Experimental Psychology* 13:78–89.

DAVIS, R.; SUTHERLAND, N. S.; AND JUDD, B. R. 1961. Information content in recognition and recall. *Journal of Experimental Psychology* 61:422–29.

DAY, R. H. 1968. Perceptual constancy of auditory direction with head rotation. *Nature* 219:501–2.

DEESE, J. 1959. Influence of inter-item associative strength upon immediate free recall. *Psychological Reports* 5:305–12.

———. 1961. From the isolated verbal unit to connected discourse. In *Verbal learning and verbal behavior*, ed. C. N. Cofer. New York: McGraw-Hill.

DEROSA, D. V., AND BAUMGARTE, R. 1971. Probe digit recall of items from temporally organized memory sets. *Journal of Experimental Psychology* 91:154–58.

DEUTSCH, D. 1969. Music recognition. *Psychological Review* 76:300–307.

———. 1970. Tones and numbers: specificity of interference in immediate memory. *Science* 168:1604–5.

———. 1972a. Octave generalization and tune recognition. *Perception and Psychophysics* 11:411–12.

———. 1972b. Music and memory. *Psychology Today* December:87–120.

DEUTSCH, J. A. 1951. A preliminary report on a new auditory after-effect. *Quarterly Journal of Experimental Psychology* 3:43–46.

DEUTSCH, J. A., AND DEUTSCH, D. 1963. Attention: some theoretical considerations. *Psychological Review* 70:80–90.

———. 1973. *Physiological psychology*. Homewood, Ill.: Dorsey Press.

DEVALOIS, K. K. 1977. Independence of black and white phase-specific adaptation. *Vision Research* 17:209–15.

DOOLING, D. J., AND LACHMAN, R. 1971. Effects of comprehension on retention of prose. *Journal of Experimental Psychology* 88:216–22.

DOSHER, B. A. 1976. The retrieval of sentences from memory: a speed-accuracy study. *Cognitive Psychology* 8:291–310.

———. 1978. The effects of delay and interference on retrieval dynamics: implications for retrieval models. Unpublished manuscript, Dept. of Psychology, Columbia University.

DUNCKER, K. 1945. On problem solving. *Psychological Monographs* 58 (whole no. 270).

EARHARD, B. 1976. Retroactive inhibition: associative loss or response suppression? *American Journal of Psychology* 89:385–401.

EFRON, R. 1963. Temporal perception, aphasia, and déjà vu. *Brain* 86:403–24.

EGAN, J. P. 1958. Recognition memory and the operation characteristic. Indiana University, Hearing and Communication Lab, AFCRC-TN-68-51, AD 152650.

EGAN, J. P.; CARTERETTE, E. C.; AND THWING, E. J. 1954. Some factors affecting multi-channel listening. *The Journal of the Acoustical Society of America* 26:774–82.

EGETH, H. 1967. Selective attention. *Psychological Bulletin* 67:41–57.

EGETH, H.; MARCUS, N.; AND BEVAN, W. 1972. Target-set and response-set interaction: implications for models of human information processing. *Science* 176:1447–48.

EGETH, H., AND SMITH, E. 1967. Perceptual selectivity in a visual recognition task. *Journal of Experimental Psychology* 74:543–49.

EKSTRAND, B. R. 1972. To sleep, perchance to dream (about why we forget). In *Human memory: festschrift for Benton J. Underwood*, ed. C. P. Duncan, L. Sechrest, and A. W. Melton. Englewood Cliffs, N.J.: Prentice-Hall.

EKSTRAND, B. R.; BARRETT, T. R.; WEST, J. N.; AND MAIER, W. G. 1977. The effect of sleep on human long-term memory. In *Neurobiology of sleep and memory,* ed. R. R. Drucker-Colin and J. L. McGaugh. New York: Academic Press.

ELLIOTT, L. L. 1971. Backward and forward masking. *Audiology* 10:65–76.

ENGELKAMP, J., AND HORMANN, H. 1974. The effect of non-verbal information on the recall of negation. *Quarterly Journal of Experimental Psychology* 26:98–105.

ENGELKAMP, J.; MERDIAN, F.; AND HORMANN, H. 1972. Semantische Faktoren beim Behalten der Verneinung von Satzen. *Psychologische Forschung* 35:93–116.

ENROTH-CUGELL, C., AND LENNIE, P. 1975. The control of retinal ganglion cell discharge by receptive field surrounds. *Journal of Physiology* 247:551–78.

ENROTH-CUGELL, C., AND ROBSON, J. G. 1966. The contrast sensitivity of retinal ganglion cells of the cat. *Journal of Physiology* 187:517–52.

EPSTEIN, W.; ROCK, I.; AND ZUCKERMAN, C. B. 1960. Meaning and familiarity in associative learning. *Psychological Monographs* 74 (whole no. 490):1–22.

ERICKSEN, C. W., AND HOFFMAN, J. E. 1974. Selective attention: noise suppression or signal enhancement? *Bulletin of the Psychonomic Society* 4:587–89.

ERICKSEN, C. W.; POLLACK, M. D.; AND MONTAGUE, W. E. 1970. Implicit speech: mechanism in perceptual encoding. *Journal of Experimental Psychology* 84:502–7.

ERVIN-TRIPP, S. 1973. Some strategies for the first two years. In *Cognitive development and the acquisition of language,* ed. T. E. Moore. New York: Academic Press.

ESTES, W. K. 1972. An associative basis for coding and organization in memory. In *Coding processes in human memory,* ed. A. W. Melton and E. Martin. Washington, D.C.: Winston.

———. 1975. The locus of inferential and perceptual processes in letter identification. *Journal of Experimental Psychology: General* 104:122–45.

ESTES, W. K., AND TAYLOR, H. A. 1964. A detection method and probabilistic models for assessing information processing from brief visual displays. *Proceedings of the National Academy of Sciences* 52:446–54.

ESTES, W. K., AND WOLFORD, G. L. 1971. Effects of spaces on report from tachistoscopically presented letter strings. *Psychonomic Science* 25:77–80.

EVANS, J. ST. B. T. 1972. Interpretation and matching bias in a reasoning task. *The Quarterly Journal of Experimental Psychology* 24:193–99.

EVANS, S. H. 1967. A brief statement of schema theory. *Psychonomic Science* 8:87–88.

EVANS, S. H., AND EDMONDS, E. M. 1966. Schema discrimination as a function of training. *Psychonomic Science* 5:303–4.

FAJNSZTEJN-POLLACK, G. 1973. A developmental study of decay rate in long-term memory. *Journal of Experimental Child Psychology* 16:225–35.

FANT, C. G. M. 1962. Descriptive analysis of the acoustic aspects of speech. *Logos* 5:3–17.

FILLENBAUM, S. 1969. Words as feature complexes: false recognition of antonyms and synonyms. *Journal of Experimental Psychology* 82:400–402.

FILLMORE, C. J. 1968. The case for case. In *Universals in linguistic theory,* ed. E. Bach and R. T. Harms. New York: Holt, Rinehart, and Winston.

FISCHLER, I. 1977. Associative facilitation without expectancy in a lexical decision task. *Journal of Experimental Psychology: Human Perception and Performance* 3:18–26.

FISHER, D. F. 1975. Reading and visual search. *Memory and Cognition* 3:188–96.

FLAGG, P. W. 1976. Semantic integration in sentence memory? *Journal of Verbal Learning and Verbal Behavior* 15:491–504.

FLAGG, P. W., AND REYNOLDS, A. G. 1977. Modality of presentation and blocking in sentence recognition memory. *Memory and Cognition* 5:111–15.

FOLKINS, J. W., AND ABBS, J. H. 1975. Lip and jaw motor control during speech: responses to resistive loading of the jaw. *Journal of Speech and Hearing Research* 18:207–20.

———. 1976. Additional observations on responses to resistive loading of the jaw. *Journal of Speech and Hearing Research* 19:820–21.

Foss, D. J. 1970. Some effects of ambiguity upon sentence comprehension. *Journal of Verbal Learning and Verbal Behavior* 9:699–706.

Foss, D. J., AND HARWOOD, D. A. 1975. Memory for sentences: implications for human associative memory. *Journal of Verbal Learning and Verbal Behavior* 14:1–16.

Foss, D. J., AND JENKINS, C. M. 1973. Some effects of context on the comprehension of ambiguous sentences. *Journal of Verbal Learning and Verbal Behavior* 12:577–89.

Foss, D. J., AND SWINNEY, D. A. 1973. On the psychological reality of the phoneme: perception, identification and consciousness. *Journal of Verbal Learning and Verbal Behavior* 12:246–57.

FRANKS, J. J., AND BRANSFORD, J. D. 1971. Abstraction of visual patterns. *Journal of Experimental Psychology* 90:65–74.

FREEDMAN, J. L., AND LOFTUS, E. F. 1971. Retrieval of words from long-term memory. *Journal of Verbal Learning and Verbal Behavior* 10:107–15.

FREIBERGS, V., AND TULVING, E. 1961. The effect of practice on utilization of information from positive and negative instances in concept indentification. *Canadian Journal of Psychology* 15:101–6.

FREIDES, D. 1974. Human information processing and sensory modality: cross-modal functions, information complexity, memory, and deficit. *Psychological Bulletin* 5:284–310.

FROMKIN, V. A. 1968. Speculations on performance models. *Journal of Linguistics* 4:47–68.

FROST, N., AND WOLF, J. 1973. How "visual" is visual memory? Paper presented at the Psychonomics Society meeting, St. Louis, Missouri.

FUNKENSTEIN, H. H.; NELSON, P. G.; WINTER, P.; WOLLBERG, Z.; AND NEWMAN, J. D. 1971. Unit responses in auditory cortex of awake squirrel monkeys to vocal stimulation. In *Physiology of the auditory system*, ed. M. B. Sachs. Baltimore: National Educational Consultants, Inc.

GAINES, B. R. 1976. Foundations of fuzzy reasoning. *International Journal of Man-Machine Studies* 8:623–68.

GAINES, B. R., AND KOHOUT, L. J. 1977. The fuzzy decade: a bibliography of fuzzy systems and closely related topics. *International Journal of Man-Machine Studies* 9:1–68.

GANZ, L., AND WILSON, P. D. 1967. Innate generalization of a form discrimination without contouring eye movements. *Journal of Comparative and Physiological Psychology* 63:258–69.

GARDNER, M. B. 1969. Distance estimation of 0° or apparent 0°-oriented speech signals in anechoic space. *Journal of the Acoustical Society of America* 45:47–53.

GARNER, W. R. 1974. *The processing of information and structure.* Potomac, Md.: Erlbaum.

———. 1976. Interaction of stimulus dimensions in concept and choice processes. *Cognitive Psychology* 8:98–123.

GARNER, W. R., AND FELFOLDY, G. L. 1970. Integrality of stimulus dimensions in various types of information processing. *Cognitive Psychology* 1:225–41.

GARROD, S., AND TRABASSO, T. 1973. A dual-memory information processing interpretation of sentence comprehension. *Journal of Verbal Learning and Verbal Behavior* 12:155–67.

GAZZANIGA, M. S. 1970. *The bisected brain.* Englewood Cliffs, N.J.: Prentice-Hall.

GEISLER, C. D.; RHODE, W. S.; AND HASELTON, D. W. 1969. Responses of inferior colliculus neurons in the cat to binaural acoustic stimuli having wide-band spectra. *Journal of Neurophysiology* 32:960–74.

GENTNER, D. 1975. Evidence for the psychological reality of semantic components: the verbs of possession. In *Explorations in cognition*, ed. D. A. Norman and D. E. Rumelhart. San Francisco: Freeman.

GENTNER, D. R. 1976. The structure and recall of narrative prose. *Journal of Verbal Learning and Verbal Behavior* 15:411–18.

GIBSON, E. J. 1965. Learning to read. *Science* 148:1066–72.

GIBSON, E. J., AND LEVIN, H. 1975. *The psychology of reading.* Cambridge, Mass.: M.I.T. Press.

GIBSON, J. J. 1933. Adaptation, aftereffect, and contrast in the perception of curved lines. *Journal of Experimental Psychology* 16:1–31.

GIBSON, J. J., AND RADNER, M. 1937. Adaptation, aftereffect, and contrast in the perception of tilted lines I. Quantitative studies. *Journal of Experimental Psychology* 20:453–67.

GLANZER, M., AND RAZEL, M. 1974. The size of the unit in short-term storage. *Journal of Verbal Learning and Verbal Behavior* 13:114–31.

GLASS, A. L.; HOLYOAK, K. J.; AND O'DELL, C. 1974. Production frequency and the verification of quantified statements. *Journal of Verbal Learning and Verbal Behavior* 13:237–54.

GLEITMAN, H. 1957. Proactive and retroactive assimilation in the successive comparison of loudness. *American Journal of Psychology* 70:117–19.

GLEZER, V. D.; BERTULIS, A. V.; IVANOV, V. A.; ROSTELYANETS, N. B.; AND PODVIGIN, N. F. 1971. Functional organization of the receptive fields of the retina. In *Sensory processes at the neuronal and behavioral levels,* ed. G. V. Gersuni, trans. Jerzy Rose. New York: Academic Press.

GLEZER, V. D.; COOPERMAN, A. M.; IVANOV, V. A., AND TSHERBACH, T. A. 1976. An investigation of spatial frequency characteristics of the complex receptive fields in the visual cortex of the cat. *Vision Research* 16:789–97.

GLUCKSBERG, S. 1964. Functional fixedness: problem solution as a function of observing responses. *Psychonomic Science* 1:117–18.

GLUCKSBERG, S., AND DANKS, J. H. 1968. Effects of discriminative labels and of nonsense labels upon availability of novel function. *Journal of Verbal Learning and Verbal Behavior* 7:72–76.

GLUCKSBERG, S., AND WEISBERG, R. W. 1966. Verbal behavior and problem solving: some effects of labeling in a functional fixedness problem. *Journal of Experimental Psychology* 71:659–64.

GOLDBERG, J. J.; DIAMOND, I. T.; AND NEFF, W. D. 1958. Frequency discrimination after ablation of cortical projection areas of the auditory system. *Federation Proceedings* 17:55.

GOLDBERG, J. M., AND GREENWOOD, D. D. 1966. Responses of neurons of the dorsal and posteroventral cochlear nuclei of the cat to acoustic stimuli of long duration. *Journal of Neurophysiology* 29:72–93.

GOLDBERG, M. M., AND NEFF, W. D. 1961. Frequency discrimination after bilateral ablation of cortical auditory areas. *Journal of Neurophysiology* 24:119–28.

GOLDMAN, D., AND HOMA, D. 1977. Integrative and metric properties of abstracted information as a function of category discriminability, instance variability, and experience. *Journal of Experimental Psychology: Human Learning and Memory* 3:375–85.

GOTTLIEB, G., AND WILSON, I. 1965. Cerebral dominance: temporary disruption of verbal memory by unilateral electroconvulsive shock treatment. *Journal of Comparative and Physiological Psychology* 60:368–72.

GOTTSDANKER, R., AND STELMACH, G. E. 1971. The persistence of psychological refractoriness. *Journal of Motor Behavior* 3:301–12.

GRAF, R. G. 1973. Speed reading: remember the tortoise. *Psychology Today* December: 112–13.

GRAVES, R. E. 1976. Are more items identified than can be reported? *Journal of Experimental Psychology: Human Learning and Memory* 2:208–14.

GRAY, C. R., AND GUMMERMAN, K. 1975. The enigmatic eidetic image: a critical examination of methods, data, and theories. *Psychological Bulletin* 82:383–407.

GREEN, D. M., AND MOSES, F. L. 1966. On the equivalence of two recognition measures of short-term memory. *Psychological Bulletin* 66:228–34.

GREEN, D. M., AND SWETS, J. A. 1966. *Signal detection theory and psychophysics.* New York: Wiley.

GREEN, D. W., AND SHALLICE, T. 1976. Direct visual access in reading for meaning. *Memory and Cognition* 4:753–58.

GREENE, J. M. 1970a. The semantic function of negatives and passives. *British Journal of Psychology* 61:17–22.

———. 1970b. Syntactic form and semantic function. *The Quarterly Journal of Experimental Psychology* 22:14–27.

GREENO, J. G. 1973. The structure of memory and the process of solving problems. In *Contemporary issues in cognitive psychology,* ed. R. L. Solso. Washington, D.C.: Winston.

———. 1977. Process of understanding in problem solving. In *Cognitive theory*, vol. 2, ed. N. J. Castellan, Jr.; D. B. Pisoni; and G. R. Potts. Hillsdale, N.J.: Erlbaum.

GROFF, P. 1975. Research in brief: shapes as cues to word recognition. *Visible Language* 9:67–71.

GROSS, C. G.; BENDER, D. B.; AND ROCHA-MIRANDA, C. E. 1974. Inferotemporal cortex: a single unit analysis. In *The neurosciences: third study program*, ed. F. O. Schmitt and F. G. Worden. Cambridge, Mass.: M.I.T. Press.

GROSSMAN, L., AND EAGLE, M. 1970. Synonymity, antonymity, and association in false recognition. *Journal of Experimental Psychology* 83:244–48.

GUTTMAN, N., AND JULESZ, B. 1963. The lower limits of auditory periodicity analysis. *Journal of the Acoustical Society of America* 35:610.

HABER, R. N., AND HABER, L. R. 1964. Eidetic imagery: I. Frequency. *Perceptual and Motor Skills* 19:131–38.

———. 1977. Word length and word shape as sources of information in reading. Paper presented at the Psychonomic Society Meeting, Washington, D.C.

HABER, R. N., AND STANDING, L. G. 1969. Direct measures of short-term visual storage. *Quarterly Journal of Experimental Psychology* 21:43–54.

HAGGARD, M. 1974. Selectivity for distortions and words in speech perception. *British Journal of Psychology* 65:69–83.

HALL, D. C. 1974. Eye fixations and spatial organization in memory. *Bulletin of the Psychonomic Society* 3:335–37.

HALLIDAY, M. A. K. 1967. Notes on transitivity and theme in English: II. *Journal of Linguistics* 3:199–244.

HARDYCK, D. C., AND PETRINOVICH, L. F. 1970. Subvocal speech and comprehension level as a function of the difficulty level of reading material. *Journal of Verbal Learning and Verbal Behavior* 9:647–52.

HARM, O. J., AND LAPPIN, J. S. 1973. Probability, compatibility, speed, and accuracy. *Journal of Experimental Psychology* 10:416–18.

HARRISON, J. M., AND IRVING, R. 1966. Visual and nonvisual auditory systems in mammals. *Science* 154:738–43.

HARTLINE, H. K. 1949. Inhibition of activity of visual receptors by illuminating nearby retinal areas in the limulus eye (abstract). *Federation Proceedings* 8:69.

HARTLINE, H. K.; WAGNER, H. G.; AND RATLIFF, F. 1956. Inhibition in the eye of limulus. *Journal of General Physiology* 39:651–73.

HAVILAND, S. E., AND CLARK, H. H. 1974. What's new? Acquiring new information as a process in comprehension. *Journal of Verbal Learning and Verbal Behavior* 13:512–21.

HAYES, J. R., AND SIMON, H. A. 1974. Understanding written problem instructions. In *Knowledge and cognition*, ed. L. W. Gregg. Potomac, Md.: Erlbaum.

———. 1976. Understanding complex task instructions. In *Cognition and instruction*, ed. D. Klahr. Potomac, Md.: Erlbaum.

HAYES-ROTH, B., AND HAYES-ROTH, F. 1975. Plasticity in memorial networks. *Journal of Verbal Learning and Verbal Behavior* 14:506–22.

HAYGOOD, R. C., AND STEVENSON, M. 1967. Effects of number of irrelevant dimensions in nonconjunctive concept learning. *Journal of Experimental Psychology* 74:302–4.

HEBB, D. O. 1949. *The organization of behavior*. New York: Wiley.

———. 1966. *A textbook of psychology*, 2nd ed. Philadelphia, Pa.: Saunders.

———. 1968. Concerning imagery. *Psychological Review* 75:466–77.

HEIDER, E. R. 1971. "Focal" color areas and the development of color names. *Developmental Psychology* 4:447–55.

———. 1972. Universals in color naming and memory. *Journal of Experimental Psychology* 93:10–20.

HEIDER, E. R., AND OLIVIER, D. C. 1972. The structure of the color space in naming and memory for two languages. *Cognitive Psychology* 3:337–54.

HELD, R., AND SHATTUCK, S. R. 1971. Color- and edge-sensitive channels in the human visual system: tuning for orientation. *Science* 174:314–16.

HENDERSON, L. 1975. Do words conceal their component letters? A critique of Johnson (1975) on the visual perception of words. *Journal of Verbal Learning and Verbal Behavior* 14:648–50.

HERNANDEZ-PEON, R., and SCHERRER, H. 1955. Habituation to acoustic stimuli in cochlear nucleus. *Federation Proceedings* 14:71.

HERNANDEZ-PEON, R.; SCHERRER, H.; AND JOUVET, M. 1956. Modification of electric activity in cochlear nucleus during "attention" in unanesthetized cats. *Science* 123:331–32.

HERRNSTEIN, R. J., AND BORING, E. G., ed. 1968. *A source book in the history of psychology.* Cambridge, Mass.: Harvard University Press.

HICK, W. E. 1952. On the rate of gain of information. *Quarterly Journal of Experimental Psychology* 4:11–26.

HINTZMAN, D. L., AND BLOCK, R. A. 1973. Memory for the spacing of repetitions. *Journal of Experimental Psychology* 99:70–74.

HINTZMAN, D. L.; CARRE, F. A.; ESKRIDGE, V. L.; OWENS, A. M.; SHAFF, S. S.; AND SPARKS, M. E. 1972. "Stroop" effect: input or output phenomenon? *Journal of Experimental Psychology* 95:458–59.

HITCH, G. J., AND BADDELEY, A. D. 1976. Verbal reasoning and working memory. *Quarterly Journal of Experimental Psychology* 28:603–21.

HOGBEN, J. H.; JULESZ, B.; AND ROSS, J. 1976. Short-term memory for symmetry. *Vision Research* 16:861–66.

HOLLOWAY, C. M. 1970. Consonant recognition with two levels of decision complexity. *The Quarterly Journal of Experimental Psychology* 22:467–74.

———. 1972. The disruptive effect of an irrelevant message in dichotic listening to word-lists. *Quarterly Journal of Experimental Psychology* 24:474–84.

HOLMES, V. M.; ARWAS, R.; AND GARRETT, M. F. 1977. Prior context and the perception of lexically ambiguous sentences. *Memory and Cognition* 5:103–10.

HOLYOAK, K. J., AND GLASS, A. L. 1975. The role of contradictions and counterexamples in the rejection of false sentences. *Journal of Verbal Learning and Verbal Behavior* 14:215–39.

HOLYOAK, K. J., AND WALKER, J. H. 1976. Subjective magnitude information in semantic orderings. *Journal of Verbal Learning and Verbal Behavior* 15:287–99.

HOMA, D.; CROSS, J.; CORNELL, D.; GOLDMAN, D.; AND SHWARTZ, S. 1973. Prototype abstraction and classification of new instances as a function of number of instances defining the prototype. *Journal of Experimental Psychology* 101:116–22.

HOMA, D., AND VOSBURGH, R. 1976. Category breadth and the abstraction of prototypical information. *Journal of Experimental Psychology: Human Learning and Memory* 2:3222–330.

HORII, Y.; HOUSE, A. S.; LI, K.; AND RINGEL, R. L. 1973. Acoustic characteristics of speech produced without oral sensation. *Journal of Speech and Hearing Research* 16:67–77.

HORNBY, P. A. 1974. Surface structure and presupposition. *Journal of Verbal Learning and Verbal Behavior* 13:530–38.

HOROWITZ, L. M., AND PRYTULAK, L. S. 1969. Redintegrative memory. *Psychological Review* 76:519–31.

HOUSTON, J. P. 1967. Unlearning of specific associations in the AB-AC paradigm. *Journal of Experimental Psychology* 74:254–58.

———. 1968. Competition in the two-factor theory of forgetting. *Journal of Verbal Learning and Verbal Behavior* 7:496–500.

HOVLAND, C. I. 1951. Human learning and retention. In *Handbook of experimental psychology,* ed. SS. Stevens. New York: Wiley.

HOVLAND, C. I., AND WEISS, W. 1953. Transmission of information concerning concepts through positive and negative instances. *Journal of Experimental Psychology* 45:165–82.

HOWE, T. S. 1969. Effects of delayed interference on list-1 recall. *Journal of Experimental Psychology* 80:120–24.

HUBEL, D. H., AND WIESEL, T. N. 1962. Receptive fields, binocular interaction and functional architecture in the cat's visual cortex. *Journal of Physiology* 160:106–54.

———. 1963. Receptive fields of cells in striate cortex of very young, visually inexperienced kittens. *Journal of Neurophysiology* 26:994–1002.

———. 1965. Receptive fields and functional architecture in two nonstriate visual areas (18 and 19) of the cat. *Journal of Neurophysiology* 28:229–89.

HUEY, E. B. 1908. *The psychology and pedagogy of reading.* New York: Macmillan. Republished by M.I.T. Press, Cambridge, Mass., 1968.

HULL, C. L. 1920. Quantitative aspects of the evolution of concepts: an experimental study. *Psychological Monographs* 28 (whole no. 123).

HUNTER, I. M. L. 1962. An exceptional talent for calculative thinking. *British Journal of Psychology* 53:243–58.

HUTTENLOCHER, J., AND BURKE, D. 1976. Why does memory span increase with age? *Cognitive Psychology* 8:1–31.

HYDE, T. S., AND JENKINS, J. J. 1969. Differential effects of incidental tasks on the organization of recall of a list of highly associated words. *Journal of Experimental Psychology* 82:472–81.

HYMAN, R. 1953. Stimulus information as a determinant of reaction time. *Journal of Experimental Psychology* 45:188–96.

HYMAN, R., AND FROST, N. 1974. Gradients and schema in pattern recognition. In *Attention and performance V*, ed. P. M. A. Rabbitt. New York: Academic Press.

INGLE, D.; SCHNEIDER, G.; TREVARTHEN, C.; AND HELD, R. 1967–68. Locating and identifying: two modes of visual processing: a symposium. *Pschologisches Forschung* 31:44–62, 299–348.

JACKSON, M. D., AND McCLELLAND, J. L. 1975. Sensory and cognitive determinants of reading speed. *Journal of Verbal Learning and Verbal Behavior* 14:565–74.

JACOBSON, J. Z. 1973. Effects of association upon masking and reading latency. *Canadian Journal of Psychology* 1:58–69.

JAKOBSON, R.; FANT, G.; AND HALLE, M. 1963. *Preliminaries to speech analysis.* Cambridge, Mass.: M.I.T. Press.

JAMES, C. T., AND ABRAHAMSON, A. A. 1977. Recognition memory for active and passive sentences. *Journal of Psycholinguistic Research* 6:37–47.

JAMES, W. 1890. *The principles of psychology,* vol. 1. New York: Holt.

JASTRZEMBSKI, J. E., AND STANNERS, R. F. 1975. Multiple word meanings and lexical search speed. *Journal of Verbal Learning and Verbal Behavior* 14:534–37.

JENKINS, J. G., AND DALLENBACH, K. M. 1924. Oblivescence during sleep and waking. *American Journal of Psychology* 35:605–12.

JENKINS, J. J. 1974. Remember that old theory of memory? Well, forget it. *American Psychologist* 29:785–95.

JENKINS, J. J., AND RUSSELL, W. A. 1952. Associative clustering during recall. *Journal of Abnormal and Social Psychology* 47:818–21.

JENSEN, A. R., AND ROHWER, W. D., JR. 1966. The Stroop color-word test: a review. *Acta Psychologica* 25:36–93.

JOHNSON, N. F. 1968. The influence of grammatical units on learning. *Journal of Verbal Learning and Verbal Behavior* 7:236–40.

———. 1970. The role of chunking and organization in the process of recall. In *The psychology of learning and motivation,* vol. 4, ed. G. H. Bower. New York: Academic Press.

———. 1975. On the function of letters in word identification: some data and a preliminary model. *Journal of Verbal Learning and Verbal Behavior* 14:17–29.

JOHNSON, P. J. 1967. Nature of mediational responses in concept identification problems. *Journal of Experimental Psychology* 73:391–93.

JOHNSON, R. E. 1970. Recall of prose as a function of the structural importance of the linguistic units. *Journal of Verbal Learning and Verbal Behavior* 9:12–20.

JOHNSON-LAIRD, P. N. 1975. Meaning and the mental lexicon. In *Studies in long-term memory,* ed. A. Kennedy and A. Wilkes. New York: Wiley.

JOHNSON-LAIRD, P. N., AND TAGART, J. 1969. How implication is understood. *American Journal of Psychology* 82:367–73.

JOHNSON-LAIRD, P. N., AND TRIDGELL, J. M. 1972. When negation is easier than affirmation. *Quarterly Journal of Experimental Psychology* 24:87–91.

JOHNSTON, C. D., AND JENKINS, J. J. 1971. Two more incidental tasks that differentially affect associative clustering in recall. *Journal of Experimental Psychology* 89:92–95.

JOHNSTON, J. C., AND MCCLELLAND, J. L. 1974. Perception of letters in words: seek and ye shall not find. *Science* 184:1192–93.

JONES, P. D., AND HOLDING, D. H. 1975. Extremely long-term persistence of the McCollough effect. *Journal of Experimental Psychology: Human Perception and Performance* 1:323–27.

JULESZ, B. 1965. Texture and visual perception. *Scientific American* 212:38–48.

———. 1971. *Foundations of cyclopean perception.* Chicago: University of Chicago Press.

JUOLA, J. F., AND ATKINSON, R. C. 1971. Memory scanning for words vs. categories. *Journal of Verbal Learning and Verbal Behavior* 10:522–27.

JUOLA, J. F.; FISHLER, I.; WOOD, C. T.; AND ATKINSON, R. C. 1971. Recognition time for information stored in long-term memory. *Perception and Psychophysics* 10:8–14.

KAHNEMAN, D. 1973. *Attention and effort.* Englewood Cliffs, N.J.: Prentice-Hall.

KANTOWITZ, B. H. 1972. Interference in short-term motor memory: interpolated task difficulty, similarity, or activity? *Journal of Experimental Psychology* 95:264–74.

———. 1974. Modality effects in recognition short-term motor memory. *Journal of Experimental Psychology* 103:522–29.

KAPLAN, R. M. 1972. Augmented transition networks as psychological models of sentence comprehension. *Artificial Intelligence* 3:77–100.

———. 1975. On process models for sentence analysis. In *Explorations in cognition,* ed. D. A. Norman and D. E. Rumelhart. San Francisco: Freeman.

KARLIN, L., AND KESTENBAUM, R. 1968. Effects of number of alternatives on the psychological refractory period. *Quarterly Journal of Experimental Psychology* 20:167–78.

KATZ, J. J., AND FODOR, J. A. 1963. The structure of semantic theory. *Language* 39:170–210.

KAUSLER, D. H., AND SETTLE, A. V. 1973. Associative relatedness vs. synonymity in the false-recognition effect. *Bulletin of the Psychonomic Society* 2:129–31.

KEELE, S. W. 1969. Repetition effect: a memory-dependent process. *Journal of Experimental Psychology* 80:243–48.

———. 1972. Attention demands of memory retrieval. *Journal of Experimental Psychology* 93:245–48.

KEELE, S. W., AND BOIES, S. 1972. Processing demands of sequential information. Paper presented at Western Psychological Association meeting, Anaheim, California.

KEELE, S. W., AND ELLS, J. G. 1972. Memory characteristics of kinesthetic information. *Journal of Motor Behavior* 4:127–34.

KEMPEN, G. 1974. Syntactic construction as retrieval plans. *Report* 74FV02, Department of Psychology, University of Nijmegen, Nijmegen, The Netherlands.

KENDLER, H. H., AND KENDLER, T. S. 1962. Vertical and horizontal processes in problem-solving. *Psychological Review* 69:1–16.

KENT, R. D., AND MOLL, K. L. 1972. Cinefluorographic analyses of selected lingual consonants. *Journal of Speech and Hearing Research* 15:453–73.

KEPROS, P. G., AND BOURNE, L. E., JR. 1966. Identification of biconditional concepts: effects of number of relevant and irrelevant dimensions. *Canadian Journal of Psychology* 20:198–207.

KEREN, G. 1976. Some considerations of two alleged kinds of selective attention. *Journal of Experimental Psychology: General* 105:349–74.

KERST, S. M., AND HOWARD, J. H., JR. 1977. Mental comparisons for ordered information on abstract and concrete dimensions. *Memory and Cognition* 5:227–34.

KIMURA, D. 1973. The asymmetry of the human brain. *Scientific American* 228:70–78.

KINCHLA, J. 1972. Duration discrimination of acoustically defined intervals in the 1- to 8-sec range. *Perception and Psychophysics* 12:318–20.

KINCHLA, R. A. 1971. Visual movement perception: a comparison of absolute and relative movement discrimination. *Perception and Psychophysics* 9:165–71.

KINCHLA, R. A., AND ALLAN, L. G. 1969. A theory of visual movement perception. *Psychological Review* 76:537–58.

KINCHLA, R. A., AND SMYZER, F. 1967. A diffusion model of perceptual memory. *Perception and Psychophysics* 2:219–29.

KING, D., AND ANDERSON, J. R. 1976. Long-term memory search: an intersecting activation process. *Journal of Verbal Learning and Verbal Behavior* 15:587–605.

KINTSCH, W. 1968. Recognition and free recall of organized lists. *Journal of Experimental Psychology* 78:481–87.

——. 1970. *Learning, memory, and conceptual processes.* New York: Wiley.

——. 1974. *The representation of meaning in memory.* Hillsdale, N.J.: Erlbaum.

——. 1975. Memory for prose. In *The structure of human memory,* ed. C. N. Cofer. San Francisco: Freeman.

KINTSCH, W.; CROTHERS, E. J.; AND JORGENSEN, C. C. 1971. On the role of semantic processing in short-term retention. *Journal of Experimental Psychology* 90:96–101.

KINTSCH, W., AND GLASS, G. 1974. Effects of propositional structure upon sentence recall. In *The representation of meaning in memory,* ed. W. Kintsch. Hillsdale, N.J.: Erlbaum.

KINTSCH, W., AND KEENAN, J. M. 1973. Reading rate and retention as a function of the number of propositions in the base structure of sentences. *Cognitive Psychology* 5:257–74.

KINTSCH, W.; KOZMINSKY, E.; STREBY, W. J.; McKOON, G.; AND KEENAN, J. M. 1975. Comprehension and recall of text as a function of context variables. *Journal of Verbal Learning and Verbal Behavior* 14:196–214.

KINTSCH, W., AND MONK, D. 1972. Storage of complex information in memory: some implications of the speed with which inferences can be made. *Journal of Experimental Psychology* 94:25–32.

KINTSCH, W., AND VAN DIJK, T. A. 1975. Comment on se rappelle et on résume des histoires. *Languages* 9:110–28.

KIRSNER, K., AND CRAIK, F. I. M. 1971. Naming and decision processes in short-term recognition memory. *Journal of Experimental Psychology* 88:149–57.

KLAPP, S. T. 1974. Syllable-dependent pronunciation latencies in number naming: a replication. *Journal of Experimental Psychology* 102:1138–40.

——. 1976. Short-term memory as a response preparation state. *Memory and Cognition* 4:721–29.

KLAPP, S. T.; ANDERSON, W. G.; AND BERRIAN, R. W. 1973. Implicit speech in reading, reconsidered. *Journal of Experimental Psychology* 100:368–74.

KLEIMAN, G. M. 1975. Speech recoding in reading. *Journal of Verbal Learning and Verbal Behavior* 14:323–39.

KLEIN, G. S. 1964. Semantic power measured through the interference of words with color-naming. *American Journal of Psychology* 77:576–88.

KOHLER, W., AND WALLACH, H. 1944. Figural aftereffects: an investigation of visual processes. *Proceedings of the American Philosophical Association* 88:269–357.

KOHN, B., AND DENNIS, M. 1974. Selective impairments of visuo-spatial abilities in infantile hemiplegics after right cerebral hemidecortication. *Neuropsychologia* 12:505–12.

KOLERS, P. A. 1968. The recognition of geometrically transformed text. *Perception and Psychophysics* 3:57–64.

——. 1970a. Three stages of reading. In *Basic studies on reading,* ed. H. Levin and J. P. Williams. New York: Basic Books.

——. 1970b. The role of shape and geometry in picture recognition. In *Picture processing and psychopictorics,* ed. B. S. Lipkin and A. Rosenfeld. New York: Academic Press.

KOLERS, P. A., AND LEWIS, C. L. 1972. Bounding of letter sequences and the integration of visually presented words. *Acta Psychologica* 36:112–24.

KONORSKI, J. 1967. *Integrative activity of the brain.* Chicago: University of Chicago Press.

———. 1972. Some ideas concerning physiological mechanisms of so-called internal inhibition. In *Inhibition and learning,* ed. R. A. Boakes and M. S. Halliday. New York: Academic Press.

KOPPENAAL, R. J. 1963. Time changes in the strength of AB-AC lists: spontaneous recovery? *Journal of Verbal Learning and Verbal Behavior* 2:310–19.

KOSSLYN, S. M. 1973. Scanning visual images: some structural implications. *Perception and Psychophysics* 14:90–94.

———. 1975. Information representation in visual images. *Cognitive Psychology* 7:341–70.

———. 1976. Visual images preserve metric spatial information. Paper presented at Psychonomic Society meeting, St. Louis, Missouri.

KOSSLYN, S. M., AND POMERANTZ, J. R. 1976. Imagery, propositions, and the form of internal representations. *Cognitive Psychology* 9:52–76.

KOZHENVNIKOV, V. A., AND CHISTOVICH, L. A. 1965. Speech, articulation, and perception. Trans. JPRS, Washington, D.C., no. JPRS 30, 543.

KROLL, N. E. A. 1975. Visual short-term memory. In *Short-term memory,* ed. D. Deutsch and J. A. Deutsch. New York: Academic Press.

KROLL, N. E. A.; PARKS, T.; PARKINSON, S.; BIEBER, S. L.; AND JOHNSON, A. L. 1970. Short-term memory while shadowing: recall of visually and of aurally presented letters. *Journal of Experimental Psychology* 85:220–24.

KRUEGER, L. E. 1970. Search time in a redundant visual display. *Journal of Experimental Psychology* 83:391–99.

———. 1976. Evidence for directional scanning with the order-of-report factor excluded. *Canadian Journal of Psychology* 30:9–14.

KRUEGER, L. E., AND WEISS, M. E. 1976. Letter search through words and nonwords: the effect of fixed, absent, or mutilated targets. *Memory and Cognition* 4:200–206.

KUFFLER, S. W. 1953. Discharge patterns and functional organization of mammalian retina. *Journal of Neurophysiology* 16:37–68.

LAABS, G. J. 1973. Retention characteristics of different reproduction in motor short-term memory. *Journal of Experimental Psychology* 100:168–77.

———. 1974. The effects of interpolated motor activity on the short-term retention of movement distance and end-location. *Journal of Motor Behavior* 6:279–88.

LACKNER, J. R., AND GARRETT, M. F. 1972. Resolving ambiguity: effects of biasing context in the unattended ear. *Cognition* 4:359–72.

LADEFOGED, P., AND BROADBENT, D. E. 1957. Information conveyed by vowels. *Journal of the Acoustical Society of America* 29:98–104.

LADEFOGED, P.; SILVERSTEIN, R.; AND PAPCUN, G. 1971. The interruptibility of speech. *Working papers in phonetics,* 17, UCLA.

LAKOFF, G. 1972. Hedges: a study in meaning criteria and the logic of fuzzy concepts. *Journal of Philosophical Logic* 2:458–508.

LANDAUER, T. K., AND FREEDMAN, J. L. 1968. Information retrieval from long-term memory: category size and recognition time. *Journal of Verbal Learning and Verbal Behavior* 7:291–95.

LAPPIN, J. S., AND DISCH, K. 1972a. The latency operating characteristic: I. Effects of stimulus probability on choice reaction time. *Journal of Experimental Psychology* 92:419–27.

———. 1972b. The latency operating characteristic: II. Effects of visual stimulus intensity on choice reaction time. *Journal of Experimental Psychology* 93:367–72.

———. 1973. Latency operating characteristic: III. Temporal uncertainty effects. *Journal of Experimental Psychology* 98:279–85.

LASHLEY, K. S. 1951. The problem of serial order in behavior. In *Cerebral mechanisms in behavior,* ed. L. A. Jeffress. New York: Wiley.

LASKY, R. E. 1974. The ability of six-year-olds, eight-year-olds, and adults to abstract visual patterns. *Child Development* 45:626–32.

LAWRENCE, D. H., AND COLES, G. R. 1954. Accuracy of recognition with alternatives before and after the stimulus. *Journal of Experimental Psychology* 47:208–14.

LAWRENCE, D. H., AND LABERGE, D. L. 1956. Relationship between recognition accuracy and order of reporting stimulus dimensions. *Journal of Experimental Psychology* 51:12–18.

LAWSON, R. 1977. Representation of individual sentences and holistic ideas. *Journal of Experimental Psychology: Human Learning and Memory* 3:1–9.

LEIMAN, A. L., AND HAFTER, E. R. 1972. Responses of inferior colliculus neurons to free field auditory stimuli. *Experimental Neurology* 35:431–49.

LEVELT, W. J. M., AND KEMPEN, G. 1975. Semantic and syntactic aspects of remembering sentences: a review of some recent continental research. In *Studies in long-term memory*, ed. A. Kennedy and A. Wilkes. New York: Wiley.

LEVY, A. S., AND HESHKA, S. 1973. Similarity and the false recognition of prototypes. *Bulletin of the Psychonomic Society* 1:181–83.

LEVY, B. A. 1975. Vocalization and suppression effects in sentence memory. *Journal of Verbal Learning and Verbal Behavior* 14:304–16.

LEWIS, C. H., AND ANDERSON, J. R. 1976. Interference with real world knowledge. *Cognitive Psychology* 8:311–35.

LEWIS, J. L. 1970. Semantic processing of unattended messages using dichotic listening. *Journal of Experimental Psychology* 85:225–28.

———. 1972. Semantic processing with bisensory stimulation. *Journal of Experimental Psychology* 96:455–57.

LIBERMAN, A. M.; COOPER, F. S.; SHANKWEILER, D. P.; AND STUDDERT-KENNEDY, M. 1967. Perception of the speech code. *Psychological Review* 74:431–61.

LIGHT, L. L., AND CARTER-SOBELL, L. 1970. Effects of changed semantic context on recognition memory. *Journal of Verbal Learning and Verbal Behavior* 9:1–11.

LINDBLOM, B. 1963. Spectrographic study of vowel reduction. *Journal of the Acoustical Society of America* 35:1773–81.

LINDSAY, P. H., AND NORMAN, D. A. 1972. *Human information processing.* New York: Academic Press.

LINDSLEY, J. R. 1975. Producing simple utterances: how far ahead do we plan? *Cognitive Psychology* 7:1–19.

LOCKHEAD, G. R. 1972. Processing dimensional stimuli. *Psychological Review* 79:410–19.

LOFTUS, E. F. 1973a. Activation of semantic memory. *American Journal of Psychology* 86:331–37.

———. 1973b. Category dominance, instance dominance, and categorization time. *Journal of Experimental Psychology* 97:70–74.

———. 1974. On reading the fine print. *Quarterly Journal of Experimental Psychology* 27:324.

LOFTUS, E. F., AND COLE, W. 1974. Retrieving attribute and name information from semantic memory. *Journal of Experimental Psychology* 102:1116–22.

LOFTUS, G. R. 1972. Eye fixations and recognition memory for pictures. *Cognitive Psychology* 3:525–51.

LONG, E. R.; REID, L. S.; AND HENNEMAN, R. H. 1960. An experimental analysis of set: variables influencing the identification of ambiguous, visual stimulus objects. *American Journal of Psychology* 73:553–63.

LONG, J. 1975. Reduced efficiency and capacity limitations in multidimensional signal recognition. *Quarterly Journal of Experimental Psychology* 27:599–614.

———. 1976. Division of attention between non-verbal signals: all-or-none or shared processing? *Quarterly Journal of Experimental Psychology* 28:47–69.

LUCHINS, A. S. 1942. Mechanization in problem solving. *Psychological Monographs* 54 (whole no. 248).

LURIA, A. R. 1970. *Traumatic aphasia.* The Hague: Mouton.

LYON, D. R. 1977. Individual differences in immediate serial recall: a matter of mnemonics? *Cognitive Psychology* 9:403–11.

McCLELLAND, J. L. 1976. Preliminary letter identification in the perception of words and non-words. *Journal of Experimental Psychology: Human Perception and Performance* 2:80–91.

McCOLLOUGH, C. 1965. Color adaptation of edge detectors in the human visual system. *Science* 149:1115–16.

McCORMACK, P. D. 1972. Recognition memory: how complex a retrieval system? *Canadian Journal of Psychology* 26:19–41.

McCULLOCH, W. S., AND PITTS, W. 1943. A logical calculus of the ideas immanent in nervous activity. *Bulletin of Mathematical Biophysics* 5:115–33.

McFARLAND, J. H. 1968. "Parts" of perceived visual forms: new evidence. *Perception and Psychophysics* 3:118–20.

McGEOCH, J. A. 1932. Forgetting and the law of disuse. *Psychological Review* 39:352–70.

McGOVERN, J. B. 1964. Extinction of associations in four transfer paradigms. *Psychological Monographs* 78 (whole no. 593):1–21.

McGUIGAN, F. J. 1973. The function of covert oral behavior ('silent speech') during silent reading. *International Journal of Psycholinguistics* 2:39–47.

MACKAY, D. G. 1966. To end ambiguous sentences. *Perception and Psychophysics* 1:426–36.

———. 1969. Forward and backward masking in motor systems. *Kybernetik* 2:57–64.

———. 1970a. Mental diploplia: towards a model of speech perception at the semantic level. In *Advances in psycholinguistics*, ed. G. B. Flores D'Arcais and W. J. M. Levelt. London: North-Holland.

———. 1970b. Spoonerisms: the structure of errors in the serial order of speech. *Neuropsychologia* 8:323–50.

———. 1971. Stress pre-entry in motor systems. *American Journal of Psychology* 84:35–51.

MACKAY, D. G., AND BEVER, T. G. 1967. In search of ambiguity. *Perception and Psychophysics* 2:193–200.

MACKINTOSH, N. J. 1974. *The psychology of animal learning.* New York: Academic Press.

MACLEOD, C. M., AND NELSON, T. O. 1976. A nonmonotonic lag function for false alarms to associates. *American Journal of Psychology* 89:127–35.

MACNEILAGE, P. F. 1970. Motor control of serial ordering of speech. *Psychological Review* 97:182–96.

McNEILL, D., AND LINDIG, K. 1973. The perceptual reality of phonemes, syllables, words, and sentences. *Journal of Verbal Learning and Verbal Behavior* 12:419–30.

MANDLER, G. 1967. Organization and memory. In *The psychology of learning and motivation: advances in research and theory*, vol. 1., ed. K. W. Spence and J. T. Spence. New York: Academic Press.

———. 1975. Memory storage and retrieval: some limits on the reach of attention and consciousness. In *Attention and performance V*, ed. P. M. A. Rabbitt and S. Dornic, pp. 499–516. New York: Academic Press.

MANELIS, L. 1974. The effect of meaningfulness in tachistoscopic word perception. *Perception and Psychophysics* 16:182–92.

MANELIS, L., AND YEKOVICH, F. R. 1976. Repetitions of propositional arguments in sentences. *Journal of Verbal Learning and Verbal Behavior* 15:301–12.

MARGOLIS, R. H., AND WILEY, T. L. 1976. Monaural loudness adaptation at low sensation levels in normal and impaired ears. *The Journal of the Acoustical Society of America* 59:222–24.

MARKMAN, E. M., AND SEIBERT, J. 1976. Classes and collections: internal organization and resulting holistic properties. *Cognitive Psychology* 8:561–77.

MARKS, D. F. 1972. Individual differences in the vividness of visual imagery and their effect on function. In *Function and nature of imagery*, ed. P. Sheehan. New York: Academic Press.

———. 1973. Visual imagery differences and eye movements in the recall of pictures. *Perception and Psychophysics* 14:407–12.

———. 1977. Imagery and consciousness: a theoretical review from an individual differences perspective. *Journal of Mental Imagery* 1:275–90.

MARKS, M. R., AND JACK, O. 1952. Verbal context and memory span for meaningful material. *American Journal of Psychology* 65:298–300.

MARTIN, E. 1967. Relation between stimulus recognition and paired-associate learning. *Journal of Experimental Psychology* 74:500–505.

MARTIN, J. G. 1968. Temporal word spacing and the perception of ordinary, anomalous, and scrambled strings. *Journal of Verbal Learning and Verbal Behavior* 7:154–57.

MASSARO, D. W. 1970a. Retroactive interference in short-term recognition memory for pitch. *Journal of Experimental Psychology* 83:32–39.

———. 1970b. Perceptual auditory images. *Journal of Experimental Psychology* 85:411–17.

———. 1973a. A comparison of forward vs. backward recognition masking. *Journal of Experimental Psychology* 100:434–36.

———. 1973b. The perception of rotated shapes: a process analysis of shape constancy. *Perception and Psychophysics* 13:413–22.

———. 1973c. Perception of letters, words, and nonwords. *Journal of Experimental Psychology* 100:349–53.

———. 1974. Perceptual units in speech perception. *Journal of Experimental Psychology* 102:199–208.

———. 1976. Auditory information processing. In *Handbook of learning and cognitive processes*, vol. 4, ed. W. K. Estes. Hillsdale, N.J.: Erlbaum.

———, ed. 1975. *Understanding language.* New York: Academic Press.

MASSARO, D. W., AND SCHMULLER, J. 1975. Visual features, preperceptual storage, and processing time in reading. In *Understanding language*, ed. D. W. Massaro. New York: Academic Press.

MELTON, A. W., AND IRWIN, J. M. 1940. The influence of degrees of interpolated learning on retroactive inhibition and the overt transfer of specific responses. *American Journal of Psychology* 53:175–203.

MERKEL, J. 1885. Die zeitlichen Verhaltnisse der Willensthatigkeit. *Philosophische Studien* 2:73–127.

MEYER, B. J. F. 1975. *The organization of prose and its effects on memory.* New York: North-Holland.

MEYER, D. E. 1970. On the representation and retrieval of stored semantic information. *Cognitive Psychology* 1:242–300.

MEYER, D. E., AND RUDDY, M. G. 1973. Lexical-memory retrieval based on graphemic and phonemic representations of printed words. Paper presented at the Psychonomic Society Meeting, St. Louis, Missouri.

MEYER, D. E., AND SCHVANEVELDT, R. W. 1971. Facilitation in recognizing pairs of words: evidence of a dependence between retrieval operations. *Journal of Experimental Psychology* 90:227–34.

MILLER, G. A. 1956. The magical number seven, plus or minus two: some limits on our capacity for processing information. *Psychological Review* 63:81–97.

———. 1962. Decision units in the perception of speech. *IRE Transactions in Information Theory* IT-8, 81–83.

MILLER, G. A.; GALANTER, E.; AND PRIBRAM, K. H. 1960. *Plans and the structure of behavior.* New York: Holt, Rinehart and Winston.

MILLER, G. A., AND HEISE, G. A. 1950. The trill threshold. *The Journal of the Acoustical Society of America* 22:637–38.

MILLER, G. A., AND ISARD, S. 1963. Some perceptual consequences of linguistic rules. *Journal of Verbal Learning and Verbal Behavior* 2:217–28.

MILNER, B. 1971. Interhemispheric differences and psychological processes. *British Medical Bulletin* 27:272–77.

———. 1973. Hemispheric specialization: scope and limits. In *The neurosciences: third study program*, ed. F. O. Schmitt and F. G. Worden. Cambridge, Mass.: M.I.T. Press.

MILNER, B.; BRANCH, C.; AND RASMUSSEN, T. 1964. Observations on cerebral dominance. In *Ciba Foundation on disorders of language,* ed. A. V. S. de Reuch and M. O'Connor. London: J. and A. Churchill.

———. 1966. Evidence for bilateral speech representation in some non-right-handers. *Transactions of the American Neurological Association* 91:306–8.

MILNER, P. M. 1974. A model for visual shape recognition. *Psychological Review* 81:521–35.

MINSKY, M. 1975. A framework for representing knowledge. In *The psychology of computer vision,* ed. P. Winston. New York: McGraw-Hill.

MISTLER-LACHMAN, J. L. 1975. Queer sentences, ambiguity, and levels of processing. *Memory and Cognition* 4:395–400.

MOESER, S. D. 1977. Recognition processes in episodic memory. *Canadian Journal of Psychology* 31:41–70.

MONAHAN, J. S., AND LOCKHEAD, G. R. 1977. Identification of integral stimuli. *Journal of Experimental Psychology: General* 106:94–110.

MOORE, J. J., AND MASSARO, D. W. 1973. Attention and processing capacity in auditory recognition. *Journal of Experimental Psychology* 99:49–54.

MORAY, N. 1959. Attention in dichotic listening: affective cues and the influence of instructions. *Quarterly Journal of Experimental Psychology* 11:56–60.

MORAY, N.; BATES, A.; AND BARNETT, T. 1965. Experiments on the four-eared man. *Journal of the Acoustical Society of America* 38:196–201.

MORAY, N.; FITTER, M.; OSTRY, D.; FAVREAU, D.; AND NAGY, V. 1976. Attention to pure tones. *Quarterly Journal of Experimental Psychology* 28:271–83.

MORIN, R. E.; DeROSA, D. V.; AND STULTZ, V. 1967. Recognition memory and reaction time. *Acta Psychologica* 27:298–305.

MORIN, R. E.; DeROSA, D. V.; AND ULM, R. 1967. Short-term recognition memory for spatially isolated items. *Psychonomic Science* 9:617–18.

MORTON, J., AND HOLLOWAY, C. M. 1970. Absence of a cross-modal 'suffix effect' in short-term memory. *Quarterly Journal of Experimental Psychology* 22:167–76.

MORTON, J., AND LONG, J. 1976. Effect of word transitional probability on phoneme identification. *Journal of Verbal Learning and Verbal Behavior* 15:43–51.

MOWBRAY, G. H. 1960. Choice reaction time for skilled responses. *Quarterly Journal of Experimental Psychology* 12:193–202.

MOWBRAY, G. H., AND RHOADES, M. U. 1959. On the reduction of choice-reaction times with practice. *Quarterly Journal of Experimental Psychology* 11:16–23.

MOYER, R. S. 1973. Comparing objects in memory: evidence suggesting an internal psychophysics. *Perception and Psychophysics* 13:180–84.

MOYER, R. S., AND BAYER, R. H. 1976. Mental comparison and the symbolic distance effect. *Cognitive Psychology* 8:228–46.

MÜLLER, G. E., AND PILZECKER, A. 1900. Experimentelle Beitrage zur Lehre vorn Gedachtniss. *Zeitschrift Psychologie Erganzungsband* 1:1–288.

MUNSTERBERG, H. 1890. Die Association successiver Vorstellungen. *Zeitschrift fur Psychologie* 1:99–107.

MURDOCK, B. B., JR. 1967. Auditory and visual stores in short-term memory. *Acta Psychologica* 27:316–24.

———. 1974. *Human memory: theory and data.* Potomac, Md.: Erlbaum.

MURRAY, D. J. 1967. The role of speech responses in short-term memory. *Canadian Journal of Psychology* 21:263–76.

MURRAY, D. J., AND NEWMAN, F. M. 1973. Visual and verbal coding in short-term memory. *Journal of Experimental Psychology* 100:58–62.

NEBES, R. D. 1974. Hemispheric specialization in commissurotomized man. *Psychological Bulletin* 81:1–14.

NEIMARK, E. D., AND CHAPMAN, R. H. 1975. Development of the comprehension of logical quantifiers. In *Reasoning: representation and process in children and adults,* ed. R. J. Falmagne. Hillsdale, N.J.: Erlbaum.

NEISSER, U. 1963. Decision-time without reaction-time: experiments in visual scanning. *The American Journal of Psychology* 126:376–85.

———. 1967. *Cognitive psychology.* Englewood Cliffs, N.J.: Prentice-Hall.

———. 1976. *Cognition and reality.* San Francisco: Freeman.

NEISSER, U., AND BECKLEN, R. 1975. Selective looking: attending to visually specified events. *Cognitive Psychology* 7:480–94.

NEISSER, U., AND HUPCEY, J. A. 1972. A Sherlockian experiment. *Cognition* 3:307–11.

NEISSER, U., AND LAZAR, R. 1964. Searching for novel targets. *Perceptual and Motor Skills* 19:427–32.

NEISSER, U.; NOVICK, R.; AND LAZAR, R. 1963. Searching for ten targets simultaneously. *Perceptual and Motor Skills* 17:955–61.

NEISSER, U., AND WEENE, P. 1962. Hierarchies in concept attainment. *Journal of Experimental Psychology* 64:644–45.

NELSON, D. L.; BROOKS, D. H.; AND BORDEN, R. C. 1973. Sequential memory for pictures and the role of the verbal system. *Journal of Experimental Psychology* 101:242–45.

NELSON, K. E., AND KOSSLYN, S. M. 1975. Semantic retrieval in children and adults. *Developmental Psychology* 11:807–13.

NELSON, T. O. 1977. Repetition and depth of processing. *Verbal Learning and Verbal Behavior* 16:151–71.

NEUMANN, P. G. 1974. An attribute frequency model for the abstraction of prototypes. *Memory and Cognition* 2:241–48.

NEWCOMBE, F., AND RUSSELL, W. R. 1969. Dissociated visual perceptual and spatial deficits in focal lesions of the right hemispheres. *Journal of Neurology, Neurosurgery and Psychiatry* 32:73–81.

NEWELL, A. 1973. Production systems: models of control structures. In *Visual information processing,* ed. W. G. Chase. New York: Academic Press.

NEWELL, A.; SHAW, J. C.; AND SIMON, H. A. 1962. The processes of creative thinking. In *Contemporary approaches to creative thinking,* ed. H. E. Gruber, G. Terrell, and M. Wertheimer. New York: Atherton Press.

NEWELL, A., AND SIMON, H. A. 1972. *Human problem solving.* Englewood Cliffs, N.J.: Prentice-Hall.

NEWPORT, E. L., AND BELLUGI, V. 1977. Linguistic expression of category levels in a visual-gestural language: a flower is a flower is a flower. In *Cognition and concepts,* ed. E. Rosch. Hillsdale, N.J.: Erlbaum.

NEWTON, J. M., AND WICKENS, D. D. 1956. Retroactive inhibition as a function of the temporal position of interpolated learning. *Journal of Experimental Psychology* 51:149–54.

NOOTEBOOM, S. G. 1967. Some regularities in phonemic speech errors. *IPO Annual Progress Report* (Instituut Voor Perceptie Onderzoek).

———. 1968. The tongue slips into patterns. In *Nomen, linguistic and phonetic studies,* pp. 114–32. The Hague: Mouton.

NORMAN, D. A. 1966. Acquisition and retention in short-term memory. *Journal of Experimental Psychology* 72:369–81.

———. 1967. Temporal confusions and limited capacity processors. *Acta Psychologica* 27:293–97.

———. 1969. Memory while shadowing. *The Quarterly Journal of Experimental Psychology* 21:85–93.

———. 1973. Memory, knowledge, and the answering of questions. In *Contemporary issues in cognitive psychology,* ed. R. L. Solso. Washington, D.C.: Winston.

NORMAN, D. A., AND BOBROW, D. G. 1975. On data-limited and resource-limited processes. *Cognitive Psychology* 7:44–64.

NORMAN, D. A.; RUMELHART, D. E.; AND the LNR Research Group. 1975. *Explorations in cognition.* San Francisco: Freeman.

NORMAN, D. A., AND WICKELGREN, W. A. 1969. Strength theory of decision rules and latency in retrieval from short-term memory. *Journal of Experimental Psychology* 6:192–208.

ÖHMAN, S. E. G. 1966. Coarticulation in VCV utterances: spectrographic measurements. *Journal of the Acoustical Society of America* 39:151–69.

OLSON, D. R. 1970. Language and thought: aspects of a cognitive theory of semantics. *Psychological Review* 77:257–73.

OLSON, D. R., AND FILBY, N. 1972. On comprehension of active and passive sentences. *Cognitive Psychology* 3:361–81.

OLSON, J. N., AND MACKAY, D. G. 1974. Completion and verification of ambiguous sentences. *Journal of Verbal Learning and Verbal Behavior* 13:457–70.

OLSON, R. K., AND ATTNEAVE, F. 1970. What variables produce similarity grouping? *American Journal of Psychology* 83:1–21.

OLTON, R. M. 1976. Incubation in problem solving: the pause that refreshes? Unpublished manuscript available from author at Xerox PARC, Palo Alto, California.

OLTON, R. M., AND JOHNSON, D. M. 1976. Mechanisms of incubation in creative problem solving. *American Journal of Psychology* 89:617–30.

ORTONY, A. 1975. Why metaphors are necessary and not just nice. *Educational Theory* 25:45–53.

ORTONY, A. 1976. Names, descriptions, and pragmatics. *Technical Report, 7,* Laboratory for Cognitive Studies in Education, University of Illinois.

OSGOOD, C. E. 1949. The similarity paradox in human learning: a resolution. *Psychological Review* 56:132–43.

————. 1971. Where do sentences come from? In *Semantics,* ed. D. D. Steinberg and L. A. Jakobovits. Cambridge: Cambridge University Press.

OSLER, S. F., AND FIVEL, M. W. 1961. Concept attainment: I. The role of age and intelligence in concept attainment by induction. *Journal of Experimental Psychology* 62:1–3.

OSLER, S. F., AND TRAUTMAN, G. E. 1961. Concept attainment: II. Effect of stimulus complexity upon concept attainment at two levels of intelligence. *Journal of Experimental Psychology* 62:9–13.

OSTRY, D.; MORAY, N.; AND MARKS, G. 1976. Attention, practice, and semantic targets. *Journal of Experimental Psychology: Human Perception and Performance* 2:326–36.

OVER, R. 1971. Comparison of normalization theory and neural enhancement explanation of negative aftereffects. *Psychological Bulletin* 75:225–43.

PACHELLA, R. G. 1974. The interpretation of reaction time in information processing research. In *Human information processing,* ed. B. Kantowitz. Potomac, Md.: Erlbaum.

————. 1975. The effect of set on the tachistoscopic recognition of pictures. In *Attention and performance V,* ed. P. M. A. Rabbitt and S. Dornic. New York: Academic Press.

PAIVIO, A. 1971. *Imagery and verbal processes.* New York: Holt, Rinehart and Winston.

————. 1975. Perceptual comparisons through the mind's eye. *Memory and Cognition* 3:635–47.

PAIVIO, A., AND CSAPO, K. 1969. Concrete image and verbal memory codes. *Journal of Experimental Psychology* 80:279–85.

PALMER, S. E. 1975a. The effects of contextual scenes on the identification of objects. *Memory and Cognition* 3:519–26.

————. 1975b. Visual perception and world knowledge: notes on a model of sensory-cognitive interaction. In *Explorations in cognition,* ed. D. A. Norman and D. E. Rumelhart. San Francisco: Freeman.

————. 1977. Hierarchical structure in perceptual representation. *Cognitive Psychology* 9:441–74.

PARDUCCI, A., AND PERRETT, L. F. 1971. Category rating scales: effects of relative spacing and frequency of stimulus values. *Journal of Experimental Psychology* 89:427–52.

PARKER, D. E.; TUBBS, R. L.; JOHNSTON, P. A.; AND JOHNSTON, L. S. 1976. Influence of auditory fatigue on masked pure-tone thresholds. *The Journal of the Acoustical Society of America* 60:881–85.

PARKS, T. E.; KROLL, N. E. A.; SALZBERG, P. M.; AND PARKINSON, S. R. 1972. Persistence of visual memory as indicated by decision time in a matching task. *Journal of Experimental Psychology* 92:437–38.

PELTON, L. H., AND SOLLEY, C. M. 1968. Acceleration of reversals of a Necker cube. *American Journal of Psychology* 81:585–88.

PENFIELD, W., AND ROBERTS, L. 1959. *Speech and brain mechanisms.* Princeton, N.J.: Princeton University Press.

PEPPER, R. L., AND HERMAN, L. M. 1970. Decay and interference effects in the short-term retention of a discrete motor act. *Journal of Experimental Psychology Monograph Supplement* 83:1–18.

PERFETTI, C. A., AND GOODMAN, D. 1970. Semantic constraint on the decoding of ambiguous words. *Journal of Experimental Psychology* 86:420–27.

PERKY, C. W. 1910. An experimental study of imagination. *American Journal of Psychology* 21:422–25.

PETERSON, G. E., AND BARNEY, H. L. 1952. Control methods used in a study of the vowels. *Journal of the Acoustical Society of America* 24:15–24.

PETERSON, L. R., AND KROENER, S. 1964. Dichotic stimulation and retention. *Journal of Experimental Psychology* 68:125–30.

PETERSON, M. J.; MEAGHER, R. B., JR.; CHAIT, H.; AND GILLIE, S. 1973. The abstraction and generalization of dot patterns. *Cognitive Psychology* 4:378–98.

PETTIGREW, J. D. 1974. The effect of visual experience on the development of stimulus specificity by kitten cortical neurones. *Journal of Physiology* 237:49–74.

PHILLIPS, W. A., AND BADDELEY, A. D. 1971. Reaction time and short-term visual memory. *Psychonomic Science* 22:73–74.

PIAGET, J. 1954. *The construction of reality in the child.* Trans. Margaret Cook. New York: Basic Books.

PISONI, D. B. 1972. Perceptual processing time for consonants and vowels. *Haskins Laboratories Status Reports on Speech Research* SR-31/32, 83–92.

POHLMANN, L. D., AND SORKIN, R. D. 1976. Simultaneous three-channel signal detection: performance and criterion as a function of order of report. *Perception and Psychophysics* 20:179–86.

POLF, J. O. 1976. The word superiority effect: a speed-accuracy analysis and test of a decoding hypothesis. Ph.D. dissertation, University of Oregon.

POLLACK, I., AND ROSE, M. 1967. Effect of head movement on the localization of sounds in the equatorial plane. *Perception and Psychophysics* 2:591–96.

POLLATSEK, A.; WELL, A. D.; AND SCHINDLER, R. M. 1975. Familiarity affects visual processing of words. *Journal of Experimental Psychology: Human Perception and Performance* 1:328–38.

POLLEN, D. A., AND RONNER, S. F. 1975. Periodic excitability changes across the receptive fields of complex cells in the striate and parastriate cortex of the cat. *Journal of Physiology* 245:667–97.

POLLEN, D. A., AND TAYLOR, J. H. 1974. The striate cortex and the spatial analysis of visual space. In *The neurosciences: third study program,* ed. F. O. Schmitt and F. G. Wordon. Cambridge, Mass.: M.I.T. Press.

POLYA, G. 1957. *How to solve it.* Garden City, N.J.: Doubleday.

———. 1962. *Mathematical discovery,* vol. 1. New York: Wiley.

POSNANSKY, C. J., AND NEUMANN, P. G. 1976. The abstraction of visual prototypes by children. *Journal of Experimental Child Psychology* 21:367–79.

POSNER, M. I. 1967. Characteristics of visual and kinesthetic memory codes. *Journal of Experimental Psychology* 75:103–7.

POSNER, M. I.; BOIES, S. J.; EICHELMAN, W. H.; AND TAYLOR, R. L. 1969. Retention of visual and name codes of single letters. *Journal of Experimental Psychology Monograph* 79:1–16.

POSNER, M. I., AND KEELE, S. W. 1967. Decay of visual information from a single letter. *Science* 158:137–39.

———. 1968. On the genesis of abstract ideas. *Journal of Experimental Psychology* 77:353–63.

———. 1970. Retention of abstract ideas. *Journal of Experimental Psychology* 83:304–8.

POSNER, M. I., AND KONICK, A. F. 1966. Short-term retention of visual and kinesthetic information. *Organizational Behavior and Human Performance* 1:71–86.

POSNER, M. I., AND MITCHELL, R. F. 1967. Chronometric analysis of classification. *Psychological Review* 74:392–409.

POSNER, M. I., AND SNYDER, C. R. R. 1975. Facilitation and inhibition in the processing of signals. In *Attention and performance V,* ed. P. M. A. Rabbitt and S. Dornic. New York: Academic Press.

POSNER, M. I., AND TAYLOR, R. L. 1969. Subtractive method applied to separation of visual and name components of multiletter arrays. *Acta Psychologica* 30:104–14.

POSTMAN, L. 1964. Short-term memory and incidental learning. In *Categories of human learning,* ed. A. W. Melton. New York: Academic Press.

POSTMAN, L.; STARK, K.; AND FRASER, J. 1968. Temporal changes in interference. *Journal of Verbal Learning and Verbal Behavior* 7:672–94.

POSTMAN, L., AND WARREN, L. 1972. Temporal changes in interference under different paradigms of transfer. *Journal of Verbal Learning and Verbal Behavior* 11:120–28.

POTTS, G. R. 1972. Information processing strategies used in the encoding of linear orderings. *Journal of Verbal Learning and Verbal Behavior* 11:727–40.

———. 1974. Storing and retrieving information about ordered relationships. *Journal of Experimental Psychology* 103:431–39.

POULTON, E. C. 1962. Peripheral vision, refractoriness and eye movements in fast oral reading. *British Journal of Psychology* 53:409–19.

PRITCHARD, R. M.; HERON, W.; AND HEBB, D. O. 1960. Visual perception approached by the method of stabilized images. *Canadian Journal of Psychology* 14:67–77.

QUILLIAN, M. R. 1966. Semantic memory. Ph.D. dissertation, Carnegie Institute of Technology. Reprinted in part in M. Minsky, 1968. *Semantic information processing.* Cambridge, Mass.: M.I.T. Press.

———. 1967. Word concepts: a theory and simulation of some basic semantic capabilities. *Behavioral Science* 12:410–30.

———. 1969. The teachable language comprehender: a simulation program and theory of language. *Communications of the ACM* 12:459–76.

RABBITT, P. M. A., AND VYAS, S. M. 1970. An elementary preliminary taxonomy for some errors in laboratory choice RT tasks. *Acta Psychologica* 33:56–76.

RASHEVSKY, N. 1938. *Mathematical biophysics,* reprint. New York: Dover.

RATLIFF, F. 1965. *Mach bands: quantitative studies on neural networks in the retina.* San Francisco: Holden-Day.

REED, A. V. 1973. Speed-accuracy tradeoff in recognition memory. *Science* 181:574–76.

———. 1976. List length and the time course of recognition in immediate memory. *Memory and Cognition* 4:16–30.

———. 1977. Discriminability spectra in bilingual word recognition. Paper presented at Mathematical Psychology Meeting, University of California at San Diego, 23 August 1977.

REED, S. K. 1972. Pattern recognition and categorization. *Cognitive Psychology* 3:382–407.

———. 1974. Structural descriptions and the limitation of visual images. *Memory and Cognition* 2:329–36.

REED, S. K.; ERNST, G. W.; AND BANERJI, R. 1974. The role of analogy in transfer between similar problem states. *Cognitive Psychology* 6:436–50.

REED, S. K., AND FRIEDMAN, M. P. 1973. Perceptual vs. conceptual categorization. *Memory and Cognition* 1:157–63.

REED, S. K., AND JOHNSEN, J. A. 1975. Detection of parts in patterns and images. *Memory and Cognition* 3:569–75.

REICH, P. A. 1976. The early acquisition of word meaning. *Journal of Child Language* 3:117–23.

REICHER, G. M. 1969. Perceptual recognition as a function of meaningfulness of stimulus material. *Journal of Experimental Psychology* 81:275–80.

REITMAN, J. S., AND BOWER, G. H. 1973. Storage and later recognition of exemplars of concepts. *Cognitive Psychology* 4:194–206.

REMINGTON, R. W. 1977. The processing of phonemes in speech: a speed-accuracy study. *Journal of the Acoustical Society of America* 62:1279–90.

REVLIS, R. 1975. Syllogistic reasoning: logical decisions from a complex data base. In *Reasoning: representation and process in children and adults,* ed. R. J. Falmagne. Hillsdale, N.J.: Erlbaum.

RIACH, W. D., AND SHEPOSH, J. 1964. Further observations on the central factor in auditory fatigue. *The Journal of the Acoustical Society of America* 36:967–68.

RIEGER, C. 1975. Conceptual memory and inference. In *Conceptual information processing,* ed. R. C. Schank. Amsterdam: North-Holland.

RIESBECK, C. K., AND SCHANK, R. C. 1977. Comprehension by computer: expectation-based analysis of sentences in context. In *Studies in perception of language,* ed. W. J. Levelt. New York: Wiley.

RILEY, C. A. 1976. The representation of comparative relations and the transitive inference task. *Journal of Experimental Child Psychology* 22:1–22.

RIPS, L. J. 1975. Quantification and semantic memory. *Cognitive Psychology* 7:307–40.

RIPS, L. J.; SHOBEN, E. J.; AND SMITH, E. E. 1973. Semantic distance and the verification of semantic relations. *Journal of Verbal Learning and Verbal Behavior* 12:1–20.

ROBERGE, J. J. 1976. Reasoning with exclusive disjunction arguments. *Quarterly Journal of Experimental Psychology* 28:419–27.

ROBSON, J. G. 1975. Receptive fields: neural representation of the spatial and intensive attributes of the visual image. In *Handbook of perception,* vol. 5., *Seeing,* ed. E. C. Carterette and M. P. Friedman. New York: Academic Press.

ROCK, I. 1973. *Orientation and form.* New York: Academic Press.

———. 1975. *An introduction to perception.* New York: Macmillan.

ROCK, I., AND GILCHRIST, A. 1975. Induced form. *American Journal of Psychology* 88:475–82.

ROCK, I., AND HARRIS, C. S. 1967. Vision and touch. *Scientific American* 216:96–104.

ROFFLER, S. K., AND BUTLER, R. A. 1968. Factors that influence the localization of sound in the vertical plane. *The Journal of the Acoustical Society of America* 43:1255–59.

ROHWER, W. D. 1966. Constraint, syntax and meaning in paired-associate learning. *Journal of Verbal Learning and Verbal Behavior* 5:541–47.

ROSCH, E. H. 1973a. Natural categories. *Cognitive Psychology* 4:328–50.

———. 1973b. On the internal structure of perceptual and semantic categories. In *Cognitive development and the acquisition of language,* ed. T. E. Moore. New York: Academic Press.

———. 1975a. Cognitive reference points. *Cognitive Psychology* 7:532–47.

———. 1975b. Cognitive representations of semantic categories. *Journal of Experimental Psychology* 104:192–233.

———. 1975c. The nature of mental codes for color categories. *Journal of Experimental Psychology: Human Perception and Performance* 1:303–22.

———. 1977. Human categorization. In *Advances in cross-cultural psychology,* vol. 1, ed. N. Warren. London: Academic Press.

ROSCH, E., AND MERVIS, C. B. 1975. Family resemblances: studies in the internal structure of categories. *Cognitive Psychology* 7:573–605.

ROSCH, E.; MERVIS, C. B.; GARY, W. D.; JOHNSON, D. M.; AND BOYES,-BRAEM, P. 1976. Basic objects in natural categories. *Cognitive Psychology* 8:382–439.

ROSCH, E.; SIMPSON, C.; AND MILLER, R. S. 1976. Structural bases of typicality effects. *Journal of Experimental Psychology: Human Perception and Performance* 2:491–502.

ROSE, J. E.; GROSS, N. B.; GEISLER, C. D.; AND HIND, J. E. 1966. Some neural mechanisms in the inferior colliculus which may be relevant to localization of a sound source. *Journal of Neurophysiology* 29:288–314.

ROSS, J., AND HOGBEN, J. H. 1974. Short-term memory in stereopsis. *Vision Research* 14:1195–1201.

ROTHKOPF, E. Z., AND COKE, E. U. 1961. The prediction of free recall from word association measures. *Journal of Experimental Psychology* 62:433–38.

ROUTH, D. A., AND MAYES, J. T. 1974. On consolidation and the potency of delayed stimulus suffixes. *Quarterly Journal of Experimental Psychology* 26:472–79.

ROWE, P. B. 1964. Three nonlogical influences on syllogistic reasoning. Master's thesis, M.I.T.

ROY, E. A., AND DAVENPORT, W. G. 1972. Factors in motor short-term memory: the interference effect of interpolated activity. *Journal of Experimental Psychology* 96:134–37.

ROZIN, P.; PORITSKY, S.; AND SOTSKY, R. 1971. American children with reading problems can easily learn to read English represented by Chinese characters. *Science* 171:1264–67.

RUBENSTEIN, H.; RICHTER, M. L.; AND KAY, E. J. 1975. Pronounceability and the visual recognition of nonsense words. *Journal of Verbal Learning and Verbal Behavior* 14:651–57.

RUMELHART, D. E. 1975. Notes on a schema for stories. In *Representation and understanding*, ed. D. G. Bobrow and A. Collins. New York: Academic Press.

RUMELHART, D. E.; LINDSAY, P. H.; AND NORMAN, D. A. 1972. A process model for long-term memory. In *Organization of memory*, ed. E. Tulving and W. Donaldson. New York: Academic Press.

RUSSELL, W. R. 1959. *Brain, memory, learning.* London: Oxford University Press.

SACHS, J. S. 1967. Recognition memory for syntactic and semantic aspects of connected discourse. *Perception and Psychophysics* 2:437–44.

SACHS, M. B., AND KIANG, N. Y.-S. 1968. Two-tone inhibition in auditory nerve fibers. *Journal of the Acoustical Society of America* 43:1120–28.

SAKITT, B. 1976. Iconic memory. *Psychological Review* 83:257–76.

SAVIN, H. B., AND BEVER, T. G. 1970. The nonperceptual reality of the phoneme. *Journal of Verbal Learning and Verbal Behavior* 9:295–302.

SCARBOROUGH, D. L. 1972. Memory for brief visual displays of symbols. *Cognitive Psychology* 3:408–29.

SCHANK, R. C. 1975a. *Conceptual information processing.* New York: Elsevier.

———. 1975b. The role of memory in language processing. In *The structure of human memory*, ed. C. N. Cofer. San Francisco: Freeman.

SCHANK, R. C., AND RIEGER, C. J. 1973. Inference and the computer understanding of natural language. *A. I. Memo* 197, Computer Science Department, Stanford University, California.

SCHARF, B. 1975. Audition. In *Experimental sensory psychology*, ed. B. Scharf. Glenview, Ill.: Scott, Foresman.

SCHILLER, P. H. 1965. Monoptic and dichoptic visual masking by patterns and flashes. *Journal of Experimental Psychology* 69:193–99.

SCHNEIDER, G. E. 1969. Two visual systems. *Science* 163:895–902.

SCHNEIDER, W., AND SHIFFRIN, R. M. 1977a. Controlled and automatic human information processing: I. Detection, search, and attention. *Psychological Review* 84:1–66

———. 1977b. Controlled and automatic human information processing: II. Perceptual learning, automatic attending, and a general theory. *Psychological Review* 84:127–90.

SCHOUTEN, J. F., AND BEKKER, J. A. M. 1967. Reaction time and accuracy. *Acta Psychologica* 27:143–53.

SCHUBERTH, R. E., AND EIMAS, P. D. Effects of context on the classification of words and nonwords. *Journal of Experimental Psychology: Human Perception and Performance* 3:27–36.

SCHVANEVELDT, R. W. 1966. Concept identification as a function of probability of positive instances and number of relevant dimensions. *Journal of Experimental Psychology* 72:649–60.

Scott, C. M., and Ringel, R. L. 1971. Articulation without oral sensory control. *Journal of Speech and Hearing Research* 14:804–18.

Segal, S. J., and Fusella, V. 1970. Influence of imaged pictures and sounds on detection of visual and auditory signals. *Journal of Experimental Psychology* 83:458–64.

————. 1971. Effect of images in six sense modalities on detection of visual signal from noise. *Psychonomic Science* 24:55–56.

Selters, W. 1964. Adaptation and fatigue. *The Journal of the Acoustical Society of America* 36:2202–9.

Selz, O. 1922. *Zur Psychologie des produktiven Denkens und Irrtums.* Bonn: Cohen.

Shaffer, L. H. 1975. Multiple attention in continuous verbal tasks. In *Attention and performance V*, ed. P. M. A. Rabbitt and S. Dornic. New York: Academic Press.

Shepard, R. N., and Metzler, J. 1971. Mental rotation of three-dimensional objects. *Science* 171:701–3.

Shepard, R. N., and Sheenan, M. M. 1963. Immediate recall of numbers containing a familiar prefix or postfix. *Perceptual and Motor Skills* 21:263–73.

Shiffrin, R. M. 1976. Capacity limitations in information processing, attention, and memory. In *Handbook of learning and cognitive processes*, vol. 4, *Attention and memory*, ed. W. K. Estes. Hillsdale, N.J.: Erlbaum.

Shiffrin, R. M., and Grantham, D. W. 1974. Can attention be allocated to sensory modalities? *Perception and Psychophysics* 15:460–74.

Shiffrin, R. M.; Pisoni, D. B.; and Castaneda-Mendez, K. 1974. Is attention shared between the ears? *Cognitive Psychology* 6:190–215.

Shockey, L. 1973. Phonetic and phonological properties of connected speech. Ph.D. dissertation, Ohio State University.

Shulman, H. G. 1970. Encoding and retention of semantic and phonemic information in short-term memory. *Journal of Verbal Learning and Verbal Behavior* 9:499–508.

Sidowski, J. B., and Nuthmann, C. 1961. Induced muscular tension, incentive, and blink rate in a verbal learning task. *Journal of Experimental Psychology* 61:295–99.

Simmons, F. B. 1965. Binaural summation of the acoustic reflex. *The Journal of the Acoustical Society of America* 37:834–36.

Simon, H. A., and Hayes, J. R. 1976. The understanding process: problem isomorphs. *Cognitive Psychology* 8:165–90.

Singer, M. 1976. Thematic structure and the integration of linguistic information. *Journal of Verbal Learning and Verbal Behavior* 15:549–58.

Skowbo, D.; Timney, B. N.; Gentry, T. A.; and Morant, R. B. 1975. McCollough effects: experimental findings and theoretical accounts. *Psychological Bulletin* 82:497–510.

Sloboda, J. A. 1976a. Decision times for word and letter search: a wholistic word identification model examined. *Journal of Verbal Learning and Verbal Behavior* 15:93–101.

————. 1976b. The effect of item position on the likelihood of identification by inference in prose reading and music reading. *Canadian Journal of Psychology* 30:228–37.

Smith, A., and Burkland, W. C. 1966. Dominant hemispherectomy: preliminary report on neuropsychological sequelae. *Science* 153:1280–82.

Smith, E. E.; Chase, W. G.; and Smith, P. G. 1973. Stimulus and response repetition effects in retrieval from short-term memory: trace decay and memory search. *Journal of Experimental Psychology* 98:413–22.

Smith, E. E., and Haviland, S. E. 1972. Why words are perceived more accurately than nonwords: inference versus unitization. *Journal of Experimental Psychology* 92:59–64.

Smith, E. E.; Haviland, S. E.; Reder, L. M.; Brownell, H.; and Adams, N. 1976. When preparation fails: disruptive effects of prior information on perceptual recognition. *Journal of Experimental Psychology: Human Perception and Performance* 2:151–61.

Smith, E. E.; Rips, L. J.; and Shoben, E. J. 1974. Semantic memory and psychological semantics.

In *The psychology of learning and motivation*, vol. 8, ed. G. H. Bower. New York: Academic Press.

SMITH, E. E.; SHOBEN, E. J., AND RIPS, L. J. 1974. Structure and process in semantic memory: a featural model for semantic decisions. *Psychological Review* 81:214–41.

SMITH, F. 1971. *Understanding reading.* New York: Holt, Rinehart and Winston.

SMITH, F.; LOTT, L.; AND CRONNELL, B. 1969. The effect of type size and case alternation on word identification. *American Journal of Psychology* 82:248–53.

SMITH, M. C. 1967a. Reaction time to a second stimulus as a function of intensity of the first stimulus. *The Quarterly Journal of Experimental Psychology* 19:125–32.

——. 1967b. The psychological refractory period as a function of performance of a first response. *Quarterly Journal of Experimental Psychology* 19:350–52.

——. 1967c. Stimulus-response compatibility and parallel response selection. *Canadian Journal of Psychology* 6:496–503.

——. 1968. Repetition effect and short-term memory. *Journal of Experimental Psychology* 77:435–39.

SNODGRASS, J. G., AND ANTONE, G. 1974. Parallel versus sequential processing of pictures and words. *Journal of Experimental Psychology* 103:139–44.

SNODGRASS, J. G.; LUCE, R. D.; AND GALANTER, E. 1967. Some experiments on simple and choice reaction time. *Journal of Experimental Psychology* 75:1–17.

SOMJEN, G. 1972. *Sensory coding in the mammalian nervous system.* New York: Plenum.

SORKIN, R. D., POHLMAN, L. D., AND GILLIOM, J. D. 1973. Simultaneous two-channel signal detection. III. 630 and 1400 Hz signals. *Journal of the Acoustical Society of America* 53:1045–50.

SORKIN, R. D.; POHLMANN, L. D.; AND WOODS, D. D. 1976. Decision interaction between auditory channels. *Perception and Psychophysics* 19:290–95.

SPELKE, E.; HIRST, W.; AND NEISSER, U. 1976. Skills of divided attention. *Cognition* 4:215–30.

SPERLING, G. 1960. The information available in brief visual presentations. *Psychological Monographs* 74 (whole no. 11).

——. 1963. A model for visual memory tasks. *Human Factors* 5:19–31.

——. 1967. Successive approximations to a model for short-term memory. *Acta Psychologica* 27:285–92.

SPERLING, G.; BUDIANSKY, J.; SPIVAK, J. G.; AND JOHNSON, M. C. 1971. Extremely rapid visual search: the maximum rate of scanning letters for the presence of a numeral. *Science* 174:307–11.

SPERRY, R. W. 1968. Hemisphere deconnection and unity in conscious awareness. *American Psychologist* 23:723–33.

SQUIRE, L. R., SLATER, P. C., AND CHACE, R. M. 1975. Retrograde amnesia: temporal gradient in very long-term memory following electroconvulsive therapy. *Science* 187:77–79.

STANDING, L. G., AND DODWELL, P. C. 1972. Retroactive contour enhancement: a new visual storage effect. *Quarterly Journal of Experimental Psychology* 24:21–29.

STEINHEISER, F. H. 1971. Rehearsal and recoding of information from visual sensory-memory. *Perceptual and Motor Skills* 33:843–48.

STERNBERG, S. 1966. High-speed scanning in human memory. *Science* 153:652–54.

——. 1967. Retrieval of contextual information from memory. *Psychonomic Science* 8:55–56.

——. 1969. Memory scanning: mental processes revealed by reaction time experiments. *American Scientist* 57:421–57.

STEVENS, A. L., AND RUMELHART, D. E. 1975. Errors in reading: an analysis using an augmented transition network model of grammar. In *Explorations in cognition*, ed. D. A. Norman and D. E. Rumelhart. San Francisco: Freeman.

STRATTON, G. M. 1917. The mnemonic feat of the 'Shass Pollak'. *Psychological Review* 24:244–47.

STROOP, J. R. 1938. Factors affecting speed in serial verbal reactions. *Psychological Monographs* 50 (whole no. 225):38–48.

SULLIVAN, E. V., AND TURVEY, M. T. 1974. On the short-term retention of serial, tactile stimuli. *Memory and Cognition* 2:600–606.

SUSSMAN, H. M. 1972. What the tongue tells the brain. *Psychological Bulletin* 77:262–72.

SUTHERLAND, N. S. 1968. Outlines of a theory of visual pattern recognition in animals and man. *Proceedings of the Royal Society* 171:297–317.

———. 1973. Object recognition. In *Handbook of perception*, vol. 3, *Biology of perceptual systems*, ed. E. C. Carterette and M. P. Friedman. New York: Academic Press.

SWINNEY, D. A. 1976. Does context direct lexical access? Paper presented at Midwestern Psychological Association Convention, 7 May 1976.

SWINNEY, D. A., AND HAKES, D. T. 1976. Effects of prior context upon lexical access during sentence comprehension. *Journal of Verbal Learning and Verbal Behavior* 15:681–89.

TANNER, W. P., AND SWETS, J. A. 1954. The human use of information: I. Signal detection for the case of the signal known exactly. *Transcripts of IRE Professional Group on Information Theory* (PGIT-4), 213–21.

TENG, E. L., AND SPERRY, R. W. 1973. Interhemispheric interaction during simultaneous bilateral presentation of letters or digits in commissurotomized patients. *Neuropsychologia* 11:131–40.

TERRY, P.; SAMUELS, S. J.; AND LaBERGE, D. 1976. The effects of letter degradation and letter spacing on word recognition. *Journal of Verbal Learning and Verbal Behavior* 15:577–85.

TEUBER, H. L. 1960. Perception. In *Handbook of physiology: Section 1, Neurophysiology*, vol. 3, ed. J. Field, H. W. Magoun, and V. E. Hall. Washington, D.C.: American Physiological Society.

THEIOS, J., AND MUISE, J. G. 1976. The word identification process in reading. In *Cognitive theory*, vol. 2, ed. N. J. Castellan and D. Pisoni. Potomac, Md.: Erlbaum.

THIOS, S. J. 1975. Memory for general and specific sentences. *Memory and Cognition* 3:75–77.

THOMPSON, M. C., AND MASSARO, D. W. 1973. Visual information and redundancy in reading. *Journal of Experimental Psychology* 98:49–54.

THOMPSON, R. F.; MAYERS, K. S.; ROBERTSON, R. T.; AND PATTERSON, C. J. 1970. Number coding in association cortex of the cat. *Science* 168:271–73.

THORNDYKE, P. W. 1977. Cognitive structures in comprehension and memory of narrative discourse. *Cognitive Psychology* 9:77–110.

THORNDYKE, P. W., AND BOWER, G. H. 1974. Storage and retrieval processes in sentence memory. *Cognitive Psychology* 5:515–43.

THURLOW, W. R. 1972. Audition. In *Experimental psychology*, vol. 1, ed. J. W. Kling and L. A. Riggs. New York: Holt, Rinehart and Winston.

THURSTONE, L. L. 1927a. A law of comparative judgment. *Psychological Review* 34:273–86.

———. 1927b. Psychophysical analysis. *American Journal of Psychology* 38:368–89.

TRABASSO, T., AND BOWER, G. 1964. Presolution reversal and dimensional shifts in concept identification. *Journal of Experimental Psychology* 67:398–99.

———. 1968. *Attention in learning*. New York: Wiley.

TRAVERS, J. R. 1973. The effects of forced serial processing on identification of words and random letter strings. *Cognitive Psychology* 5:109–37.

———. 1974. Word recognition with forced serial processing: effects of segment size and temporal order variation. *Perception and Psychophysics* 16:35–42.

———. 1975. Forced serial processing of words and letter strings: a reexamination. *Perception and Psychophysics* 18:447–52.

TREISMAN, A. M. 1960. Contextual cues in selective listening. *Quarterly Journal of Experimental Psychology* 12:242–48.

———. 1964a. The effect of irrelevant material on the efficiency of selective listening. *American Journal of Psychology* 77:533–46.

———. 1964b. Monitoring and storage of irrelevant messages in selective attention. *Journal of Verbal Learning and Verbal Behavior* 3:449–59.

————. 1964c. Verbal cues, language, and meaning in selective attention. *The American Journal of Psychology* 77:206–19.

TREISMAN, A. M.; RUSSELL, R.; AND GREEN, J. 1975. Brief visual storage of shape and movement. In *Attention and performance V,* ed. P. M. A. Rabbitt and S. Dornic. New York: Academic Press.

TREISMAN, A. M.; SQUIRE, R.; AND GREEN, J. 1974. Semantic processing in dichotic listening? a replication. *Memory and Cognition* 2:641–46.

TRESSELT, M. E., AND MAYZNER, M. S. 1960. A study of incidental learning. *Journal of Psychology* 60:339–47.

TULVING, E. 1962. Subjective organization in free recall of "unrelated words." *Psychological Review* 69:344–54.

————. 1964. Intratrial and intertrial retention: notes toward a theory of free recall verbal learning. *Psychological Review* 71:219–37.

————. 1968. When is recall higher than recognition? *Psychonomic Science* 10:53–54.

————. 1974. Cue-dependent forgetting. *American Scientist* 62:74–82.

TULVING, E., AND PEARLSTONE, Z. 1966. Availability vs. accessibility of information in memory for words. *Journal of Verbal Learning and Verbal Behavior* 5:381–91.

TULVING, E., AND PSOTKA, J. 1971. Retroactive inhibition in free recall: inaccessibility of information available in the memory store. *Journal of Experimental Psychology* 87:1–8.

TULVING, E., AND THOMSON, D. M. 1971. Retrieval processes in recognition memory: effects of associative context. *Journal of Experimental Psychology* 87:116–24.

TULVING, E., AND WATKINS, M. J. 1973. Continuity between recall and recognition. *American Journal of Psychology* 86:739–48.

————. 1974. On negative transfer: effects of testing one list on the recall of another. *Journal of Verbal Learning and Verbal Behavior* 13:181–93.

TURVEY, M. T. 1973. On peripheral and central processes in vision: inferences from an information-processing analysis of masking with patterned stimuli. *Psychological Review* 80:1–52.

TURVEY, M. T.; MICHAELS, C. F.; AND PORT, D. 1974. Visual storage or visual masking? an analysis of the "retroactive contour enhancement" effect. *Quarterly Journal of Experimental Psychology* 26:72–81.

UNDERWOOD, B. J. 1957. Interference and forgetting. *Psychological Review* 64:49–60.

————. 1965. False recognition produced by implicit verbal responses. *Journal of Experimental Psychology* 70:122–29.

UNDERWOOD, B. J., AND SCHULZ, R. W. 1960. *Meaningfulness and verbal learning.* Chicago: Lippincott.

VAN DER HEIJDEN, A. H. C. 1975. Some evidence for a limited capacity parallel self terminating process in simple visual search tasks. *Acta Psychologica* 39:21–41.

VAN DIJK, T. A. 1972. *Some aspects of text grammars.* The Hague: Mouton.

VON HELMHOLTZ, H. 1962. *Treatise on physiological optics,* vol. 3. Trans. and ed. J. P. C. Southall. New York: Dover.

VON WRIGHT, J. M. 1968. Selection in visual immediate memory. *Quarterly Journal of Experimental Psychology* 20:62–68.

————. 1970. On selection in visual immediate memory. *Acta Psychologica* 33:280–92.

————. 1972. On the problem of selection in iconic memory. *The Scandinavian Journal of Psychology* 13:159–71.

WAGNER, H. G.; MACNICHOL, E. F.; AND WOLBARSHT, M. L. 1963. Functional basis for "on"-center and "off"-center receptive fields in the retina. *Journal of the Optical Society of America* 53:66–70.

WALLEY, R. E., AND WEIDEN, T. D. 1973. Lateral inhibition and cognitive masking: a neuropsychological theory of attention. *Psychological Review* 80:284–302.

WANG, M. D. 1977. Frequency effects in the abstraction of linguistic ideas. *Bulletin of the Psychonomic Society* 9:303–6.

WANNER, E. 1974. *On remembering, forgetting, and understanding sentences.* The Hague: Mouton.

WARD, W. D. 1967. Adaptation and fatigue. In *Sensorineural hearing processes and disorders,* ed. A. B. Graham. Boston: Little, Brown.

WARDLAW, K. A., AND KROLL, N. E. A. 1976. Autonomic responses to shock-associated words in a nonattended message: a failure to replicate. *Journal of Experimental Psychology: Human Perception and Performance* 2:357–60.

WARREN, R. E. 1972. Stimulus encoding and memory. *Journal of Experimental Psychology* 94:90–100.

———. 1974. Association, directionality, and stimulus encoding. *Journal of Experimental Psychology* 102:151–58.

WARREN, R. E., AND WARREN, N. T. 1976. Dual semantic encoding of homographs and homophones embedded in context. *Memory and Cognition* 5:586–92.

WARREN, R. M. 1970. Perceptual restoration of missing speech sounds. *Science* 167:392–93.

———. 1971. Identification times for phonemic components of graded complexity and for spelling of speech. *Perception and Psychophysics* 9:345–49.

———. 1974a. Auditory pattern recognition by untrained listeners. *Perception and Psychophysics* 15:495–500.

———. 1974b. Auditory temporal discrimination by trained listeners. *Cognitive Psychology* 6:237–56.

———. 1976. Auditory perception and speech evolution. *Annals of the New York Academy of Sciences* 280:708–17.

WARREN, R. M., AND ACKROFF, J. M. 1976. Two types of auditory sequence perception. *Perception and Psychophysics* 20:387–94.

WARREN, R. M., AND OBUSEK, C. J. 1971. Speech perception and phonemic restorations. *Perception and Psychophysics* 9:358–63.

———. 1972. Identification of temporal order within auditory sequences. *Perception and Psychophysics* 12:86–90.

WARREN, R. M.; OBUSEK, C. J.; FARMER, R. M.; AND WARREN, R. P. 1969. Auditory sequence: confusion of patterns other than speech or music. *Science* 164:586–87.

WARRINGTON, E. K., AND JAMES, M. 1967. Disorders of visual perception in patients with localized cerebral lesions. *Neuropsychologia* 5:253–66.

WASON, P. C. 1965. The contexts of plausible denial. *Journal of Verbal Learning and Verbal Behavior* 4:7–11.

———. 1966. Reasoning. In *New horizons in psychology,* ed. B. M. Foss. Harmondsworth: Penguin.

WASON, P. C., AND JOHNSON-LAIRD, P. N. 1972. *Psychology of reasoning: structure and content.* Cambridge, Mass.: Harvard University Press.

WATKINS, M. J. 1974. When is recall spectacularly higher than recognition? *Journal of Experimental Psychology* 102:161–63.

WAUGH, N. C. 1970. Retrieval time in short-term memory. *British Journal of Psychology* 61:1–12.

WAUGH, N. C., AND NORMAN, D. A. 1965. Primary memory. *Psychological Review* 72:89–104.

WEBER, R. J., AND CASTLEMAN, J. 1970. The time it takes to imagine. *Perception and Psychophysics* 8:165–68.

WEBER, R. J., AND HARNISH, R. 1974. Visual imagery for words: the Hebb test. *Journal of Experimental Psychology* 102:409–14.

WEBSTER, W. R., AND AITKIN, L. M. 1975. Central auditory processing. In *Handbook of psychobiology,* ed. M. S. Gazzaniga and C. Blakemore. New York: Academic Press.

WEINER, B. 1966. Effects of motivation on the availability and retrieval of memory traces. *Psychological Bulletin* 65:24–37.

WEISKRANTZ, L. 1966. Experimental studies of amnesia. In *Amnesia,* ed. C. W. M. Whitty and O. L. Zangwill. London: Butterworths.

WERTHEIMER, M. 1923. Untersuchung zur Lehre von der Gestalt. II. *Psychologische Forschung* 4:301–50.

———. 1945. *Productive thinking.* New York: Harper and Row.

WEVER, E. G. 1949. *Theory of hearing,* reprint. New York: Dover, 1970.

WHEELER, D. D. 1970. Processes in word recognition. *Cognitive Psychology* 1:59–85.

WHITFIELD, I. C. 1967. Coding in the auditory nervous system. *Nature* 213:756–60.

———. 1969. Response of the auditory nervous system to simple time-dependent acoustic stimuli. *Annals of the New York Academy of Sciences* 156:671–77.

WHITFIELD, I. C., AND EVANS, E. F. 1965. Responses of auditory cortical neurons to stimuli of changing frequency. *Journal of Neurophysiology* 28:655–72.

WICKELGREN, W. A. 1964. Size of rehearsal group and short-term memory. *Journal of Experimental Psychology* 68:413–19.

———. 1965a. Acoustic similarity and retroactive interference in short-term memory. *Journal of Verbal Learning and Verbal Behavior* 4:53–61.

———. 1965b. Distinctive features and errors in short-term memory for English vowels. *Journal of the Acoustical Society of America* 38:583–88.

———. 1965c. Short-term memory for phonemically similar lists. *American Journal of Psychology* 78:567–74.

———. 1965d. Short-term memory for repeated and non-repeated items. *Quarterly Journal of Experimental Psychology* 17:14–25.

———. 1966a. Distinctive features and errors in short-term memory for English consonants. *Journal of the Acoustical Society of America* 39:388–98.

———. 1966b. Associative intrusions in short-term recall. *Journal of Experimental Psychology* 72:853–58.

———. 1967a. Rehearsal grouping and hierarchical organization of serial position cues in short-term memory. *Quarterly Journal of Experimental Psychology* 19:97–102.

———. 1967b. Exponential decay and independence from irrelevant associations in short-term recognition memory for serial order. *Journal of Experimental Psychology* 73:165–71.

———. 1968. Unidimensional strength theory and component analysis of noise in absolute and comparative judgments. *Journal of Mathematical Psychology* 5:102–22.

———. 1969a. Context-sensitive coding, associative memory, and serial order in (speech) behavior. *Psychological Review* 76:1–15.

———. 1969b. Context-sensitive coding in speech recognition, articulation, and development. In *Information processing in the nervous system,* ed. K. N. Leibovic. New York: Springer-Verlag.

———. 1969c. Learned specification of concept neurons. *Bulletin of Mathematical Biophysics* 31:123–42.

———. 1969d. Auditory or articulatory coding in verbal short-term memory. *Psychological Review* 76:232–35.

———. 1969e. Associative strength theory of memory for pitch. *Journal of Mathematical Psychology* 6:13–61.

———. 1972a. Context-sensitive coding and serial vs. parallel processing in speech. In *Speech and cortical functioning,* ed. J. H. Gilbert. New York: Academic Press.

———. 1972b. Trace resistance and the decay of long-term memory. *Journal of Mathematical Psychology* 9:418–55.

———. 1974a. Single-trace fragility theory of memory dynamics. *Memory and Cognition* 2:775–80.

———. 1974b. Strength/resistance theory of the dynamics of memory storage. In *Contemporary developments in mathematical psychology,* vol. 1, ed. D. H. Krantz, R. C. Atkinson, R. D. Luce, and P. Suppes. San Francisco: Freeman.

———. 1974c. *How to solve problems.* San Francisco: Freeman.

———. 1975a. Alcoholic intoxication and memory storage dynamics. *Memory and Cognition* 3:385–89.

———. 1975b. Dynamics of retrieval. In *Short-term memory,* ed. D. Deutsch and J. A. Deutsch. New York: Academic Press.

———. 1976a. Phonetic coding and serial order. In *Handbook of perception: language and speech,* vol. 7, ed. E. C. Carterette and M. P. Friedman. New York: Academic Press.

————. 1976b. Memory storage dynamics. In *Handbook of learning and cognitive processes,* vol. 4., ed. W. K. Estes. Potomac, Md.: Erlbaum.

————. 1976c. Subproblems of semantic memory: a review of Human Associative Memory (by J. R. Anderson and G. H. Bower). *Journal of Mathematical Psychology* 13:243–68.

————. 1976d. Network strength theory of storage and retrieval dynamics. *Psychological Review* 83:466–78.

————. 1977a. Speed-accuracy tradeoff and information processing dynamics. *Acta Psychologica* 41:67–85.

————. 1977b. *Learning and memory.* Englewood Cliffs, N.J.: Prentice-Hall.

WICKELGREN, W. A., AND CORBETT, A. T. 1977. Associative interference and retrieval dynamics in yes-no recall and recognition. *Journal of Experimental Psychology: Human Learning and Memory* 3:189–202.

WICKELGREN, W. A., AND NORMAN, D. A. 1966. Strength models and serial position in short-term recognition memory. *Journal of Mathematical Psychology* 3:316–47.

WICKELGREN, W. A., AND WHITMAN, P. T. 1970. Visual very-short-term memory is nonassociative. *Journal of Experimental Psychology* 84:277–81.

WICKELGREN, W. O. 1968a. Effect of state of arousal on click-evoked responses in cats. *Journal of Neurophysiology* 31:757–68.

————. 1968b. Effects of walking and flash stimulation on click-evoked responses in cats. *Journal of Neurophysiology* 31:769–76.

————. 1968c. Effect of acoustic habituation on click-evoked responses in cats. *Journal of Neurophysiology* 31:777–84.

WICKENS, D. D.; MOODY, M.; AND SHEARER, P. W. 1976. Lack of memory for nonattended items in dichotic listening. *Journal of Experimental Psychology: Human Learning and Memory* 2:712–19.

WILKENS, A. J. 1971. Conjoint frequency, category size, and categorization time. *Journal of Verbal Learning and Verbal Behavior* 10:382–85.

WING, A., AND ALLPORT, D. A. 1972. Multidimensional encoding of visual form. *Perception and Psychophysics* 12:474–76.

WINKELMAN, J. H. 1974. The repetition effect in mental arithmetic. Ph.D. dissertation, University of Oregon.

WINOGRAD, T. 1972. *Understanding natural language.* New York: Academic Press.

————. 1973. A procedural model of language understanding. In *Computer models of thought and language,* ed. R. C. Schank and K. M. Colby. San Francisco: Freeman.

WITTGENSTEIN, L. 1953. *Philosophical investigations.* New York: Macmillan.

WOLFORD, G. 1971. Function of distinct associations for paired associate performance. *Psychological Review* 78:303–13.

WOLFORD, G., AND HOLLINGSWORTH, S. 1974. Evidence that short-term memory is not the limiting factor in the tachistoscopic full-report procedure. *Memory and Cognition* 2:796–800.

WOOD, C. C. 1974. Parallel processing of auditory and phonetic information in speech discrimination. *Perception and Psychophysics* 15:501–8.

WOODS, W. A. 1970. Transition network grammars for natural language analysis. *Communications of the ACM* 13:591–606.

————. 1975. What's in a link: foundations for semantic networks. In *Representation and understanding,* ed. D. G. Bobrow and A. Collins. New York: Academic Press.

WOODWORTH, R. S. 1938. *Experimental psychology.* New York: Holt.

ZADEH, L. A. 1965. Fuzzy sets. *Information and Control* 8:338–53.

————. 1976. A fuzzy algorithmic approach to the definition of complex or imprecise concepts. *International Journal of Man-Machine Studies* 8:249–91.

ZADEH, L. A.; FU, K. S.; TANAKA, K.; AND SHIMURA, M., eds. 1975. *Fuzzy sets and their application to cognitive and decision processes.* New York: Academic Press.

ZWICKER, E., AND SCHARF, B. 1965. A model of loudness summation. *Psychological Review* 72:3–26.

INDEXES

NAME INDEX

Abbs, J. H., 141–42
Abells, M., 105, 106, 107
Abrahamson, A. A., 319
Ackroff, J. M., 115
Adams, N., 182 (Smith et al.)
Adamson, R. E., 380
Ainsworth, W. H., 138
Aitkin, L. M., 107n
Allan, L. G., 70
Allard, F., 274
Allport, D. A., 62–63, 173, 182, 184
Alluisi, E. A., 45
Altman, Y. A., 105
Anderson, J. A., 263
Anderson, J. R., 7, 8, 24, 223, 225–26, 229, 237, 287, 318, 319, 322, 325, 327, 335, 337, 338, 339, 340, 351, 352n, 356, 364n
Anderson, R. C., 286, 340
Anderson, W. G., 145
Anglin, J. M., 313, 315
Anisfeld, M., 279
Antone, G., 24
Antonis, B., 173
Archer, E. J., 246, 304, 305
Arnold, D., 165–66 (Carr et al.)
Asch, S. E., 232
Ashcraft, M. H., 338, 339
Asso, D., 154
Astor-Stetson, E. C., 165–66 (Carr et al.)
Atkinson, R. C., 265, 266
Attneave, F., 21n, 45, 49, 50, 55, 60, 61, 62, 69, 300
Austin, G. A., 303

Ausubel, D. P., 289–90
Averbach, E., 179, 191–93, 194

Baddeley, A. D., 201, 211–12, 265
Bahrick, H. P., 259
Ball, F., 176
Ball, G. G., 305
Banerji, R., 379
Banks, W. P., 369
Barclay, J. R., 321
Barlow, H. B., 30, 46, 51
Barnett, T., 198–99
Barney, H. L., 127, 133
Baron, J., 156
Barresi, J., 310
Bartlett, F. C., 326
Bates, A., 198–99
Baumgarte, R., 266
Bayer, R. H., 369
Beck, J., 49
Becklen, R., 186
Begg, I., 280, 319
Bekesy, G. von, 109
Bekker, J. A. M., 274
Bellugi, V., 314
Bendler, D. B., 57
Bennett, D. C., 138
Berrian, R. W., 145
Bertelson, P., 182, 278
Bertulis, A., 29, 30 (Glezer et al.)
Besner, D., 274
Bever, T. G., 136, 176, 336
Bieber, S. L., 201–2

Biederman, I., 62
Birch, H. G., 380
Birnbaum, I. M., 243
Bitterman, M. E., 30n
Blakemore, C., 46, 51
Blechner, M. J., 116
Block, G., 62
Block, R. A., 222–23
Blumenthal, A. L., 325
Boakes, R., 325
Bobrow, D. G., 175, 326
Boies, S., 182, 274 (Posner et al.)
Bongartz, W., 180, 181
Borden, R. L., 24
Boring, E. G., 29
Bourne, L. E., Jr., 304
Bousfield, W. A., 267
Bower, G., 7, 8, 24, 75, 80, 229, 231, 232, 237,
    304, 305, 309, 310, 319, 322, 335, 337, 339,
    340, 346, 347, 349, 350
Boyes-Braem, P., 297–98, 314 (Rosch et al.)
Bradshaw, J. L., 150n, 151, 185
Branch, C., 22
Bransford, J. D., 307, 308, 319, 320, 321, 349
Bregman, A. S., 113–14, 307, 308
Broadbent, D. E., 133, 138, 177
Brooks, D. H., 24
Brooks, L. R., 23, 310n
Brookshire, K. H., 305
Brown, K. T., 47, 48
Brown, R., 288
Brownell, H., 182 (Smith et al.)
Bruner, J. S., 303
Budiansky, J., 164, 170, 174, 180, 194 (Sperling
    et al.)
Bugarella, R., 304
Burke, D., 212
Burkland, W. C., 22
Burrows, D., 264
Butler, R. A., 103
Butterworth, G., 104–5

Cairns, H. S., 336
Campbell, D. T., 381, 383, 384
Campbell, F. W., 35n, 46
Campbell, J., 113
Capps, M. J., 110
Carr, T. H., 155–56
Carre, F. A., 170 (Hintzman et al.)
Carterette, E. C., 177–78
Carter-Sobell, L., 287
Carver, R. P., 158
Casteneda-Mendez, K., 183
Castillo, M., 104–5
Castleman, J., 84
Cattell, J. M., 153
Caussé, R., 110
Cavanagh, P., 263
Ceraso, J., 232
Chabot, R. J., 237, 238n
Chace, R. M., 241
Chafe, W. L., 341
Chait, H., 308 (Peterson et al.)
Chapman, R. H., 364n
Chase, W. G., 278
Charness, N., 307, 308
Chavasse, P., 110
Checkosky, S. F., 62
Cherry, E. C., 177

Chistovich, L. A., 133
Chomsky, N., 129, 321, 356
Chow, S. L., 195
Clark, H. H., 341, 343, 365, 367
Clarkson, J. K., 111
Cleland, B. G., 30
Cofer, C. N., 267
Cohen, B. D., 22
Cohen, B. H., 267
Cohen, G., 24, 176
Cohen, R. L., 22, 212
Coke, E. U., 267
Cole, R. A., 132
Coles, G. R., 182
Collins, A. M., 7, 265–66, 279, 326, 338, 339
Collins, W. F., 110
Coltheart, M., 90, 149, 274, 339
Conrad, R., 204, 336, 338
Cooper, F. S., 129, 132, 140, 147 (Liberman et
    al.)
Cooper, L. A., 89–90
Cooperman, A. M., 35n, 36 (Glezer et al.)
Corballis, M. C., 199, 260n, 264
Corbett, A. T., 261, 269, 271, 272, 273, 274, 277,
    328
Corcoran, D. W. J., 274
Coriell, A. S., 179
Cornell, D., 308 (Homa et al.)
Craft, J. L., 72
Craik, F. I. M., 264
Cronnell, B., 149
Cross, J., 308 (Homa et al.)
Crothers, E. J., 232–33
Crowder, R. G., 198, 199–200, 201
Csapo, K., 24
Cutting, J. E., 116

Dallas, M., 185
Dallenbach, K. M., 245
Dallett, K. M., 239
Dallos, P. J., 109
Daniloff, R., 145
Danks, D. H., 380
Dannenbring, G. L., 113
Dark, V. J., 238
Darwin, C. J., 199
Davelaar, E., 339
Davenport, W. G., 72
Davies, G. M., 24
Davis, G. A., 279
Davis, R., 181, 267
Day, R. H., 105, 116
Deese, J., 267
Dennis, M., 22
DeRosa, D. V., 264, 266
Deutsch, D., 23, 99n, 107n, 108, 117, 118–19, 165
Deutsch, J. A., 99n, 107n, 108, 111, 165
DeValois, K. K., 46
DeValois, R., 36, 37
Diamond, I. T., 107
Dodwell, P. C., 196
Dooling, D. J., 349
Dosher, B. A., 261, 265, 271, 272, 274, 279, 322,
    337, 338
Dumpty, H., 343n
Duncker, K., 377, 378, 380

Eagle, M., 279
Earhard, B., 244

Ecob, J. R., 265
Edison, T., 383
Edmonds, E. M., 307
Efron, R., 135
Egan, J. P., 177–78, 257
Egeth, H., 182, 183, 266
Eichelman, E. H., 274 (Posner et al.)
Eimas, P. D., 157
Ekstrand, B. R., 245
Ells, J. G., 71
Engelkamp, J., 324n, 366
Enroth-Cugall, C., 40, 41
Epstein, W., 232
Ericksen, C. W., 145, 181
Ernst, G. W., 379
Ervin-Tripp, S., 315
Eskridge, V. L., 170 (Hintzman et al.)
Estes, W. K., 8, 156, 194
Evans, E. F., 106
Evans, J. St. B. T., 362
Evans, S. H., 307

Fant, C. G. M., 129, 132
Farmer, R. M., 115, 134 (Warren et al.)
Favreau, D., 184
Felfoldy, G. L., 55n
Filby, N., 344
Fillenbaum, S., 279
Fischler, I., 339
Fisher, D. F., 149
Fitter, M., 184
Fitzhugh, R., 30
Fivel, M. W., 304
Flagg, P. W., 321
Flora, J., 369
Fodor, J. A., 350
Folkins, J. W., 141–42
Foss, D. J., 136, 176, 336, 340
Franks, J. J., 307, 308, 319, 320, 321
Fraser, J., 244, 261
Freedman, J. L., 262, 265, 266
Freeman, R., 149
Freibergs, V., 295
Freides, D., 24
Friedman, M., 307, 308
Fromkin, V. A., 146
Frost, N., 92, 307–8
Fu., K. S., 297 (Zadeh et al.)
Funkenstein, H. H., 116
Fusella, V., 80, 81

Gaines, B. R., 297
Galanter, E., 356, 358, 360
Ganz, L., 59
Gardner, M. B., 102
Garner, W. R., 55
Garrett, M. F., 336
Garrod, S., 318, 351
Gary, W. D., 297–98, 314 (Rosch et al.)
Gazzaniga, M. S., 20n
Gentner, D., 315, 350, 351
Gentry, T. A., 46 (Skowbo et al.)
Gibson, E. J., 148n, 149, 150n, 151, 153
Gibson, J. J., 45, 71
Gilchrist, A., 65
Gillie, S., 308 (Peterson et al.)
Gilliom, J. D., 184
Glanzer, M., 231
Glass, A. L., 80, 364, 366, 368

Glass, G., 319
Glezer, V. D., 29, 30, 35n, 36
Gleitman, H., 117
Glick, M. J., 90
Glucksberg, S., 380
Goetz, E. T., 286 (Anderson et al.)
Goldberg, J. J., 107
Goldman, D., 308 (Homa et al.)
Goldstein, M. H., 105, 106, 107
Goodman, D., 287, 308, 310
Goodnow, J. J., 303
Gottlieb, G., 22
Gottsdanker, R., 172
Graf, R. G., 158
Granström, K., 22
Grantham, D. W., 182
Graves, R. E., 194
Gray, C. R., 81
Green, D. M., 257, 267
Green, D. W., 150n, 151
Green, J., 183, 185, 198
Greene, J. M., 365
Greeno, J. G., 377, 378
Greenwood, D. D., 107
Groff, P., 149
Gross, C. G., 57
Grossman, L., 279
Gummerman, K., 81
Guttman, N., 200

Haber, L. R., 81, 149
Haber, R. N., 81, 149, 193
Hafter, E. R., 104
Haggard, M., 182
Hakes, D. T., 336
Hall, D. C., 75
Halle, M., 129
Halliday, M. A. K., 341
Hardyck, D. C., 150
Harnish, R., 77–79, 84, 85
Harrison, J. M., 105
Hartline, H. K., 42
Harwood, D. A., 340
Hastie, R., 287
Haviland, S. E., 156, 182 (Smith et al.), 341, 343
Hayes, J. R., 377
Hayes-Roth, B., 369
Hayes-Roth, F., 369
Haygood, R. C., 304
Hebb, D. O., 52n, 54, 55, 74, 77, 78, 300
Heider, E., 298
Heimer, W., 232
Heise, G. A., 112–13
Held, R., 45, 69 (Ingle et al.)
Henderson, L., 153, 274
Henneman, R. H., 182
Herman, L. M., 72
Hernandez-Peon, R., 108
Heron, W., 54, 55
Herrnstein, R. J., 29
Hick, W. E., 181
Hinrichs, J. V., 72
Hintzman, D. L., 170, 222–23
Hirst, W., 173
Hitch, G., 211–12
Hochberg, J. E., 30n
Hoffman, J. E., 181
Hogben, J. H., 198
Holding, D. H., 46

Hollingsworth, S., 194
Holloway, C. M., 182, 184, 199–200
Holyoak, K. J, 364, 366, 368, 369
Homa, D., 308, 310
Horii, Y., 142
Horman, H., 324n, 366
Hornby, P. A., 342
Horowitz, L. M., 233, 325
Houston, J. P., 246, 261
House, A. S., 142 (Horii et al.)
Hovland, C. I., 294
Howard, J. H., Jr., 369
Howe, T. S., 246
Hubel, D. H., 31–34, 36, 37, 51
Huey, E., 153
Hull, C. L., 305–7
Hunter, I. M. L., 357n
Hupcey, J. A., 347
Hurtig, R., 336
Huttenlocher, J., 212
Hyde, T. S., 237
Hyman, R., 181, 182, 278, 307–8

Ingle, D., 69
Isard, S., 138, 139
Irving, R., 105
Irwin, J. M., 243
Ivanov, V. A., 29, 30, 35n, 36 (Glezer et al.)

Jack, O., 203
Jackson, J. Z., 153
Jackson, M. D., 153
Jakobson, R., 129
James, C. T., 319
James, M., 21, 68
James, W., 278
Jastrzembski, J. E., 288
Jenkins, C. M., 336
Jenkins, J. G., 245
Jenkins, J. J., 236, 237, 267
Jensen, A. R., 280
Johnsen, R. A., 74, 76, 80
Johnson, A. L., 201–2
Johnson, D. M., 297–98, 314, (Rosch et al.), 381
Johnson, M. C., 164, 170, 174, 180, 194
Johnson, M. K., 349
Johnson, N. F., 153, 231
Johnson, P. E. J., 305
Johnson, R. E., 347
Johnson-Laird, P. N., 352, 362, 363n, 364n, 365, 367, 368
Johnston, C. D., 237
Johnston, J. C., 156
Johnston, L. S., 111 (Parker et al.)
Johnston, P. A., 111 (Parker et al.)
Jones, P. D., 46
Jorgensen, C. C., 232–33
Jouvet, M., 108
Judd, B. R., 267
Julesz, B., 49, 195, 198, 200
Juola, J. F., 237, 238n, 265, 266

Kahneman, D., 75
Kamerman, J., 336
Kantowitz, B. H., 72
Kaplan, R. M., 335, 356
Karlin, L., 167–68, 169
Karlin, M. B., 237
Katz, J. J., 350

Kausler, D. H., 279
Kay, E. J., 150n
Keele, S. W., 71, 170, 182, 201, 202, 307, 308, 311, 321, 347
Keenan, J. M., 325n, 345, 347 (Kintsch et al.)
Kempen, G., 322, 324n
Kendler, H. H., 305
Kendler, T. S., 305
Kent, R. D., 140
Kepros, P. G., 304
Keren, G., 180
Kerst, S. M., 369
Kestenbaum, R., 167–68, 169
Kiang, N. Y.-S., 107
Kimura, D., 20
Kinchla, R. A., 70, 117
King, D., 339
Kintsch, W., 232–33, 267, 319, 321, 322, 325n, 345, 347, 349, 350, 351–52
Kirby, J., 264
Kirsner, K., 264
Klapp, S. T., 145
Kleiman, G. M., 152
Klein, G. S., 280
Knapp, M., 279
Kohler, W., 45
Kohn, B., 22
Kohout, L. J., 297
Kolers, P. A., 75, 152–53, 154, 157
Konick, A. F., 71, 72
Konorski, J., 37, 41
Koppenaal, R. J., 243
Kosslyn, S. M., 79, 84–86, 338
Kottas, B., 165–66 (Carr et al.)
Kozhevnikov, V. A., 133
Kozminsky, E., 325n, 345, 347 (Kintsch et al.)
Krauskopf, J., 30n
Kroener, S., 211
Kroll, N. E. A., 201–2, 211
Krueger, L. E., 154, 176
Kuffler, S. W., 29, 30

Laabs, G. J., 70, 72–73
LaBerge, D. L., 154, 182
Lachman, R., 349
Lackner, J. R., 336
Ladefoged, P., 133, 138, 144–45
Lakoff, G., 291
Landauer, T. K., 265
Lashley, K. S., 143, 144, 385–86
Lasky, R. E., 307, 308
Lawrence, D. H., 182
Lawson, R., 369
Lazar, R., 174
Lehmkuhle, S. W., 155–56 (Carr et al.)
Leiman, A. L., 104
Lemnie, P., 41
Levelt, W. J. M., 322, 324n
Levick, W. R., 30
Levin, H., 149, 150n, 151, 153
Levy, B. A., 152
Lewis, C. H., 226, 325
Lewis, C. L., 152–53
Lewis, J. L., 185
Li, K., 142 (Horii et al.)
Liberman, A. M., 129, 132, 140, 147
Light, L. L., 287
Lindblom, B., 140
Lindig, K., 136, 176

Lindsay, P. H., 7, 101n, 103
Lindsley, J. R., 145n
Lockhead, G. R., 55, 63–64
Loftus, E. F., 7, 185, 262, 266, 279, 339, 340
Loftus, G. R., 75, 238
Long, E. R., 182
Long, J., 138, 139, 157, 184
Lott, L., 149
Luchins, A. S., 380
Luria, A. R., 21
Lyon, D. R., 212

McClelland, J. L., 149–50, 153, 156
McCollough, C., 46
McCormack, P. D., 260n
McCulloch, W. S., 7, 338
McFarland, J. H., 54
McGeoch, J. A., 245
McGovern, J. B., 224, 225, 244
McGuigan, F. J., 150
Mach, E., 40
MacKay, D. G., 144, 146, 287–88, 336
Mackintosh, N. J., 305
McKoon, G., 325n, 345, 347 (Kintsch et al.)
MacLeod, C. M., 280
MacLeod, D. I. A., 46
MacNeilage, P. F., 140, 143
McNeill, D., 136, 176, 288
MacNichol, E. F., 40
Mandler, G., 267
Manelis, L., 156, 325n, 345, 346, 347
Marcus, N., 266
Markman, E. M., 295
Marks, D. F., 75, 76, 81
Marks, G., 184
Marks, M. R., 203
Martin, E., 239
Martin, J. G., 138, 139
Massaro, D. W., 60, 111, 117, 134–35, 148n,
    150n, 151, 156, 157, 182, 198, 199
Mayers, K. S., 57
Mayes, J. T., 199–200
Mayzner, M. S., 237
Meagher, R. B., Jr., 308 (Peterson et al.)
Melton, A. W., 243–44
Merdian, F., 324n
Merikle, P. M., 185
Merkel, J., 181
Mervis, C. B., 297–98, 311, 314 (Rosch et al.)
Metzler, J., 86–89
Meyer, B. J. F., 347
Meyer, D. E., 151, 265, 339, 368
Michaels, C. F., 196
Miller, A., 264
Miller, G. A., 8, 45, 112–13, 135, 138, 139, 203,
    227, 356, 358, 360
Miller, R. S., 298
Miller, T. J., 237, 238n
Milner, B., 21, 22
Milner, P. M., 52n
Minsky, M., 326
Mistler-Lachman, J. L., 336
Mitchell, R. F., 274
Moeser, S. D., 345
Moll, K., 140, 145
Monahan, J. S., 64
Montague, W. F., 145
Moody, M., 211
Moore, J. J., 182

Morant, R. B., 46 (Skowbo et al.)
Moray, N., 178, 181, 184, 185, 198–99
Morin, R. E., 264
Morton, J., 138, 139, 157, 198, 199–200
Moses, F. L., 267
Mowbray, G. H., 181
Moyer, R. S., 367, 369
Muise, J. G., 153
Müller, G. E., 239
Müller, J., 28, 29
Muncey, J. P. J., 46
Munsterberg, H., 201–2
Murdock, B. B., Jr., 195, 199
Murray, D. J., 22, 201–2

Nagy, V., 184
Nebes, R. D., 20n
Neff, W. D., 107
Neimark, E. D., 364n
Neisser, U., 58n, 173–74, 186, 191, 198, 295, 347
Nelson, D. L., 24
Nelson, K. E., 338
Nelson, P. G., 116 (Funkenstein et al.)
Nelson, T. O., 211, 237, 238, 280
Neumann, P. G., 307, 308, 310
Newcombe, F., 21, 68
Newell, A., 356, 371, 375
Newman, F. M., 22
Newman, J. D., 116 (Funkenstein et al.)
Newport, E. L., 314
Newton, J. M., 246
Noblin, C. D., 22 (Cohen et al.)
Nooteboom, S. G., 146
Norman, D. A., 7, 101n, 103, 113, 175, 211, 235,
    257, 258, 266, 267, 278, 322, 334, 335, 339,
    344, 350
Novick, R., 174

Obusek, C. J., 115, 134, 139
O'Dell, C., 368
Öhman, S. E. G., 140
Okada, R., 264
Olivier, D. C., 298
Olson, D. R., 344
Olson, J. N., 336
Olson, R. K., 49, 60
Olton, R. M., 381
Ortony, A., 287, 352
Osgood, C. E., 239, 344
Osler, S. F., 304
Ostry, D., 184
Owens, A. M., 170 (Hintzman et al.)
Over, R., 47

Pachella, R. G., 183
Paivio, A., 24, 232, 369
Palmer, S. E., 64, 74, 80, 91, 92, 326
Papcun, G., 144–45
Parducci, A., 45
Parker, D. E., 111
Parkinson, S., 201–2
Parks, T., 201–2
Pasteur, L., 381
Patterson, C. J., 57
Pauling, L., 389
Pearlstone, Z., 267
Pelton, L. H., 48
Penfield, W., 21
Penick, S. B., 22 (Cohen et al.)

Pepper, R. L., 72
Perfetti, C. A., 287
Perky, C. W., 81
Perrett, L. F., 45
Peterson, G. E., 127, 133
Peterson, L. R., 211
Peterson, M. J., 308
Petrinovich, L. F., 150
Pettigrew, J. D., 51
Phillips, W. A., 201
Piaget, J., 312–13, 314
Pickert, J. W., 286 (Anderson et al.)
Pilzecher, A., 239
Pisoni, D. B., 134–35, 183
Pitts, W., 7
Podvigin, N. F., 29, 30 (Glezer et al.)
Pohlmann, L. D., 184
Polf, J. O., 274–76
Pollack, I., 105
Pollack, M. D., 145
Pollatsek, A., 155–56
Pollen, D. A., 35n
Polya, G., 371
Pomerantz, J. R., 86
Poritsky, S., 147
Port, D., 196
Posnansky, C. J., 307, 308
Posner, M. I., 71, 72, 186, 201, 202, 274, 280, 307, 308, 311, 381
Postman, L., 236, 244, 246, 261
Potts, G. R., 369
Poulton, E. C., 158
Pribram, K. H., 356, 358, 360
Pritchard, R. M., 54, 55
Prussin, H. A., 199–200
Prytulak, L. S., 233, 325

Quillian, M. R., 7, 266, 279, 338, 361

Rabinowitz, H. S., 380
Radner, M., 45
Raeburn, V. P., 199–200
Rashevsky, N., 7, 338
Rasmussen, T., 22
Ratliff, F., 40, 42
Razel, M., 231
Reder, L. M., 182 (Smith et al.)
Reed, A. V., 261, 265, 274
Reed, S. K., 74, 76, 80, 92, 307, 308, 379
Reich, P. A., 313
Reicher, G. M., 155–56
Reid, K. W., 60
Reid, L. S., 182
Reitman, J. S., 309, 310
Remington, R. W., 135
Renkin, A., 182, 278
Reynolds, A. G., 321
Reynolds, P., 173
Rhoades, M. U., 181
Richter, M. L., 150n
Ridley, R. M., 46
Rieger, C., 261
Riesbeck, C. K., 336
Riley, C. A., 369
Ringel, R. L., 142
Rips, L. J., 291, 368
Robbins, D., 310
Roberge, J. J., 367
Roberts, L., 21

Robertson, R. T., 57
Robson, J. G., 29, 40
Rocha-Miranda, C. E., 57
Rock, I., 48, 58n, 60, 65, 232
Roffler, S. K., 103
Rohwer, W. D., 232, 280
Ronner, S. F., 35n
Rose, M., 105
Rosenblith, W. A., 109
Ross, J., 198
Rostelyanets, N. B., 29, 30 (Glezer et al.)
Rothkopf, E. Z., 267
Routh, D. A., 199–200
Rowe, P. B., 363
Roy, E. A., 72
Rozin, P., 147
Rubenstein, H., 150n
Rudnicky, A. I., 113–14
Ruddy, M. G., 151
Rumelhart, D. E., 7, 322, 335, 339, 344, 349, 350
Russell, R., 198
Russell, W. A., 267
Russell, W. R., 21, 68, 240

Sachs, J. S., 237
Sachs, M. B., 107
Sakitt, B., 194, 195–96
Samuels, S. J., 154
Sandberg, R. L., 212
Savin, H. B., 136, 176
Scarborough, D. L., 195
Schallert, D., 286 (Anderson et al.)
Schank, R. C., 322, 336, 350, 361
Scharf, B., 102, 111
Scheerer, E., 180, 181
Scherrer, R., 108
Schiller, P. H., 196
Schindler, R. M., 155–56
Schmuller, J., 148n
Schneider, G. E., 69
Schneider, W., 170, 174–75
Schouter, J. F., 274
Schuberth, R. E., 157
Schulz, R. W., 231
Schvaneveldt, R. W., 294, 339
Scott, B., 132
Scott, C. M., 142
Segal, S. J., 80, 81
Seibert, J., 295
Selters, W., 110
Selz, O., 326
Settle, A. V., 279
Shaff, S. S., 170 (Hintzman et al.)
Shaffer, L. H., 173
Shain, K., 310
Shallice, T., 150n, 151
Shankweiler, D. D., 129, 132, 140, 147 (Liberman et al.)
Shattuck, S. R., 45
Shaw, J. C., 375
Shearer, P. W., 211
Sheenan, M. M., 204
Shephard, R. N., 55, 86–90, 204
Shiffrin, R. M., 170, 174–75, 182–83, 194
Shimura, M., 297 (Zadeh et al.)
Shoben, E. J., 291
Shockey, L., 133
Shwartz, S., 308 (Homa et al.)
Silverman, A. J., 22 (Cohen et al.)

430

Silverstein, R., 144–45
Simmons, F. B., 109
Simon, H. A., 371, 375
Simon, J. R., 377
Simpson, E., 298, 307, 308
Singer, M., 342
Skowbo, D., 46
Slater, P. C., 241
Sloboda, J. A., 157
Smith, A., 22
Smith, E. E., 156, 176, 182, 183, 278, 291
Smith, F., 149, 153, 158
Smith, M. C., 169, 170, 171–72, 182, 278
Smith, P. G., 278
Smyzer, F., 117
Snodgrass, J. G., 24
Snyder, C. R. R., 186, 280
Solley, C. M., 48
Somjen, G., 99n, 107n, 108
Sorkin, R. D., 184
Sotsky, R., 147
Sparks, M. E., 170 (Hintzman et al.)
Spelke, E., 173
Sperling, G., 164, 170, 174, 179, 180, 190,
    191–93, 194
Sperry, R. W., 20n
Spivak, J. G., 164, 170, 174, 180, 194 (Sperling et
    al.)
Squire, L. R., 241
Squire, R., 183, 185
Standing, L. G., 193, 196
Stanners, R. F., 288
Stark, K., 244, 261
Steinhauser, F. H., 194
Stelmach, G. E., 172
Sternberg, S., 261–64, 265, 266
Stevens, A. L., 335
Stevens, K. V., 286 (Anderson et al.)
Stevenson, M., 304
Stratton, G. M., 82
Streby, W. J., 325n, 345, 347 (Kintsch et al.)
Stroop, J. R., 280
Studdert-Kennedy, M., 129, 132, 140, 147
    (Liberman et al.)
Stultz, V., 264
Sussman, H. M., 140
Sutherland, N. S., 48n, 52, 58n, 267
Sutton, P., 46
Swets, J. A., 257
Swinney, D. A., 136, 176, 336

Tagart, J., 362
Tanaka, K., 297 (Zadeh et al.)
Tanner, W. P., 257
Taylor, D. W., 380
Taylor, H. A., 194
Taylor, J. H., 35n
Taylor, R. L., 274
Teng, E. L., 20n
Terry, P., 154
Teuber, H. L., 55n
Theios, J., 153
Thios, S. J., 325
Thompson, M. C., 156
Thompson, R. F., 57
Thomson, D. M., 287
Thorndyke, P. M., 337, 346, 347, 349, 350
Thurlow, W. R., 111
Thurstone, L. L., 156, 257

Thwing, E. J., 177–78
Timney, B. N., 46 (Skowbo et al.)
Trabasso, T., 304, 305, 318, 351
Trautman, G. E., 304
Travers, J. R., 153, 154–55
Treisman, A. M., 177, 178, 181, 183, 185, 198,
    200
Tresselt, M. E., 237
Trevarthen, C., 69 (Ingle et al.)
Tridgell, J. M., 365, 367
Trollip, S. R., 286 (Anderson et al.)
Tsherback, T. A., 35n, 36 (Glezer et al.)
Tubbs, R. L., 111 (Parker et al.)
Tulving, E., 239, 267, 268, 269, 287, 295
Turvey, M. T., 196, 199

Ulm, R., 264
Underwood, B. J., 231, 239, 244, 246, 279

Van der Heijden, A. H. C., 174
Van Dijk, T. A., 349, 350
Van Meeteren, A., 46
Von Wright, J. M., 180
Vosburgh, R., 308

Wagner, H. G., 40, 42
Walker, J. H., 369
Wallach, H., 45
Walley, R. E., 41, 165
Wang, M. D., 319
Wanner, E., 346
Ward, W. D., 110
Wardlaw, K. A., 211
Warren, J. M., 305
Warren, L., 246
Warren, N. T., 336
Warren, R. E., 280, 336
Warren, R. M., 115, 117, 134, 136, 139, 176
Warren, R. P., 134 (Warren et al.)
Warrington, E. K., 21, 68
Wason, M. J., 362, 363n, 364n, 365, 368
Watkins, M. J., 239, 268, 269
Waugh, N. C., 266, 278
Weber, R. J., 76–79, 84, 85
Webster, W. R., 107n
Weene, P., 295
Weiden, T. D., 41, 165
Weiner, B., 236n
Weiskrantz, L., 241
Weiss, M. E., 176
Weiss, W., 294
Well, A. D., 155–56
Wertheimer, M., 48
Wever, E. J., 110
Wheeler, D. D., 156
Whitfield, I. C., 99, 106, 107n, 108
Whitman, P. T., 197
Wickelgren, W. A., 8, 117, 125, 136, 143, 145,
    176, 197, 204, 205, 206, 207, 209, 224n, 229,
    236n, 239, 240, 241, 244, 246, 257, 258, 259,
    260n, 261, 265, 266n, 267, 269, 271, 272,
    273, 274, 276n, 278, 279, 280, 319, 322, 338,
    352, 373, 374, 375, 377, 378, 379, 380, 381
Wickelgren, W. O., 108
Wickens, D. D., 211, 246
Wiesel, T. N., 30–34, 36, 37, 51
Wilkens, A. J., 265
Wilson, I., 22
Wilson, P. D., 59

Wing, A., 62–63
Winograd, T., 335
Winter, P., 116 (Funkenstein et al.)
Wittgenstein, L., 301
Wolbarsht, M. L., 40
Wolf, J., 92
Wolford, G., 194, 269
Wollberg, Z., 116 (Funkenstein et al.)
Wood, C., 176
Wood, C. C., 116
Woods, D. D., 184

Woods, W. A., 290n, 296, 327, 335, 344n, 350, 356, 363n
Woodworth, R. S., 300
Wyke, M., 154

Yekovich, F. R., 325n, 345, 346, 347

Zadeh, L. A., 297
Zuckerman, C. B., 232
Zwicker, E., 111

SUBJECT INDEX

Absolute judgment, 44–45, 269
Absolute pitch, 117–18
Abstract, 289–90, 313–14
Abstraction, 302, 304–12
Accessible information, 220
Acoustic reflex, 109, 110
Action, 357–60. See also Operations
Activation, 6–7, 13–15, 28–29, 38, 42–43, 52–53, 57, 62–64, 75–79, 82–86, 100–106, 114–17, 133–39, 143–45, 152–57, 165–66, 175–76, 189–212, 216, 219, 228, 235–37, 260, 274, 278–80, 288, 292–94, 324–26, 334–39, 343–45, 356–64, 387
    halo, 279, 326. See also Attentional set, Schema
    spread, 278–79, 337–39. See also Attentional set, Schema
Activational memory. See Active memory
Active memory, 166, 189–212, 326–27, 338–39. See also Attentional set, Priming
Acuity, 40–41, 51
Adaptation, 30, 40–48, 108–11, 133, 138
Aesthetics, 95–96, 119–20
Afterimage, 75, 179, 190–91. See also Iconic memory
Agraphia, 21
Alexia, 21. See also Dyslexia
Allophone, 19, 125–27, 132–39, 142–47
All-or-none
    recall, 319
    retrieval, 272
    storage, 276
Ambiguity
    figural, 47–48, 50
    phrase label, 335–36
    phrase structure, 316, 335
    words (lexical), 185, 286–88, 336
Analysis, 2–3, 11, 25
AND gate, 35, 106
Aphasia, 21
Apprehension span, 153, 164, 173–75, 178–79, 193–95, 272, 326
Arousal, 163, 235–37, 245
Articulation, 18, 115, 116, 124, 126–29, 139–47, 204, 357–58
Association, 7–16, 22–25, 55, 64, 75, 81, 86, 109, 143–45, 153, 156–57, 166, 169–72, 175, 178, 181, 189, 196–97, 202–11, 215–46, 267–70, 276–79, 297–99, 302, 309–12, 324–26, 334, 337–40, 342, 346–48, 363–66, 382
    backward, 225, 233–34, 260, 269, 339–40
    forward, 225, 233–34, 260, 269, 339–40
    horizontal vs. vertical, 8–11, 25–26, 55, 144, 227–34

Associative memory, 216–34, 253–54, 259–62, 273, 340–41, 358–60, 385, 387
Asymptote, 167–68, 271, 274–77
Attention, 15, 41–42, 49–50, 53–54, 56, 75–79, 83–85, 108, 113–14, 161–76, 194–95, 235, 278, 304–5, 342–43, 361, 363
Attentional set, 16–17, 42, 161–66, 171–72, 174, 176–86, 195, 298, 326–27, 380. See also Priming
Attribute. See Feature
Auditory stream segregation, 112–14
Automatization, 174–75, 276–78
Available information, 220

Ballistic, 140–42
Branching, 356–60

Canonical form, 350–52
Capacity, 212
Case, 321–25
Cell assembly, 55
Choice. See Decision making
Chunking, 8–12, 51–52, 55–58, 115–16, 189, 202–4, 207–9, 211–12, 227–34, 239, 243, 254, 272–73, 289, 352, 354, 360, 361, 364, 378–79
Class, 295–96
Coarticulation, 142–43
Coding, 4–11, 23–24, 73–74, 124–31, 216–34, 236–37, 273–78, 331, 371, 373, 376–381
    analogue, 92
    cross-classification, 208–9
    hierarchical, 209, 357–60
    procedural, 356–60
    propositional, 288–357
    specific node (element), 7, 28–29, 57, 80, 101–7, 114–16, 134–35, 216–34
Cognitive maps, 18, 65, 68–69
Cognitive-sensory-motor, 4, 17–20, 25, 28, 127–29
Collection, 295–96
Comparative judgment, 44–45, 70, 269
Competition, 243–44, 261
Comprehension. See Understanding
Concept, 8–11, 52, 56–62, 114, 119, 124, 147, 150–51, 158–59, 189, 202, 209, 217–18, 227–30, 284–315, 331–32, 336, 339, 341–46, 350–53, 360–70, 377, 385–86
    basic, 312–15
    family, 296
    learning, 289–290, 301–15
    subordinate, 312–15
    superordinate, 312–15
Concrete, 289–90, 313–14
Confounding, 268

Conjunction, 28, 31–36, 56–57, 106, 293–94, 301, 324
Consciousness, 175, 235, 239, 276–79, 308–9
Consolidation, 12, 234–35, 239–42, 245–46
Constancy, 58–62, 105
Constituent, 3, 8–11, 51–56, 73–74, 76, 79, 83, 91–92, 108, 113–15, 124–131, 136, 143, 145–47, 156, 175–76, 228, 230, 233–34, 254, 288–301, 308–12, 315–18, 320–25, 339, 357–59, 361–64
Content addressable, 219
Context, 13–14, 59, 64, 80–81, 113, 116–17, 131–32, 136–39, 156–57, 166, 178, 185, 316, 334, 336, 342–48, 349–50, 352–53
Context-sensitive coding, 385–86
    in articulation, 125–26, 142–47, 357–58
    in audition, 114–16
    of concepts, 310–11
    of forms, 52–55
    of music, 118
    in phonetic short-term memory, 210–11
    of plans, 143–45, 356–60
    of propositions. See Fuzzy case theory
    in reading, 129–30, 149–50, 153–57
    of serial order, 114–16, 125–26, 133–39, 142–47, 149–50, 153–55, 357–60
    in speech recognition, 125–26, 132–39
Contradiction, 17, 279–80, 333, 361, 364–68, 378
Creativity, 356, 381–87

d', 256–58, 271–72
Deafness, 151
Decay, 12–13, 234–35, 245–46
Decibel, 97–98
Decision, 14, 158, 164–65, 169–73, 254–59, 261, 269–70. See also Attention
    criterion rule, 255–57, 261
    maximum rule, 165, 255, 257–58, 261
    threshold rule, 255, 258–59, 261
Declarative knowledge. See Image, Proposition
Definite description, 286–87, 316, 341, 342, 343, 360
Déjà vu, 250
Detection of signals, 97–98
Detector, 29–36, 99
    allophone, 132–33
    angle, 52–54, 129
    corner, 34, 52–54, 129
    grating, 34–36
    line, 31–33 51–54, 129
    location, 102–5
    loudness, 100, 102
    movement, 105
    pitch, 100–101, 105–6
    ray, 33–34
    segment, 33–34, 51–54
    spot, 29–30
Development, 312–15
Dialect, 133, 138
Dimensions, 62–64, 71, 148, 293, 303–5. See also Feature
    integral, 55–56
    separable, 55–56
Direct access, 217–20, 259–67, 269, 368
Discrimination, 42–47, 60, 62–64, 102, 104, 110–11, 116, 117, 138, 183, 185, 242, 311–12
Disjunction, 28, 32–36, 56–58, 106, 293–94, 366–67
Distraction, 161–63

Distractor, 258
Divided attentional deficit, 184
Duration, 117, 137–38
Dyslexia, 147. See also Alexia

Echoic memory, 190, 198–201
Electroconvulsive shock, 241
Embedding, 316, 325, 357, 365, 366
Expectation, 13–14, 16–17, 42, 64, 116–17, 119, 136–39, 156–57, 163, 180–82, 278–80, 295, 326, 365
Eye movements, 74–76, 81, 158, 173, 178, 179

False alarm, 184
Family resemblance, 301, 307, 311
Feature, 18–19, 28–36, 58–62, 70, 74, 99–106, 117, 126–29, 131–33, 139–40, 147–49, 204–5, 288–93, 302–5, 311–12, 314–35
    characteristic, 291–92
    defining, 291–92
    semantic, 350–52
Feedback, 14, 41–42, 64, 109, 116–17, 136–39, 156–57, 176, 274, 358–60
    sensory, 69–70, 140–42
Figural aftereffects, 45–46
Figure-ground, 49–50
Fixation, 152–53, 158, 173, 179
    span. See Apprehension span
Forgetting. See Storage
Form perception, 30–36, 52–64, 112, 114. See also Object perception
Fourier analysis
    in audition, 99–101
    in vision, 34–36
Fragility of memory, 239–42, 245–46
Frame of reference, 60–61, 70
Frequency, 97–101
Functional fixedness, 380
Fuzzy
    case theory, 323–25
    concepts, 296–300, 360–61
    sets, 296–300

Gamma feedback loop, 140–42
Generalization, 32, 100–101, 110, 308, 310–12, 313
Generation of images, 74–77, 82–83, 90
Generator potential, 29, 43–44, 96, 100, 195–96
Given vs. new information, 340–43
Grammar. See Syntax
Graphic, 18–19, 125, 129–31, 147–59
    memory, 190, 201–2
Grating detectors, 34–36
Grouping, 48–56, 80, 92, 111–14, 207–9, 335

Habituation, 108, 162–63, 166
Hemisphere specialization, 19–22
Hertz, 97
Hierarchical coding. See Levels of coding/processing
Hypothesis, 302–5

Iconic memory, 189–98
Image, 18, 21–24, 54, 64, 68–69, 73–92, 231–34, 277, 285, 302, 356, 368, 377
    eidetic, 81–82
    operations, 58–62, 82–92
    stabilized, 53–54
    synthesis, 91–92

Incubation, 380–81
Inference, 14–15, 292, 301–5, 321, 332, 334, 340, 345–49, 350–52, 356, 360–70, 377
  analytic, 351
  coimplication, 363–65, 367–68
  constituent implication, 361
  contradiction, 364–66
  disjunction, 366–67
  equivalence, 360
  expansion, 360–63
  linear ordering, 368–70
  negation, 364–66
  quantifier, 367–68
  set inclusion, 360–63
  synthetic, 351
  transitive, 368–70
Information gathering responses, 28
Information processing, 136, 164, 167–76. See also Activation, Inference, Parallel processing, Process, Retrieval, Serial processing, Thinking
Inhibition, 6, 16–17, 29, 31–42, 53–54, 63, 82–83, 101, 105, 107–9, 153, 165–66, 169, 170, 186, 184–85, 279–80, 311–12, 326, 336, 339, 360, 364
  proactive, 223
Instantiation, 316–17, 320, 322, 386
Intelligence, 212
Intensity, 97–98, 100
Intent to learn, 235–37
Intercept, 271, 274–75, 277
Interference, 11–13, 22–23, 70, 72–73, 170, 189–90, 193–96, 199–200, 204, 207, 222–27, 229, 233–35, 239–40, 242–45, 261, 319, 324–25, 339, 340, 346
  proactive, 223–24, 238–39, 244–45
  retroactive, 223–25, 242–44
Interval scale, 257

Kinesthetic, 69–73, 140–42, 150–51

Lateralization. See Hemisphere specialization
Learning, 12, 119–20, 158–59, 211, 228–39, 289–90, 324–25, 332, 335, 340–48. See also Chunking
Lesion, 21–22
Letter, 147–59
Level of coding/processing, 3–4, 13, 123–31, 135–39, 155–59, 175–76, 212, 237–38, 273–78, 336, 337–40, 357–60
Link, 7–11, 25, 138, 166, 210, 260, 276, 322–25, 337–40, 346–48, 369–70
Localization, 95, 102–5, 177, 179–81
Location, 68–73, 177, 179–81, 196–99
  addressable, 218–19
Logic, 293–301, 362–68
Looping, 356–60
Loudness, 102, 104, 107, 109–11, 117, 177–78

McCollough effects, 46
Mach bands, 38–40
Masking, 62, 111–12, 135, 155, 196, 274–76
Matching, 280
  name, 201–2, 273–74
  physical, 201, 273–74
  semantic, 273–74
Mathematics, 21, 242, 277–78, 279, 357, 370–80
Meaning, 286–301, 313, 316–27
  constituent, 288–90, 294

  extensional, 290–91, 294
  intensional, 290–91, 294
  propositional, 288–90, 294
  referential, 288–94
Memory, 12–13, 15–16, 81, 189–212, 215–389. See also Association, Storage, Retrieval
  item, 205–6, 253–54
  order, 205–9, 253–54. See also Order
  preattentive. See Echoic memory and Iconic memory
  redintegrative, 233
  sensory. See Echoic memory and Iconic memory
  simultaneous span, 193–95
  successive span, 203–9, 227
  trace, 215
  working, 211–12
Metaphor, 352–53
Modality, 3–4, 17–25, 68–70, 72–73, 81, 96, 164, 182–83, 199, 285
Monitoring, 195, 277
Motivation, 119–20, 162, 177, 185, 235–37
Motor. See also Response
  control, 68–73, 139–47, 170–73, 175
  memory, 68–73
Movement perception, 32–33, 47
Music, 18–19, 23, 95–96, 106, 111–15, 117–19, 123

Negation, 17, 279–80, 294–95, 364–67
Nervous system, 7, 13, 16–17, 28–42, 46, 51, 57, 97, 98–109, 133, 140–42, 176, 191, 195–96, 215, 219, 245
Network, 7–11, 22, 216–19, 230, 319–27, 331–32, 337–48, 363–64
Node, 7–17, 22–24, 25, 52–58, 76, 91, 114–15, 138–39, 148, 150–59, 165–66, 186, 189, 194–95, 210–11, 216–19, 224, 227–31, 233–34, 260, 272–73, 286–87, 316–17, 318, 322–26, 335–40, 342, 344–45, 348, 358–59, 360–66
Nonassociative memory, 189–212, 216–27
Nonverbal, 18–24

Object perception, 36, 38, 39, 47–65, 116. See also Form perception
Operation, 16, 358, 365, 371–75, 377, 380. See also Action, Process, Transformation
Order, 112–16, 125–26, 133–39, 216–17, 221–22, 357, 368–70. See also Context-sensitive coding
OR gate, 35, 106
Orienting reaction, 163

Paired associates, 223–27, 231–34, 236, 238–39, 243–46, 252, 255, 258–59, 269, 271, 273, 277, 279
Parallel processing, 24–25, 62–64, 74–79, 83–84, 115–16, 133–39, 152–53, 170–75, 182–85, 194, 261, 272–73, 279, 335–36, 337–39
  chain, 135–36, 155–57, 175–76, 273–76, 337–39, 369–70
  divergence, 337
  multiple access, 337
Parsing, 80, 315–16, 334–36, 360. See also Constituent, Syntax
Partial report, 179–81, 192–93, 195
Perceptual learning, 51–52, 54, 81

Perceptual recognition, 13–14, 57, 74–75, 80–81, 252–53, 316–17, 332, 333–40, 340–46, 360, 364. *See also* Recognition (memory), Retrieval, Scanning of text
Perceptual response, 64–65, 104–5, 117
Perceptual tuning, 182–85
Persistence
  of activation. *See* Active memory
  of audition. *See* Echoic memory
  of vision. *See* Iconic memory
Phase, 97–98
Phoneme, 19, 106, 124–27, 131–32, 142
Phonetic, 14, 18–19, 124–47, 150–52
  memory, 190, 202–11
Phrase, 315–16, 335
Pitch, 100–101, 105–6, 107, 111, 117–19, 177
Plans, 143–46, 204, 332, 334–36, 356–60, 363, 364, 365, 366, 367, 368, 370, 384, 385. *See also* Problem solving
Precedence effect, 105, 108
Predicate, 14, 317, 321–25
Presupposition, 334, 340–44
Primary memory. *See* Short-term memory
Priming, 6–7, 15–16, 64, 136–39, 143–45, 156–57, 163, 165–66, 178, 185–86, 211, 260, 278–80, 308, 326–27, 338–39, 343, 345, 346, 349, 358–59. *See also* Attentional set
Probe technique, 198–99, 252
Problem tree, 372–75, 377
Problem solving, 14, 302–5, 356, 370–81
  analogy, 379
  contradiction, 378
  equivalent operation sequence, 373
  heuristic, 373
  representation, 373, 376–81
  search reduction, 373–75, 379
  similar problem, 379–80
  special case, 373–74
  state evaluation, 373–74
  subgoals, 375
  working backward, 374–75
Problem tree, 372–75, 377
Procedural knowledge. *See* Plan
Process, 4–6, 11–17, 175–76, 330–89. *See also* Operation, Transformation
Production system, 356, 364. *See also* Plan
Proposition, 8–11, 21, 124, 158–59, 221, 229–30, 233, 285, 288–91, 302, 314–15, 317–25, 331–36, 339–48, 356, 360–70, 371–72, 377, 383–84
Prototype, 297–301, 305–15
  plus correction, 300
Psychological refractory period, 167–71

Qualification, 296, 362
Quantification, 296, 362–63, 366, 367–68
Questions, 11, 333–34, 348, 382–83, 384–85, 387

Reaction time, 167–76, 181–82, 185, 226, 263–67, 270, 273–76, 280
Reading, 123, 147–59, 272–73, 274–76
  speed, 157–58
Recall, 14, 72, 224, 244–45, 250–52, 255, 258–62, 266–70, 272–73, 324–25, 332–34, 339–40, 342, 345–50
  yes-no, 269
Recency judgment, 221–22, 241–242, 250
Receptive field, 29–36, 107
Recognition (memory), 14, 71–72, 224–27,

244–45, 250–80, 318–21, 333–40, 340–46, 360
Recovery of function, 21–22
Reduction,. 133
Redundancy (gain), 56, 62, 116, 143, 148, 156, 157, 174, 175–76, 294, 301, 305
Reference, 286–93, 313–17, 343–46, 360
Rehearsal, 84, 193–94, 212, 235, 239, 264
Relation, 7, 9–11, 24, 58, 61–62, 114, 118, 218, 295–96, 310–11, 317, 322, 339, 350–52, 361, 377, 379, 382
Repetition
  effect, 181–82, 278–79
  and learning, 238
Response, 165–173, 231. *See also* Decision, Motor
  bias, 166
  set, 244–45, 248
Retention. *See* Storage
Retrieval, 12, 14–16, 23, 75–80, 82–86, 91, 211, 216–21, 234–35, 243–44, 250–80, 332–34, 335–47, 351–52, 356
  cues, 220–21, 255, 259, 269, 347
Retrograde amnesia, 240
Rotation of images, 59–62, 86–90

Salience, 305
Scanning
  of images, 82–86
  of text, 157–58, 173–75, 193–95, 202
Schema, 119, 285, 300, 325–27, 334, 336, 343–46, 349–50, 382, 383
Search of memory, 217–20, 259–67
Segmentation, 112, 131–33
Segments, 19, 124–31, 145–47, 149–50, 156–57
Selective attentional deficit, 184–85
Semantic congruity effect, 369
Semantic distance effect, 368–70
Semantic integration, 319–20, 344–47
Semantic memory, 8–11, 14, 19, 24, 124, 130, 139, 157–59, 178, 180–81, 225–30, 237, 280, 283–89
Sentence, 124
Serial order. *See* Order
Serial Processing, 24–25, 62–63, 74–79, 83–90, 116, 135–36, 164, 167–71, 173–75, 184, 194, 205, 261–67, 337–39, 369, 370–81
Set. *See* Attentional set
Shadowing, 123, 177, 178, 200
Short-term memory, 15–16, 117, 152, 189–212, 232–33, 262–66, 278–80, 343
  motor, 71–73
Similarity, 148, 222–27
Simultaneous processing. *See* Parallel processing
Singing, 111
Skimming, 157–58
Sleep, 245
Sound, 96–98
Spacing judgment, 222
Spatial, 18, 20–24, 64, 68–73, 285
Spatial frequency analysis, 34–36
Spectrographic analysis
  in audition, 99–100
  in speech, 131–32
  in vision, 34–36
Speech errors, 144–46
Speech production. *See* Articulation, Planning
Speech recognition, 106, 112, 116–17, 131–39, 189, 203
Speed-accuracy tradeoff, 135, 265, 269–77, 370

Split brain, 19–21
S-R compatibility, 171–73
State, 358–59, 372–75
Statistical decision theory (SDT), 256–69. *See also* Decision
Stereotype, 300
Storage, 12–13, 216, 234–35, 239–46, 268, 319
Strategy, 212
Strength (of association), 12–13, 171, 175, 181, 216, 222–27, 234–46, 253–61, 263, 265–66, 271–72, 276–77, 297–99, 302, 309–12, 324–25, 334, 339–40, 369–70
Stress, 341
Stroop effect, 170, 280
Structural description, 80. *See also* Constituent
Subvocalization, 150–51
Successive processing. *See* Serial processing
Syllable, 125, 129–30, 137, 145–47
Synapse, 36, 46, 176
Syntax, 4, 8–11, 23–24, 138, 157, 178, 231, 315–16, 318–19, 321–25, 334–36, 341–44, 360
Synthesis, 2–3, 25

Temporal order. *See* Order
Temporary threshold shift, 109–11
Tests, 358
Texture, 36, 48–50, 112
Thinking, 14–15, 57, 235, 273, 284, 356–87
Threshold, 97–98, 165, 184–85

Tip of the tongue, 288
Token, 218, 322–23, 342, 386
Top-down processing, 13–14, 16–17, 42, 136–39
Topic vs. comment, 341, 343–44
Transfer, 223, 239
Transformation, 61–62. *See also* Operation
Transition network, 356. *See also* Plan
Tuning curve, 33, 35, 100–101, 107
Type, 218, 322

Unconscious, 7, 279, 306, 380–81, 387
Understanding, 2–3, 11, 13–15, 157–59, 277, 316–17, 318–21, 325–26, 330–54, 360, 361, 376–81
Unlearning, 224–25, 243–44

Verbal, 18–24, 285
Verification, 318, 320–21, 333–34, 338, 345–46, 350–52, 367–68
Visual search, 173–76

Words, 9, 17, 123–31, 138–39, 143–59, 202, 274–76, 284–88, 312–18, 344–46
  superiority effect, 155–56, 274–76
Writing, 131. *See also* Graphic

Yankee Doodle phenomenon, 118–19

Zooming, 82–86